Social psychology
Attitudes, cognition and social behaviour

Social psychology

Attitudes, cognition and social behaviour

A revised and updated edition of *Cognitive Social Psychology: a Guidebook to Theory and Research* (McGraw-Hill, 1980)

J. Richard Eiser

University of Exeter

CAMBRIDGE
UNIVERSITY PRESS

Published by the Press Syndicate of the University of Cambridge
The Pitt Building, Trumpington Street, Cambridge CB2 1RP
40 West 20th Street, New York, NY 10011-4211, USA
10 Stamford Road, Oakleigh, Melbourne 3166, Australia

(First edition published under the title *Cognitive Social Psychology:
a Guidebook to Theory and Research*
by McGraw-Hill Book Company (UK) Limited, 1980)
This edition first published 1986
Reprinted 1988, 1990, 1992, 1994

Printed in Great Britain
by Athenæum Press Ltd, Gateshead, Tyne & Wear

British Library cataloguing in publication data
Eiser, J. Richard
Social psychology: attitudes cognition and
social behaviour. – Rev. and updated ed.
1. Social psychology
I. Title   II. Eiser, J. Richard. Cognitive social psychology
302   HM251

Library of Congress cataloguing in publication data
Eiser, J. Richard.
Social psychology.
'A revised and updated edition of Cognitive social
psychology . . . 1980.'
Bibliography.
Includes index.
1. Social psychology.   2. Cognition.   3. Attitude.
I. Eiser, J. Richard. Cognitive social psychology.
II. Title.   [DNLM: 1. Attitude.   2. Cognition.
3. Psychology, Social.   4. Social Behavior.
HM251 E36S]
HM251.E4292   1986   302   86–6093

ISBN 0 521 32678 8 hardback
ISBN 0 521 33934 0 paperback

WV

For Chris,
for David and Benjamin,
and for my friends everywhere

Contents

Preface

Social psychology is a lively, growing discipline. Writing a textbook about it is therefore a bit like trying to take a still photograph of a bird in flight. Just to get the target in focus is hard enough. To achieve a balanced composition, and a clear picture of the background, as well, needs a good measure of luck. In this book, I have tried to present a glimpse of where social psychology is going, a hopefully balanced, though undeniably selective, insight into the perspectives which different researchers have adopted, and a broader view of the various empirical and theoretical traditions from which contemporary work derives.

In 1980 my previous textbook, *Cognitive Social Psychology: A Guidebook to Theory and Research*, was published by McGraw-Hill. The present volume includes both a thorough revision and reorganization of my previous work and much completely new material. The change of title is deliberate too. At the end of the seventies, most apparently successful theories in social psychology were placing a heavy emphasis on the primacy of cognition, information-processing and decision-making. The term 'cognitive' took on an imperialistic breadth of application, and a consequential looseness of meaning. In the last six or seven years, however, a noticeable reaction has set in, and some of my own views have changed too. 'Social cognition' has re-emerged as a strong, but more narrowly defined, field of research within social psychology, and at the same time much more attention has been paid to issues such as the impact of mood and emotion and the limitations of human memory and reasoning. In short, cognition is not the only form of psychological functioning upon which an understanding of social behaviour depends. Whereas my own approach remains broadly cognitive, it is by no means exclusively or narrowly so.

Social psychology is an international discipline, although not as international as it ought to be. The literature is still predominantly North American, but not nearly as exclusively so as it was fifteen or twenty years ago. Most North American textbooks contain lamentably little coverage of work conducted outside North America. In this book readers will find accounts of a fair, but not disproportionate, amount of research by authors who happen to work in other countries. However, I have not adopted this approach out of any deliberate attempt to introduce a self-consciously European flavour, but simply because such research deserves inclusion on its merits. Ingroup favouritism is no substitute for critical appraisal when it comes to judging the value of scientific contributions, whatever their origin. Even so, the health of any discipline depends on an openness to new ideas and on cross-fertilization from different, even sometimes older, traditions. In this respect, I hope that this book will have something distinctive to offer to readers on both sides of the Atlantic (or the Pacific). I have attempted to write an international book, but doubtless it is still not as international as it ought to be.

Whilst European social psychology has gained in prestige and productivity, in the last few years it has sadly lost two of its most eminent and influential figures. Henri Tajfel died in 1982. He first introduced me to social psychology when I was an undergraduate at Oxford. He persuaded me to do postgraduate research at the London School of Economics, and he helped me to my first position at the University of Bristol. He had a vision and a sense of purpose that could truly inspire. I am proud to call myself his student. Jos Jaspars died in 1985. Whereas Henri always seemed to be burning the candle at both ends, Jos was younger and apparently strong and healthy. His sudden death left all who knew him stunned. His was a genuine and generous intellect. He was a devoted teacher, the most constructive of critics, a good friend and a most dependable colleague. This book is a small thank you to each of them.

My thanks are also due to all those who have helped me with my writing of this book: to Marian Gowen for typing the manuscript; to the students of the University of Exeter over the last six years for their comments and questions; and finally to Michael Billig, Rick Budd, Connie Kristiansen, Stephen Reicher, Russell Spears, Arnold Upmeyer, Joop van der Pligt and Paul Webley, and many other friends and colleagues for stimulating discussions.

J. RICHARD EISER
November 1985

1
Aims and approaches

The topics of social psychology

Often the closer something is to everyday experience, the more difficult it can be to convince people of the need for its scientific study. The study of the extraordinary has always had a glamour not usually accorded to the study of the ordinary. What happens at the other end of a telescope or microscope, that is the stuff of science. What happens in front of our naked eyes, that is just common knowledge. This is not just a problem for the social and behavioural sciences, although it is now our turn to deal with it: the physical and biological sciences have suffered acutely from this difficulty in the past, and no doubt continue to do so. Yet, if we look at the history of these sciences, we can see that the most revolutionary advances were made when scientists sought directly to explain the obvious. Concepts such as gravity, evolution, infectious disease, were all attempts to account for experiences which were very familiar to scientists and non-scientists alike. These concepts are now themselves so familiar that it is difficult to imagine how the world could have been perceived in any other way, yet already science has moved further on, through questioning once again the basis of what has now become 'obvious'.

Human social behaviour is about as familiar an object of study as one could possibly imagine. We perceive it and participate in it constantly. Even without the help of social psychologists, we feel we know a very great deal about it, and often with very good reason. We are taught about right and wrong, about human nature, about what is done and what is not done, and the lessons we learn bear more than a fortuitous correspondence to our experience. So where does social psychology fit in? Ideally, what social psychology can do is try to answer questions like *why* people feel and act towards one another in the ways they do, why they hold particular attitudes, why they explain each other's behaviour in particular ways, and why they accept particular roles and rules of conduct. But once again the problem of 'obviousness' reappears. If one looks at the traditional topic areas of social psychology, it seems almost as though social psychologists are welcomed only as trouble-shooters, called in to help out when things go wrong, to answer questions to which conventional wisdom has no obvious answer. As social psychologists, we are asked why people are racially prejudiced, attack one another, act destructively and self-destructively, are easily led and persuaded, fail to help one another and get 'carried away' in a crowd. In short, we are asked to explain apparently *irrational* behaviour.

In many respects, this is fair enough. Interactions between human beings have their uglier aspects, and if these can be understood, then possibly some contribution can be made to the prevention or alleviation of human misery. Indeed, one could argue more strongly that researchers have a real responsibility to try and make such a contribution. But there is still a danger. To be asked, 'Why do people behave irrationally?' is to be asked a leading question. It assumes that the behaviour in question *is* irrational, not only in comparison to some logical ideal (for, as we shall see, most social behaviour would have to be called irrational from this standpoint), but in the sense of requiring a different kind of explanation from non-problematic 'sensible' behaviour. In addition, it assumes that, whatever explanations social psychologists come up with, these will *not* be applicable to contexts where conventional wisdom seems confirmed.

If these assumptions are accepted, then the ordinary and everyday – the territory of conventional wisdom – are protected from scrutiny. Yet neither evidence nor logic requires that they be accepted, and hence social psychology has no obligation to submit to the restrictions which they imply. Rather, one could argue that it is these very assumptions, and others which form the basis of so-called common knowledge, that social psychology must challenge and examine, if it is to make any real contribution, either practical or conceptual. The topics of social psychology, then, are not merely different categories of social acts, but also and more vitally the common everyday assumptions which underly such acts and give them meaning.

Theory and data

Before one starts any investigation, one should have in mind some question that one wants to answer. This sounds so obvious as not to be worth stating, but sadly it seems often to be ignored in many research endeavours. The motto, 'If it moves, measure it', characterizes an unfortunately large proportion of what has passed for research in social psychology and related disciplines. In the short term, following this motto allows one to seem and feel busy, but in the longer term, it is a recipe for disappointment. But having said that, it is not always easy to decide on a question. It takes a little thought. It takes a little theory.

To collect data about how human beings interact with one another is so easy that it is almost impossible. It is easy because human social interactions are going on almost all the time, almost anywhere one cares to look. The streets, so to speak, are paved with gold. The complexity of information potentially available can be quite overwhelming. To get anywhere, one must select and categorize, one must act on hunches, one must decide where the analysis should start and when it should end, in short, one must theorize. As Coombs (1964: 5–6) has put it: 'All knowledge is the result of theory – we buy information with assumptions – "facts" are inferences, and so also are data and measurement and scales . . . there is no necessary interpretation of any behavioral example as some particular kind of data.'

In this book I shall be describing a great number of studies where researchers have deliberately set out to test hypotheses derived explicitly from some theory or other. But this is neither the only, nor arguably the most important, aspect of the role of theory in the acquisition of knowledge. Researchers from different theoretical factions may disagree about whose predictions are most accurate, but may still agree about what the measurements they obtain are measurements *of*. Such agreement is by no means universal, but it is often much more widespread than is agreement over the predictive accuracy of any single model. For example, there have been numerous theories of attitude change, but little questioning of the assumption that attitude change can be measured in terms of changes in individuals' responses on an attitude scale. Yet it is precisely here, in the attribution of meaning to particular scores and measurements, that the fundamental theoretical assumptions are made. Without any such assumptions, we cannot even make a start; but neither can we make real progress unless we recognize such assumptions for what they are.

Experimentation and observation

Just as the questions which researchers ask depend on their theoretical assumptions, so do the methods which they use. Thus, many of the controversies which present themselves as disagreements over methods are in fact disagreements at the level of theory. One of the most heated of these controversies has been over the value of laboratory experimentation in social psychology. On the one side, there are those who argue that the purpose of research is to determine the effects of independent variables on dependent variables, and that the most efficient way to do this is to perform an experiment in a laboratory where the independent variables can be accurately recorded and measured. On the other side are those who argue that laboratory experiments involve situations which bear no relation to any 'real-life' social interactions, and impose artificial restrictions on unrepresentative samples of subjects: to find out what 'really' happens, observations of naturally occurring behaviour are the answer.

There is considerable merit in both these positions, and the fairest conclusion one can reach is the unsurprising one that both experimental and observational studies have a great deal to contribute. Nonetheless, it is important to understand the basis of the disagreement. What are experimentalists trying to do? In spite of accusations and occasional protestations to the contrary, they usually are trying to answer questions about 'real-life' social interaction. They choose aspects of 'real-life' behaviour and attempt to reproduce them within a laboratory setting. They also choose situational variables which they suspect might influence such behaviour, and create experimental analogues for these. Of course, the end-product is artificial, but does such artificiality matter, if what one is trying to do is to discover lawful relationships between independent and dependent variables which are generalizable across contexts and often even across cultures? Of course, the subject sample (usually students) is not demographically representative of the general population, but does such unrepresentativeness matter if one is looking for relationships which are generalizable across different kinds of individuals? Such generalizability, however, is more often assumed as an act of faith than put directly to an empirical test.

Generalizability can be just as much of a problem for the observational approach. The data yielded by an observational study are directly relevant to the 'real-life' situation in question, and are less likely to be distorted by the subjects' knowing that they are being observed. This is fine if all one is interested in is just the one particular situation, but once the researcher attempts to extrapolate to other 'similar' situations, the conceptual difficulties reappear. How does one decide if two 'real-life' situations are in fact similar? Just as in the experimental approach, one needs to make *theoretical* assumptions about which variables are relevant, and which are the relevant dimensions of similarity. At this point, experimentalists would claim that they are in a better position than observationalists to make such decisions of relevance, since the experiment allows one to look at the effects of a number of variables independently, and assess their relative effectiveness and the degree to which they interact, i.e. depend upon one another. Without intervening to control the different variables in turn, the observationalists have less basis on which to judge which variables are most important.

Where possible, a happy compromise can be the 'field experiment'. In studies of this kind, subjects do not know that their behaviour is being observed, and instead have to react to what they believe is a naturally occurring event. The problem of extrapolating from the laboratory to the outside world therefore does not arise. At the same time, the experimenter can stage the 'naturally occurring event' so that aspects of it are different for different groups of subjects, and so control and manipulate independent variables at least as effectively as in a laboratory. The main limitations of this method are that it is more difficult to obtain these base-line measures of subjects' attitudes and behaviour before any manipulation takes place, and that the number of responses one can hope to obtain from any single subject is usually quite restricted. These limitations, however, are not necessarily insuperable, granted a certain amount of ingenuity, and, from another point of view, might be positive advantages. The relative value of a field-experiment approach depends to a large extent on how much it matters, in a specific context, that subjects should be unaware that they are participating in a piece of research.

The important issue, however, is not so much how researchers obtain their data, but how they interpret them. Whether one looks at observational, experimental, or field-experimental studies, what researchers attempt to do is usually to treat the observed behaviour of their subjects as an exemplar of a more general class of behaviour, and to treat features of the specific situations as exemplars of more general classes of situational influences. In a large number of cases, they have then attempted to infer causal relationships between these classes of situational variables and the class of behaviour. Thus, researchers will try to say something about the relationships between, for instance, 'attitude similarity' and 'interpersonal attraction', between 'threat' and 'cooperation', between 'ambiguity' and 'helping', or between 'status' and 'discrimination'. Such terms are the building blocks of much social psychological theory, but how good a foundation do they provide? This is an empirical question, which needs to be answered separately for each specific construct. In an experimental approach, it will depend on how well the relevant variables are 'operationalized'; in other words, how well the variables which the experimenter has chosen to manipulate and measure represent the more general classes of situational influences and the more general classes of behaviour with which the theory is concerned. In an observational approach, it will depend on how well the specific situation and behaviour observed can be classified into the established theoretical categories. The problem is really the same for both approaches; it is merely tackled from opposite sides.

Theoretical advances come when data of any kind force us to rethink such situational and behavioural classifications, and to challenge prior assumptions about their interrelationships, so that our theoretical terms and constructs come to be refined, differentiated, or replaced. Observational studies provide such a challenge by showing what happens 'out there'. Experiments do so by demonstrating relationships which are more subtle and interdependent than our initial preconceptions would have enabled us to envisage.

Theory and application

The relationship between experimental or observational evidence on the one hand and theory on the other, then, is one of mutual clarification. Theories clarify our understanding of events, whilst empirical findings clarify our explanatory concepts. The very nature of the subject matter being dealt with means that it is vain to look for 'proof' or 'disproof' of theorems in the kind of absolute categorical sense we might suppose to be more applicable in a discipline like pure mathematics. Even in what conventionally are called the more 'exact' sciences, negative findings do not necessarily lead to the rejection of a theory, if no better alternative theory is yet available. The phenomena studied by social psychologists are by definition the outcome of an interaction between personal, interpersonal, social and environmental factors. The significance of this is not so much that it makes our science more 'uncertain' or 'inexact' (though this may be true). Rather, it means that we must accept variability as a fact of life, as an intrinsic property of mind, behaviour and society, and not simply as a consequence of measurement error. If we start from the position that *all* social psychological theories will be correct under *some* conditions, but that *no* social psychological theory will be correct under *all* conditions, we shall not go too far astray. The more generalizable a theory is, the better, by and large. Wider applicability, though, merely establishes greater explanatory usefulness within the context of the problems currently seen as in need of explanation. Whether it constitutes a closer approximation to some idealized universal Truth, is altogether a more metaphysical question.

If we view theories as tools, and improved understanding as the product or at least the goal of research activity, we can dispense with a false dichotomy that has distracted many previous discussions of the nature of social psychology. This is the distinction between 'basic' and 'applied' research. Search for long enough and you can find extreme examples of studies that seem 'purely' theoretical or 'purely' applied. The more important question, though, is how to conceptualize the generality of research that is carried on between these two extremes. Where there is variation in proportionate emphasis on theory and application, this is by and large a difference in degree, not in kind. Most applied studies worth talking about are shaped by theory at some level, and most people whose concern is with the refinement of theoretical models hope that such models have something to say about real-life practical issues.

More applied studies, however, need not, and perhaps often should not, be set up with the aim of 'testing' one theory or another. Very often, what is needed is straightforward descriptive evidence of what is happening, and how people think and talk about what is happening, within a specific concrete situation. The answers we get hopefully will enable us to understand that situation more fully. They *may* give us more insight into how to change that situation for the better, but we cannot depend on this, nor should we blame ourselves if the forces that inhibit change are beyond our control. Social psychology *may* sometimes enable us to design or implement interventions for some purpose of human betterment, but we should not fall into the trap of assuming that this will always be the case, or that our interventions will be the most effective ones.

Take, for example, the issue of deterring young people from taking up smoking, drug-use or other damaging activities. Yes, social psychology does have something to say about the kinds of information, and styles of presentation of information, that might be more persuasive. Yet the size of any change in behaviour we might expect through informational persuasion may be very small so long as environmental factors, such as ease of availability of the substances in question, remain unchecked. It is no failure if the outcome of research is a demonstration of the relative *un*importance of particular variables like individual attitudes and personality in a wider scheme of things. It is no failure if what we gain is a better understanding of why change is often *difficult* to bring about. Such an understanding can be very useful practically in helping direct resources where they may have the greatest chance of effectiveness. It may also contribute directly to the advancement of theory.

What this points to is a conclusion that application does not just need theory, but that theories need application. Confining one's attention mainly to the responses of introductory psychology students at English-speaking universities is not something that a science would *choose* to do, except on grounds of convenience. For many purposes, this restriction may not matter as much as is often supposed. Replicated findings cannot simply be dismissed. On the other hand, doing research in this way may be like living on a small island where there is less and less left to be discovered. It is not so much that *effects* may prove ungeneralizable (at least where other factors remain reasonably constant) in the transition to applied settings. Rather, it may be that the kinds of questions that are important in one setting may be radically different from those that are important in another. We may have little difficulty in designing an experiment or observational study to look at students' concern with physical attractiveness in their choice of partner. We may have greater difficulty in designing research on the psychological effects of the fear of starvation.

It may be just such uncomfortable questions that need to be asked, both for their own sake, and as a spur to new theoretical development. Social psychological theories do not come from thin air, but from a concern with understanding social problems, even if these problems are beyond our power alone to solve. Attention to new issues and problems in the outside world may be the source from which new developments in theory can spring. For these reasons, I have deliberately resisted the idea of splitting this book into 'basic' and 'applied' parts, or worse, having a separate chapter at the end called 'Applications'. Instead, studies that some would call 'applied' are described alongside other studies using traditional experimental procedures, the connection being their shared relevance to common theoretical concerns.

The individual and the social

Social psychology is a discipline which is wide in its scope, but modest in its claims. In that it attempts to study human social behaviour from a scientific viewpoint, it is potentially relevant to an immense variety of phenomena. Yet it is not the only discipline which seeks to study such phenomena, and for this reason the contribution of social psychology to their understanding can only be partial, and complementary to what we can learn from other fields of academic inquiry.

More than a few times during its development, social psychology has faced criticism from two sides at once. General experimental psychologists have seen social psychology as too 'soft', as sacrificing rigour of experimental design in a search for greater realism. At the same time, more qualitatively oriented social scientists have accused us of doing exactly the opposite – sacrificing realism in the search for rigour. Up to a point, both accusations are correct, but this is not something for which we need feel guilty. Compromises are probably inevitable in any attempt to reconcile and integrate different spheres of knowledge, and this is precisely what social psychology aims to do. When it comes down to a choice between defending disciplinary boundaries and gaining a fuller understanding of the human condition, the direction should be clear.

In fact, many of these boundaries are showing signs, if not of crumbling, then at least of opening. Within general psychology, in such fields as cognitive development, personality, memory and psycholinguistics, there is a growing acknowledgement that the processes being studied take the form that they do because of the inherently *social* nature of human behaviour. To take just one example, language reflects more than the acquisition of vocabulary and syntactic rules. It is a means of *communication* that involves the ability to take account of the contextually based assumptions likely to be held by *other* people by whom a verbal message is received. In short, it involves the ability to consider other people as thinking beings.

From the other side, it is sometimes argued that it is not enough for social psychology to study groups and individuals within a given social, geographical, historical, economic and political context: it is up to social psychology also to provide an analysis of that context. This criticism is unfair, and does little justice to what other disciplines, such as sociology, geography and so on, have to offer in their own right. On the other hand, to say that we cannot offer a complete analysis of social context is an inadequate excuse for ignoring that context completely. Social psychology *does* aim to say something about human social behaviour which transcends the particularities of context, but it cannot succeed if it pretends that such particularities do not exist. There is often a danger of regarding the concerns and preconceptions of a single culture as universal. This danger cannot be ignored in a discipline where so much of the published empirical research derives from what is not just a single culture, but a selected subcategory of members of that culture.

How, then, can the 'social context' be brought into psychology? There are two main complementary approaches. The first is to take the view of the individual as 'perceiver' or 'information-processor', interpreting information *provided by* the social context. In crude terms, the social context is viewed as a stimulus configuration to be judged, interpreted and remembered much like any other stimulus configuration. As will be seen, a long tradition of social psychological research has pointed to the applicability of 'basic' principles of judgement and cognition to more 'social' phenomena.

The second approach is to view people as *participants* in the social context on which they themselves can have an influence, either as individuals, or as members of groups. What this leads to is a view, on the one hand, of individual experience as a social product (we think and feel as we do because we are social beings) and, on the other hand, of the social context as the product of human thought and action (the world we live in is partly the product of the way we think).

Whereas the first of these approaches provides the main bridge with general experimental psychology, the second provides an invitation for interchange with other social sciences. Traditionally, such interchange has occurred most frequently with sociology, but other opportunities are also promising. A good deal of social psychological research involves people's attitudes towards, and interpretation of, political issues. Work on inter-group relations is also relevant, directly or indirectly, to questions of the involvement of people within a political process (e.g. Billig, 1976, 1978). The role of individuals as participants in an economic system, and indeed the implicit psychological assumptions of economic theories, are further important topics for study (Lea, Tarpy and Webley, 1986). Social health and preventive medicine is another field where social psychology has its part to play (e.g. Eiser, 1982).

Social psychology, then, *is* relevant to social issues, and to a potentially even wider range of issues than those that have so far been studied in depth. This relevance does not depend just on some vague expression of concern. It derives from the distinctive methods and theoretical ideas that social psychology has developed, and that this book attempts to describe.

PART II
ATTITUDES

2
Attitudes, attraction and influence

What are attitudes?

The study of attitudes is both the most natural and the most dangerous point from which to start a book on social psychology. The term 'attitude' is probably used more frequently than any other in social psychology. There are few theories in which the concept is not explicitly or implicitly introduced, and few experiments in which attitudes are not involved somewhere among the dependent variables. But is it, as Allport (1935) once claimed, social psychology's most distinctive and indispensable concept?

At one level, we all have a rough idea of what attitudes are. To say that we have a certain attitude towards something or someone is a shorthand way of saying that we have feelings or thoughts of like or dislike, approval or disapproval, attraction or repulsion, trust or distrust and so on. Such feelings will tend to be reflected in what we say and do, and in how we react to what others say and do.

The difficulty is one of sorting out our various intuitions about attitudes into assumptions that are logically essential to the concept of attitude itself, as distinct from those that involve empirical predictions about how attitudes are related to other observable events. Kiesler, Collins and Miller (1969: 4) have said 'all too often, social psychologists have tried to make their definition of attitude both a definition and a theory of the concept'. To this it might be added that some researchers have attempted to treat logical problems as though they were merely problems of empirical observation.

Let me therefore outline some of the main assumptions implicit in the use of the term 'attitude'.

(1) *Attitudes are subjective experiences.* This assumption is basic to most definitions, although some writers, notably Bem (1967, see chapter 4, pp. 101–6), regard people's statements about their attitudes as inferences from observations of their own behaviour.

(2) *Attitudes are experiences of some issue or object.* This point is rarely acknowledged explicitly. Not all experiences qualify as attitudes. Attitudes are not simply 'moods' or 'affective reactions' presumed to be somehow *caused* by external stimuli. Reference to some issue or object is *part of* the experience.

(3) *Attitudes are experiences of some issue or object in terms of an evaluative dimension.* If we have an attitude towards an object we do not simply

experience it, we experience it as more or less desirable, or better or worse, to some degree. Whilst it is accepted that attitudes involve evaluations, there is less than unanimity over whether attitudes are *only* evaluative. Even among those who define attitudes more inclusively, though, there is a preparedness to allow attitudes to be measured along an evaluative continuum.

As Thurstone (1928: 530) wrote in his early defence of the idea that attitudes can be measured:

> It will be conceded at the outset that an attitude is a complex affair which cannot be wholly described by any single numerical index. For the problem of measurement this statement is analogous to the observation that an ordinary table is a complex affair which cannot be wholly described by any single numerical index. Nevertheless, we do not hesitate to say that we measure the table. The context usually implies what it is about the table that we propose to measure. We say without hesitation that we measure a man when we take some anthropometric measurements of him. The context may well imply without explicit declaration what aspect of the man we are measuring, his cephalic index, his height or weight or what not. Just in the same sense we shall say here that we are measuring attitudes. We shall state or imply by the context the aspect of people's attitudes that we are measuring. The point is that it is just as legitimate to say that we are measuring attitudes as it is to say that we are measuring tables or men.

(4) *Attitudes involve evaluative judgements.* This is pretty well a rephrasing of the third proposition above. However, we should be careful what we read into the term 'judgement'. It is an *empirical* question how much a particular person's attitude to (or evaluative judgement of) some object in some situation involves deliberate, conscious appraisal of that object, as opposed to, say, an overlearned conditioned response.

(5) *Attitudes may be expressed through language.* Attitudes *may* be expressed non-verbally to some extent, but we could only apply a very impoverished conception of attitude to a species which did not have speech. Ordinary language is replete with words containing an element of evaluation (Osgood, Suci and Tannenbaum, 1957).

(6) *Expressions of attitude are in principle intelligible.* This is both the most obvious and most mysterious fact about attitudes. When other people express their attitudes, we can understand them. We may not know *why* they feel as they do, but, within limits, we know *what* they feel. The question of how language can make public what otherwise would be a private experience, is too broad a philosophical issue to be dealt with here (see, e.g., Ayer, 1959). Part of the key, however, may be provided by proposition 2, that, whereas attitude statements express subjective experiences, such subjective experiences have a *public* reference.

(7) *Attitudes are communicated.* Expressions of attitudes are not simply intelligible, they are typically made so as to be perceived and understood by others. In other words the expression of attitude is a social act that

presupposes an audience by whom that expression may be understood. How the presence, kind and size of the audience may affect the expression of attitude is an empirical question.

(8) *Different individuals can agree and disagree in their attitudes.* This proposition is dependent both on the notion that attitudes can be expressed in language (since language permits negation) and on the notion that attitudes have a public reference. An analogy may be drawn with colour perception. A statement like 'that rose is red' presupposes that the speaker has certain perceptual sensations which would be different if, say, the rose was white. The statement does not just imply: 'I see red' (which would qualify as a description of private experience which no-one could easily challenge), but also: 'what I see is a red rose' (which is a description of, or existential statement concerning, an external object which *could* be challenged by another person). Indeed these last two statements are logically distinct, in that one could make, say, the second statement (e.g. if one knew oneself to be colourblind, or if one was pointing to a black-and-white photograph) without having to endorse the first. In the same way a statement like 'that rose is beautiful' does not just imply: 'I have a beautiful visual experience', but also: 'what I see is a beautiful rose' – again a statement about an external object. The point is not whether people disagree more about beauty than about redness. It is that, logically, they *can* disagree.

(9) *People who hold different attitudes towards an object will differ in what they believe is true or false about that object.* The possibility of attitudinal agreement and disagreement implies that people will interpret attitude statements as having truth values that are in principle determinable through interaction with the attitude object. However, it is *not* necessarily the case that attitudes are formed on the basis of prior investigation of relevant facts. The relationship between factual beliefs and evaluation is an empirical question.

(10) *Attitudes are predictably related to social behaviour.* This is the most troublesome assumption concerning attitudes – so much so that the whole of Chapter 3 will be devoted to examining it. For the present it is enough to point out that: (a) if people *generally* showed no consistency between their verbally expressed attitudes and other social behaviour, it would be difficult to know what such verbal expression *meant*; (b) though people may be motivated to obtain, approach, support, etc., objects they evaluate positively, this is unlikely to be the only motive relevant to social behaviour, and its relative importance in any context is an empirical question; (c) to talk of attitudes *causing* behaviour (or vice versa) can often beg questions concerning the nature of the intervening processes.

Attitude organization

An attitude, then, is a subjective experience involving an evaluation of something or somebody. That something or somebody is represented within the experience but also has a *public* reference: public in the sense that, if we express our attitudes, another person should, in principle, be able to identify the something or somebody to which our evaluation refers. We distinguish attitude statements from other kinds of descriptive statements primarily because they imply a value judgement of some kind, not because they describe different kinds of phenomena. This point is of central importance for our conception of attitudes, since it suggests a picture of individuals actively perceiving, interpreting and evaluating their external world. It is only because attitudes have a public reference that we can describe attitudes as consistent or inconsistent, stable or changeable, normative or deviant and related or unrelated to nonverbal behaviour.

This picture of the individual as an active perceiver and interpreter of events is fundamental to one of the central concepts of social psychology, the notion of *cognitive consistency*. The basic idea is that people are predisposed to organize their attitudes and beliefs into internally consistent structures. Although defined in slightly different ways by later writers, the essential features of this idea are best introduced by considering Heider's (1946, 1958) theory of cognitive balance.

Balance theory

Balance theory is an attempt to describe part of what Heider refers to as the 'subjective environment' of an individual 'perceiver'. This 'subjective environment', analogous to Lewin's (1936) concept of a 'life-space', consists of certain *entities*, and certain *relations* between these entities, *as perceived by the individual*. The classic example consists of three entities, p, o and x, where p is the individual 'perceiver', o is another person and x is an impersonal object or issue. (If this third entity is another person, it is conventional to use the symbol q rather than x.) Each of the three relations between each pair of entities can consist of *positive* or *negative* 'sentiment' (e.g. likes/dislikes; approves of/disapproves of). Heider also distinguishes between positive and negative 'unit' relations (e.g. has some sort of bond or relationship with/ has no sort of bond or relationship with), but there are some conceptual and empirical ambiguities surrounding the status of a negative unit relation (Jordan, 1953; Cartwright and Harary, 1956). With two possible relations between each pair of entities, there are eight possible triads that can be constructed, as shown in Figure 2.1.

Heider defines as 'balanced', triads containing either three positive relations, or one positive and two negative relations. These four triads represent those situations in which either p perceived agreement with someone he or she likes, or disagreement with someone he or she dislikes. The remaining four triads, containing either three negative or one negative and two positive relations, are defined as 'imbalanced' (although the triad with three negative relations was initially considered by Heider to be 'ambiguous'). These all represent situations in which p perceives agreement

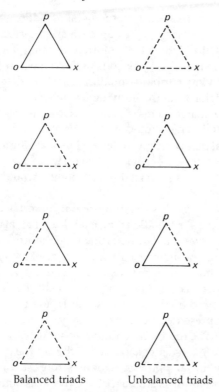

Balanced triads   Unbalanced triads

Figure 2.1. Balanced and unbalanced triads as defined by Heider (1946). Positive
relations are represented by continuous lines, negative relations by
broken lines.

with someone he or she dislikes, or disagreement with someone he or she
likes.

Heider defines balance as 'a harmonious state, one in which the entities
comprising the situations and the feelings about them fit together without
stress' (1958: 180); in other words, it is a kind of *Gestalt*. This definition
implies a number of predictions that have been taken up by later research.
First, balanced structures are more stable, in the sense that an individual
will be motivated to change an imbalanced structure into a balanced one,
but not vice versa. Second, if an imbalanced structure cannot be changed
into a balanced one, it will produce 'tension'; hence, balanced states are
preferred to imbalanced ones. Third, if people are required to predict the
third relation in a triad from a knowledge of the other two (e.g. 'A likes B and
A approves of X. Does A think B approves or disapproves of X?'), they are
more likely to *predict* a state of balance than imbalance (e.g. 'A thinks B
approves of X'). Finally, since balanced states are more predictable than
imbalanced ones, they are *simpler* to learn or recognize.

There is quite a literal sense in which balanced states are simpler than imbalanced ones, as can be seen if one applies attitude-scaling notions to the theory of balance (Jaspars, 1965). In terms of the approach taken by Coombs (1950, 1964), one can conceptualize judgements of preference and evaluation as depending upon: (1) the perceived positions of the judged items in terms of one or more underlying attributes or dimensions and (2) the perceived distances of these items from the individual's own *ideal point* on the dimensions. Positively evaluated items should be close to this ideal point, and negatively evaluated items should be further away. Thus if p represents an individual's ideal point on a given dimension or attribute, and o and x represent the positions of two evaluated items, Figure 2.2 would represent a situation in which o was preferred to x. Coombs would term such a representation a '*J*-scale'.

If we wished to extend this approach so as to represent, in terms of the same schema, not only people's evaluations of o and x, but also p's perception of o's evaluation of x, we could do so by treating a short distance between o and x as representing a positive relation (o is seen as liking x), and a long distance as representing a negative relation. Figure 2.2 would therefore also imply that o disliked x. Applying this to the distinction between balanced and imbalanced triads, one can see in Figure 2.3 that all four balanced triads can be represented unidimensionally. The triad with three negative relations can also be represented unidimensionally, but only in the special case where the individual's ideal point is at the neutral point of the dimension, and o and x are at opposite extremes (e.g., a political 'moderate' might hate both communists and fascists, and also assume that communists and fascists would hate each other). With this single special

$$o \quad P \qquad\qquad\qquad\qquad\qquad x$$

Figure 2.2. Example of a *J*-scale.

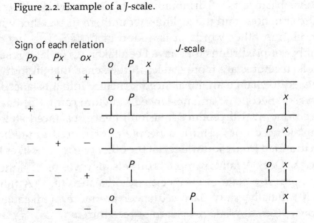

Figure 2.3. Representation of triads in a unidimensional preference space.

exception, imbalanced triads cannot be represented unidimensionally. The 'preference space' required to map imbalanced situations would require more than one dimension.

This approach carries a number of important implications. First, the preference for balanced structures is a preference for cognitively simpler structures which can be represented in terms of a single evaluative dimension. Second, imbalanced situations require more than one dimension for their representation, but if people are prepared to use more than one dimension (base their evaluations of different entities on independent criteria) they can conceptualize such situations quite adequately. Heider's concept of balance therefore only applies to cases where individuals see all three relations of a triad as interdependent and relevant to each other; where, in other words, they are disposed to make their evaluations in simple unidimensional terms (Stroebe, Thompson, Insko and Reisman, 1970). Finally, the above definitions of balance and imbalance apply only where people evaluate themselves positively (i.e. close to their ideal point). In other words, the basic formulation of balance theory assumes a positive self-concept, and the hypothesized preference for balance may be viewed as a preference for situations in which this positive self-concept is unchallenged.

Balance theory, then, has very little to do with any preference people may have for strict *logical* consistency. Instead it implies that people are *biased* towards perceiving their social environment in such a manner that they can make simple evaluative judgements in terms that enable them to maintain a positive view of themselves. Consistency in this sense is primarily a form of cognitive bias, rather than the achievement of perfect rationality. The main empirical questions to be asked therefore concern the relative strength of this bias compared with *other* biases which may also influence perceptions of the social environment, and the extent to which this bias may be dependent upon the stimulus context and the particular mode of response employed. Indeed, even some of the earliest research in this area contained strong hints of the presence of biases other than balance, as originally defined by Heider.

Jordan (1953), for example, presented subjects with verbal descriptions of different triads, e.g. 'I like o, I dislike x, o dislikes x', and obtained ratings of the 'pleasantness' of each triad. As predicted, balanced triads overall were rated as more pleasant than imbalanced ones. However, Jordan also noticed a preference for positive sentiment relations (e.g. 'positivity bias'), particularly between p and o. That is, situations in which the interpersonal relationship was one of liking rather than disliking tended to be rated as more pleasant, irrespective of any effects due to the presence or absence of balance.

In view of the importance of the po relation, Newcomb (1968) proposed a modification of Heider's theory, based on the assumption that the balance principle applies only when the po relation is positive. Newcomb suggests that the individual does not feel 'engaged' in situations where the *po* relation is negative, and therefore the issue of a preference for balance does not arise. This accords with findings that balanced triads do not tend to be rated as more pleasant than imbalanced ones if the *po* relation is negative, particularly when the third entity is another person (*poq* triads) rather than an impersonal object or issue (Price, Harburg and Newcomb, 1966; Rodrigues, 1967).

Other evidence has pointed to the importance of an *agreement* bias, whereby situations in which *p* and *o* agree are preferred to situations in which they disagree (Gerard and Fleischer, 1967; Rodrigues, 1968; Whitney, 1971; Zajonc, 1968b). Crockett (1974) found consistent evidence of an agreement bias when subjects were required to rate the pleasantness of situations where the third entity was a political issue, regardless of whether or not *p* liked *o*. This argues against Newcomb's (1968) approach, since no such effects should occur if subjects were only 'engaged' in those situations where the *po* relation was positive. Crockett also found that balanced situations tended to be those which subjects rated as having a higher likelihood of occurrence, suggesting that pleasantness ratings may not always be the best test of Heider's theory (see also Anderson, 1977; Gollob, 1974; Rossman and Gollob, 1976).

Other studies have asked subjects to predict which relations, if any, between the entities in a triad are likely to change over time. Burnstein (1967) found that such predictions tended to be in the direction of balance, i.e. imbalanced situations were predicted to change so as to become balanced. In addition, negative relations between *p* and *o* were predicted by the subjects to change so as to become positive. Where subjects have to predict the value of a missing relation in a triad, balance effects have been shown by Rodrigues (1968) and Mower White (1974, 1982). Additional evidence of a positivity bias was demonstrated by Mower White, but in the Rodrigues study, presumably because of instructions that may have emphasized the importance of agreement in the hypothetical situations described, an agreement bias was found to be more influential than balance.

Studies on the learning of balanced and imbalanced situations, however, have not produced consistent evidence that balanced structures are easier to recall (Cottrell, Ingraham and Monfort, 1971; Gerard and Fleischer, 1967; Rubin and Zajonc, 1969; Zajonc and Burnstein, 1965; Zajonc and Sherman, 1967), although these studies have generally shown that positive relations are more easily recalled than negative ones.

Mower White (1974, 1982) has also pointed out that an important prerequisite for the occurrence of balance effects may be that the subject identifies with, or takes the role of, the entity *p* in the triad (as in studies by Aderman, 1969; Jordan, 1953; Rodrigues, 1967), as opposed to viewing the triad from the standpoint of an uninvolved observer (as in studies by Rubin and Zajonc, 1969; Whitney, 1971; Zajonc and Sherman, 1967).

The notion of cognitive balance, therefore, remains an important principle of attitude organization. However, it does not operate precisely as predicted by Heider for all people or all situations. As Crockett has appealed (1974: 110): 'we ought to ask no longer whether one principle or another predominates in people's constructions of social situations. Instead, let us begin to map out how balance, agreement, positivity, and other principles operate with respect to different dimensions of judgment, in different circumstances, and for different kinds of people.'

Although its fashionability has waned, balance theory continues to stimulate a certain amount of research, of which that by Insko (1984) is the most notable. Insko rejects the idea that positivity, attraction and agreement biases are something *other than* balance, arguing instead that they are special forms of balance. For instance, an expectation of future contact between p and o (in Heider's terms, a positive unit relation) would be balanced with a positive *po* sentiment relation. In other words, the preference for situations where p likes o can be considered a preference for balance between a positive *po* sentiment relation and a positive *po* unit relation. Similarly, if the *px* and *ox* relations share the same sign (if there is perceived agreement), this again can be seen as a form of balance if future contact between p and o, and hence a positive *po* unit relation, is expected (Insko, Songer and McGarvey, 1974). Furthermore, if a person's self-concept is treated as an element in the cognitive structure, then the attraction bias can be treated as a special case of balance, with 'being liked' as something linked to a positive self-concept. The idea that 'being right' is also linked to a positive self-concept similarly allows for a prediction of an agreement bias (Insko, Sedlak and Lipsitz, 1982).

Cognitive complexity

Crockett's (1974) appeal to consider 'different kinds of people' highlights the fact that balance theory does not deal with differences between individuals in how motivated they are to reduce inconsistency, particularly in their evaluative impressions of others. In fact, a number of researchers have found fairly reliable differences between individuals, in the extent to which they will make fine or gross distinctions in their judgements of others, will use simpler or more complex ways of categorizing and will consider a smaller or greater number of attributes or dimensions simultaneously. On the basis of these findings, various tests have been devised to measure a construct (or set of constructs) known generally as *cognitive complexity–simplicity*. It should be stressed that these tests do not all necessarily measure exactly the same tendency or trait, nor are they based on exactly the same theoretical assumptions (Streufert and Streufert, 1978; Vannoy, 1965).

Whatever the precise definitions and measures employed, however, a common prediction is that balance theory and its derivatives should more adequately describe the behaviour of cognitively simple than of cognitively complex individuals. Support for this prediction comes from a number of studies. Press, Crockett and Rosenkrantz (1969) found that cognitively simple subjects were quicker at learning balanced than imbalanced structures when presented with a set of like–dislike relationships among groups of four hypothetical persons. Cognitively complex subjects showed no consistent differences in the speed with which they learned the two kinds of structures. Similar results were obtained by Delia and Crockett (1973). Ware and Harvey (1967) found that cognitively simple subjects were more prepared to make generalizations about a person's behaviour, and were more certain of their impressions, when presented with evaluatively consistent information about the stimulus person. Cognitively complex subjects were more prepared to generalize when the information contained evaluative inconsistencies. Harvey and Ware (1967) gave subjects information about a stimulus person, whose present behaviour was apparently inconsistent with his previous behaviour. When asked to write explanations for this inconsistency, cognitively simple subjects seemed more troubled by it, and tended to explain it away as due to a temporary change in the person. In comparison, cognitively complex subjects were more likely to try and make sense of the inconsistency, in the form of an integrated account.

Cognitive complexity can also be viewed, not just as an individual difference variable, but as a motivation in its own right, reflected in tendencies to seek out novelty and variety, and explore unfamiliar situations (e.g. Berlyne, 1960; Maddi, 1968). Although this seems to be a direct contradiction of balance theory, there seems reason to suppose that both the motive to seek out incongruity and the motive to reduce it may co-exist (McGuire, 1968). The need to view one's world as relatively stable and predictable seems basic to any behavioural decision, but the need to find out more about one's world would also seem to have obvious survival value. An organism that expected the environment to be *completely* predictable would be as poorly adapted to the needs of survival as one that expected the environment to be completely unpredictable. Much the same considerations apply to the advantages of categorization as opposed to differentiation between exemplars of a category (Billig, 1985; see also Chapter 5, pp. 143–4). The real issue seems to be one of the *level* of congruity or incongruity a person will tolerate or seek to attain.

Streufert and Streufert (1978) have attempted to integrate the different findings in this area through the use of a concept which they term the 'general incongruity adaptation level', or GIAL. (The concept of adaptation level will be discussed in Chapter 5.) Broadly, what they propose is that individuals form, on the basis of experience, certain expectations about the level of incongruity they are likely to encounter in any given area. If individuals experience incongruity above their GIAL, they will act in accordance with the precepts of consistency theory, and seek to reduce the incongruity (though they will not necessarily go so far as completely to restore balance). On the other hand, if they experience less incongruity than expected, i.e. below their GIAL, they will actively search out incongruity. An example of this could be when a person is described to us so as to be 'too good to be true' and our suspicions are aroused as a result.

Streufert and Streufert allow for the fact that individuals may have different GIALs for different areas of their experience. For instance, one might have learned to expect considerable unpredictability in the performance of one's favourite sports team, but still expect highly predictable relationships between, say, the political attitudes and patterns of friendship among one's neighbours. It remains a possibility, though, that some individuals may have generally higher GIALs across different areas than other individuals. Indeed the notion of cognitive complexity–simplicity as a stable personality characteristic implies just this. At present, though, the measures used provide only a weak basis for any such generalizations beyond the area of interpersonal judgements.

Attraction and similarity of attitudes

One of the first attempts to develop a social theory of attraction was made by Newcomb (1956; 1968). Newcomb's theory, for most relevant purposes, may be considered a restatement of Heider's (1946) theory of cognitive balance, applied to the specific issue of the prediction of positive and negative interpersonal attitudes from agreement and disagreement about an attitude object and vice versa. At its simplest, Newcomb's theory predicts that interpersonal agreement and attraction should facilitate each other. As already mentioned, Newcomb predicts that there will be little motivation to reduce imbalance through attitude change in situations where one person dislikes another. Whereas Heider does not differentiate systematically between the three relationships of the *pox* triad in terms of their importance for balance or imbalance, Newcomb places especial emphasis on the interpersonal links. For example, if p likes o, p will be concerned that their attitudes should be in agreement; but if p dislikes o, o's attitudes will have little or no psychological significance for p and will not, as Newcomb puts it, induce any 'strain toward symmetry'. Heider, however, would predict that people would be just as motivated to disagree with others whom they dislike, as to agree with others whom they like.

An important difference between Newcomb and Heider is that Newcomb does not claim to derive his theory from any *Gestalt* principle, but rather from a consideration of the conditions which facilitate interpersonal communication. Thus, one may avoid communicating with others whom one dislikes, or choose to communicate with others whom one likes, as a means of reducing the 'strain' produced by disagreement. This difference is reflected in the kind of data Newcomb sought as support for his theory. Rather than the abstract paper-and-pencil tasks used by researchers such as Jordan (1953) to test Heider's theory, Newcomb looked for evidence in the patterns of attitude similarity and friendship which developed as members of 'real-life' groups became acquainted with each other. In an early investigation of this process, Newcomb (1943) described how female students attending a small private college in Vermont in the thirties (Bennington College) espoused the liberal attitudes of their lecturers and fellow-students, even though they came from predominantly conservative backgrounds, and stuck to their new attitudes long after leaving college. In another study, the attitudes of male college students who shared a house provided by the experimenter were monitored over a sixteen-week period. As the house-members' acquaintance with each other increased, patterns of friendship became more predictable from similarity of attitudes on various issues, including liking for other house-members (Newcomb, 1961). More recently, however, Newcomb (1981) has reanalysed these data in terms of the patterns of agreement and attraction within dyads rather than just considering balance as an intrapersonal phenomenon. His surprising finding is that only a subgroup of students (predominantly engineers) showed the predicted pattern of mutual liking and agreement. For another subgroup (predominantly liberal arts students), agreement and liking were negatively associated.

There is evidence from many sources pointing to the interrelationship between friendship and communication. In the classic study of housing communities by Festinger, Schachter and Back (1950), physical proximity was found to be an important predictor of friendship patterns, with next-door neighbours most likely to become friends. Friendship has also been shown to be predictable from actual (Gullahorn, 1952) and anticipated (Darley and Berscheid, 1967) amounts of interaction. The converse relationship also holds true, with individuals who are attracted to, or friendly with, each other being more likely to talk to each other in group discussions (Lott and Lott, 1961), keep especially close to each other (Byrne, Ervin and Lamberth, 1970), and maintain eye-contact (Exline, Gray and Schuette, 1965; Goldberg, Kiesler and Collins, 1969). Although such findings taken individually are perhaps not all that surprising, cumulatively they add up to a case for looking at interpersonal liking, not simply as an abstract evaluative response, but as functionally related to processes of communication and cooperative interaction. A large part of 'being friendly' seems to involve putting oneself (or being put) into situations which facilitate communication, the exchange of information, and the mutual transmission and reception of stimulation generally.

In spite of these considerations, a powerful research tradition has attempted to look at interpersonal attraction, and its relation to attitudinal similarity in particular, by using experimental situations which deliberately exclude the possibility of any such interaction or communication. A short research note by Byrne (1961) described a procedure which was to serve as a paradigm for a long series of subsequent studies. Students were presented with an attitude scale to measure their positions on 26 different issues (e.g. God, premarital sex relations, classical music, politics). They also had to indicate which of the issues they considered to be the 13 most and the 13 least important. Two weeks later they were told that they had completed the scale as part of a study of interpersonal perception. They were then shown an anonymous questionnaire, supposedly of a student in another class, to 'determine how much they could learn about one another from this information alone' (Byrne, 1961: 714). The questionnaire of this 'other student' was faked so that the responses were: (1) identical to the subject's own on all issues, (2) opposite to the subject's own on all issues, (3) similar on important and dissimilar on unimportant issues, or (4) dissimilar on important and similar on unimportant issues.

When the 'other student' held similar as opposed to dissimilar attitudes on all issues, subjects indicated that they felt they would like and enjoy working with the other more, and rated the other as more intelligent, knowledgeable, moral and well-adjusted. Smaller differences in the same direction were found when comparing the conditions where attitude similarity occurred on important as opposed to unimportant issues.

Following this first experiment, Byrne proposed that the degree of interpersonal attraction towards another is directly and linearly related to the proportion of attitudinal items on which this other holds similar, as opposed to dissimilar, attitudes to the subject (Byrne and Nelson, 1965). The observed linear relationship seems to be generalizable beyond paper-and-pencil presentations of the attitude of the 'other' to conditions involving sound and/or visual recordings (Byrne and Clore, 1966) and beyond the use of college students as subjects (Byrne and Griffitt, 1966). Nonetheless, the 'other' in these studies remains an object of perception, rather than a partner in any real interaction.

Byrne and Clore (1967) claim that, by demonstrating that attitude similarity can lead to attraction for a complete stranger, towards whom one has no pre-existing positive orientation of the kind implicitly required by Newcomb's model, 'it has become possible to place the relationship between attitude similarity and attraction in an antecedent-consequence framework' (p. 2). This claim is justified only within the narrowest of contexts. By definition, the subject's liking or disliking can have no consequences for future interaction with the other, as no such interaction can occur.

Using a very different approach, Duck (1973) obtained evidence relevant to the attraction–similarity hypothesis by studying the patterns of friendship that developed among students of the same sex within their first six months at university, who shared the same hall of residence or were taking the same course. Similarity was defined in terms of responses on the Kelly repertory grid test (Kelly, 1955), and, in general, was positively related to friendship development. However, Duck makes two important points: first, that the *kind* of similarity in the responses of any pair of individuals is more predictive of their relationship than just the *amount* of similarity, with closer personal relationships being associated with greater similarity in the use of 'psychological' as opposed to 'role' constructs – a finding which has parallels to the developmental data on children's interpersonal descriptions reported by Peevers and Secord (1973); and second, that similarity of any kind should be regarded as a cue or 'filter' which individuals use as a criterion for selecting potential friends from a wider circle of possible acquaintances. Such 'filtering' is assumed to be continuous with the impli- cation that different kinds of cues may have different degrees of importance at different stages in the development of a relationship.

Physical attractiveness and the 'matching hypothesis'

Apart from similarity of attitudes, the kind of similarity most often studied in terms of its relation to interpersonal attraction has been similarity along the dimension of physical attractiveness. The attention given to this variable reflects the fact that most experiments are done on students, among whom the choice of 'dating partner' provides researchers with a convenient dependent variable. Walster, Aronson, Abrahams and Rottman (1966) argue that the probability of being accepted by the partner of one's choice may be thought of as analogous to the probability of succeeding at a task, and should be inversely related to the attractiveness of one's partner, and directly related to one's own attractiveness. The higher one aims, therefore, the greater should be the probability of being rejected. There are likely to be wide individual differences in how far people are prepared to put them- selves at risk in this context. (See Stroebe, 1977, for a fuller discussion of the influence of self-esteem.) Moreover, situational factors will determine the benefits that may accrue from being accepted, and the costs, in terms of loss of face, disruption to existing relationships, etc., of being rejected by the partner of one's choice. With such factors remaining constant, however, one would expect that individuals seeking to maximize both their own chances of being accepted, and chances that the partner who accepts them will be 'worth having', should choose partners who neither far exceed, nor fall short of, themselves in terms of estimated attractiveness and desir- ability. In other words, they should choose others roughly comparable in attractiveness to themselves.

Walster *et al.* (1966) tested this 'matching hypothesis' by exploiting a popular event in American universities – the computer dance. The pro- cedure involved first-year students filling in a questionnaire, the results of which were then supposedly fed into a computer, which matched them with compatible partners of the opposite sex for the dance. Walster *et al.* in fact had the computer generate matchings on a completely random basis. All subjects were rated surreptitiously for physical attractiveness and, during an intermission in the dance, filled in individual questionnaires, supposedly as an evaluation of the computer selection, which asked them how much they liked their partner and would like to go out with him or her in future. Walster *et al.* found that more attractive participants of either sex were liked more by their partners, but that the partners' own attractiveness had little influence on their ratings. Furthermore, there was no evidence that subjects liked partners who liked them more. This study therefore failed to provide evidence for reciprocity of liking, or for liking being dependent on matching in terms of physical attractiveness.

Subsequent tests of the matching hypothesis have yielded mixed support at best. In a study asking for *hypothetical* ratings of a supposed member of the opposite sex, Stroebe, Insko, Thompson and Layton (1971) found a general preference for more physically attractive others (judged from facial photographs). Subjects who rated themselves as more attractive chose more attractive others as hypothetical dating (but not potential marriage) partners. Stroebe *et al.* also manipulated attitude similarity (along the lines of Byrne's, 1961, procedure), with more consistent positive effects. Huston (1973) examined the possibility that the negative findings of Walster *et al.* (1966) might have been due to even unattractive individuals having little fear of rejection. (Those whom a computer hath joined together, etc.) Huston showed male students photographs of potential dating partners who in one condition had, and in another had not, supposedly already seen the subject's own photograph and indicated that they would accept him. Where acceptance was thus assured, more attractive partners were preferred. Where acceptance was not assured, subjects who rated themselves as less attractive rated their chance of acceptance by their chosen partner as lower, but were still no less likely to choose a more attractive partner.

Despite such negative findings, it is worth saying that, *had* these experiments supported the matching hypothesis, such a result might well have been dismissed by some as 'just common sense'. If the matching hypothesis retains any intuitive appeal, this may be derived from judgements of real relationships, where covariation of age and habits (e.g. fashion, diet) between partners may enhance the impression of covariation in attractiveness. More generally, the study of hypothetical first dates may be far removed from the reality of long-term relationships.

Whatever the reasons for the failure of the matching hypothesis in such experiments, however, physical attractiveness *per se* emerges as a powerful variable. It not only affects liking, but many other indicators of social influence. For instance, Chaiken (1979) conducted a field study in which students were trained to deliver persuasive arguments to other students, and elicit support for a petition, in favour of meat-free meals in the university canteens. Communicators of either sex who were independently rated as more attractive elicited more agreement and behavioural compliance. Benson, Karabenic and Lerner (1976) found that help was more likely to be given to attractive individuals, and in a study of criminal trials in Pennsylvania (Stewart, 1980) more attractive male defendants received lighter sentences, and were twice as likely as less attractive defendants to avoid imprisonment. An unpublished study by Efran and Patterson (1976; cited by Cialdini, 1984: 21) found that the votes cast in the 1974 Canadian federal elections were strongly related to the candidates' attractiveness. Walster *et al.* (1966) seem, with their matching hypothesis, to have been hunting for a rather subtle effect (an interaction between the perceiver's and target's attractiveness) whereas the data are generally better explained by the more straightforward hypothesis that more attractive others elicit more liking as well as more attitude and behaviour change.

Reactions to personal evaluations

The notion that individuals seek consensual validation for their attitudes and beliefs implies that other people may also be an important source of the views one holds about oneself. The notion that one tends to perceive oneself as others see one can be traced historically through the writings of James (1968), Cooley (1968) and Mead (1968) to the more recent literature on self-attribution processes (see Chapter 6). The scope of such self-evaluation may be quite general (e.g., the extent to which one sees oneself as a good and pleasant person), or quite specific (e.g. the extent to which one's most recent essay or course assignment was creative, accurate, or uninspired). In either case, there will be some occasions when other people appear to evaluate one in the same way as one evaluates oneself, and other occasions when other people's evaluations differ from one's own, in either a more positive or more negative direction. When such discrepancies occur, they may provide an impetus for a change in either one's self-concept, or one's attitude towards the other person by whom one has been evaluated, or both. For instance, students who received a lower mark than they expected for an essay or an examination might respond by lowering their estimate of their own ability or of the adequacy of their preparation, or they might persist in the belief that they had really done a brilliant piece of work, the merit of which their lecturers or examiners were too perverse or stupid to recognize. Either way, it seems reasonable to suppose that some kind of cognitive resolution of the discrepancy would frequently be sought.

It is intuitively highly plausible, therefore, that one's liking or disliking for another person will be influenced by the extent to which one feels this other person regards one's personality, or performance at some task, in a favourable or unfavourable light. But at this point a less obvious question arises: do we prefer others who merely say favourable things about us, or do we prefer others whose views of us coincide with, and hence validate, our own self-perceptions, be they favourable or unfavourable?

The latter view is that held by Secord and Backman (1965) in what they refer to as their 'social congruity theory'. Balance theory predicts that we should evaluate more positively a person who makes a favourable remark about something of which we approve, or an unfavourable remark about something of which we disapprove, than a person who contradicts our own approval or disapproval. The extension embodied in 'social congruity theory' is merely the observation that this 'something' can be oneself, or some aspect of one's behaviour (see also Insko, 1984; Insko *et al.*, 1982). If we evaluate ourselves positively, that is, have relatively high self-esteem, the theory predicts simple reciprocity of liking: we should prefer others who evaluate us favourably and thus validate our own favourable opinion of ourselves. On the other hand, if we are relatively low in self-esteem or have a relatively low opinion of ourselves, or of our performance on some task, we should, according to the theory, prefer others who evaluate us negatively. Evaluations by others, in other words, should lead to liking only if they are perceived as accurate.

One of the main studies cited in support of this position is that by Deutsh and Solomon (1959). Subjects in their study were female telephone operators who performed a task individually, but supposedly as members of a team, and were led to believe that they had either done well or poorly at the task. They were then shown an evaluation of their performance, supposedly by another subject, which was designed to be either very favourable or very unfavourable. Their own evaluations of this 'other subject' on the basis of this feedback were then recorded. When subjects believed that they had succeeded, they clearly preferred others who evaluated their performance positively, whereas this preference disappeared in the condition where subjects believed that they had failed. Deutsch and Solomon interpret these results as indicating both the presence of a congruity effect, or preference for accurate evaluations, and a positivity effect, or preference for favourable evaluations.

Although one might be tempted to ask which of these two 'biases' or preferences is the more important, this is not the kind of question that is likely to yield any sensible answer which is generalizable beyond a specific situation. A more fruitful enterprise is to examine the variables that may make sometimes accuracy, and sometimes positivity, the more important factor. Skolnick (1971) introduced only minor variations into the Deutsch and Solomon procedure but found results that strongly supported the prediction of positivity effect. Whether subjects were led to believe that they had failed, or if they were given no feedback about their own performance, they clearly preferred a positive to a negative evaluation from the simulated fellow-subject. There was even an interaction of marginal significance ($p < 0.09$) in the direction opposite to that predicted by social congruity theory, indicating that this preference for positivity was somewhat stronger when subjects believed that they had failed. On the basis of these results, Skolnick tentatively proposes a viewpoint which he calls 'signification theory', which predicts that individuals will prefer positive to negative evaluations *especially* when their own opinion of themselves is low. Essentially, what is being argued is that positive evaluations from others are welcomed insofar as they boost one's morale, but if one's morale is already high, it is less in need of a boost.

Skolnick goes into some detail in discussing the implications of differences between his own procedure and that of Deutsch and Solomon. His subjects were students rather than telephone operators, and he suggests, rather patronizingly, that 'telephone operators may be less likely to become aroused by a test that purports to measure their intelligence and leadership ability than would college students' (p. 66). Apart from arousal or involvement, there may have been differences in self-concept stability, and feedback credibility. He speculates that the manipulation of subjects' self-esteem through feedback concerning their own success or failure 'would not have as strong an effect on telephone operators, who probably have more stable self-concepts, than on college students, who are very tuned into identity problems and are in the process of modifying their self-image constantly' (p. 66). Also, in contrast to the students, who were deliberately selected so that they did not know each other, 'the telephone operators might have been friends and/or thought each other unlikely to evaluate them incongruously' (p. 66). How idyllic it must be to be an uninvolved, unambitious, simple, stable, non-neurotic, non-introspective, friendly telephone operator!

If Skolnick is right in suggesting that the credibility of incongruous evaluations differed between his own and the Deutsch and Solomon studies, the reason may lie in the task itself, rather than in the subjects' backgrounds. Skolnick used tests of logical reasoning in which it was probably quite difficult for subjects to be absolutely sure how well or poorly they had done. Following up this possibility, Dutton (1972) manipulated both perceived task importance and stability of positive or negative self-evaluations. When the task was made to seem important, senders of positive evaluations were preferred in all conditions except when subjects had formed stable negative self-evaluations. When the task was made to seem unimportant, a congruency effect was found, with subjects who had formed positive self-evaluations preferring the positive evaluator, and those who had formed negative self-evaluations (particularly when stable) preferring the negative evaluator. There was no evidence of the processes suggested by Skolnick's 'signification theory'.

The importance of others' perceived sincerity was examined in a study by Stroebe, Eagly and Stroebe (1977). Student subjects were classified as high or low in chronic self-esteem on the basis of a personality test (as opposed to

having their self-evaluations manipulated experimentally). Having completed the questionnaire which was to provide this measure, subjects were
told that their responses would be shown to another person, who would be
asked to describe their character. The subjects were told that the other
person had either been instructed to record 'sincere' impressions, or had
been acting under 'role-playing' instructions to write a description of the
subjects' character so as to be convincingly positive or negative. After some
delay, subjects were then all given hand-written notes, actually made up by
the experimenters. Just two such notes were used, one favourable and one
unfavourable in content, and each about 100 words long. Subjects were then
asked to say how likely or unlikely it was that the person supposedly
evaluating them had produced the description of them under the 'role-
playing' rather than 'sincere' instructions. The results indicated that high
self-esteem subjects felt that the description was less likely to be sincere if it
was negative, whereas the low self-esteem subjects felt that it was likely to
be sincere if it was positive. Apparently, therefore, subjects in this study,
presented with evaluations of themselves by others which were incongruent with their own self-evaluations, resolved this incongruity by seeing
their evaluator's behaviour as due to the experimental instructions. (This
study thus provides an example of self-serving biases in attribution, as
described in Chapter 6, pp. 199–201.)

Consistency and change

Whereas the main interests of researchers such as Newcomb (1956, 1968)
and Secord and Backman (1965) were with the prediction of interpersonal
attraction, other extensions of the notion of cognitive consistency have been
more concerned with the prediction of changes in attitude and statements of
belief. Chapter 4 will describe the most distinctive and important of these,
Festinger's (1957) theory of cognitive dissonance. Two other influential
contributions are the theories of 'affective-cognitive consistency'
(Rosenberg and Abelson, 1960), and of 'congruity' (Osgood and Tannenbaum, 1955).

Affective–cognitive consistency theory

Rosenberg and Abelson's (1960) theory deals specifically with the question
of consistency between an individual's evaluations of attitude objects or
'elements' and beliefs concerning the relations between them. A 'cognitive
unit' or 'band' consists of two evaluated 'elements' connected by a 'relation'.
Elements are treated as either positive (+) or negative (−), relations as either
positive (p), negative (n), or null (o). For instance, the situation, 'My friend
disapproves of my political party', would be represented as a band consisting of two positive elements (my friend and my political party) connected by

a negative relation $(+n+)$. One of the most important differences between this theory and that of Heider is in the way Rosenberg and Abelson use the term 'relation'. Positive and negative relations express not only positive and negative sentiment (e.g. 'likes–dislikes') but also facilitatory and inhibitory causal relations (e.g. 'helps–hinders', 'brings about–prevents'). Balanced bands thus also include situations in which positive agents are seen as *instrumental* in producing positive consequences or negative agents in producing negative consequences. Positive agents should similarly be seen to inhibit negative consequences and negative agents to inhibit positive consequences. Thus, 'My friend gave me a winning tip for the 3.30 at Doncaster', would be an example of a $+p+$ band [My friend $(+)$ helped (p) my winning $(+)$].

Rosenberg and Abelson predict 'as a major consequence of imbalance (when the person is *attending* to that imbalance) that the cognitive band will be unstable: that it will be comparatively likely to undergo change in a balancing direction' (1960: 120). They are thus concerned mainly with predicting changes in how someone evaluates elements or perceives the relation between elements, as a consequence of imbalance. At the same time, however, they are well aware that there are other available strategies for coping with imbalance (Abelson, 1959). People may simply not attend to the imbalance, or may differentiate or redefine the concepts or elements, e.g. 'Smoking $(+)$ may damage (n) my health $(+)$' can become differentiated into '*Lifelong-heavy-smoking* $(-)$ causes (p) cancer $(-)$ but *smoking-the-way-I-do* $(+)$ has no effect (o) on my health $(+)$'; or they may attempt to 'bolster' their existing attitude by relating one or other of the elements in a balanced way to other valued elements, e.g. 'Smoking $(+)$ may damage (n) my health $(+)$, but it improves (p) my concentration $(+)$'.

The translation of triads into bands allows also for the easy description of more complex 'structures' containing numbers of interconnected bands. Such larger structures can themselves be thought of as balanced or imbalanced, depending on whether the component bands are consistent or inconsistent. Rosenberg and Abelson hypothesized that, when subjects are presented with an imbalanced structure, they will tend to follow the 'least effortful' path towards the restoration of balance, that is, they will try to keep the number of changes in their evaluations of individual entities and relations to a minimum.

Congruity theory

Osgood and Tannenbaum's (1955) congruity theory is an application of the consistency principle to the specific question of how a person's attitude may change when exposed to a persuasive message of communication. The variables considered are: (1) the individual's initial attitude towards the *source* of the message, (2) the individual's initial attitude towards the *concept* evaluated by the source, and (3) the nature of the evaluative *assertion* about the concept contained in the message. Both (1) and (2) are defined in terms of a single evaluative scale of approval–disapproval from $+3$ to -3, which is essentially the 'good–bad' scale of the semantic differential (Osgood, Suci and Tannenbaum, 1957). The assertion is treated simply as either *associative* (the source approves of the concept) or *disassociative* (the source disapproves of the concept). These three variables are analogous to the three relations of a Heider triad, corresponding respectively to the *po, px* and *ox* relations. Whereas Heider treated all three relations as dichotomies, Osgood and Tannenbaum treat the first two, but not the third, as continua. The fact that the value of the assertion is treated as a simple dichotomy indicates that congruity theory applies strictly only to those cases where the source advocates full, unambiguous approval or disapproval of the concept. The theory is not concerned with changes in a person's perception of the content of the message, but is concerned with changes in how the concept and the source are evaluated.

The basic congruity principle is that 'changes in evaluation are always in the direction of increased congruity with the existing frame of reference' (Osgood and Tannenbaum, 1955: 43). If there is an *associative* bond between source and concept, maximal congruity obtains if both occupy the same positive on the evaluative scale. If the bond is a *dissociative* one, maximal congruity obtains if source and concept occupy symmetrical positions on opposite sides of the neutral point on the evaluative scale, e.g. if the source is evaluated at $+2$ and the concept at -2. In a state of incongruity the person's evaluations of *both* source *and* concept are predicted to change in the direction of increased congruity. Osgood and Tannenbaum also assume that the amount a person's evaluation of either source or concept will change will be inversely proportionate to the extremity of that evaluation. This is compatible with the notion that extreme judgements are made with greater confidence and are therefore less liable to change.

In the basic formulation, both source and concept are referred to simply as 'objects of judgement' and are treated as equivalent as far as predictions of change are concerned. However, since the attitude change effects observed in empirical studies did not show a perfect correspondence with the predictions of this model, Osgood and Tannenbaum introduced two modifications. The first of these is a 'correction for incredulity', based upon the assumption that 'the amount of incredulity produced when one object of judgement is associated with another by an assertion is a positively accelerated function of the amount of incongruity which exists' (1955: 47). 'Incredulity' is used as a blanket term in this context, and can best be regarded as a general resistance to communications which are incompatible with one's previous beliefs about the relation between source and concept. The second modification is an 'assertion constant' which embodies the prediction that, over and above any effects due to the person's evaluation of the source, the concept will become slightly more positively evaluated if praised and slightly more negatively evaluated if denounced by the source.

Osgood and Tannenbaum are careful to point out that their model does not attempt to account for all the variables which could produce or inhibit attitude change. To consider the function of a persuasive communication merely to be that of establishing an associative or disassociative bond between source and concept, is clearly an oversimplification. The model establishes a conceptual bridge between the notion of cognitive consistency and the associationist learning principle that stimuli come to take on the valence of other stimuli with which they are associated. At the same time, the predictions of congruity theory apply only to attitude change which occurs within 'the existing frame of reference'. How such a frame of reference becomes established is an important question which the theory leaves unanswered.

The notion of cognitive consistency can therefore be used to predict changes in attitude in response to persuasive communications. The question of the success of such predictions is largely a question of the limiting conditions of the consistency principle, and the relationship between this principle and other cognitive biases. In this connection, some of Newcomb's (1981) conclusions in relation to balance and attraction are salutary:

> There are exceptions to the balance principle. Forces toward balance may or may not be compatible with other forces. Commitment to values, regardless of others' opinions, may outweigh the satisfaction of matching agreement with attraction. Subgroup membership and norm formation appear to be the stronger forces that can outweigh preferences for balance. (p. 866)

Conformity and social influence

Against the prediction of consistency theories that we will tend to accept the opinions of others we like or respect, may be set the simpler notion that we will tend to conform with what others say and do, and particularly when others say and do things as a group. In one of the classic studies of social psychology, Sherif (1935) demonstrated that individuals would rely upon the responses of other people, albeit no more expert than themselves, when making judgements about an ambiguous perceptual stimulus, so that judgements made in a group setting would show a convergence towards a collective norm. His study made use of the optical illusion known as the autokinetic phenomenon, first noted by astronomers. If a stationary point of light is shown against a completely dark background, so that there is no visible frame of reference, it will appear to wander or waver. Subjects will then be found to give varying estimates of the amount the point of light has moved. Sherif compared two conditions, one where subjects first made judgements individually, and then were brought together into a group, and another where the order of sessions was reversed. In the first condition, subjects modified their initial individual judgements so as to lessen the discrepancy between themselves and the other group members. In the second condition, the collective norm established in the group session still affected subjects' judgements when made individually. There was even evidence of some influence due to the collective norm when subjects were re-tested one year later.

One legacy of this study has been the work described in Chapter 8 on the role of situational ambiguity on bystander intervention in emergencies. Other research, based more directly on Sherif's paradigm, has examined whether the emergence of a collective norm is inevitable in such situations, or whether it depends upon subjects' expectations about the stimulus, and their relationships with one another. Sperling (1946) compared Sherif's original situation, in which subjects were led to believe that the point of light really would move, with a situation in which they were told that: 'This is just an optical illusion and the only truth is what each of you sees.' While replicating Sherif's results in the first condition, Sperling found that 60 per cent of the subjects in the second condition showed no convergence either towards the judgements of the other group members, or to those made by an experimental confederate.

In a similar vein, Alexander, Zucker and Brody (1970) informed subjects that the phenomenon was in fact an illusion, before asking them to make judgements of the apparent movement of the point of light over a series of trials, first individually and then in pairs. Neither set of responses showed any convergence, remaining as variable at the end as at the beginning of the session. In a second experiment, subjects were not informed about the nature of the illusion, but were instead paired with a confederate of the experimenter who made increasingly convergent and stable responses over time, or alternatively made judgements that became increasingly divergent and variable. In the former condition, subjects' responses became increasingly close to those of the stooge, whereas in the second they appeared to give up the attempt to make their responses either internally consistent or consistent with those of the stooge.

Other studies have explored the effects of subjects' attraction towards others in a group (or dyadic) judgement situation, and have suggested a greater tendency for judgements to converge when the interpersonal relationships are positive. Sampson and Insko (1964) found that subjects' judgements converged towards those of a likeable confederate, but diverged from those of an objectionable confederate. Pollis (1967) found that pairs of subjects who were friends made judgements closer to each other, and stood by their initial responses more when afterwards paired with a stranger, than did pairs of subjects who initially did not know each other. Similarly Pollis and Montgomery (1968), using the autokinetic phenomenon, had subjects make judgements either individually, partnered by a friend, or partnered by a stranger, before making judgements individually

in a second phase of the experiment. The subjects who were initially partnered by a friend showed less change between the two phases, and less
variability of judgement within the second phase.

Status as well as friendship can also affect such judgements. Sampson
(cited by Sherif and Sherif, 1969: 169) used members of a monastery as
subjects. Each subject was paired with another whose initial judgements of
the autokinetic phenomenon showed an average discrepancy of about
twelve centimetres from their own. Within this restriction, three kinds of
couples were formed: (1) couples of young novices after only one week of
noviciate who barely knew each other; (2) couples of novices who had been
together for a year and therefore knew each other well (account was also
taken of their sociometric choices, so that one member of each pair was the
first choice of his partner, but had not placed his partner among his top three
choices); (3) unequal couples consisting of novices and non-novices. In the
first condition, subjects were influenced by each other and tended to
converge over time. In the second condition, they also converged, but the
less preferred member of each pair shifted his judgements most. In the final
condition, the higher status non-novices showed the greater stability in
their judgements, while the novices initially shifted their judgements
towards those of their partner, before going back to their original position.
(For a more general discussion of the maintenance of orthodox beliefs
within religious communities, see Deconchy, 1984.)

There seems reasonable evidence, therefore, that individuals will tend to
be influenced by one another when making judgements of ambiguous
perceptual stimuli in a dyad or group setting. Nonetheless, the emergence
of a 'collective norm' is by no means as automatic as Sherif may have
originally supposed. Convergence of judgement is generally more marked
when the others are more liked, or perceived as more similar to oneself. Also
of critical importance is the extent to which subjects are, or are not, led to
believe that the phenomenon they have to judge is objective or illusory.
Whereas disagreement over the size of an illusion is quite tolerable,
disagreement over objective reality is far less so. Some initial disagreement
is nonetheless to be expected, even when judging objective reality, where
the judgement task is difficult. In such situations, the adoption of a
'collective norm' is by no means an irrational solution, but on the contrary
may be seen as a quite efficient way of estimating the correct answer.

If Sherif's (1935) results depend partly on the ambiguity of the stimulus
presented for judgement, the same cannot so clearly be said of the experiments by Asch (1951, 1956) which established the term 'conformity' as a
major part of the social psychologist's explanatory repertoire, but which still
have subtleties which resist easy explanation. His basic paradigm was as
follows: imagine you are one of a group of subjects numbering somewhere
between four and ten seated together in front of a screen, and asked to judge
the lengths of sets of lines. The judgements require a comparison of a

standard line with a simultaneously presented set of three comparison lines, of which one is equal in length to the standard. Each subject in turn has to say out loud which of the three comparison lines is equal to the standard. The discrimination is so easy that mistakes are quite implausible. On two-thirds of the trials, however, you hear all the others unanimously give a response which is blatantly wrong. Usually it is your turn to respond last. In fact, the other subjects are all confederates of the experimenter responding in accordance with instructions. As the experiment progresses you exhibit growing nervousness. Sometimes you get out of your seat to go and look at the lines from the same angle as the other subjects; sometimes you hesitate before responding; sometimes you make the correct response; sometimes you conform to the incorrect response given by the rest of the group; and sometimes you even give a response which is incorrect but different from the group response.

Over a variety of conditions, the proportion of incorrect conformist responses made by naive subjects averages out at about one in three. This proportion is lower if there are fewer than four people in the group, but remains essentially unchanged for groups containing from three to sixteen confederates in addition to the single naive subject. Beyond a certain point, therefore, the absolute size of the majority does not seem to matter. What does seem to matter very considerably, however, is if the naive subject has an 'ally' among the confederates. If this ally responds correctly throughout, the subject's level of conformity to the majority response is very drastically reduced. If the ally starts by giving correct judgements, but then adopts the majority norm, the subject tends to conform at the typical level (one trial in three) on later trials. On the other hand, if the ally starts giving correct responses only on the later trials, the subject shows greater independence as the experiment goes on. It should be stressed that Asch does not claim that incorrect conformity is the predominant or typical response. Indeed, only a minority of subjects contributed the majority of the errors (Harris, 1985). However, for Asch, the important finding was that there was any conformity at all. Although very few of his subjects showed total conformity, about three-quarters of them gave at least one incorrect response.

The importance of unanimity is underlined by Mouton, Blake and Olmstead (1956), who seated subjects in separate cubicles where they were asked to estimate the number of metronome clicks in sequences of 14, 32, or 49 clicks played back to them through earphones at the rate of 180 per minute. This was, therefore, a rather more ambiguous situation than that used by Asch, but less so than that used by Sherif. Before making their responses, each subject also heard what were supposedly the responses of four other subjects. These responses were in fact pre-recorded, and either under- or over-estimated the correct number of clicks on each trial by one, two or three. In one condition, when the responses of the pre-recorded majority were unanimous, more than half the total number of subjects' responses conformed to the majority norm. However, when the majority was not unanimous, the subjects accepted the normative response on only one occasion out of eight.

How is this importance of unanimity to be interpreted? Is what is crucial the lack of consensus within the majority, or the fact that the subject has direct support for his or her own judgement from another person? An experiment which allows us to distinguish these two possibilities was performed by Allen and Levine (1968). In one of their conditions, the majority responded incorrectly, apart from one confederate who gave the correct responses. In another condition, this confederate disagreed with the majority, but in fact gave a response which was even more incorrect than the majority norm. In both these conditions, the number of trials on which the naive subject conformed to the majority norm was greatly reduced, suggesting that the lack of consensus within the majority, rather than the presence of social support for the naive subject, is the crucial factor.

Such an interpretation makes a number of assumptions. It assumes that if you are the naive subject you regard the other subjects as making their responses in good faith, which implies that you do not see through the experimental deception. Conformity experiments are now so much a part of the folklore of social psychology that this might appear a risky assumption. However, it has to be remembered that, at the time, these were novel procedures, and subjects were less hypersensitive to deceptive manipulations generally. Other cultural changes may also have occurred that make any contemporary replication more difficult (Perrin and Spencer, 1981). Another assumption is that the naive subject's response is also made in reasonably good faith. You may not know what's up with your eyesight, but if *everyone* else agrees on a different answer, perhaps they are right and you are wrong. In other words, this interpretation assumes that the main influence of the group is at a cognitive level – the unanimous opposition of the other members of the group makes you less certain of your own judgement.

Such feelings of uncertainty might be quite confusing and distressing. Indeed, the problem is one to which there is no easy solution. Sometimes your perceptions do coincide with the judgements of the other group members, but there seems no way in which you can predict when this will happen. If anything, things get worse rather than better as the experiment progresses. (The confederates in fact gave correct responses on trials 1, 2, 5, 10, 11 and 14 of the 18 trials in the Asch, 1956, experiment.) Such confusion and distress, however, is, as described, still a personal affair. You ask yourself, 'What's happening to me?' and cannot find an answer.

This is very different from an alternative interpretation, which assumes that you fear ridicule or rejection by the group if you make a deviant response. In other words, the question you ask yourself is not, 'What's happening to me?' but instead, 'What will happen to me?' In support of this possibility, it should be remembered that the naive subject is typically readily identifiable by the other members of the group. In the Asch studies, you would be sitting together with them in the same room. In the Mouton *et al.* (1956) study you would have to speak your name before giving your response. If you make a deviant response, everyone will know.

There is also evidence, in a different situation, that deviants are rejected by other group members. Schachter (1951) had groups of students discuss a short case history concerning a juvenile delinquent, and recommend alternative courses of action, varying in harshness or leniency. A confederate who stubbornly defended a punitive recommendation, to which the majority was opposed, was clearly rejected by the other subjects, and was rated as an undesirable group-member. The largest proportion of remarks made during the discussion was also addressed to this confederate. In comparison, a confederate who adopted the modal position of the group was not rejected, and was addressed less frequently in the discussion, whereas another who moved from a deviant to a modal position in the course of the discussion received fewer communications after changing his position.

Possibly Asch's subjects feared a similar kind of rejection if they disagreed with the majority. This seems less likely in view of the fact that no group discussion took place, and is not easily reconciled with the findings that the unanimity of the majority was far more important than its sheer numerical preponderance. Nonetheless, one needs to know what would happen if subjects were able to make their responses in private, unobserved by other members of the group. Deutsch and Gerard (1955) found that subjects made, on average, just over 7 out of 13 conforming responses in an Asch line-judgement situation when responding publicly. Significantly fewer conforming responses were made when the naive subject responded in private, but the level (just under 6 out of 13) is still very high for any attempt to 'explain away' Asch's results as purely the results of a fear of rejection. Similar conclusions come from a study by Raven (1959), who presented subjects with the same case description used by Schachter (1951). Having made initial recommendations individually, subjects were presented with false information that the other members of the group, unlike them, were mostly in favour of an extremely punitive solution. Each subject was then asked to write an account of the case, either anonymously, or so that it could be passed round for the other group members to see. Having done so, the subjects again made individual recommendations. Of those who expected their accounts to be passed around, 39 per cent yielded to the bogus majority, as compared with 26 per cent of those who had no such expectation. Once again, fear of being an *identified* deviate appears to have some effect, but not to be the whole story.

On balance, the evidence from studies of group influence on individual judgements, both in cases where the stimulus is ambiguous, and more dramatically even when it is not, suggested that a conforming response is best seen as an attempted solution to a dilemma that is essentially cognitive in nature. How do you deal with the fact that your perceptions appear to be different from those of other people who appear similar to yourself? There is no real problem if the others' responses are in any way an unstable variable. The stimulus is simply not the kind of stimulus where one gets inter-observer consensus. But if everyone else is in consensus, some cognitive work has to be done: cognitive, that is, but not necessarily perceptual. There is an important middle ground between viewing a conforming response as a deliberate lie, and supposing that naive subjects begin to actually 'see' the stimuli in accordance with the majority norm. This is perhaps a reasonable possibility in the case of the autokinetic phenomenon, but rather less so in the Asch experiments. But we do not need to go nearly this far. It is enough to say that the violation of expectations can make you uncertain as to which *response* is correct. Such uncertainty is likely to be even greater if your perceptions remain veridical, since then your expectations will remain violated. The problem is not whether your perceptions are in fact accurate, but whether you have confidence that they are. If such confidence is undermined, you may respond, even in private, in accordance with what you think you *ought* to see. That is, you may give the response which you regard as the best estimate of the correct answer, even if it does not correspond to what you *actually* see.

Groupthink

Despite the cognitive functions that conformity may serve, social psychologists have often, and perhaps predominantly, emphasized the dangers for individuals and society at large of simply going along with the group. This is probably nowhere more evident than in Janis's (1972, 1983) identification of the phenomenon of 'groupthink' as a feature of bad political decision-making. Janis (1983: 41) lists eight symptoms of groupthink:

1. An illusion of invulnerability, shared by most or all the members, which creates excessive optimism and encourages taking extreme risks;
2. Collective efforts to rationalize in order to discount warnings which might lead the members to reconsider their assumption before they recommit themselves to their past policy decisions;
3. An unquestioned belief in the group's inherent morality, inclining the members to ignore the ethical or moral consequences of their decisions;
4. Stereotyped views of rivals and enemies as too evil to warrant genuine attempts to negotiate, or as too weak and stupid to counter whatever risky attempts are made to defeat their purposes;
5. Direct pressure on any member who expresses strong arguments against any of the group's stereotypes, illusions, or commitments, making clear that this type of dissent is contrary to what is expected of all loyal members;

6. Self-censorship of deviations from the apparent group consensus, reflecting each member's inclination to minimize to himself the importance of his doubts and counterarguments;

7. A shared illusion of unanimity concerning judgements conforming to the majority view (partly resulting from self-censorship of deviations, augmented by the false assumption that silence means consent);

8. The emergence of self-appointed mindguards – members who protect the group from adverse information that might shatter their shared complacency about the effectiveness and morality of their decision.

Among the historical events that Janis suggests reveal these symptoms are Chamberlain's policy of appeasement of Hitler in 1937–1938, the failure of the US Navy to anticipate the Japanese attack on Pearl Harbour and various blunders by US Presidents and their advisers: by Truman over escalation of the Korean war, by Kennedy over the Bay of Pigs, by Johnson over escalation of the Vietnam war and by Nixon over Watergate (Raven, 1974). From analysis of the public statements on foreign policy issues by those involved in decisions that did or did not manifest groupthink, Tetlock (1979) found evidence of more positive references to the US and its allies, and more simplistic perceptions of issues, among groupthink decision-makers.

A question raised by such research is whether it is merely the pressures of an immediate crisis that produce groupthink, or whether institutional factors may help select for positions of responsibility individuals who may be most liable to show these kinds of biases. In a discussion of military competence and incompetence, Dixon (1976) has proposed that military institutions have often helped promote individuals whose personalities *least* suit them for high command, so that the creative military commander is not just the exception, but someone who succeeds *despite* the system.

Types and techniques of influence

A number of researchers have attempted to classify the ways in which people influence others. Of particular importance is the description by French and Raven (1959) of different bases of 'social power'. These consist of: (1) *Coercive power*, stemming from the ability of the influencing agent to dispense or permit punishment of the target; (2) *Reward power*, stemming from the agent's ability to dispense or allow rewards; (3) *Legitimate power*, which depends on the target's acceptance of role obligations to follow the agent's instuctions or advice; (4) *Reference power*, which occurs when the target uses the agent (or others) as a frame of reference (see Chapter 5, pp. 128–30) for evaluating his or her own behaviour, and identifies with the agent; (5) *Expert power*, stemming from the agent being seen by the target as having superior knowledge and ability; and (6) *Informational power* (not originally distinguished as a power base in its own right), which depends on the persuasiveness of the information conveyed by the agent.

Raven and Haley (1982) have applied this framework to the problem of how to reduce the incidence of infections contracted in hospitals. Their research considers the role of specialist 'Infection Control Nurses' (ICNs) entrusted with the task of enforcing compliance by hospital staff with approved hygienic precautions. When asked how they would try and influence physicians and staff nurses, the ICNs claimed they would predominantly rely on informational and expert power in their interactions with physicians, and on informational power in their interactions with staff nurses. Coercive power was much more likely to be used towards staff nurses than physicians. However, the staff nurses themselves denied that they would comply just because of the ICNs' coercive power.

A conceptual difficulty with this classification concerns the independence or interdependence of the different bases. Could an agent claim expert power for long without providing information? The invocation of coercive or reward power may be interpreted very differently if the agent is also seen as having legitimate power than if legitimacy is perceived to be lacking. Podsakoff and Schriesheim (1985) have reviewed a large number of field studies that relate outcomes such as subordinates' job performance to their ratings of the bases of power used by their supervisors. Podsakoff and Schriesheim conclude that the measures used typically involve inadequate operationalizations of the French and Raven (1959) categories, so that a conclusive study of the interrelationships between the different power bases within the context of organizational behaviour has yet to be conducted.

Cialdini (1984) has documented a number of the techniques used by members of 'compliance professions' (e.g. advertising, direct sales) and discusses the relationship of these to psychological processes. Cialdini's strategy involved personally undertaking training or employment in such professions, with his immediate colleagues (at least) being unaware that he was anything other than an ordinary employee. The principles identified by Cialdini as underlying the most frequent, adaptable and widespread of such techniques include:

> Consistency. Many tactics involve trying to make potential customers feel inconsistent if they do not buy the product or services on offer. If one is induced to commit oneself to a position (e.g. that one cares about one's child's education or one's family's security), then one will subsequently be more likely to comply with requests for behaviour consistent with such commitment (e.g. buying encyclopaedias or life-insurance). Special offers can elicit commitment to buy at a particular store, even when the special offers are 'sold out' and only more expensive goods are available (termed 'bait-and-switch'). Similarly the 'low-ball' technique involves inducing early commitment by offering goods for sale at an apparently low price that then fails to include expensive extras.

Reciprocity. This is most evident in the use of 'free' samples and gifts in promotion. Also dealers may offer 'special' discounts.

Social validation. This involves persuading customers that others similar to them have chosen the product on offer. Reingen (1982), for instance, found that people were more likely to donate to a charity when shown a long list of previous donors.

Authority. This essentially involves a claim by the influence agent to have what French and Raven (1959) would term legitimate and/or expert power.

Scarcity. This relies on customers placing a higher value on what they believe to be in short supply ('limited edition') or only available for a short time ('while stocks last').

Friendship/liking. This capitalizes on people's tendency to comply with requests from others whom they like. Sales staff are therefore trained to present themselves as the customer's 'friend'. (I still remember being sold a car in Canada by a salesman who insisted on calling me 'John'. He'll never know how near he came to losing the sale!)

Cialdini refers to such techniques as forms of 'automatic influence', by which he does not mean that their effectiveness is inevitable, but rather that they exploit the tendency of people, faced with a request for compliance, to rely on overlearned routines, rules-of-thumb or 'heuristics' (see Chapter 7), that enable behavioural decisions to be made 'automatically' without a full processing of the relevant information. This re-emphasizes the point that principles of psychological consistency, and similar notions, should not be viewed necessarily as a reflection of any precisely logical rationalism, but rather as devices for making thoughts easier and simpler.

Persuasive language

Simplification and selectivity are thus *not* incompatible with the principle of consistency. They are the other side of the same coin. This is implied by Osgood and Tannenbaum's (1955) formulation of congruity theory to predict attitude change 'within the existing frame of reference'. The concept of 'frame of reference' will recur frequently in this book (particularly in Chapter 5). For the time being, it may be taken to refer to those stimuli and specific attributes of stimuli (or aspects of issues) that form the *context* within which, and relative to which, an object is evaluated. Objects are not evaluated relative to *everything*, but relative to *selected* standards of relevant comparison.

From this one can derive the prediction that attitude change may be produced by inducing people to think of an issue in terms of one 'frame of reference' rather than another. One way of doing this may be to have subjects structure their own views on an issue in terms of language that contains a definite evaluative bias, one way or another. Two studies, by

Eiser and Ross (1977) and Eiser and Pancer (1979), have examined the hypothesis that, when this is done, subjects will change their reported attitudes towards greater congruity with the evaluative implications of the language they are obliged to use.

The main experiment reported by Eiser and Ross (1977) consisted of a comparison between a *pro-bias* condition, in which subjects were induced to use words consistent with a pro attitude, and an *anti-bias* condition, in which they were induced to use words consistent with an anti attitude. The prediction was that those in the former condition should shift their attitudes in a more pro direction, as compared with those in the latter condition, who should shift their attitudes in a more anti direction. The subjects for this experiment were Canadian introductory psychology students, who had completed a questionnaire during a lecture period to measure their attitudes on a number of topics, including the critical issue, capital punishment. About one week later, they were contacted by telephone and asked to take part in an ostensibly unconnected experiment in psycholinguistics. On their arrival, they were instructed to write an essay on the topic of capital punishment, incorporating as many words as possible from a list of 15, the supposed aim being to see how this affected the 'stylistic structure and verbal fluency' of their essays. In the pro-bias condition, all the words in the list implied a negative evaluation of the abolitionist position (e.g. over-sentimental, starry-eyed). In the anti-bias condition, they all implied a negative evaluation of capital punishment (e.g. callous, sadistic). Subjects were *not* told to write either for or against capital punishment, but only to use the words provided.

After writing the essay, subjects had to rate their own opinion towards capital punishment. They were also divided into a pro and an anti group on the basis of their attitudes towards capital punishment expressed in the previous questionnaire. As can be see from Table 2.1, the pro group rated themselves much more pro than the anti group in both conditions, indicating that their attitudes on this issue were reasonably stable. Nonetheless, the predicted effect, for the self-ratings to be more positive in the pro-bias condition, achieved significance. Table 2.1 also shows the mean number of words out of 15 incorporated in the essays by each group of subjects, and, as can be seen, subjects used more words if they were given a list which was evaluatively congruent with their own attitude.

Eiser and Pancer (1979) used a similar design, with British teenagers as subjects, the issues being that of adult authority over young people. The attitude shifts found by Eiser and Ross were replicated with biased word lists which included both evaluatively positive and evaluatively negative labels. No change in attitude was observed in a control condition, in which subjects also wrote an essay but were given no words to incorporate. However, one week later it was found that these shifts had largely disappeared. Thus, although the initial changes were consistent with predic-

Table 2.1. *Mean self-ratings of attitude following essay-writing, and mean number of words from list of 15 incorporated by each group of subjects, in the Eiser and Ross (1977) study*

	Pro-bias		Anti-bias	
Initial attitude	Pro	Anti	Pro	Anti
Self-rating	88.5	29.3	61.0	19.6
Number of words	11.0	8.3	8.7	11.3

Note: 0 extremely unfavourable, 100 extremely favourable.

tion, no claim is made that this kind of manipulation (or at any rate a single trial of it) can produce long-term shifts in attitudinal responses.

An additional question concerns the relationship between evaluative language and what Abelson (1976, 1981) has referred to as 'scripts' (see Chapter 7, pp. 239–40). Basic to the notion of scripts is the idea that individuals organize their cognitions in terms of interrelated propositions which may be expressed linguistically. Changes in such organization, and hence in attitude, could follow if individuals are led to use particular kinds of scripts, or to modify their existing scripts in particular ways. It is possible that repeated exposure to (and/or use of) evaluatively biased language might have this effect, but when Eiser and Ross required subjects to incorporate short arguments (e.g. 'Capital punishment is primitive') instead of single words, no attitude change was observed.

There is considerable evidence of a less experimental nature, however, that points to the fact that evaluatively biased labels or slogans are used to change people's attitudes. Even if the claimed effectiveness of such techniques may sometimes be exaggerated, the concept of a product's 'image' is basic to most commercial advertising. What is being communicated is typically a positive evaluation. Political propaganda contains many examples of slogans whose purpose is hardly to convey 'information', but rather to suggest a way of categorizing uncertain events and situations. For evidence of the explicit assumptions behind one of the most obscene, but effective, campaigns of political persuasion in recent history, we need to look no further than the following remarkable passage by Hadamovsky (1933), a deputy to Goebbels:

> The unsophisticated man, and even more so the broad masses, will almost invariably yield to the power of the word, without concern for its inner truth. It is not the truth inherent in the word itself which gives the lie to that has been said, but rather a new word pitted against the old . . . Politics avails itself of the technique of creating expressions to win over the masses and to hold new followers forever within the spell of a definite conception and *Weltanschauung* . . . The French revolution set in motion the era of the struggles of the masses . . . The refined old language of diplomacy yielded to the earthy and impetuous terminology of political mass propaganda . . .

Liberty, equality, fraternity, capitalism, socialism, communism, profit, surplus value, proceeds, world economy, Soviet Germany, nationalism, blood, soil, race, autarchy, the Third Reich, these are some of the slogans of this language, slogans which by themselves as well as in their derivations encompass entire *Weltanschauungen*. They beat down on the adversary, pound him, create doubt, fear, repulsion and agreement. To those who believe in these slogans they appear as positive promises of a brighter future . . . The political system is suddenly confronted by an enigmatic linguistic ogre, a flood of alien concepts through which he receives a strictly one-sided impression of a world mysteriously confined and stupefying. Thus he is faced by a linguistic monster manifesting itself through words – recruiting and organizing.

Whilst remembering the horrific effects of such 'recruiting and organizing', however, we should not assume that it was merely 'the power of the word' alone that was responsible for the Nazis' rise to power and the behavioural compliance of the German people as a whole. Techniques of persuasion may be effective in producing attitude change without *directly* producing behavioural compliance.

A tamer and more recent example of behavioural compliance on a national scale involves legislation that has made the use of seat-belts compulsory in Britain for car-drivers and front-seat passengers. The suggestion of earlier research (e.g. Cliff, Catford, Dillow and Swann, 1980) was that health education aimed at persuading drivers to use seat-belts was largely ineffective at a behavioural level, despite public acceptance at an attitudinal level of the advantages of seat-belts and even of the desirability of making their use compulsory. When such legislation was eventually passed, despite the opposition of those who regarded it as an infringement of personal liberty, the new laws produced a very high degree of compliance. Thus, attitude change may have been needed for the coercive legislation to be publicly acceptable, but without such coercion, attitude change did not translate into behavioural compliance.

Cognitive responses to persuasion

Attitude change, then, can be observed in many different kinds of situations, inside and outside the laboratory. But *how* does such change occur? What psychological processes are involved? In the opinion of many researchers (e.g. Himmelfarb and Eagly, 1974), these are the kind of questions to which we should not expect a single answer. Nonetheless, some recurrent themes are emerging in contemporary research, of which one of the most important is a consideration of what people think about when they are exposed to a persuasive communication, and how they process the information to which they are exposed.

The 'elaboration-likelihood model'

One of the most ambitious attempts to integrate such research is the 'elaboration-likelihood model' of Petty and Cacioppo (1985). The name derives from the central importance they attach to variables affecting the likelihood that recipients of a message will 'elaborate', in their own minds, the information conveyed to them in the message and scrutinize carefully the arguments that the message contains. Persuasion, in other words, is mediated by the thoughts in which people engage on exposure to a communication. The extent of such thought or 'elaboration' is measured in various ways, for instance by having subjects list any thoughts that come to mind (Brock, 1967; Greenwald, 1968a) or through the recording of physiological correlates of cognitive activity (Cacioppo, 1979).

Of special importance is the assumption that such elaboration (production of thoughts and arguments) is *self-generated*, so that the recipient is viewed as an active processor of information. For instance, Cialdini, Petty and Cacioppo (1981: 359–60) interpret the Eiser and Ross (1977) and Eiser and Pancer (1979) studies as showing that, when subjects have to generate their *own* arguments, this produces attitude change, but when they are given ready-made arguments no elaboration and hence no attitude change occurs.

Basic to Petty and Cacioppo's model is a distinction between what they call the 'central' and 'peripheral' routes to persuasion. The central route involves thoughtful, though possibly biased, weighing up of relevant arguments (a high 'elaboration likelihood'). The peripheral route involves affective associations and simple inferences from cues in the 'persuasion context', but little consideration of arguments *per se* (a low 'elaboration likelihood'). Petty and Cacioppo hypothesize that attitude change via the central route is more persistent, resistant to counter-argument and predictive of behaviour than change produced via the peripheral route.

Empirical tests of the model have often involved looking for interactions between message quality and other variables, the logic being that, if a message contains strong arguments, more detailed thought about it will produce greater attitude change, whereas if the arguments are weak, more thought will produce less change. Different studies have therefore employed different manipulations to produce high versus low likelihood of elaborated thought regarding the content of communications.

Petty, Wells and Brock (1976), for instance, found that if subjects were *distracted* during presentation of a message, this impeded persuasion (and facilitated the subsequent production of counter-arguments) if the arguments in the message were strong, but increased persuasion (and inhibited the subsequent production of counter-arguments) if the arguments were weak. *Repetition* of messages similarly has been found to enhance persuasion if arguments are strong but to impede it if they are weak (Cacioppo and Petty, 1979).

Petty and Cacioppo (1979) manipulated subjects' *involvement* with the issue of a communication by using topics which were or were not personally relevant. This was achieved by using messages proposing policy changes (regarding visiting restrictions, or examinations) relating either to the students' own or another university. The idea was that subjects would be more motivated to process the arguments carefully if they were personally relevant than if they were irrelevant. Consistent with this, more acceptance of the message was found under conditions of high involvement if the arguments presented were strong, but under conditions of low involvement if the arguments were weak. Petty and Cacioppo (1985), however, add the warning that, for real issues, involvement is likely to be confounded with the amount of prior thinking a person has done about an issue.

Petty, Harkins and Williams (1980) demonstrated that the degree of *personal responsibility* for evaluating a message produced analogous effects to those of involvement. If subjects were led to believe that they were the only people responsible for evaluating a message (supposedly an editorial written by a journalism student), they gave more positive evaluations of strong messages, than in a condition where they believed that they were only one of a group of ten evaluators.

Attributes of the individuals presented with a message may also influence the kind and amount of processing that the message receives. Cacioppo and Petty (1982) and Cacioppo, Petty and Kao (1984) have developed a scale for the measurement of individual difference in what they term *'need for cognition'*. Among the items included are: 'I like tasks that require little thought once I've learned them', 'Thinking is not my idea of fun' and 'I would prefer complex to simple problems'. There would seem to be a good case for a more complete investigation of the discriminant validity (Campbell and Fiske, 1959) of this scale – that is, the extent to which it is tapping an attribute which is *not* being measured by other tests of cognitive style (Cacioppo and Petty, 1982, report a positive association here) or of cognitive complexity. Nonetheless, taken at face value, the scale does seem to predict the extent to which individuals will think deeply about arguments, so that, once again, there is evidence of message acceptance depending on an interaction involving message quality. High 'need for cognition' enhances acceptance of stronger arguments and inhibits acceptance of weaker arguments.

Petty and Cacioppo (1985) also discuss factors that may bias a person's thoughts about an issue. Here differences in *prior knowledge* and initial *attitude* are predicted to lead to differential processing of information, depending on whether it confirms or contradicts a person's existing opinion. *Forewarning* of the content of a message can also lead to people generating either counter-arguments (Petty and Cacioppo, 1977) or changing their opinions towards one they feel more able to defend (termed 'anticipatory belief change' by McGuire and Millman, 1965). Closely related is McGuire's (1964) suggestion that one can 'inoculate' people against the effects of persuasion by first presenting them with weak arguments on an issue, against which they are able to generate their own counter-arguments to defend their own position. Petty and Cacioppo (1977) found that student subjects who were forewarned about the content of a message (advocating an unpopular proposal on student residence) and/or had to write down their own thoughts on the issue before hearing the message, showed less change than those who were unwarned. The inference they draw is that it is not forewarning *per se* that inhibits persuasion, but the generation of counter-arguments to bolster one's existing opinion. Petty and Cacioppo (1979) also found that the effects of forewarning were stronger under conditions of greater personal relevance.

Unresolved issues in the 'cognitive response' approach

The elaboration-likelihood model can certainly claim applicability to a wide range of attitude change phenomena. However, a number of ambiguities remain. The question of *how* attitude change occurs is only partly answered by saying that it depends on the thoughts that subjects generate in response to persuasive message. We are still left with the question of how *thoughts* produce change. The assumption is that what is involved is a kind of search for consistency and truth. Petty and Cacioppo (1985) adopt Festinger's (1950) statement that 'people are motivated to hold correct attitudes' as the first postulate of their model. But how does someone decide that an attitude is correct or incorrect? By thinking? Yes, but what *kind* of thinking?

Then there is the distinction between 'central' and 'peripheral' routes to persuasion. It is difficult, also, to think of 'elaboration likelihood' as a continuum, and still allow for the plausible possibility that many persuasion contexts elicit both 'central' and 'peripheral' responses; which leads to the trickier question of how such responses interact.

The compliance techniques described by Cialdini (1984) presumably fall under the 'peripheral' heading, but these still seem to involve the use of consistency and similar principles. There are still questions to answer relating to *how* people's evaluations of objects are influenced by 'peripheral' cues of the persuasion context. A number of similar criticisms have been raised by Eagly and Chaiken (1984), who argue that the elaboration-likelihood model 'lacks clear implications regarding the persuasive impact of variables that are less obviously related to recipients' abilities or motivations to engage in message-relevant thinking' (p. 285). 'Nor, for that matter', they continue, 'do cognitive response researchers' assumptions regarding *why* variables such as involvement, multiple sources and recipients, message repetition, and rhetorical questions influence the extent of processing stem directly from the cognitive response approach. Rather, such assumptions require the importation of extratheoretical postulates and concepts' (pp. 286–7).

A variable such as the credibility of the source could well influence the kind of message-relevant thinking in which people engage (and so surely cannot be dismissed as just a peripheral cue), but on what grounds would one expect the arguments of a credible source to be subjected to more detailed appraisal, rather than taken on trust? Heesacker, Petty and Cacioppo (1983) propose that credibility should increase elaboration of arguments for more involving issues, but their data are ambiguous (see Eagly and Chaiken, 1984: 286). Furthermore, one can reasonably speculate that there may be interactions with yet other factors, such as recipients' ability to process messages – i.e. their relative expertise compared with the source. If one regards one's own expertise as low it may be a good strategy simply to accept the viewpoints of a credible source. However, processing ability has typically been manipulated experimentally (e.g. by increasing distraction) rather than by seeing how well predictions hold up using real issues concerning which people may have greater or less expertise (the safety of nuclear power plants, for instance). Indeed, a great deal of the experimental work on cognitive responses to persuasion has confined itself to somewhat parochial or small-scale attitudinal issues.

A more immediate difficulty with the 'elaboration-likelihood' treatment of variables like source credibility, however, is that emphasis on the *extent* of message-relevant thoughts may partly overlook the extent to which such thoughts are favourable or unfavourable. It may be the *favourability* of such cognitive responses, rather than their number, that is crucial (e.g. Cook, 1969). For sure, the elaboration likelihood model would have no difficulty with any finding that showed attitude change to be associated with the generation of favourable as opposed to unfavourable thoughts. The problem is one of prediction. When does one predict an effect on extent of thought and when on favourability?

As for processes involved in the 'peripheral' route to persuasion, Petty and Cacioppo (1985) adopt an eclectic theoretical approach that incorporates principles of conditioning, identification (Kelman, 1961), impression-management (Schlenker, 1980, see also Chapter 4, pp. 100–1) and 'reactance' – i.e. resistance to persuasive attempts interpreted as a threat to personal freedom (Brehm, 1966).

A different approach has been suggested by Chaiken (1980). Without denying the importance of such motivational factors, she emphasizes a distinction between 'systematic' and 'heuristic' information-processing. Systematic processing is essentially the same as the kind of cognitive responses Petty and Cacioppo hypothesize to be involved in the 'central' route to persuasion. Heuristic processing is a special subclass of the kind of process involved in the 'peripheral' route. More will be said of heuristics generally in Chapter 7. However, Cialdini's (1984) discussion of 'automatic influence' draws heavily on the same notion – that even if people do not process information thoroughly, they may do so in a predictable and rule-governed way, by using rules-of-thumb (heuristics) of the form that, if certain source or message cues are present, it is more (or less) reasonable to accept what the message says. It is one thing, though, to show that people react to such cues, another to say that they use subjective rules to guide their reactions, and yet another to say that they can report introspectively on the rules that they are using. Nonetheless, 'heuristic' approaches seem to have much to offer to a more general understanding of persuasion processes. At the very least they avoid the too-frequent assumption that social cognition can only be described in terms of quasi-logical inference and complex cerebration.

Taking a general view of the cognitive responses, there can be no doubt that the whole attitude-change field has been revitalized by it, to the extent that there is a new optimism in the search for theoretical principles, and less concern with just pointing out the limiting conditions of classic notions such as consistency. Ambiguities over the roles of particular variables (e.g. credibility) remain. Their resolution demands not just the search for higher-order interactions, but a more detailed conceptual analysis of the relationship between the content of the message itself, the thoughts about, and the thoughts stimulated by, the message, and changes in the evaluation of the attitude object and (not forgetting Osgood and Tannenbaum, 1955) of the source.

As for what should go into such a conceptual analysis, I would not hazard a bet, but I would make a bid. I should like to see more attention paid to the language in terms of which both the message itself and recipients' responses to the message are expressed. Linguistic expression is fundamental to the concepts of attitude and of attitude change. It has received rather scant attention in attitude *theory*.

Secondly, whilst researchers such as Petty and Cacioppo have looked at attitude change on issues that have *some* apparent real-life relevance for their subjects, there has been a tendency to avoid 'hotter' issues of more direct ideological conflict. Yet such issues are not hard to find. If we are asked what generalizations we can draw from this literature to provide insights into the effects of political propaganda, or into the psychological underpinnings of differences in values or ideologies, we may well *want* to say something about cognitive (and other) processes. However, on the data to hand, we would have to do a lot of extrapolating. Rather too much has to be taken on trust regarding the generalizability of conclusions to different attitude domains.

Conclusions

The research reviewed in this chapter has considered attitudes as subjective evaluative experiences, and has looked at how these experiences are organized, how they may relate to interpersonal attraction, and how they may change. Throughout this research a recurrent theme has been the notion of *consistency*. This notion implies that individuals are concerned to make sense of the world around them, and generally prefer to be able to make relatively simple evaluative judgements. As used in attitude theory, therefore, consistency is not a principle of logic, but a bias that influences the way in which our thoughts, experiences, and perhaps friendships, are organized. The precise definition of the form this bias takes, and its relative strength in different contexts and for different people, are therefore matters for empirical research. Not everyone will want to be consistent, certainly not all the time, and even when they do, the *kind* of consistency they seek may be different and dependent on the aspects of the situation that have most subjective relevance.

A brief look at research on interpersonal attraction indicates that similarity of attitudes may be an important factor in the formation and maintenance of relationships. Physical attractiveness, whether 'in person' or merely conveyed by photographs, has a simple powerful effect on initial personal evaluations. Such results should make one hesitate before trying to interpret the effect of physical attractiveness as a special case of a similarity-attraction relationship and hence as a close cousin of cognitive balance.

Attitudes and judgements (including judgements of physical stimuli) are liable to the influence of other people. In this chapter, I have only considered conformity from the perspective of how individuals may be influenced by a group, or a person in authority. The reciprocal question of how minorities can influence majorities will be held over to Chapter 9, in which I shall discuss intergroup behaviour. Even so, the message to come out of this research is that individuals do not simply conform out of fear of some unspecified consequences. Rather they use what others say as a source of information concerning what the correct judgement should be.

The concept of information-processing is fundamental to much contemporary research on persuasion and attitude change. This has looked at how the attitude change a message can produce is mediated by a person's cognitive responses – the thoughts that the message elicits. Attitude change from this perspective is an active process, involving the recipient making sense of the message received in relation to existing knowledge and values. Against this 'rationalistic' picture, however, is set the evidence that much attitude change may involve less thought-through reactions to features of the environment, of the message, or of the person who delivers it. The fact that we *can* process information in a deliberately and closely attentive way does not mean that we always do so, nor that we always need to do so.

Because of this, we remain somewhat at the mercy of persuasion by those who will use devices that are less than completely factual or logical. Since attitudes themselves are neither completely factual nor logical, we should not regard this as a cause for surprise, though it remains a cause for concern.

What, then, of the questions that remain? The first is that of the relationship of attitudes to behaviour. What differences do attitudes make to what people *do*? This will be considered in Chapter 3. Looking further ahead, there is the issue of how cognitive and motivational accounts of attitude and behaviour change interrelate (Chapter 4). The concept of attitude will also reappear in later chapters in discussions of social judgement, attributions, decision-making, equity, and intergroup relations.

Yes, the concept of attitude is indispensable to social psychology, but that does not make it easy to define. I have defined attitude as subjective evaluative experience. This makes it a psychological concept. What makes it a *social* psychological concept is the fact that such experience can be *communicated*. Because of this, attitudes can be the focus of agreement and disagreement between individuals and groups, and the touchstone for social relationships.

3
Attitudes and behaviour

Predicting behaviour from attitudes

At the beginning of Chapter 2, I said that the study of attitudes is a dangerous starting point for a book on social psychology. Probably the greatest danger concerns the predictive utility of the attitude concept. Sophisticated techiques of attitude measurement can be devised, impressive theories of attitude organization can be proposed, but if, at the end of it all, we are no more able to predict what á person will or will not do in a given situation, what use are our measurements and theories?

Some of the most surprising studies in social psychology, therefore, are those that have claimed to find little or no relation between people's behaviour and their verbally expressed attitudes. When one looks at those studies that have attempted directly to compare verbal expression of attitude towards a group or issue with other attitude-relevant behaviours, a rather confused picture emerges. Sometimes the verbal measures provide quite good predictors of the specific kinds of behaviour under investigation, but very often they seem to allow no such prediction at all. In his review of such research, Wicker (1969) concluded that only in a minority of cases was a close relationship found between verbally expressed attitudes and overt behaviour, the typical result being one of only a slight association, or no association at all. The classic study in this field is that by LaPiere (1934), who travelled across the United States over a period of two years accompanied by a Chinese couple, and noted the reactions of hoteliers and restaurateurs. During the course of their travels, 'we met definite rejection from those asked to serve us *just once*. We were received at 66 hotels, auto camps and "Tourist Homes" . . . We were served in 184 restaurants and cafes . . . and treated with . . . more than ordinary consideration in 72 of them' (p. 232). This apparent lack of prejudice at a behavioural level, however, contrasted sharply with the responses of the managers of the same establishments to a questionnaire sent out by LaPiere six months later, which asked the question, 'Will you accept members of the Chinese race as guests in your establishment?' Of the 81 restaurants and 47 hotels that replied, 92 per cent said 'No', the remainder saying, 'Uncertain; depends upon circumstances'.

A similar pattern of results was found by Kutner, Wilkins and Yarrow (1952). Their study involved two white men entering a restaurant and shortly after being joined by a black woman. In the eleven restaurants visited, the black woman was never refused admission, and the service was completely satisfactory. Later, the same restaurants received a letter asking for a reservation for a racially mixed group and when none had replied 17 days later, all received telephone calls making the same request. Only five of the restaurants then accepted the reservation (reluctantly) and six gave clear refusals. Somewhat more positive results were obtained by DeFleur and Westie (1958), who obtained verbal indices of white college students' racial attitudes during the course of an interview, and then asked them if they would be willing to have their photographs taken in the company of a black person of the opposite sex, for a range of specified purposes. Of the 23 subjects classified as 'prejudiced' on the basis of their verbal attitudes, 18 refused to be photographed, while 14 of the 23 'unprejudiced' subjects agreed to be photographed. Thus, a clear association was found between the verbal and behavioural indices of prejudice, but there were still 14 subjects (30 per cent of the sample) whose behaviour appeared discrepant from their verbally expressed attitudes.

The three-component view of attitudes

There have, therefore, been many examples where measures of attitude and behaviour fail to correlate, or where correlations are found which are ambiguous with respect to the direction of causality. Nonetheless, such results have generally failed to shake the conviction on the part of most attitude theorists that attitudes are an important, if not the major, cause of the kinds of behaviour which interest social psychologists. The most common defence is that embodied in the *three-component* view of attitudes. According to this view, 'attitudes are predispositions to respond to some class of stimuli with certain classes of response' (Rosenberg and Hovland, 1960: 3), the three major types of response being defined as *affective* (evaluative feelings and preferences), *cognitive* (opinions and beliefs), and *behavioural* or conative (overt actions and statements of intent). The relationship between these three components is represented in Figure 3.1.

Assuming that the arrows in Figure 3.1 denote the direction of causality (although the *kind* of causality that is at issue here is rarely discussed), it can be seen that the concept of attitude is being used to intervene between observable antecedent stimuli and observable subsequent responses. It is situated in the middle of the causal chain, simultaneously an *effect* and a *cause* of external observable events. The most ambiguous part of the diagram is the set of three arrows leading from the box labelled 'attitudes' to those labelled 'affect', 'cognition', and 'behaviour'. It is unclear whether the same set of 'attitudes' simultaneously causes specific affective, cognitive and behavioural effects; whether affect, cognition, and behaviour are separate components of the 'attitudes' box (i.e. the arrows should be replaced by brackets) simultaneously caused by the same antecedent stimuli; or

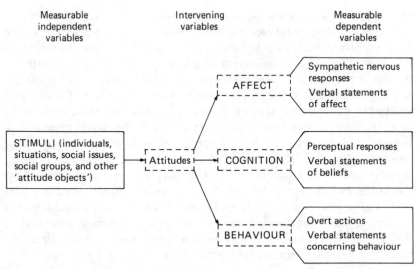

Figure 3.1. Schematic conception of attitudes in terms of three components. (Reproduced with permission of the Yale University Press, from C. I. Hovland and M. J. Rosenberg (eds.), *Attitudes, organization and change: An analysis of consistency among attitude components.* New Haven, Conn.: Yale University Press, 1960, p.3.)

whether affect, cognition and behaviour are separate components caused by separate antecedent stimuli. Finally, nothing is implied in the diagram about how affect, cognition and behaviour may directly influence one another.

This ambiguity allows attitude theorists either to treat attitudes as internally consistent structures, or as conglomerations of essentially distinct components. If one finds an apparent discrepancy between verbal attitudes and overt behaviour, this is because one is dealing with distinct components, and any complete description of a person's attitude requires that one should obtain measures of all three classes of responses, and not simply infer attitudes from the affective component alone. On the other hand, if one succeeds in predicting behaviour from a person's statements of affect or opinion, this just goes to show how closely the three components of attitude are related to one another. Thus, research on the three-component view of attitudes has alternatively emphasized the independence and interdependence of the different components. Triandis (1967) has proposed that instruments of attitude measurement should incorporate indices of all three components, and has also argued, with the support of factor-analytic data (Triandis, 1964), that the behavioural component may itself be multidimensional. For example, personal attributes that might lead others to exhibit 'friendship' towards one, would be distinct from those attributes which would elicit 'respect', 'marital acceptance', or 'deep emotional involvement'.

Ostrom (1969) constructed three types of attitude scales (Thurstone, Likert and Guttman) from each of three sets of statements concerning attitudes towards the Church, which had been previously categorized by judges as referring primarily to either affect cognition or behaviour. A three-item self-rating scale was also incorporated, with one item representing each component. In comparing the responses of subjects to the different parts of the questionnaire, Ostrom noted that the correlations between the *different* measures of any *single* component were higher than the correlations between the measures of the three *different* components by any *single* method, implying that somewhat different areas of content were being tapped by the different components (see Campbell and Fiske, 1959, for a discussion of the rationale behind this kind of analysis). For each scaling method, however, the correlations between the three components were still high (averaging approximately 0.6, 0.8, 0.5 and 0.7 on the Thurstone, Likert, Guttman and self-rating scales respectively, for a sample of 189 subjects). In addition, Ostrom asked subjects to indicate their own behaviour towards the Church in terms of seven separate criteria, which were then intercorrelated with the 12 previously derived attitude scores. The attitude–behaviour correlations were almost all positive but generally very low. The only behaviour that could be predicted from the attitude measures with reasonable confidence was the number of days per year on which subjects attended church services, and even this was not appreciably more predictable from the verbal measures of the behavioural component than from the other verbal measures. The main conclusion of Ostrom's study is nonetheless that there is support for the idea that affect, cognition and behaviour operate as distinct, though interrelated components. Using a similar application of the Campbell and Fiske (1959) procedure, Kothandapani (1971) arrived at the same conclusion from a study of attitudes towards contraception.

Since these earlier studies, powerful computer programmes have been developed for multivariate statistical analysis, and have permitted more sophisticated tests of the three-component model. One particular package, with frequent up-dates, called LISREL (Jøreskog and Sorbom, 1981), is designed specifically for looking at the relationships between inferred or 'latent' variables of which one has separate multiple measures or 'indicators'. Basically, this allows one to see whether the pattern of intercorrelations between the different indicators is compatible with a given hypothetical set of distinctions and relationships between the specified latent variables (e.g. affect, cognition, and behaviour). Breckler (1983) reanalysed the Ostrom (1969) and Kothandapani (1971) studies, and confirmed Ostrom's conclusions with reservations (although the three-component model was statistically supported, the intercorrelations between the components came out as very high – in the 0.95 region), but failed to find statistical confirmation of the three-component model in Kothandapani's data.

Breckler (1984) proposes five conditions that need to be met for a strong test of the validity of the three-component view:

(1)   Both verbal and non-verbal measures of affect and behaviour are required.

(2)   Dependent measures of affect, cognition and behaviour must take the form of responses to a *physically present* attitude object. If subjects can only respond to a symbolic or mental representation of the attitude object, one may suspect that *all* their responses will be mediated by the cognitive system, thus spuriously inflating estimates of the intercorrelations between affect, cognition and behaviour.

(3)   Multiple indicators of the three-components should be used.

(4)   A confirmatory rather than exploratory method of analysis is required (i.e. one testing *a priori* conceptual distinctions).

(5)   All dependent measures must be scaled along a common evaluative dimension.

Although some previous studies had met some of these conditions, Breckler argues that insufficient attention had been paid in particular to the importance of the verbal–non-verbal distinction and the presence/absence of the attitude object. Breckler corrects these omissions in two studies of people's attitudes towards snakes. In the first of these, student subjects provided affect, cognition and behaviour in the presence of a live snake. Affect was measured both by verbal measures and by heart rate, and behaviour by actual approach to the snake as well as reported intention. (All measures of cognition were verbal.) The results of this first study showed a very good statistical fit with the three-component model, and moderate intercorrelations between the three components (0.38 for the affect/cognition, 0.50 for affect/behaviour, and 0.70 for cognition/behaviour).

In Breckler's second study, a similar procedure was followed, with the exceptions that only verbal measures were included, and no live snake was shown to the subjects (they were instructed instead to imagine that a live snake was present). The results showed a relatively good fit to the three-component model, but not good enough for the model to be statistically accepted, and the intercorrelations between the components were higher (0.81 to 0.86).

Such findings allow us to attribute a degree of validity to the *a priori* distinctions between affect, cognition and behaviour. Such distinctions also have parallels in other branches of psychological theory, notably animal learning (e.g. Tarpy, 1982), where operant behaviour may be conceptually distinguishable from, but still influenced by, conditioned emotional states ('affect') and expectancies concerning the consequences of stimuli and response ('cognition'). What neither such findings, nor any statistical analysis using LISREL or such like, can tell us is whether these *a priori* distinctions are the best way, in general, of thinking about attitudes. The possibility always remains that some other model, incorporating alternative distinctions, could fit the data even better.

However, even if, with such reservations, we accept the three-component model as valid, it still does not provide a complete explanation of why verbal measures of attitude have often apparently failed to predict behaviour. Even the 'moderate' intercorrelations between components found by Breckler in his first study (that permit the components to be distinguished statistically) are still very high by comparison with those found in studies taken to imply an attitude-behaviour discrepancy. Breckler found behaviour to be highly predictable (even though distinguishable) from affective and cognitive measures of attitude. Distinguishability need not amount to discrepancy.

Generality versus specificity

Most attitude scales require subjects to state their agreement or disagreement with numbers of separate statements, or items. But what do these items look like? A glance at the impressive collection of attitude scales compiled by Shaw and Wright (1967) can be quite revealing. Suppose we were interested in designing a research project around a title such as 'Attitudinal factors influencing law-abiding and law-breaking'. We might not feel able to design our own scale, and so might select the Rundquist and Sletto (1936) 'Law Scale' (Shaw and Wright, 1967: 253) – a scale with quite respectable levels of reliability. We could then ask our subjects how much they agreed or disagreed with statements such as: 'The Law protects property rights at the expense of human rights'; 'On the whole, policemen are honest'; and 'A hungry man has a right to steal.' Using this scale, we might then find that right-wing students scored more 'pro-law' than left-wing students; police constables more 'pro-law' than croupiers; and magistrates more 'pro-law' than second-hand car dealers (with apologies to all honest croupiers and car-dealers). At one level, such data (of which there is a considerable amount in the early attitude scaling studies) could be taken as evidence that the scale *did* discriminate between groups of people who exhibited different kinds of behaviour. In other words, one might well discover differences in very *general* kinds of law-related behaviour which were not too unrelated to the *general* measure of attitude employed. But suppose one set oneself a different kind of task. Suppose one had in mind, not law-breaking in general but a *specific* form of law-breaking, say drunken driving. It is more than likely that one would find *no* relationship between people's attitudes towards the law, as measured by this scale, and their tendency to drive when drunk. Why not?

Many of the explanations may by now have a familiar ring. It might be said that a measure of attitudes towards the law is incomplete without items of a more behavioural nature. To compensate for this, we might return to

Shaw and Wright, turn over three pages (p. 256), and find the Gregory (1939) 'Law-Abidingness Scale', which contains 14 items designed to measure people's indulgence in various kinds of illegal activity, including traffic offences. Out goes the new questionnaire, but still it fails to discriminate drunken drivers from anyone else. So we start thinking about the behaviour a little more directly – suppose law-abidingness is only one of the relevant variables, and not nearly as important as people's attitudes towards the possibility of inflicting physical injury on oneself or others. Back to Shaw and Wright we go, and on page 481 we find the Yuker, Block and Campbell (1960) 'Attitude toward Disabled People Scale'. With this we can ask subjects how far they agree with statements like, 'Disabled people are often unfriendly', or 'Most severely disabled persons are just as ambitious as physically normal persons'. Still no luck, so still the search can continue, leading us further and further away from where we started. Finally, frustrated and fatigued, we might take the trouble actually to read the attitude scales we have been using. Then, probably for the first time, it might strike us that nowhere, in any of the scales, was there any specific mention of drunken driving.

Does this mean that the scales we used were invalid? Not necessarily, since they were never intended to be *specifically* concerned with drunken driving. It was merely an assumption on our part that a more positive evaluation of the law in general would be predictive of an avoidance of this particular kind of law-breaking. In choosing to use the scales in question for purposes of this kind of prediction, we implicitly reified the construct of a generalized attitude-towards-the-Law dimension. We proceeded as though everyone possessed such an attitude at some level of favourability or unfavourability, and this attitude motivated their specific actions.

But where did this construct of a generalized attitude-toward-the-Law come from? From people's behaviour, or researchers' presuppositions? If from peoples' behaviour, 'attitude–behaviour discrepancies' of the kind we have been discussing would have to be the exception rather than the rule. But if from researchers' presuppositions, how can such a subjective factor still be influential after the rigorous procedures of item selection and scale construction have been scrupulously completed? The answer is that it is precisely these procedures which serve to reify the construct in question. Items which yield responses which are compatible with the assumption of a general unidimensional attitude continuum may be selected for inclusion in the final scale. Items which yield responses incompatible with the unidimensional assumption will not be selected, but this does not mean that these latter responses are random or meaningless. It just means that they come between researchers and their presuppositions, and are therefore simply removed.

Even so, this does not mean that scales so constructed are necessarily invalid. They can provide perfectly adequate measures of *those aspects* of attitudes towards the Law or any other such issue which *can* be treated in terms of a generalized unidimensional continuum. It is then an empirical question how many specific aspects remain which cannot be treated in this way. Thus, if we found that generalized attitudes towards the Law did not predict drunken driving, this would *not* entitle us to speak of discrepancy between attitudes and behaviour. If we took the trouble specifically to measure attitudes towards drunken driving, we might well find much higher levels of predictability of behaviour. If this were so, we would have to say, not that we had previously failed to predict behaviour from attitudes, but that we had failed to predict a specific attitude from a more general attitude which we had *presumed* encompassed it.

If we reconsider the literature in this area, it is apparent that most studies have used relatively specific indices of behaviour and relatively general indices of attitude (Ajzen and Fishbein, 1977). The host of studies in which college students were assessed along a *general* attitudinal dimension of prejudice against blacks, and then presented with a specific behavioural option involving interaction with one or more black persons, exemplifies this problem to a marked extent. This is even more unfortunate in view of the proportion of the total number of attitude–behaviour studies for which they account (Wicker, 1969). Even in the LaPiere (1934) study, which is by no means the most transparent from this point of view, the hoteliers and restaurateurs may have seen the choice before them as that of whether or not to create a scene by refusing custom to a specific, well-dressed, well-behaved, middle-class Chinese couple (no doubt quite unlike their stereotype of the 'typical' Chinese), who were obviously not out to make trouble, were just passing through, and were in the company of a non-Chinese American, and had also actually arrived at their establishment and so could not be politely diverted with: 'Sorry, we're fully booked tonight.' The measure of 'attitude' used by LaPiere, however, involved a commitment to serve 'members of the Chinese race' in unspecified numbers, at unspecified times, for unspecified periods, and regardless of whether they presented themselves in a socially accommodating manner, even assuming that this attitude measure was elicited from exactly the same individuals whose behaviour had been recorded (which is far from certain). The method of measuring attitudes in this study may well have involved just the kind of situation which would maximize the effect of the respondents' stereotypes about the Chinese, and the method of assessing behaviour may have involved just the kind of situation in which the effect of these stereotypes would be minimal.

Fishbein (1967) and Fishbein and Ajzen (1975) have emphasized an important distinction between attitudes towards a specific object, and attitudes towards specific behaviour performed with respect to that object. The implication of this distinction is that there is no more reason to assume a one-to-one relationship between someone's general attitude on some issue and their performance of any specific act, than there is to assume such a relationship between their general attitude and their endorsement of any specific attitude statement. Many statements of apparent relevance to a given issue are not suitable for inclusion in an attitude scale, in that they do not discriminate between people with different positions on the attitude continuum measured by the researcher. This could be because of the base rate of agreement to the statement in question. The statement could be so implausible or offensive that everyone would reject it, or so obvious that everyone would accept it. Alternatively, the statement could yield a range of responses which was not predictable from subjects' responses to other items in the scale. This would be taken to imply that it was affected by factors other than those which the attitude scale was designed to measure. So much is well-known with respect to verbal indices of attitude. Exactly the same argument, however, can be applied to *behavioural* indices of attitude. One can imagine many specific acts which might be supposed to reflect a person's attitude on a particular issue, but which do *not* in fact discriminate between people with different 'attitudes', either because of response base rates, or because they are affected by factors other than the people's positions on the attitude continuum measured by the researcher.

The 'attitude–behaviour discrepancy' is essentially an artefact of the haphazard selection of specific behavioural indices which researchers have tried to relate to general verbal measures of attitudes. If the selection of specific verbal indices (for inclusion in an attitude scale) were as lax and arbitrary, we would quickly have a situation in which we had to talk of an 'attitude–attitude discrepancy': attitudes would not simply fail to predict behaviour, they would have to be considered self-contradictory even at the level of verbal expression (and indeed ordinary language expressions of attitudes may contain many apparent self-contradictions). On the other hand, if we are as selective in our choice of behavioural indices as we are at present in our choice of verbal indices, the 'attitude–behaviour discrepancy' may disappear as a substantive problem.

Fishbein and Ajzen (1974) have demonstrated that it is possible to construct 'behavioural' attitude scales by applying the same scaling and item selection procedures to series of behavioural criteria as are conventionally applied to verbal expressions of sentiment and approval. Using the issue of religious behaviour, they had subjects complete both 'behavioural' and standard attitude scales. Their most important finding was that the standard attitude scales, designed to measure whether people were generally favourable or unfavourable towards religion, correlated quite highly with the overall behavioural scores, which indicated how favourably or unfavourably subjects said they behaved or would behave *in general* with respect to religion. At the same time, there was considerable variability in the extent to which specific acts could be predicted from scores on the verbal attitude scales, and Fishbein and Ajzen discuss possible reasons for this.

The Fishbein and Ajzen (1974) data have been reanalysed by Bagozzi and Burnkrant (1979). They claim to find evidence for a distinction between affective and cognitive components of attitude, which make separate contributions to the prediction of behaviours. In a subsequent debate deeply steeped in the details of LISREL analysis, Dillon and Kumar (1985) dispute Bagozzi and Burnkrant's claim that the different attitude scales are indicators of separate latent variables ('affect' and 'cognitive' components), rather than a single latent variable ('attitude'). Bagozzi and Burnkrant (1985) argue in reply that the distinction between the two components cannot simply be put down to measurement error or method variance, although they acknowledge that affect and cognition are highly correlated with each other. Despite these finer points of disagreement, however, the agreed message is clear. With suitable matching of levels of specificity, high correlations between measures of attitude and behaviour can be found.

The theory of reasoned action

The empirical findings of Fishbein and Ajzen (1974) do not simply restore confidence in the utility of attitudes as a predictor of behaviour; they form the basis for a conceptualization of the supposedly causal links between attitudes and behaviour termed the 'theory of reasoned action' (Ajzen and Fishbein, 1980). The basic assumptions of this theory are represented in Figure 3.2.

According to the theory, behaviour (to the extent that it is under 'volitional control') is determined by intention, whereas intention is determined by a weighted additive function of 'attitude toward the behaviour' (often termed the 'attitudinal component') and 'subjective norm' (often termed the

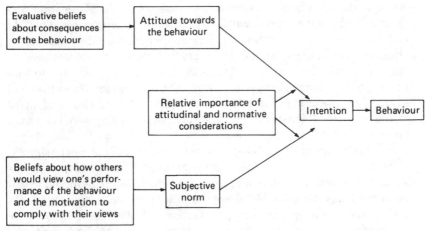

Figure 3.2. The 'theory of reasoned action'. (Adapted from Ajzen and Fishbein, 1980.)

'normative component'). The definition of these two components is given by considering the cognitive elements that combine to make them up. 'Attitude towards the behaviour' is defined as the sum of 'evaluative (behavioural) beliefs' about the *consequences* of performing the behaviour in question. Such beliefs are specific to *oneself* performing the behaviour towards a defined *target* at a defined *time* and *place*. Any evaluative belief contains both an expectancy element (will this consequence be made more or less likely by my performance of this behaviour?) and a *value* element (how good or bad would such a consequence be?) The expectancy and value elements are combined multiplicatively. (The theory is thus an example of an 'expectancy-value' model of decision-making, see Chapter 7, pp. 214–17.)

'Subjective norms' are composed of qualitatively distinct beliefs about how *other people* will view one's performance of the behaviour. Again, these contain both an expectancy element (will this significant other be more or less likely to approve of me if I perform this behaviour?) and a value element, referred to as the 'motivation to comply' (how much do I value this significant other's approval?). Again, these elements are presumed to combine multiplicatively. The 'motivation to comply' term, seems the least indispensable variable in the model. There is some indecision over whether it is best to measure it as a unipolar construct (do I care what this other thinks of my behaviour, or not?) or as a bipolar construct (do I want to obtain this other's approval or do I want to obtain this other's *dis*approval?). (See Bowman and Fishbein, 1978, and Davidson and Jaccard, 1979, for alternative measures.) Schlegel, Crawford and Sanborn (1977) even found that inclusion of the 'motivation to comply' variable, however measured, *worsened* the prediction of behavioural intention. Saltzer (1981) draws a similar conclusion, and recommends calculation of the subjective norm component without multiplication by the 'motivation to comply' term. Although not all researchers who have used the model are quite so pessimistic, the status of this particular variable is questionable. Possibly much may depend on who the others whose opinions the subject is asked to anticipate are. The model has been applied to a very wide range of behaviours including smoking (Fishbein, 1982), alcohol use (Budd and Spencer, 1984, 1985; Schlegel *et al.*, 1977), contraceptive use (Davidson and Jaccard, 1975, 1979; Pagel and Davidson, 1984), mothers' choice of infant feeding method (Manstead, Proffitt and Smart, 1983) and consumer behaviour (Fishbein and Ajzen, 1980).

One of the ways in which the theory of reasoned action is most helpful is in directing attention to the relative contributions of attitudinal and normative factors as predictors of intention. Is the behaviour in question one that people tend to perform for the sake of what they personally will get out of it, or is it performed mainly because people are mindful of others' approval or disapproval? This question can have considerable practical relevance, for instance in the field of health education.

Fishbein (1982) found that young women's intentions regarding whether or not to take up or give up smoking were more importantly determined by attitudinal factors (i.e. beliefs about consequences) than by normative factors, although the latter were also influential especially among non-smokers. Manstead *et al.* (1983) found that women who breast-fed their babies differed from those who only bottle-fed them in terms of a number of beliefs relevant to the attitudinal and normative components of the model. For example, the outcome consequence 'allows baby's father to be involved in feeding' was rated as more important (higher value) and as truer of bottle-feeding (higher expectancy) by those who bottle-fed only, than by those who breast-fed. On the other hand, the two groups of mothers did not differ in terms of how much they valued convenience, lack of trouble and of restriction on social life, but differed in their expectancies linking such consequences to a particular feeding method. Among normative beliefs, the perceived preference of the baby's father emerged as a very strong predictor. The 'motivation to comply' variable did not distinguish between the two groups, with the exception that those who breast-fed were more motivated to comply with their medical adviser.

Davidson and Jaccard (1975) found that both attitudinal and normative considerations were important in family planning decisions. Within a sample of married women considered as a whole, the attitudinal and normative components were of comparable importance in predicting intentions to have a two-child family; the attitudinal component was somewhat more important in predicting intentions to have a child in the next two years; but the normative component was more important in predicting intentions to use contraceptive pills. This last result contrasts with that previously found by Jaccard and Davidson (1972), that among unmarried women college students intentions to use contraceptive pills were rather more strongly determined by the attitudinal component.

Within a very different context, Songer-Nocks (1976) attempted to predict cooperation and competition in a two-person laboratory game from subjects' attitudes (measured by ratings of how foolish–wise, bad–good and harmful–beneficial the cooperative move could be) and normative beliefs (measured as assessments of the percentage of cooperative moves the partner expected of the subject). Songer-Nocks found that the influence of such normative beliefs was strong when subjects were given non-competitive instructions, but negligible when they were given competitive instructions. The influence of attitudes was far greater when subjects had been given prior experience with the game. Songer-Nocks tries to argue that such a demonstration of the importance of situational factors questions the generality of the Fishbein–Ajzen model. However, it has to be said, firstly, that her operationalization of the model's variables was unconventional and incomplete and, secondly, that Fishbein and Ajzen have no objection to the idea that the relative importance of the attitudinal and normative components will vary from context to context.

Another strategy is to consider structural aspects of a person's attitudes and subjective norms that help predict the relative weighting of the two components. In a study of students' attitudes towards social drinking, Budd and Spencer (1984) included measures of how certain subjects were of their own attitudes, or of others' approval/disapproval, and of the centrality of such attitudes and subjective norms (e.g. 'drinking alcoholic drinks is a central concern of mine'). A third moderator variable, 'latitude of rejection' (cf. Sherif and Hovland, 1961), was derived from the number of attitude or normative-belief statements with which subjects indicated that they strongly disagreed. The correlation between attitudes and intentions was significantly higher for subjects with wider latitudes of rejection, and greater certainty with regard to their attitudes, and the correlation between subjective norms and intentions was significantly higher for subjects who were more certain, and more centrally concerned, about others' approval or disapproval of their drinking.

Originally Fishbein (1967) included in his model a term representing *personal* normative beliefs, representing what subjects thought they *should* do in the situation, as distinct from *social* norms (others' perceived opinions). This term was soon dropped from the model, on the grounds that it functioned simply as an alternative measure of behavioural intention. (Ajzen and Fishbein, 1969, 1970). Pagel and Davidson (1984), however, found that inclusion of a personal norm measure ('I feel a moral obligation to do/not do . . .') substantially improved prediction of intentions concerning contraceptive use. Budd and Spencer (1985) included a slightly different measure of personal norms in relation to alcohol use (e.g. 'I think that I should drink beer in pubs'), and argued that personal norms should be seen mainly as an indicator of *ideal* behavioural intentions.

The attitudinal–normative distinction, therefore, has been applied to a wide variety of contexts in which researchers have attempted to predict behavioural intentions. This does not mean that it is the *only* distinction that can be made between different kinds of beliefs (cf. Bagozzi and Burnkrant, 1979), nor even that it is necessarily the *best* in any given context. From some points of view, one could argue that others' approval or disapproval is a *consequence* of behaviour, and hence that normative beliefs (or at any rate *social* normative beliefs) are not ultimately that different from other kinds of behavioural beliefs. Nonetheless, it has proved a *useful* distinction, and one that has directed researchers' attention to issues that might not otherwise have been raised.

Habits and past behaviour

Despite its success as a predictive model, the theory of reasoned action has not gone unchallenged, particularly with respect to the assumptions it makes concerning the causal links between attitudes, subjective norms, intentions and behaviour. In simple terms, according to Fishbein and Ajzen, attitudes and subjective norms jointly determine intention, and intention determines behaviour. It is accepted that behaviour can produce feedback which will influence later attitudes and subjective norms (Fishbein and Ajzen, 1975: 16), but in other respects the model is relentlessly unidirectional in its causal assumptions.

It is a familiar adage that correlations do not establish causality. A simple correlation between attitude and behaviour could mean that attitudes have a causal influence on behaviour, or that behaviour has a causal influence on attitude, or that both attitudes and behaviour are influenced by some other antecedent variable. Indeed, these possibilities are not mutually exclusive. However, we may have more than simple correlations to work with, and when this is so, comparative tests of different causal assumptions can be made using more sophisticated statistical techniques (notably LISREL).

The theory of reasoned action is also ahistorical, in the sense that it purports to describe the decision processes underlying the formulation of a behavioural intention at one point in time. It does not deal with the development or stability over time of attitudes, subjective norms, intentions and behaviour (beyond making the point that intentions may be unstable, and that this may attenuate intention–behaviour correlations). Whatever the value of the model in describing the formulation of *new* behavioural decisions, therefore, it may not necessarily provide an accurate account of the relationship of attitudes to *habitual* behaviour.

Bentler and Speckart (1979) tested the theory of reasoned action in the context of students' use of three classes of drug: alcohol, marijuana and 'hard drugs' (such as amphetamines, barbiturates, cocaine, LSD, but without specific mention of heroin). A time interval was built into the study, so that, at time 1 subjects indicated the current attitudes, subjective norms and intentions (to use the drugs over the next two weeks), as well as reporting how often they *had* used the drugs in the two weeks before. At time 2, two weeks later, the behavioural report measure was repeated with equivalent wording. Thus Bentler and Speckart were able to predict subsequent behaviour not only from attitudes, subjective norms and intentions but also from recent past behaviour.

The variant of the Fishbein and Ajzen model that Bentler and Speckart put to the test is represented in Figure 3.3. What the arrows imply are the possibilities that:

(a)   Past behaviour, attitudes and subjective norms can mutually influence one another.

(b)   Attitudes can influence subsequent behaviour both *indirectly*, through influencing intention (as assumed by Fishbein and Ajzen), and *directly* i.e. over and above any effect mediated by intention.

(c)   Subjective norms can have only an indirect effect on subsequent behaviour.

(d)   Past behaviour can influence subsequent behaviour both directly and indirectly.

The findings of this study directly challenged the basic assumption of the

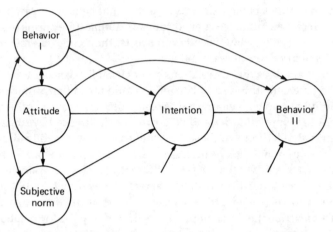

Figure 3.3. A model of the attitude–behaviour relation incorporating previous
     behaviour. (From P. M. Bentler and G. Speckart, 'Models of attitude–
     behavior relations', *Psychological Review*, 86 (1979), 455. Copyright 1979
     by the American Psychological Association. Reprinted with permission.)

theory of reasoned action, namely that the influence of attitudes on
behaviour is mediated by intention. Although the path from intention to
subsequent behaviour had positive regression weights in the analyses
relating to use of alcohol and marijuana, it had a negative regression weight
in the hard drugs analysis (contrary to what Fishbein and Ajzen would
require). Consistent with Fishbein and Ajzen, there were positively
weighted paths from attitudes and subjective norms to intention for all three
behaviours. (Interestingly, of the three behaviours, marijuana use showed
the greatest dependence on the attitudinal component, and the least
dependence on the normative component.) However, intentions were also
positively linked to past behaviour and, what is more troublesome for
Fishbein and Ajzen, both attitudes and past behaviour had *direct* positive
influences on subsequent behaviour in all three analyses. Bentler and
Speckart (1979: 461) conclude:

> For this sample it is apparent that attitudes and past behaviour, or some
> other factor(s) linearly related to these antecedents, are contributing strongly
> to the occurrence of behavior without the regulation of intentions.

A possible counter to this argument is that Bentler and Speckart (1979)
were studying addictive behaviours (and indeed, the predictive power of
intentions was weakest for the 'hard drugs' category) whereas the theory of
reasoned action assumes that the behaviour in question is under 'volitional
control' – i.e. people are *able* to carry out their wishes and intentions. On the
other hand, it is by no means clear what exactly is meant by saying that
addictive behaviours are beyond volitional control (Eiser, 1982; see also

Chapter 6, pp. 207–10). Furthermore, other studies have found various forms of drug use to be predictable from intentions (e.g. Fishbein, 1982; Schlegel *et al.*, 1977). Nonetheless, there may be problems with self-reports of intentions where people feel unable to put their intentions easily into effect. In such contexts, one may be tapping 'ideal' behavioural intentions (Budd and Spencer, 1985) rather than anything more immediately tied to ongoing behaviour.

Fredricks and Dossett (1983) tested the Bentler and Speckart (1979) model against that of Fishbein and Ajzen (1975) with respect to the prediction of students' classroom attendance. Their findings confirmed that recent past behaviour (over a time interval of two to three weeks) had a direct predictive effect on subsequent behaviour that was not mediated by intention. There was no direct effect of attitudes on behaviour, however. Consistent with Fishbein and Ajzen, the influence of attitudes on behaviour was mediated by intention. Attitudes and prior behaviour were positively associated. Subjective norms, however, showed little relationship either to intentions or to prior behaviour.

Bentler and Speckart (1981) tested a number of alternative causal models with respect to three classes of behaviour: dating, studying and exercise. They found a complex pattern of relationships that varied across the three behaviours. For dating and for studying, the data broadly support the conclusion reached by Fredricks and Dossett (1983) that prior behaviour can directly influence subsequent behaviour, and that intention mediates the influence of attitudes and subjective norms. However, this pattern is disrupted by a *negative* association between attitudes to studying and studying behaviour (which Bentler and Speckart try to interpret in terms of less diligent students feeling under greater pressure due to impending examinations). Subjective norms were quite important in the case of studying, but not dating. For exercise, however, intention failed to retain its mediating role. Both prior behaviour and attitudes had direct effects on subsequent behaviour. Additional analyses on the attitude–behaviour correlations allowed Bentler and Speckart to conclude that, for dating and exercise, behaviour was dependent on attitude, rather than attitude being a consequence of behaviour. A consistent positive association between attitude and *prior* behaviour, however, was found for studying.

Such findings lead to the conclusion that there is no single causal model that is likely to prove superior in all behavioural domains. Whilst the theory of reasoned action provides good predictions of behaviour on the basis of a few variables, expansion of the model by the inclusion of additional variables seriously questions the generality of the assumptions made by Ajzen and Fishbein (1980) concerning the causal relationships involved.

There is clearly a need for more longitudinal studies of the stability of attitudes, normative beliefs, behaviour, and their interrelationships over time (cf. Himmelweit, Humphreys, Jaeger and Katz, 1981). The step taken in this direction by Bentler and Speckart (1979) is small in time-scale but important theoretically. Attitudes and behaviours persist for longer than the decision moment that the theory of reasoned action appears to describe.

Salience and attitude differences

Another problematic feature of the theory of reasoned action concerns the relationship between separate evaluative beliefs and the attitudinal component considered as a whole. Mathematically, the hypothesized relationship is quite simple – attitude is predicted from the sum of the products of probabilistic beliefs weighted by evaluation. What is more difficult theoretically is the question of *what* evaluative beliefs are entered into the formula.

It is important to distinguish here between how the theory of reasoned action applies to the question of attitude formation or decision-making and how it applies to attitude *change*. A persuasive communication may change a person's attitude by introducing a completely *new* evaluative belief concerning a behavioural consequence or an attribute of the attitude object which the individual previously had not considered. However, in the prediction of attitudes from *existing* beliefs, the theory of reasoned action assumes that only a *selection* of the beliefs people may hold will influence their attitude. These Fishbein and Ajzen (1975) refer to as *salient* beliefs. Taking into account earlier work on attention and memory (e.g. Miller, 1956), they assume that an individual is unlikely to be holding more than five to nine beliefs in mind at any given time. Researchers are therefore recommended to elicit only this number of beliefs from a given individual concerning a particular action or object.

At this point a separation of emphasis occurs, depending on whether researchers are primarily interested in the content of beliefs underlying a person's attitude, or in the relationship of attitude (and other variables) to intention and behaviour. Thus, whereas it is acknowledged that different individuals may hold different beliefs as salient, no hypotheses are offered about the nature of such individual differences, and in practice most research has followed the procedure of presenting a standard set of belief statements to all subjects. Fishbein and Ajzen (1975: 219) recommend that one selects those beliefs that occur most frequently when elicited from a given population. These they refer to as *modal salient beliefs*.

This procedure seems quite reasonable if what one is concerned with is finding belief measures that *on average* are predictive of attitudes and intentions within a subject population as a whole. The difficulty arises if one tries to interpret the regression equations that describe this predictive relationship as accurate representations of the decision processes of any single individual. The theory of reasoned action claims to represent individual decision processes, but it is difficult to see how such a claim can be tested without taking into account individual differences in the salience of particular beliefs for particular people.

One way of doing so would be to take each individual in turn, and find out which aspects of the behaviour or attitude object he or she *personally* regarded as critical or salient. Some of these might correspond to ones that would be chosen as modal salient belief items, but others might be more idiosyncratic. If one was trying to predict attitudes towards the Conservative government in Britain in 1985, beliefs that the government 'stands up to trade unions' and 'is responsible for the rise in unemployment' might be regarded as true or false, and good or bad, to different extents by different people. Nonetheless, it seems unlikely that a set of modal salient beliefs would be constructed from which these were excluded. On the other hand the belief that the government 'favours the building of a third London airport at Stansted' might be very salient for residents of the Stansted area (and those living near rejected alternative sites) but not at all salient for residents of many other parts of the country. However, the objection to eliciting separate belief items for each individual is that comparison of results *across* individuals becomes much more difficult where not everyone has answered the same questions.

Another strategy is to present all subjects with a common set of belief items, and then ask them to identify those that are most important or salient to them personally. One can then compute the correlations between individuals' attitudes and the particular evaluation beliefs that are salient to them personally. When such correlations are compared with equivalent calculations on the remaining belief items, the typical finding is that personally salient beliefs predict attitudes far better than personally non-salient beliefs. This has been found in the context of the expected conse-quences of nuclear power developments (Eiser and van der Pligt, 1979; van der Pligt, Eiser and Spears, 1986). In addition, Budd (1986), whose study more closely followed the standard procedure for tests of the Fishbein and Ajzen model, obtained measures from students concerning their beliefs, attitudes, subjective norms, intentions and behaviour with respect to cigarette smoking. Subjects were presented with 18 behavioural belief items, and also indicated the five of these most important to them per-sonally. For the 144 subjects who completed the relevant measures, a semantic-differential measure of attitude correlated 0.615 with an evaluative belief score based on the five items salient for each subject. This compared with a correlation of 0.556 when the whole set of 18 items was used, and a non-significant one of 0.073 when the calculation used only the 13 items that were *least* salient for each individual.

Not only do individuals differ in the belief items they choose as personally salient, but such differences are systematic and predictable. *People with different attitudes tend to regard different aspects of an issue as salient*. The kinds of differences observed make considerable intuitive sense. For instance, Budd (1986) found that non-smokers were more likely than smokers to regard the risks of cancer and of heart disease, expense and offensiveness to others as salient to them personally. Smokers were more likely to choose relaxation, relief of tension and anxiety, and taste. Very similar conclusions were reached by Eiser, van der Pligt and Friend (1983) in an analysis of 15-year-olds' free discussions about cigarette smoking. Non-smokers were more likely to introduce into the discussion themes concerned with health risks and social and personal costs, whereas smokers tried to produce arguments against the seriousness of such risks and emphasized personal and social benefits.

Eiser and van der Pligt (1979) had pro- and anti-nuclear subjects rate how likely eleven separate effects would be as a consequence of the building of a nuclear fuel reprocessing plant, and then identify the five possible effects they personally thought were most important. A score was calculated for each subject, conceptually equivalent to the sum of beliefs weighted by evaluation in the Fishbein and Ajzen model. When this score was calculated on the five 'important' items, the correlation with subjects' attitude was nearly twice what it was when only the 'unimportant' items were used in the calculation. What is striking, though, is the qualitative separation between pros and antis in the possible effects they regarded as important. Whereas the anti-nuclears emphasized restrictions on individual civil liberties, the risks of nuclear terrorism and of military nuclear proliferation, the pro-nuclears chose the country's ability to meet future energy demands, the strength of the economy, and the *relative* safety, as they saw it, of nuclear as opposed to other forms of energy. Similarly, when asked to choose factors that they felt would contribute most to 'overall' quality of life', pro-nuclears were more likely to emphasize factors relevant to material well-being.

In another study on the nuclear issue (van der Pligt, Eiser and Spears, 1986), residents of communities close to sites under consideration for a new nuclear power station rated how much a number of consequences would change for the better or the worse if a nuclear power station were built nearby, and they indicated which consequences they thought most important. Broadly, pro-nuclears were more likely than anti-nuclears to select local economic impact (employment opportunities, new roads and facilities) whereas anti-nuclears tended to stress various forms of possible environmental damage, health hazards, and 'personal peace of mind'. The correlation between attitudes and a score based on these consequence ratings showed that as good predictions of attitude were obtained by confining the calculation to personally salient consequences as by including a large number of less salient predictors.

Thus, the relationship between evaluative beliefs and overall attitude is generally closer for beliefs that are *personally* salient for the individuals concerned. Furthermore, the *kinds* of belief that tend to be chosen as salient or important are those that are *evaluatively consistent* with the individual's own attitude. Quite simply, the benefits of smoking will be more salient to smokers than non-smokers and the costs of smoking will be more salient to non-smokers than smokers. Similarly, pro-nuclears not only see nuclear power as more beneficial than do anti-nuclears, they also assign greater importance to the benefits than to the costs.

This relationship between salience and evaluative consistency is one to which I shall return later (Chapter 5, pp. 159–65). As regards the implications for the theory of reasoned action, however, the main message is this: there is no more reason to assume that people's attitudes depend on the beliefs they choose as salient, than to assume that the choice of salient beliefs is dependent on their attitudes. Fishbein and Ajzen assume that people arrive at an overall evaluation by adding up some balance sheet of expected benefits and costs. The contrary possibility is that people form an overall evaluative impression first, and then choose an accounting system that provides the 'right' answer in terms of costs and benefits. The latter alternative requires one to look for factors other than antecedent evaluative beliefs as determinants of attitude, but this is not an overriding objection.

The theory of reasoned action assumes not only that attitudes and evaluative beliefs are consistent with each other, but that beliefs have *causal precedence* over attitude. In disputing this assumption, there is no need to make the contrary claim that attitudes *always* have causal precedence over beliefs, but only that they *sometimes* may. It may happen that individuals sometimes adopt beliefs that *justify* their attitude, rather than deriving attitudes from their beliefs. This possibility is suggested by evidence that subjects may be motivated to present themselves as self-consistent when required to complete questionnaires. Budd and Spencer (1986) showed subjects attitude questionnaires supposedly completed by other students, and asked them to rate how much they believed the questionnaires had been completed honestly. Patterns of responses that were internally consistent – i.e. that conformed to the relationships posited by the theory of reasoned action – were rated as more believable. This may imply that people are aware of a social expectation that their beliefs, subjective norms, attitudes and intentions should be consistent with each other.

Budd (1987) provides another challenging result from a study in which students completed a questionnaire containing items measuring the components of the Fishbein and Ajzen model in relation to three behaviours: smoking, brushing teeth, and exercising. In one condition, the order of presentation of the items followed the systematic order observed in previous research using the Fishbein and Ajzen model, and with the items relating to the three behaviours separated into different sections. In this condition, the correlations predicted by the model were all highly positive, for all three behaviours. In another condition the items were presented in a random order, with the three behavioural domains intermixed. Here, none of the correlations predicted by the model achieved significance, with the exception of that between subjective norms and intentions regarding smoking (and this may have been due to the fortuitous juxtaposition of related items).

The theory of reasoned action assumes a consistency in the cognitive structures underlying attitudes, beliefs and behavioural decisions. One possible interpretation of Budd's (1987) results is that this underlying consistency was still 'there' (somewhere) but subjects could not express it, due to the distracting demands of the random questionnaire. However, an interpretation more damaging to the theory is that such consistency is only produced at the time of *response*, and *cannot* be so easily produced if the format of the questionnaire impedes people's ability to monitor the internal consistency of their answers.

Attitude accessibility

The theory of reasoned action therefore posits a special relationship between a person's overall attitude and component beliefs about an object or action: attitudes are *derived from* individual evaluative beliefs summed together. The possibility that attitudes can also shape beliefs, and the salience of beliefs, in the direction of enhanced consistency, is not represented in the Fishbein and Ajzen model. This objection does not apply, however, to a quite different conceptualization of the attitude–behaviour relationship proposed by Fazio (1985; Fazio, Powell and Herr, 1983).

According to Fazio, attitudes should be regarded as a *learned association* between a given object and a given evaluation. Such an evaluation may range from one of strong emotional affect through to a more rationalistic kind of cogitive inference. Thus, a form of affective–cognitive distinction is incorporated but this is used merely to describe qualitative differences between attitudes. No assumption is made that affect, cognition and behaviour will necessarily be consistent with each other.

Whereas attitudes are the product of learned associations, behaviour depends directly on the individual's *definition of the event:*

> Approach behaviors are promoted by a definition of the event that consists primarily of positive perceptions of the attitude object in the immediate situation. Likewise, avoidance behaviors are prompted by a negative definition of the event. (Fazio, 1985).

People are assumed to behave in the ways they do because of the *meanings* they assign to their environment and objects and events within it. Fazio acknowledges the link between this view and notions embodied in symbolic interactionist perspectives (see, e.g., Deutscher, 1984; Manis and Meltzer, 1972; Mead, 1934). However, Fazio does not go into the question of how individuals define *themselves* within a situation of context of relationships – a major concern for symbolic interactionists (although the issue of self-perception of attitudes is considered by Fazio, Herr and Olney, 1984). Rather, the point he is making is simply that to understand how behaviour occurs in response to events, one needs to know how the events are defined or interpreted by the individual.

The 'definition of the event' is seen by Fazio as a joint function of 'immediate perceptions of attitude object' and the 'definition of the situation' within which the event occurs (see Figure 3.4). This may be considered as a kind of 'figure–ground' distinction. The 'ground', or situational context, is interpreted in the light of normative expectations, whereas the 'figure', that is the attitude object, is experienced through a process of *selective perception* that in turn is shaped by the person's attitude. Although there is still some vagueness about the precise nature of the links connecting the different components in the model, Fazio is forthright in the causal primacy he assigns to attitudes in shaping the process of interpretation and decision-making:

> According to the proposed model, this influence of attitudes upon behavior occurs as a result of the impact that attitudes have upon perceptions of the attitude object in the immediate situation and upon definitions of the event. The model implies that without such selective perception attitudes would not affect behavior. (Fazio, 1985).

Fazio's model has yet to receive thoroughgoing empirical testing in its totality. However, there is a fair amount of research relating to particular assumptions that it makes, notably the definition of attitude as the product of learned evaluative associations to the attitude object. Fazio assumes that the stronger the 'object-evaluation associations' the more 'accessible' a person's attitude will be from memory in response to any questioning and the more likely it will be to be 'automatically activated' upon presentation of the attitude object – in other words, the more likely it will be to be spontaneously experienced, or to occur as a conditioned response.

Fazio, Chen, McDonel and Sherman (1982) manipulated the strength of the attitude association by simply requiring subjects to copy out their evaluations onto additional response sheets. (The task involved rating the attractiveness of different puzzles.) After this repetition procedure, subjects responded quicker when their evaluative associations to the stimuli were tested, and behaved in ways more consistent with their attitude (were more likely to choose to work with the puzzles they had evaluated more

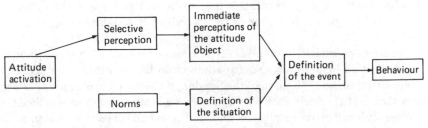

Figure 3.4. Fazio's model of the influence of attitude on behaviour. (Adapted from Fazio, 1985.)

positively), in comparison to subjects who had not had to copy out their initial ratings. Powell and Fazio (1984) replicated the effect of repeated attitude expression on subsequent response latency in an attitude survey on twelve separate social issues (e.g. legalized abortion, gun control, nuclear power plants).

Attitude–behaviour consistency has been shown to be enhanced by procedures that lead subjects to see their attitudes and behaviour as relevant to each other. Snyder and Swann (1976) presented male students with a description of an invented sex-discrimination case (in which a university had appointed a male over a female candidate). In an 'attitude salient' condition, subjects were encouraged to organize their 'thoughts and views on the affirmative action issue', before writing an essay to say what they thought of the court case; whereas those in an 'attitude not salient' condition wrote essays without such an instructional set. These essays were then coded to provide measures of support for the female plaintiff (an index of 'behaviour' that Snyder and Swann admit to be rather arbitrary). The correlation between this 'behavioural' measure of support for the plaintiff and previous attitudes towards affirmative action was high when subjects' attitudes were made salient and non-significant when they were not.

Snyder and Kendzierski (1982) found a similar result using the same case description, but distinguishing between 'attitude availability' (equivalent to Snyder and Swann's manipulation of 'attitude salience') and 'attitude relevance', which was manipulated by having the judge in the case supposedly inform the jury that their decision might set a legal precedent for other affirmative action cases. The results showed that both manipulations increased correspondence between attitudes on the general issue and verdicts in the specific case. The effects were somewhat different as a function of subjects' scores on Snyder's (1974) Self-Monitoring Scale, which measures individual differences in people's concern with controlling the impressions that others will form of them.

In a second experiment, Snyder and Kendzierski (1982) found greater correspondence between subjects' attitudes towards psychological research and their decisions whether or not to participate in an experiment following a staged interaction between two confederates (supposedly other subjects) designed to make subjects feel that they really had a choice, and that this choice boiled down to a question of 'how worthwhile you think experiments are' (p. 177).

Fazio (1985) interprets such results in terms of the selective perception processes that he assumes to occur when attitudes are made more accessible. He reports a replication of the Snyder and Swann (1976) study (Fazio and Herr, 1984) which showed that increased attitude salience enhanced correspondence between attitudes and verdicts when subjects were instructed to try and reach a decision, but not in a 'memory set' condition when subjects were told to try and remember 'all the factual details' in the case.

Fazio infers that this was because the memory set instructions 'prevented selective perception from occurring'.

Other studies have considered the manner in which evaluative associations to an attitude object are formed. Fazio and Zanna (1981) review evidence in support of the notion that *direct experience* of the attitude object leads to more strongly formed associations and hence, they observe, to greater attitude–behaviour consistency. For instance, Regan and Fazio (1977) used the issue of a campus housing shortage, during which many students had to put up with emergency sleeping accommodation for the first few weeks of term. A survey showed, as would be expected, that students held negative attitudes towards the shortage, more or less regardless of whether they had been assigned temporary accommodation or had proper rooms. Those who had been personally inconvenienced, however, were more prepared to agree to undertake a number of behavioural options consistent with their attitude. By the time the study was conducted (one month into term) 64 per cent of those who were in the temporary accommodation group had found more permanent housing.

A similar conclusion was reached by Fazio and Zanna (1978), who found that the correlation between students' attitudes towards participation in psychological experiments and their willingness to join the departmental subject pool was higher the more previous experience they had had as experimental subjects.

Other studies have looked at interactions between direct or indirect experience and other manipulations of attitude accessibility. Fazio *et al.* (1983) concluded that mere observation of an attitude object (the puzzles used in the Fazio *et al.*, 1982, experiment already described) can lead to subjects bringing their evaluation of the object immediately to mind, but only if they had direct experience of the object themselves (had personally played with the puzzles). Indirect experience did not lead to attitudes being so accessible, unless subjects had had to give repeated evaluative ratings of the objects.

Borgida and Campbell (1982) gave students the opportunity to sign a petition for more car-parking spaces on the campus. A questionnaire measured their attitudes on a number of issues, including environmental pollution, and also their personal direct experience of the parking shortage. Subjects also had to take part in a 'person perception' task in which they rated their impressions of a participant in a tape-recorded conversation. The critical manipulation involved the nature of this conversation which in the 'belief relevant' condition turned round to the conclusion that increasing campus parking facilities could lead to more pollution. There were thus four basic cells to the design – those with greater or less experience of being inconvenienced by the lack of parking spaces, and those for whom the link between the parking issue and general environmental issues had or had not been made salient. A significant *negative* association between environmental attitudes and petition signing (hence attitude–behaviour consistency) was observed *only* for subjects in the 'belief relevant' condition who had experienced *little* personal inconvenience due to the parking shortage.

Fazio's approach thus addresses the question of how attitudes are called to mind and 'guide' subsequent cognitive and behavioural processes. Fishbein and Ajzen may be seen as concerned primarily with the formulation of behavioural intentions, *granted* certain antecedent behavioural and normative beliefs, as input to the decision-making process. Fazio, on the other hand, treats the nature of that input as the central problem – hence the importance he assigns to the role of selective perception. But do these differences amount to a fundamental theoretical divide, or rather to a separation of emphasis and research strategy, with the two models concentrating on different stages of a common process?

The weakest aspect of the theory of reasoned action is its ahistorical nature – its lack of specificity concerning where salient beliefs come from. Fazio's model is more explicit in how antecedent attitudes can influence later cognitions, and hence can incorporate findings on the relationship of attitudinal differences to differences in salient beliefs. However, the final links in the attitude–behaviour chain are not defined with anything like the precision to which Fishbein and Ajzen at least aspire. Fazio talks in general terms about approach and avoidance behaviours, and positive and negative definitions of the event. There is some methodological as well as conceptual ambiguity with regard to whether behaviours merely follow from a positive or negative definition or are chosen by the actors as being *instrumental* in changing the event in a more desirable direction. Consider the fact that a third of Regan and Fazio's (1977) temporarily housed students were *still* temporarily housed when measures of attitude-related behaviour were obtained.

Fazio is almost studious too, in his avoidance of the term 'intention'. This has the advantage of allowing the model to be applicable, in principle, to habitual as well as non-habitual behaviours. Nonetheless, if the concept of intention belongs anywhere in Fazio's model, it must be part of the 'definition of the event'. Fazio's concept of learned evaluative associations is also basically quite similar to Fishbein's concept of evaluative beliefs. The difference is that we think of 'associations' in terms of basic learning processes, and 'beliefs' in terms of higher order cognitions.

Assuredly, then, there are *some* differences between the models, particularly in the assumptions made concerning the causal direction of the link between attitudes and selective perception and cognition. How important this difference is depends on whether one thinks the causality issue amounts to more than whether chickens come before eggs. Fazio also avoids terminology that implies a restricted applicability to rationalistic 'reasoned action' rather than more habitual or less reflective forms of learned behaviour. The importance of this distinction depends on whether or not one treats 'cognition' and 'learning' as fundamentally different spheres of psychological activity.

Learning and attitude–behaviour consistency

There is nothing especially new about the suggestion that learning processes may be involved in attitude formation and expression (see e.g., Greenwald, 1968b). Concepts of habit, association and reinforcement abound in many earlier theories. However, the popularity of such concepts has been somewhat eclipsed in recent years by a reliance on notions of information-processing. As a consequence, possibly relevant principles of learning have sometimes been overlooked in the search for 'new' principles of social cognition. Perhaps one reason for this is that it is easy to think of 'principles of learning' as making only reluctant distinctions between human beings and other animals, whereas we think of 'attitudes' as peculiarly human. In fact, much recent research on animal-learning uses conceptual language that can be surprisingly familiar, even congenial, to social psychologists (e.g. Dickinson, 1980). In a word, such conceptual language is frequently *cognitive*. Following a tradition that may be traced back to Tolman (1959), learning may be viewed as the *acquisition of expectancies* (Tarpy, 1982). One advantage of the expectancy notion is that it enables stimulus learning (Pavlovian conditioning) and response learning (instrumental conditioning) to be explained in terms of common principles. The principles assume that the function learning serves is to enable animals to *predict* important events in their environment. Such predictions can be made either on the basis of stimulus events, or response events (how the animal has behaved). In addition to changes in measurable responses, such expectancies may be associated with different affective or emotional states (e.g. fear).

A crucial assumption of this 'cognitive' approach to animal learning is the idea that conditioned stimuli and response acquire *information value*, so that the strength of conditioning depends not simply on the number of previous associations or reinforcements, but on whether a given outcome can be predicted better following a given stimulus (or response) than if this stimulus (or response) has not occurred (Rescorla, 1968). Phenomena such as 'blocking' (Kamin, 1969) are interpreted as showing that once an animal can adequately predict a particular outcome, it does not look for extra predictions, and so may fail to learn about further contingencies associated with that outcome that, from its point of view, would be redundant. There are thus indications of selective processing, cognitive 'miserliness' (cf. Nisbett and Ross, 1980) and possibly even the use of heuristics (see Chapter 7, pp. 220–6) in animal cognition that have demonstrable effects on behaviour.

The essential unity of processes of stimulus and response learning is further shown by studies of 'stimulus–response interactions', where emotional reactions to stimuli produced by Pavlovian conditioning can influence instrumental responding to other stimuli – e.g. superimposing a fear stimulus on an avoidance reaction will increase the intensity of avoidance (Martin and Riess, 1969; Rescorla and Solomon, 1967). Tarpy (1982) argues strongly for an interpretation of such results in terms of interacting conditioned emotional states. This testifies to the close interrelationships between behavioural, cognitive, and affective systems in animals – a message that is interesting not simply in terms of Rosenberg and Hovland's (1960) classification of attitudes into three analogous components, but also in relation to more recent work on the influence of affect and emotion on social cognition (Clark and Fiske, 1982), and of the priming effects of mood and affectively loaded stimuli on memory and judgement (Bower, 1984; Fazio, Powell and Herr, 1983; Higgins, Rholes and Jones, 1977), to be described in Chapter 7 (pp. 232–7).

The point of all this is that, whereas we tend to think of attitudes as something distinctively human, the *responses* we take as indicative or expressive of attitudes may be acquired through processes that we seem to share, to a large extent, with other animals.

What the animal literature appears to tell us is that expectancies, emotional states, and adaptive or goal-oriented behaviours, tend to be acquired in a closely interrelated manner, but also in relation to very specific stimulus contexts. Put differently, the same stimulus conditions can give rise together to effective, cognitive and behavioural responses. In more human terms, consistency between affect, evaluative beliefs, and behaviour is likely to be high so long as one is dealing with the *same* specific attitude object under the *same* stimulus conditions. This is exactly the point that Fishbein and Ajzen (1975) make when they demand precise matching of levels of specificity and content among 'attitudinal' and 'behavioural' measures. On the other hand, when affective, cognitive and behavioural responses are elicited under different stimulus conditions, a lack of correspondence, or, in social psychological terms, an apparent attitude–behaviour discrepancy, may be typical. One would of course expect similar stimulus conditions to elicit similar patterns of response through processes of generalization. However, similarity may not always be easy to quantify outside the laboratory independently of the dependent variables it is presumed to influence.

So we can expect consistency between what Rosenberg and Hovland (1960) would have called the three 'components' of attitude, to the extent that the different responses measured are responses to the same stimulus conditions – not because of any process of balance, but because such responses *share a common learning history*. We can, however, expect apparent inconsistency as soon as the stimulus conditions differ, and they may not have to differ by very much. Although it will be remembered that Breckler

(1984) found *weaker* associations between affect, cognition and behaviour in the physical presence of an attitude object (a live snake), his experiment did not ensure that affective, cognitive and behavioural responses to snakes had been acquired together. More relevant is the evidence of greater attitude–behaviour consistency when attitudes are acquired through direct (i.e. behavioural) experience (Fazio and Zanna, 1981).

We need to be careful, however, over what might be meant by 'consistency' in the context of animal studies. Here we are talking primarily of events, such as animals approaching stimuli associated with food (or some other attractive unconditioned stimuli) and avoiding stimuli associated with aversive states. In the human context, we *can* scale behaviours on a single evaluative dimension analogous to approach-avoidance, as Fazio's (1985) model arguably requires. Indeed, many measurement techniques do essentially this. However, we are clearly losing information through such a simplification – information that may be vital to any assessment of consistency.

The real conceptual difficulty in the human context, though, is not with relating changes in adaptive or goal-directed action to changes in expectancy or emotional state, but with relating any of these to linguistic behaviour. Whilst the Rosenberg and Hovland (1960) 'three-component' model may provide a quite useful taxonomy of non-linguistic attitudinal responses, for some purposes it disguises what may be a crucial distinction by dispersing linguistic behaviour across the three components according to its content.

Consistency and the meaning of expressive behaviour

Before examining how linguistic behaviour may differ from other forms of response, however, it must be stressed that it is not *necessarily* very different in all contexts. It is perfectly reasonable to think of people making particular kinds of verbal statements about an issue either out of habit, or to produce a desired effect on their audience. People may well acquire, for instance, the habit of talking about members of an outgroup in a pejorative fashion, through imitation or whatever, but without necessarily having direct contact with individual outgroup members. Indeed the use of racist rhetoric may coexist with friendly interpersonal relationships with individuals of other ethnic groups, as Billig (1985) points out. How much such verbal behaviour 'truly' expresses the speaker's subjective evaluative experiences cannot be determined without taking other evidence and situational factors into account.

Just as verbal behaviour can be conditioned, so it can be instrumental. It is easy enough to think of examples of where people 'say things for effect' or conversely refrain from stating a position because of the company they are in. This essentially amounts to considering such verbal behaviour as an intentional act that may be largely shaped by normative expectations. Here again, one requires additional information to determine the sincerity of such verbal behaviour.

There is a sense, therefore, in which we can account for the fact that attitude statements are *made* (though not for how such statements are *understood*) without needing to assume any necessary relationship between such statements and the speaker's subjective evaluative experience of the attitude object to which the statements refer. Nonetheless, it is also an important fact that people will *in general* interpret such statements as expressive acts, and furthermore that any instrumental effectiveness of such statements within a social context (be they sincere, insincere, or simply empty) derives from this fact. What then is really meant by saying that statements *express* a person's attitude?

As already mentioned, much of the methodology of attitude measurement and research makes the assumption that attitude statements express positive to negative evaluations, and thus attitudes are scaled on an evaluative dimension from favourable to unfavourable. However, if *all* that attitude statements expressed was positive to negative evaluations, the use of *language* for this purpose would be an extravagant complexity. Any other range of displays, from smiles to frowns, or gurgles to growls would suffice, provided (and it is quite a big 'provided') that the identity of the attitude object that stimulated such evaluative responses could be clearly discerned. In other words, if *all* that we require of attitudes is that they involve subjective evaluative experience, and *all* that we require of an expressive repertoire is that it communicates such evaluations, there is no reason in principle to insist that attitudes are inherently human. In terms of such a perspective, animals can have attitudes, and express them, too.

If this perspective strikes you as too limited, too reductionist, then you must ask: what exactly has been left out? What can language do that shrieks or barks cannot? Many things, obviously, but among the functions of language most relevant to attitude expression are: the possibility of *reference* to objects and abstractions that are not physically present, the possibility of *negation*, and hence expression of disagreement, and the possibility of *argumentation*, whereby evaluations may be defended and their implications for beliefs and behaviour articulated.

What is crucial is that these functions of reference, negation and argumentation are only meaningful within a *social* context which assumes the possibility of another person by whom such expressive behaviour may be interpreted. There is thus a fundamental dialectical opposition between attitudes as subjective individual experience and attitude expression as an objective social activity. Justice cannot be done to this dialectic by ignoring either one side or the other. People have subjective experiences, whether or not they express them. At the same time, the statements people make *have meaning* in their own right, whether or not they accurately communicate subjective experience. Yet still we would not have the concept of attitude that we do, were it not for our use of language to communicate what we feel. As for causality, it is just as reasonable to think of subjective experiences becoming structured through the cognitive and social processes involved in their expression as it is to assume that expressive behaviour is always shaped by antecedent experiences. Furthermore, the relationship of meaning to expression is logical, not causal: the meaning of a statement does not 'cause' the statement to be made.

An important part of socialization seems to be learning how one may be *held accountable* for things one says and does. This involves partly the learning of normative expectations concerning if–then contingencies (e.g., 'If you make a promise, other people will expect you to keep it'). If one violates such normative expectations, one renders oneself less predictable and thereby less intelligible. This in turn means that the way others will behave towards oneself will be less predictable and controllable. Consistency is thus a *social product*, born of *others'* expectations concerning what follows from the performance of a specific expressive act. Similarly, *social* factors can make such expectations sometimes more salient, and sometimes less so. Because attitudes involve communication as well as subjective experience, one can look *outside* the individual for the origins of many of the processes supposedly involved in attitude formation and change. To say that people may elaborate their own arguments in response to persuasive communications (Petty and Cacioppo, 1985) comes close to saying that they will rehearse a kind of dialogue with the communicator or an imaginary other. Fazio, Lenn and Effrein (1984) found shorter response latencies suggestive of more accessible attitudes when subjects expected to have individual discussions about their evaluations of the attitude object (types of puzzles) or to have opportunities to act out their evaluations (i.e. work with the puzzles) later.

Accountability may not only produce pressures towards consistency, but also towards complexity. Tetlock (1983) had subjects report their attitudes on controversial issues (affirmative action, defence spending and capital punishment) under conditions where they expected to be anonymous or to have to justify their viewpoints to another person with liberal, conservative, or unknown attitudes. Subjects shifted towards more liberal standpoints when expecting to interact with a liberal other, and to more conservative standpoints when they expected the other to be conservative. The most interesting results, however, came from the condition where the other's views were unknown. Here subjects produced arguments of greater evaluative *inconsistency* and 'integrative complexity'. In other words, they came to think about the issues in more multidimensional terms 'thus preparing themselves for arguments that could be raised against the positions they had taken' (Tetlock, 1983: 80).

Such a view contrasts with the more traditional definition of balance or consistency as depending on some kind of intrapsychic aesthetic sense or *Gestalt* principle of cognitive organization. Even so, there is every reason to suppose that a person's subjective evaluative experiences of attitude objects can be based on more than raw emotional reactions, and can instead involve comparisons, selections, categorizations, inferences, associations, expectancies and so on, all of which may be directly influenced by the manner in which the person has learned to communicate such experiences to others. The language of attitude expression does not simply reflect a set of devices for engineering social approval, it can feed back into the nature of the subjective experience itself. Words like nice, nasty, clean, dirty, safe, dangerous, contain as strong connotations of 'do' and 'don't' as of 'good' and 'bad'. If attitudes become coded in terms of such categories, they acquire a behavioural imperative as part of the experience itself. Feeling that something is bad carries with it a feeling that it ought somehow to be avoided, prevented or corrected if at all possible.

That is why the question of the relationship of attitudes to behaviour is not *simply* an empirical, but also partly a logical, one. Through socialization we also learn the power of language to produce behavioural effects. Expressions of evaluation are not simply like ratings on a scale from good to bad – they can convey a *gerundive* message: this is something that ought or ought not to be done, whether for ethical reasons or as a means to achieve a desired goal (Nowell-Smith, 1956). Evaluative 'definitions of the event', to borrow Fazio's (1985) phrase, if coded linguistically, contain implicit plans for action, that is, implications about what should or should not be done. The arguments people construct to defend their evaluations can thus also be used to justify their behaviour. Evaluative language contains within itself implicit directives for potential action.

Conclusions

Attitudes, in short, have behavioural implications. The question of which specific behaviours are implied by a particular attitude, however, will depend on circumstances, and is therefore an empirical one. What Fishbein and Ajzen (1975, 1980) demonstrate empirically is the closer correspondence of evaluative and behavioural measures where the measures themselves have a closer linguistic and logical relationship to each other. The establishment of common reference in terms of target, time and place is as much a technique of refinement of *meaning* as anything else.

Work by Bentler and Speckart (1979, 1981) and others demonstrates that behavioural decisions have a history, and that to understand the relationship of present attitudes to present behaviour, we must look back to see how stable such attitudes and behaviour have been over time. Fazio's work shows the importance of learned evaluative associations to the attitude object, and the way such associations may guide cognitive and behavioural processes. His emphasis on the concept of selective perception helps to take account of the differential salience of specific beliefs for individuals with different attitudes observed in our own research.

Attitudes involve not only the acquisition of affective, cognitive and behavioural responses, but also the communicative skills to express one's subjective experience. To understand attitudes, we must attempt to understand not simply processes of learning but processes of communication.

4
Motivation, incentive and dissonance

Intrinsic and extrinsic motivation

A central place in psychology has always been accorded to the study of the effects of reward and reinforcement on behaviour. The 'law of effect', that the probability of a response being emitted varies as a function of its consequences for the subject, is one of psychology's most basic postulates. But does this 'law' adequately describe the effects of rewards and incentives on more complex forms of human social behaviour? Is a simple manipulation of reward and punishment, incentive and deterrent, all that is required to change people's behaviour in a 'desired' direction? The answer to this question has profound implications for educational, clinical, criminological, industrial and marketing psychology, and indeed for any applied area of psychology one could think of. It also raises more general issues concerning the potential abuse of psychological techniques for political purposes. It is not just an abstract theoretical question. Nonetheless, it is in social psychological research that some of the clearest evidence can be found concerning how this principle may and may not usefully be applied.

A distinctive feature of a social psychological approach to this issue is a concern with how incentives and deterrents are interpreted by those to whom they are offered. Confronted with incentives and deterrents, individuals might ask themselves: 'Am I behaving in this way because of my own feelings towards what I am doing, or because of what I hope to get out of it?' A person who performs a task believing it to be interesting or enjoyable in itself is said to be 'intrinsically' motivated, whereas someone for whom the task is merely a means of achieving some ulterior goal or reward is said to be 'extrinsically' motivated.

How do these two types of motivation affect each other? A common assumption is that a trade-off relationship operates between intrinsic and extrinsic sources of motivation, so that an individual may be less likely to find an activity intrinsically motivating if there are strong extrinsic reasons (such as a large monetary reward, or the threat of punishment) for performing the activity. Extrinsic rewards, in other words, may undermine intrinsic interest, at least if one is dealing with behaviour which the individual might have been happy to perform anyway. Someone offering an excessive incentive to perform such behaviour may produce the feeling 'I'm just doing this for the money', or 'I have to do this or else I'll get punished', rather than

'I'm doing this because I want to'. If this happens, then one would expect the person to stop performing the activity as soon as the intrinsic rewards or threats were withdrawn.

A number of studies have supported this 'overjustification hypothesis'. Deci (1971) had college students play with a commercially produced puzzle during each of three experimental sessions. During the second of these three sessions, the experimental group received payment for their solutions to the puzzle, while the control group did not. Deci found, as predicted, that the experimental group spent less time playing with the puzzle of their own free choice in the third session when the incentive for performance had been removed, whereas the control group spent slightly more time.

Kruglanski, Friedman and Zeevi (1971) found that high-school students who were unexpectedly promised a tour of the university psychology laboratory after volunteering for a problem-solving task showed less intrinsic motivation for the task than a group who received no such promise, as reflected by a number of measures of performance, including the strength of the Zeigarnik (1927) effect (the tendency to recall interrupted problems more than completed ones). Calder and Staw (1975) had male undergraduates solve a series of 15 easy jigsaw puzzles, designed so as to be either fairly interesting (consisting mainly of pictures from *Life* and *Playboy* magazines) or fairly boring (of exactly the same shape, but without any pictures), under conditions where they either received no payment, or collected $1 which was left for them beside the last of the puzzles. When subjects were asked to rate their enjoyment of the task, those who had solved the blank puzzles gave higher ratings when they had received payment, whereas those who had solved the more interesting picture puzzles rated their enjoyment less when they had been paid.

Similar effects have been found using much younger subjects. Lepper, Greene and Nisbett (1973) had nursery-school children (aged three to five years) draw with felt-tip pens either under a 'no award' condition, or an 'expected award' condition where they were promised a 'Good Player Award' (a brightly decorated certificate) for drawing pictures, or an 'unexpected award' condition, where they received the same award but had not been promised it beforehand. One or two weeks later, independent observers counted the time spent by the children playing with the felt-tip pens during a free-play period. The amount of time so spent by subjects in the 'expected award' condition was approximately half that spent by those in the other two conditions. The interpretation is that subjects in the 'expected award', but not the 'unexpected award' condition, could put their interest in the drawing activity down to their eagerness to obtain the promised reward, rather than to the enjoyability of the task itself.

Lepper and Greene (1975) found a similar difference between unexpected and expected award conditions, with an interesting puzzle as the experimental activity, and access to a variety of toys as the reward. Children who had been promised a reward showed less subsequent interest in the puzzle, as did another group who were told that their activity was being monitored by a television camera.

In the two experiments just described, subjects who expected a reward also knew what that reward would be. An experiment by Ross (1975) compared instead a no-reward condition with a 'non-salient' reward condition in which nursery-school children were promised a reward, but not told what it would be, and a 'salient' reward condition, in which a box was put in front of them throughout their performance of the experimental activity (beating a drum) with the unknown reward underneath. Subsequent measures showed that intrinsic interest in the drum-beating was lowest in the salient reward condition. In a second experiment, Ross established that decrease of intrinsic motivation as a result of expected rewards is not simply due to the possibility, suggested by Reiss and Sushinsky (1975), that the thought of reward might distract subjects from the experimental activity. In the experimental conditions of this second study, subjects were all told the reward that they would receive (some marshmallows). The crucial comparison was between a 'think-reward', condition, in which subjects were told to 'think about the marshmallows' while they were playing the drum, and a 'distraction' condition, in which they were told to 'think about snow'. Subjects who had been in the distraction condition on average spent more than twice as much time as those who had been in the 'think-reward' condition playing with the drum in a later free-play period.

Ross, Karniol and Rothstein (1976) examined the possibility that the apparent decrease in intrinsic motivation in conditions where subjects anticipate a reward for performing the experimental task might be due to the frustration of having to wait for the reward, making the task itself, by association, seem more unpleasant. This suggestion is very plausible in view of the relative lack of tolerance by young children for delayed gratification (Mischel, 1974). As in previous studies, Ross et al. found that an anticipated reward reduced subsequent intrinsic motivation, but only when subjects were told that the reward depended on their performing the activity in the absence of the experimenter. When the reward was dependent only on their waiting for the experimenter's return, intrinsic interest in the activity was actually enhanced.

Reiss and Sushinsky (1975, 1976), however, have raised a more basic objection to this body of research, on the grounds that it is frequently unclear exactly what is being rewarded in the 'reward' conditions of the experiments just described. It would presumably make a difference if subjects felt that they had to show special care rather than creativity, or creativity rather than persistence, to obtain the reward. Also, it is possible that the rewards given might reinforce responses other than those in which the experimenter was interested. There is, however, no consistent evidence that the quality of subjects' performance during the experimental sessions as opposed to subsequent free-play periods is typically any worse under reward than under no-reward conditions (though obviously this may sometimes be difficult to measure). In other words there is no consistent evidence that subjects are being reinforced for 'low-quality play'.

Reiss and Sushinsky (1975, 1976) also take issue with the assumption that subjects *explain* their own performance by reference to the rewards they receive (an assumption derived from attribution theory – see Chapter 6). They point out that there is little direct evidence that subjects verbalize their reasons for performing the rewarded task by saying, 'I did it to get the reward'. Bearing in mind both the age of the subjects in most of these studies, however, as well as possible demand characteristics of the experimental situation, such lack of evidence should not be regarded as crucially damaging. As Nisbett and Wilson (1977) have argued, people may often have difficulty in verbalizing the reasons for their own behaviour. A study by Kruglanski, Alon and Lewis (1972), for instance, which showed decreases in reported task enjoyment after subjects (10- to 11-year-olds) had been unexpectedly rewarded for winning a team game, showed that a proportion of those who had been rewarded mistakenly named the prize (of which they had been unaware at the time) as their reason for participating in the game. The conclusion that overjustification manipulations can produce changes at a behavioural level without corresponding changes in attitude and cognition has been challenged by Quattrone (1985), however. He points out a number of conceptual and methodological difficulties with such findings, particularly in relation to different kinds of self-report procedures, and possible interference with cognitive processing due to the distraction of the behaviour itself.

One of the main reasons why Reiss and Sushinsky object so strongly to the overjustification hypothesis seems to be their interest in defending the use of behaviour-modification techniques, such as token economies. One of the most important points that they make is that the experiments described have used single-trial reinforcements, whereas behaviour-modification techniques rely generally on a series of reinforcements for continued performance of the activity which the experimenter wishes to produce. Somewhat belatedly, perhaps, Greene, Sternberg and Lepper (1976) have attempted to deal with this objection by demonstrating overjustification effects following multiple-trial reinforcements of an intrinsically interesting activity. However, as Lepper and Greene (1976) points out, there remains an equally important difference between the situations studied in the behaviour modification and the overjustification literatures. The former body of research is primarily concerned with influencing subjects to acquire and maintain *new* patterns of behaviour that they would not have consistently performed of their own accord without such intervention. Whereas the effects of such treatments may not always generalize to other forms of behaviour or necessarily survive for long after the complete withdrawal of reinforcement, at least they provide many psychiatric patients, autistic children, and other groups of clients, with much-needed success experiences (and presumably subsequent gains in self-esteem) which they would otherwise not have had. By contrast, the overjustification literature is concerned explicitly with undermining motivation for behaviour in which the subject is *already* keen and able to engage, before any experimental intervention. It is also important to consider what rewards are perceived as being rewards *for*. Ross (1976) makes the distinction between extrinsic rewards that are made contingent simply on performance of an activity (which typically undermine intrinsic interest) and those that are made contingent on the quality or success of performance (which may not). Harackiewicz, Manderlink and Sansone (1984) compared students' intrinsic motivation on a pinball game under different reward conditions. They argue that even reward procedures that are contingent on quality of performance may contain negative as well as positive features. On the positive side, the reward may be desirable in itself (have 'positive cue value') as well as providing informational feedback about success. However, on the negative side, knowing that one's performance is being evaluated may lead one to see it as under extrinsic control. Harackiewicz *et al.* conducted three experiments in order to unconfound these features. In the first experiment, subjects who received a reward showed greater intrinsic interest (both attitudinally and behaviourally) than those who experienced the same evaluation expectancy and informational feedback but without a reward (the latter group showing *less* intrinsic interest than controls). In the second experiment, unexpected rewards were found to enhance intrinsic interest more than expected rewards. In the third experiment it was found that the negative effect of evaluation expectancy on intrinsic interest could be counteracted by telling subjects beforehand what target score would count as success, thereby allowing them to evaluate their own performance while the game was in progress.

A study by Miller, Brickman and Bolen (1975) provides evidence that subjects' intrinsic motivation can be increased by influencing the attributes they ascribe to themselves. In the first experiment which they report, classes of pupils around ten years of age were submitted to schedules designed to make them be tidier and clean up litter in their classroom. One class was assigned to an 'attribution' condition, in which their teacher repeatedly told them how neat and tidy they *were*. Another class was assigned to a 'persuasion' condition, in which the teacher continually told them that they *should be* neat and tidy. Pupils in the 'attribution' class were considerably tidier than both the 'persuasion' class and a control class who received no special treatment. This was assessed by the percentage of litter put into a waste-paper basket, rather than left on desks or on the floor, shortly after the training phase had been completed. A delayed assessment two weeks later (after the period in which no further mention was made of tidiness by the teacher) showed the 'attribution' group at least as tidy as on the previous assessment, but the 'persuasion' group had returned to the level of the control group.

In their second experiment, Miller *et al.* (1975) generalized this approach to performance at mathematics among pupils of about seven years old. Pupils who received comments from their teacher such as: 'You are doing very well in arithmetic', or 'You really work hard in arithmetic', showed sustained improvement as compared with those who were told: 'You should be good at arithmetic', or 'You should work harder at arithmetic'. Miller *et al.* suggest that 'persuasion often suffers because it involves a negative attribution (a person should be what he or she is not), attribution generally gains because it disguises persuasive intent' (1975: 430). It may be that 'overjustification' procedures similarly imply negative attributions, such as, 'I know that you wouldn't want to do this for nothing, so this is what I'm offering you.'

The predominant concern in the literature with how subjects might *explain* their own performance, however, may have distracted attention from the question of how they *feel* about what they do and the feedback they receive. In the Miller *et al.* study, for instance, being told that they *were* neat and tidy would surely have made the pupils feel happier and better about themselves than being told that they *should be* neat and tidy. Pretty and Seligman (1984) have proposed that manipulations found to undermine intrinsic motivation may also create more negative moods. In an experiment similar to Deci's (1971), in which student subjects were presented with a number of puzzles, Pretty and Seligman found that subjects' reports of their own mood states increased and decreased in parallel to manipulated changes in intrinsic motivation (as reflected in both self-reports and behavioural persistence). In a second experiment, subjects' mood was directly manipulated by having them read and think about cheering or depressing statements about themselves (a technique developed by Velten, 1968). An indication of negative mood further undermined intrinsic interest in the task, whereas an induction of positive mood produced an increase in intrinsic interest sufficient to cancel out any 'overjustification' effect produced by an expected reward.

Despite the apparent contradiction between overjustification effects and a simple notion of reinforcement, therefore, it is by no means clear that such findings are incompatible with general principles of learning. If people do not persist at tasks that have become associated with a negative mood state, this is easily interpretable as a special case of secondary negative reinforcement. What matters is not just what rewards people *receive*, but the thoughts and feelings to which such rewards give rise.

Cognitive dissonance theory

In between those kinds of behaviour in which people would be eager to engage spontaneously, and those which they would refuse, or feel unable, to perform except in the presence of powerful and consistent reinforcements, there lie a large number of behaviours which people might be prepared to undertake, but still have doubts about whether they were doing the right thing. It is this last category that has been the prime focus of probably the most influential theory in social psychology, Festinger's (1957) theory of cognitive dissonance. According to this theory, any decision between alternative courses of action will lead to a state of psychological tension or 'dissonance' to the extent that the net attractiveness of the two alternatives is similar. This state of dissonance, moreover, does not immediately dissipate once the individual has embarked on the chosen course of action. For it to do so, the individual must usually engage in some 'cognitive work' which will lead to a re-evaluation of the relevant 'cognitive elements'.

To see how this might apply, imagine the case of a student (male for purpose of this example) who finds that yet another week is staggering to its close, and has to make a decision as to how he is going to spend his Saturday evening. Being someone of fairly simple tastes, at least by Saturday evening, his choice boils down to one between just two alternatives: either his peak experience of the evening is going to be watching the football match on the college television, or he could go off to a party that some friends of his are having. Whichever way he decides, there is always the risk that the next morning someone could greet him with, 'You missed a great party last night', or 'Wasn't it a fantastic match last night? What? Didn't you see it?'. Any doubt that he might feel as to whether he made the right choice would be an example of what is meant by cognitive dissonance. Any reassessment that convinced him that he had chosen rightly after all would provide a means of resolving such dissonance.

Since this example assumes that the choice is initially one between two attractive alternatives, it can be seen that dissonance will increase to the extent that our student learns about positive aspects of the rejected alternative or negative aspects of the chosen alternative. Similarly, any negative aspects of the rejected alternative, or positive aspects of the chosen alternative would allow him to reduce dissonance. The main game might have been a goalless draw between two inferior teams in which he had no interest, rather than the five–one victory by his favourite team that he had hoped to see. Or he might find out the next day that a girl he had been quietly fancying had been at the party unaccompanied and had been asking after him – until she went off with someone else.

In terms of dissonance theory, the cognition that he stayed behind to watch the football is inconsistent with other cognitions that the match was dull, or that he missed a good party. In much the same way that balance theory predicts that individuals will be motivated to resolve cognitive imbalance, dissonance theory (as formulated by Festinger) predicts that he will be motivated to resolve this inconsistency. Since he is stuck with the fact that he did stay behind (cannot change the cognition that he behaved in such a way), he therefore has to try and justify his decision. There are any number of ways in which he could do so, and dissonance theory as such (i.e. as opposed to experimental tests of the theory) does not require that any single method of dissonance resolution should be preferred over others. Indeed, it is likely that a person might use any number of strategies in combination with each other. Most strategies we could imagine, however, relate to central concepts of the theory, and there is a large body of experimental research that testifies to their importance.

One strategy would be to re-evaluate the two alternatives, so that the chosen alternative (the football match) appeared, on reconsideration, even more positive than the rejected one (the party). This might take the form of either a more positive evaluation of the chosen alternative, or a more negative evaluation of the rejected alternative, or both. In the first case, our student could convince himself that he really found the game quite exciting. In the second case, he could convince himself that the party would not really have been worth going to after all – it would have meant a long cold walk in the rain, then having to talk to all those boring people, and he didn't really fancy her, anyway. Experimental evidence for this kind of process of re-evaluating alternatives to reduce any doubt about the correctness of one's choice was found by Brehm and Cohen (1959) in a situation which involved children having to choose between toys of comparable attractiveness. The data suggest an increase in the relative perceived attractiveness of the chosen toy, after the choice was made.

Another strategy would be to recall selectively those aspects of the chosen alternative which were compatible with the decision, and suppress the more negative aspects ('I know there weren't any goals, but there was some superb defensive play'). Although not researched as fully as some other aspects of the theory, this is again a process that has received some experimental support. Brehm (1962) had pairs of friends (college students) perform a rating task, and then compare their completed questionnaires with each other. (In fact, the experimenter did not show subjects their friends' actual questionnaires, but ones which were specially completed so as to be the same as the subjects' own on 30 out of 40 responses, but discrepant on the remaining 10.) The assumption was that the information that one's friend had responded differently on certain items would be relatively dissonance-arousing. As predicted, these discrepant responses were less accurately recalled when subjects were re-tested one week later.

Another strategy would be to deny freedom of choice. It is conceivable that our student could say to himself, 'I heard about the party, but no-one really invited me, so I didn't think I could go.' In such a situation, he can admit that the football on the television was really boring, and that he would have really enjoyed the party, but such feelings of envy or whatever do not constitute a state of dissonance – since he is perceiving the situation as one in which he did not have a decision to make. Possibly this may be a very common dynamic in situations where a person can say fairly plausibly that he 'can't help himself'. One such instance might be that of the large proportion of cigarette smokers who claim that they would like to give up smoking if they could do so easily, but see themselves as 'addicts' who are unable to do so (Eiser, 1978; see also pp. 207–10). Such smokers also tend to be those most prepared to acknowledge the health hazards of smoking, but it cannot necessarily be concluded that such fears for their health, however distressing, constitute a state of dissonance. Rather, it may be that the denial that one could stop smoking of one's own free choice provides a mode of dissonance resolution.

Finally, another strategy to be considered is that of denying the foreseeability of the consequences of the decision. He could say to himself, 'I never thought it would be such a dreadful match' – but in this case it would have to be considerably worse than he expected, or was entitled to expect, for this justification to be plausible, as he should have been aware of some risk of disappointment when he made his decision. (It would be more plausible to use this strategy, for instance, if the television broke down in the middle of the game.) A more promising application of this strategy in this instance would be along the lines of, 'I never thought she'd have been at the party'. As Wicklund and Brehm (1976) have pointed out, the foreseeability of consequences of one's decision, the perceived freedom of that decision, and one's personal responsibility for it, are some of the most crucial variables shown by more recent research to govern the occurrence of cognitive dissonance phenomena.

Forced compliance

The term 'forced compliance' is that given to the most common of the wide range of experimental situations to which cognitive dissonance theory has been applied. Such experiments involve 'compliance', in that a crucial part of the procedure involves inducing the subject to comply with some request. Such compliance is said to be 'forced' in the sense that it is assumed that subjects would not normally wish to undertake the requested behaviour of their own free will. Specifically, it is assumed that the decision to comply with the experimenter's request arouses dissonance, in that the behaviour requested is designed to run counter to subjects' pre-existing attitudes. Whereas, the example in the previous section was a choice between two fairly attractive alternatives, here subjects have to choose what seems to be the lesser of two evils. Either they must refuse what is an unusual, but typically polite, request and risk the embarrassment of appearing antagonistic to the experimenter, or they must commit themselves to behaving in a way which they know to be inconsistent with their true feelings. In fact, the situations devised are ones in which a practised experimenter can elicit almost universal compliance. (Where this is not so, one needs to be very cautious over interpreting any results. If a substantial number of subjects refused to perform the counter-attitudinal behaviour requested of them, one could be less sure that those subjects who did comply were in fact behaving counter-attitudinally; see Chapanis and Chapanis, 1964.) The experimenter's main interest, therefore, is not just in whether subjects will comply, but in the conditions that enhance or minimize any dissonance associated with such compliance, and in how such dissonance will be resolved.

To take the last point first, it has already been mentioned that dissonance theory does not require that any specific mode of dissonance reduction be employed by all individuals in a given situation. However, the situations are so devised that a possible means of resolving dissonance is to change one's attitudes so as to be more consistent with the way in which one has behaved. Thus someone induced to deliver a speech against their previously held beliefs could resolve such dissonance by changing those beliefs. In formal terms, if a person holds the two cognitions, 'I have argued in favour of X' and 'I am opposed to X', one way of resolving the dissonance that this typically produces is by changing the latter cognition to, 'I am now in favour of X'. This prediction that attitudes can change as a consequence of behaviour is the vital intuitive step that separates cognitive dissonance theory from other formulations of the consistency notion. It does not follow from the theory that dissonance has to be resolved in this way. Hence, subjects who do not show such attitude change cannot necessarily be said to be acting in a manner contrary to the tenets of the theory – a consideration which has prompted some critics (e.g. Chapanis and Chapanis, 1964) to regard the theory as incapable of disproof. A more constructive point of view, however, is that any experiment that tests the prediction of the theory for any specific single effect, such as a change in post-compliance attitudes, provides a conservative test of the theory: the predicted effect could fail to occur even if the theory was correct, but would not occur (according to dissonance theorists) if the theory was wrong. Suffice it to say that a large number of studies have succeeded, as will be seen, in producing changes in post-compliance attitudes, and the more serious challenges to dissonance theory have been in terms of the interpretation of such effects, rather than over the question of their occurrence.

With regard to the conditions that are assumed to enhance or minimize dissonance, one of the variables most commonly considered is the monetary or other incentive that the subject is offered for performing the counter-attitudinal task. As in the overjustification literature, it is assumed that a large extrinsic incentive, such as money, may provide a justification for behaviour so that it need not be regarded as attractive for any other reason. In terms of the theory, performing the counter-attitudinal task will arouse dissonance, but this dissonance can be largely resolved if doing so produces adequate extrinsic rewards for the individual. With such dissonance reduced there is then less pressure to change the cognition concerning one's initial attitude. Although the cognition: 'I have argued in favour of X' is still inconsistent with the cognition: 'I am opposed to X', it is *in a sense* consistent with the cognition: 'I have been very well paid for arguing in favour of X.'

I say 'in a sense' because *logical* consistency is not what seems to be at issue here. Rather, what seems to be implied is more a kind of 'balance sheet' of positive and negative consequences (reinforcements even). The point is simply that the amount of dissonance a person will experience is assumed to be a function of the strength and/or frequency of cognitions under the heading of: 'What is bad about my decision?', *minus* that of cognitions under the heading of: 'What is good about my decision?'. The fact that the behaviour was counter to one's attitudes comes under the first heading, but the resulting dissonance can be cancelled out by the fact that the behaviour produced a large reward, which comes under the second heading. The intriguing implication, therefore, is that, since it is predicted that dissonance from counter-attitudinal behaviour can motivate the individual to change the cognition concerning his or her attitude, and since large incentives will reduce this dissonance, *there will be less attitude change when the individual is given a large, rather than a small, incentive for performing the counter-attitudinal behaviour.*

A classic study by Festinger and Carlsmith (1959) was the first to test this prediction directly, and is worth describing in some detail. Subjects, male introductory psychology students, volunteered for a two-hour experiment on 'measures of performance' from among other options open to them to enable them to fulfil a course requirement, which meant that they had to spend a specified total number of hours as experimental subjects. It was explained that the psychology department was also conducting a study to evaluate these experiments with a view to their future improvement, and that a sample of the students would be interviewed independently after they had served as subjects. On arrival at the laboratory, subjects were all told that the experiment for which they had volunteered, although scheduled for two hours, would in fact take only slightly over an hour, so that they would possibly be in the sample to be interviewed afterwards ('Since we have that extra time, the introductory psychology people asked if they could interview some of our subjects . . . I gather that they're interviewing some people who have been in experiments. I don't know much about it. Anyhow, they may want to interview you when you're through here' (p. 204)). For one hour, the subject was then required to perform what was designed to be an extremely boring task.

At the end of this period, when the experiment was ostensibly over from the subjects' point of view, the experimenter then continued with what seemed to be a full explanation of the purpose of the study. Subjects were told that there were two conditions to the study. In the condition to which they had been assigned, subjects performed the tasks with no prior expectations:

> But in the other group, we have a student that we've hired that works for us regularly, and what I do is take him into the next room where the subject is waiting – the same room you were waiting in before – and I introduce him as if he had just finished being a subject in the experiment. That is, I say, 'This is so-and-so, who's just finished being a subject in the experiment, and I've asked him to tell you a little of what it's about before you start.' The fellow who works for us then, in conversation with the next subject, makes these points: (The E then produced a sheet headed 'For Group B' which had written on it, 'It was very enjoyable, I had a lot of fun, I enjoyed myself, it was very interesting, it was intriguing, it was exciting . . .'). Now, of course we have the student do this, because if the experimenter does it, it doesn't look as realistic, and what we're interested in doing is comparing how these two groups do on the experiment – the one with this previous expectation about the experiment, and the other, like yourself with essentially none. (Festinger and Carlsmith, 1959: 205)

Subjects in the control condition were then told that, 'that fellow from the introduction psychology class' was due to arrive to interview them, and were asked to wait for him. For subjects in the two remaining conditions, however, the experimenter then continued, with much hesitation and embarrassment:

> Now, I also have a sort of strange thing to ask you. The thing is this. The fellow who normally does this for us couldn't do it today – he just phoned in, and something or other came up for him – so we've been looking for someone that we could hire to do it for us. You see, we've got another subject waiting who is supposed to be in that other condition. Now Professor —, who is in charge of this experiment, suggested that perhaps we could take a chance on you doing it for us. I'll tell you what we have in mind: the thing is, if you could do it for us now, then of course you would know how to do it, and if something like this should ever come up again, that is, the regular fellow couldn't make it, and we have a subject scheduled, it would be very reassuring to us to know that we had somebody else whom we could call on who knew how to do it. So if you would be willing to do this for us, we'd like to hire you to do it now and then be on call in the future, if something like this should happen again. We can pay you — for doing this for us, that is, for doing it now and then being on call. Do you think you could do that for us? (ibid.)

In one of the conditions the amount offered was $1. In the other condition it was $20. Subjects were then taken in and introduced to the 'next subject' (a female undergraduate hired for the role), and were left to tell her how interesting and enjoyable the tasks had been. When they had finished, they were told that 'that fellow from introductory psychology' was probably waiting to interview them, and on the way to find this interviewer, the experimenter thanked them, as he had the control subjects, with the words, 'Thanks very much for working on those tasks for us. I hope you did enjoy it. Most of our subjects tell us afterwards that they found it quite interesting. You get a chance to see how you react to the tasks and so forth' (p. 206).

In the post-experimental interview, subjects in the $1 condition rated the tasks as significantly more interesting and enjoyable than subjects in either of the other two conditions. A similar, but less statistically reliable, pattern of results was evident in responses to a question concerning willingness to participate in a similar experiment in the future.

Although this experiment is probably the most frequently cited of all dissonance studies, I have described it in such detail because it both provides the archetype for many subsequent experiments, and contains a number of important subtleties that would be missed in a more cursory account. First, what provides the hypothesized state of dissonance? Although the task itself was boring, this boredom in itself was not assumed to be a source of dissonance. Although it was boring, the 'performance' task in fact lasted only slightly over half the time they had initially anticipated. The experimenter then appears to be concerned, through the debriefing, to provide the subject with some kind of learning experience. So far so good. The subject is now ready to leave the experiment after a less-than-fruitful experience, but one that at least provided him with a credit towards his course requirement. But then (except in the control condition), the experimenter asks him, as a special favour, if he would be willing to help him by standing in for the missing assistant. Note that the experimenter has now: (1) told the subject the supposed design of the study, together with details of the assistant's task, (2) told the subject that the assistant would get paid for what he did (but not how much), (3) appealed to the subject to help him out in an emergency, (4) implied that this was the first time he had made such a request of a subject, and (5) put the request on a contractual basis through the mention of money and through asking for a fairly open-ended commitment on the part of the subject to be available to stand in, in any future emergency, until the completion of the study. Note also that the experimenter has not said that he suspects that the task was in fact very boring, and so does not put the request in terms of explicitly asking the subject to tell the waiting subject something which, in the experimenter's eyes, would be untrue. Boredom, after all, is pretty relative, and social psychologists have rarely had difficulty in devising 'boring' tasks which are still credible as procedures within the range of general psychological practice.

In fact, it is an interesting speculation what response such a request might have had if subjects had been promised no money whatsoever. It is quite possible that the apparent confidence of the experimenter in the subject's ability to play the role might have been flattering enough to elicit substantial compliance without any further inducement. What would seem to militate against this is the fact that subjects know: 'They normally pay someone to do this', so that once the question of payment is introduced they can then ask themselves whether they consider this payment to be equitable, bearing in mind the continuing nature of the commitment.

In terms of the theory, dissonance is produced by virtue of the inconsistency between the cognition: 'I found the tasks boring' and the cognition: 'I told the next subject that the tasks were interesting'. How should such dissonance be resolved? By avoiding the latter cognition? Apart from a few discarded subjects, the cognition within this situation can be assumed to be fairly resistant to change. The open-ended commitment to repeat such action in the future is also extremely relevant here (and not just as a variable influencing the perceived adequacy of any reward). Even when he leaves the experiment proper, and is being interviewed by the 'fellow from introductory psychology', he has not fulfilled his commitment. On the contrary, for all he knows, he could be called in the next day to play the same role again. So, the choice for him is either to find compensating elements in his contrast with the experimenter, or to change his cognition that the tasks were boring. The plausibility of this latter alternative is increased by the fact that the experimenter himself genuinely regards the tasks as quite interesting, and tells the subject after his role-playing, but before the post-experimental interview, that previous subjects found the experiment quite enjoyable. By implication, the experimenter is saying, 'You told the next subject the truth'. Subjects in the $1 condition, without any other obvious way of justifying their recent action and future commitment, turn out to be comparatively willing to accept this construction of events. Subjects in the $20 condition, however, can regard their sizeable monetary bonus as adequate compensation for the otherwise negative aspects of their contract with the experimenter. They are thus prepared to give the independent interviewer a different account of their experience than they gave to the waiting 'subject'. Thus we have the paradoxical, but predicted, finding that larger rewards for counter-attitudinal role-playing produce less change in independently measured attitude.

The magnitude of incentive

A number of experiments have been designed to test the prediction that attitude change following counter-attitudinal role-playing will be inversely proportionate to the size of any incentive or payment for such role-playing, within the context of attitudinal issues that might be assumed to have greater personal significance than the situation used by Festinger and Carlsmith (1959). Typically, these have capitalized on controversies of topical significance to their subject populations.

The first of these was conducted by Cohen (1962) at Yale, at a time when the students there were accusing the New Haven police of brutality in quelling a recent campus demonstration. The experimenter approached subjects individually, explained that he was a student doing a research project in 'human relations' on the issue of the police action, hinted that he assumed the subject was opposed to the police action, but explained that, in trying to study this problem, it was important to obtain a full list of possible arguments on both sides of the issue. He went on to explain that an ample number of anti-police arguments had already been collected, but that there was a need for more pro-police arguments. The subject was therefore asked to write the 'strongest, most forceful, most creative and thoughtful essay you can, unequivocally against your own position and in favour of the police side of the riots'. (Note that, unlike the Festinger and Carlsmith study, the subject is aware that the experimenter knows that compliance with this request would indeed be counter-attitudinal.) The experimenter then said he could pay the subjects a specified amount (ranging from $0.50 to $10) for doing so, but that it was entirely their own choice whether or not they were willing to take part in the study. (There is no report of how many refused in the different conditions. Hopefully this was not a function of the size of the incentive.)

Immediately after they had written the essay, subjects were asked, by the same experimenter, to complete a questionnaire which included a critical item on how much they felt the police action was justified. It was suggested to subjects that they might like to look at the issue 'in the light of' the reason they had just considered. As predicted by dissonance theory, the larger the monetary incentive, the less justified they rated the police action.

The Cohen study has been severely criticized by Rosenberg (1965), who sees its results as running counter to his own application of cognitive consistency theory (Rosenberg and Abelson, 1960). His major argument is that the 'dissonance' effect reported by Cohen could be a function of either, or both, of two research contaminants, which he labels 'evaluation apprehension' and 'affect arousal'. The first of these refers to the possibility that the subject could have been nervous about the conclusions the experimenter might draw about his honesty and integrity: 'They probably want to see whether getting paid so much will affect my own attitude, whether it will influence me, whether I am the kind of person whose views can be changed by buying him off' (Rosenberg, 1965: 29). The second, related, possibility is that large rewards might make the subject suspicious of the experimenter and for that reason resentful towards him, with the consequence that the subject might 'find emotional release' for such resentment in refusing to show the change in attitude that the experimenter is seen to be trying to achieve. Rosenberg's argument, therefore, is that Cohen's results reflect experimenter bias (cf. Orne, 1962) rather than dissonance reduction, and that the so-called 'dissonance' effect should disappear if the source of such bias, specifically the fact that the same experimenter elicits both the counter-attitudinal behaviour and the final attitude measure, is removed. Rosenberg does not explain how this would apply to the Festinger and Carlsmith (1959) study, in which these two phases were separated as he recommends.

Rosenberg, therefore, attempted a modified replication of the Cohen study. As before, the issue was one of topical significance for the student subjects – whether the university governing body would allow the university football team to enter a national competition. Subjects arrived as scheduled at the experimenter's office to find him still busy with another 'student'. At this point, the experimenter apologized that they would have to wait 15 or 20 minutes, but then 'remembered' that he had had a call from a graduate student in the education department, who needed some subjects in a hurry for 'some sort of study he's doing – I don't know what it's about exactly except that it has to do with attitudes and that's why he called me, because my research is in a similar area as you'll see later . . . I gather they have some research funds and are paying people.'

Having agreed to go over to investigate this 'second' experiment, subjects were put through a procedure very similar to that used by Cohen, with the 'education–graduate student' appealing for an essay opposed to the university team's participation in the competition. They were then paid $0.50, $1 or $5, and returned to the first experimenter, who explained that the purpose of his study was a continuing survey of student attitudes, and then administered a questionnaire which included an item on the critical issue. As predicted by Rosenberg, subjects in the $0.50 condition showed the least, and those in the $5 condition the most, shift in favour of a ban on the team's participation (the position for which they had argued) as compared with a base-line control condition.

However, there are a number of difficulties with Rosenberg's explanation. From a design point of view, he only shows that, with 'evaluation apprehension' removed, dissonance effects did not occur. He does not show that Cohen's results would have been replicated if evaluation apprehension had been reintroduced into his situation. In other words, since he did not manipulate what he considered to be the most important variable differentiating his own study from Cohen's, he cannot be certain that this variable was responsible for the difference in the pattern of results (but see Nuttin's, 1975: 228–30, comments on this point). Also, as Wicklund and Brehm (1976: 40) note, the essays written by Rosenberg's subjects were later scored for persuasiveness and those by the $5 group were rated as most persuasive. Since writing a persuasive essay against one's own position should give rise to greater dissonance than writing an unpersuasive essay, it could be that subjects in the $5 group thereby experienced greater dissonance than the other subjects. If this were so, the greater attitude change shown by this group would not be incompatible with dissonance theory.

Impression management

Despite these difficulties, the notion of 'evaluation apprehension' proposed by Rosenberg (1965) persisted and was developed by Tedeschi, Schlenker and Bonoma (1971) into a more general approach termed 'impression-management theory'. Tedeschi *et al.* argued that the effects produced by dissonance manipulations are not genuine instances of attitude change, but merely arise from subjects deliberately pretending to hold a particular opinion to improve the impression they feel will be formed of them by the experimenter. Their motivation is to be thought well of by the experimenter, rather than to reduce any internal state of tension.

Notions of impression management have potentially wide applicability in many areas of social psychological research (see Baumeister, 1982; Tetlock and Manstead, 1985, for reviews). Applied to the forced-compliance paradigm, the suggestion is that subjects are afraid that the experimenter will think badly of them if they can be seen to have acted counter-attitudinally for a small reward. One way to protect themselves against the accusation that they have been easily bribed is to *pretend* that their compliant behaviour reflected their true attitude. From this it follows that, if one removes the need for such pretence, there should be no attitude change.

Experiments in which the final attitude measure is collected by someone other than the experimenter who elicited the compliant behaviour, therefore, should not give rise to attitude change as predicted by dissonance theory. However, as has been seen, this prediction is contradicted by the Festinger and Carlsmith (1959) study, where manipulation and measurement phases were separated. Hoyt, Henley and Collins (1972) also found dissonance effects when subjects wrote counter-attitudinal essays anonymously. While there is the faint possibility that subjects might have mistrusted such precautions, an impression-management interpretation of such findings appears rather far-fetched.

Another way of tackling the 'pretence' suggestion is by making subjects believe that attempts at pretence are pointless. This is the rationale behind the 'bogus pipeline' technique proposed by Jones and Sigall (1971). This involves wiring subjects up to a piece of imitation electronic gadgetry that supposedly can tell the experimenter the subject's 'true' evaluation of an object or concept. It seems ironic that experimenters may go to such lengths in deceiving their subjects so as to inhibit their subjects from deceiving them. Nonetheless, the relevant prediction is that, if impression-management theory is correct, dissonance effects should not occur with a bogus pipeline in place.

There are findings on both sides. Cooper (1971), for instance, found that a bogus pipeline manipulation actually strengthened effects predicted by dissonance theory, whereas Gaes, Kalle and Tedeschi (1978) found that such a manipulation eliminated attitude change. It is likely that the bogus pipeline is a rather impure device for persuading subjects to be honest. The experimenter's claims regarding the apparatus need to be accepted as genuine for a start. Perhaps it would not take too much knowledge of brain function (bearing in mind that many, if not most, subjects could be psychology students), let alone of electronics, for subjects to have had some suspicions about the genuineness or at least reliability of the apparatus. What is more, the apparatus may itself, by virtue of its novelty, make subjects feel nervous and aroused in a way that might be confused with dissonance arousal itself. If subjects then interpreted any arousal as due to the equipment, this would remove the motivation for attitude change. Stults, Messé and Kerr (1984) found that a bogus pipeline manipulation eliminated attitude change when they used a standard procedure, but not when they provided subjects with more time to habituate to the apparatus.

More recent impression-management interpretations of dissonance phenomena have placed less emphasis on the notion of attitude as merely feigned. Tedeschi and Rosenfeld (1981) stress the notion of social anxiety or embarrassment as an important mediator of attitude change. Since the same conditions that are said to give rise to dissonance could be said to give rise to anxiety or embarrassment, this proposal looks very like an attempt at reconciliation. Schlenker (1982) somewhat similarly argues that people are motivated to protect positive views of their own identity, and that this can involve *not* regarding themselves as responsible for negative events. As with the earlier suggestion by Aronson (1968) that dissonance primarily involves a threat to self-esteem, there is no implication that attitude change, motivated by a desire to protect a positive identity, is anything but genuine.

Self-perception

Another interpretation of cognitive dissonance phenomena emphasizes the inferences people may draw concerning their *own* attitudes, rather than how they think others may regard them. This is the approach proposed by Bem (1965, 1967) and termed 'self-perception theory'. According to Bem, any self-report of attitude is an *inference* from observation of one's own behaviour, that takes account of the situational constraints, if any, under which such behaviour occurs. If our attitude-relevant behaviour occurs under situations of minimal constraint, this allows us to infer that our attitudes correspond to the way in which we have behaved. On the other hand, if we can interpret our behaviour as a response to situational demands, we cannot use it as a basis for inferring how we really feel. This is essentially the same idea as that which will be discussed in Chapter 6 in terms of 'self-attribution'.

General support for the notion that attitudinal responses may be influenced by processes of self-observation comes from a number of sources. For instance, Ross, Insko and Ross (1971) had subjects complete a questionnaire requiring ratings of agreement or disagreement with a large number of statements on a number of issues, and then at a later session returned these initial questionnaires to the subjects, but with some of the statements replaced by new ones, and with fictitious responses marked in against these, so as to appear to the subjects as though they were ratings that they themselves had made. When their attitudes on these new items were then assessed, subjects behaved as though the ratings assigned to them accurately reflected their 'true' opinions.

Kiesler, Nisbett, and Zanna (1969) found that subjects who had committed themselves to trying to persuade passers-by to sign a petition against air pollution, using arguments prepared by the experimenter, expressed attitudes more strongly against air pollution when the relevance of their own attitudes to such behaviour was emphasized, as compared with when they were led to believe that the reason for their commitment was a concern for the scientific value of the study. This was achieved by having a confederate agree immediately beforehand, in the subject's presence, to a similar request to present arguments on the topic of road safety by saying, in the first condition, 'Okay, I wouldn't mind convincing people about something I really believe in', and in the second condition, 'Okay, it would be good to be in a study that really shows something.' Other studies that have employed similar manipulations of the perceived relevance of general attitudes to specific behaviours include Snyder and Swann (1976), Snyder and Kendzierski (1982) and Borgida and Campbell (1982), all described in Chapter 3 (pp. 72–6).

Applied to the forced compliance paradigm, Bem's argument is that conditions which are designed to compensate for the dissonance supposedly incurred in any counter-attitudinal act, the prime example being the provision of a large incentive, are just the conditions which would allow the behaviour to be explained by reference to situational factors ('I decided to do it for the money'), rather than by reference to one's attitude ('I decided to do it because that's what I believed'). The prediction is therefore that high dissonance (e.g. low incentive) conditions lead to subjects reporting attitudes more closely in line with their behaviour (cf. 'correspondent inferences', Jones and Davis, 1965; see Chapter 6, pp. 175–6).

Bem presents his proposition, however, in a very extreme form. He does not simply say that dissonance-reduction may involve inferring one's attitude from one's behaviour. Instead, he says that the inferences one makes concerning one's own attitudes are the same as those that would be made by an independent observer with access to the same information. To substantiate this thesis, Bem (1965, 1967) presents evidence from a procedurally novel set of experiments, which he calls 'interpersonal simulations'. Such simulations typically take the form of presenting observer-subjects with a summary description of the experimental situation used in a well-known study supporting dissonance theory, telling them of the agreement by an individual subject to perform the counter-attitudinal act requested by the original experimenter, with information about the incentive provided in a given condition, and then asking them to predict the original subject's final attitude response. Among the studies so simulated are those by Cohen (1962) and by Festinger and Carlsmith (1959). Superficially, the results seem to offer good support for Bem's position, with the predictions of the observer-subjects closely paralleling the responses of the actual subjects of the original experiments.

Before one hastens to commend such simulations as an easy, cheap and non-deceptive method of testing social psychological theories, two questions need to be asked. The first is simply: so what? Even if exact simulations produce exact replications of results, does this discriminate between different theoretical explanations? Not at all – it is quite conceivable that states of dissonance arousal and reduction could be experienced vicariously by empathetic observers if the simulations were at all realistic, just as we may experience other emotions vicariously whenever we watch a convincing film. Second, do exact simulations in fact produce exact replications? Jones, Linder, Kiesler, Zanna and Brehm (1968) point out that Bem's (1965) observer-subjects, for instance in the simulation of the Cohen (1962) study, were told of the agreement of just one actual subject with the experimenter's request, and so may have concluded that many of those approached may have refused. They may thus have concluded that any subject who did agree to write a pro-police essay already had pro-police attitudes, especially where there would have been no other obvious reason, such as a large monetary reward, for doing so.

Jones et al. (1968), therefore, compared the results of a replication of the Cohen study (with $0.50 and $1 incentives) run with Bem's instructions (where observer-subjects were told that the 'actual' subject had been selected at random) with conditions where observer-subjects were told that the original experimenter had contacted a number of students, all of whom had indicated negative attitudes towards the police. The idea behind this was to prevent observer-subjects from inferring that an accident of random sampling had given them an exceptional case, who was pro-police and had agreed to write the essay. When Bem's instructions were used, the same pattern of results was obtained as in Bem's and Cohen's original study. However, with these new instructions, the results were reversed.

Jones et al. (1968) also included conditions which included fuller details of the instructions given to subjects in the Cohen study (which enumerated a variety of reasons for writing the essay) than the more abbreviated summary used by Bem. Here again, Bem's findings were not confirmed – observer-subjects gave, on average, the same estimate of the actual subject's attitude response regardless of the level of incentive that had supposedly been offered. An even more complete simulation of Cohen's procedure by Piliavin, Piliavin, Loewenton, McCauley and Hammond (1969) again found no differences among observer-subjects' estimates as a function of incentive level ($0.50, $1, and $5).

The implication of these findings seems to be that observer-subjects do not generally reproduce the responses of actual subjects when the conditions of the original experiment are replicated precisely. Bem's results appear to be the product of the deletion of details from the original procedures that were judged by him to have been non-essential, on intuitive rather than empirical grounds. An important deletion seems often to have been anything that allows the observer-subjects to infer what the actual subject's attitude was, prior to the act of compliance, and this might lead one to expect that self-perception theory generally will only be able to predict attitude change in forced-compliance situations when subjects ignore, or are unaware of, their initial attitudes.

A small number of experiments have therefore attempted to contrast dissonance and self-perception theories by investigating the effect on subjects' attitudes of making their initial attitudes prior to compliance more salient. The argument, as put forward by Bem and McConnell (1970), is that stressing the counter-attitudinal nature of any essay-writing or similar task, by reminding subjects of their prior attitudes, should lead to greater dissonance and hence more attitude change according to dissonance theory, but to less attitude change from a self-perception theory point of view, since subjects would be more likely to use this extra information as a basis for 'inferring' their true beliefs. Implicit in this position is the notion that subjects in a typical forced-compliance study are not normally too attentive to what their prior attitudes may have been, unless the experimenter goes out of his or her way to make these salient.

Bem and McConnell had subjects write counter-attitudinal essays (on the issue of student control of curricula) under conditions of apparent freedom or absence of choice. (As will be described shortly, a consistent finding is that dissonance effects only occur when subjects believe that they have chosen freely.) After writing the essay, half the subjects were simply asked to record their final attitudes, whereas the remainder were asked to say what their previous attitudes had been prior to the experiment, before they recorded their final attitudes. (Actual measures of subjects' initial attitudes had been obtained one week earlier.) The results showed clearly that subjects' estimates of their initial attitudes were practically the same as their ratings of their final attitudes and were more highly correlated with final attitudes than with actual initial attitudes.

Two subsequent studies employed the same issue and basic procedure as Bem and McConnell, but with an additional manipulation to increase the salience of prior attitudes for half the subjects. Snyder and Ebbesen (1972) accomplished this by telling some of their subjects, prior to 'choice' or 'no-choice' instructions, to write a counter-attitudinal essay, to 'take a few minutes to think about and organize your thoughts and views on the issue'. Their results showed more attitude change under 'choice' than 'no-choice' instructions, except when subjects were made to think about their own views beforehand. The choice manipulation had no reliable effect after their initial attitudes had been made salient in this way. Ross and Shulman (1973) instead contrasted a 're-instatement' condition, in which subjects re-read a questionnaire they had completed one week earlier and which contained a response to the critical issue now singled out for special attention, with a 'non-reinstatement' condition in which subjects were not allowed to examine their previous response. The results of this study showed more attitude change under choice than no-choice conditions, regardless of the reinstatement manipulation. Although subjects in the reinstatement condition, as was intended, were able to recall their prior attitudes significantly more accurately than those in the non-reinstatement condition, they showed no less attitude change as a result.

But would these studies have allowed a crucial test to be made of the two theories, whatever the results had been? The finding that subjects do not accurately recall their earlier attitudes after engaging in counter-attitudinal behaviour (Bem and McConnell, 1970) may show that such initial attitudes are irrelevant to later responses, or it may reflect the selective forgetting of dissonant cognitions. Shaffer (1975) has since found greater error in recall of prior attitudes following counter-attitudinal rather than pro-attitudinal advocacy. Moreover, dissonance theory predicts attitude change as a function of counter-attitudinal advocacy only to the extent that cognitions concerning one's attitudes are less resistant to change than other relevant cognitions. Making initial attitudes more salient might simply make them more resistant to change and hence, according to dissonance theory, impel the subject to explore alternative modes of dissonance reduction other than a change in attitude. Greenwald (1975) has even proposed that self-perception theory could be used to predict greater 'attitude change' following increased salience of initial attitudes. Essentially, the argument is that an observer of a person's counter-attitudinal behaviour could interpret the emphasis on the person's previous attitudes as a 'situational demand' which should militate against the occurrence of the behaviour – in Kelley's (1971) terms, it would count as an inhibitory condition. Under such circumstances, the observer might infer that the person's present attitude corresponded even more closely with his behaviour, and the same should apply to self-attribution of attitude.

Greenwald's intention is to show that a truly crucial test of the two theories is impossible. Others have been prepared to distinguish between dissonance-reduction and self-perception processes, whilst disputing Bem's claims that the latter can provide a complete account of the former. Fazio, Zanna and Cooper (1977) propose that self-perception processes may operate where subjects comply with a request to perform a behaviour that is still reasonably close to their initial attitude. One example could be the Kiesler, Nisbett and Zanna (1969) study referred to earlier. Fazio *et al.* suggest, though, that attitude change following behaviour that is more clearly counter-attitudinal is better explained in terms of dissonance reduction. In support of this, Fazio *et al.* found that subjects were more aroused when complying with requests to perform more counter-attitudinal behaviours.

Fazio, Herr and Olney (1984) report two experiments in which subjects showed shorter response latencies to questions about their attitudes where their previous behaviour was more freely chosen. In the first experiment, students completed 90 items concerning religious behaviour, taken from Fishbein and Ajzen (1974). Half the subjects responded to these items in terms of their behaviour up to the age of twelve, the remainder responding in terms of their behaviour over the last year. They then had to evaluate the concept 'being religious' (by pressing a 'yes' or 'no' button in response to the items 'Being Religious': Good? and 'Being Religious': Foolish?). Relative to responses to filler items, subjects showed shorter latencies (hence greater accessibility of attitudes, see Chapter 3, pp. 72–6) when they had previously described their recent, but not their childhood, behaviour. Presumably childhood religious behaviour is more under parental influence, and this, together with its greater remoteness in time, may have meant it was a less relevant cue to attitudinal self-perception. (Response latencies were also shorter when subjects had completed two questionnaire items measuring the favourability of their own attitude, and their own religiosity.) In the second experiment, students' evaluations of increases in tuition fees similarly showed shorter response latencies after they had written an essay on the issue under high- rather than low-choice conditions. Although subjects were told that for experimental purposes the position they should defend in their essay had been assigned to them, it is important to note that in all cases this position was the one most congruent with their own attitudes.

In summary, then, it is difficult (and unnecessary) to say that self-perception processes do not often contribute to attitude change in forced-compliance studies; but the evidence falls far short of requiring us to abandon dissonance theory in favour of Bem's alternative.

Response-contagion

Another important challenge to cognitive dissonance theory is that by Nuttin (1975). In what he calls a 'response-contagion' theory of persuasion, Nuttin argues that so-called 'dissonance' effects (specifically within the forced-compliance paradigm) do not arise from any strictly *cognitive* dissonance, but are to be attributed to the general arousal effects of any novel or unusual situation. The first part of his argument is to deny that varying levels of incentive work in the manner that dissonance theory assumes. According to dissonance theory, the performance of counter-attitudinal acts arouses dissonance by virtue of the inconsistency between cognitions of the form, 'I have argued in favour of X' and, 'I am opposed to X'. The provision of a large, but not a small, incentive is then assumed to cancel out, or compensate for, this inconsistency (what Nuttin calls 'central dissonance'), so that the motivation for attitude change is removed in the former, but not the latter, case. The assumption is that low incentives are not large enough to provide a justification for such compliance, but are *just sufficient* to deter subjects from refusing to comply with the experimenter's request.

Nuttin argues that this last assumption is essentially devoid of empirical support. In previous forced-compliance studies, the decision on what constituted an appropriate low incentive has been made generally on the basis of intuition or precedence, rather than through any systematic attempt to reduce the level of incentive to the minimum. In fact, there are many reports of compliance under conditions of *no* reward, notably in studies where researchers have sought to vary the level of dissonance by manipulating variables other than incentive magnitude (e.g. perceived freedom of choice – see below, pp. 112–14). If subjects comply without an incentive, then, what happens to 'central dissonance'? According to dissonance theory, it should be even greater among compliant subjects in a zero than a low-reward condition, so that subjects who are given no reward should show even greater attitudinal shifts in the direction of the position they are required to advocate than those who receive low rewards.

Apparently, things are not so simple. In one of a number of experiments reported by Nuttin (1975), Belgian students were approached by a female experimenter, who posed as a reporter from the national broadcasting company, and complied with her request to record arguments against reform of the university examination system for use in a radio programme. This, of course, was directly contrary to their own position. The experiment included two conditions comparable to the low- and high-incentive conditions of other dissonance experiments (20 Belgian francs and 200 Belgian francs). Measures of subjects' attitudes after they had recorded their speech revealed the expected 'dissonance' result, with those who received the smaller reward showing the greater shift in favour of the traditional examination system. However, the experiment also included a zero-reward condition. Here, subjects failed to show the shift found in the 20Bfr. condition, giving instead a mean response which was almost the same as that in the 200Bfr., as well as that in a control condition, where subjects were given no reward but argued in favour of their own position (Nuttin, 1975: 87). Thus we have the paradoxical result, apparently inconsistent with dissonance theory, that a low reward leads to more attitude change (presumably as a result of greater dissonance arousal) than no reward at all.

Another condition of the same experiment brings us a little nearer to an explanation. This was a 'relative-deprivation' condition, in which subjects were told that those students who had taken part so far (among whom, by implication, there would be many who would have been allowed to argue in favour of reform) had been paid for doing so, but that the broadcasting company's funds allocated for these payments were now used up, so that they themselves would not receive any payment. These subjects showed the most anti-reform attitudes of any of the groups, even more than those in the 20Bfr. condition. As also found by Cooper and Brehm (1971), not being paid for a task for which others have been paid arouses dissonance, or, less interpretatively, can lead to 'dissonance-reducing' attitude change. But this suggests a crucial departure from the assumptions of earlier studies such as that by Festinger and Carlsmith (1959). It is not that a large reward necessarily reduces dissonance, but that the inequitable withholding of a reward gives rise to dissonance. If the subjects are not led to expect that the task is one for which they should be paid – if, in other words, the question of payment never arises – they may well show no evidence of 'central dissonance' or consequent attitude change. Presumably, in such cases they construe their behaviour as a personal favour, or as a contribution to scientific inquiry, but its counter-attitudinal aspects, according to Nuttin, are essentially irrelevant. If, however, the question of payment arises, subjects then have to assess whether the payment is appropriate or equitable.

Such an assessment of 'appropriateness' may depend on many factors – how difficult the task was (which may be related to whether pro- or counter-attitudinal advocacy was required), how much other participants were paid, as well as the resources of the person who gives the payment. What would be appropriate as a token of appreciation from a fellow-student might be seen as quite derisory from a national broadcasting company, and it is an interesting speculation how many student experimental projects, aimed at replicating standard dissonance results, may have 'failed' because 'low' rewards were seen by subjects as all that the experimenter could afford. Thus, whereas the dissonance theory account is that large rewards compensate for 'central dissonance' but small rewards leave it unaffected, Nuttin argues that so-called large rewards are typically not too much more than the subjects would expect, granted that they are to be paid for the task at all, but that small rewards are perceived as inappropriately low. It is, according to Nuttin, this inappropriateness of the *reward*, rather than the counter-attitudinal nature of the *task*, that produces whatever psychological tension or arousal may be experienced, and that leads to the observed changes in attitudinal responses.

Nuttin goes on to provide additional data aimed at clarifying this notion of 'inappropriateness'. In these later experiments, the same female experimenter, now in the true role of a junior member of staff in Nuttin's department, elicited counter-attitudinal arguments from male psychology students on the same general issue of examination reform, under conditions which departed from subjects' expectations in a number of ways.

In the first of these experiments (Nuttin, 1975: 119), very marked 'dissonance-reducing' shifts were produced when the experimenter supposedly altered the rather bad mark obtained by the student in a recent examination in the student's favour – clearly a most unusual but very welcome reward. This effect was even stronger when the experimenter did this (offering the student money as an alternative) before the student prepared the counter-attitudinal speech. So here a reward which was probably inappropriately generous, and certainly violated role expectations in the kind of generosity involved, produced shifts of the same order as those produced by an inappropriately low, or inequitably withheld, reward in the previous experiment.

Next, Nuttin added a condition which was inappropriately aversive from the subjects' point of view. Here the experimenter unjustly accused the student of disrupting a lecture she had recently given, before he started on the counter-attitudinal task. Again, a shift was found in the direction of making subjects' final attitude responses more consistent with the speech they had produced (Nuttin, 1975: 136). This result is reminiscent of a finding by Zimbardo, Weisenberg, Firestone and Levy (1965), that students and army reservists who were asked to 'volunteer' to eat grasshoppers subsequently rated grasshoppers as less unpleasant to eat when the experimenter had made the request in an unfriendly, as compared with a friendly, manner.

Finally, Nuttin (1975: 150) found comparable shifts following a very different kind of 'inappropriateness', which he terms the 'dissonant-dress' condition. This involved the student, on arrival at the experimental room, finding the experimenter, his lecturer, 'dressed in very short hot-pants and an exceptionally low-necked T-shirt' – definitely not the normal outfit for a Belgian lady academic!

Nuttin argues that what all the experimental conditions which produce shifts in the 'dissonance-reducing' direction have in common is that they confront the subject with a novel or incongruous situation, and that it is this incongruity or novelty, rather than the presumed inconsistency between initial attitudes and compliance with the experimenter's request – the so-called 'central-dissonance' – which produces the arousal that is the precursor of changes in attitude response. This analysis, however, does not so far explain why such arousal should lead to attitude change rather than to any other response, since it is difficult to see how changing one's attitude reduces the incongruity of the experimental situation. Nuttin's answer is an intriguing one – arousal does not lead to a change in attitude response unless the response is elicited.

The main evidence for this assertion comes from a comparison between conditions where subjects' post-advocacy attitudes were measured first at the time of the original experimental session, and then again about five weeks later, and conditions where the first of these measurement phases was omitted. The stability of the shifts produced in the first set of conditions after this intervening period is impressive (Nuttin, 1975: 169). Where the first measurement phase was omitted, however, subjects' responses, assessed for the first time five weeks after the experiment, showed no evidence of any shift. 'There appears to be no trace of any attitude change effect in a situation where the attitude response was not emitted in close temporal contiguity with the ongoing counterattitudinal verbal responses' (Nuttin, 1975: 170–1).

On the strength of these data, Nuttin puts forward his purportedly *non-cognitive* interpretation of cognitive dissonance phenomena. Arousal tends to stabilize ongoing behaviour, so that when someone is induced to produce particular verbal responses, such as a counter-attitudinal plea, under highly arousing conditions, there is an increased probability of their making a qualitatively similar response on a verbal rating scale if questioned about their attitude immediately afterwards. This is derived from the notion that arousing conditions (e.g. social facilitation, Zajonc, 1965) tend to increase the probability of a response that is 'dominant' in an individual's repertoire, i.e. one that already, as a function of previous learning, has a high probability of occurrence. Whether this derivation is authentic depends on whether one accepts that what normally applies to dominant responses also applies to ongoing responses, since the subject's counter-attitudinal behaviour would not have had a high probability of occurrence prior to the experiment. Nonetheless, it is interesting that arousing conditions, all involving some violation of expectations, but not all intentionally related to the manipulation of cognitive dissonance, may produce shifts that appear at least as stable as those resulting from more conventional manipulations.

At the same time, it would be premature to regard Nuttin's results as damaging dissonance theory beyond the point of repair or compromise. Nuttin succeeds in demonstrating that subjects' attitudes, as measured by verbal-response scales, change in the direction of the position they were induced to advocate if they either received an inequitably low reward, received a large but unethical reward (the extra examination marks), were confronted by an unjustly accusing and hostile experimenter, or had to prepare and present their speech with the experimenter dressed in such a way that it must have been very difficult for them to give their full attention to the task in hand. In addition to the studies already mentioned, unethical counter-attitudinal behaviour has been claimed to be particularly dissonance-arousing (Aronson, 1968, 1969), and the effort of performing a task is supposed to be directly predictive of the magnitude of dissonance produced (Aronson and Mills, 1959; Lawrence and Festinger, 1962). Nuttin's manipulations, therefore, need not be regarded as necessarily beyond the scope of a dissonance framework. There are also other manipulations, notably the perception of decision freedom, which certainly are predictive of the magnitude of 'dissonance' effects, but which seem less obviously interpretable within Nuttin's approach (unless one makes additional assumptions about how manipulations of perceived freedom influence arousal). Finally, Nuttin deals only with the forced-compliance paradigm, and it remains to be seen if his theory can account for different paradigms, such as the free-decision situation when an individual has to choose between attractive alternatives.

In a direct attempt to compare dissonance and response contagion interpretations, Verhaeghe (1976) has shown that situations may be emotionally arousing but still not lead to the attitude-change effects predicted by Nuttin. In a variation on the Festinger and Carlsmith (1959) study, subjects were induced to persuade two stooges to spend an extra amount of time performing a boring task. In addition to replicating the standard dissonance effect with a low-incentive and a high-incentive condition, Verhaeghe introduced a 'compensation' condition and a 'retaliation' condition. In the first of these, each subject was given the opportunity, after apparently successfully persuading the stooges, of compensating them for the deception. In the second, the stooges acted unpleasantly towards the subject during the period between the counter-attitudinal advocacy and the elicitation of the final attitude response. In other respects these two conditions followed the procedure of the 'low-incentive' condition and, therefore, should have produced the same degree of emotional arousal at the time the subjects performed their counter-attitudinal behaviour, and hence the same amount of attitude change according to response contagion theory. In fact, no attitude change was produced in either of these two conditions – a result which Verhaeghe interprets as showing that dissonance was reduced through the cognition that the stooges would be compensated for the aversive consequences of the subjects' deception of them, or that they had acted in such a way that they deserved these consequences.

The most important conclusions to be drawn from Nuttin's results relate to the denial of the concept of 'central dissonance' and the specificity of the kind of 'attitude change' produced. It does seem that we should move away from a concept of dissonance as aroused by counter-attitudinal behaviour *per se*, but compensated for by high rewards or the denial of personal responsibility, and think instead of dissonance as produced only under specific conditions. Also, one should hesitate before assuming that one is witnessing changes in general social attitudes rather than specific expressive responses. As Nuttin points out (1975: 178–9), there is evidence from other studies (Festinger and Carlsmith, 1959; Carlsmith, Collins and Helmreich, 1966) that 'dissonance' effects may only be found on scales that incorporate the specific words used in the counter-attitudinal argument.

Choice, foreseeability and responsibility

Tedeschi, Bem and Nuttin all put forward their ideas as alternatives to cognitive dissonance in at least some of its applications. A number of other researchers have considered dissonance in general, and the problem of the relationship between incentive magnitude and attitude change in particular, by looking for other variables which may be crucial for the occurrence of the state of dissonance hypothesized by Festinger. Essentially, the argument is that one should only expect an inverse relationship between attitude change and incentive magnitude if the counter-attitudinal behaviour produced dissonance in the first place. If, for any reason, such behaviour did not produce dissonance, it would be reasonable to expect a direct relationship between incentive magnitude and attitude change. Linder, Cooper and Jones (1967) reasoned that a necessary condition for the arousal of dissonance should be that people can construe the situation as one in which they chose *freely* to perform the counter-attitudinal behaviour. If 'forced' compliance was perceived by subjects to be truly forced, it should not produce dissonance. In other words, dissonance is not dependent on the cognition, 'I did X' (where X is a counter-attitudinal act), but on the cognition, 'I *chose* to do X'. If this is so, one would expect an inverse relationship between attitude change and incentive magnitude under conditions of perceived freedom of choice. In the first of two experiments, they performed a modified replication of the Cohen (1962) study, using the issue of proposed legislation in the state of North Carolina which would have forbidden communists and similar groups to address meetings at state-supported institutions. The subject population (psychology students at Duke University) were strongly opposed to this legislation. Subjects arrived individually at the laboratory to meet the experimenter, who asked them to write essays in favour of the proposed legislation, but before making the request said to subjects in the 'free-decision' condition, 'I want to explain to you what this task is all about. I want to make it clear, though, that the decision to perform the task will be entirely your own.' To subjects in the 'no-choice' condition, however, he merely said, 'I want to explain to you what this task that you have volunteered for is all about.'

After explaining the purpose of the task, the experimenter told subjects in the 'free-decision' condition that the association that was supposedly sponsoring the research would pay them either $0.50 or $2.50 for writing the essay, over and above their experimental course credit, but stressed again that the decision was entirely the subjects' own, and that they would not forfeit the credit if they refused. In the 'no-choice' condition, subjects were simply told in an off-hand way that the association would be paying them either of the two amounts. In both choice conditions, the money was then paid to the subjects before they started to write. As predicted, the results showed that the free-decision subjects who received only $0.50 subsequently indicated, on a brief questionnaire administered by the experimenter, a more favourable attitude towards the legislation than those who had received the $2.50 payment, whose responses were close to those of control subjects who did not perform the essay-writing task. In the no-choice condition, however, the results were reversed, with subjects who received the low reward giving responses close to those of the control group, and those who received the larger amount showing more favourable attitudes towards the legislation.

In the second experiment, Linder *et al.* (1967) applied the same notions to an interpretation of the Rosenberg (1965) results. If a direct relationship between incentive magnitude and attitude change applies under no-choice conditions, perhaps Rosenberg's finding of such a relationship was due to his procedure having somehow reduced subjects' perceived freedom of choice. Although Rosenberg did not pressurize his subjects to go and help out the 'other' experimenter, subjects might well have found it difficult to refuse by the time they had gone to the trouble of finding their way to this 'other' experiment, and had received fairly obligating instructions as to what they then had to do. The procedure for this experiment closely followed that of Rosenberg, with subjects being asked if they were willing to help out 'some graduate student in education' while they were waiting. In the 'prior-commitment' condition, subjects went off to find this second experimenter without any extra comment by the first experimenter other than what was said in the Rosenberg study. In the 'free-decision' condition, however, the first experimenter added: 'All I told this fellow was that I would send him some subjects if it was convenient but that I couldn't obligate my subjects in any way. So, when you get up there, listen to what he has to say and feel free to decide from there.' On arrival at the 'second' experiment, all subjects then received identical instructions, up to the mention of either a $0.50 to $2.50 payment, for writing an essay in favour of university regulations to which they were strongly opposed. As predicted, subjects in the prior-commitment condition subsequently indicated more favourable attitudes on this issue after receiving the larger rather than the smaller reward, thus replicating Rosenberg's finding. In the free-decision condition, however, the results were in the reverse direction, in accordance with dissonance theory.

The implication of this last experiment is that Nuttin's (1975) finding of a 'dissonance' rather than an 'incentive' effect in his attempted replication of Rosenberg's study might have been due to his presenting the possibility of participation in the 'second experiment' rather less coercively. One can only speculate about differences in the non-verbal aspects of experimenter–subject communication in the two studies, but two more tangible differences might have been crucial. First, Rosenberg's subjects were obliged to participate in what was ostensibly the 'proper' experiment of his study as part of a course requirement, whereas Nuttin's subjects attended entirely voluntarily, and without expectation of credit or payment. Second, there are slight differences in the wording of the instructions. After mentioning the 'second' experiment, Rosenberg told his subjects: 'So if you care to go down there you can', whereas Nuttin said to his subjects: 'Perhaps you would like to help him' (Nuttin, 1975: 29). Nuttin's 'second' experimenter was also presented as a graduate in psychology (hence there was less commitment involved in a journey to another location), and seems to have reassured subjects that their choice was still a free one: 'Of course, I do not want to force you to write the essay, but you certainly would do me a favour . . .' (Nuttin, 1975: 31).

In case such differences in instructions are considered too subtle to influence perceived decision freedom, it is worth mentioning a study by Holmes and Strickland (1970). Subjects were instructed in groups to write a counter-attitudinal essay for a reward of either one or two experimental credit points under either 'free' choice, ('we'd like your discussion group to write . . .') or 'no choice', ('we're going to have your group write . . .') conditions. The results confirmed the interaction found in the Linder *et al.* (1967) study, free-choice subjects showing a 'dissonance' effect, no-choice subjects an 'incentive' effect. Perceived freedom of choice also mediates dissonance effects in other situations. Frey and Wicklund (1978) found that 'selective exposure' – i.e. the selective search for information supportive rather than non-supportive of a previous decision – depended on subjects perceiving their decision as freely made.

Research has also shown that an important prerequisite for dissonance arousal is that individuals should be aware of possible negative consequences of their decision at the time the decision was made. In an early study in this tradition, Freedman (1963) investigated the effects of giving subjects high or low justification for performing a boring task before or after the task was performed. When subsequently asked to rate their enjoyment of the task, those subjects who received high justification before the task rated it as less enjoyable than those who received low justification before, whereas those who received high justification afterwards rated it as more enjoyable than those who received low justification afterwards. The implication is that the dissonance analysis of the effects of differential levels of justification (or reward) is relevant only to cases where subjects are aware of such justification at the time they commit themselves to the behaviour. Unexpected consequences of one's behaviour seem to operate more in accordance with a kind of secondary reinforcement principle – more positive consequences producing more positive evaluations of the behaviour.

A number of subsequent studies have produced results consistent with this conclusion. Two such experiments are reported by Cooper and Brehm (1971). In both of these, dissonance was manipulated by leading subjects to feel greatly or slightly deprived relative to other subjects, who supposedly had received high or low compensation in terms of course credits or money for performing a tedious task. Cross-cutting this manipulation, through the instruction letter, subjects (a) either were given no choice over whether to perform the task, but were told about the credit/payment system beforehand, or (b) were told about the credit/payment system beforehand and were given the right to refuse to participate or (c) were given a letter, implying the same right of refusal but with no mention of the credits or payments until after they had performed the task. In both experiments, when subjects were required afterwards to rate their satisfaction with the task, those who had the right to refuse and knew about the credits beforehand (condition b) gave more positive ratings when they thought that they were more deprived relative to the other subjects. Those who had been given no choice, or who were not told about the credit/payment system until after the task (conditions a and c) rated the task more negatively when they felt themselves to be more relatively deprived (though significantly so only in the second experiment reported).

Closely related to this line of research are studies that have manipulated the extent to which subjects might feel responsible for persuading others through advocating a position with which they personally disagreed. Cooper and Worchel (1970) conducted an experiment based on that of Festinger and Carlsmith (1959), which involved male student subjects performing a dull task (actually, one of those used by Festinger and Carlsmith) and then being induced, for either an extra half-hour or one-hour experimental credit, to tell the 'next subject' how interesting it had been. This 'next subject' (a male confederate) then either played the part of becoming increasingly persuaded that it would indeed be interesting, or remained unconvinced. Subjects who felt that they had convinced the 'next subject' through the false information they had given him showed more positive evaluations of the task. Also, the difference between the two levels of incentive, which was in the same direction as that found by Festinger and Carlsmith, came out clearly only when the confederate appeared to be persuaded. Subsequently, Cooper and Goethals (1974) showed that what is important is whether subjects expect their counter-attitudinal advocacy to lead others to change their views. Subjects who expected a recording of their counter-attitudinal advocacy to be played to another group still changed their attitudes in spite of later news that the recording would not be used after all.

There are, however, examples of attitude change following consequences that were unforeseen at the time the decision was made (Sherman, 1970; Sogin and Pallak, 1976). Sherman reports two experiments involving counter-attitudinal advocacy. In the first, an offer of a $2.50 incentive, whether foreseen or unforeseen, reduced attitude change so long as subjects had chosen freely. In the second, the unforeseen negative consequence for subjects, of being told that their counter-attitudinal essays would be published in a student newspaper, increased attitude change under conditions of high choice. Sogin and Pallak had students attempt to generate series of random numbers under different conditions of choice and fore-warning of possible negative consequences (that their random number tables would be useless for research and that their time would therefore have been wasted). Subjects evaluated the task more positively when their apparent freedom of choice of task had been high rather than low, after being told that their list would not be used, and regardless of whether they had been forewarned of this possibility. However, this shift in the high-choice condition *only* occurred if subjects were induced to feel responsible for the quality of their lists.

Goethals, Cooper and Naficy (1979), however, have argued that it is important to distinguish between consequences that are merely *unforeseen* and those that can reasonably be regarded as *unforeseeable*. If the unforeseen consequences are still of the kind which, with the benefit of hindsight, might reasonably have been anticipated, then these should be regarded as foreseeable. Reasonably foreseeable consequences, whether or not actually anticipated, can give rise to dissonance and the kind of attitude-change effects that dissonance theory predicts. This is what may have happened in the Sherman (1970) and Sogin and Pallak (1976) studies.

In support of this argument, Goethals *et al.* (1979) found attitude change following the writing of counter-attitudinal essays, if subjects were told beforehand that their essays would be sent to a committee who might use them for undesirable purposes (foreseen consequences) *or* if they were told afterwards that their essays would go to this committee, having previously been told simply that some other people might be interested in their essays (foreseeable consequences). In contrast, when subjects had previously been assured that their essays would be treated confidentially by the experimenter and shown to nobody else, they showed no attitude change towards the position they were asked to advocate, despite being told afterwards that the essays were in fact going to be passed on to the committee (unforeseeable consequences).

The importance of the distinction between consequences that are unforeseeable and those that are merely unforeseen is that we do not tend to hold ourselves or others *responsible* for the former, whereas we may do so for the latter. We can be held responsible for unforeseen, and unintended consequences, if these consequences could reasonably have been anticipated (see Chapter 6, pp. 180–3). Similarly, denial of freedom of choice involves a negation of responsibility. If subjects can deny responsibility for their counter-attitudinal behaviour, therefore, dissonance theory predictions of attitude change should not apply. Collins and Hoyt (1972) manipulated subjects' feelings of personal responsibility for the consequences of their counter-attitudinal behaviour through the simple device of having subjects sign a receipt for their payment (either $0.50 or $2.50) for writing an essay. For half the subjects, this receipt stated, 'Responsibility for its contents is mine'; for the remainder, it stated, 'I am in no way responsible for its contents.' The perceived importance of the consequences of their behaviour was also varied. Both immediately after writing the essay and also two weeks later, the only subjects to show a strong shift in attitude were those who felt that their essay could have important consequences, had received only the low ($0.50) payment, and had accepted responsibility for its contents.

Within the forced-compliance paradigm, therefore, attitude change occurs only if subjects see themselves as having chosen to perform the counter-attitudinal task with reasonable foreknowledge of its likely negative consequences, and hence with personal responsibility for their decision.

What is dissonance?

Throughout the history of dissonance research, and despite the ability of dissonance theory to generate novel predictions, a remarkable vagueness has surrounded the definition of dissonance itself. This vagueness stems from a typically unreconciled contest between two very different conceptualizations. The first of these involves a definition predominantly in terms of *cognitive* inconsistency. Awareness of implicit contradiction anywhere within one's beliefs, preferences, or thoughts about behaviour should prompt attempts to change cognitions so as to restore a kind of balance. Festinger (1957) clearly endorsed this first definition, but he also talked about the subjective experience of dissonance being one of 'discomfort'. This notion was later developed into the second conceptualization of dissonance in primarily *motivational* terms, as a drive state involving unpleasant arousal (e.g. Brehm and Cohen, 1962).

The impression-management and self-perception approaches were both developed in explicit opposition to this latter conceptualization. The line of argument adopted by Bem initially was a kind of Occam's razor – one shouldn't invent superfluous hypothetical constructs for the sake of it, and arousal seemed just such a construct. If one could explain the results of dissonance experiments without postulating any change in arousal, then, it seemed, dissonance theory should be rejected on grounds of parsimony. At a time when cognitive viewpoints were gaining popularity in many branches of psychology, it seemed easy to treat arousal as something that, at best, could only be indirectly inferred. More cognitive processes of self-presentation and observation, on the other hand, could be accepted as 'real' rather than 'hypothetical', without any special pleading. In fact, though, constructs such as impression-management and self-perception are just as hypothetical as any of the postulates of cognitive dissonance theory.

The traditional defence of dissonance theorists against such critiques was to attempt to discover patterns of attitude change (or resistance to change) that could not be precisely predicted by the alternative theories in question. Effective though this tactic often was, it is surprising how long it took researchers to adopt the more forthright strategy of looking directly for evidence of arousal as a result of dissonance manipulations. It is partly for this reason that Nuttin's (1975) critique provides a refreshing contrast – for him, arousal was the central construct that he sought to manipulate and in terms of which he sought to explain changes in response. Even so, Nuttin's experiments fall some way short of relating dissonance to any kind of physiological arousal. What Nuttin found was that various situations, all of which seem intuitively to have been likely to make subjects aroused, but not all of which bore any close relationship to dissonance theory proper, produced changes in attitudinal response of the kind we would expect of subjects experiencing a 'state of dissonance'.

Is there more direct evidence, though, that the 'state of dissonance' in fact involves tension or arousal? A study by Zanna and Cooper (1974) provides some important information on this point. They had subjects write a counter-attitudinal essay under conditions of high or low perceived choice (hence, high or low dissonance), but in addition gave all subjects a placebo pill before they wrote the essay. Subjects were either told that it would make them feel tense, that it would make them feel relaxed, or were given no information. The results are shown in Table 4.1. When subjects were not led to expect any side-effects from the drug, the typical dissonance results were obtained (with the important additional information that these subjects reported greater feelings of tension under high-choice instructions). However, this effect was eliminated when subjects were able to attribute any experienced tension to the drug, and significantly enhanced when they were given 'relaxation' instructions, the effect of which was intended to make them think: 'If I'm feeling this tense writing the essay after taking a drug to make me relaxed, I must be really tense.'

These findings are complemented by a study by Cooper, Zanna and Taves (1978). Again, subjects had to write a counter-attitudinal essay (defending President Ford's pardoning of Richard Nixon) under high- or low-choice instructions. There were also three drug conditions, with the difference that this time one-third actually received a tranquillizer (phenobarbital), one-third an amphetamine, and one-third a placebo, but all subjects were told that the pill they had taken was in fact a placebo. Subjects given an amphetamine, therefore, should feel most aroused, but not attribute their arousal to the drug. On the other hand, the tranquillizer should suppress any dissonance-produced arousal, and subjects should not attribute such lack of arousal to the drug. The results are shown in Table 4.2. As can be seen, the results confirmed the predictions, with the additional finding of change in the low-choice amphetamine condition. It should be noted that in this same condition, possibly because they felt so aroused, subjects (wrongly) reported that the choice to write the essay had been a free one.

Croyle and Cooper (1983) found even more direct evidence of physiological arousal associated with dissonance by recording subjects' spontaneous electrodermal activity during and after an essay-writing task. Three condi-

Table 4.1. *Mean agreement with the position defended in the counter-attitudinal essay in each condition of the Zanna and Cooper (1974) study*

	Potential side-effect of the drug		
	Tenseness	None	Relaxation
High choice	3.4	9.1	13.4
Low choice	3.5	4.5	4.7

Note: Higher scores indicate greater agreement, 31-point scale, *n* 10 per cell.

Table 4.2. *Mean agreement with the position defended in the counter-attitudinal essay in each condition of the Cooper, Zanna, and Taves (1978) study*

	Type of drug administered		
	Tranquillizer	Placebo	Amphetamine
High choice	8.6	14.7	20.2
Low choice	8.0	8.3	13.9

Note: Higher scores indicate greater agreement, 31-point scale, *n* 10 per cell.

tions were included: (a) high-choice/counter-attitudinal essay, (b) low-choice/counter-attitudinal essay and (c) high-choice/pro-attitudinal essay. The essay-writing task produced elevated electrodermal activity in all three conditions, but it was only in the first condition that elevated arousal persisted during a rest period. A previous experiment, involving the same conditions without physiological recording, had confirmed that the first condition – the only one hypothesized to involve dissonance – produced attitude change predicted by dissonance theory.

Is dissonance experienced as arousal or more specifically as an unpleasant affective state? Studies by Zanna, Higgins and Taves (1976) and Higgins, Rhodewalt and Zanna (1979) have attempted to answer this question by following the Zanna and Cooper (1974) procedure of giving subjects contrasting expectations of the effects of a placebo pill. Zanna *et al.* found that attitude change was inhibited if subjects were led to expect feelings of 'tension' due to a pill, but not if they expected 'pleasant excitement'. Higgins *et al.* expanded this design with two additional suggestions of affective state: 'relaxation' and 'unpleasant sedation'. Consistent with the Zanna and Cooper (1974) and Zanna *et al.* (1976) studies, an expectation of 'tension' inhibited attitude change, whereas expectations of 'relaxation' and 'pleasant excitement' did not. Interestingly, the new condition where subjects expected 'unpleasant sedation' also inhibited attitude change, suggesting that unpleasantness is a more crucial attribute of dissonance than heightened arousal.

This last result suggests that one should be careful not to treat different emotional states as though distinguished only in terms of arousal-sedation, or to regard arousal itself as a unitary concept. Such a conclusion is compatible with more recent research on emotion and arousal, but (as will

be discussed in more detail in Chapter 6, pp. 193–8) earlier social psychological work on this question was heavily influenced by Schachter and
Singer (1962), who proposed that emotion depends both on a state of
arousal and on a cognitive labelling of such arousal, taking account of
situational cues. From Schachter and Singer also comes the idea that the
subjective intensity of an emotion will be reduced if the arousal can be
'misattributed' to an irrelevant or external source.

Leaving until later the issue of the more general validity of Schachter's
theory of emotion, the research reviewed in this chapter supports the
conclusion that dissonance is experienced as an *unpleasant* affective state,
probably associated with heightened physiological arousal (though the
Higgins *et al.*, 1979, data invite some caution here). In Nuttin's (1975)
research, the 'relative deprivation' and other less orthodox conditions that
led to shifts in attitudinal response may have led to general bad feelings
being associated with the compliant behaviour. This assumes, of course,
that in those conditions where Nuttin's subjects received inappropriate
generosity they felt bad about it, and that those faced with the 'dissonant-
dress' experimenter experienced distraction and/or embarrassment rather
than what subjects in the Zanna *et al.* (1976) and Higgins *et al.* (1979) studies
would have accepted as 'pleasant excitement'. (The point is not a frivolous
one. What is involved is not just the nature of a visual stimulus, but that of a
powerfully ambivalent social relationship.)

In other studies, it seems that bad feelings and/or arousal may have been
produced by more standard dissonance manipulations, but the typical
changes in attitudinal response were reduced or blocked because subjects
were able to interpret such feelings as caused by factors other than their
counter-attitudinal behaviour. Pills, placebo or otherwise, have been used
in the studies just cited, but dissonance effects have also been reduced
where subjects have been able to put their bad feelings down to fluorescent
lighting (Gonzalez and Cooper, cited by Zanna and Cooper, 1976),
unpleasant seating (Fazio, Zanna and Cooper, 1977) or, as has already been
mentioned, the paraphernalia of 'bogus pipeline' equipment (Stults *et al.*,
1984).

The 'arousal' conceptualization of dissonance, therefore, is alive and well,
but what of the 'consistency' conceptualization? The question may be
rephrased as whether dissonance arousal is primarily the consequence of
the experience of inconsistency or of other factors. Cooper and Fazio (1984:
234) are uncompromising in their statement of position: 'dissonance has
precious little to do with inconsistency between cognitions *per se*, but rather
with the production of a consequence that is unwanted'.

According to Cooper and Fazio (1984; see also Fazio and Cooper, 1983),
the experience of dissonance is essentially a conditioned emotional
response, acquired through socialization, contingent on the acceptance of
personal responsibility for aversive consequences. Such consequences must

have been foreseeable, and the behaviour freely chosen, for responsibility to be so accepted. Attitude change reduces or eliminates such arousal through allowing one to see the consequences of one's (previously) counter-attitudinal behaviour as not so aversive.

Aversive consequences and learning

Cooper and Fazio (1984) offer an elegant integration of a varied research tradition. However, a number of conceptual as well as empirical issues still require attention. They concentrate, as do most previous researchers, on the forced-compliance paradigm. However, dissonance theory makes predictions about other paradigms in which people may question the decisions they have made. Do people generally devalue rejected decision options, or only where they feel their choice may have had aversive consequences for which they could hold themselves responsible (as Cooper and Fazio would predict)? And how should we decide if particular consequences are more or less aversive? Does it matter more if such consequences are aversive for *others* (as is typical in forced-compliance studies) or for *oneself* (e.g. in studies manipulating degree of effort, such as Aronson and Mills, 1959)? The answer is probably that there is no general answer – it depends on the individual's history of socialization.

Once we open the door to individual differences in socialization, however, there is no real possibility of reimposing the consistency formulation of dissonance as a general principle. Some people may be socialized to have bad feelings if they believe they have been inconsistent or illogical, even if no-one has suffered. Others may worry less about inconsistency unless specifically challenged on account of it. Some may be socialized so as to view counter-attitudinal behaviour as a form of play-acting, others as a form of dishonesty. Some may just feel worse about wasted effort or inadequate payment, others may be less concerned with the accumulation of credits or small monetary payments.

The little words 'unwanted' and 'aversive', on which so much depends for Cooper and Fazio, thus hide a multitude of new questions. Anything can be experienced as aversive if we have learned to find it so. At the same time, culturally shared values will contribute to a consensus over the aversiveness of particular kinds of consequences, and over what constitutes acceptable mitigation. Dissonance experiments exploit part of such a cultural consensus, but only a part. We can expect there to be very many other kinds of situations that are consensually experienced as aversive, and such aversive experience may well lead to attitudinal and behavioural change.

There may be those who are tempted to produce a taxonomy of the kinds of situations consensually experienced as 'dissonant' in this more general sense of 'aversive'. Others may prefer to document the limiting conditions that confine any such consensus. From the point of view of psychological *process*, however, the specific content of such situations does not matter. The issue may be considered more generally as one of conditioned emotional states on attitudes and behaviour.

Dissonance theory achieved early popularity by appearing to contradict accepted notions of reinforcement and the law of effect. Typically, the relationship between levels of incentive and attitude change was viewed as one of the effects of *positive* reinforcement, and it was for this reason that the Festinger and Carlsmith (1959) findings, and their numerous replications, appeared so paradoxical. However, if dissonance is experienced as an unpleasant affective state, then the issue is one of negative, not positive reinforcement. The more negative the experience of dissonance, the more the individual should be motivated to avoid cognitions or behaviours associated with this negative experience. High incentives do not increase the individual's level of motivation under such circumstances – they reduce it. This line of reasoning is compatible with research in the field of animal learning that indicates that different reinforcers and learned associations can have additive effects on animals' emotional reactions to stimuli. For instance, positive rewards can reduce classically conditioned fear, whilst such fear can enhance the learning of avoidance of novel stimuli or inhibit the acquisition of approach behaviours (Tarpy, 1982). Far from challenging notions of reinforcement and conditioning, dissonance research can be interpreted as an illustration of more general learning principles.

Conclusions

This final argument is not meant to sound dismissive of nearly three decades of research. As with the smaller literature on intrinsic and extrinsic motivation reviewed at the beginning of this chapter, much has been learned of the dangers of applying reinforcement concepts too simplistically to human social behaviour. What must be remembered is that we are not just dealing with environmental stimuli and behavioural reactions, but with cognitive and emotional responses, too. Stimuli and responses are open to alternative interpretations. Such interpretations will be emotionally toned, and will themselves be the product of previous learning. People do not just learn to do what pays most, but learn to interpret rewards and their absence or withdrawal as *information* about discriminable features of their behaviour. Interpreting one's actions in particular ways can also provoke emotional reactions which may motivate changes in expressed attitudes and other behaviour. *How* such learning takes place is a question of the greatest importance, but more the business of developmental psychology and theories of socialization than the main focus of this volume. For better or (far more probably) for worse, social psychologists have tended to concern themselves with the products rather than the processes of socialization. So be it – no discipline can consider all questions simultaneously, and the products of socialization are important in their own right. As the research reviewed in this chapter implies, one of the more important of such products is the ability to form evaluative judgements and inferences concerning complex social situations. It is with this that the next three chapters are more specifically concerned.

5
Social judgement

Basic principles of judgement

The question of how people judge stimuli is one of the oldest in psychology. Judgement tasks can take many forms, and they can crop up in any branch of psychology. Deciding whether a stimulus is present or absent, similar to or different from a standard, larger or smaller, better or worse – all these are kinds of judgement; so too is the decision that a stimulus belongs to a particular category, or that stimuli within one category resemble each other more than they resemble stimuli within another category. In short, the term 'judgement' refers to all those processes whereby any piece of information on perceptual input is *compared* to some criterion. Theories of judgement essentially try to describe how such processes of comparison operate.

Are the ways we judge 'social' stimuli – such as other people and things they say and do – the same as the ways we judge physical objects? This question has received considerable attention since, historically, the tendency has been to take theories developed to account for simple perceptual judgements and to see how well they apply to social judgements. On the whole, this approach has been quite successful. To a remarkable extent, principles that account for how people judge the heaviness of cylindrical weights, or the brightness of lights, have been found to be highly predictive of how people judge the desirability of some outcome, or the extremity of somebody's opinion on some issue. Yet there are still a number of important effects that cannot be understood without consideration of more social factors. To a large extent, such differences as there are between social and more simple perceptual judgements derive from the greater complexity of social stimuli, their value-laden nature, and the fact that they are interpreted within the context of social relationships.

Although it is dangerous to describe theoretical debates in terms of simple dichotomies, a distinction can be drawn between those researchers whose primary interest in judgement has been in what it allows one to say about mechanisms of sensory *perception*, and those whose primary interest has been in how subjective experience is *expressed* by means of various kinds of response language. For the present purpose I shall call the first approach 'psychophysical' and the second approach 'integrationist'.

The psychophysical approach has a rather longer tradition within experimental psychology. The term *psychophysics* derives from a concern with identifying lawful relationships between the 'physical' (objective) magnitude or intensity of a stimulus and the 'psychological' (subjective) magnitude or intensity of the sensation it produces. The problem is that sensation and subjective experience can only be measured indirectly, by getting the subject to make a *response* (e.g. by marking a category on a rating scale). There is, therefore, a whole set of questions to be asked concerning the relationships between experience and judgemental response, over and above those concerned with perceptual input. It is with these questions that the integrationist approach is more concerned.

The psychophysical approach and the concept of adaptation

The classic achievement of the first approach was the Weber–Fechner law. Over 150 years ago, Weber proposed that the detectability of any change in a stimulus was a simple logarithmic function of its initial magnitude. For a stimulus of small size or low intensity, a relatively small change would be noticeable, whereas, for a larger or stronger stimulus, any change would have to be larger in order to be noticed. In other words, the size of the just noticeable difference (JND) is directly proportionate to the size of the stimulus. Fechner (1860) extended this notion in order to relate differences in stimulus magnitude to differences in sensation, by assuming that each JND corresponded to a subjectively equal difference in sensation.

Fechner's principle received little serious challenge for the best part of a century. Although his own work was concerned mainly with refining methods for measuring JNDs, it provided the starting point for Thurstone's (1928, 1931) work on attitude measurement, and also for Helson's (1947, 1964) theory of adaptation level. Stevens (1957, 1975), however, proposed that the logarithmic law should be replaced by a power law, in terms of which 'equal stimulus-ratios produce equal sensation-ratios' (Stevens, 1958: 636). He also claims that this principle is applicable to symbolic and social psychological continua such as perceived social status, seriousness of offences, and national power (Stevens, 1966).

For both Fechner and Stevens, the main aim was to discover a stable psychophysical law to relate psychological magnitude, or sensation, directly to physical magnitude. Helson (1947, 1964), on the other hand, was far more concerned with explaining why variations in response to the same stimulus tended to occur when it was presented under different conditions, and to this end proposed his theory of adaptation level (AL). According to AL theory, whenever we are presented with a stimulus we compare it with a subjective average or neutral point. Thus, if we are dealing with judgements of people's height, we might consider a height of 5ft 6in. to be average. If we then saw someone of 5ft 9in., we would probably judge such a person to be fairly tall, whereas someone of 5ft 3in. would be judged as fairly short. In Helson's terms, our AL for judgements of people's height would be

5ft 6in., and the two people whose height we judged would be respectively above and below his AL. A straightforward extension of this notion is that, if different people have different ALs for judging the same stimuli, their judgements will also differ. Someone whose AL is 5ft 9in. will judge more people to be short than will someone whose AL is 5ft 3in. Similarly, our AL for a given stimulus dimension may change over time (indeed, it is predicted to do so as a result of a variety of conditions), and where this happens our judgements will change accordingly: as our AL becomes higher, our judgements of a given set of stimuli will become lower, and vice versa.

How such changes will occur is implied by Helson's definition of AL as a weighted logarithmic mean of all past and present stimulation on a given dimension. As each new stimulus is presented, it will be averaged into the computation of a new AL. Thus, with every new stimulus above the prevailing AL, AL will rise, and with every new stimulus below the prevailing AL, AL will fall. For example, if a subject is judging the heaviness of a series of weights and the experimenter intersperses a new, very heavy weight after each of the original stimuli, the original stimuli will be judged as lighter than they were before. Alternatively, if this new stimulus (conventionally termed either an 'anchor', comparison, or standard stimulus) was much lighter than the other stimuli, the other stimuli would be judged heavier than before. This phenomenon, known as a *contrast effect*, is the single most important predictor of AL theory.

Experience of stimuli prior to the judgement task is also predicted to lead to similar contrast effects. Tresselt (1948) presented the same series of weights to a group of professional weightlifters and a group of watchmakers. At least in the earlier stages of the experiments, the professional weightlifters judged the stimuli to be lighter than did the watchmakers. The direction of this effect is consistent with AL theory, although it is uncertain whether its magnitude could have been predicted.

Helson goes further than just saying that stimuli are judged relative to their prevailing context and that changes in this context tend to lead to contrast effects in judgement. In addition, he makes a number of contentious assumptions. First, in the Fechner tradition, he uses a logarithmic mean formula in his definition of AL. This has been challenged by Stevens (1958). Next, he insists that he is dealing with changes, not merely in the labels which subjects ascribe to stimuli, but in the intensity of the sensations which these stimuli produce. Judgemental contrast effects, according to Helson, are essentially perceptual contrast effects produced by processes at least analogous to those of physiological adaptation. True perceptual contrast effects undoubtedly occur (as can easily be demonstrated by putting your left hand in a bowl of cold water and your right hand in a bowl of hot water, and then, after a minute or so, putting both hands together into a bowl of tepid water – it will feel hotter to your left hand than to your right). It is Helson's assertion that such perpetual shifts are the basis of all contrast effects in judgement.

The objection to this is that generally the same results could be predicted on the basis of the more parsimonious assumption that subjects are attempting to apply an arbitrary response language to a novel and restricted range of stimuli. If the stimulus distribution changes, as with the introduction of a new anchor stimulus, they may change their ideas of what kind of weight it is *appropriate to call* heavy without necessarily perceiving the stimulus weights any differently.

A further implication of Helson's reliance on the notion of perceptual adaptation is that all stimuli on a given dimension within a given modality should influence AL, including those that are irrelevant to the judgement task. The difficulty with this is that it is quite clear that we use words like 'heavy' and 'light' differently depending on the kind of object we are describing. A light suitcase, for instance, would probably weigh considerably more than a heavy book. Helson (1964: 126) struggles to deal with this problem by suggesting that it is all a matter of the number of muscles involved – he refuses, in other words, to allow a cognitive principle such as the notion of perceived relevance into the formulation of his theory. The experimental evidence is quite clear, however. Anchor stimuli, which are made to seem relevant to the other stimuli being judged, produce the contrast effects predicted by Helson's model. Stimuli of the same physical magnitude as these anchors, presented in such a way that they seem to be irrelevant to the judgement task, have no such effects (Bevan and Pritchard, 1963: Brown, 1953).

The concept of frame of reference

Whereas theorists such as Helson seem to assume that the perceiver takes an essentially passive role *vis-à-vis* incoming stimulation, the integrationist tradition treats the perceiver as a far more active processor and interpreter of stimulus information. The roots of this approach can be traced back to the *Gestalt* concept of a frame of reference. Instead of assuming that each stimulus is judged singly in relation to a single standard, be it AL, an absolute threshold value, or a comparison stimulus, the assumption is that perceivers categorize stimuli as belonging to a particular class, and then, if required to judge them, do so in relation to the implicit or perceived distribution of stimuli within that class. An early model in this tradition was that proposed by Volkmann (1951) who claimed that judgements of stimuli were largely predictable from a knowledge of the stimuli at either extreme of the stimulus distribution. Thus, if a subject had to judge a series of lines in terms of a scale from 'very short' to 'very long', a line of 12 inches would be judged as 'very long' if the lengths ranged from 2 inches to 12 inches, but as 'medium' if they ranged from 2 inches to 22 inches (see Figure 5.1). In many

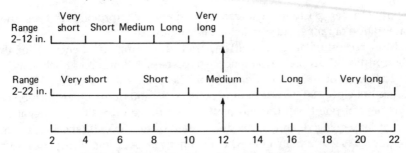

Figure 5.1. Shift in judgement resulting from extension of stimulus range. Arrow indicates predicted rating of a stimulus of 12 in. within two stimulus ranges. (According to Volkmann's 1951 model.)

situations, this model makes much the same prediction as AL theory on the basis of fewer assumptions.

Although adding extra stimuli beyond the end of the stimulus range will generally alter the predicted AL as well as the end-points of the range, it is possible to devise stimulus distributions which differ on a number of parameters but share the same AL according to Helson's formulation. If one wanted a predictor of the stimulus value judged as medium, the mean (or logarithmic mean in Helson's formula) is only one of a number of plausible alternatives. If Volkmann's model were correct, the midpoint between the two end-stimuli would be the better predictor. Or again, if subjects were to employ an ordinal principle, so as to make the number of stimuli they judged as greater than medium equal the number they judged as smaller than medium, the median stimulus value would become the best predictor.

Pointing out that, for typical stimulus distributions, the mean will tend to lie between the midpoint and the median, Parducci (1963) proposed that one could account for the predictive success of Helson's model by assuming that subjects' judgements reflect a compromise between two distinct tendencies. The first is a tendency to use each category of the judgement scale to cover a fixed proportion of the range between the two end-stimuli. The second is a tendency to use each category to cover a fixed proportion of the total number of stimuli. There is by now a considerable body of evidence establishing the predictive superiority of the *'range–frequency compromise'* over AL theory (Birnbaum, 1974; Parducci, 1974; Parducci and Perrett, 1971). Anderson (1975) has incorporated Parducci's ideas into a more generalized 'functional measurement' approach, according to which judgements obey a simple 'cognitive algebra', in terms of which a response to any stimulus is the outcome of a process of averaging the available relevant information about that stimulus. Thus, the range–frequency compromise is incorporated by assuming that the subject averages information about the relative location of each stimulus within the range, with information about its rank-order position. The range–frequency compromise is thus the integration of range and frequency information.

More recently, Parducci (1984) has applied his range-frequency notion to the question of people's experience of happiness. His argument is that one's overall level of happiness depends on the proportion of events that are above or below a subjective neutral point (analogous to AL). The position of this neutral point will depend both on the range of positive or negative events experienced, and on the distribution of such events (specifically the degree of skew). Someone who experiences occasional very negative events, according to Parducci, should derive more happiness from everyday events of average positivity (since these will fall above this person's subjective neutral point), than will someone who escapes negative events, but occasionally experiences events of exceptional positivity. In other words, someone whose aspirations are raised unrealistically will find everyday experiences less satisfactory. This approach does not, however, take account of how people *explain* exceptional experiences to themselves. As will be seen in the next chapter, people's explanations (attributions) for success or failure relate both to their subjective emotional reactions, and to their motivation to perform demanding tasks.

Parducci's ideas relate, too, to what still ranks as one of the most elegant theoretical approaches in social psychology, that of Thibaut and Kelley (1959). According to them, power and satisfaction among participants in a relationship can be conceptualized in terms of the *exchange* of rewards and costs. Of most relevance here is what Thibaut and Kelley say about satisfaction with an interpersonal relationship. This depends on the key concept of *comparison level* (CL), which is directly analogous to the concept of adaptation level (AL), without taking on board Helson's (1964) mathematical or physiological assumptions. The CL is the personal standard against which participants evaluate their satisfaction with a relationship. Outcomes above CL will lead to satisfaction, outcomes below CL to dissatisfaction. The CL is defined as 'some modal or average value of all the outcomes known to the person (by virtue of personal or vicarious experience), each outcome weighted by its salience' (p. 81).

Satisfaction, however, is carefully distinguished from dependence on a partner and any decision to stay within or leave a relationship. Such decisions are made with reference to the *comparison level for alternatives* (CL_{alt}). This 'will depend mainly on the quality of the best of the member's available alternatives, that is, the reward–cost positions believed to exist in the most satisfactory of other available relationships' (p. 22). Thus, if someone's outcomes fall below CL, that is, below 'what he feels he "deserves"' (p. 21), this will result in dissatisfaction, but *not* necessarily a decision to leave the relationship, unless the outcomes are also below the person's CL_{alt}. A person's CL and CL_{alt} will tend to influence each other, since 'the more satisfactory any given relationship has been found to be, the higher will be the comparison level for evaluating any new relationship' (p. 95).

Categorization and judgements of valued objects

In their concern with finding conditions in which judgements could be taken as relatively unbiased measures of sensation, traditional psychophysicists have been meticulous in their attempts to use stimuli which differ from each other only in terms of the single attribute which subjects are required to judge.

In social psychology, however, we are constantly coming across multi-attribute stimuli. Indeed, even when social psychologists attempt to devise stimuli which differ only in terms of a single attribute, they fail to do so. This is so especially in the case of attitude measurement, where attitude statements are constructed, and judgements typically obtained, along a single pro–anti continuum. Consider, for example, the following two items from a scale to measure attitudes towards birth control, devised by Wang and Thurstone in 1930 (Thurstone, 1931): 'The practice of birth control evades man's duty to propagate the race', and 'Uncontrolled reproduction leads to over-population, social unrest, and war.' Nobody could seriously claim that these two items differed only in terms of the degree to which they express favourable or unfavourable attitudes towards birth control, even though judges may be asked to conceptualize the differences between them in terms of such a construct.Even the simplest of social psychological dimensions are already simplifications of something much more complex. It is therefore very important to know how judgements of a stimulus in terms of one attribute or dimension may be influenced by its other, unjudged attributes.

Some of the earliest research relevant to this question stems from what was called the 'New Look' hypothesis, that basic processes, such as perception and memory, are susceptible to influence by emotional and motivational factors. In accordance with this approach, Bruner and Goodman (1947) proposed that physical objects associated with some kind of emotional significance or value should be seen as larger than physical objects of the same size without such associations. To test this hypothesis, they asked 10-year-old children to estimate the size of a series of coins. Compared with a control group, who were presented with grey cardboard discs of equivalent size, subjects over-estimated the sizes of the coins, particularly those of greater value.

This effect was broadly replicated by Carter and Schooler (1949) and by Bruner and Rodrigues (1953), with more marked over-estimation again being found in the case of the more valuable, i.e. larger, coins. In a particularly well-controlled study, Holzkamp and Perlwitz (1966) showed that the same stimulus may be judged differently, depending upon assumptions about its value. They glued a circular disc to the back of a ground-glass screen, and illuminated this from behind so that all that subjects saw was its silhouette. Subjects then adjusted a circular light spot until it seemed to match the silhouette. Subjects who were told that the silhouette was made by a 5 DM. coin (the largest German coin) give significantly larger estimates than those who were told that it was made by a cardboard disc. Holzkamp (1965) also found greatest over-estimation in the case of children from poorer backgrounds, and Ashley, Harper and Runyon (1951) found that subjects hypnotized to believe that they were very poor gave larger estimates of the sizes of coins than when hypnotized to believe that they were very rich. The argument is that money has greater subjective value if one is poor than if one is rich, and this greater subjective value should produce greater over-estimation.

Although coins have been the stimuli most frequently used in such experiments, Bruner and Postman (1948) found discs bearing a dollar sign were over-estimated; so too were discs bearing another 'emotionally relevant' symbol – a swastika – but less reliably. Two later studies failed to confirm these results in the case of discs bearing a swastika (Klein, Schlesinger and Meister, 1951; Solley and Lee, 1955). On the other hand, Lysak and Gilchrist (1955) found that the sizes of dollar bills were not reliably over-estimated in comparison with rectangles of the same size.

Tajfel (1957) was able to synthesize these and other experimental data by pointing out that those studies which showed over-estimation effects used stimuli, such as coins, where size and value were explicitly or implicitly correlated, so that the larger stimuli also tended to be those of greatest value. In other cases, where the size of a stimulus was irrelevant to its emotional significance, as in the case of the swastika, reliable over-estimation was not observed. Moreover, where over-estimation occurs, it is by no means constant over the continuum, but increases steadily as one moves up the scale of size and value. Thus, for stimuli where size and value are correlated, one finds an accentuation of the judged differences between adjacent stimuli in the experimental as compared with the control series. This, Tajfel argues, is nothing to do with the effects of value as such, but is part of a more general principle concerned with what happens when stimuli vary concurrently on more than one dimension. If subjects are required to judge a series of stimuli along a single 'focal' dimension, but the stimuli presented also vary along a second 'peripheral' dimension which is correlated with the focal dimension, they may use the perceived position of each stimulus on the peripheral dimension as a cue to its position on the focal dimension. They thus have additional information on the basis of which to discriminate it from the other stimuli in the series, which they would not have if such peripheral variation had been eliminated by experimental control, or was only randomly related to the positions of stimuli on the focal dimension.

This notion is discussed more fully by Tajfel (1959a, b) and by Eiser and Stroebe (1972). For the present, it is enough to view this as part of the more general integrationist position, that judgements are the product of a systematic combination and integration of relevant available stimulus information. The visual angle subtended by a coin is only one piece of information relevant to a judgement of its size. If it can also be seen to be a coin of higher value, this too is a piece of information which can be taken into account so as to make a more definite inference that the coin is large, provided that one has learned that size and value are predictably related to each other in the case of coins.

A special case of this phenomenon is where stimuli can be separated into distinct classes or categories in terms of some peripheral attribute. If the class-membership of a stimulus is predictably related to its position on the focal continuum, an accentuation of the judged interclass differences is predicted. To test this hypothesis, Tajfel and Wilkes (1963) required subjects to estimate the length in centimetres of eight lines of different lengths. In the experimental condition, each of the four shortest lines had a large A printed above its centre, while each of the four longest lines had a B (the labelling being reversed for half the subjects). The labels A and B constituted what Tajfel and Wilkes call a 'superimposed classification'. As predicted, this produced an accentuation of the judged differences between the two classes (i.e. the interval between the fourth and fifth longest lines was overestimated) as compared with estimates by control subjects, who judged the lines either in the absence of any alphabetic labels, or with the labels being randomly associated with the lengths of the lines.

Similar results are reported by Lilli (1970) and Marchand (1970). In none of these three studies, however, is there significant confirmation of an additional hypothesis proposed by Tajfel and Wilkes. This is that stimuli belonging to the same class should be judged as closer to each other: in other words, that the accentuation of *interclass* differences should be accompanied by a reduction of *intraclass* differences. On the other hand, an earlier study by Campbell (1956), on memory for the visual position of two classes of stimuli, found a reduction of intraclass differences, as well as a reduction in the perceived overlap between the classes, without the two classes on average being seen as further apart.

Categorization and stereotyping

Despite the lack of consistent support for the hypothesis of a reduction of intraclass differences, this question was one of wider significance for Tajfel, since his more general concern was with laying a foundation for a cognitive approach to the study of stereotypes and prejudice (Tajfel, 1969). According to Tajfel, one aspect of prejudice is a tendency to react to members of an alien group simply in terms of group membership, without due regard to individual differences within the group. Thus, an individual's group membership is analogous to a classification superimposed upon the particular focal dimension one is judging – be it educability, trustworthiness, arrogance, skin colour, or whatever. When this happens, the outcome is predicted to be a subjective accentuation of the difference between the alien group and one's own (usually involving devaluation of the alien group) and a subjective minimization of individual differences within the alien group (so that such devaluation applies more or less without exception). Such a way of dealing with interpersonal perceptions has precisely the same appeal that cognitive consistency has as a way of dealing with interpersonal and other attitudes – it maximizes the chances for positive self-regard and minimizes the need to make complex differentiations.

Evidence from interpersonal judgements, in fact, shows more positive support for the hypothesis of a reduction in intraclass differences. In judgements of photographs of people who are labelled as belonging to particular ethnic groups, more prejudiced subjects, at least, can fail to distinguish adequately between members of the alien group (Secord, 1959; Secord, Bevan and Katz, 1956). The same has been found for facial recognition, with white subjects being much poorer at distinguishing between black faces than between white faces (Malpass and Kravitz, 1969). Using a group discussion situation, Hensley and Duval (1976) led subjects to believe that their co-discussants fell into two subgroups, whose opinions were respectively similar or dissimilar to their own. The greater the supposed difference between the subgroups, the smaller were the perceived differences within each subgroup.

What seems crucial for stereotyped judgements to occur is that the attribute being judged should be believed to be distinctively associated with the group in question. Tajfel, Sheikh and Gardner (1964) compared subjects' ratings of two Indians and two Canadians on a number of scales. The two Indians were judged to be more similar to each other on traits which formed part of the Indian stereotype, and the two Canadians on traits which formed part of the Canadian stereotype. But how do beliefs in the association of particular attributes with particular groups come about? Obviously this is a very broad question, and if one demands an explanation for the content of specific stereotypes, it is unlikely that one will be satisfied without a sociological and historical, as well as a social psychological, analysis of the relationships between the groups in question. At a general level, however, two suggestions seem reasonable. The first is that stereotypes *exaggerate* differences that actually exist between an alien group and one's own, although these differences may be slight and involve a great deal of overlap between the groups. Brigham (1971) refers to this as the 'kernel-of-truth' idea. This is plausible enough when one is considering relatively easily observed characteristics such as skin colour (though even in this case it is unnecessary to assume that a person has to have 'observed' a representative sample, or indeed any member, of another group before he can form or accept a stereotyped view of the group as a whole). It is less plausible when one considers other components of the stereotype, such as personality and intelligence. The second possibility is that stereotypes at least partly reflect an *illusion* of difference, that is, a bias towards attributing distinctive characteristics to an alien or minority group, more or less regardless of their validity. These possibilities may be complementary rather than mutually exclusive.

A study that deals mainly with the first of these possibilities is that by Taylor, Fiske, Etcoff and Ruderman (1978). Its theoretical contribution consists, partly at least, of a restatement of the ideas contained in Tajfel's (1959a, b, 1969) earlier writings, for which more explicit acknowledgement might have been appropriate, even though the experiments by Tajfel and Wilkes (1963) and Tajfel *et al.* (1964) are described. Taylor *et al.* start from the assumption that 'there is no theoretical or empirical reason to assume that forming generalizations about ethnic groups is radically different from forming generalizations about other categories of objects' (p. 778). They then develop the following seven hypotheses:

(1)   People use physical and social discriminators such as race and sex as a way of categorizing people and organizing information about them.

(2)   As a result of this categorization process, within-group differences become minimized and between-group differences become exaggerated.

(3)   As a result of this categorization process, within-group members' behaviour comes to be interpreted in stereotyped terms.

(4)   The social perceiver pays more attention to, and makes more discriminations, within a subgroup, the fewer members of the subgroup there are.

(5)   The social perceiver pays more attention to, and makes more discriminations, within more familiar subgroups, such as those to which he or she belongs, than less familiar ones.

(6)   Group members are stereotyped depending on the number of other members of the subgroup present.

(7)   Social units are stereotyped as a function of the proportion of different subgroup members.

The experimental situation used by Taylor *et al.* involved subjects listening to a sound recording of a group discussion between six people, synchronized with a slide projector so that, as each voice spoke, a picture (supposedly) of the speaker was projected onto a wall. Subjects were then asked to recall which suggestions had been made by which participants in the discussion, and the main dependent variable was the pattern of errors obtained. In the first of their experiments, three of the participants were presented as white, and three as black. As predicted, it was found that intraracial confusion was higher than interracial confusion. In other words, a suggestion actually made by one of the black participants was more likely to be misattributed to one of two other blacks than to one of the three whites, and vice versa for the suggestions of the white participants, after correcting for the fact that interracial errors would be expected to exceed intraracial errors in a 3:2 ratio on a chance basis. All subjects were white, but, contrary to prediction, were no more likely to confuse the contributions of the different blacks with each other than those of the different whites.

A second experiment found essentially the same results, this time using sex rather than race as the basis for categorization, with three males and three females in the recorded discussion group. Again, proportionately fewer of the errors than would be expected by chance involved misattributing a suggestion to a participant of a different sex, but subjects were no better at recalling the contributions made by members of their own than of the opposite sex.

In a third experiment, the sex composition of the group was varied continually from all male to all female, and the dependent variable consisted of ratings of the individual group members, rather than accuracy of recall. The results of this last experiment were somewhat mixed, but there was a tendency for female participants to be rated as more stereotypically feminine, and male participants as more stereotypically masculine, the fewer the other members of their own sex there were taking part in the discussion. At the same time, both male and female participants were seen as more assertive and influential in the discussion, the fewer the other members of their own sex there were in the group. This finding is taken to show that observers pay more attention to persons or events that are less frequent and hence more distinctive (see also Taylor and Fiske, 1975, 1978).

These results, therefore, reinforce the view that characteristics such as race and sex can function as a basis for categorizing information about other people, and support a cognitive interpretation of stereotyping. In contrast to many other studies, however, no support was found for the prediction that people are better at discriminating among members of their own group than among members of another group. One factor not included in this study was the personal emotional significance or 'salience' of the classification for the individual subjects (as opposed to 'salience' in the sense of stimulus distinctiveness or infrequency). According to Tajfel (1959a), accentuation effects should be more pronounced on more personally salient dimensions (cf. Tajfel and Wilkes, 1964). If, as one suspects, the Harvard students who served as subjects were neither particularly racist nor sexist, the tendency to stereotype members of another race or sex would not be expected to be very strong.

Illusory correlation

Other researchers have emphasized the role of biased information-processing in the formation of stereotypes, in the absence of 'real' group differences. Hamilton (1976) has argued that stereotyping may reflect a cognitive bias termed 'illusory correlation'. Chapman (1967) used this term to refer to certain systematic biases he found in his subjects' responses on a paired associate learning task. Subjects over-estimated the frequency (in the experiment) of co-occurrence of pairs of words whose meanings were strongly associated (e.g. lion–tiger, bacon–eggs), and also over-estimated the co-occurrence of the longest word in one list with the longest word in the other list. It is suggested that stimuli which are distinctive within their respective sets are more likely to be seen as paired with each other. Hamilton extends this notion to suggest that people are biased towards seeing an illusory correlation between uncommon or distinctive attributes and membership of a distinctive group.

Hamilton and Gifford (1976) report two experiments in support of this interpretation. In the first of these, subjects were presented with a series of statements describing behaviour performed by a male member of either Group A or Group B, and were told that, 'In the real-world population, Group B is a smaller group than Group A' (p. 395). Two-thirds of the statements referred to a Group A member, and one-third to a Group B member. The desirability of the behaviours described was also varied, and the statements were distributed so that, within both Group A and Group B, there was 9:4 ratio of desirable to undesirable behaviours. Thus Group B was more distinctive than Group A, and undesirable behaviours were more distinctive than desirable behaviours, but there was no actual correlation between group membership and desirability in the statements presented. However, when asked to recall how many statements concerning members of each group had described undesirable behaviours, subjects over-estimated the co-occurrence of distinctive attributes, i.e. they recalled Group A members as having performed more of the desirable behaviours and Group B members as having performed more of the undesirable behaviours. In their second study, Hamilton and Gifford used a similar procedure, but with two-thirds of the statements describing undesirable behaviours. Since desirable behaviour was now more distinctive, their hypothesis was supported by the finding that subjects over-estimated the frequency with which desirable behaviours were performed by Group B and undesirable behaviours by Group A.

Hamilton's explanation for such effects is based on the assumption that, where infrequent events co-occur (e.g. distinctive behaviour by a minority group member), this will attract more attention during encoding and hence will be more easily available from memory when subsequent estimates and evaluations are made (see Hamilton, Dugan and Trolier, 1985, for evidence that this effect is due to differential encoding). As regards frequency estimates, the hypothesis is that subjects assume that classes of events they can remember more easily must have occurred more frequently.

One difficulty with accepting that these findings reflect the same processes underlying stereotyping in real life is the hypothetical nature of the groups and behaviours concerned. What would happen if one used real-world issues where subjects might identify more closely with one side rather than another? Spears, van der Pligt and Eiser (1985) found evidence of illusory correlation effects using the issue of attitudes towards nuclear power stations. At the time of the study, the British electricity industry was investigating a number of sites as possible locations for a new nuclear power station. Student subjects were presented with a series of slides containing either pro- or anti-nuclear statements, supposedly made by residents of each of two towns, identified as 'Town A' and 'Town B', but described as being under investigation for possible power stations. They then had to recall which town each statement came from and estimate the percentage of pro and anti statements from each town.

Of the total of 36 statements, 24 were presented as from Town A and 12 as from Town B. Subjects were told that this distribution reflected the fact that Town A was bigger than Town B. Half the subjects received a distribution with a 2:1 majority of pro-nuclear statements (so that there were only 4 anti-nuclear statements from Town B), whereas for the others the proportions of pro and anti items were reversed.

The crucial difference from the Hamilton and Gifford (1976) experiment was the fact that Spears *et al.* included a measure of subjects' *own* attitudes on the issue. Specifically, illusory correlation effects (shown by exaggerating the extent to which the smaller town was identified as being the more likely to hold the minority position) occurred only for those subjects whose own attitudes were congruent with the minority position (whether pro or anti). Furthermore, among these 'minority-congruent' subjects, the illusory correlation effects were stronger among subjects with more extreme attitudes. However, among those whose attitudes were congruent with the majority of statements presented, those with more extreme attitudes showed *least* evidence of illusory correlation in their responses. Spears *et al.* (1985) concluded that these results reflect the fact that statements congruent with one's own position are more personally relevant or 'salient', and hence (like more distinctive stimuli generally) are more thoroughly encoded.

Spears, van der Pligt and Eiser (1986) followed up this study with a series of experiments varying critical aspects of the instructions and distribution of pro and anti statements. First, the distribution of statements was changed so that Town A contained 12 pro and 12 anti items, and Town B 6 pro and 6 anti items. The prediction was that subjects should see residents of the smaller town as more likely to hold opinions similar to their own. This prediction was upheld, but only for anti-nuclear subjects. Subsequent findings, however, suggested that subjects had reliable prior assumptions that smaller towns (on any short-list for a new power station) would tend to be more intensely anti-nuclear than larger towns, and hence that subjects' estimates were biased towards these prior expectations (see Alloy and Tabachnik, 1984, for a more general discussion of how prior expectations influence covariation judgements). This prior expectation of a relationship between attitude and town size was strong enough to get subjects to over-estimate the number of anti statements from the smaller town even when the numbers of statements presented within each of the four categories (Town A/B × pro/anti) were *equal* (subjects were told that Town B was smaller, but had been more heavily sampled). However, when subjects were presented with the same distribution as in the first experiment of this paper, but were told that both towns were of equal size (although Town A had been more heavily sampled) pro as well as anti subjects showed illusory correlation effects. For both attitude groups, these effects were stronger for those with more extreme attitudes.

Spears *et al.* concluded that biased information-processing can lead to illusory group stereotypes. However, before one can draw any simple inferences concerning intergroup perception in the real world on the basis of findings such as those of Hamilton and Gifford (1976), one needs to take account (at least) of (a) people's prior expectations of group differences within the particular social context, and (b) how people's own attitudes and levels of involvement can lead them to pay more attention to certain classes of stimuli rather than others.

Accentuation, integration and intraclass differences

People, then, may come to see groups as different from one another either through accentuation of actual interclass differences, or through perceiving an illusory correlation between different kinds of stimulus distinctiveness. However, no cognitive account of stereotyping is complete if it does not address the issue of the reduction of *intraclass* differences – what determines whether someone will view another person simply as 'just another' member of a group, as opposed to an individual differentiated from other group members.

Let us review the judgemental principles mentioned so far. First, there are *contrast* effects, where stimuli are judged relative to a particular standard. Next, we have *accentuation* effects, whereby classes of stimuli become judged as more separate from one another. Finally, though mentioned so far only in passing, judgements may be *assimilated* to prior expectations. Although research has typically studied these principles in isolation from one another, this does not mean that they necessarily reflect mutually incompatible processes. However, there is relatively little evidence on how such processes might act in combination.

Let us consider for the moment simply the last two effects – accentuation and assimilation-to-expectation. How might they combine in a situation where stimuli fall into two different classes? To try and answer this question, let us consider the kind of 'cognitive algebra' (Anderson, 1974) a person might use to incorporate information about the class-membership of a stimulus to produce a judgement of the position of each stimulus along a defined focal dimension. Let us suppose that the subject is presented with two distinct or partially overlapping classes of stimuli $(a_1, a_2 \ldots a_{na}, b_1, b_2 \ldots b_{nb})$, and that the judgement of each stimulus is a function of sensory information concerning the actual position of each individual stimulus on the focal dimension, and of the position that the subject would predict on the basis of the class-membership information alone. By definition, this latter position would be the same for all members of a given class, so in our example it can take only two values (A or B, for the two classes respectively). For present purposes, it does not matter whether this predicted position is a result of unsubstantiated prejudice, or experimental learning. In either case, we can express the response R to each stimulus as a weighted sum of the experienced position of each stimulus and the predicted position of the 'class-type'. Thus:

$$Ra_i = w_1a_i + w_2A$$

and (5.1)

$$Rb_i = w_3b_i + w_4B$$

If the weights w_1 and w_3 both equalled 1 (and w_2 and w_4 were both greater than 0), the outcome woud be an accentuation of interclass differences but no change in the size of intraclass differences. If w_1 and w_3 both exceeded 1, the outcome would be an accentuation of both interclass and intraclass differences. If one assumed that $w_2 = 1 - w_1$ and that $w_4 = 1 - w_3$, one would have an averaging model of the kind discussed by Anderson (1970). A variety of effects could then be predicted, depending on the size of weights and on the values taken by A and B relative to the individual stimuli within each class. If A equalled the mean of the stimuli in class a and B the mean of the stimuli in class b, there would be a reduction of intraclass differences and a consequential reduction in overlap (or increase in the separation of adjacent stimuli) at the boundary between the classes, but without the two classes on average being judged as further apart (e.g. Campbell, 1956). The larger the weights w_2 and w_4, the more pronounced would be these effects. Any differences between w_2 and w_4 would result in asymmetrical reductions of intraclass differences (as may happen in interpersonal judgements of members of one's own and an alien group).

If A and B were further apart than the means of classes a and b, the outcome would be the commonly observed accentuation of interclass differences, together with a reduction of intraclass differences. At the same time, the possibility of a reduction of interclass differences, though not commonly reported, is not precluded, since A and B could be closer together than the means of classes a and b. Thus, changes in interclass and intraclass differences would depend on the extremity of the 'class-types' A and B, and their relative weights.

It is a short step from here to the more general case of stimuli which vary concurrently along two or more correlated dimensions. (Class-membership as described above can be thought of simply as a dichotomous peripheral attribute.) If s_i represents the experienced position of a stimulus i on the focal dimension, and t_i the position that would be inferred from its other (peripheral) attributes, then we have the following general formula, which is equivalent to that presented by Anderson (1970: 155):

$$R_i = w_1 s_i + w_2 t_i \tag{5.2}$$

Assuming again that $w_2 = 1 - w_1$, the judgements given to each stimulus would depend on the value of t_i compared with s_i. If the t values had a wider range than the s values, the outcome would be accentuation of each interstimulus interval, as seems to occur with estimates of the size of coins. Anderson assumes that the weights w_1 and w_2 should remain constant for all stimuli in a series, but no such assumption is made here.

This way of looking at accentuation effects, however, makes no allowance for contrast effects. The reason for this is that Anderson's (1970) formula, and the derivations made here, assume a common frame of reference for *all* stimuli being judged, whereas contrast effects are assumed to be the result of a *change* in frame of reference. Indeed, this highlights a basic tenet of most judgement methods, that stimuli that are judged on the same scale are judged relative to the same frame of reference. But suppose that this tenet is sometimes wrong. After all, as I mentioned earlier, not *all* stimuli within a given modality will lead to shifts in adaptation level (AL) or frame of reference (e.g. Brown, 1953). Subjects only compare stimuli with other stimuli they regard as *relevant*. It is quite conceivable that *different* standards, or frames of reference, may be seen as relevant for stimuli in different regions of the scale, and in particular for stimuli belonging to different *classes*.

This line of reasoning leads to a prediction that, when a classification is superimposed on a series of stimuli, ratings of the stimuli will (at least partly) reflect their positions *relative to other stimuli in their own class*. Suppose one had stimuli of different sizes falling into two classes, A and B, of which A was the larger. The prediction would be that the smallest Ss would be called 'small' and the largest Bs 'large' even if they were of comparable size to each other. This would be directly contrary to the kind of effect predicted by Tajfel (1959a). Even so, direct evidence of such intraclass contrast comes from a recent study by Manis, Paskewitz and Cotler (in press).

The series of experiments reported by Manis *et al.* involved judgements of the apparent psychopathology of a series of target persons ('patients') from various records such as test responses and handwriting samples. The basic procedure was for subjects to undergo an induction phase, in which they were presented with a number of behavioural items both clearly low and clearly high in the degree of pathology they appeared to indicate. Subjects then went on to judge a series of 'midscale' items intermediate in terms of indication of pathology. Responses involved paired comparison and certainty ratings of the likelihood of the target persons being schizophrenic.

The crucial manipulation was that, during the induction phase, all high-pathology items were identified as belonging to one class, whereas the low-pathology items were identified as from another class (e.g. they were presented as coming from patients from two different hospitals). What happened was that midscale items were rated as *less* pathological if they belonged to the group that was identified as *more* pathological in the induction phase, and vice versa. However, if the items were presented as all coming from two *individuals* (rather than from two hospitals), judgements of midscale items were closer to judgements of the induction items from the same individual. A neutral behaviour from an individual who had already given signs of pathology was interpreted as more compatible with a diagnosis of schizophrenia than if the same or similar behaviour came from someone who had given no such signs.

How can one reconcile these results with those of Tajfel and Wilkes (1963)? One possibility considered by Manis *et al.* is that interclass accentuation effects and a reduction of intraclass differences are primarily aspects of how we judge single individuals rather than groups. From the literature already reviewed, however, one can conclude that interclass accentuation effects *can* occur when *groups* of persons or other stimuli are being judged: attribution to single individuals is not normally a necessary condition for such effects. In fact, although Manis *et al.* regard their study as a conceptual replication of the Tajfel and Wilkes (1963) experiment, there are potentially important differences of procedure.

In the Manis *et al.* experiments, the analyses reported concern *only* the 'midscale' test items, i.e. those items where the two stimulus classes are not reliably distinguishable. These items are presented separately and after the more extreme 'induction' items. They are also discrepant from the 'induction' items in the sense of being clear *outliers*, compared with the distribution of remaining items from their own class. In other words, there is quite a gap (in terms of apparent pathology) between any of the 'midscale' items and the least extreme of the 'induction' items. This may well have made it more likely that the 'midscale' items would be contrasted away from other items in their class. By comparison, the stimuli in the Tajfel and Wilkes (1963) study constituted a continuous distribution without any sudden gap between extreme and moderate items. (The same could be said of the stimuli used by Campbell, 1956, where the classes actually overlapped, and where evidence of reduction of intraclass differences is quite strong.)

We are still some way from defining, in more general terms, the limiting conditions within which one would expect different kinds of judgemental effects as the result of superimposed classifications. However, even if Manis *et al.* would have found different effects with different stimuli, their study provides an important message: contrast effects can still occur, even when stimuli fall into separate classes, and the direction of these effects suggest that *different* standards of comparison may be applied to different classes of stimuli, even when the different classes are being judged together with one another.

Viewed in this way, it may be a false question to ask: when do we get accentuation and when do we get intraclass contrast? Perhaps *both* processes are operating whenever stimuli are judged in the presence of any superimposed classification predictably related to a focal attribute. Researchers in the accentuation tradition have not looked for the kind of 'local contrast' process observed by Manis *et al.*, but it is quite possible that this process is operating all the time, mostly just strongly enough to stop categorization leading to the predicted reduction of intraclass differences, but usually too weakly to produce a reliable effect opposite to this prediction.

Categorization, particularization and prejudice

Although this discussion might appear to be narrowly focussed on details of experimental procedures, in fact many of the same considerations apply in the context of ethnic and other forms of prejudice. Billig (1985) points to the worrying apparent implication of most cognitively-oriented work on prejudice, that stereotyping is a 'natural', almost inevitable, consequence of our limited cognitive capacity and our biased strategies of information-processing. At the extreme, describing prejudice as 'natural' might seem to condone it, and to legitimate societies where racial and other divisions are institutionalized.

The crux of Billig's argument, however, is that the emphasis on categorization provides a one-sided account both of prejudice in particular and human thinking in general. Whilst it is certainly functional for organisms to be *able* to categorize, it can also be functional for them to be able to differentiate between exemplars of a category – that is, to particularize. It is too simplistic to argue that it is *always* in the organisms' interest to categorize. In many instances, it may be more advantageous to particularize. As far as prejudice is concerned, Billig points to the paradox in conventional theorizing – that, on the one hand, prejudiced thinking supposedly is different in *form* from tolerant thinking (Allport, 1958), but, on the other hand, the supposed hallmark of prejudiced thinking – the use of simplifying categories – is regarded as a universal feature of cognitive processes.

Billig responds to this paradox by asserting that prejudiced and tolerant thinking differ in context but *not* in form. The important difference between prejudiced and tolerant thinkers is not how much they group people into categories, but *which* categories they use, and *which* differences they empha-size. The problem of *category selection*, in other words, has been largely overlooked in attempts to explain prejudice by reference to categorization. Someone who wants to resist the argument that, for instance, blacks are inherently different from whites, may well do so by emphasizing categories that either cut across the ethnic distinction (e.g. religion or citizenship), or are superordinate to it (e.g. 'the human race'). Similarly, someone who wants to maintain that there are fundamental differences between blacks and whites, Jews and non-Jews, etc., may need to show willingness to particularize in other respects. As Billig puts it:

> Categories do not exist in isolation, but a category, if it is to be applied, must be particularized or selected from other categories. As such it is conceivable that an inflexible use of one category might necessitate a flexible use of other categories, and in this way a rigid categorization would not lead to further rigidities but to subtle particularization. (Billig, 1985: 93)

As an example, Billig cites this quotation from a respondent in the classic study *The Authoritarian Personality* (Adorno *et al.*, 1950: 624):

> There are good and bad amongst all races . . . the trouble is that there are two types of Jews. There are the white Jews and the kikes. My pet theory is that the white Jews hate the kikes as much as we do.

Thus, confronted by the knowledge that one's friends and associates include members of other races, religion or whatever, the prejudiced person can differentiate such known and liked individuals from the *real* Jews, blacks, Irish or whatever:

> The point is that the authoritarian, far from using global unsophisticated categories, will be seeking to make distinctions in order to defend a categori-cal usage . . . This implies that a certain inventiveness will be required to maintain categorical distinctions: it is precisely this sort of inventiveness that can lead the serious racist to formulate complex theories about hidden racial conspiracies and concealed qualities of blood, which 'prove' that under the skin all Aryans, blacks or whatever really do have 'essential' racial qualities. (Billig, 1985: 94)

Billig concludes that prejudice should not be seen as a form of 'perception' but in terms of the *arguments* where prejudiced and tolerant people defend their positions. The study of prejudice must focus on linguistic content, and more specifically, the everyday *rhetoric* that prejudiced people *use*, since, without language, the concept of prejudice makes little sense.

The judgement of attitudes

Another important area of social judgement where language plays an influential part is that concerned with how we appraise one another's attitudes. Just as research on the judgement of physical stimuli started from a concern with questions of the validity and reliability of psychophysical measurement, so a concern with equivalent questions in the field of attitude measurement gave rise to research on the judgement of attitudes. Most of such research has been concerned with the technique of attitude-scale construction known as Thurstone's (1928, 1931) method of equal-appearing intervals. This method is aimed at selecting a series of short attitude statements, varying along an interval scale from extremely unfavourable to extremely favourable towards a given issue. The 'scale value' of each item, or statement (i.e. its assumed position on the scale of favourability) is calculated from the ratings of a group of independent 'judges', who are required to say how favourable or unfavourable towards the issue they consider the item to be, typically in terms of an 11-point scale. Originally Thurstone proposed using the median of judges' ratings of a given item as the scale value of that item. However, with an adequate number of judges, the arithmetic mean is a defensible substitute, and can be simpler to compute. These scale values can be then used to calculate the attitude scores of respondents who indicate their agreement or disagreement with items in the final scale, in a variety of ways. Following Thurstone, one can take the median scale value of the items with which a person strongly agrees or disagrees as that person's attitude score on the 11-point scale. However, statements chosen by the Thurstone method can be scored in other ways. For instance, Likert (1932) proposed a scoring method that simply treats items as pro or anti, but takes account of respondents' levels of agreement *and* disagreement. More recently, Monk and Eiser (1980) have proposed a scoring method, based on the likelihood of a respondent preferring pro items to anti items, so as to control for response biases that may affect Likert scores.

However, the main emphasis of judgement research has been on the scaling phase, i.e. with how statements are rated as more pro or anti. When proposing their method, Thurstone and Chave (1929: 92) stated boldly that 'if the scale value is to be regarded as valid, the scale values of the statements should not be affected by the opinion of the people who help to construct it'. In other words, different judges should agree with each other as to the degree of favourability expressed by each statement, even if their own personal attitudes on the issue are different. The majority of research in this field has therefore been concerned with whether judges' own attitudes affect their ratings, and if so, how.

The first test of Thurstone's assumption was by Hinckley (1932), using what has become the classic issue in such research, that of 'attitude toward the social position of the Negro'. Hinckley presented a series of statements on this issue to three groups of college student judges: whites with pro-black attitudes, whites with anti-black attitudes, and blacks. On the basis of a 0.98 correlation between the scale values obtained from the ratings of the two white groups separately, and a 0.93 correlation between the scale values of the blacks and anti-black whites, Hinckley concluded that his scale was 'not influenced in its measuring function by the subjects used in the construction' (p. 203). There followed a number of studies on different attitude issues, which found the same kind of high correlations between the ratings of different judges, and drew essentially the same conclusions (Beyle, 1932; Eysenck and Crown, 1949; Ferguson, 1935; Pintner and Forlano, 1937). Hinckley's conclusion thus remained essentially unchallenged for twenty years, even though during this period increasing evidence was being accumulated which pointed to the effects of attitudes and values on the perception of physical stimuli.

Struck by the paradox that perceptions of physical stimuli were supposedly influenced by perceivers' attitudes, but perceptions of attitudes were not, Hovland and Sherif (1952) conducted an extended replication of Hinckley's study. At the same time, they examined the effects of a methodological device, suggested by Thurstone and used by Hinckley, called the 'carelessness criterion', according to which judges who lumped together too many items in a single response category were excluded for presumed 'carelessness'. Analysing their data without the use of this criterion, Hovland and Sherif found that both black and pro-black white judges lumped a large proportion of the items together close to the 'unfavourable' extreme of the scale, with a small minority of the items being judged as 'extremely favourable', and with the intermediate scale categories being used only very occasionally. The ratings of the anti-black group were distributed more evenly over the scale, with a higher proportion of items being judged as close to the 'favourable' extreme. The 'average' white judges (students from various colleges in south-east Oklahoma) sound, from the description given by Hovland and Sherif, as if they may have held fairly anti-black attitudes, and their ratings in fact correspond quite closely with those of the anti-Negro group. When the same 'carelessness criterion' employed by Hinckley was used, this had the effect of excluding a disproportionate number of pro-black subjects, and of producing scale values closely resembling those obtained by Hinckley (see Figure 5.2).

Although Hovland and Sherif were concerned mainly with demonstrating that judges' attitudes could have an effect, and less with describing the precise kind of effect involved, an impressive feature of their data is the apparent tendency of judges to 'displace' large proportions of the item series towards the extreme of the scale opposite to their own position. In other words, favourable judges tended to rate more of the statements as 'unfavourable' and unfavourable judges more of the statements as 'favour-

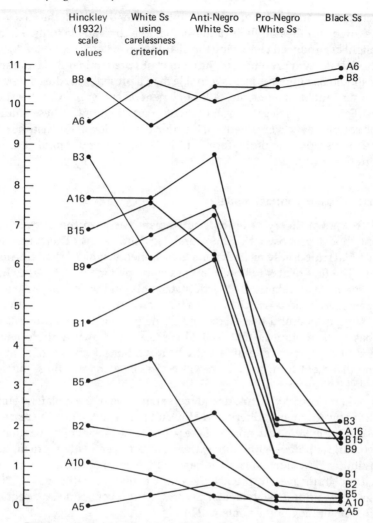

Figure 5.2. Scale values for selected items obtained from the ratings given by different groups of subjects. (Adapted from Hovland and Sherif, 1952.)

able'. The apparent similarity of this phenomenon to the kind of contrast effects found in judgements of physical stimuli did not escape notice, and in subsequent research both the terminology and the theoretical explanations of psychophysics were eagerly adopted.

The ability of AL theory to explain such contrast effects was asserted by Helson (1964), on the assumption that more favourable judges have ALs closer to the more favourable extreme. This could either be because they may have had more experience of statements congruent with their own attitude, or because they use their own attitude as a kind of 'anchor' or subjective comparison stimulus. One implication of this is that the effects of judges' own attitudes on their ratings should be comparable to the effects that might be produced by varying the distribution of items presented to the judges. A statement presented in the context of a predominantly favourable series should be judged as less favourable than if presented in the context of more unfavourable statements. Although general evidence exists for such effects (Fehrer, 1952; Segall, 1959; Upshaw, 1962), in none of these studies are the contrast effects obtained as a function of variation in the distribution of statements precisely of the form which AL theory would predict (Eiser and Stroebe, 1972).

The assimilation–contrast model

The best-known theory of attitude judgement has been the *assimilation–contrast* model proposed by Sherif and Hovland (1961). There are two distinct, but supposedly related, parts to their theory, which I shall consider in turn. The first relates to how a judge's own opinion will influence their ratings of the favourability of attitude statements, and the second relates to how people's opinions will change as a function of the discrepancy between their own position and that advocated in the persuasive communication. The basic assumption is that individuals use their own attitude as an 'anchor' or comparison stimulus, with the result that statements of attitude not too divergent from their own will be 'assimilated' and those further away will be 'contrasted'.

Thus, in the context of attitude judgement, instead of the unilateral shifts predicted by AL theory, Sherif and Hovland predict a bilateral increase in the use of the extreme categories of the scale, that is, greater polarization of judgement, for judges with more extreme, as compared with more moderate, attitudes. Two questions, therefore, need to be asked about this model. First, does it adequately predict the effect of judges' attitudes on their ratings of the attitude statements? Second, does it constitute an adequate explanation of the findings obtained?

If the Hovland and Sherif (1952) study were the only one to find differences in polarization as a function of judges' attitudes, it is doubtful whether one would need to take the 'assimilation' part of the assimilation–contrast model very seriously. Although the blacks and pro-black whites appear to assimilate a few pro-black statements, the number of such statements is not particularly large. This objection, however, can be quickly dismissed by inspecting some of the items actually used (Shaw and Wright, 1967: 360–2), and comparing them in terms of the selected scale values shown in Figure 5.2. The two examples, in this figure, of items already very favourable in terms of their original (Hinckley) scale values, which become rated as even more extremely favourable (i.e. are 'assimilated') by blacks and pro-Negro whites, in fact read as follows:

Item A6: 'The Negro should be given the same educational advantages as the white man.'

Item B8: 'I believe that the Negro is entitled to the same social privileges as the white man.'

Historical and cultural relativity notwithstanding, this is enough to lead one to question how extremely favourable the supposedly 'extremely favourable' items really were. Other items yield a similar picture. Item A16, with an original scale value of 7.7 (i.e. to the favourable side of neutral) expresses a straight segregationist position: 'The Negro should have the advantage of all social benefits of the white man but be limited to his own race in the practice thereof.' Similarly, Item B3, which is even more favourable in terms of its original scale value (8.7), reads: 'Although the Negro is rather inferior mentally, he has a fuller and deeper religious life than the white man, and thus has an emphatic claim upon our social approval.' Both these items are 'contrasted' by pro-black and black judges, so as to be judged as fairly close to the unfavourable extreme. For comparison purposes, it is also worth citing the two more extremely anti-black items listed in the same figure. These are:

Item A10: 'No Negro has the slightest right to resent, or even question the illegal killing of one of his race.'

Item A5: 'I place the Negro on the same social basis as I would a mule.'

There seems every reason to suppose, therefore, that if the item pool had contained a higher proportion of clearly favourable statements, the assimilation effects found for subjects with pro-black attitudes would have been far stronger – perhaps even as strong as the contrast effects found with the less favourable statements. Yet curiously this very asymmetry in the strengths of the assimilation and contrast shifts, which may be more than an artefact of a biased item pool, becomes for Sherif and Hovland an integral part of their model, and particularly of its extension to the field of attitude change. According to them, the relative strengths of assimilation and contrast effects depend upon the relative sizes of a person's *'latitudes of acceptance, non-commitment* and *rejection'*. A person's latitude of acceptance is simply the range of opinions that are accepted and the latitude of rejection the range of opinions that are rejected, with the latitude of non-commitment containing attitude positions that are neither accepted nor rejected. Basically, Sherif and Hovland assume that the statements which fall within a person's latitude of acceptance will tend to be assimilated and others will tend to be contrasted. They also assume that people with extreme opinions will tend to have narrow latitudes of acceptance (i.e. agree with very few opinions at all different from their own) and hence will tend to assimilate relatively few items.

Another feature of the Hovland and Sherif data is less easy to reconcile with their assimilation–contrast model. Although judges with pro-black attitudes seem to show the predicted polarization effects, the same effect should also occur in the cases of extremely anti-black judges: they should assimilate unfavourable and contrast favourable statements and so show greater polarization than more moderate judges. There is no evidence that this occurred. In fact all that seems clear is that the 'average' and anti-Negro whites gave less polarized ratings than the blacks and pro-black whites. The similarity in the ratings given by the former two groups could mean that no really anti-black subjects were included in the sample, and that those labelled anti-black were in fact really moderate. If this were so, the data would not allow a test of the assimilation–contrast model for judges with opinions at the unfavourable extreme.

With a changing cultural context, the difficulty of finding really anti-black judges within a random sample of college students cannot be entirely ruled out as a contributory factor, and Manis (1964) used this argument in order to defend the assimilation–contrast model against the results of a study by Upshaw (1962), which also found that anti-Negro judges polarized less than neutral judges. Manis (1960, 1961) himself found results more supportive of the assimilation–contrast model when using the issue of fraternities. Two further studies on the issue of attitudes towards blacks, however, by Zavalloni and Cook (1965) and Selltiz, Edrich and Cook (1965), again found that anti-black judges gave the least polarized ratings. In these studies, the researchers were apparently careful to find some who were 'really' anti-black. The second of these studies also added new items at the pro-black end of the scale to compensate for the bias in the original Hinckley pool.

To summarize these studies, then, there is fair evidence of a tendency for more favourable judges to rate statements, on average, as more unfavourable than do unfavourable judges. This overall contrast effect, however, is very much a function of where the statements fall on the pro–anti continuum. The evidence on polarization of judgement seems to point to a direct relationship between polarization and favourability of attitude on this issue, with pro-black judges giving the most, and anti-black judges the least, polarized ratings (see Figure 5.3).

As far as the explanatory value of the assimilation–contrast model is concerned, I have already mentioned that Sherif and Hovland based their predictions on the assumption that judges use their own position on an issue as an 'anchor'. The more conventional (e.g. AL theory) application of this notion would be that judgements should be inversely related to the position of the anchor, and so contrast effects should be observed for all items in a series. Sherif and Hovland, however, claim to use this same principle to predict that items near to the judge's own position (anchor) will be assimilated and items further away will be contrasted. In other words, within the same item series, the same anchor can produce judgemental shifts in opposite directions.

Sherif and Hovland (1961) do not discuss this discrepancy between their own predictions and the typical findings in psychophysical judgement, but

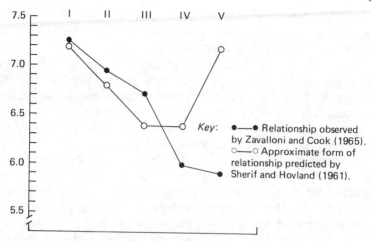

Figure 5.3. Relationship between judges' attitudes and polarization (mean differences between ratings of favourable and unfavourable items). Attitude groups: I: Black students, actively involved; II: Pro-black white students, actively involved; III: Pro-black white students, not actively involved; IV: Anti-black white students, not actively involved; V: Anti-black white students, actively involved.

instead cite a single study of their own involving judgements of the heaviness of lifted weights (Sherif, Taub and Hovland, 1958). In this study, they found the typical contrast effects in conditions where a series of weights was judged in the context of an anchor stimulus lying outside the range of the original series. In one condition only, where the anchor was of exactly the same weight as the heaviest stimulus in the original series, assimilation and not contrast occurred: in other words, all the stimuli were judged as somewhat heavier than when they were presented without the anchor. No comparable assimilation occurred to an anchor equal in weight to the lightest of the other stimuli. The possible influence of non-standard features of the experimental procedure in producing the exceptional assimilation effect in the one condition has been discussed by Parducci and Marshall (1962).

Even if we take these results as completely reliable, however, they bear absolutely no resemblance to the 'assimilation–contrast' effects observed, or at least predicted, in attitude judgement. The hypothesis, which Sherif *et al.* interpret their results as supporting, is that anchor stimuli at, or near to, the extreme of a stimulus series will produce assimilation of the total series, and that anchors further away will produce contrast of the total series. What matters, therefore, is the relation between the anchor and the series *as a whole*, not that between the anchor and each stimulus taken *by itself*. There is simply no way in which these results, concerning shifts of the total series as a function of different anchors, can be used to generate the prediction of *simultaneous* assimilation and contrast of different stimuli within a single series as a function of a single anchor.

The transition from the 'attitude-judgement' to the 'attitude-change' part of the assimilation–contrast model is also beset by difficulties. The attitude-change effect that the model attempts to explain is that people, exposed to a communication advocating a position somewhat discrepant from their own, may change their viewpoint in the direction of that advocated, i.e. they will be persuaded by the communication to a greater or lesser extent. On the other hand, if the advocated position is extremely discrepant from their own, an opposite 'boomerang' effect may sometimes occur. Sherif and Hovland bridge the gulf that separates such results from the attitude-judgement data by treating normal persuasion effects as equivalent to 'assimilation' and 'boomerang' effects as equivalent to 'contrast', but the bridge they build is perilously unsteady. As before, the individual's own position is the anchor, whereas the persuasive communication takes the role of the attitude statement in the judgement task; but now, instead of predicting changes in the judged favourability of the statement, the model starts trying to deal with changes in the actual favourability of the anchor. Moreover, whereas in attitude and (certainly) psychophysical judgement, contrast is the typical effect and assimilation the exception, in attitude change 'boomerang' effects generally occur only under fairly exceptional conditions of extreme discrepancy between a person's initial attitude and that advocated by a communicator.

This last point is troublesome for one of the substantive predictions of the model, namely that the direction of any attitude-change effects will be determined by whether a communication falls within a person's latitude of acceptance or rejection. As in the judgement situation, 'assimilation' should only occur to communications which advocate positions within, or just beyond, the latitude of acceptance. Communications falling within the latitude of rejection should make a person more extreme in the direction contrary to that advocated. This model has merit in helping to explain the resistance to persuasion often observed among people whose initial attitudes are extreme. According to Sherif, Sherif and Nebergall (1965) such people will tend to have high 'ego-involvement' with regard to the issue in question, and hence will have relatively narrow latitudes of acceptance (Hovland, Harvey and Sherif, 1957). In other respects, though, its contribution is very limited. It takes no account of the possibility that the discrepancy of an advocated position from a person's own may be taken as a cue to the credibility of the communication, and that it may be credibility rather than discrepancy *per se* which is important. In addition, when the direction of attitude-change effects can be related to an individual's latitudes of acceptance and rejection, direct persuasion effects have been found as a result of communications well within the latitude of rejection (e.g. Dillehay,

1965). Also Miller (1965) failed to decrease the width of subjects' latitudes of acceptance by experimentally increasing their levels of involvement.

The variable-perspective model

Although it is completely established that Thurstone and Chave (1929) were incorrect in their assumption that judges' ratings would be unaffected by their attitudes, it does not necessarily follow that this invalidates Thurstone scales as a measure of relative differences along a specified attitude continuum. An experiment by Upshaw (1962), therefore, aimed to show that the scale values obtained by the Thurstone method could still be regarded as constituting an interval scale, even though they were clearly influenced by judges' attitudes. Comparisons between ratings obtained from different attitude groups, and between conditions in which the range of items presented was experimentally varied, revealed significant differences in the derived scale values, but these differences did not lead to significant departures from linearity when the different sets of scale values were correlated with each other. Upshaw infers from these results that the basic function of an interval scale, that of comparing the relative sizes of differences in different parts of the continuum, is still fulfilled by Thurstone scales, even though no absolute meaning can be attached to the scale value of any item considered singly.

Upshaw (1965) interprets the high linear correlations between different sets of scale values as evidence against the assimilation–contrast model. Sherif and Hovland predict that statements near the centre of the scale will show the greatest shifts, on the assumption that these statements are the most 'ambiguous' and hence the most liable to biased or distorted interpretation when presented to judges with strong emotional involvement in an issue. If this were so, the relationship between the scale values obtained from judges with different attitudes would be less than perfectly linear.

While this argument is correct, it is still possible that departures from linearity might occur, but have little effect on the value of the correlation coefficient. As Ager and Dawes (1965) have pointed out, as long as two sets of values have a high rank-order correlation with each other, the product-moment correlation coefficient tends to be very insensitive to departures from linearity. Assuming that the relationships are in fact linear, however, Upshaw proposed that differences in judgement can be conceptualized in terms of differences in *'perspective'*. The concept of perspective is essentially the same as that of 'frame of reference' in the sense it was used by Volkmann (1951). In other words, judges anchor the two ends of the judgement scale to two subjective values, the one corresponding to their perception of an extremely unfavourable position, and the other to their perception of an extremely favourable position. Their perspective – the distance between the two end anchors – is then divided up between the different categories of the judgement scale into what normally can be assumed to be equal intervals. The width of each interval – in Torgerson's (1958) terms, the width of the scale '*unit*' – will then be inversely related to the degree of polarization, since the wider each interval or unit, the more items will fall within fewer scale categories (see Figure 5.4).

In his 1962 paper, Upshaw predicts that a judge's perspective will correspond to the range of items presented for judgement, plus the judge's own position. As can be seen from Figure 5.4, this implies that a judge's attitude will alter his perspective so as to produce a contrast effect in judgement only when it lies beyond the range of items presented. This last prediction is not supported by the many studies in which fairly moderate differences in judges' attitudes have produced significant judgemental shifts. One has to conclude that, if such shifts are to be thought of as resulting from changes in perspective, perspective must be determined by factors other than simply the range of items presented, expanded to include own position, if necessary.

Another implication of Upshaw's variable-perspective model has received more support, however. This is that the way judges rate their own position will depend not only on the 'content' of their attitude (where it falls on the underlying continuum), but also on their perspective, that is, how they apply the response language. In other words, self-ratings should be liable to context effects following changes in perspective in the same way as ratings of any other item (Ostrom and Upshaw, 1968). Thus, if something happens to make judges extend their perspective at the pro extreme on some issue they will then rate their own attitude as more anti, even though the content of their attitude (the position they endorse) may not have changed at all. This prediction is supported in studies by Ostrom (1970) and

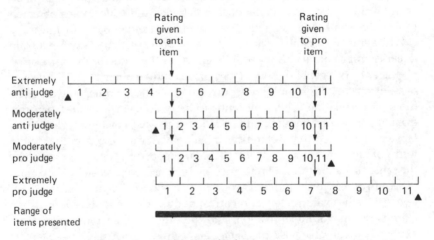

Figure 5.4. Perspective as a function of judges' own position. Upshaw's (1962) variable perspective model.

Upshaw, Ostrom and Ward (1970), in which subjects' perspectives were changed by giving them differing information concerning the expected range within which their own positions might fall. A study by Kinder, Smith and Gerard (1976) is presented as inconsistent with this prediction, but, as Upshaw (1976) points out, fails to operationalize the crucial variables, such as perspective, in a way that provides an adequate test of his model. The distinction between attitude content and self-rating implies, too, that, in certain circumstances, individuals may be even more committed to a particular self-label, such as 'unprejudiced', 'fair-minded', 'radical', or whatever, than to any specific position or policy.

Ostrom (1970) attempted to look at differential effects of commitment to attitude content or self-rating. Subjects read about a fictitious case of a bomb threat in a hospital, selected the prison sentence they thought appropriate for the person found guilty (attitude content) and rated their own leniency/ sternness (self-rating). They then wrote essays justifying either their sentence or their rating. They were then exposed to a manipulation of perspective in terms of information concerning the presiding judge's views about the range of appropriate sentences and what would count as lenient or severe. As predicted, those committed to a particular sentence (by having defended it in an essay) changed their self-rating more than their sentence, whereas those committed to a particular self-rating (e.g. as 'lenient') changed the sentence they recommended more than their self-rating. More recently Upshaw (1978; Upshaw and Ostrom, 1984) has introduced into perspective theory the notion of *congeneric scales* (cf. Jøreskog, 1971). The essential idea following from this notion is that *any* response language is arbitrary, and therefore that attitude content is essentially a latent variable for which multiple indicators may be sought. 'Congeneric scales' are defined as measures yielding scores that are all linear functions of the same 'true scores'. From this it follows that rated agreement or disagreement is not necessarily a 'truer' measure of attitude content than any other response. This leads to a reinterpretation of the Ostrom (1970) distinction between 'content-involvement' and 'rating-involvement': both sentences and self-ratings are indicators of subjects' attitude towards the guilty person.

There are also implications for the issue of attitude–behaviour relations. As Upshaw and Ostrom (1984: 31) argue:

> We find it difficult to distinguish between attitude and behaviour as many have done. Given our conception of attitude content as a latent variable, we view the person as seeking ways to express the latent attitude. Any expression is a behaviour, and it is also a judgement. In this sense, one can learn about attitude content only by inference from behaviour.

Illustrative of this view is a study of Roth and Upmeyer (1985). Subjects rated their amusement at a series of cartoons (verbal attitude measure), while their facial reactions to the cartoons were secretly videotaped. The videotapes were later content-analysed to provide 'non-verbal behavioural' measures of subjects' amusement. Correlations between the two measures were generally high but tended to be higher still when subjects had a mirror placed in front of them, and were instructed to take account of their own facial expressions. The main conclusion is that evaluations can be expressed in terms of alternative modalities (including what could normally be designated as a 'behavioural' rather than an 'attitudinal' response dimension), and that different instructions can influence the extent to which subjects seem to try deliberately to control their expressive output within a particular modality.

Accentuation theory

Although a number of related explanations have been suggested for the overall contrast effects first noted by Hovland and Sherif (1952), the polarization effects found in a number of studies are not predicted at all by AL theory, and are only partly predicted by the assimilation–contrast model. Although describable in terms of differences in perspective, they are not specifically predicted by Upshaw's (1962) model either. In all these approaches, some kind of continuity has been assumed between psychophysical and social judgement, but in none has attention been paid to those physical judgement effects which might seem to correspond most closely to the polarization effects observed in judgements of attitude statements. These are the accentuation effects produced by peripheral stimulus attributes, discussed earlier in this chapter.

In a study designed to demonstrate that comparable accentuation effects could be produced in judgements of attitude statements (Eiser, 1971c), students were presented with a series of 64 statements concerned with the non-medical use of drugs, which had to be rated in terms of an 11-point scale from 'extremely permissive' to 'extremely restrictive'. The study was presented as to do with the role of the mass media in shaping attitudes, and subjects in the control condition were informed that the statements were 'drawn from newspapers'. In the experimental condition, subjects were (falsely) told that all the statements in fact came from two newspapers, and each statement was presented in quotation marks with one of two newspapers' names (*The Gazette* and *The Messenger*) typed underneath it on the questionnaire. Subjects were told that these fictitious names were substitutes for the real names of the two newspapers ('to control for any personal biases'). In fact, the 32 more permissive items were attributed to *The Gazette* and the 32 more restrictive to *The Messenger*. This manipulation is thus a direct analogue of the superimposed classification used in the Tajfel and Wilkes (1963) study.

The results showed a clear-cut accentuation of interclass differences, as well as a non-significant reduction of intraclass differences, in the experimental as compared with the control condition. This accentuation principle is then used to re-interpret the effects predicted by the assimilation–contrast model. If judges assimilate items within their latitude of acceptance and contrast items within their latitude of rejection, this need not have anything to do with the supposed anchoring effects of their own attitudes. Instead, what may be happening is that judges *use their own acceptance or rejection of the items as an additional cue*, superimposed upon the focal dimension of favourability towards the issue. Judges with, say, extremely favourable attitudes will tend to agree with favourable items and disagree with unfavourable items, so, for them, the subjective acceptable–unacceptable distinction will be superimposed on the favourable–unfavourable distinction and should lead to an accentuation of the judged differences between favourable and unfavourable items – in other words, increased polarization in comparison to more neutral judges, for whom the acceptability and favourability of the items are unlikely to be monotonically related.

Up to this point, this interpretation makes basically the same prediction as the assimilation–contrast model, and so is open to the same empirical objections. Most importantly, in the previous studies on attitudes towards blacks, it can still only account for the ratings of the more pro-black judges. Like the assimilation–contrast model, it fails to explain the fact that anti-black judges give less polarized judgements than neutral judges. Moreover, when the subjects in the Eiser (1971c) study were split into a 'permissive' and a 'restrictive' group in terms of their own attitudes on the drug issue, it was found that polarization was directly related to permissiveness of own position, with no evidence that the most restrictive subjects gave more polarized ratings than more neutral judges. Figure 5.5 shows the mean differences between the two item groups as a function of judges' attitudes and the superimposed classification.

To account for these results, as well as those of the previous studies mentioned, an additional principle is introduced. This relates to the *value connotations* of the words used to label the response scale. It is that terms such as 'anti-black' and 'restrictive' may carry relatively negative value connotations for most of the subjects used. In other words, even people who endorsed anti-black statements might be reluctant to describe such statements (or themselves) as 'anti-black', since they would still recognize this as a term which implied a negative evaluation. Thus, for pro-black judges, but not for anti-black judges, the value connotations of the response language would be congruent with the acceptability and unacceptability of the items to the judges personally. If pro-black judges were to rate an anti-black statement as 'extremely anti-black', they would be attaching a 'bad' label to a statement with which they disagreed – something which they presumably would be only too happy to do. Anti-black judges, on the other hand, would be in the position of having to attach a 'bad' label to statements with which they agreed, and a 'good' label to statements with which they

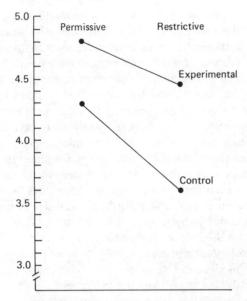

Figure 5.5. Mean item group differences (polarization of judgement) as a function
of judges' attitudes (permissive versus restrictive) and superimposed
classification (experimental versus control). (Data from Eiser, 1971c.)

disagreed. This presumably would be something they would not be happy
to do, so they might try to avoid making extreme discriminations on the
particular scale provided. The same argument should apply to the Eiser
(1971c) data, if one can assume that 'restrictive' was a relatively 'bad' label
and 'permissive' a relatively 'good' label for most subjects.

This interpretation, however, does not rule out the possibility that other
factors may contribute to the asymmetry between the patterns of judgements shown by pro and anti judges, at least on the issue of attitudes
towards blacks. When ratings are required on a scale labelled 'unfavourable/
favourable', there is the real possibility of some semantic confusion between
saying a statement is 'favourable' and finding oneself personally 'in favour'
of it. Since anti judges would be 'in favour' of items that are 'unfavourable'
(e.g. towards blacks), they would be the ones most at risk of mixing up the
ends of the scale, and hence (on average) of showing less polarization. In
fact, in yet another of the studies on the issue of attitudes to blacks, Ward
(1966) deliberately excluded judges he regarded as having possibly confused the ends of the scale. Having done so, he found an overall contrast
effect due to judges' own attitude, with no differences in polarization
between pros and antis. The criterion used by Ward may have led to the
exclusion not just of judges who genuinely reversed the scale, but also of
those who simply gave more neutral ratings (Eiser, 1971b). Whatever the

interpretation, though, it is noteworthy that anti judges were disproportionately represented among those whom Ward excluded from his analysis.

More recently, Romer (1983) has argued that scale labels such as pro/anti,
or favourable/unfavourable have 'connotatively unstable meanings'. While
he accepts that a label like 'anti-Negro' will have value connotations, he
disputes the idea that these connotations will be broadly stable across
attitude groups. In other words he argues that anti-blacks may find a term
like 'anti-Negro' *positive*, whereas I have usually argued that they should
mostly see it only as *less negative* than would pro-black judges.

Romer presents data from two experiments on the issue of abortion, in
which he attempts to classify judges in terms of their individual patterns of
response, and in terms of how well they understood the standard rating
instructions. When considering only those who clearly understood the
instructions (i.e. that they were to rate the favourability expressed by each
item towards the issue, *not* their own levels of agreement/disagreement),
neutral judges gave less polarized ratings than *both* pro and anti judges. If
value connotations are unstable across attitude groups, this is precisely
what accentuation theory would predict. There were more anti than pro
judges, however, among those who misinterpreted the instructions as
requiring them to record their own agreement/disagreement with each
statement.

In view of all this, one needs to be careful to distinguish between the
reinterpretation of previous findings in terms of notions of accentuation and
value connotations of scale labels, on the one hand, and empirical tests of
predictions concerning the effects of evaluative language on judgement, on
the other. The latter will now be described, but two points should be borne
in mind in view of Romer's arguments. First, these studies will be using
judgement scales where the labels have what Romer would call 'connotatively *stable* meanings' (i.e. both pros and antis are in fair agreement
about whether a label is positive or negative, even if they differ over *how*
positive or negative they consider it to be). Second, the instructions given to
judges avoid some of the ambiguities of the previous studies here reviewed.
Generally, judges are given a kind of 'person perception' set, in which they
are asked to imagine, and then describe, the kind of *person* who might have
made each of the statements presented.

Evaluative language and salience

When the notion of the value connotations of the response language is
incorporated into accentuation theory, the basic prediction becomes that
judges will only accentuate the differences between items they accept and
those they reject on judgement scales where the value connotations of the
scale labels are *congruent* with their own evaluations of the items they are
judging. In other words, more extreme judges should *not* give more

polarized ratings, if their 'own end' of the scale is defined by a label with evaluatively negative connotations. As for the observed effects of judges' attitudes on the polarization of their ratings these are a function of experimenters unwittingly requiring responses to be made in terms of an evaluatively biased judgemental language: biased, that is, so as to accord more with the attitudes of judges on one side of the issue than on the other.

This leads to the prediction that changing the judgemental language may alter the relationship between judges' attitudes and polarization of judgement. In a further study on the drug issue (Eiser, 1973), students rated a modified series of 30 items on five scales. These included the permissive–restrictive scale, which showed the same relationship between judges' attitudes and polarization which had been found by Eiser (1971c). The same relationship was also found on two other scales (liberal–authoritarian and broad-minded–narrow-minded) where the more pro-drug term was more positive in connotation and the more anti-drug term more negative. However, this relationship was reversed, with the more anti-drug subjects giving more polarized ratings, on two scales (immoral–moral and decadent–upright), where the anti-drug term was the more positive.

Even more clear-cut results were obtained in a subsequent study (Eiser and Mower White, 1974) in which 14- to 15-year-olds judged ten short communications, supposedly comments made by young people concerning the issue of adult authority, in terms of ten scales in which an attempt was made to balance the implicit evaluative connotations of the judgement scale labels. Five of the statements, which were longer and more informally worded than conventional attitude sale items (see Eiser and Stroebe, 1972: 159–60, for the complete text), represented positions broadly favourable towards the idea that parents and teachers should have authority over teenagers, for example:

> I think life can be just as exciting if you do what you're told. Teachers and parents generally know best and they often have good ideas. Also if you're polite and do what they say you usually come off best in the end. I think you should support them because they've probably done quite a lot for you.

The remainder were chosen to represent broadly anti-authority positions, for example:

> Nobody has the right to tell anybody else what to do with their lives. It's up to each individual to decide what he wants to do, and what he wants to be, and to discover life in his own way. You have to break free from authority if you want to discover your true self, even if this means offending people in the process. If you think your parents or teachers are wrong, you shouldn't be afraid of saying so.

The ten scales included five which were chosen so that the pro-authority extreme would be the more positive in connotation (e.g. disobedient–obedient), and five chosen so that the anti-authority extreme would be the more positive (e.g. adventurous–unadventurous). Subjects were split into three attitude groups on the basis of their agreement with the ten statements. Taking as a measure of polarization the mean difference between the two groups of five statements, the results showed that the pro-authority judges gave more polarized ratings than the anti-authority judges on scales such as disobedient–obedient, but less polarized ratings than the anti-authority judges on scales like adventurous–unadventurous. In other words, judges seem to try to maintain evaluative consistency between their ratings and their agreement with the items.

A further study by Eiser and Mower White (1975) was designed to look for more general evidence, not restricted to the case of evaluative consistency, for the hypothesis that 'polarization of judgement depends both on the correlation between the focal and peripheral continua and on the degree of congruity between the peripheral cues and the response scale labels' (p. 770). To this end, a peripheral cue was superimposed on the same series of ten statements, consisting of the supposed sex of the young person by whom each statement was made, resulting in three conditions. In the *'direct condition'*, the five pro-authority statements were presented as having been made by girls (with a different girl's name printed under each of these statements), and the five anti-authority statements were presented as having been made by boys. In the *'reverse'* condition, the pro-authority statements were presented as having been made by boys, and the anti-authority statements as having been made by girls. In the *control* condition, the statements appeared without either boys' or girls' names attached. Subjects were also split into three attitude groups (pro, neutral, and anti) on the basis of their agreement with the statements.

Subjects had to rate the statements on eight scales, chosen to produce a 2×2 design. The effects of the value connotations of the scales were determined by comparing four scales where the pro-authority extreme was the more positive (P+ scales) with four where the anti-authority extreme was the more positive (A+ scales). Figure 5.6 shows the predicted interactive effect, on polarization, of judges' attitudes and value connotations of the scales, replicating the main finding of Eiser and Mower White (1974).

Independently of value connotation, four of the scales (*'marked* scales') were chosen, on the basis of a pilot study, so that the anti-authority term was seen as more applicable to boys, and the pro-authority term as more applicable to girls. For instance, boys were seen as more likely to be 'bold', and girls to be 'timid'. The remaining four (*'unmarked'*) scales were chosen so that neither term would be perceived as more applicable to boys or to girls. The hypothesis was that subjects in the direct condition should show more polarization than the control subjects on both types of scales, but those in the reverse condition should do so only on the unmarked scales. On the unmarked scales, the question of the congruity between the response language and the superimposed classification does not arise, so both direct

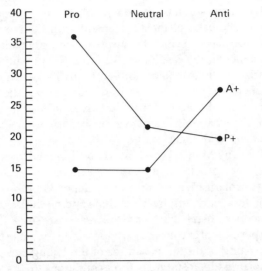

Figure 5.6. Mean item group differences (polarization of judgement) as a function
of judges' attitudes (pro, neutral, anti) and value connotations of scales
(P+ scales; pro and positive versus A+scales anti end positive). (Data
from Eiser and Mower White, 1975.) Ratings of items scored from 0
(anti end) to 100 (pro end).

and reverse conditions should show more polarization. 'The terms used to
label the marked scales, on the other hand, would be congruent with the
superimposed classification in the direct condition but incongruent for the
reverse subjects; on these scales, therefore, only the direct subjects should
show greater polarization than the control subjects' (p. 772).

As can be seen from Figure 5.7, this hypothesis was confirmed, although
the data also show an unpredicted effect of greater polarization on the
marked than on the unmarked scales. The situation of the reverse subjects
using the marked scales is comparable to that of the pro-subjects using A+
scales, or anti-subjects using P+ scales. The direct subjects, on the other
hand, believed the authors of the pro-statements to be girls, and the authors
of the anti-statements to be boys, and so could attach feminine and
masculine labels to each respectively without incongruity.

The main thesis of the Eiser and Mower White (1975) paper is that the two
principles of categorization and cognitive consistency should be regarded as
alternative ways of conceptualizing the same fundamental process. The
central notion of cognitive consistency theory is that individuals attempt to
organize their cognitions and evaluations, as Osgood and Tannenbaum
(1955: 43) put it, 'in the direction of increased congruity with the existing
frame of reference'. In other words, there is a search for a subjective
representation of reality in terms of which objects, people and events can be
evaluated with maximal simplicity and minimal ambivalence. Similarly,

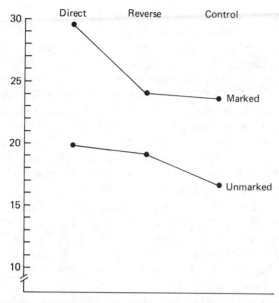

Figure 5.7. Mean item group differences (polarization of judgement) as a function of superimposed classification (direct, reverse, control) and congruency of scales with classification (marked versus unmarked scales). (Data from Eiser and Mower White, 1975.)

throughout the literature on accentuation and categorization processes (e.g. Bruner, Goodnow and Austin, 1956; Rosch and Lloyd, 1978), there has been an equivalent acknowledgement of people's need to simplify their perceptual and social environment so as to make it conceptually manageable (although the ability to differentiate exemplars of a category should not be underestimated). Such simplification is achieved primarily through an exploitation of the redundancy which one learns to recognize in one's perceptual experience, so that a conglomeration of a multitude of separate items of stimulus information come to be treated as a single category.

Normally, the presence of a clearly detectable peripheral attribute which is correlated with the focal attribute will lead to greater accentuation of inter-stimulus differences. In terms of an integrationist approach (see Formula 5.2, p. 141) the extent to which one stimulus will be rated higher on a given scale than another stimulus (i.e. the $R_i - R_j$ difference) will be a joint function both of the perceived difference on the focal attribute $(s_i - s_j)$, and of the differences which would be predicted on the basis of peripheral stimulus information $(t_i - t_j)$. However, it may be the case that the sign of the $t_i - t_j$ difference is opposite to that of the $s_i - s_j$ difference, which is precisely what happens if there is incongruity between the peripheral cue and the response language.

There is likewise no reason to suppose that the principle of cognitive consistency is independent of the language in terms of which an individual expresses and conceptualizes the relationship between different attitude objects. It is all very well to talk of 'increased congruity with the existing frame of reference', but how is this frame of reference to be defined? The implication of the Jaspars (1965) interpretation of balance theory is that this frame of reference consists, in the case of a typical balanced state, of a unidimensional preference space in terms of which the perceivers are also able to evaluate themselves positively. The hypothesized motivation towards balance may be interpreted, therefore, as a search for cognitive dimensions in terms of which attitude objects can be appraised in a way which presents the least challenge to a positive self-evaluation.

Stemming from the factor-analytic and multidimensional scaling traditions, the conventional definition of a cognitive dimension is based heavily on correlational techniques. If different rating scales are highly intercorrelated, they are generally taken to represent the same underlying dimension, factor, construct or latent variable. In terms of this general approach, what is crucial is the question of which attributes a person uses to distinguish between different objects in his or her experience.

In the studies described in this section, however, the different scales tend to be very highly intercorrelated, in spite of being chosen so as to differ in this implicit value connotation. In a strictly positivistic sense, these scales may reflect the same underlying dimensions, but they are nonetheless used very differently by judges with different attitudes. Intuitively, it appears that some judges 'prefer' to use some scales, and others 'prefer' to use other scales.

The basis for this intuition is the extent to which judges seem prepared to commit themselves to extreme discriminations along a given scale, or alternatively to cluster their ratings around the more neutral categories. In short, polarization may be a sign of preference. This would be broadly consistent with the view that greater extremity of response is an index of greater confidence (Cantril, 1946), or of greater salience or personal relevance to individuals of the judgement they are required to make (Bonarius, 1965; Cromwell and Caldwell, 1962; Landfield, 1968; Tajfel and Wilkes, 1964). Salience is certainly not the most clearly defined of concepts (Eiser, 1971a), but it seems to have much in common with the notion of ego-involvement (Sherif *et al.*, 1965) – the idea that one's self-esteem has been brought into play and may require protection.

Direct evidence for the relationship between polarization and preference for particular labels has been provided by van der Pligt and van Dijk (1979). When subjects were given a choice of labels with which to describe statements on the drug issue, the labels they chose were evaluatively congruent with their own positions. Also, when these same labels were combined in the form of rating scales, greater polarization was again shown by judges whose own positions were closer to the positively labelled extreme. Similarly, in a study of attitudes towards a nuclear-waste reprocessing plant, Eiser and van der Pligt (1979) had pro- and anti-nuclear subjects select from a list of adjectives they considered applicable to the pro- and anti-nuclear lobbies. The pro-nuclear lobby was described most frequently as realistic, rational and responsible by pro subjects but as materialistic, complacent and elitist by the antis. Conversely, the anti-nuclear lobby was described as emotional, alarmist and ill-informed by the pros, but as far-sighted, humanitarian and responsible by the antis. These findings demonstrate the limitation of the conventional 'positivistic' definition of a cognitive dimension in terms of an underlying attribute, rather than the person's own description of such an attribute. Even in situations where individuals have little or no control over the stimulus variation they experience, language may allow them many ways of describing, interpreting and evaluating such variation. It is therefore only to be expected that, when it comes to attitudinal issues, individuals will prefer to use language which is evaluatively congruent with their own attitude. It is such language, rather than the underlying attribute *per se*, which defines the 'existing frame of reference' in terms of which congruity is achieved. As Billig (1985) would put it, we are dealing with differences in the *content of the rhetoric* used by different sides on an issue, rather than with cognitive structure as such.

Value and perspective

Although most research stemming from the assimilation–contrast and accentuation theory approaches has been concerned with differences in polarization, changes in overall mean judgement (what Upshaw, 1969, calls changes in scale *origin* rather than scale unit) can also be observed as a result of manipulations of response language. It may be useful to think of these in terms of differences in perspective, even though they are not specifically predicted by Upshaw's (1962, 1969) model.

In particular, there was a very clear 'positivity' effect in the Eiser and Mower White (1974, 1975) studies for judges' ratings of the series of statements as a whole to be 'displaced' towards the evaluatively positive extreme of each scale. A possible interpretation of this effect is that judges tend to use the different scales to cover different regions of the underlying attitude continuum. Evidence in the field of personality trait inferences (Peabody, 1967; and see Chapter 6) implies that more extreme positions on a given trait tend to be evaluated negatively, and more moderate positions positively. This notion in fact dates back well over two thousand years, and Aristotle gives an excellent example in Book Two of his *Nicomachean Ethics*: 'In agreeableness in social amusement, the man who hits the mean is "witty" and what characterizes him is "wittiness". The excess is "buffoonery" and a man who exhibits that is a "buffoon". The opposite of the buffoon is the "boor" and his characteristic is "boorishness"' (translation by Thomson, 1955, p. 70).

In the Eiser and Mower White studies, therefore, a statement would not have to be particularly extreme on the pro-authority side to be rated as 'obedient', but would have to be quite extreme on the anti-authority side to be rated as 'disobedient'. Similarly, a moderately anti-authority statement could be rated as 'adventurous', but only extremely pro-authority statements would be rated as 'unadventurous'.

This 'positivity' effect is an instance of how scale origin can depend on the value connotations of the response language. However, such connotations may also influence scale unit, i.e. polarization of judgement, in a manner that does not depend on judges' own positions. The scales used by Eiser and Mower White (1974, 1975) were all ones where the value connotations of the two extremes were opposed, or asymmetrical; in other words, one extreme was relatively negative in connotation. Eiser and Osmon (1978), however, compared scales where both extremes were evaluatively negative (EN) with those where both extremes were evaluatively positive (EP). The same ten statements concerned with adult authority used in the Eiser and Mower White studies were presented to a final sample of sixty 13- to 14-year-olds for judgement on four EN and four EP scales. An example of an EN scale was resentful–timid, and of an EP scale, bold–polite.

The hypothesis was that, if evaluatively negative labels tend to denote more extreme positions on a descriptive continuum, the EN scales should cover a wider perspective, and hence show less polarization, than the EP scales. This can be seen from Figure 5.8, which shows the hypothetical differences in perspective and judgement that could be expected between EN and EP scales, as well as on scales of the kind used by Eiser and Mower White (1974, 1975), viz: P+ scales where the pro-end was the more positive (e.g. disobedient–obedient) and A+ scales where the anti-end was the more positive (e.g. adventurous–unadventurous). As can be seen, the difference in connotations between P+ and A+ scales should produce the 'positivity effect' observed by Eiser and Mower White (1974, 1975), whereas EN and EP scales should differ in terms of polarization. This last prediction was strongly supported by the Eiser and Osmon results, the effect being independent of judges' own positions.

This interpretation could also be applied to the results of a study by Dawes, Singer and Lemons (1972). Using the issue of the Vietnam war, they found in one experiment that 'hawk' statements were judged as more extreme by 'hawks' than by 'doves'. In a second experiment students had to write statements which they considered to be typical of 'hawk' and 'dove' positions. 'Hawk' statements written by students who were in fact 'doves' were rejected by genuine 'hawks' as too extreme, and similarly 'dove' statements written by 'hawks' were rejected as too extreme. Dawes et al. interpret these findings as instances of 'contrast effects' which are not dependent on changes in perspective, i.e. in how judges interpret descriptive labels. However, a semantic interpretation is clearly applicable if one assumes that extremity is negatively evaluated and hence that, in the first

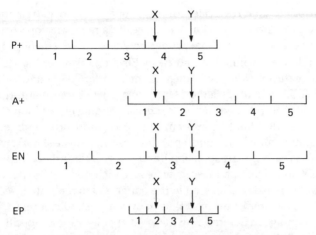

Figure 5.8. Differences in item ratings as a function of the value connotations of the response scale: hypothetical example to show ratings given to a relatively anti-authority item X and a relatively pro-authority item Y on four five-point scales assumed to represent different regions of the underlying continuum from anti- to pro-authority. P+: Asymmetrical value connotations, pro end positive (e.g. disobedient–obedient); A+: Asymmetrical value connotations, anti end positive (e.g. adventurous–unadventurous); EN: Symmetrical value connotations, both ends negative (e.g. resentful–timid); EP: Symmetrical value connotations, both ends positive (e.g. bold–polite). (From J. R. Eiser and B. E. Osmon, 'Judgemental perspective and the value connotations of response scale labels', *Journal of Personality and Social Psychology, 36* (1978), 494. Copyright 1978 by the American Psychological Association. Reprinted with permission.)

experiment, negatively evaluated positions were judged as more extreme than positively evaluated positions and, in the second experiment, labels which subjects evaluated negatively were seen by them as applicable to more extreme positions.

This connection between value extremity implies, as has been seen, that the overall mean judgement of a series of statements will generally be more pro on P+ scales than A+ scales. One can also derive predictions of differences in polarization of P+ and A+ scales, over and above any effects due to judges' own position. One way of interpreting the findings of studies that have manipulated judgemental language is that polarization of judgement largely reflects the extent to which a given scale is regarded as *appropriate* to the distinctions between the items presented. Pro judges will regard P+ scales as more appropriate ways of expressing their discriminations between items than will anti judges, and vice versa for A+ scales. In a similar way, different response scales might be seen as more appropriate to different ranges of stimulus values, e.g. it is difficult to think of ants as varying in size from 'huge' to 'gigantic', or of elephants from 'minuscule' to 'tiny'. From what has been said, we might expect P+ scales also to be seen as more appropriate than A+ scales for *ranges* of items from extremely anti to moderately pro, and for A+ scales to be seen as more appropriate than P+ scales for ranges of items from moderately anti to extremely pro.

This possibility was explored in a study by Eiser and van der Pligt (1982), that included manipulations both of judgemental language and of item range, in a way directly modelled on Upshaw's (1962) experiment. Judges were presented with statements about drug-use ranging either from anti to pro (whole-range condition), from neutral to pro (short-pro condition) or from anti to neutral (short anti condition). Judges rated these statements on an A+ scale (responsible–irresponsible) and a P+ scale (unadventurous–adventurous). (An EN and an EP scale were also included but the results of these, for possible reasons discussed in the paper, fail to replicate Eiser and Osmon, 1978.) The prediction was that item range should interact with judgemental language in determining the level of polarization. Specifically, on the A+ scale there should be most polarization in the short-pro and least in the short-anti condition, whereas on the P+ scale the trend should be reversed. Figure 5.9 shows that this prediction was strongly upheld. Also shown in this figure is the standard interaction between attitude and judgemental language. (Note though, that the 'anti' judges were so designated only on the basis of a median split. In absolute terms they were probably much less extreme in their attitudes than the pro group, which would explain why they did not show a clear preference for the A+ scale.)

The intention of the Eiser and van der Pligt (1982) paper was to build a bridge between accentuation theory and Upshaw's variable perspective model. However, in terms of the more recent developments in perspective theory, it remains somewhat unclear whether A+ and P+ scales, even if related to the same issue, can be properly regarded as congeneric scales. Upshaw and Ostrom (1984: 37–8) are dubious, on the grounds that if such scales denote different positions as well as connoting different evaluations, they cannot be seen as measures of the same attitude content. A counter-argument could be that, while A+ and P+ scales differ in denotation, they still can be assumed to denote regions of the same content dimension. There may be differences in the means and standard deviations of ratings on the different scales, but the scales may still intercorrelate. If this is so, there is no reason why the different scales should not be regarded as 'congeneric'.

This issue is not just one of terminology. The question is whether the judgemental effects predicted by accentuation theory reflect preferences of different judges for different ways of *labelling* the same attitude distinctions, or whether they reflect differences in the *attributes* of the attitude objects to which judges are attending. While it would be foolish to deny that the latter process may often be importantly involved, I have tended to emphasize the former process, and to this extent accentuation theory and perspective theory share many common assumptions. However, both approaches are likely to yield at best ambiguous predictions in situations where there is no clear ordering of items along some simple pro/anti continuum.

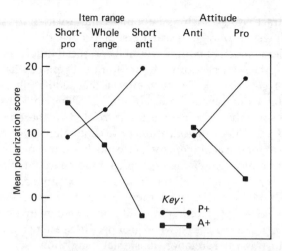

Figure 5.9. Mean polarization scores on P+ (pro end positive) and A+ (anti end positive) scales as a function of item range and of attitude. (From J. R. Eiser and J. van der Pligt, 'Accentuation and perspective in attitudinal judgment', *Journal of Personality and Social Psychology*, 42 (1982), 232. Copyright 1982 by the American Psychological Association. Reprinted with permission.)

It is no accident that research in this field has used attitude issues that in one way or another are controversial. What attitudinal judgements reflect are really ways of representing the *controversy* – the distinctions between opposing points of view. If there is no controversy, it is difficult to know how to judge one attitude statement in relation to any other. Judgements of attitudes – like judgements of anything – can only be relative. More complex situations may nonetheless arise, where a number of separate controversies become intertwined within the context of a single issue.

Conclusions

The origins of social judgement research go back to early work on psychophysics, where the aim was to discover lawful principles relating subjective sensation to the physical magnitude or intensity of a stimulus. One thing that this work showed is that judgements of sensation are dependent on the stimulus context. This dependence on context has a number of features, but the most important is that so-called 'absolute' judgements are in fact *relative*. The same stimulus can be judged as 'large' in the context of other stimuli that are smaller, and 'small' in the context of other stimuli that are larger. This constitutes an effect known as *contrast*.

Explanations for the contrast effect have alternatively emphasized the role of changes in sensation, or changes in the way people define the sensory equivalents of certain verbal labels. However, contrast effects are not confined to simple perceptual judgements, but appear widespread in judgements of abstract issues, such as happiness and a variety of social stimuli. Such findings encourage researchers to believe that common principles may underlie much of both perceptual and social judgement.

Another principle that can be shown to apply in both perceptual and social fields is that of *categorization*. The basic effect is that people will tend to accentuate the judged differences between stimuli falling into distinct classes, where class-membership is predictably related to the stimulus attribute being judged. This categorization or accentuation principle is particularly important for social judgement, since much of our experience of events, people, communication, etc., comes to us, to some extent, already classified. Membership of social or ethnic groups is an example of classificatory information and for this reason there has been a good deal of attention paid to the idea that stereotyping and prejudice may involve the subject exaggeration of differences between groups. There are two important qualifications to this interpretation of stereotyping, however. First, people can gain an illusion of difference between separate groups of classes, even where there is no real difference to exaggerate. Second, even prejudiced people do not always lump members of an alien group together for all purposes – they may be as prepared to differentiate individuals as are more tolerant individuals. Tolerance and prejudice may therefore need to be distinguished more in terms of the content of beliefs, than in terms of extent of reliance on a cognitive principle of categorization.

Applied to the issue of judgements of attitude statements, the accentuation principle predicts ways in which the same statements may be judged differently as a function both of the attitude of the person making the judgements, and of the particular response language provided by the experimenter. From this viewpoint, social judgement becomes very much a process whereby subjects *communicate* the evaluative distinctions which they personally consider most important. Different patterns of judgements therefore reflect differences in the kinds of distinctions people wish to communicate, and the language in which they prefer to do so.

6
Attribution

Impression formation

The question of how we make judgements in a social context involves many issues apart from those considered in the previous chapter. In particular there is the question of how we perceive one another, on the basis of observed behaviour and the context in which that behaviour occurs. This question has been approached from a variety of different standpoints, some of which I shall mention only in passing. Notably, there is a large literature on how visual communication and non-verbal cues such as facial expression, posture and movement, can influence social interaction both in human beings (e.g. Rutter, 1984) and other primates (e.g. von Cranach and Vine, 1973).

Another important tradition, usually termed 'impression-formation' research, is based on the use of personality trait descriptions as stimulus material. The phrase 'personality trait' is not restricted to technical terms such as 'neurotic' or 'introvert', but includes any adjective that can be used as a description of someone's character – and ordinary language is full of these (Allport and Odbert, 1936). Anderson (1968b) for instance, lists 555 such adjectives, scaled in terms of 'likeableness'.

Typically, studies in this tradition have presented subjects with lists of such adjectives that supposedly describe a single hypothetical person. Subjects are then required to make an overall rating of their composite impression of the target person, or to infer whether or not the target person possesses some other trait, not on the original list.

Among the many questions considered in this literature are issues of whether some traits may be more 'central' (more heavily weighted) than others in terms of their influence on composite impressions (Asch, 1946; Wishner, 1960), and particularly what mathematical rules best describe how information concerning separate traits is combined or integrated (e.g. Anderson, 1965; Warr and Smith, 1970; Wyer, 1974). Other issues addressed have been the relative importance of primacy and recency effects (Anderson, 1968a; Jones and Goethals, 1971) and of positive as opposed to negative information (Kanouse and Hanson, 1971; Warr and Jackson, 1975).

Related to some of the work (on response language effects) described in Chapter 5 (pp. 159–69) is research that attempts to unconfound evaluative and descriptive similarity between traits (e.g. Felipe, 1970; Peabody, 1967,

1968, 1970; Rosenberg and Olshan, 1970). Peabody (1968), for instance, conducted a study in the Philippines in which ratings of four ethnic groups, i.e. Chinese living in the Philippines, Filipinos, Americans and Japanese, were obtained from members of the first two groups. There were 14 pairs of scales, each pair constructed so as to unconfound descriptive and evaluative similarity. Thus one pair of scales was 'thrifty–extravagant' and 'generous–stingy'. The results showed that the two groups of judges tended to disagree about their evaluations of each other's group, but to agree about the descriptive attributes which they considered to be characteristic of each group. Thus, for example, both groups agreed that the Filipinos were more generous/extravagant than the Chinese. However, whereas the Filipinos preferred to label themselves as generous and the Chinese as stingy, the Chinese preferred to label themselves thrifty and the Filipinos as extravagant. For a more recent, larger-scale study of perceived national characteristics, see Peabody (1985).

Another question considered within the impression formation literature concerns how consistent and inconsistent trait information is combined. Anderson (1965) proposes that all trait combinations can be combined in terms of a weighted-average model. However, Cohen (1971) has argued that the weighted-average approach may only predict subjects' responses to inconsistent trait combinations when one forces subjects to make their responses in terms of the dimension which contains the inconsistency. Thus, a typical situation might involve selecting two evaluatively negative traits (e.g. dishonest, arrogant), and then asking subjects a question in the form, 'How good or bad is someone who is dishonest, clever, affectionate and arrogant?' In such a situation, the subjects will generally give relatively neutral responses in terms of the good–bad dimension. On the other hand, if subjects were simply asked, 'How would you describe someone who was dishonest, clever, affectionate and arrogant?', they might well be able to report quite definite impressions, but not ones which could be adequately conceptualized in terms of the good–bad dimension.

In support of this position, Cohen reports the results of an experiment in which subjects were required to make ratings of consistent and inconsistent pairs of traits in terms of a large number of rating scales (36 in all). Factor analyses revealed that the majority of the variance of ratings of consistent trait combinations fell on the same dimension as that which accounted for most of the variance of the ratings of the single traits in isolation. Combining consistent information, therefore, does not require major cognitive restructuring. However, for ratings of contradictory trait combinations, most of the variance fell on dimensions other than that which accounted for most of the variance of the single-trait judgements. These results were confirmed in later studies using more realistic behavioural descriptions as stimulus information.

An important feature of Cohen's data is that, when subjects 'switch dimensions' in response to contradictory information, they tend to show considerable agreement among themselves over which dimensions they should switch to. In other words, the qualitative changes in impressions generated by such trait combinations are consistent across subjects. What experimenters have defined as contradictory information is in fact information that is contradictory in terms of the specified response dimension (e.g. likeableness), but which need not necessarily be inconsistent in terms of some other dimension. Osgood and Tannenbaum (1955) predicted that changes in evaluation should be such as to produce increased congruity within 'the existing frame of reference'. An alternative strategy open to subjects, rather than to compromise on a neutral impression as both Anderson's model and congruity theory suggest, is to find another dimension, or frame of reference, in terms of which the information is no longer contradictory. The need for cognitive simplicity implied by cognitive consistency theory might, then, lead to a search for an appropriate cognitive restructuring.

Cohen's (1971) conclusions are echoed in a paper by Asch and Zukier (1984) that addresses the question of how people may process information provided by inconsistent trait combinations, as in the early study by Asch (1946). Subjects received pairs of trait adjectives, and were asked to imagine someone with the two attributes, describe the person briefly and state how the two attributes might be related. Asch and Zukier report that subjects complied easily with these instructions, and almost always succeeded in providing a characterization of a person in which the inconsistency in question was resolved. For instance, when required to deal with the combination *brilliant–foolish*, a typical interpretation was that the person was brilliant intellectually but foolish in terms of practical common-sense. A *sociable–lonely* person was characterized as appearing sociable whilst being lonely 'inside'. A *cheerful–gloomy* person was characterized as 'moody'. As in Cohen's study, so-called inconsistent information was still treated as meaningful and interpretable, with the process of interpretation depending on restructuring rather than simple averaging.

The Peabody (1968) and Cohen (1971) studies stand apart from much of the literature on impression formation and trait inference in that both attempted to embed the rating tasks in real-life contexts (ethnic relations and clinical diagnosis, respectively). In many other studies, though, there had been little attempt to present subjects with the kind of information which they would be likely to receive about real people in real life. The problem is not just that the information provided is minimal but that it has already been linguistically structured. Every personality trait adjective is in itself already an attempt at explaining behaviour. As Asch and Zukier (1984) show, people can imagine 'real' instances of behaviour corresponding even to inconsistent trait descriptions. However, the inference *from* behaviour *to* trait description is more problematic. We cannot observe traits, we can only observe behavioural and physical cues and then, if we wish, summarize our impressions in words which purport to describe personality traits. We cannot observe arrogance, we can only observe people behaving in ways which we may choose to label arrogant. Alternatively, we may hear one person describing another as arrogant, but here we are only receiving impressions at second hand. To assume that person perception is the perception of personality traits (with traits assumed to be observable entities) is to beg so many questions that it is doubtful whether any remain that are really worth asking. (For a critique of how trait descriptions have sometimes been used in personality research, see Mischel, 1968.)

This tradition of research is therefore valuable so long as it is not overinterpreted. However, it is also important to consider *why* we form impressions of others, and the answer suggested by much other research is that we do so in order to render our social world – other people, ourselves, and the events of which we are a part – intelligible, predictable and explicable.

The process, or set of processes, whereby we seek to understand our social world, primarily through attributing various characteristics and intentions to the actors within it, is termed *attribution*. Attribution research, the focus of the remainder of this chapter, encompasses both work derived specifically from an approach known as *attribution theory*, and other work concerned more generally with people's subjective theories and representations of events.

Attribution theory

Attribution theory differs from the impression-formation tradition just described by treating trait descriptions as a possible output from, rather than as a possible input to, the person perception process. It is concerned explicitly with how people try to find appropriate *causal* explanations for one another's behaviour, and more generally for any event in their social environment. Its origins can be traced to Heider's (1944, 1958) work on the notion of phenomenal causality. Heider assumes that individuals are motivated to see their social environment as predictable and hence controllable, and that they apply the same kind of logic to the prediction of social events as to the prediction of physical events; they look for the necessary and sufficient conditions for such events to occur. Such conditions may either be situational or impersonal factors, external to the person whose behaviour one is trying to predict and explain, or factors regarded as internal to the person, such as his ability or personality. In Heider's words, 'Attributions in terms of impersonal and personal causes, and with the latter, in terms of intent, are everyday occurrences that determine much of our understanding of and reaction to our surroundings' (1958: 16).

Heider goes on to stress the importance of the concept of intentionality, arguing that behaviour should only be attributed to personal causes if its outcome is seen to have been intended by the actor (1958: 101–2). There is assumed to be a kind of 'trade-off' relationship between the assumed influence of personal and impersonal factors, so that attributions to a person's character will not be so likely to be made if the behaviour is seen to be under the control of external constraints. Personality-trait descriptions are thus an attempt to explain behaviour which cannot be clearly attributed to external conditions. Even so, Heider argues, the effect of such environmental conditions may not be fully taken into account: 'It seems that behaviour in particular has such salient properties it tends to engulf the total field rather than be confined to its proper position as a local stimulus whose interpretation requires the additional data of a surrounding field' (1958: 54). In other words, we may be biased towards explaining behaviour in terms of personal factors – a bias which may be reflected in the readiness to treat problematic behaviour as a disorder of individual personality.

On the basis of these notions, Jones and Davis (1965) propose a model of how individuals make inferences about a person's dispositions or character, which they explain as follows:

> It is assumed that the perceiver typically starts with the overt action of another; this is the grist for his cognitive mill. He then makes certain decisions concerning ability and knowledge which will let him cope with the problem of attributing particular intentions to the actor. The attribution of intentions, in turn, is a necessary step in the assignment of more stable characteristics to the actor (p. 222)

Ability and knowledge are relevant in that it is assumed that the actor must be seen as knowing that his or her action could have the consequences produced, and being able to produce these consequences intentionally by the action, before an attribution can be made to his or her intentions. When the perceiver infers that the actor's behaviour is 'in character', this is termed a 'correspondent' inference. For example, if the actor shows aggressive behaviour, the most 'correspondent' inference is that this is because of the actor's aggressiveness, which also involves the assumption that the actor intended to act aggressively.

At a conceptual level, there are a number of serious difficulties with this model. At its most mechanistic, it implies that personality causes intentions and intentions cause behaviour. Yet we do not assume that stupid people necessarily intend to act stupidly, or that forgetful people necessarily intend to forget things. Nor can we assume that anyone who adapts their behaviour to the constraints of external circumstances has acted unintentionally. Nor again, in the absence of external constraints, can people be said to have acted unintentionally just because their actions produce unintended consequences. As Anscombe (1963) has argued, to say that someone acted intentionally does not entail that they acted with the intention of bringing about any of the actual consequences of their action.

Notwithstanding these difficulties surrounding the concept of intentionality, the Jones and Davis model contains empirical predictions concerning the conditions most likely to lead to correspondent inferences. The likelihood of a correspondent inference is assumed to be less if the consequences of the actor's behaviour are high in 'social desirability': unusual or deviant behaviour is more likely to lead to inferences about an actor's personality. Also correspondent inferences are more likely if an action produces a larger number of consequences ('non-common effects') which would not have been produced if the actor's traits or intentions had been different. For instance, if we had to decide whether a new acquaintance was 'shy' or 'unfriendly', there would be no point in just considering behaviour which could be interpreted as a sign of either characteristic.

The important question thus appears to be that of the distinctiveness of the behaviour on the basis of which perceivers base their attributions. This notion is developed more explicitly by Kelley (1967, 1971), who assumes that attributions are based on a 'naive version' of J. S. Mill's 'method of differences': the effect is attributed to that condition which is present when the effect is present and absent when the effect is absent. This is most easily understood if we take as the 'effect' the specific impression that a perceiver has formed concerning an actor on the basis of the actor's behaviour. This effect could be said to lack distinctiveness if the perceiver described almost everyone in the same way, so that if we heard person A described by person B as 'unfriendly', we could assume nothing about person A's real personality if it turned out that person B described everyone as unfriendly. The question of consensus is also important, in that we would be more likely to accept person B's assessment if it were shared by persons C, D, E, etc. In this example, one can thus think of one effect (the impression 'the person is unfriendly') and two sets of conditions (the person being perceived, and the person doing the perceiving). One will attribute the impression to the true characteristics of the target person, if different target persons are perceived differently, and if different perceivers report the same impressions.

Other criteria dealt with by Kelley are those of consistency over time, and consistency over modality. If continued observation of the target person over time confirms the same impression, it is more likely to be regarded as accurate. On the other hand, if the target person sometimes appears friendly and sometimes unfriendly, his or her occasional 'unfriendliness' cannot be attributed to a characteristic of 'unfriendliness', but instead to whatever external condition is seen to covary with such changes in behaviour over time. The criterion of consistency over modality can be interpreted literally in the terms of sensory modalities in the case of simple perceptual judgements (e.g. for an object to be round it must both look round and feel round), or metaphorically in terms of the kinds of information one considers about a target person.

Attribution theory therefore assumes that individuals attempt to weigh up different kinds of explanations for behaviour by looking for covariation between presumed causes and effects. For behaviour to be seen as reflecting stable characteristics of the actor, perceivers have to feel able to assume that others would share their impression, that their impression would be confirmed by varied and repeated observations, and that they might have formed a different impression if the actor had behaved differently.

Kelley's (1967) version of attribution theory is often termed the ANOVA model of attribution, in that the criteria of consensus, distinctiveness, and consistency can be regarded, in terms of their predicted separate and combined effects, as analogous to independent variables in a factorial design analysis of variance. Since the three criteria are presumed to be orthogonal, i.e. mutually independent, their possible combinations can be represented graphically as a cube – hence 'Kelley's cube'. In support of this model, there have been a number of studies, of which that by McArthur (1972) is prototypical, in which subjects have been presented with short descriptions of hypothetical behavioural events, in which consensus, distinctiveness and consistency information have been systematically varied. However, this line of research is open to some basic criticisms.

> Although the original formulation of Kelley's ANOVA model of attribution processes always refers to the observation of covariation of conditions and effects, most studies have not presented subjects with actual events which can be seen to covary with certain conditions. Instead subjects have merely been informed about covariation in terms of consistency, consensus and distinctiveness. . . One should first ask whether subjects are in fact able to extract consensus, consistency and distinctiveness information from observed covariation and secondly one might ask whether this is the only information they obtain when observing the occurrence of natural events. (Jaspars, Hewstone and Fincham, 1983: 19)

Jaspars *et al.* (1983) provide evidence (including a replication of the McArthur, 1972, experiment) suggesting negative answers to both these questions. Furthermore, they indicate how departures from predictions of Kelley's model observed in previous studies are compatible with a view that subjects rely more on probabilistic inference processes, and on more 'natural' causal categories appropriate to the specific events to be explained.

Internal versus external attributions

An experimental situation commonly used by attribution theorists involves presenting subjects with a description of some behaviour by another ('target') person, together with additional information which implies that the target person stood either to gain or to lose by such behaviour, and either chose freely, or was compelled, to act in such a way. Subjects' assessments of the intentions or character of the target person are then the dependent variable.

An early study within this tradition was that by Jones, Davis and Gergen (1961), in which student subjects listened to a tape-recording of a simulated job interview, where it was clear which characteristics would, or would not, be desirable in the candidate. They were then asked what they felt the interviewee was 'really like as a person'. When the behaviour shown by the interviewee was such as to imply that he was suitable for the job in question, he received only moderate ratings on the relevant attributes, and subjects expressed little confidence in their judgements. However, when the interviewee responded so as to imply unsuitability for the job, subjects made more extreme and confident inferences, since the behaviour could not be attributed to an attempt to create a favourable impression in terms of the criteria specified by the interviewer. In terms of the Jones and Davis (1965) model, this is an example of more 'correspondent inferences' occurring where the target person's behaviour has fewer 'non-common effects', i.e. where there would be little reason to behave in such a way if it did not correspond with the person's 'real' character. All this, of course, assumes that the candidate was seen as supposedly trying to get the job, and Messick and Reeder (1972) have shown, not too surprisingly, that the results of this study can be reversed if subjects are led to assume that the candidate is trying to avoid getting the job.

A related procedure is involved in studies where subjects are presented with statements about some controversial issues made by the target person, and are asked to infer the target person's true attitude in the light of additional information concerning the circumstances under which such statements were supposedly elicited. Jones and Harris (1967) report two experiments using the issue of attitudes towards Cuba, and a third using the issue of segregation, in which the target person was supposedly either free to choose what side of the issue to support, or was instructed to defend a specific point of view (by a course instructor, or as part of a debating contest). As predicted, the target person's real opinions were seen as being more in line with those actually expressed under the former, 'free-choice', conditions. Even under 'no-choice' conditions, however, there was a tendency to assume some degree of correspondence between real and expressed attitudes, particularly when the expressed attitudes were in line with subjects' prior expectations. This may be thought of as an example of what Heider (1958: 54) meant when he talked of behaviour 'engulfing the field'.

Jones, Worchel, Goethals and Grumet (1971) followed up this study with an experiment in which subjects were presented with an essay that was either strongly favourable, moderately favourable, moderately unfavourable, or strongly unfavourable towards the legalization of marijuana, supposedly either by someone who had been allowed a free choice over what position to support, or had been specifically instructed to write on the side he did. Subjects were also given additional information about the writer's supposed attitudes on other issues. These were so constructed as to give an impression of someone with clearly radical or conservative views, which could be expected to generalize to the issue of legalization of marijuana. The results for the strongly favourable and strongly unfavourable essays were in line with those of the Jones and Harris (1967) study. The moderate essays were seen as corresponding to the writer's real opinion under 'free-choice' conditions, but a moderately favourable essay written in response to instructions calling for a favourable essay was seen as reflecting a moderately unfavourable attitude, and a moderately unfavourable essay in response to instructions calling for an unfavourable essay was seen as reflecting a moderately favourable attitude. Apparently, these moderate essays were seen as a sign of 'foot-dragging' under 'no-choice' condition.

A more subtle manipulation of apparent freedom of choice was involved in a study by Kruglanski and Cohen (1973), in which subjects were presented with an essay arguing either for, or against, the broad issue of cooperation 'in human affairs'. This essay had supposedly been written in response to a request by a survey worker that allowed the writer free choice as to whether to argue for cooperation or competition, but at the same time made it clear that an essay supporting one side of the issue (depending on the condition) would be preferred 'because we are particularly interested in the kinds of argument people bring up on this side of the issue'. Subjects thus rated either a pro-cooperation or a pro-competition essay which either conformed to, or deviated from, the preferences supposedly stated by the survey worker, and they were also provided with background information about the target person which would lead them to expect either a pro-cooperation or a pro-competition essay to be 'in character'. When the essay was 'in character', it was assumed to reflect the writer's true opinion, regardless of the survey worker's preference. When the essay was 'out of character', it was more likely to be seen as reflecting the writer's true opinion when it went against the survey worker's preference.

The persuasiveness of a message has also been shown to depend on the attributions subjects make about the communicator and the situational constraints under which the message is delivered. From an attributional perspective, the perceived truth, and hence persuasibility, of a message should depend on its content being seen as 'caused' by external reality, rather than by the personal biases of the communicator or his intended audience. The less predictable a message is from these latter factors, therefore, the more persuasive it should be.

Support for this hypothesis was found by Eagly and Chaiken (1975) and by Eagly, Wood and Chaiken (1978). In the first of these studies, students listened to a recorded interview, supposedly with a university employee, who was made to seem either attractive (pro-student) or unattractive (anti-student), and who then argued in favour of either a desirable or undesirable attitudinal position. Ratings indicated that the more attractive communicator was seen as more likely to support the desirable position, and the unattractive communicator the undesirable position. Although the more attractive communicator produced much more attitude change when the advocated position was undesirable, this difference in persuasiveness was eliminated when the position was desirable. In the second study, students read a transcript of a defence of an environmentalist position in front of what was supposedly a pro-business or pro-environment audience, and were given information about the communicator suggesting that his own background was pro-business or pro-environment. Again, support was found for the prediction that the message would be more persuasive when it went against the subjects' prior expectations, regardless of whether these expectations were based on the presumed bias of the communicator, of his audience, or of both combined.

Attribution of responsibility

The manipulation of perceived freedom of choice has also been central to those studies which have looked at attributions of responsibility for behaviour. Much of this research has stemmed from Walster's (1966) hypothesis that the more serious the consequences of a person's behaviour, the more likely it is that he or she will be seen as 'responsible', even if these consequences were unintended. Walster found support for this prediction by asking subjects to make judgements about the central character in a story involving a car accident. Later research, however, has generally failed to confirm the simple relationship between outcome severity and responsibility attribution predicted by Walster (Shaver, 1970a, b; Shaw and Skolnick, 1971; Walster, 1967). Moreover, as pointed out by Wortman and Linder (1973), there has generally been insufficient care taken to unconfound severity and perceived likelihood of consequences.

Most of the experimental work using such accident scenarios has been concerned with testing the *defensive attribution* hypothesis, that one is motivated to avoid blaming oneself for accidental occurrences, particularly if the outcomes are severe. As a consequence, experimenters have tended to concentrate on variables directly relevant to this hypothesis such as outcome severity and personal relevance of the situation to the subject (e.g. Shaver, 1970a). Personal relevance is assumed to influence the extent to which subjects will identify with the character or characters in the story. Where they identify with the perpetrator of the accident, less responsibility should be attributed, but where they can think of themselves as the victim, they will be more likely to blame the perpetrator (assuming that the perpetrator and victim are different characters, which is often not the case). Particularly damaging, though, to the generalizability of such conclusions is the finding that other variables can be much more influential than those derived from the defensive attribution notion. Arkellin, Oakley and Mynatt

(1979) found that outcome severity had no influence on attributions for a road accident when subjects were given varying information concerning factors such as vehicle speed, traffic conditions, driver's record, etc. One can imagine that this is precisely the kind of information that one would look for in the context of a real accident.

A more general criticism of the attribution of responsibility literature is that the dependent variables (e.g. responses to questions like, 'To what extent is this person responsible?') are an uncertain mixture of causal inference and moral judgement, and differences in response may largely reflect differences in the sense in which the experimenter's questions are interpreted under different conditions. Fishbein and Ajzen (1973) point out that researchers in this area (with the exception of Shaw and Sulzer, 1964) have often ignored the distinctions recognized by Heider (1958) between different 'levels' of responsibility. At the first level, people might be said to be responsible for all effects with which they were associated (Association); at the next level, only for effects they were instrumental in producing (Commission); at the next level, only if they could have foreseen the effects (Foreseeability); at the next level, only if the effects were foreseen and intended (Intentionality); and, at the final level, only if their intended behaviour was not constrained by external factors beyond their control (Justification). Just asking subjects to say whether a target person was responsible, without stating the level of responsibility with which one is concerned, is to ask a question which different subjects are likely to interpret in different ways. A person could be responsible for the effects of a car accident at the level of commission, but presumably not at the level of intentionality, and differences in response may simply reflect differences in the level chosen. In most of these studies, there is no implication that the consequences were intended by the target person. What seems to be mainly at issue is whether the consequences could have been foreseen and prevented. Thus, any value that these studies have for an understanding of attribution processes is with respect to inferences concerning the knowledge and ability of the target person, not inferences about intentions.

In spite of these conceptual difficulties, an attempt to impose some order on the attribution of responsibility literature has been made by Brewer (1977). Starting from what she calls an 'information-processing' approach, she suggests that attribution of responsibility (AR) is related to just two independent subjective probability estimates: (1) the prior expectancy (PE) that the outcome would have occurred anyway without any action by the target person, and (2) the congruence (C) between the action and its outcome, i.e. the expectation that the action would lead to the outcome without any prior knowledge of the situation. AR is assumed to be inversely related to PE, but directly related to C.

Walster's (1966) findings can be fitted into this interpretation, if it is assumed that the more severe consequences had a lower PE. The failures to replicate Walster's findings may also be interpreted, albeit *post hoc*, if it is assumed that different outcomes varied not only in PE but also in C. For example, part of what Shaw and Skolnick (1971) found was that a description of a low PE positive outcome led to a lower AR than a higher PE positive outcome (respectively a major discovery or a pleasant smell accidentally produced by a chemistry student). It seems plausible that there would have been an even larger difference in C between these outcomes, with the former being seen as a very unlikely result of the student's behaviour.

Regarding the issue of levels of responsibility, Brewer treats the levels not as qualitatively different, but simply as 'determinants of judgements made along a continuous dimension, that of the degree of congruence between action and outcome' (p. 60). Essentially, the more intended the consequences, the higher should be C and hence AR. However, Brewer does not really deal with the Fishbein and Ajzen (1973) point that subjects may give different AR ratings depending on the level of responsibility they consider relevant. This implies that subjects may require different 'threshold levels' of C before making positive AR ratings, depending, for example, on their interpretations of the experimenter's instructions. At the very least, this seems to require a modification of Brewer's position.

Perhaps the crux of the difficulty, though, is Brewer's attempt to equate 'responsibility judgements with cause, rather than praise or blame' (p. 63). If all that subjects were asked in these studies was whether the actor 'caused' the outcome, Brewer's analysis might be perfectly adequate. However, subjects are asked to assign responsibility, and so what matters is not how responsibility is defined in terms of an information-processing model, but how the concept is used by the subjects. The fact is that the concept of responsibility, as ordinarily used, is not completely synonymous with causality, and does carry evaluative connotations of praise and blame. It is precisely for this reason that attribution of responsibility can be so difficult to interpret.

In sharp contrast to Brewer's (1977) purely information-processing approach, attempts have been made to consider attribution of responsibility more in terms of concepts borrowed from legal theory and practice. Legal philosophers such as Hart and Honoré (1959) carefully distinguish causation and responsibility under the law, the latter being based ultimately on 'common-sense' notions of when someone can reasonably be held morally accountable for particular outcomes. From this point of view the 'naive' or 'common-sense' psychology involved in such attributions is not that of a naive scientist as proposed by Kelley (1967) but rather that of a naive lawyer, jurist or moralist (Fincham and Jaspars, 1980). The notion of levels of responsibility has parallels in legal distinctions, for instance between murder and manslaughter. Similarly, one may be held liable to compensate another person whose property one damages, even if the damage is not intended (if it were intended, it could be the basis of a criminal charge).

Similarly, judgements of degrees of negligence involve concepts of foresee-ability and of responsibility to others (e.g. employees, customers) who may be entitled to have expected greater care to have been taken.

Although legal judgements of responsibility are by no means devoid of their own ambiguities and inconsistencies, as Lloyd-Bostock (1983) points out, they are in many ways more 'social' than the ratings made in typical attribution experiments. Such judgements occur within the context of social obligations, and have real consequences for the participants. They may also depend on contextual factors, such as whether anyone can be sued for damages, and if so whether the defendant or an insurance company will pay. Lloyd-Bostock interviewed victims of different kinds of accidents and found them less likely to attribute fault or responsibility in the case of domestic or leisure accidents than in the case of road or industrial accidents, where compulsory liability insurance can be assumed.

One disturbing consequence of all this is that apologies, if construed as admissions of responsibility, can have financial costs. Thus motor-insurance companies may advise their clients against saying 'sorry' if they are involved in an accident, and medical defence lawyers may advise doctors against admitting any mistake or miscalculation to their patients or their patients' relatives lest this form the basis for a malpractice suit. (It is probably no coincidence that malpractice litigation appears more wide-spread under a private health care system.) The repercussions of such advice on doctor–patient communication are not hard to imagine.

Actor–observer differences

The central tenet of attribution theory – that interpersonal descriptions are the outcome of an attempt to explain observable behaviour – applies just as much to the descriptions one may make about oneself as those one may make about others. The information on the basis of which we make self-descriptions may be somewhat different from that to which we have access when judging others, but, according to attribution theory, the processes of inference are essentially the same. In other words, *self-attribution* – the attribution of characteristics to ourselves – should be subject to the same criteria of consensus and distinctiveness, and influenced by the same kind of trade-off relationship between internal and external factors, as are important in the attribution of characteristics to other people.

Nonetheless, a major area of attribution research is explicitly concerned with *differences* between how people attribute characteristics to themselves and others. According to Jones and Nisbett (1971: 80), 'there is a pervasive tendency for actors to attribute their actions to situational requirements, whereas observers tend to attribute the same actions to stable personal dispositions'. Put another way, one is less inclined to account for one's own behaviour in terms of underlying personality traits, and more inclined to see oneself as responding to circumstantial factors, whereas one is more likely to see other people's behaviour as emanating from aspects of their personality than as contingent upon transient features of the situation.

In support of this hypothesis, Nisbett, Caputo, Legant and Maracek (1973) asked people to predict the future behaviour of subjects whom they observed responding to a request to volunteer for a social service task. These observers were relatively willing to generalize from what they saw to predict how the subjects (actors) would react to a similar request in the future, thus making an implicit assumption that the actors' behaviour was indicative of stable dispositions. The actors themselves, when asked to make the same prediction about their own behaviour, made no such assumption of cross-situational consistency. In addition, Nisbett *et al.* found that students tended to ascribe more personality trait descriptions to others than to themselves, and that when asked to account for their own, and their best friend's, choice of girl friend, they would tend to concentrate on the girl-friend's attributes when considering their own choice, and on their best friend's attributes when describing his choice. The same bias was observed in accounts which students gave for their choice of major course subject: comparatively speaking, one chooses one's own course because of what the course has to offer, whereas other students choose their courses because of the kind of people they are.

Differences between attributions of freedom made by actors and observers have also been reported by Gurwitz and Panciera (1975). Their experiment involved testing subjects in pairs, with one subject in each pair taking the role of a 'teacher' and the other student taking the role of a 'student'. Depending on the 'student's' performance on an anagrams' task, the 'teacher' either rewarded him by giving him money, or punished him by taking money away. Both 'teachers' and 'students' viewed their partner's behaviour during the experiment as more indicative of their behaviour in general than they viewed their own, and the 'students' saw the 'teachers' as having more freedom than the 'teachers' saw themselves. Similarly, Harvey, Harris and Barnes (1975) employed a situation in which subjects either had to play the part of a 'teacher', supposedly having to give mild electric shocks to another person (in fact an accomplice of the experimenters) whenever he made a mistake on a paired-association learning task, or alternatively were assigned to an observer condition, in which case, they sat alongside the 'teacher' and observed his behaviour. The more the apparent distress caused by these punishments, the greater was the amount of freedom and responsibility attributed by the observers to the 'teacher'. However, the 'teachers' attributed less freedom and responsibility to themselves, the more severe the apparent consequences of their behaviour. This result is worth remembering when considering Milgram's (1974) experiments on obedience (see Chapter 8, pp. 275–80).

The Jones and Nisbett hypothesis was also supported by West, Gunn and

Chernicky (1975), who employed what must rank as one of the most extreme forms of deception in the history of social psychology. A random sample of criminology students was approached by the experimenter, 'who was known to most of the subjects as a local private investigator', with news that he had 'a project you might be interested in'. All those approached agreed to a later meeting to discuss the project, which in fact turned out to be a proposal to burgle a local advertising firm, for which the experimenter had produced elaborate plans. Subjects were then each given one of four different justifications to entice them to agree to take part in the burglary. In the first two conditions, they were told that the burglary was to be committed for a government department (the Inland Revenue Service) for the purpose of microfilming an allegedly illegal set of accounting records which would provide evidence of a large tax fraud by the firm. The microfilm was supposedly required so that a search warrant and subpoena could be obtained and the original records seized. In the first condition, subjects were told that the government would guarantee their immunity from prosecution if they were arrested, while, in the second condition, they were given no such promise of immunity. In the third condition, they were told that another local advertising firm had offered $8,000 for a copy of a set of designs prepared by the first firm, and that their own fee would be $2,000 if they participated. Finally, in the fourth condition, subjects were told that the only purpose of the burglary was to see if the plans the experimenter had devised would work, and that nothing would in fact be stolen.

Subjects were told that the burglary team would consist of four people, including themselves, the experimenter, a confederate present at the meeting, and a lock-and-safe expert, not present at the meeting, but described as having an extensive background in military intelligence. Subjects were then shown elaborate plans for the burglary, and were encouraged to ask questions (most of these were concerned with technical details of the plan). They were then asked to come to a final planning meeting at the experimenter's office. If they refused, they were asked to reconsider their decision, and if they refused again, the experiment was terminated. The confederate recorded the subject's decision to take part or not, and his expressed rationale for doing so. The percentages of subjects agreeing to take part in each condition were 45 per cent, 5 per cent, 20 per cent, and 10 per cent, respectively. Clearly, the promise of immunity from prosecution had a powerful effect.

These results were then compared with the responses made by a group of 238 psychology students, who were each given a mimeographed booklet which described one of the four conditions in great detail, and were asked to say how many students out of 100 they thought would agree to participate (this yielded no significant differences between conditions), and whether they themselves would do so, responses being in the form 'Yes', 'No', or 'Maybe'. West *et al.* (1975) take both 'Yes' and 'Maybe' responses as indicative of self-estimated compliance, and report rates of 28.1 per cent, 14.0 per cent, 12.2 per cent, and 18.2 per cent for the four conditions, respectively. In addition, subjects were asked to give reasons why another student might have agreed or refused to participate after hearing the proposal. The reasons attributed by these subjects (observers) were then compared with the rationale offered by those who had actually been confronted with the proposal (actors), and were coded in terms of whether they emphasized the attitudes or personality of the actor, or in terms of an environmental factor, such as the justification or inducement given. As predicted, observers made more dispositional attributions than did the actors themselves.

West *et al.* present their study as relevant to an understanding of phenomena such as the Watergate break-in, which sections of the American press attributed to such factors as: 'the paranoid style of the Nixon administration, and the recruitment of an amoral staff of non-political administrators'. In other words, such 'observers' of the event sought to explain it in terms of the internal characteristics of those who perpetrated it. On the other hand, members of the Nixon administration, the 'actors', were more inclined to see the break-in as necessitated by circumstances. The results of this study imply that normally law-abiding citizens may be more likely than might be supposed to commit illegal activities in the name of a government agency when offered the safeguard of immunity from prosecution. Cook (1975) rightly draws attention to the serious ethical considerations involved in this study, since subjects were not simply asked to indulge in some mildly counter-attitudinal behaviour, but actually enticed into what, for all they knew, was a conspiracy to commit a criminal offence. Whether the 'real-life relevance' of these results justifies the means by which they were obtained is a matter of opinion.

If the research of West *et al.* (1975) implies that actor–observer differences in attribution can occur outside the experimental laboratory, a much more experimentally oriented study by Storms (1973) contributes more directly to an understanding of the cognitive processes underlying the phenomenon. Before labelling actor–observer differences as a manifestation of a 'bias' with a presumably motivational rather than rational basis, it needs to be asked whether actors and observers do in fact make their inferences on the basis of the same information. At the simplest level, actors know more about how they behaved in the past in similar and dissimilar situations, than do observers, who have typically nothing else to go on apart from what the actors' present behaviour implies if taken in isolation. Actors are therefore in a far better position to assess the extent of any covariation between their own behaviour and features of the external situation, and hence make a situational rather than an internal disposition inference. By comparison, observers have to take what they see in the here-and-now as being typical. (And anyway, if it were atypical, why should the experimenter be interested in their impression of another's personality?) In addition, and it is this aspect of a difference in available information to which Storms's experiment is more directly addressed, actors cannot see themselves in the same literal, physical sense that they appear to others. Actors see the situation as more important because it is the situation which they are looking at, whereas observers see the actors themselves as more important since they are the focus of attention. The same behaviour, therefore, will be perceived from different physical perspectives by actors and observers.

Storms was able to overcome this physical constraint by the simple device of videotaping two-person conversations simultaneously through two separate cameras, positioned so as to record the interactions from the physical perspectives of each of the two participants. When actors were allowed to view the recording of the conversation from what had been the other person's (the observer's) orientation, they became more 'internal' in their attributions to themselves – in fact even more than the observer had been. Similarly, when observers viewed the conversations from the actors' orientation, they attached far more importance to the situation in explaining the actors' behaviour. Another study, by Regan and Totten (1975), which also used videotape recording of a two-person conversation (though with less clear-cut results as a function of a different kind of camera-position manipulation), managed to elicit more situational and less dispositional attributions from independent observers who were not themselves participants in the conversation, but were instructed to 'empathize' with one of the participants in particular.

Taylor and Fiske (1975, 1978) have also shown that those participants in an interaction who are most 'salient', i.e. attract more attention, whether because of the position in which they are seated, or because of some distinctive characteristic such as race or sex, tend to be seen as disproportionately 'causal' or influential – in other words, they attract particularly internal attributions. Such results reinforce the viewpoint that actor–observer differences may be a function of differences in the kind of information available to, or attended to by, actors and observers respectively.

Research on actor–observer differences also has implications for the question of how individuals process information concerning base-rate probabilities, which will be considered in more detail in Chapter 7. If actors see their own behaviour as more situationally appropriate, rather than personally distinctive, they should attach a relatively higher probability to others behaving in the same way as themselves, than should independent observers of their behaviour. Ross, Greene and House (1977) found that students overestimated the commonness of their own responses on a number of criteria (from questionnaire items, to compliance with a request to walk round the campus wearing a sandwich-board). In other words, whatever their own responses, they tended to believe that the 'typical' student would respond in the same way as they themselves did. Similar conclusions were reached by Hansen and Donoghue (1977). This tendency, which Ross *et al.* call a 'false consensus' effect, may have implications for processes of stereotyping discussed in Chapter 5, and for intragroup and intergroup relations, to be discussed in Chapter 9.

It is also interesting to set this finding alongside that of McGuire and Padawer-Singer (1976), who found that children tended to describe themselves more often in terms of those traits which serve to distinguish them from their classmates. Also, in a subsequent study, ethnicity was mentioned more by children whose own ethnic group was in a minority (McGuire, McGuire, Child and Fujioka, 1978). Distinctive rather than normative characteristics are thus regarded as more personally informative, even though individuals may underestimate their own distinctiveness.

When combined with a possible bias towards self-enhancement, actor–observer differences in attribution may raise important methodological problems in other areas of psychology, whenever individuals are asked to offer explanations for life-events – particularly good and bad events considered in contrast to one another. Farr (1977a, 1977b) has argued that Herzlich's (1973) analysis of social representations of health and illness, according to which the self is seen as the source of health and the environment as the source of illness, may be an 'attributional artefact' whereby good events are attributed internally and bad events externally, and that the same 'artefact' may be present in the two-factor theory of work motivation proposed by Herzberg, Mausner and Snyderman (1959), according to which the self is seen as the source of job satisfaction and the environment as the source of job dissatisfaction.

This evaluative aspect of attribution is considered more fully by van der Pligt (1981) in an extensive critique of the measurement technique used in research on actor–observer differences in attribution. van der Pligt points out that the choice between making a dispositional and situational attribution is frequently confounded with evaluation. This can result in a bias towards attributing good consequences to characteristics of the target person (so long as the target person is not negatively evaluated) and bad consequences to the situation. Furthermore, following Goldberg (1978), van der Pligt points out that a 'situational' attribution may frequently just reflect response uncertainty (e.g. 'it depends'). This reinforces the view, suggested by much other research described in this chapter, that attributions reflect much more than mere *causal* inference processes of the kind postulated in the earlier formulations of attribution theory.

Further evidence of the importance of evaluation comes from two field studies reported by van der Pligt (1984) concerning behaviour related to environmental conservation in the Netherlands (different laundry and home-heating practices). On the one hand there was clear evidence of 'false consensus' in subjects' overestimation of the commonness of their own habits. However, trait ratings of the typical person engaging in the different practices were determined primarily by how subjects evaluated such practices – positively evaluated behaviour provoked more confident *dispositional* attributions, whether or not subjects showed such behaviour themselves. Thus, it was only when subjects evaluated their own habits negatively (e.g. they regarded their use of home heating as wasteful) that they accounted for their own behaviour more situationally than the behaviour of dissimilar others, as Ross *et al.* (1977) would predict.

Attributions of cooperative and competitive intentions

Further evidence of how we may underestimate the role of situational factors in others' behaviour comes from experimental studies of cooperation and competition. What is especially interesting is that this occurs even when our *own* behaviour forms part of the 'situation' by which the other person's behaviour is affected.

This literature has been more generally reviewed elsewhere (Colman, 1982; Pruitt and Kimmel, 1977). For present purposes, it is enough to mention that the typical experiment in this field has involved a two-person game known as the Prisoner's Dilemma game (PD). This game owes its name to an imaginary situation in which two prisoners are awaiting trial, and each is considering informing on the other, with the hope of receiving a lighter sentence for himself. If neither of them informs, both their sentences are likely to be moderate; if one informs but the other does not, the informer receives only a light sentence, but the other receives a severe one; but if both inform, they will both receive moderately severe sentences, and so be worse off than if they had both kept quiet. Since they have to make their decisions independently, the dilemma for each of them is whether they can trust the other not to inform.

The laboratory version of this dilemma is a two-person game in which each player has a choice between two alternative responses on each trial, referred to as cooperation (C) and defection or competition (D). The outcomes each player receives on each trial depend both on his own behaviour and on the behaviour of the other player. These outcomes, which often are in the form of small monetary rewards, can be represented in terms of the matrix shown in Figure 6.1, where the number above the diagonal in each cell of the matrix represents the outcomes of person A and the number below the diagonal the outcomes of person B. In the example given, if A and B both choose C, both receive 3 units; if both choose D, both receive 1; if one chooses C and the other D, the one who chooses C loses 1; and the other receives 5. (These numbers can have real money equivalents, e.g. pence, but this has only a slight effect on subjects' behaviour.) The pay-offs do not have to be the same as those shown in the matrix, but their rank ordering has to be the same. The two rules that distinguish the PD from other games

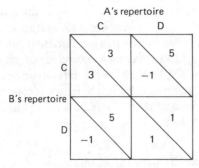

Figure 6.1. Example of pay-off matrix for a Prisoner's Dilemma game.

are: (a) that individual outcomes from highest to lowest should obey the following order: D if other goes C, C if other goes C, D if other goes D, and C if other goes D; and (b) that the combined outcomes of mutual cooperation should be higher, and those of mutual competition lower, than those of one person cooperating and the other competing.

The relative sizes of the pay-offs have important implications for the players' decisions to cooperate or compete. From the point of view of individual outcomes, on any given trial person A will receive more points by choosing D rather than C, whatever person B chooses. The problem is that if person B thinks the same way, they both are likely to choose D and receive relatively low pay-offs. Even from the point of view of their maximum joint outcomes, they should each choose C, but by choosing C they each leave themselves open to exploitation if the other switches to D.

Kelley and Stahelski (1970b) have proposed that the extent to which players in the PD or any similar game will see their partner as having cooperative or competitive intentions will be related to their own intentions in the interaction. In what they call the 'triangle hypothesis', they propose that cooperative individuals may see their partner as likely to be either cooperative or competitive, but that competitive individuals will predominantly interpret their partner's intentions as competitive. If one were to test a group of subjects, and then plot their own intentions against their expectations of their partner's intentions, a triangular shape should result (see Figure 6.2).

Of most significance are the attributions made by subjects when the other player chooses D. Such a choice might represent either an attempt at exploitation (if the other player felt the subject would choose C) or an attempt at self-defence (if the other player felt the subject would choose D). Thus if one subject competed, the other might be forced to choose D, even if the other's original intentions were cooperative. Kelley and Stahelski argue that competitive individuals make an 'attributional error' in taking insufficient account of the causative influence of their own behaviour in forcing the

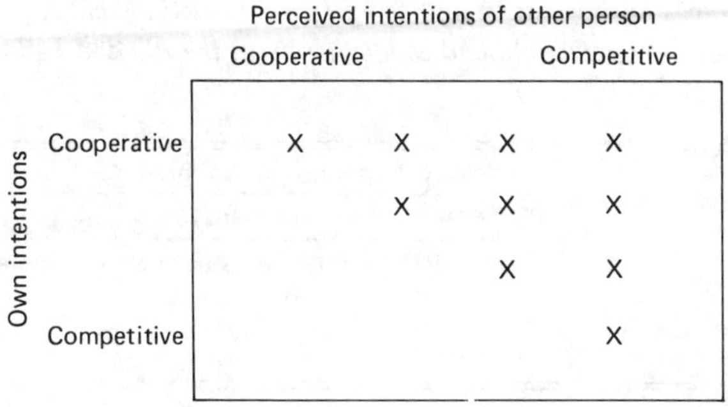

Perceived intentions of other person

		Cooperative		Competitive	
	Cooperative	X	X	X	X
Own intentions			X	X	X
				X	X
	Competitive				X

Figure 6.2. The 'triangle hypothesis' concerning relation between own intentions and perceived intentions of the other person. (Adapted from Kelley and Stahelski, 1970b.)

other to act competitively. Thus, by attributing competitive intentions to their partner, they force the other to act competitively, and so their attributions become self-fulfilling.

In support of this hypothesis, Kelley and Stahelski (1970a) show that, whilst the intentions of a competitive player in the PD tend to be accurately perceived, a player whose original intentions are cooperative tends to be seen as cooperative by a cooperative partner and competitive by a competitive partner. This is largely because the subject is forced to behave competitively, if faced with a competitive partner. Kelley and Stahelski see the differences in the attributions made by cooperators and competitors as evidence that they 'have different views of their worlds' (1970b: 66), which reflect differences in personality, particularly in authoritarianism, generalizable to other interactions, and not specific to their behaviour in the PD or mixed-motive games generally.

Following the many other writers who have pointed out the very specific situational factors present in the PD as compared with other mixed-motive interactions (e.g. Sermat, 1970), Miller and Holmes (1975) have argued strongly against an interpretation of such findings in terms of player's general dispositions. They compared a standard PD with an 'expanded Prisoners' Dilemma' (EPD). The additional feature of the EPD was that both the subject and the other player had an extra response option, termed a 'defensive' move. If the other player acted competitively, a cooperative move by the subject would result in a high profit to the other and a serious loss to oneself. However, by acting 'defensively' the subject could prevent both these consequences if the other acted competitively, without penalizing the other for cooperating. The importance of this additional option is that a competitive move in the EPD cannot be construed as an attempt at self-defence, as it can be in the PD. Miller and Holmes had subjects both declare their own intentions as cooperative or competitive, and also predict

Table 6.1. *Percentages of cooperative and competitive predicting that the 'typical person' would respond cooperatively and competitively in the PD and EPD games used by Miller and Holmes (1975)*

	Predicted behaviour of 'typical person'			
	PD		EPD	
	Cooperative	Competitive	Cooperative	Competitive
Own intentions				
Cooperative	60	40	65	35
Competitive	10	90	32	68

whether the 'typical person' would play cooperatively or competitively. As shown in Table 6.1, these data confirmed the Kelley and Stahelski prediction of a 'triangular' relationship in the case of the PD, but not of the EPD.

Miller and Holmes do not dismiss the idea that attributions of intentions to the other person can operate as self-fulfilling prophecies, but stress the importance of specific situational variables in such attributions to a far greater extent than do Kelley and Stahelski. These conclusions are reinforced by Kuhlman and Wimberley (1976), who also compare subjects' expectations of others' intentions in the PD and other experimental games. Whereas the data from the PD are consistent with the triangle hypothesis, the data from the other games (which allow 'individualistically' oriented subjects to be distinguished from those who are cooperative or competitive) show that subjects tend to assume that others will have broadly similar intentions to their own, whatever these happen to be.

This last conclusion, though, is by no means without its broader implications. Although competitors may not be generally more prone to attributional errors than are competitors (as hypothesized by Kelley and Stahelski), both may make predictions compatible with a false consensus effect (Ross *et al.*, 1977). When this happens, one can consider people's attributions of intentions to others as providing justifications for their own behaviour, be this cooperation, competition, or individual self interest (see also pp. 180–3).

Snyder and Swann (1978) provide further evidence of the behavioural effects of attributions and expectations concerning hostility or non-hostility. Their experiment involved a target subject in two successive encounters, the first with another person who had been led to expect that the target subject would act in a hostile or (in another condition) non-hostile manner, and the second with another person who had no such expectations. The interactions consisted of a competitive reaction time task where each subject in turn was provided with the opportunity to distract the other by delivering bursts of noises of controllable intensity. In addition, the *target* subjects (only) were led to make either dispositional or situational attributions for their *own* level of use of the noise weapon. Thus, they were informed that previous research had indicated that the loudness of the noise bursts people choose to deliver 'depends on the type of person they are' or 'depends on how their opponent uses his noise weapon against them', and that the best strategy for a subject to use would be one that 'uniquely fits his capabilities and personality' or that takes account of 'the strategy that their opponent has used and might use in the future'. Male student subjects were used throughout.

During the first interaction, target subjects behaved as more hostile, and were so perceived by their opponent, when their opponent had been given expectations of hostility rather than non-hostility. These differences were almost as strong when the target subjects had received situational as opposed to dispositional attributional sets. The most striking effects, though were found in the second interaction, where target subjects who had previously been labelled as hostile continued to act in a hostile manner towards a 'naive' opponent, but *only* when they had been led to make dispositional attributions for their own behaviour.

Cognition, arousal and emotion

Another important line of research is that concerned with the involvement of attributional processes in the *experience* of emotion. One might suppose that we 'know' how to describe our own emotional states simply through some process of introspection, or that emotional states are a direct result of internal physiological conditions, unmediated by any cognitive interpretation; but the results of a number of studies have shown that situational factors can influence how we choose to describe the way we feel. The classic study in this field is that of Schachter and Singer (1962), in which subjects had to fill out a questionnaire containing a number of potentially offensive questions in the presence of another person (supposedly another subject, but in fact a confederate of the experimenters) who either behaved increasingly angrily as the session progressed, or behaved in an increasingly lighthearted fashion, practising basket-ball shots with balls of paper, and such like. Cross-cutting this manipulation, some subjects had been injected with epinephrine (a synthetic form of adrenalin which causes general physiological arousal), but were not led to expect that they would feel aroused. Another group received the same injection, but were forewarned about its effects, and a control group received a placebo injection. Subjects in the first group behaved more emotionally than those in the other two groups, but the form of their behaviour, and the way in which they labelled their emotions was determined by the behaviour of the other 'subject'. When he behaved angrily, they did so also, and when he behaved in a lighthearted fashion, so did they. Schachter and Singer interpret these results as showing that subjects labelled their emotional states in terms of the situational cues provided by the other 'subject's' behaviour – they were aroused because of the offensive or farcical nature of the task, and hence either angry or euphoric – but only when they could not explain their arousal as the normal expected result of the injection which they had received. Subjects who were told to expect to feel aroused could explain their arousal as a drug effect without having to label it as anger or euphoria.

The design of this study unfortunately fails to control for an alternative interpretation; namely, that, provided the stooge's behaviour is seen as a genuine reflection of his mood, a kind of 'contagion' effect occurs, whereby the subject's own mood is directly influenced by the other's behaviour. Such contagion could well be enhanced by physiological arousal, but this does not mean that the subject is necessarily using the other's behaviour as a cue to help explain his own arousal.

This distinction between internal (physiological) and situational cues has remained an important theme in Schachter's subsequent work. Applied to the problem of obesity, it is used to generate the prediction that obese people overeat because situational cues, such as the availability of food, the sight of other people eating, or the passage of time (Nisbett, 1968; Schachter and Gross, 1968) are more likely to make them feel hungry (i.e. label their emotional state as 'hunger') than in the case of less obese people, whose appetites tend to be more regulated by physiological cues. Thus, fat Jews were found to be more likely to fast on Yom Kippur, and the less exposure they had to food-relevant cues during this period (especially, the longer the time they spent in the synagogue), the less unpleasant they found the fasting. As another example, overweight pilots working for air France were less likely than those who were not overweight to complain about 'jet-lag' disrupting their eating habits, suggesting that 'internal clocks' were less important in comparison to 'local time' as cues for eating in the case of the former rather than the latter group of pilots (Goldman, Jaffa and Schachter, 1968). Tom and Rucker (1975) also found that obese students, in comparison with those of normal weight, ate more crackers, and intended to buy more crackers, after viewing slides of food dishes as opposed to slides of scenic views. Also, obese subjects ate more, and intended to buy more food, if they had been 'preloaded' with ham sandwiches at the start of the experiment than if they had not eaten, the reverse being true for those of normal weight.

Moving to another health behaviour, Schachter, Silverstein, Kozlowski, Perlick, Herman and Liebling (1977) have suggested a contributory reason for the fact that many cigarette smokers claim that smoking 'steadies their nerves'. They argue first that heavy smokers tend to regulate their smoking so as to maintain a relatively constant level of nicotine in their bloodstream (Russell, 1976), and second that stress alters the pH balance of the urine so that more nicotine is excreted (without reaching the brain). In stressful situations, therefore, the heavy smoker will attempt to compensate for the resultant fall in blood-nicotine level by smoking more, but this change in behaviour will be interpreted as a means of coping with the stressful situations, rather than as a compensation for loss of nicotine. This, of course, does not preclude the possibility that nicotine may have pharmaco-logical effects of the kind which smokers claim, so that any such misattribu-tions may simply enhance the perceived effects of a cigarette.

Other studies have used false feedback concerning a person's state of arousal as a means of influencing self-attributed emotion. Valins (1966) showed male students film slides of a number of *Playboy* nudes, while they were connected to an apparatus that supposedly amplified the sound of their own heart-beat. In fact, the sound of the heart-beat was pre-recorded so that each subject appeared to hear his heart-beat change on half the slides (determined at random), remaining constant on the other half. Subjects tended to judge the nudes that had apparently produced a change in heart-beat as more attractive, and these tended to be those most frequently chosen when subjects were told that they could take some away to keep for themselves. In a later study, Valins (1972) showed that such preferences persisted even after the full details of the experimental deception were disclosed. He interpreted this finding as implying that subjects looked harder at those slides which produced an apparent change in heart-beat to discover what was so special about them!

Evidence that arousal can be *mis*attributed comes from Cantor, Zillmann and Bryant (1975), who argued that aspects of the physiological arousal produced by physical exercise decay relatively slowly, so that there is a recovery period after exercise when one can feel one is back to normal but during which one is still relatively aroused. Male students were shown four parts of an erotic film either immediately after, five minutes after, or nine minutes after, pedalling on an exercise bicycle. The middle of these three groups rated the film more sexually arousing, exciting, aesthetic, entertain-ing and involving than did the other two groups. The reasoning is that the middle group were in the intervening recovery phase when they viewed the film, whereas the first group still attributed their arousal to the exercise, and the last group were no longer experiencing any residual arousal that could be misattributed to the film.

The notion of misattribution of arousal is central to the ideas of Berscheid and Walster (1974) concerning the antecedents of romantic love. They hypothesize that stress and frustration intensify romantic attachment since the arousal produced by such stress is misinterpreted by the partners in a relationship as evidence of their intense feelings for each other.

Probably the most creative study bearing on this idea is that by Dutton and Aron (1974). The subjects for the first of three experiments they reported were male tourists, unaccompanied and appearing to be between 18 and 35 years old, who were visiting a canyon area in British Columbia. The most dramatic condition involved their being approached individually by an attractive young female interviewer who introduced herself as a student who was doing a psychology project on the 'effects of exposure to scenic attractions on creative expression'. The unsuspecting male then had to fill in a questionnaire which contained a Thematic Apperception Test (TAT) item designed to provide a projective measure of sexual arousal. All this took place as subjects were crossing a 5-foot-wide, 450-foot-long wooden suspension bridge described as having the following features: '(a) a tendency to tilt, sway, and wobble, creating the impression that one is about to fall over the side; (b) very low handrails of wire cable which contribute to this impression and (c) a 230-foot drop to rocks and shallow rapids below the bridge' (p. 511). The control condition consisted of the same interviewer approaching unaccompanied males crossing a shorter, wider and firmer wooden bridge 10 feet above a small rivulet further up the canyon. These two conditions were also repeated with a male interviewer approaching male subjects.

The results of this first experiment showed that approximately two-thirds of subjects approached by the female interviewer agreed to fill in the questionnaire, as compared with about half those approached by the male interviewer, regardless of the bridge being used as the location. The scores for sexual imagery on the TAT item were low in the male interviewer conditions, higher with the female interviewer on the safe bridge, and highest of all with the female interviewer on the dangerous bridge. To provide an additional measure, the interviewer tore off a corner of each subject's questionnaire, and wrote on his or her name and phone number, and invited the subject to phone, 'if he wanted to talk further'. The rate of acceptance of the phone numbers was more than twice as high when the interviewer was female, and of those subjects who accepted her number, 9 out of 18 subsequently phoned her if they had been interviewed by her on the dangerous bridge, as compared with 2 out of 16 in the safe bridge condition.

Such findings provide only tentative support for the Berscheid and Walster (1974) approach, however. One anyway has to stretch a point to accept that 'romantic love' was what was being measured. More basically, enhanced attraction can occur without subjects failing to recognize the cause of their arousal. Manipulation checks included by Dutton and Aron (1974) showed clearly that subjects described themselves as anxious about crossing the bridge. For such reasons Kenrick and Cialdini (1977: 385), arguing in favour of a 'reinforcement view' of the effects of arousal on attraction, suggest that 'Lovers not only provide increases in arousal for one another, but they also provide reductions of that arousal . . . it is our major hypothesis that it is more often the reduction of that arousal, rather than its labelling, that intensifies the relationship.'

The studies just described represent a very small selection of the procedures used to study the question of how we experience emotion. Broadly, they are consistent with a view that emotion can be influenced both by arousal and by cognitive appraisal of the situation. However, Schachter claims more than this. His theory requires that both cognition and arousal are *necessary* for the experience of emotion. It is assumed that physiological arousal 'by itself' is rather diffuse and determines the intensity, but not the quality, of an emotional state. For the emotion to be experienced qualitatively as of one kind rather than another, inferences must be drawn from the situation in which the arousal occurs. Although such inferences were originally considered in terms of social comparison (Schachter, 1959) rather than attribution processes, a function of such inferences is to *explain* the nature of the arousal.

Most empirical work on Schachter's theory has concerned three specific predictions:

(1)   If someone misattributes artificially induced arousal to an emotional source, the emotional state will be intensified. Examples of 'artificial' arousal are that produced by drugs as in the original Schachter and Singer (1962) study, and by the exercise bicycle in the Cantor *et al.* (1975), study.

(2)   If physiological arousal or feedback during an emotion is reduced, the intensity of the emotional state will be reduced.

(3)   If someone misattributes emotionally induced arousal in whole or part to some non-emotional or irrelevant stimulus, the intensity of the emotion will be reduced.

In a thorough review of the experimental literature, Reisenzein (1983) concludes that there is adequate support for the first of these predictions; there is little support for the second, and support for the third is ambiguous in view of possible confounds (e.g. when experimenters try to get subjects to consider a neutral stimulus as the source of emotional arousal, they may divert attention away from the emotional stimulus). Moreover, none of the studies reviewed by Reisenzein support Schachter's view that diffuse peripheral arousal is a *necessary* condition for emotion. Schachter's claim that no qualitative tone is attached to emotional arousal in the absence of social labelling has also come under heavy criticism. Maslach (1979) and Marshall and Zimbardo (1979) argue that the unexplained arousal induced in misinformed subjects following epinephrine injections (as in the original Schachter and Singer, 1962, study) is not experienced as 'emotional plasticity' but rather as a kind of *negative* affect. Schachter and Singer (1979) partly concede this point when admitting that *high* arousal is a noxious stimulus.

Leventhal's (1980, 1984) theoretical approach allows for the fact that cognitive appraisal may influence emotion without assuming that labelling processes always precede emotion. As he argues (1980: 151) 'According to cognition-arousal theory, neither infants nor children should experience emotion until given social labels for their body states. However, this conjectured sequence of events poses a near insuperable barrier to learning emotional labels. The alternative view, that emotional experience precedes labelling, provides a more reasonable account of the developmental sequence.'

The concept of learning is crucial to Leventhal's theory, which allows both for unconditioned and conditioned emotional reactions and for the learning of social labels for different emotional states. He postulates, among other things, an 'emotional memory mechanism', in terms of which subjective emotions, autonomic, expressive and instrumental reactions and situational memories are integrated together. As a result of this, situations and stimuli can be experienced emotionally in specific qualitative ways, rather than, as Schachter would have it, causing diffuse arousal which then needs to be *explained* in terms of some label.

The idea that emotional experience is reducible to a special kind of self-attribution is therefore no longer acceptable as a general explanation. Indeed, the pendulum has swung so far that Zajonc (1980) has argued for the *primacy* of emotion over cognition. Leventhal (1980: 193) distances himself slightly from such enthusiasm, pointing out that: 'To assign emotion priority (either in time, or in importance) to cognition as a determinant of behaviour is to treat emotional and cognitive processes as unitary events, which they are not.'

In sharp contrast to the earlier attempts to explain emotion through attribution, a number of researchers are now busy showing that emotional experience can influence the affective quality of attributions and of social cognition and behaviour generally (e.g. Bower, 1981; Clark and Fiske, 1982).

Attributions for success and failure

Another research question involving an interplay between emotional and cognitive processes, and one that is of great practical relevance in the fields of education and of clinical psychology, is that of how people explain the achievement, or lack of achievement, shown by themselves and others. If one succeeds, is it because the task was easy, because one was lucky, because of superior skill, or because of extra effort? The answer is likely to affect how much personal credit one should be given for such success, and whether one would expect such success to be repeated.

The question of whether success or failure should be internally or externally attributed is basic to social learning theory approaches to personality (Rotter, Chance and Phares, 1972). According to Rotter (1966), individuals differ in the extent to which they expect 'reinforcements' to occur, as a function of their own behaviour ('internal control'), or as a function of luck or forces beyond their personal control ('external control'). The I–E scale devised by Rotter to measure individuals' positions on this dimension of 'locus of control' consists of pairs of statements such as: 'Becoming a success is a matter of hard work, luck has little or nothing to do with it' versus 'Getting a good job depends mainly on being in the right place at the right time', subjects having to indicate which statement in each pair is closer to their own opinion. (In this example, endorsement of the first alternative would be taken as indicative of an internal orientation.)

Although attempts have been made to develop comparable measures for use with younger subjects (e.g. Crandall, Katkovsky and Crandall, 1965; Gammage, 1974), most of the large literature on locus of control has used college students as subjects (Lefcourt, 1972). The most common research strategy has been to look for differences between 'internals' and 'externals' in their responses on a variety of judgement and performance tasks. For example, Jones, Worchel, Goethals and Grumet (1971) found that 'internals' were more sensitive than 'externals' to whether essays on a controversial issue had been supposedly elicited under free-choice or no-choice conditions, when asked to assess the real attitudes of the writers of the essays. With very few exceptions (e.g. McArthur, 1970), there has been little attempt to relate changes in an individual's generalized expectancies for locus of control to specific learning experiences. Mirels (1970) has since disputed the unidimensionality of the I–E scale, distinguishing items concerned with personal control from those concerned with potentiality for influence in a political context. There have also been attempts to identify 'defensive externals' who adopt external attitudes so as to protect themselves from the implications of accepting personal responsibility for failure, but may be rather similar to internals in other respects, such as motivation for academic achievement (Prociuk and Breen, 1975).

Research of this kind is also important when it comes to evaluating the assumption, originally made by Heider (1958), that, for an event, to be seen as attributable to a given reason 'the reason has to fit the wishes of the person' – in other words, that individuals generally appear to be biased towards explaining events in a manner congruent with a positive self-evaluation. A study frequently cited as support for Heider's assumption is that by Johnson, Feigenbaum and Weiby (1964), who examined the attributions made by student teachers in a simulated teaching situation. When a child performed badly at a task over two sets of trials, the student teachers blamed the child and denied personal responsibility for his lack of improvement, but when he improved from the first set to the second, they saw this improvement as due to the success of their teaching. Schopler and Layton (1972) found a similar effect when student subjects evaluated the simulated performance of a fellow-student. Subjects were more likely to see themselves as having influenced the other's behaviour when the other's performance improved over two sets of trials, and also when it remained at a high level over both sets of trials, as compared with a condition where the other's performance started at a low level, and failed to show improvement.

Reviewing these and other similar studies, Miller and Ross (1975) argue that it is important to distinguish between 'self-protection' effects, or attributions which involve denying responsibility for negative consequences, and 'self-enhancement' effects, or attributions which involve claiming responsibility for positive consequences. Miller and Ross conclude that there is only minimal evidence in the literature for self-protection effects. Schopler and Layton (1972), for instance, included a condition in which the target person's performance started at a high level, and then deteriorated over the two sets of trials. There is no evidence that subjects in this condition were inclined to deny responsibility for the target person's decline in performance.

The evidence for self-enhancing attributions is more consistent with Heider's (1958) assumption, but even here, according to Miller and Ross, there is no general need to favour a motivational orientation. Kelley's (1967, 1971) formulation of attribution theory assumes that individuals will attribute effects to causes which are seen to covary with changes in such effects. In other words, a change in the target person's behaviour over time is likely to be attributed to a factor which also is seen to change over time. In studies such as those by Johnson et al. (1964), the influence of the subjects' instruction of the target person would be assumed to increase over time, and hence would covary with any increase (or decrease) in the person's performance. Conversely, if the target person's performance shows no change (for the better or the worse), Kelley's covariation principle would imply that subjects should look for a cause which could be assumed to remain constant over time, such as the target person's lack of ability.

Bradley (1978), on the other hand, has argued against the 'non-motivational' interpretation proposed by Miller and Ross. He points out that studies which show evidence of self-serving biases in attribution use situations where subjects' performance is publicly observable, and hence where one might expect motives of self-esteem maintenance to be operative. Emphasizing subjects' observability can increase their tendency to make self-serving attributions. This was shown by Federoff and Harvey (1976), who had subjects attempt to give therapy to another person, the success or failure of which was indicated by supposed feedback concerning the person's state of muscular relaxation. Subjects were more likely to see themselves as responsible for the outcome of the therapy when they appeared to succeed in relaxing the client than when they failed, but only in a 'high self-awareness' condition in which they administered the therapy in front of a camera.

Why should the tendency to disclaim responsibility for failure be less consistent than the tendency to claim responsibility for success? Bradley's suggestion is that the subjects realize that their own 'interpretative activities' are also being observed and evaluated, and so they will be less likely to deny responsibility for failure if such a denial would appear implausible. If there is a plausible alternative reason for failure, responsibility may be denied. Thus Snyder, Stephan and Rosenfield (1976) report that players in a competitive game attributed their outcomes more to bad luck if they lost, and more to skill or effort if they won. However, subjects may sometimes attribute their failure to bad luck even in conditions where such denials are barely plausible, e.g. when one repeatedly fails at a task at which others succeed (Stevens and Jones, 1976).

Rather less direct evidence of self-enhancement comes from studies concerned with the issue of how individuals evaluate others who yield to their point of view in an argument. Cialdini (1971) and Lombardo, Weiss and Buchanan (1972) produced evidence that individuals report greater liking for others whom they manage to persuade to come round to their own point of view. Also, when an attempt is made to hold subjects' liking for the other person constant, subjects tend to rate someone who yields to their point of view as more intelligent than someone who does not, whereas observers of the subjects' attempts at persuasion rate those who yield to persuasion as less intelligent than those who do not (Cialdini, Braver and Lewis, 1974).

Cialdini and Mirels (1976) have examined such effects in relation to individual differences in attributional style. Student subjects were classified as high or low in 'personal control' on the basis of their scores on the nine items of Rotter's (1966) I–E scale which were differentiated by Mirels's (1970) factor analyis. Those subjects who were high in 'personal control' (responded more 'internally' on these items) rated a target person who yielded to their arguments as more intelligent and attractive, and one who did not yield as less intelligent and attractive, than did observers of their influence attempts. However, for subjects low in personal control, these differences were completely reversed.

If expectations for success and failure can be biased, this further fuels the concern, felt particularly by educationalists, that such expectancies can be self-fulfilling. For many years, Rosenthal (e.g. Rosenthal and Jacobson, 1968) has defended the view that teachers' expectancies can influence student performance. The important social psychological question is how such expectancy effects are mediated by aspects of teachers' behaviour. Rosenthal (1973) suggested that the crucial aspects of teachers' behaviour could be grouped in terms of four factors or categories: *climate*, the extent to which teachers create an atmosphere of interpersonal warmth with students for whom they have high expectations; *feedback*, the extent to which such students receive more differentiated praise or blame, contingent on their performance; *input*, the extent to which teachers give such students more, and more difficult material; and *output*, the extent to which such students are given greater opportunities for responding. Harris and Rosenthal (1985) report the results of a meta-analysis of 135 relevant studies and conclude that the effects of teachers' expectancies are indeed mediated by a great number of behavioural variables. However, in terms of a broad overview, climate and input are the most, and feedback the least, important of these four factors.

How, then, do people's attributions for success or failure influence their expectancies for future success? The attributional distinction to which most attention has been paid in the research so far described is that between internal and external causes. Weiner (1979) has proposed that causes may also be classified as controllable or uncontrollable, and as stable or unstable over time. Thus, a person's ability would be an internal but uncontrollable cause, stable over time, the amount of effort expended on a task would be an internal, controllable but unstable cause, the difficulty of the task would be external, controllable and unstable. The difference between the two internal causes, ability and effort, is important when evaluating other people's performance. Weiner and Kukla (1970) found that subjects, instructed to play the role of school-teachers giving rewards and punishments for pupils' examination performance, rewarded pupils more for greater effort than for greater ability. Where pupils of different ability achieved the same level of performance, the one with less ability received the greater reward.

In the context of attributions for one's own success or failure, Weiner incorporates these distinctions to revise Atkinson's (1957) concept of achievement motivation. According to Atkinson, the amount of 'pride' obtained from the attainment of some goal is related to the subjective difficulty of the task, so that success at a more difficult task leads to a greater sense of achievement. In terms of the attributional model of achievement motivation (Weiner and Kukla, 1970; Weiner, Frieze, Kukla, Reed, Rest and Rosenbaum, 1971), what is crucial is the degree of perceived personal responsibility for success or failure. Thus individuals high in achievement motivation are assumed to be attracted to achievement-related activities, which allow the attribution of success to ability and effort; to persist in the face of failure, which they tend to attribute to lack of effort rather than ability; to select tasks of intermediate difficulty (since too easy a task will give no sense of achievement, but too difficult a task is likely to lead to failure); and to tend to try hard, in accordance with their assumption that success is at least partly a function of effort. By comparison, individuals low in achievement motivation are assumed to be less attracted to achievement-related activities, since they would tend to attribute success externally even if they succeeded; to give up in the face of failure, which they are more likely to attribute to lack of ability than to lack of effort; to select either extremely easy or extremely difficult tasks, since these provide the least information on which to base a self-evaluation; and to tend not to try hard, since success, particularly at the kinds of tasks they choose, is assumed to be largely unrelated to effort.

In contrast to Atkinson, therefore, who defines achievement motivation as 'capacity for experiencing pride in accomplishment' (1964: 214), Weiner distinguishes the affective component of achievement motivation (e.g. pride in success or shame at failure) from expectancy for future success or failure. Expectancy is seen to depend primarily on stable versus unstable causes. Attribution of success to a stable cause, or of failure to an unstable cause, leads to a higher expectancy of success than attribution of failure to a stable cause, or of success to an unstable cause (Weiner, 1979). Attributions to internal versus external, or controllable versus uncontrollable causes, by comparison, have their main influence on the affective component. However, as shown by Weiner, Russell and Lerman (1978, 1979) they are not the only influence. Weiner *et al.* identified a number of distinctive kinds (or descriptions) of affective reactions that seemed dependent on outcome, but independent of attributions. In addition, different kinds of attributions for success or failure (comprising more distinctions than just internal versus external) were associated with particular classes of described emotion (e.g. success following stable effort could lead to feelings such as 'relaxation'). Feelings related to self-esteem are particularly influenced by attributions. At the same time, emotional reactions can provide a basis for inferring the attributions made by a person for success and failure.

With regard specifically to expectancy for success, a number of studies have supported Weiner's emphasis on the stability dimension where attributions for one's *own* success or failure are concerned (Meyer, 1970; Weiner, Heckhausen, Meyer and Cook, 1972; McMahan, 1973). In addition, the attributions to stable or unstable causes which *others* make for their success or failure can affect one's own expectancy of success on a similar task (Fontaine, 1974; Pancer and Eiser, 1977).

In the context of attributions for failure, Weiner and Sierad (1975) argue that high achievement needs lead to an ascription of failure to lack of effort, which leads in turn to an increase in performance (greater effort). By comparison, low achievement needs lead to an ascription of failure to a lack of ability, which leads in turn to a decrease in performance. In support of this interpretation, they report an experiment in which subjects received a placebo pill before performing a task involving the substitution of symbols for a group of numbers. The pill was described as likely to interfere with hand–eye coordination, and the experiment was explained as being concerned with assessing the extent of this interference. Subjects were then randomly assigned either to a 'pill' or 'no-pill' (control) condition, unless they objected to taking the pill. All subjects who refused to take the pill were assigned to the control condition but excluded from subsequent analysis. Subjects had previously completed a measure of individual differences in achievement motivation (Mehrabian, 1969), and on the basis of this measure were divided into those 'low' and 'high' in achievement motivation. As predicted, those low in achievement motivation performed better in the 'pill' than the 'no-pill' condition (since they did not have to attribute their failure to lack of ability), whereas those high in achivement motivation performed worse in the 'pill' condition (since they did not have to attribute their failure to lack of effort).

Helplessness, adjustment and depression

A closely related notion to that of expectancy for failure is 'learned helpless-ness'. The origin of this notion can be seen in an experiment by Seligman and Maier (1967), who found that dogs who had received a series of shocks from which they were unable to escape, later failed to learn a simple operant response for avoiding shock in a different situation. The interpretation is that the dogs develop an expectancy that responding will be ineffective and so fail to initiate new behaviours that may lead to the termination of shock; or, if they make an occasional response that turns off the shock, fail to repeat it. Seligman has since argued (1972, 1975) that this situation may be analogous to depression in humans. An inability to respond effectively may reflect a learned expectancy that any response will be ineffective.

Hiroto and Seligman (1975) found that exposing human subjects to inescapable aversive stimuli, or presenting them with insoluble discrimi-nation problems, produced deficits in subsequent performance at tasks involving avoidance behaviour or anagram solving, analogous to the 'learned-helplessness' effects found with dogs. Benson and Kennelly (1976) have pointed out that these results show only that uncontrollable negative reinforcements can produce learned helplessness in humans. In a modified replication of the Hiroto and Seligman study, they failed to find deficits in performance following uncontrollable positive reinforcements, which, according to Seligman, should produce similar feelings of helplessness.

To give one example of experimental work inspired by this model, Klein, Fencil-Morse and Seligman (1976) showed that patterns of behaviour similar to those shown by depressives could be produced in subjects who under-went the sort of learning experiences assumed to underly the development of depression. In other words, helplessness can be taught as well as learned. Depressed and non-depressed college students were recruited to take part in a problem-solving experiment. In the first phase, subjects performed a discrimination task consisting of a series of either four soluble or four insoluble problems, a control group receiving no problems. Among those who received insoluble problems, some received no instructions on how to attribute their failure, some were told 'most people are able to get three or four of the problems correct' ('internal attribution for failure' instructions), and the remainder were told 'the problems are very difficult and almost no one has been able to solve them' ('external attribution for failure' instruc-tions). All subjects were then given an anagram task, at which depressed subjects performed worse than non-depressed subjects, and those who had been given insoluble problems in the previous phase performed worse than those who had been given soluble problems. The performance of non-depressed subjects given insoluble problems in the previous phase resem-bled that of the depressives who had been in the control or soluble-problem groups. The instructions on how to attribute their failure on the insoluble problems had little effect on non-depressed subjects. However, depressives, given instructions which allowed them to attribute their failure externally to the difficulty of the task, performed much better than depressives who were given insoluble problems, but were led to expect that the problems would be easy, or were given no such instructions.

The learned-helplessness model of depression was reformulated by Abramson, Seligman and Teasdale (1978) so as explicitly to include attributional concepts. According to Abramson *et al.*, for depression to occur individuals must not only experience uncontrollable outcomes, they must develop expectations that future outcomes will also be uncontrollable. Such expectations are seen to depend on the attributions made for *why* such non-contingent outcomes occur. The hypothesized causal chain consists of *objective* non-contingency, leading to *perception* of non-contingency, leading to *attribution* for non-contingency, leading to *expectation* of future non-contingency, leading to *symptoms* of helplessness. Depressives are predicted to attribute negative outcomes to internal, global and stable factors, and it was subsequently suggested that depressives may also attribute good outcomes to external, specific and unstable factors (Seligman, Abramson, Semmel and von Baeyer, 1979).

Alloy, Peterson, Abramson and Seligman (1984) provide further evidence on the role of the global versus specific distinction. They compared students who tended to attribute negative outcomes to global factors with those who tended to attribute such outcomes to specific factors. Subjects were then given one of three pre-treatments designed to manipulate helplessness (loud bursts of white noise which were either controllable or uncontrollable, plus a control condition without noise). About one week later subjects were tested on one of two tasks used by Hiroto and Seligman (1975), one (a hand shuttlebox) involving a similar setting to the pre-treatment task, and the other (anagrams) being dissimilar. As predicted, when tested on the similar tasks, those who had been subjected to noise showed deficits in performance, regardless of whether they had a 'global' or 'specific' attributional style. However, when the test situation was dissimilar to the pre-treatment phase only those with a 'global' attributional style still showed such deficits as a consequence of the helplessness manipulation.

Just as feelings of lack of control may be implicated in depression, so feelings of positive control may play a part in adjustment to a variety of adverse circumstances. Taylor, Lichtman and Wood (1984) observed that, among women being treated for breast cancer, those who showed better adjustment had more positive beliefs in either their own ability, or that of physicians, to control their cancer. Although the great majority of the women made attributions for why they had developed cancer, neither the particular attributions offered, nor whether responsibility was internally or externally attributed, made a difference to level of adjustment. Bulman and Wortman (1977) interviewed a sample of patients with severe spinal cord injuries as a result of a recent accident (mainly male, mean age 27 years). They found a complex association between adjustment and attribution of responsibility for the accident, with those who blamed others rather than themselves showing worse adjustment. Independently of degree of self-blame, those who felt the accident could have been avoided showed worse adjustment. Attributions were affected by the circumstances of the accident (e.g. whether another person was present).

Despite the superficial discrepancy between these findings and those of Taylor *et al.*, there are some obvious but important differences between the kinds of patients being studied. While the accident victims may not have considered their condition as life-threatening, their prognosis for anything approaching complete recovery would have been very much poorer than for the cancer patients. At the same time, the cancer patients could at best speculate about the circumstances that may have given rise to their present condition, whilst the accident victims knew the event for which responsibility might be ascribed. More generally, there is a case for looking at the ways in which different medical treatments may not simply interact with, but contribute to, patients' levels of psychological adjustment. Raps, Peterson, Jonas and Seligman (1982) conclude that longer periods of hospitalization can produce symptoms of depression in patients, as well as deficits on cognitive tasks. Raps *et al.* ascribed such effects to the perceived lack of control learned by patients as a direct result of their experience in hospital (although perceived lack of control was not measured; see Baltes and Skinner, 1983; Peterson and Raps, 1984, for subsequent discussion).

The reformulated learned-helplessness model is not alone in proposing that cognitive processes play a causally antecedent role in the onset of depression. The other main 'cognitive' approach is that of Beck (1967, 1976). Instead of considering attributions directly, Beck concentrates on the misinterpretations of experience he suggests that depressives may make through faulty information-processing and dysfunctional schemata (see Chapter 7, pp. 237–43), in terms of which meanings are attached to particular events. Thus, depressives may selectively attend to more negative aspects of a situation, interpret neutral or negative events as more extremely negative, and resist alternative, more positive interpretations of the same events. It follows from this that depressives should show excessive self-blame for negative events. This is different from the original (Seligman, 1975) notion of helplessness, which stated that depressives should perceive such events to be uncontrollable. However, the Abramson *et al.* (1978) reformulation seems to remove this contradiction.

There is considerable evidence that depressed and non-depressed people report their life experiences in different terms – indeed this is probably a large part of what one *means* by depression – but the assertion that particular kinds of cognitive style necessarily *cause* depression is not without its critics (e.g. Wortman and Dintzer, 1978). Coyne and Gotlib (1983) take issue both with Beck's model and the reformulated learned-helplessness model on precisely this point. The life-events experienced by clinically depressed people can indeed be quite difficult to interpret very positively (Brown and Harris, 1978), lending support to the idea that greater importance should be attached to environmental factors. This goes against Beck's assertion that depressives routinely distort facts to fit negative assumptions or schemata. It also points to an important methodological difficulty – many studies have simply compared non-depressed and mildly depressed college students, and generalization to clinic samples may be problematic. From the point of view of measurement, too, while depressives show somewhat lower measures of self-esteem on questionnaires than non-depressed people, it is not established that such effects are specific to depression.

Similar conclusions are reached by Brewin (1985) in a review that concentrates on clinical as opposed to experimental evidence. He argues that attributions of helplessness may often be a consequence of depressed mood, and that there is little evidence that depression is dependent on the attributions people make for specific life events. On the other hand, Brewin suggests that attributions may reflect positive and negative coping styles that may be quite important predictors of recovery from depressive episodes.

All in all, therefore, Abramson *et al.* (1978) appear to be making an inflated claim for the causal importance of attributions when they propose that 'chronicity, generality, and intensity of depression fall inexorably, "rationally" from the attributions made and the importance of the outcomes' (1978: 68).

Attribution and addiction

Another practical field in which attributional concepts have been applied is the study of addiction. Addictive behaviours of any kind pose a particularly severe challenge to any cognitive approach. The typical view of addicts is of people whose behaviour is beyond their own voluntary control, being instead completely determined by physical craving. The normal criteria for saying that a user of a drug is addicted include the development of *tolerance* to the effects of the drug (so that larger doses are required for intoxication, and the user becomes habituated to initial noxious effects) and the likelihood of *withdrawal* effects and consequential experiences of craving if the user is deprived of the drug for any length of time. One of the most straightforward criteria, though, is a simple behavioural one – how difficult would the user find it to give up?

Although the pharmacological properties of a substance obviously play a major part in determining whether its use will lead to addiction, it is not easy to say why some substances are more addictive than others. One suggestion is that opiates are similar chemically to substances naturally occurring within the central nervous system ('endorphins'), associated with habituation to pain (Kosterlitz and Hughes, 1977). However, the search for natural analogues of other commonly used addictive substances, such as alcohol and nicotine, has a long way to go. In other words, if we wait just for psychopharmacologists to tell us why a drug is addictive, we may often have a long wait.

More successful have been approaches incorporating conditioning concepts, of which the most influential is that of Solomon (1980). Solomon proposes that there is a characteristic pattern of change over time in the affective reactions shown to any stimulus. This results from the fact that any stimulus produces both a primary reaction, and an 'opponent process', the function of which is to shut down the primary reaction. However, with repeated exposure to the stimulus (and particularly repeated exposure before or during which the person's affective state is dominated by the opponent process) the strength of the opponent process increases. The eventual consequence is that the person experiences little net positive reaction to the stimulus itself (e.g. the drug) but a very strong negative reaction (withdrawal) when the initial effect wears off. A vital additional feature of Solomon's theory is the hypothesis that different parts of this pattern of affective change over time can become conditioned to environmental stimuli. For instance, particular places, people, or situations may elicit withdrawal or craving experiences, even in 'reformed' addicts, as conditioned responses.

So long as addictive behaviour is interpreted deterministically, there seems little reason to introduce more cognitive or social psychological concepts. However, there is considerable evidence of drug users' ability, *under certain conditions*, to give up drugs spontaneously and without professional help. The most striking example is a study by Robins, Davis and Goodwin (1974) of American servicemen returning from Vietnam, where opiate use was extremely widespread. Even among a sample identified by urine tests as being opiate users at the time of their discharge, only 7 per cent were still addicted to opiates eight to twelve months later. This is compatible with Solomon's (1980) theory if we assume that, for these men, the environmental cues associated with craving had mostly been left behind with the other horrors of war. In the context of other drugs, there is a similar contrast between, on the one hand, studies on clinic samples that show very high rates of relapse among, for instance, alcoholics and cigarette smokers treated in clinics (e.g. Hunt and Matarazzo, 1973), and, on the other hand, the fact that many smokers and others are able to give up their habits without professional assistance (Schachter, 1982).

Addiction, therefore, may not be the *automatic* life (or death) sentence that is commonly assumed, and for such reasons, increased attention is being paid to cognitive and motivational factors influencing addicts' determination to give up (e.g. Robinson, 1972 for alcohol; Eiser and Gossop, 1979 and Gossop, Eiser and Ward, 1982, for heroin and other 'hard drugs'). Cigarette smoking is the addiction that has been studied most by social psychologists, if only for reasons of ease of access to large numbers of users prepared to talk openly about their behaviour. The work of Schachter *et al.* (1977) in this context has already beer. mentioned. Other work has looked more specifically at smokers' difficulty in giving up.

One of the earliest attempts to apply social psychological concepts to smoking was in a British survey by McKennell and Thomas (1967). They proposed a distinction between 'consonant' and 'dissonant' smokers on the basis of responses to the question, 'Would you like to give up smoking if you could do so easily?' Those who answered 'no' were considered 'consonant' in the sense that they were happy with being smokers, whereas those who answered 'yes' were presumed to be in a state of 'dissonance' (cf. Chapter 4), because of the inconsistency between the cognitions that they were continuing to smoke and that they would like to stop.

What this leaves out is the role of perceived freedom of choice (e.g. Linder *et al.*, 1967), which as we have seen (pp. 111–17) is a necessary condition for the experience of dissonance. These so-called 'dissonant' smokers would *not*, in the light of such research, be predicted to experience dissonance if they perceived themselves as *unable* to give up smoking (Eiser, 1978). What this suggests is that it may be functional for smokers to see themselves as unable to give up – i.e. as addicted – as a way of *resolving* dissonance. Eiser, Sutton and Wober (1978) observed that those smokers classified as 'dissonant' by the McKennell and Thomas (1967) criterion were much more likely to be prepared to label themselves as 'addicted'. In a later study it was found that more 'dissonant' smokers were also prepared to endorse the statement: 'I don't think I'm really prepared to give up smoking if it proves too difficult or distressing' (Eiser, 1982). What this points towards is a rather more ambivalent motivation to give up among smokers who characterize themselves as addicted. They may want to give up if it's easy, but may be less sure if it proves difficult (which of course is quite likely).

Motivation to quit smoking thus appears to be undermined by perceptions of task difficulty and personal inability, two concepts that feature prominently in Weiner's (1979) attributional approach to achievement motivation. The relevance of Weiner's model to smoking cessation was investigated by Eiser, van der Pligt, Raw and Sutton (1985) in a study of smokers who responded to a television company offer of free anti-smoking assistance (see also Eiser, 1982). Included were measures of self-attributed *addiction*, of *confidence*, or expectancy of succeeding in giving up if one tried, of *intention* to give up or cut down (which was later compared with self-reports of *behaviour*, in terms of having given up or cut down by the time of a one-year follow-up), and an *attribution* measure. This required subjects to answer the question, 'Why do you think so many smokers fail when they try to give up smoking?' by ranking the following five alternatives:

(a) Because its just too difficult for them
(b) Because they don't try hard enough

(c)   Because they don't know the best way to set about it
(d)   Because of the kind of people they are
(e)   Because of bad luck.

These rank scores were combined to form two indices (after discarding the 'luck' option, which few endorsed): 'stable' reflected preference for stable over unstable causes, i.e. (a) and (d) over (b) and (c); and 'internal' reflected preference for internal over external causes; i.e. (b) and (d) over (a) and (c). (Knowledge, (c), was treated as 'external' for these purposes, in that the context of this study was one where smokers were asking for others to give them advice.)

The results showed strong support for predictions derived from Weiner's model, although it should be noted that the attribution measure involved attributions for *others'* failures. The 'stable' index correlated significantly, but negatively, with confidence. In other words, those who attributed others' failure to stable factors had lower expectancies of their *own* success. Consistent with Weiner's model, the 'Internal' index was not correlated with confidence. Confidence predicted intention, and intention predicted later behaviour.

Among the other findings, those who described themselves as more addicted made more stable and (somewhat less strikingly) external attributions, and had lower confidence than those who described themselves as less addicted. Also, when at the time of follow-up, those who were still smoking answered the same attribution question with respect to their *own* failure, the stability and internality of their self-attributions correlated with their earlier attributions for others' failure. However, these self-attributions tended to be more stable and internal on average, a result that goes against a suggestion that individuals make more defensive attributions for their own failure (Shaver, 1970a).

Research on how attributions may relate to smokers' motivation to quit therefore provides good evidence of the importance of confidence, or expectancy of success, and its relationship to the self-attribution of addiction and to explanations for others' failure. The notion of confidence as an intervening variable between cognitions and behaviour is much the same as Bandura's (1977) concept of self-efficacy, and may be critical in predicting the effectiveness of interventions (Sutton and Eiser, 1984).

A word of caution is necessary, though, before interpreting such relationships in terms of a one-way causal chain. Attributions may function as rationalizations for behavioural decisions to which someone is already inclined, as well as providing informational input to the decisions themselves. Feelings of lack of ability or determination to give up, expectations of craving, withdrawal, and (which should not be underestimated) pleasure, are *learned* both on the basis of personal experience, and socially from one's peers and others during adolescence (Eiser, 1985). What people say about their smoking reflects much the same learning process as is involved in the acquisition of the habit itself.

What are attributions and when are they made?

Attribution research has held a dominant position within social psychology over the last 15 years or so, and, as I have attempted to show, is relevant to many practical fields. Kelley and Michela (1980) attempt to distinguish between *attribution* research, concerned primarily with processes of causal inferences and the antecedent conditions and information on which such inferences are based, and *attributional* research concerned primarily with the consequences of attributions in terms of expectancy, emotion and behaviour. In this chapter, I have rather blurred this distinction, which I feel could be used as a rather artificial barrier to defend attribution theory 'proper' from the often critical implications of research conducted from a more 'attributional' perspective. It is when one tries to *use* attribution theory, rather than just *test* it, that its road-worthiness begins to look a little suspect. Hence, even after all these years of work, there is less than perfect consensus among social psychologists on the basic question of what attributions are and when they are made. Heider's (1944, 1946) early work derived from an interest in the notion of 'phenomenal causality' – how objects (and by extension, people) come to be seen as *causal origins*, e.g. as capable of causing change and movement in other objects and people. Heider regards attribution as just a close relative of perception (Harvey, Ickes and Kidd, 1976: 12), but 'perception' is, for Heider, something to be seen in *Gestalt* terms. Notions of probabilistic information-processing have less influence on the development of attribution theory than do notions of balance and consistency. As a consequence, research on cognitive schemata and social decision-making, to be reviewed in the next chapter, has developed separately, so that there is rather a gap between what may well be complementary approaches to similar questions.

The legacy of this concern with phenomenal causality is that there has been a bias towards interpreting attributional responses as *causal* explanations of events that have already occurred. Awareness of this bias has prompted a debate over whether attributions are to do with 'causes' or 'reasons' (Buss, 1978, 1979; Harvey and Tucker, 1979; Kruglanski, 1979). It is a valid point that the word 'cause' can be used in alternative ways to refer not just to mechanistic effects but also to purposeful actions and goals. This is not a new point, though: Aristotle said it better. The whole notion of intentionality is likewise made simultaneously more trivial and more complex by trying to consider it in terms of inferring 'causes' or 'going beyond the information given'. As Anscombe (1963: 8) points out, 'if you want to say at least some true things about a man's intentions, you will have a strong chance of success if you mention what he actually did or was doing'.

But if attributions are not (just) explanations what (else) are they? One possibility is that they are a response to a particular form of question, typically asked by psychologists, but not so typically by anybody else. A rider to this is the implication that, when people are asked to explain their *own* behaviour, they engage in rationalizations of a self-justificatory nature (see Baumeister, 1982, and Tetlock and Manstead, 1985, for more general discussions of notions of self-presentation and impression-management).

From a different starting point, Tversky and Kahneman (1980) discuss the question of how people draw inferences from information presented in the form of conditional probabilities. They provide evidence that subjects will attach higher probabilities to the occurrence of an effect, granted the existence of an antecedent cause, than *vice versa* (i.e. if given information that an effect has occurred, they are less confident in inferring the occurrence of a specified antecedent cause). Rather confusingly, they call predictions from cause to effect 'causal inferences', and postdictions from effect to cause 'diagnostic inferences'. (It is 'diagnostic', not 'causal' inferences that are the same as what we have considered as causal attributions.) The important implication for attribution theory is that people are more disposed to think in terms of predictions than explanations. Jones and Davis (1965), for instance, argue that we start with observed behaviour (and its consequences) and infer dispositions and personal characteristics. However, the Tverksy and Kahneman findings suggest that such inferences go directly contrary to people's preferred forms of thought, which in this context would involve predicting behaviour from a knowledge (however acquired) of personal characteristics (cf. Eiser, 1983).

As a defence against such criticisms, some recent research has tried to identify conditions under which people spontaneously engage in attributional activity – that is to say, look for explanations for events without being asked to do so. Winter and Ulema (1984) tested subjects' recall for short descriptions of behaviour and found this to be best when subjects had been cued with disposition words (e.g. 'generous') describing traits that corresponded to the behaviour. From this they inferred that subjects were spontaneously encoding the behaviour in trait terms. However, they deliberately restricted their attention to behaviours that were particularly suggestive of 'correspondent inferences' (Jones and Davis, 1965). As a result it is unclear exactly what form of 'encoding' was taking place. Saying that words like 'generous' can function as convenient shorthand categorizations of *behaviour* is different from claiming that, whenever a word like 'generous' is used, a causal attribution for the behaviour has been made in terms of a stable trait or disposition of the *actor*. Winter and Uleman provide good evidence for the spontaneity of the first kind of encoding activity, but no real evidence of the second.

A different tack has been taken by Weiner (1985; Wong and Weiner, 1981), who concentrates on the kinds of situations in which attributional activity is likely to occur – with the implication that there are many events that we allow to pass us by without bringing our attributional faculties to bear. Weiner (1985) reviews 17 publications showing that people will spontaneously engage in a search for explanations without the intervention of a questioner. Most of these studies indicate that such 'causal search' is stimulated primarily by *unexpected* events, particularly ones involving loss or failure. Hastie (1984) similarly argues that unexpected events elicit causal reasoning, and that such reasoning can lead to a more elaborate representation of such events in memory.

This conclusion, that attributional activity occurs to deal with the unwanted or unexpected, is not only intuitively compelling, but consistent with Heider's (1958: 25) own view that: 'Attribution serves the attainment of a stable and consistent environment . . . and determines what we expect will occur and what we should do about it.' However, what is troublesome for many attribution theorists (with the exception of Weiner, but to a great extent including Heider), is the implication that phenomenal causality is of secondary importance compared with expectancy and prediction.

Attribution theory starts from a concern with causal explanations and hypothesizes ways in which information must be weighed and compared in order to make such explanations possible. If, however, people appear prepared to let many events occur without asking *why* they occur, the generality of the theory looks more questionable.

Conclusions

When one considers the research reviewed earlier in this chapter, there is good evidence for the central importance of expectancy in relation both to attributions and to subsequent behaviour. People will also make attributional statements in a wide range of contexts. What is far less clear is where such statements come from. Are they the outcome of some process of inductive logic, or are they just another indicator of an internal psychological state, be it an attitude, an evaluation, an emotion, a feeling of dependence or depression, or whatever, that is acquired through interaction with the environment? Attributions of responsibility may reflect, as much as cause, evaluations of actions. Emotions may influence self-descriptions and behaviour as much as being an inference from self-observation. The same events that may make people feel they have little control over their lives may also make them feel desperately unhappy. The same package of experiences that makes addicts crave for a drug may also make them pessimistic about their chances of giving up.

It is one thing to say that the study of attributions helps us to understand the different kinds of feelings and behaviour involved in such contexts. This is most definitely so. It is quite another thing to say that such feelings and behaviours generally *depend* on the kinds of attributions a person makes. For this, the evidence is far less convincing.

7
Decisions and representations

'Rational' decision-making

A recurrent issue in social psychological research is whether human social behaviour can be said to obey 'rational' rules. The term 'rational' is a dangerous one, and may be used in different contexts to imply 'reasonable', 'ethical', 'involving conscious thought', 'sensible', and such like. The notion of rationality as used by psychologists does not necessarily make any assumptions about ethics or consciousness, but is applied to the relationship between *decisions* and *expected consequences*. It is very much a utilitarian concept, based on the comparison of expected costs and benefits. For this reason, many of the theoretical assumptions used in this field have been borrowed directly from economics, and mathematical models of economic desirability have been adopted as working hypotheses about how everyday decisions are made.

The cornerstone of utilitarian conceptions of rationality is the notion of *expected value* (EV). Quite simply, to calculate the expected value of any choice, one evaluates the possible consequences, multiplies these evaluations by the probability that each consequence will occur, and adds up the products. If all that one wants to do is to maximize one's profits and minimize one's losses over a long sequence of choices, the strategy to adopt is always to choose options with the highest EV. This is not at all the same thing as choosing the option that *could* produce highest profits. If high profits are very improbable, the product of high profit and low probability could be lower than the EV for an option that provides a smaller profit with greater certainty.

For instance, consider the decision to buy a lottery ticket. Since lotteries are run for profit, it follows that it is never objectively 'rational' to buy a lottery ticket, since the probability of winning a prize will be set so low that the organizers will never have to pay out as much as they receive. To take a very simple case, where 1,000 people each buy a single ticket for £1, and this gives them one chance of winning £500 (minus the £1 for the winning ticket itself).

The EV for buying a ticket in such a lottery would then be:

$$(0.001 \times £499) - (0.999 \times £1) = -50p$$

What this means is that the EV is a loss of 50p. Of course, no one individual will lose exactly 50p. This is just the average over all tickets. Put another way, the profits to the organizers would be 50p × 1,000 = 500.

If lotteries are so 'irrational', why are they so popular? One reason may be that people are quite happy with the knowledge that the lottery organizers will make a profit – for example, if the lottery is intended to raise money for charity. Personal profitability then becomes no longer the main criterion for decision-making. Another reason may be that people's *estimates* of the probability of winning are far higher than the actual probability – they may underestimate the number of other tickets in the draw, or they may have superstitious beliefs concerning lucky numbers, or whatever. Finally, they may hardly care at all about losing their stake of £1, but be intensely motivated to have the chance of winning £500. In mathematical terms, they may personally *want* to win £500 more than 500 times as much as they want to keep £1.

The shift from *objective* probabilities and values to *subjective* estimates and wants is fundamental to the application of EV concepts in psychology. 'Expectancy-value' theories crop up in many fields, but one of the best-known examples is Fishbein's model of attitudes as the sum of beliefs about consequences weighted by evaluation (Fishbein, 1967; Fishbein and Ajzen, 1975; and see Chapter 3). However, since such beliefs and evaluations are subjective, this model does not strictly depend on EV but on what is called *subjective expected utility* (SEU). The term 'subjective' identifies the fact that one is dealing with personal estimates of what may happen, rather than with objectively known probabilities. In many decision contexts, the pro-babilities will not be known exactly, but still may be influenced by factors other than random chance, concerning which different people may have, or feel they have, different levels of knowledge. That is why, for instance, serious gambling on horse races or football pools is different from buying lottery tickets or playing roulette. The punters may feel that they have enough special expertise to enable them, on average, to predict outcomes better than chance, and (with horse races) better than the bookmakers who fix the odds.

The term 'utility' is differentiated from 'value' in that it allows for the same objective outcome to be evaluated differently by different people or in different situations. Most importantly, the relationship of (subjective) utility to (objective) value may be non-linear. For example, the relative attractive-ness of winning £20 over winning £10 may be far greater than the relative attractiveness of winning £520 over winning £510. If one compares utilities with values over a range of possible outcomes, the mathematical relation-ship is called the *utility function*. For money, the utility function is typically assumed to be concave rather than linear. In other words, for higher amounts, the increase in utility is proportionality less than the increase in value, as in the example just given. This idea is traditionally attributed to Bernoulli (1738; translated 1954). The difference between SEU and EV highlights the fact that, for many decisions, different individuals may differ in their conceptions of the 'rational' thing to do. For instance, if cigarette smokers were to accept the evidence that smoking causes lung cancer, giving up smoking ought to be seen as the 'rational' or 'sensible' course to follow. However, some smokers may minimize their subjective estimate of this risk, and even if they do not, may have so little confidence in their ability to give up, anyway, that they see no point in trying to do so. If the choice before them is whether or not to try to give up, the decision to continue smoking may be *subjectively* 'rational' for smokers who feel that they would be bound to relapse (Eiser and Sutton, 1977). Similarly, the impact of persuasive communications on smokers' intentions may be mediated by changes in subjective confidence, or expectation of success in giving up (Sutton and Eiser, 1984).

Apart from experiments that present subjects with hypothetical decision problems incorporating stated probabilities, most psychological research relates more closely to notions of SEU rather than EV. Nonetheless, whether one is dealing with subjective or objective probabilities and evaluations, the same basic assumption applies. The 'best' decision in a utilitarian sense is the one that maximizes the sum of the products of probabilities and evaluations. What has come to be known as SEU 'theory' may therefore be interpreted in two separate, but often confused, senses. First, it proposes a *prescriptive* model of how decisions ought to be made, if they are to be maximally profitable on the average. (This has implications for management training, for example.) Second, it may be taken as a *descriptive* hypothesis of how decisions actually tend to be made.

There is a considerable literature on how people take account of perceived probabilities and consequences in making decisions. Slovic, Fischhoff and Lichtenstein (1977) refer to this literature as 'behavioural decision theory' but the name, of itself, adds nothing and could give a misleading picture of theoretical unity. Much of this work has great practical relevance. Schwartz and Griffin (1986), for instance, apply this approach to the evaluation of diagnosis and treatment decisions in medicine.

Not all of this literature by any means concerns itself with discriminating between alternative models of decision-making. Just as many researchers in the field of attitudes and behaviour (see Chapter 3) have used the Fishbein and Ajzen (1975) model as a predictive tool without putting it to comparative test, so many researchers have used SEU theory to predict how individuals will make decisions under conditions of risk and uncertainty. For this reason a large amount of evidence has accumulated that supports the general notion that people are attracted to options that offer more assured and/or higher profits. Such findings match the predictions of SEU theory quite closely, but this may be because the decision problems used do not typically discriminate the predictions of SEU theory from those of any other model to any marked extent.

The general predictive success of SEU theory, therefore, has not deterred a minority of researchers from proposing alternative accounts of choice behaviour, and devising experiments where the assumptions of SEU theory can be directly challenged. Many of these experiments involve hypothetical choices or gambles, where probabilities and outcomes can be specified. Coombs and Huang (1970, 1976), for example, find consistent patterns of preference between gambles of equivalent EV, that violate assumptions of SEU theory but are compatible with an alternative model termed 'portfolio theory'. This assumes that 'a choice between risky decisions is a compromise between maximizing expected value and optimizing the level of risk' (Coombs, 1975: 66): 'With expected value fixed, then, a gamble reflects a conflict between greed and fear, an approach-avoidance conflict, and this condition means that for each individual there is an optimum level at which greed and fear are in unstable balance' (Coombs, 1975: 71).

Prospect theory

Although Coombs and Huang demonstrate violations of the axioms of SEU theory, their concern has been with preferences for different levels of risk, rather than with attempting to provide a more general theory of decision-making under uncertainty. Such an attempt, however, has been made by Kahneman and Tversky (1979). What they call *'prospect theory'* relies on the following main assumptions:

(1)   Decisions are made not with regard to the desirability of consequences or end-states as such, but with regard to how such end-states relate to some reference point (such as the present). In other words, outcomes are not evaluated as *absolute* costs or benefits, but as *relative* losses or gains.

(2)   Expected losses and gains influence decisions in direct *but not exact* proportion to their (subjective) probability. The probability terms in the calculation of SEU are therefore replaced by 'decision weights' reflecting the importance of each possible consequence on the decision.

These assumptions enable prospect theory to account for a number of empirical observations of discrepancies between choice behaviour and SEU theory predictions. For instance (from a formal prescriptive point of view), people tend to overemphasize the importance of certain outcomes as compared with those that are merely probable (as first noted by Allais, 1953). At least partly as a result of this, they will tend to be 'risk averse', i.e. cautious, with respect to gains, but 'risk seeking' with respect to losses. For example, people may consistently prefer a certain profit, rather than a higher profit that is not guaranteed – even when the EV for the uncertain option is higher than for the certain one. By contrast, when faced with choices between possible losses, people may prefer an option involving a chance of escaping loss combined with a high probability of a higher loss, over the certain consequence of an intermediate loss. (This may have implications for the circumstances under which people do or do not choose to take out insurance.)

Another important set of findings relates to the *sequential* structure of decision processes. Here prospect theory incorporates notions developed from Tversky's (1972) model of 'elimination by aspects' (EBA). As its name implies, the EBA model represents the process of choice as one of selecting between options on the basis of criterial aspects, considered one at a time. For instance, if you needed to book an air ticket you might go through a sequence of questions like: (1) What airlines operate on the route I want to take? (Eliminate all airlines that don't fly to the right place.) (2) What are the flight times? (Eliminate all airlines that don't fly at the right times.) (3) What are the different airlines' rules regarding booking, stopovers, length of stay, etc? (Eliminate all airlines that impose impossible or inconvenient restrictions.) (4) How much will it cost? (Eliminate all airlines that charge more than is reasonable or affordable.) (5) What are the different airlines' reliability/safety records? (Avoid airlines with a recent history of suspected unreliability/negligence.) (6) What aircraft will be used? (Eliminate any airlines that fly aircraft that are too old, cramped, or unsafe, presuming one has a choice. (7) How good is the cabin service? (Eliminate any whose food is more than conventionally revolting.) And so on. The list is not exhaustive, and neither is the order fixed. A student going on holiday will have a very different set of priorities from a business executive needing to be in time for an urgent meeting. The important assumption, though, is that these aspects are not just 'salient beliefs' (Fishbein and Ajzen, 1975) that can be lumped together to yield an overall evaluative index, but that they *define a structure*. This structure can be represented as a tree diagram with the nodes between the branches representing different choice points (Tversky and Sattath, 1979).

Prospect theory incorporates the basic assumptions of the EBA model: 'In order to simplify the choice between alternatives, people often disregard components that the alternatives share, and focus on the components that distinguish them' (Kahneman and Tversky, 1979: 271). Consistent with this is the idea that choices may ultimately depend on aspects or attributes that make only a marginal contribution to the overall absolute evaluation. For instance, in the example above, if many airlines fly the same kind of aircraft to the same destinations at the same price, and so on, it is perhaps not too surprising that promotion campaigns may depend on trivial extras, such as the appearance of the cabin staff or redesigned insignia.

The hypothesis that individuals will tend to ignore non-discriminating aspects of choice alternatives is supported by studies that manipulate the manner in which decision problems are presented or 'framed'. For example, when subjects were offered a hypothetical choice between a 20 per cent chance of winning 4,000 units and a 25 per cent chance of winning 3,000 units, nearly twice as many chose the first as the second option. However, in another condition the same choice was recast in the form of a two-stage game. In stage 1, one had a 75 per cent chance of finishing the game without winning anything, and a 25 per cent chance of proceeding to the second stage. In stage 2, one would be faced with a choice between an 80 per cent chance of winning 4,000 units, and a certain gain of 3,000 units. When presented with the problem in this latter form, more than half the subjects preferred the second alternative, even though this had the lower EV (750 as opposed to 800). What is going on here, according to Kahneman and Tversky (1979), is that subjects in the second condition disregard the first stage, which looks the same whatever one chooses, and then represent the choice as one between an uncertain and a lower but certain gain. Since certainty has a powerful effect, this tips the balance of preference.

Framing

Subsequent work by Tversky and Kahneman (1981) and Fischhoff (1983) provides further insight into the relationship between preference and the 'framing' of a decision problem. Since prospect theory deals with gains and losses relative to a reference point, rather than with absolute outcomes, the same outcomes can be represented alternately as gains or losses, depending on the reference point. One of the hypothetical problems reported by Tversky and Kahneman (1981) asks subjects to imagine that the US is threatened with an unusual disease, expected to kill 600 people. A choice then has to be made between two alternative interventions, concerning which subjects have to assume the following estimates to be exact:

> If Program A is adopted, 200 people will be saved.
> If Program B is adopted, there is 1/3 probability that 600 people will be saved, and 2/3 probability that no people will be saved. (p. 453)

When presented with the choice in this form, 72 per cent of subjects opted for 'Program A'. However, a second group were presented with the same problem in the following terms:

> If Program C is adopted, 400 people will die.
> If Program D is adopted, there is 1/3 probability that nobody will die, and 2/3 probability that 600 people will die. (p. 453)

In this second group, the great majority (78 per cent) chose 'Program D'. Thus when the choice was framed in terms of gains (lives saved), most people opted for the certain outcome, but when the identical choice was framed in terms of losses (lives lost) most people avoided the option of the certain loss. This confirms the principle that people tend to be risk-averse for gains and risk-seeking for losses: sure gains are popular, sure losses unpopular.

Preference, therefore, is not deterministically constrained by the prescriptive 'rationality' of SEU theory, but can be strongly influenced (at least in examples of the kind described) by the *frame of reference* in terms of which a problem is defined. Outcomes are judged as gains or losses relative to a 'reference outcome' that Tversky and Kahneman (1981: 456) talk of in the same terms as an aspiration level, or, one might add, adaptation level (Helson, 1964), or comparison level (Thibaut and Kelley, 1959). Familiar concepts of social judgement are brought right up to the decision-making front line.

Despite the promise of these ideas, however, many difficulties still remain. Although subjects presented with a problem framed in a particular way will show predictable patterns of preference, it is very much more difficult to show how people would frame such problems for themselves, or that their preferred ways of thinking about a problem can be inferred from their subsequent choice (Fischhoff, 1983). Furthermore, the dilemmas with which subjects have been faced in most of these experiments have not only been hypothetical, but in some instances quite exotically so. The ecological validity of almost all this research has yet to be established. The experiments may tell us a great deal about how abstract probabilistic information may be processed, but it is almost certainly hazardous to assume that factors which influence such processing will have impacts of comparable strength on the behaviour of real decision-makers, confronted with more familiar choices, the outcomes of which have tangible effects on them personally.

Cognitive heuristics

Whatever the ultimate verdict on the validity of studies of framing, such research carries forward what has become a prominent theme in research on social decision-making – that, rather than relying on formal prescriptive models drawn from other disciplines, psychologists should try to account for the rules people actually seem to *use* when faced with uncertainty, however informal, inexact and error-prone these may be. In earlier writings, Kahneman and Tversky (1972, 1973; Tversky and Kahneman, 1974) introduced the term *heuristic* to refer to an informal rule-of-thumb used by people in order to simplify information processing and decision-making. If one were to map the concepts of SEU, framing and heuristics in relation to one another, one could regard framing research as having something to say (principally) about the subjective definition of utilities, whereas heuristics research speaks to the subjective definition of expectancies.

Heuristics are most noticeable when they lead people to deal with probabilistic information in ways that show departures or 'biases' away from normative principles of statistical reasoning. As a consequence, much of the research could be read as showing that human reasoning is essentially errorful, and that we need to devise methods to guard against the biases to which we are prone (Nisbett and Ross, 1980). A different emphasis is provided by researchers who argue that, in the contexts in which they are typically used, heuristics are by no means as stupid as they may seem within the psychological laboratory (Hogarth, 1981).

Tversky and Kahneman (1974) place special emphasis on three informal reasoning biases or heuristics. The first, termed the *representativeness* heuristic (Kahneman and Tversky, 1972), refers to the tendency to judge the probability that a stimulus belongs to a particular class on the basis of how representative or 'typical' of that class it appears to be, with little regard for the base-rate probability of a stimulus belonging to the class. For example, imagine that one found some wild mushrooms, and wanted to decide if they were edible or poisonous. The representativeness heuristic implies that one should base one's decision on how similar the wild mushrooms appear to be to other mushrooms which one knows to be edible, that is, ordinary cultivated mushrooms, as compared with toadstools, which one knows to be poisonous. The weakness of this kind of judgement is that it fails to take account of the probability of any wild fungus, chosen at random, being edible rather than poisonous, with the result that a great number of unfamiliar but edible fungi will be avoided. In this example, of course, the costs of eating a poisonous mushroom outweigh those of avoiding an edible one, and most people would be unaware of the statistical probability of fungus being edible. The same kind of bias, however, can be demonstrated experimentally when subjects are given incentives for accuracy and are told about the base-rate probabilities. A slightly different example of the representativeness bias is the so-called 'gambler's fallacy'. If one knows that a sequence of events is randomly generated, one expects it to *look* random, even if it is very short. So, with spins of a coin, a sequence of heads (H) and tails (T) such as HHTHTTHT is judged to be more probable than HHHHTHHH.

The availability heuristic (Tversky and Kahneman, 1973) refers to the tendency for an event to be judged more probable to the extent that it is more easily pictured or recalled. A headline such as 'Child taken to hospital after eating wild mushrooms' might increase the 'availability' of information that wild mushrooms can be poisonous. An important practical instance of this is when people have to make comparisons between different kinds of risks. Risks from more easily pictured accidents, such as explosions, may contribute more to the judgement that an industrial process is dangerous, even though they may happen extremely rarely, than continuous and cumulative hazards, such as contaminated atmosphere, which have less immediate dramatic effects. Lichtenstein, Slovic, Fischhoff, Layman and Combs (1978) provide evidence that, when people judge the frequencies of death from various causes, they over-estimate small frequencies whilst relatively over-estimating large ones, and exaggerate some specific causes, due possibly, they suggest, to disproportionate media exposure or imaginability. Similarly, certain kinds of risks of mechanical failure may be under-estimated, if it is difficult to imagine a particular component going wrong (see Slovic, Fischhoff and Lichtenstein, 1976).

Finally, the anchoring bias refers to people's failure to revise their estimates adequately when new information is presented. This may happen when they made an initial estimate which they then adjusted to give the final answer. However, even with the same information presented, a higher initial estimate will tend to lead to a higher final answer than a lower initial estimate.

The rather unflattering impression of human cognitive processes con-veyed by these earlier studies has not gone unqualified or unchallenged. The implication that people will disregard information regarding base-rate probabilities (e.g. when relying on representativeness) accords with studies derived from Kelley's (1967) model of attribution processes (see Chapter 6, pp. 176–7). Kelley's criterion of *consensus* essentially refers to base-rate infor-mation (do other people generally react the same way?) There is evidence that relatively little weight is given to consensus information (McArthur, 1972, 1976; Nisbett and Borgida, 1975; Nisbett, Borgida, Crandall and Reed, 1976). Wells and Harvey (1977) on the other hand showed that people may pay more attention to sample frequencies when given to believe that a sample is statistically representative of the population.

A particularly constructive approach to this issue has been made by Ajzen (1977). He argues that base-rate information tends to be neglected when it has no apparent causal relationship to the attribute being judged or predic-ted. For example, in an experiment described by Kahneman and Tversky (1973), subjects had to predict whether a given individual was an engineer or a lawyer, having been told that 70 per cent of the sample were engineers and 30 per cent were lawyers, or vice versa. This base-rate information was almost totally ignored when subjects were given brief character sketches of the individual target cases. Ajzen argues that this base-rate information, though statistically informative, was not *causally* relevant, in that the different proportions would not have caused an individual to become a lawyer or engineer. Even the most randomly constructed character descrip-tion, however, might encourage subjects to look for causal antecedents of occupational choice. To complement the heuristics identified by Tversky and Kahneman (1974), therefore, Ajzen proposes what he calls a 'causality heuristic':

> When asked to make a prediction, people look for factors which cause the behaviour or event under consideration. Information that provides evidence concerning the presence or absence of such causal factors is therefore likely to influence predictions . . . Statistical information is used mainly when no causal information is available. p. 304

This is supported by evidence that, when asked to predict the academic performance of students, subjects took account of their IQs and of the number of hours per week spent studying, both of which were intuitively expected to affect academic performance, but ignored information that appeared causally irrelevant, such as amount of money earned in part-time jobs or living distance from campus, even though this last information was presented in a form which would have allowed an equally powerful statistical inference. Also, information about examination pass rates influenced predictions on the performance of a particular candidate, when calculated on the basis of all those taking the examination, but not when based on a non-random sample (cf. Wells and Harvey, 1977). Ajzen interprets the former type of base-rate information as causal, in that it allows an inference to be drawn about the difficulty of the examination, which in turn will be a causal factor influencing each candidate's success.

Relevant to Ajzen's (1977) notion of a causality heuristic is a paper by Hastie (1984), already mentioned (Chapter 6, p. 213) because of its support for the notion that people tend to engage in causal reasoning primarily in response to unexpected events. Hastie goes on to show that such causal reasoning leads to the more elaborate encoding of such events in memory, so that events for which people have developed causal explanations are more likely to be remembered.

The availability heuristic is supported by evidence that more vivid information is better recalled. However, as pointed out by Taylor and Thompson (1982), it is by no means typically the case that more vividly presented information has greater impact, for instance in producing attitude change, than the equivalent information presented in a duller or more abstract form. Reviewing the experimental literature, they conclude:

> The available evidence indicates that concrete descriptions have no consistently greater impact on judgments than do more pallid and dull ones; pictorially illustrated information is no more persuasive than is equivalent information that is not pictorially illustrated; videotaped information has no consistent impact on judgments compared with equivalent oral and written information; and personal contact is not inherently more impactful than vicarious experience. Case histories appear to be more persuasive than base-rate information, but this effect may be due to the underutilization of base-rate and other statistical information or inadequate understanding of statistical inference. (p. 170)

In attempting to reconcile this pattern of negative results with the finding that *salient* information has a greater impact on cognitions (e.g. Taylor and Fiske, 1978), Taylor and Thompson conclude that manipulations of vividness have not typically succeeded in directing subjects' attention *differentially* to some aspects of a message or stimulus situation rather than others. Furthermore, subjects in a psychology experiment are likely to attend reasonably to the information presented to them, whatever the form of that presentation. This leaves open the possibility that, in one's normal environment, more vivid stimuli will indeed attract greater attention than less vivid stimuli against which they may be contrasted. There is certainly room for more research examining the cognitive impact of differentially presented information in terms of the contrast effects which particular forms of presentation may create (e.g. Harding, Eiser and Kristiansen, 1982).

There have been frequent demonstrations of ordinary people's apparent misconceptions concerning statistical principles of randomness and probability (Nisbett and Ross, 1980). Even here, though, people's inferences may be more defensible than often supposed. Schaffner (1985) examines how people may acquire erroneous beliefs about the relative effectiveness of reward and punishment on another's performance through a failure to take account of the statistical principle of regression. Suppose a teacher rewards improvements and punishes decrements in a student's level of performance. Suppose too that the student's performance level fluctuates from trial to trial, either due to random variation or unreliable measurement. What will then tend to happen is that improvements after poor performance, and lapses after good performance (that are in fact due to the fact that more extreme deviations from the mean are unlikely to be immediately repeated) will be attributed respectively to the effectiveness of punishment and to the counter-effectiveness of reward or praise. The teacher would then have an 'illusion of control' (Langer, 1975) over the student's performance.

Schaffner had subjects play a computer simulation game in which they imagined themselves in the role of teachers attempting to improve the punctuality with which each of two schoolboys arrived at school. They were presented with a series of 'arrival times' for each 'boy', and on each trial could respond in terms of strong or mild 'praise' or 'reprimand' or 'no comment', in any way they felt would make the boys arrive at school as early as possible. In fact, subjects had no control over the arrival times. For one of the 'boys', the arrival times varied randomly around a mean that was stable over time, and for the other, the arrival times showed an improvement over time, but still with random trial-by-trial fluctuations. As predicted, subjects tended to use praise after improvement and reprimand after lapses, as a result of which the 'boy' who showed a steady improvement tended to receive more praise on later trials. For both 'boys', however, subjects believed reprimand to be more effective than praise. For the boy who showed no overall improvement, praise was rated as mildly or highly effective by 45.0 per cent of subjects, and reprimand as mildly or highly effective by 69.4 per cent. For the boy who improved over time, the corresponding percentages were 54.1 per cent and 80.9 per cent.

It is easy to use such findings to support the conclusion that people tend to make irrational inferences that ignore statistical principles such as chance variation. Schaffner, however, distances himself from such an interpretation. He agrees that his subjects came to their conclusions about the relative effectiveness of praise and reprimand without having experimented with different reinforcement schedules in such a way as to put their hypotheses to the test. On the other hand, he argues that it was not 'irrational' of subjects to assume that the simulated behaviour of the 'boys' would be systematic rather than random, and potentially influenced by reinforcement.

This raises the more general point that experimental demonstrations of human 'irrationality' may depend to a large extent on the use of hypothetical problems that violate assumptions that people might reasonably make about apparently similar situations in everyday life. Whilst people may seem to use informal decision rules and simplificatory heuristics rather than normative principles of logic or statistics, it is far from obvious that it is maladaptive to do so, at any rate once one takes account of the time and effort involved in double-checking every decision or inference one makes. Inductive inference does not need the guarantee of logical entailment to be accepted as reasonable (von Wright, 1965).

Hogarth (1981) argues forcibly that cognitive heuristics may not only be functional, but even a valid basis for decision-making in natural contexts. Whilst it is important for human beings (and other animals) to be able to predict events in their environment with reasonable accuracy, accuracy *per se* is not the only or even always the most important goal, since different kinds of errors can involve different costs. Is it, for instance, 'irrational' to accept the necessity for safety precautions without bothering to test what would happen if no precautions were taken? Furthermore, 'judgment is primarily exercised to facilitate action' and 'most actions induce feedback that is often immediately available . . . Receiving and acting on feedback in continuous fashion increases the number of cues and responses available to the organism and thus their intersubstitutability' (Hogarth, 1981: 199).

Whereas most experiments on heuristics involve discrete judgement tasks at a single point in time, in more natural contexts judgements and actions evolve and influence each other continuously over time. Because of this, the kind of information with which we are best adapted to deal is continuous, redundant and patterned over time. There is therefore a great difference between, on the one hand, showing that people process abstract information about base-rate probabilities inappropriately and, on the other hand, showing that they fail to make reasonable inferences from a sampling of their own previous experiences. Recent and earlier experiences will not typically be independent of each other. On the contrary, recent experiences may be the outcome of actions that themselves were a reflection of interpretations of previous experiences.

Judgements, then, are typically made on a data base that is redundant rather than randomly generated, and that can constantly be updated. Moreover, because of the possibility of correction through feedback, judgements do not generally have to be made once-and-for-all. It is more typical for people to evaluate decisions with respect to relatively short- or medium-term 'decision horizons' where the link from action to outcome is clearer. This is relevant to much of the research on framing, where people's preferences may reflect a tendency to take one step at a time, postponing the point at which they need to commit themselves to a critical choice in favour of one option or another. This may mean that some kinds of judgements can be biased by the form in which a problem is presented. On the other hand, it may be a quite 'rational' strategy to adopt in situations where the probabilities of particular outcomes may *not* be fixed in advance for all time, and where one can expect one's data-base for decision-making to improve, both as a result of feedback from one's own actions, and as more features of the choice come into focus.

It is therefore precisely because many experiments fail to simulate the natural context of judgement and action that 'errors' and 'biases' can be experimentally demonstrated with such relative ease. Such errors and biases are real enough, and testify to people's tendencies to resolve problems on the basis of rules-of-thumb rather than recourse to first principles. However, such evidence falls short of demonstrating that such rules-of-thumb, strategies or heuristics are irrational, unreasonable or invalid with respect to the contexts in which they are more typically used.

Mindfulness/mindlessness

One function that heuristics and rules-of-thumb serve is to allow people to make quick and easy distinctions without having to attend thoroughly to all the information they receive. Research on the distinction between peripheral and central routes to persuasion (Chapter 2, pp. 45–9), as well as on the conditions that give rise to attributional search (Chapter 6, pp. 211–13), leads similarly to the conclusion that people do not always (or even usually) bring the full force of their cognitive capacities to bear upon the interpretation of incoming information. Routine, unremarkable information in particular may elicit well-practised reactions, but such reactions may be performed almost automatically, without obvious evidence of much conscious thought. Many models in social psychology seem to deal with contexts in which people are engaged in a great deal of deliberation. If it can be shown that much social behaviour is performed with little or no deliberation, the generality of such models becomes more questionable.

Central to this debate is Langer's (e.g. 1978) proposal of a distinction between 'mindful' and 'mindless' behaviour. Mindful behaviour is characterized by a high level of conscious planning and monitoring, and by more complex and differentiated attention to the various aspects of the behavioural context (including other people). Novelty and high personal relevance are among the factors that can induce people to respond in a 'mindful' rather than a 'mindless' way. By comparison, 'mindlessness' is elicited by routine, familiar and boring episodes of little personal relevance, where overlearned behaviour can be performed in response without any need for a detailed analysis of the stimulus information.

Research on this distinction between 'mindfulness' and 'mindlessness' has followed two main directions. The first consists simply of the demonstration that a sizeable proportion of apparently consciously intended behaviour may in fact involve rather 'automatic' responses enacted in a way that involves a 'reduced level of cognitive activity', in Langer's terms. A prime example of the first style of research is a paper by Langer, Blank and Chanowitz (1978). The second concerns how *later* cognition and behaviour is affected by whether information is initially processed mindfully or mindlessly.

The first study reported by Langer *et al.* (1978) involved one of the experimenters approaching people using a university photocopier, and asking to be allowed to go first. The experimental manipulations consisted of the form in which the request was made. One factor was the size of favour requested – the experimenter asked to be allowed to copy just 5 or 20 pages. The second factor depended on whether a reason was offered for the request. In the *request only* condition, the experimenter said simply, 'Excuse me, I have 5 (20) pages. May I use the xerox machine?' In the *placebic information* condition, this was followed by the phrase 'because I have to make copies'. In the *real information* condition the supporting reason offered was 'because I'm in a rush'.

The dependent variable was the proportion of people granting this request in the various conditions. For the small request (i.e. 5 pages) the percentages were 60, 93 and 94 across the request only, placebic and real information conditions respectively. For the large request the figures were 24, 24 and 42. Langer *et al.* infer that requests that (a) sound polite and (b) involve little inconvenience are processed and complied with without any great deal of thought. In such circumstances, it is enough that a 'reason' has been offered. It does not matter whether or not this 'reason' makes sense, since, so Langer *et al.* imply, the information will not be processed that thoroughly. Thus, placebic information is as good as real information when the request is small. A large request, however, is something that needs thinking about – i.e. that elicits mindful processing of information and discrimination of what really can count as a reason for such a request. In two further studies, Langer *et al.* (1978) produced more evidence of higher compliance with polite 'requests' than 'demands', either to complete a postal questionnaire, or to send a memo through internal mail.

Folkes (1985) has attempted to bring such results back within the fold of attribution theory. Taking the photocopying experiment as her focus, she argues that Langer *et al.* (1978) have only inferred mindlessness indirectly, and speculates that subjects might well process the placebic information, even in the small favour condition, to the point that they realize that nothing is really being said, but still decide to comply with the request. In attempted replications of the photocopying experiment, Folkes tested the alternative notion that what is important is whether subjects attribute the state of need of the person making the request to controllable or uncontrollable factors. An uncontrollable reason ('because I feel really sick') elicited very high compliance, whereas a controllable reason ('because I want to go see my boyfriend') reduced compliance somewhat.

Interpretation of Folkes's data is made more difficult by generally high levels of compliance throughout, including in 'request only' conditions. There is every reason to suppose that perceived legitimacy of a request influences compliance (see Chapter 8, pp. 261–4) and that perceived legitimacy may depend at least partly on attributions of controllability. However, this does not really require rejection of the Langer et al. (1978) conclusion that some behaviour in social interactions occurs without evidence of clear deliberation. Compliance or non-compliance per se is not the major issue. As Langer, Chanowitz and Blank (1985: 606) point out in reply: 'It was never our belief that anything could be used as a reason for any request to obtain mindless compliance. Indeed, one could probably set up the experiment using a belligerent reason that could result in mindless noncompliance.'

A further cautionary remark about methodology is in order. Both in the first experiment of Langer et al. (1978) and in Folkes's (1985) replications, we are dealing with crude outcome measures on the one hand (subjects comply or not) and with subtle manipulations on the other. These manipulations are described in terms of a few words, but what is really at issue is the whole presentational style adopted by the person making the request. How such style might vary across conditions is a matter open to speculation, but it is perhaps surprising that Folkes (1985: 606) says that the experimenters in the first study she reports 'were informed of both cognitive and mindlessness hypotheses'. When so much seems to turn on whether subjects' suspicions, and hence attention, were aroused, it is difficult (in both studies) to be certain about exactly what cues may have been emitted by the experimenters, and how spontaneous their behaviour may have appeared.

An important application of the mindfulness/mindlessness concept concerns people's preparedness to react to others on the basis of stereotypes and prejudiced assumptions. The hypothesis is that more mindful attention to individual characteristics of a target person will inhibit prejudiced judgements and behaviour. Langer and Imber (1980) found that people recalled more special characteristics of a person they had observed on a videotape when this person was supposedly 'deviant' (mental patient, cancer patient, homosexual, divorced or millionaire) rather than 'normal'. This is consistent with the notion that the knowledge that a person is 'deviant' in some way makes an observer more mindful and attentive to detail.

Langer, Bashner and Chanowitz (1985) found that school children trained to think 'mindfully' rather than 'mindlessly' about handicapped people were less likely to hold stereotyped beliefs about handicapped people as a group or to avoid contact with a handicapped person. The intervention consisted of presentations of slides depicting handicapped people, about which subjects were required to think either superficially or more deeply. Thus, subjects in the 'mindless' condition would be asked to give one reason why the person depicted would do well or badly at work, whereas the 'mindful' group listed four reasons. Likewise, the 'mindful' group were asked to consider *how* particular practical problems could be solved (e.g. how someone in a wheelchair could drive a car), whereas the 'mindless' group were only asked *whether* the problem could be solved. These findings are taken by Langer *et al.* to show that prejudice can be decreased by getting people to think what *specific* things individuals with *specific* disabilities may or may not do, and why. Such 'appropriate discrimination', as Langer *et al.* term it, is very much the same as Billig (1985, see Chapter 5, pp. 143–4) refers to as 'particularization'.

Memory for context

Other research has considered how the way information is initially encoded affects its later accessibility from memory. Chanowitz and Langer (1981) propose the notion of *'premature cognitive commitment'*, according to which 'the way the information is initially processed will determine the limits of its subsequent use' (p. 1,052). For instance, if a piece of information is initially accepted in an unconditioned and non-discriminating way (i.e. mindless), it is unlikely to be easily subjected to scrutiny at a later stage. On the other hand, information that is initially processed in a mindful fashion can be used later to make more complex decisions.

A factor hypothesized to increase mindful processing is the personal relevance of the information. Greater personal relevance will prompt the individual to realize that there are exceptions to any rule, and the most appropriate way of responding to any stimulus cue depends on its context. On the other hand, low personal relevance can lead to mindless learning of a rule that a given situation or stimulus requires a specific fixed response: 'the person is prepared with one response and then does not seriously consider alternatives. The original "interpretation" of the situation is taken for granted and left unexamined, since the entire situation seems irrelevant' (p. 1,053).

In the first experiment reported by Chanowitz and Langer, subjects were informed that they had a fictitious perceptual deficit, that they had previously been given to believe was comparatively rare or widespread, and that they either had or had not thought about in a mindful fashion. (The mindful thinking manipulation involved having subjects think about how a sufferer could cope with such a deficit.) They then underwent a perceptual test supposedly relevant to the deficit in question. As predicted, the worst performance came from the group who had initially been told that the deficit was rare and had not thought about it in detail. In other words, this group was unprepared cognitively to question the negative implications of the label attached to them. A second experiment by Chanowitz and Langer demonstrated that performance on a visual search task could be improved by mindless acceptance of a label that implied *superior* aptitude.

Langer and Imber (1979) conducted two experiments on female air passengers waiting for their planes. Each experiment involved subjects learning a pencil-and-paper task (coding or proof-reading) under conditions designed to induce either mindful or mindless processing of the different task elements. Subjects were then split into pairs, within which one person was assigned the label 'boss' and the other the label 'assistant'. (Controls were not given status labels.) After a collaborative task, they were then re-tested on the original type of task. Those who had been assigned the inferior status label ('assistant') performed at an inferior level, but only so long as their initial learning of the task was under mindless conditions.

Chanowitz and Langer (1981) discuss how people may learn about category labels, e.g. 'cancer patient' or 'elderly person', under conditions where the information may seem of low personal relevance, and is hence accepted uncritically. They argue that, when people who have acquired such stereotypes in a mindless way find themselves within these self-same categories, they are more likely themselves to act and think in accordance with the stereotypes, since '*it will not occur to these individuals that they could think otherwise*' (p. 1,052, emphasis in original). Such self-stereotyping may then exacerbate cognitive and/or behavioural deficits, such as, it is suggested, memory loss among the elderly. Langer, Rodin, Beck, Weinman and Spitzer (1979) reported greater improvement in the memory performance of elderly residents of nursing homes following interventions designed to make them engage in greater degrees of cognitive activity (e.g. conversations involving reciprocal self-disclosure).

Langer and Imber (1979) and Chanowitz and Langer (1981) provided subjects with descriptions to apply to themselves. Higgins and Lurie (1983), however, looked at how the labels one applies to a target can persist even when the context has changed. In the first part of their experiment, subjects were presented with supposed records of sentencing decisions in criminal trials by four different judges. Through a manipulation of the sentencing patterns shown for three of the judges, simple contrast effects were produced in terms of how 'lenient' or 'harsh' the fourth judge (Judge Jones) was rated as being. In other words, along the lines of a previous study by Ostrom (1970), and almost all the research reviewed in Chapter 5, Judge Jones was rated as 'lenient' if the other judges gave longer sentences and as 'harsh' if the others gave shorter sentences. One week later, all subjects were presented with a further series of sentencing patterns for three more judges. Again, these were predominantly harsh or lenient by comparison with 'Judge Jones'. Half the subjects who had been presented with a lenient series in the first part received a second lenient series and half now received a harsh series; the same applied to those who initially had been shown a harsh series.

Subjects then had to recall the sentences passed by 'Judge Jones' for each of three offences. The results showed that, if Judge Jones had been rated as 'lenient', he was recalled as making more lenient decisions, and if rated as 'harsh', as making harsher decisions, *relative to the norms established over both sessions*. If Judge Jones was harsher than the three other judges in the first session, he would be rated as 'harsh'. If the context then shifted, so that the second session presented predominantly longer sentencing decisions, subjects would recall Judge Jones's sentences as *longer* than they were. If the change was from a harsh to a lenient context, Judge Jones's sentences were underestimated. In other words, subjects recalled how they had categorized Judge Jones, *but not the context in which the categorization was made*. They remembered that Judge Jones was 'lenient' or 'harsh', but not what these terms denoted in terms of years of sentence. To substitute a quantity for the qualitative label, they had to refer to the current norm or standard of leniency/harshness. This standard, whether conceptualized in terms of perspective (Upshaw and Ostrom, 1984) or adaptation level (Helson, 1964) incorporated information from both the previous and ongoing sessions of the experiment.

Failure to correct for changes in the context of attitude expression has also been demonstrated. Higgins and Rholes (1978) had subjects read an essay containing positive, negative and ambiguous descriptions of a target person. They were told that they would have to summarize this essay for the benefit of another person who either liked or disliked the target person, but only half were actually required to write such a summary. As expected, those who had to write a summary 'tailored' it to fit more with what they expected the recipient of their summary would like to read: that is, they produced a more favourable summary for a recipient who was a friend of the target person, and a more unfavourable summary of a recipient who disliked the target person. The important finding, though, was that this bias persisted (and even increased over the following two weeks) when subjects were later asked to reproduce the original essay, word-for-word, for the experimenter. Subjects were apparently unable to discount the effect of the anticipated audience on the previous attitude expression. No such bias was observable in the reproduction given by subjects who were not required to write a summary.

Higgins and McCann (1984) expanded this design so as to compare the effect of the anticipated recipient of the message being of either higher or equal status to the subjects (a senior postgraduate versus a second-year undergraduate). Subjects' levels of authoritarianism were also measured.

When the message recipient was of equal status, subjects distorted their summary to be more consistent with the recipient's attitude towards the target person, regardless of their level of authoritarianism. When the recipient was of higher status, high but not low authoritarians showed distortions of the kind that might please the recipient. As in the Higgins and Rholes (1978) study, subjects' own reproductions of the original information and their evaluations of the target were distorted in the direction of the summaries they produced. Higgins and McCann (1984) conclude that 'people's attitudes, impressions and memory of a person can be influenced by their prior description of the person even though their description was biased by the social context in which it was produced' (p. 38).

Mood and cognition

There is ample evidence, from the research described so far in this chapter, that many social judgements and decisions are based on a less than complete analysis of available information. People rely on heuristics and categorizations and respond to superficial cues without always checking their relevance to the current context. Such biases can lead to error, but, as Hogarth (1981) reminds us, need not generally be dysfunctional or irrational in a practical sense. Nonetheless, it is no longer a tenable view that social cognition involves *simply* the cool calculation of consequences.

But if social cognition consists of processes other than 'cool calculation', what exactly *are* these processes? If mindfulness is close to 'cool calculation', for example, what exactly is mindlessness? For the most part, mindlessness is defined negatively, in terms of cognitive activity or behaviour that is *not* mindful. Heuristics are similarly defined for the most part in terms of deviations from prescriptive models. Different heuristics have been identified, but they are still mainly defined in terms of their *effects* rather than in terms of *how* such effects are produced.

Some writers have attributed this state of conceptual uncertainty to the relative neglect of the concepts of affect and emotion in much social psychological research of the sixties and seventies. Zajonc (1980) expresses this reaction in an especially provocative form. He argues that affective reactions tend to be rapid and spontaneous, rather than 'based on a prior cognitive process in which a variety of content discriminations are made and features are identified, examined for their value, and weighted for their contributions' (p. 151), as he takes the predominant theoretical tradition to imply.

This imbalance is somewhat corrected by the demonstration that mood and emotional arousal can influence cognition and social behaviour (e.g. Clark and Fiske, 1982). Clark and Isen (1982), for instance, review a number of studies indicating that individuals are more likely to act helpfully and react more favourably towards others when in a positive than when in a negative mood. Less intuitively predictable is the finding by Isen and Daubman (1984) that the induction of positive feeling states can lead subjects to use categories more inclusively in a rating task. This is interpreted as the result of people being able to call more material, and more diverse material, to mind when in a positive mood. A marginal tendency was also found for a *negative* mood to lead to more inclusive categorization, a finding that Isen and Daubman attribute to a process of 'affect-repair', i.e. cognitive work in which people engage so as to make themselves feel better.

Johnson and Tversky (1983) report evidence that complicates interpretation of the availability heuristic. According to Tversky and Kahneman (1973), the ease with which an event can be called to mind is taken as a cue to its frequency or probability of occurrence. Because of this, it is suggested, some risks may be overestimated because of the extensive media coverage they receive (Lichtenstein *et al.*, 1978). Johnson and Tversky had subjects estimate the frequencies of deaths from various causes after reading a depressing story about the death of a student as a result of either leukaemia, homicide or fire. Compared with subjects who read a control story, subjects in all three 'depressing story' groups gave higher estimates of the frequency of death *across the whole range of different risks*. Neither in the first experiment, nor in any of the replications they report, was there any evidence of a generalization gradient related to the similarity between the story and the cause of death being rated (e.g. subjects did not rate other cancer deaths as more frequent if they had read the leukaemia as opposed to the homicide story). The findings point to a *global* increase in risk estimates as a result of the induction of a negative feeling state.

As the pendulum of research activity swings away from an emphasis on 'cool calculation', then, we can expect many more demonstrations of the influence of emotional and affective states on other psychological processes. There will no doubt be many findings of which the explanation is not immediately obvious. This is all the more reason for the development of theoretical approaches in which affective, cognitive and behavioural processes are treated as interacting parts of a single system, rather than as discrete compartments of psychological functioning. Significant steps have already been taken in this direction, for instance in more 'cognitive' versions of animal learning theory (Tarpy, 1982), and Leventhal's (1980, 1984) theory of emotion. Another important advance concerns the influence of mood on memory. According to Bower (1981):

> Human memory can be modeled in terms of an associative network of semantic concepts and schemata that are used to describe events. An event is represented in memory by a cluster of descriptive propositions. These are recorded in memory by establishing new associative connections among instances of the concept used in describing the event. The basic unit of thought is the proposition; the basic process of thought is the activation of a proposition and its concepts. The contents of consciousness are the sensa-

tions, concepts, and propositions whose current activation level exceeds some threshold. Activation presumably spreads from one concept to another, by associative linkages between them. (p. 134)

The idea of activation spreading through an associative network provides the vital key. What it means is that if one is already thinking about a concept X (if that concept has been activated), one is then more likely to think about, recognize, or remember additional concepts (Y, Z, etc.) with which X has stronger associative links, than other concepts (A, B, etc.) which are more distantly associated with X. If we assume that concepts are more closely associated if, among other things, they share the same evaluative sign, then it follows that the activation of one positive thought or feeling is likely to lower the threshold for other positive thoughts and feelings, whereas the activation of one negative thought or feeling will spread to other negative thoughts and feelings. Bower (1981) reports a number of studies showing greater recognition and/or recall of information congruent with a person's mood. For instance, hypnotizing people to feel happy or sad will make them recall more happy or sad incidents in a story they have read.

Memory and priming

The level of activation of a concept can also be manipulated experimentally by a technique known as *priming*. As an example, consider an experiment by Neely (1976), in which subjects had to categorize visually presented letter sequences as words or non-words, as fast as possible. Immediately before each letter sequence was presented, subjects were briefly exposed to a 'priming' stimulus. If the target stimulus was a word, the prime was either a neutral warning stimulus, a word semantically related to the target, or a word semantically unrelated to the target. Reaction times were fastest to words that had been preceded by a semantically related prime, and slowest to words that followed a semantically unrelated prime.

Stimuli can have a priming effect even if not 'consciously' processed. Gabrielcik and Fazio (1984) exposed subjects to a series of 20 words tachistoscopically for 4 msec. each (i.e. subliminally). All these 40 words, but not the 20 in the first set, contained the letter T. A control group received 40 presentations of strings of asterisks. As a result of this, subjects in the primed condition gave higher estimates of the relative frequency of the letter T (compared with D, M, P, R and S) in the English language. Gabrielcik and Fazio take this as evidence of the availability heuristic as an effect of associative memory.

Evaluatively positive and negative words can serve as primes for favourable or unfavourable attitude judgements, so long as they are descriptively applicable to the attitude object. Higgins, Rholes and Jones (1977) had subjects read a story about a man 'Donald' who was keen on dangerous sports, and give their impressions of 'Donald'. Previously they had participated in a supposedly unconnected perception experiment which involved them having to recite, among other words, adjectives which were either positive and applicable to Donald (adventurous, self-confident, independent, persistent); negative and applicable (reckless, conceited, aloof, stubborn); positive but inapplicable (obedient, neat, satirical, grateful); or negative but inapplicable (disrespectful, listless, clumsy, sly). Higgins *et al.* found that subjects gave more favourable characterizations of Donald when primed with positive rather than negative trait adjectives, but only when these were applicable.

Fazio, Powell and Herr (1983, see also Chapter 3, pp. 72–6) found a similar result. Subjects attributed another's participation in an experiment more to intrinsic interest when primed with words which were both positive and applicable to such a task (e.g. 'entertaining') than negative and applicable (e.g. 'dull'). Priming with inapplicable positive (e.g. 'romantic') as opposed to negative ('noisy') words produced no such effect. There are similarities in both these studies to research reviewed in Chapter 5 (pp. 159–69) on the influence of evaluative and descriptive response scale labels on attitudinal judgements (Eiser and Mower White, 1974, 1975; Eiser and van der Pligt, 1982). Furthermore, demonstrations that the use of evaluatively biased words can lead to attitude change (Eiser and Pancer, 1979; Eiser and Ross, 1977; see Chapter 2, pp. 41–3), although not designed with this thought in mind, may also be amenable to a priming interpretation.

Herr, Sherman and Fazio (1983) found that priming can produce contrast as well as assimilation effects. Their first experiment used the Higgins *et al.* (1977) recitation procedure to prime subjects with one of five sets of four animal names. These sets varied from being extremely ferocious (grizzly bear, tiger, lion, shark) through to extremely non-ferocious (dove, kitten, rabbit, puppy). Following this procedure, subjects took part in 'another' experiment which required them to rate the ferocity of different animals. Included in the list were both real and fictitious (and therefore ambiguous) animals (e.g. jabo, lemphor). Apart from a tendency for unreal animals to be rated as more ferocious, the results showed a three-way interaction, depending on whether or not the target animal was real, and on the extremity and ferocity of the priming set. Herr *et al.* interpret this pattern as showing an assimilation effect (target rated as more ferocious following a more ferocious prime) only when the target stimulus was ambiguous (unreal) *and* when the prime was moderate. Otherwise, contrast effects occurred (lower ratings of ferocity following a more ferocious prime).

Herr *et al.* (1983) replicated this finding using size rather than ferocity as the critical dimension. The primes varied from extremely large (whale, elephant, hippo, rhinoceros) to extremely small (snail, flea, minnow, ant). Unreal animals were rated as smaller overall. Otherwise, the pattern was as predicted. Moderately large primes (e.g. cow) led to unreal animals only being judged as larger, whereas moderately small primes (e.g. cat) led to unreal animals only being judged as smaller. Otherwise larger primes led to smaller ratings of the target stimuli.

A different approach to the question of how primes cause assimilation and contrast has been taken by Martin (1985, 1986). He points out that, in previous research, the priming stimuli have been presented subtly or subliminally, so that subjects have no reason to believe that any activation of a concept that they experience is anything other than their own reaction to the incoming stimulus. Under such conditions, what is most important is the discrepancy between the incoming stimuli and the primed concept: the greater the discrepancy, the more the contrast. Martin, however, used manipulations where the connection between the priming task and the rating of the target was far less hidden. For this reason his study is particularly interesting in terms of the possible links it suggests between priming processes and assimilation and contrast effects of standards or anchors in absolute judgement (e.g. Sherif, Taub and Hovland, 1958; see Chapter 5, pp. 148–52).

Instead of concentrating on the discrepancy between the target stimulus and the prime, Martin manipulated the extent to which primed concepts would still be activated whilst the target stimulus was being judged. To this end he applies the principle that, when a task is interrupted before completion, thoughts and memories relevant to that task will perseverate for longer than if the task had been completed (Zeigarnik, 1927). His main manipulation, therefore, consisted of interruption or non-interruption of the priming task. In the first two of three experiments he reports, this task consisted of reading phrases descriptive of behaviour, and indicating which of a choice of trait terms corresponded most closely to the behaviour described. In the *completed-task* condition, subjects were given eight phrases to categorize. In the *interrupted-task* condition they were given twelve phrases, but as soon as they had completed eight, they were told to stop and move on to the next task. After two distractor tasks, subjects then proceeded to the critical 'impression formation' task. This consisted of reading the story of Donald (the dangerous sportsman) taken from Higgins *et al.* (1977), and rating Donald on a number of scales. The third experiment used the same impression formation (with some changes to the scales), but a different priming procedure, in which subjects had to read statements describing positive or negative moods, try to determine the mood of the writer of the statement, and make up a statement of their own to match that statement. In the *completed-task* condition, subjects had four such statements to read, in the *interrupted-task* condition, subjects had eight, but were stopped without explanation after they had completed four.

Taken as a whole, these three experiments showed that impressions of the target (Donald) were assimilated to primed concepts when the priming task had been interrupted, but contrasted away from the primed concepts when it had been completed. What constitutes assimilation and contrast depends on the nature of the priming stimuli, and the rating scales used in the impression formation and/or priming task. For instance, in Martin's third experiment subjects were primed in the direction of positively or negatively valued concepts, and this was reflected in Donald's being seen as more adventurous, self-confident, independent and persistent in the interrupted-positive prime and completed-negative prime conditions, but as more reckless, conceited, aloof and stubborn in the interrupted-negative prime and completed-positive prime conditions. These results clearly resemble those achieved in Martin's first experiment, where positive evaluation was primed by having subjects give ratings of the traits bold and self-assured, and negative evaluation by having them give ratings of the traits foolhardy and egotistical. Martin's second experiment represented a partial attempt to unconfound descriptive and evaluative similarity between primed and rated trait terms.

Martin interprets his results in terms of what he calls a 'set/re-set' process. 'Set' refers to the tendency to use a primed concept during the formation of an impression, and 're-set' to the suppression of that concept. He suggests that 'blatant' priming manipulations may be seen by subjects as a source of bias, for which they overcompensate (re-set), but that more 'subtle' manipulations (including perseveration of activated concepts due to task interruption) leave subjects unaware, or less aware, of any such bias. Another way of looking at these data is in terms of whether the priming task was treated as a comparison standard (thereby producing contrast) or as not really distinct from the impression formation task itself. This leads on to the more general question of when incoming stimuli are interpreted as part of an established category, and when they are not.

Schemata

A concept of special relevance to social cognition and memory is that of *schemata*. Despite its recent surge of popularity, this concept has in fact been around in psychology for a long while. It is the central concept in Bartlett's *Remembering* (1932), and features prominently in Neisser's *Cognitive psychology* (1967).

In simple terms, a schema is a cognitive structure, stored in memory, that can influence the encoding, storage and recall of information. In Neisser's (1967) words:

> cognition is constructive, and . . . the process of construction leaves traces behind. The schemata themselves are such constructions, elaborated at every moment in the course of attentive activity. Recall is organized in terms of these structures because the original experiences were elaborated in the same terms . . . they are integral parts of the memories themselves. (pp. 287–8)

Crocker, Fiske and Taylor (1984) provide a good account of how the concept has been applied within social psychology:

> A schema is an abstract or generic knowledge structure, stored in memory, that specifies the defining features and relevant attributes of some stimulus domain, and the interrelationships among those attributes . . . Social schemas may be representations of types of people, social roles, or events . . . They help us to structure, organize and interpret new information; they facilitate encoding, storage, and retrieval of relevant information; they can affect the time it takes to process information, and speed with which problems can be solved. Schemas also serve interpretative and inferential functions. For example, they may fill in data that are missing or unavailable in a stimulus configuration. (p. 197)

The critical aspect of this account is the notion that a schema 'specifies the defining features', or relevant attributes of an object or category. In other words, knowledge structures are to be thought of in terms of stimulus *attributes* and their interrelationships. From this, various things follow.

(1)   Specific values or variables can be substituted for such attributes in the case of any instance of a schema. For example, one's schema for wine could include the attribute (dimension) of dryness, and a particular wine might have the 'value' of 'medium-dry' on that attribute.

(2)   Such variables have 'default values', in the sense of a 'best guess' estimate of the value of a given attribute if no information is given. (If someone just gave you a glass of wine, how dry or sweet would you expect it to be?) Obviously, sometimes such expectations are stronger than at other times.

(3)   Such variables have 'constraint values', in the sense that an object that lies too far away from the expected value of some attribute will not be accepted as an instance of the schema. (Vinegar is not wine.)

(4)   Such variables are interrelated, in the sense that the value of a stimulus on one attribute has implications for its value on the other. Thus, sweet wines may be believed to go better with dessert, dry white wines better with fish, French wines to cost more than Spanish wines, and so on.

(5)   Schemata differ in terms of both vertical and horizontal structure. Crocker *et al.* (1984) use the term 'vertical structure' to refer to the different hierarchical levels of a schema. For instance, the schema 'wine' could be seen as hierarchically below the object class 'alcoholic drink', which itself is below the more inclusive class 'drink'. Going the other way, the schema 'wine' is hierarchically above subordinate classes such as 'red wine', 'white wine', etc., which in turn can be subdivided more specifically. The term 'horizontal structure' is used to specify the number of subcategories at a given level of abstraction. For instance, the 'horizontal structure' of the schema (or sub-

schema) 'French red wine' could consist of the subcategories Burgundy, claret, etc.

(6)   Schemata may be partly defined in terms of, or evoke, 'prototypical' or particularly familiar or memorable examples. This is particularly important, since concrete instances may be more easily recalled or imagined. A somewhat hazy issue is whether such prototypes are necessarily average or normative instances of a schema, as opposed to some 'ideal' type, or a type that provides greatest distinctiveness in terms of comparison with other schemata. (Someone who offered you a *'real'* Burgundy, for instance wouldn't be claiming that it was an 'average' Burgundy.)

One of the most important aspects of schemata is their resistance to change. In other words, people tend to change their preconceptions only rather reluctantly in the face of new information. Research has therefore concentrated on the issues of how incoming information is assimilated to existing schemata, and how information that is particularly discrepant from schematic expectations is discounted, or leads to cognitive restructuring.

There is a clear overlap in this regard between the concept of schemata and other somewhat less inclusive concepts, such as categories and stereotypes. For instance, statements concerning the interrelationships between different variables of a schema seem to refer to much the same phenomena as those dealt with under an accentuation theory approach in terms of relationships between focal and peripheral dimensions (Tajfel, 1959a; Eiser and Stroebe, 1972; see Chapter 5, pp. 139–42). It is well-known, too, that stimulus information can be better remembered when it is grouped together in 'chunks' or categories (Miller, 1956). Furthermore, the kind of superimposed classifications that lead to judgemental accentuation can also provide aids to memory. Eiser, van der Pligt and Gossop (1979) presented subjects with a series of statements concerning drug-use, supposedly drawn from two different newspapers and subsequently tested their recognition-memory for the sources from which different statements were drawn. When the classification in terms of newspaper sources was systematically related to the favourability of the statements (as in the Eiser, 1971c, study), subjects' recognition-memory was very significantly higher than when the relationship between source and favourability was random. These findings have been confirmed by Arcuri (1984), in an extended design using three sources, two of which were consistently, and one of which was inconsistently, related to item favourability.

Another area of research closely related to the notion of schemata is that concerned with the theory of *cognitive scripts* (Schank and Abelson, 1977; Abelson, 1981). Essentially, scripts are schemata of sequences of related behavioural events. They are a way of organizing our 'world knowledge' or understanding of events and situations. The structure of this 'world knowledge' is represented in terms of sets of action rules, and much work has been directed towards defining such rules in ways that will allow computer simulation of behavioural decision-making. Scripts make direct reference to the classes of situations in which they apply. A frequently used example is that of a 'restaurant script', that includes features such as ordering food from the waitress, and sitting at one's table until it arrives. Besides its applications in the field of artificial intelligence, therefore, script theory has proved useful in the field of psycholinguistics and particularly in relation to work on comprehension and memory for textual material describing behavioural events (e.g. Bower, Black and Turner, 1979). Script theory also bears closely upon Langer's (1978) distinction between mindful and mindless behaviour. Actions that conform to an established normative script may be enacted and responded to mindlessly. 'Unscripted' behaviour, that either violates such norms, or is performed in unfamiliar contexts, requires and elicits more mindful processing.

Person memory and prototypes

One of the main social psychological applications of the concept of schemata relates to how we interpret and remember information about people. Hastie and Kumar (1979) present evidence suggesting that information that is inconsistent with an established schema of another person is more memorable than schema-congruent information. Their first experiment involved subjects memorizing six sets of behavioural descriptions. Each set supposedly described the behaviour of a separate individual, concerning whom they had been given a short character sketch. Each sketch consisted of eight trait adjectives which were near synonyms of each other. For instance, in the sketch that was designed to set up a schema of an intelligent person, the traits were intelligent, clever, bright, smart, quick, wise, knowledgeable and decisive. Each set of behavioural descriptions contained twelve descriptions of behaviour congruent with the schema (e.g. intelligent), four incongruent (e.g. unintelligent) behaviours, and four behaviours unrelated to intelligence–unintelligence. Overall, behaviours incongruent with the previously established schemata were best recalled. Hastie and Kumar report two further experiments varying the composition of the lists of behavioural descriptions, and found that incongruent information was more memorable, the smaller the proportion of incongruent compared with congruent items.

These findings have been qualified by other studies using similar procedures. O'Sullivan and Durso (1984) conclude that information that is incongruent with a schema may make the schematic information itself more memorable. Crocker, Hannah and Weber (1983) show that descriptions of incongruent behaviours are better recalled only if they are attributed to dispositional rather than situational factors. Crocker *et al.* also show that subjects prefer to make situational attributions for schema-incongruent behaviour and dispositional attributions for schema-congruent behaviour.

Rothbart, Evans and Fulero (1979), however, report superior recall for descriptions of behaviour that were *congruent* as opposed to incongruent with an established schema, where the schema referred to attributes of a group, and the behaviours were supposedly performed by *different* individuals from that group. This apparent contradiction seems to have been resolved by Stern, Marrs, Millar and Cole (1984) who compare the effect of describing the behaviours as those of a single individual (as in the Hastie and Kumar study) or as those of separate individuals within a single group (as in the Rothbart *et al.* study). Representing the task as that of processing information about a single individual produced better recall overall, and particularly for schema-incongruent behaviours. Stern *et al.* go on to show that incongruent information may elicit longer periods of cognitive processing, and suggest that this may involve a search for explanations of the inconsistency. In support of the intuition that less consistency is expected among different members of a group than within the behaviour of a single individual, Stern *et al.* report more spontaneous attempts to explain inconsistency among subjects presented with information about single individuals than about groups.

A related question is that of how we develop *prototypes* of particular kinds of individuals and groups. Schneider and Blankmeyer (1983) illustrate the connection between personality prototypes and people's implicit theories of personality. They propose that, when a particular prototype has been made salient, people will infer stronger implicational links (i.e. greater consistency) between behaviours that are consistent rather than inconsistent with that prototype. For instance, when subjects had been asked to rate trait combinations in terms of 'maturing' and been asked to 'think about the concept of psychological maturity', they were more likely to take the view that someone who performed one 'mature' behaviour (e.g. studying instead of going to a party) would also perform other 'mature' behaviours. Conversely, when subjects had to think about 'immaturity' and use the concept in previous ratings, 'immature' behaviours were seen as implying each other more strongly.

Lord, Lepper and Mackie (1984) applied the notion of prototypes to the question of consistency between stereotypic attitudes and behaviour towards members of particular groups. They argue that demonstrations of apparent attitude–behaviour discrepancy (e.g. LaPiere, 1934) might partly reflect the simple fact that verbal measures reflect people's attitudes towards *prototypical* members of a group, whereas individual members of the group may not match the prototype. Lord *et al.* present findings from two studies in which students' stereotypes about members of particular groups (dining clubs, or homosexuals) were assessed. Some months later, they indicated their willingness to interact with a member of the group in question, who was described so as either to show a perfect or only partial match with each subject's stereotype profile. As predicted, there was greater liking and willingness to interact with non-prototypical outgroup members. However, presenting subjects with personality descriptions of outgroup members who showed only a partial match with the stereotype was not enough to lead them to change their stereotype significantly.

Self-schemata

Research on the self-concept has similarly been influenced by the notion of schemata. According to Markus (1977), information concerning oneself is processed in terms of its relevance to one's *self-schemata*. Self-schemata are defined as cognitive structures embodying networks of meaning associated with particular attributes, that together coalesce to form the self-concept. Individuals are hypothesized to differ in the intensity with which they are concerned with various aspects of themselves. This is very much the same idea as that referred to in other contexts as salience or ego-involvement. Markus, however, uses this idea to distinguish between individuals who are *schematic* or *aschematic* with respect to a particular domain or set of attributes. People who are schematic with respect to a particular aspect of themselves are said to be more intensely concerned with that aspect and hence have well-developed cognitive structures in terms of which relevant information may be interpreted. Aschematics, by comparison, are less involved and have less differentiated and elaborated cognitive structures.

One application of this has been with respect to the importance of masculinity or femininity for people's self-concepts (Bem, 1981). Markus, Crane, Bernstein and Siladi (1982) distinguished males and females who were schematic, androgynous or aschematic with regard to their gender identity. Thus, 'masculine schematics' were males whose self-concept included attributes that were stereotypically male, but excluded those that were stereotypically female, and vice versa for 'feminine schematics'. Markus *et al.* had subjects rate themselves on 60 trait adjectives and then asked them to list as many of these adjectives that they could remember. These traits were those selected by Bem (1974) as a test of 'psychological androgyny'. Masculine schematics recalled more words with stereotypic associations of masculinity and feminine schematics recalled more stereotypically feminine words. Similar differences were found in a second experiment measuring confidence and response latency of self-ratings using the same 60 adjectives. Among the remaining subjects, those whose self-concepts showed an 'androgynous' combination of masculine and feminine traits were more confident in their self-ratings than those who were more simply neutral (i.e. 'aschematic') in terms of the masculinity–femininity of their self-concepts.

Miller (1984) has applied the notion of self-schemata to the field of social comparison. People may evaluate their own ability or performance by comparison with others, but it is not entirely clear why they should choose particular kinds of other people as standards for comparison. Research has tended to show that subjects will choose to compare themselves with others who are more similar to themselves. This can lead to a tendency for men to compare themselves more with other men, and for women to compare themselves more with other women (e.g. Zanna, Goethals and Hill, 1975), if they believed sex to be a relevant predictor of performance. Miller found no overall difference between conditions where sex was supposedly relevant or irrelevant to performance in the extent to which subjects made same-sex comparisons. Schematic subjects – whether they identified with the stereotypic traits of their own sex, the opposite sex, or had highly andro-gynous self-schemata – made at least as many same-sex comparisons when sex was unrelated as when it was related to performance. Aschematic subjects, however, were comparatively *unlikely* to make same-sex com-parisons unless they believed sex to be predictive of performance. Thus, the frames of reference individuals use for social comparisons can depend on two factors that influence the salience of particular attributes: first, whether the attributes are generally of personal importance to the individuals, and, second, whether the attributes are predictably related to the focal dimension of comparison.

Social representations

Despite the schema concept's wide applicability and inclusiveness, the basic question of where schemata come from has often been avoided. *Granted* that a person has a schema of a particular type of object, person or event, we can predict a fair amount concerning how incoming information will be inter-preted and assimilated, and how the schema may itself be changed. What is far less clear from research of the kind so far reviewed is how any such schema comes to be 'granted'.

To say that social schemata are acquired through learning is not particu-larly informative, and may even be potentially misleading in that the kind of learning involved may be vicarious and indirect. One may have schemata of countries one has never visited, people one has never encountered, or events one has never experienced. Yet such schemata may shape many other beliefs and attitudes. Take for example how one might imagine 'the aftermath of a global nuclear war'. Arguments for or against the possibility of survival will be accepted or rejected in terms of their match with a schema of an event which no-one has experienced. Where these arguments are strong enough, the schema may be changed.

Whereas schemata are considered as cognitive structures within an individual, therefore, individual learning and experience is insufficient to account for many of the schemata that we hold. Many of our schemata are acquired *from* other people and shared *with* other people. They depend on communication, and communication requires systems of meanings and symbols that are held in common by different members of a community or culture.

Such considerations lie behind a growing interest in the concept of *social representations*. Thanks largely to the work of Moscovici (e.g. 1976a, 1981, 1984), it has become the dominant theme in contemporary French social psychology, and is attracting increasing attention from further afield. The concept is close to that of 'collective representations' (Durkheim, 1898), but Moscovici prefers the term 'social' so as to emphasize that he is not simply referring to systems of knowledge and belief that are held by different members of a society, but to ones that are socially *constructed* and communicated: 'Social representations are phenomena that are linked with a special way of acquiring and communicating knowledge, a way that creates realities and common sense' (Moscovici, 1981: 186).

The kind of 'psychology of common-sense' offered by Moscovici overlaps only slightly with that of Heider (1958). In particular, the *content* (rather than the form) of 'common-sense' is a matter of prime importance, and indeed the focus of most empirical work that this approach has generated (Farr and Moscovici, 1984). Furthermore, a 'common-sense' acceptance of a proposition as 'real' creates a kind of 'reality' to which other experiences must be related. Such socially created realities are referred to by Moscovici as *'consensual universes'*.

Moscovici's theory contains a tension, never entirely satisfactorily resolved, between the functions that social representations serve for individuals, and those that they serve for society as a whole. Indeed, social representations are defined largely in functional terms. For instance: 'the purpose of all representations is to make something unfamiliar, or unfamiliarity itself, familiar' (Moscovici, 1984: 24).

On the other hand:

> To form a representation is not to select and complete an entity objectively given by reference to its subjective aspects. It is to go beyond this, to construct a theory to facilitate the task of identifying, programming or anticipating acts or sets of events. Rather than a kind of shadow cast upon society by a particular kind of experience or knowledge, a social representation is a system of values, ideas and practices with a twofold function, first, to establish an order which will enable individuals to orientate themselves in their material and social world and to master it; and secondly to enable communication to take place among the members of a community by providing them with a code for social exchange and a code for naming and classifying unambiguously the various aspects for their world and the individual and group history. (Moscovici, 1973: xiii)

Moscovici identifies two main sets of processes whereby social representations become generated within a society. These he calls *anchoring* and *objectification*. Anchoring, in Moscovici's use of the term, refers to the assimilation of an unfamiliar event to an existing knowledge structure.

It allows something unfamiliar and troubling, which incites our curiosity to be incorporated into our own network of categories and allows us to compare it with what we consider a typical member of this category. (Moscovici, 1981: 193)

Anchoring depends on classification and naming:

By classifying what is unclassified, naming what is unnamable, we are able to imagine it, to represent it. Indeed representation is, basically, a system of classification and denotation, of alloting categories and names. (Moscovici, 1984: 30)

Or, slightly rephrased:

representation is basically a classifying and a naming process, a method of establishing relations between categories and labels. (Moscovici, 1981: 193)

(Note that Moscovici's 1984 chapter is essentially a longer version of the 1981 reference, most of which it incorporates more or less verbatim. Differences between the two may therefore be mainly editorial.) Classifying is not merely a denotative system, but an evaluative one, and through this, Moscovici implies, representations constitute not simply theories given and constructed *by* society, but theories *of* society.

Neutrality is forbidden by the very logic of the system where each object and being must have a positive or a negative value and assume a given place in a clearly graded hierarchy. When we classify a person among the neurotics, the Jews or the poor, we are obviously not simply stating a fact but assessing and labelling him. And in so doing, we reveal our 'theory' of society and of human nature. (Moscovici, 1984: 30)

Here Moscovici does not simply seem to be saying that categories *can* carry connotations of value and status inequality. He appears to assert that they *always* do so. For this reason, he has little patience with (or perhaps it would be fairer to say *for*) empirical research that considers *how* the denotative aspects of categorization can be influenced by such connotations of value and/or status. Rosch and Lloyd (1978), for instance, are accused of having 'largely disregarded' the embodiment of theories of society and human nature within the systems of classification prevalent within cultures. Similarly (and choosing the softer of the two versions), he asserts:

existing studies of the phenomena of evaluation, classification, categorisation (Eiser and Stroebe, 1972) and so forth, fail to take into account the substrata of such phenomena or to realise that they presuppose a representation of beings, objects and events. (Moscovici, 1984: 30)

Fail to realise? When the vast preponderance of classical social judgement research (and, in view of other remarks he makes, *American* social judgement research at that) has dealt with attitudes towards ethnic minorities, particularly blacks? Not for the only time, Moscovici's allusions to other traditions of research take on an element of caricature, the function of which, in terms of preserving the distinctiveness of his own approach, is not hard to discern. On the other hand, concern with *prototypes* is seen as a welcome new development within social cognition. Prototypes, for Moscovici, are to be construed in terms of 'images', and it is in this context that he mentions what is essentially the notion of availability:

> The ascendancy of the test case is due, I believe, to its concreteness, to a kind of vividness which leaves such a deep imprint in our memory that we are able to use it thereafter as a 'model' against which we measure individual cases and any image that even remotely resembles it. Thus, every test case, and every typical image, contains the abstract in the concrete, which further enables them to achieve society's main purpose: to create classes from individuals. (Moscovici, 1984: 32)

Identification of an object as similar or dissimilar to a prototype – i.e. as belonging or not belonging to a class – is again assumed to be based on values and subjective conceptions of social relations. Categorizations express attitudes:

> what determines the type of generalization or individualization is not a purely intellectual choice but the expression of an attitude towards a thing or a person and the desire to view it as normal or deviant. (Moscovici, 1981: 196)

Supposedly, this has been ignored:

> The process of generalization and individualization in social representations goes beyond the processes of assimilation *vs* contrast studied by cognitive and social psychologists (Neisser, 1967; Hastie and Kumar, 1979). (ibid)

Naming is assumed to be an inextricable part of classification, so that the latter process is 'impossible' (Moscovici, 1981: 196) without the former. This has important methodological implications, in that it allows language to be taken as indicative of representations. The emphasis shifts from 'images' to 'concepts, statements and explanations' (1981: 181). Furthermore, it is through language that representations may be communicated and reproduced.

The combined effect of classification and naming is illustrated in studies of how unfamiliar objects or people are rendered familiar through assimilation to existing named classes. For instance, Jodelet (1984) describes how when psychiatric patients were housed in a village, the villagers classified them by reference to a more familiar category known locally as *bredins* – that is half-wits, tramps or mental defectives of varying degrees of harmlessness. Consensus over the nature of such prototypes, however, was higher than that over the match of any individual patient to a prototype.

The concept of *objectification* is possibly the most powerful component of the theory of social representations. This refers to a hypothesized process whereby initially abstract ideas come to be treated as though they denoted 'objective' facts and reality, and are perceived as everyday aspects of common-sense, 'obvious' experience. There are points of contact here with Berger and Luckmann's (1967) views on the 'social construction' of reality. Social representations can produce a bridge between scientific thought and common-sense. Notions such as gravity, magnetism and electricity become commonplace not because they are understood, but because they become assimilated to a class of physical properties that supposedly can be directly experienced – they appear 'obvious'. In this way, representations do not simply allow us to interpret our experience, they define the reality that we experience and about which we can communicate. Representations act *upon* our experience and our patterns of social relationships. Moscovici speculates that their effect may be even more important nowadays, with the advent of mass media, and channels for popularizing ideas, than it may have been in earlier times.

There is a price to be paid for this power that is gained by thought over experienced reality, however. The translation of theoretical ideas into common-sense involves the objectification of the abstract into something more concrete. Moscovici (1976a) provides a convincing account of how the concepts of psychoanalytic theory have become public property, but in the process have undergone transformations, so that they appear as if they were objective entities in their own right, independent of the system of which they are a part. Terms used to refer to different kinds of processes, such as ego and id, become represented as spatially distinct *parts* of 'the mind'. Similarly, 'complexes', 'repressions', 'inhibitions', 'neurosis' and the like become understood as particular 'conditions' that people 'have', much as they may 'have' a cold or a broken leg, and almost as easily recognizably so.

Abstract concepts do not need to emanate from scientific theory in order to become objectified as social representatives. Herzlich (1973) provides an interpretation of ordinary people's conceptions of health and illness, in terms of which the contrast of health to illness is enmeshed with another contrast of individual to society. Staying healthy or falling ill are seen as outcomes of a conflict between a 'reserve of health' within the individual, and the way of life imposed on the individual by society, with its stresses, environmental hazards and so on.

Moscovici is firm in his view that the proper topic of study for social psychology must be the social representation through which 'consensual universes', or socially agreed realities are constructed. To ignore the collective aspect of social cognition is, in his view, to produce a psychology that is 'social' only in name. Nor does he resist 'objectifying' the distinction between 'social' and 'individualistic' forms of psychological theory through assimilation to the geographical separation of Europe from America. As a result, it has become almost an article of faith among researchers within the social representations tradition that (whatever the potential points of contact with other kinds of work) their approach is prototypically 'European'.

For some of those outside the inner circle of this tradition, however, a concern has been to identify more precisely areas of common ground and/or divergence in the use of explanatory concepts and the interpretation of empirical findings. In this context, a fundamental question deserves more of an answer than has hitherto been provided: what is the appropriate unit of analysis for research that seeks to identify social representations?

Moscovici (1976a) is clear enough that it must be above the level of the individual, and in this respect *does* differentiate himself from much of the predominantly North American 'mainstream' tradition of experimental social psychology. But how far above the individual level? Codol (1984) argues for the admissibility of the concept of social representations to an understanding of the behaviour of experimental groups in artificial laboratory settings. Moscovici, however, tends to talk more generally of representations that are held in common by members of communities, cultures and societies. But here we run into a real danger of circularity. What constitutes a group (indeed, what keeps a group together as a group) is supposedly the sharing of representations of reality. Representations become social rather than individual if they constitute a group consensus, but at the same time a 'group' is not simply a collection of individuals but a collec*tive* defined by a shared consensus. It thus becomes almost impossible, within the *strict* terms of the theory, to ask how far different members of a group (which is something that needs to be defined according to extrinsic criteria) do in fact share the same social representations of important objects and concepts, even though, in his own experimental research Moscovici (1980; see Chapter 9, pp. 327–31) is directly concerned with the power of minorities to influence group consensus.

The emphasis placed upon linguistic discourse as the depository of such representations has also sometimes failed to convince those for whom discourse analysis is a more primary interest. Potter and Litton (1985) advocate the concept of 'linguistic repertoires' as an alternative to that of social representations, arguing that Moscovici and others have failed to distinguish between the cognitive accessibility of a linguistic construct and the way it is used within specific contexts. In simple terms, 'meaning' cannot be properly ascribed to words or phrases without reference to the context of their use. Potter and Litton's critique prompted a succession of rejoinders. Moscovici's own is far from abrasive, but, significantly, he seeks to distance the concept of social representations from that of linguistic discourse, through reasserting the notion of 'image': 'a discourse is not a representation, even if every representation is translated into a discourse. All that is image or concept does not entirely pass into language' (Moscovici, 1985: 92).

Litton and Potter (1985) back up their argument with a detailed analysis of alternative representations of 'riot' behaviour contained in data collected by Reicher (1984b; see Chapter 9, pp. 300–1), following street disturbances in the St Paul's district of Bristol in 1980. Their analysis concentrated on the distinction between accounts of the disturbances in terms of *race* (St Paul's is the centre of the black community in Bristol) or *government cuts and amenities*. They show that, whereas some respondents showed consensus in that they applied the same explanatory schemata in the *same* way, others showed consensus at the level only of which schemata they used, not of *how* they used them, and others still showed consensus at the level of recognizing the availability of alternative schemata, but rejecting them as mistaken. Thus, 'even where an explanatory schema is shared in general terms it can be interpreted in highly disparate ways in practical situations' (Litton and Potter, 1985: 383).

These analyses, then, support the idea that unfamiliar events may be interpreted by reference to pre-formed explanatory schemata. However, these schemata do not seem to produce the kind of 'consensual universe' which Moscovici claims. Rather 'they appear to form an arena in which disagreements emerge; the schemata create boundaries for conflict but do not eradicate it' (Litton and Potter, 1985: 383).

All this points towards a more complex view of the relationships between labelling, discourse, representation, common-sense and society. If a sharper distinction is drawn between conventional forms of thought (social representations) and conventional forms of talk (discourse), the possibility of studying the former solely by means of the latter becomes more problematic. Moscovici's hypotheses regarding the construction and reproduction of common-sense through processes of anchoring and objectification nonetheless remain extremely important insights. Whilst the match between these notions and those contained in other theoretical approaches could do with being more clearly articulated, there are many good reasons to heed Moscovici's plea for a less exclusive focus on the cognitive structures of *individuals*, if one's interest is in the psychological processes involved in *social* relationships and behaviour. Even so, there is room to challenge Moscovici's assumptions concerning the kinds of 'consensual universes' that social representations may create. Communities may require schemata in terms of which they can represent disagreement and uncertainty at least as much as they require schemata through which they can reproduce consensus and certainty. A community that can allow for the possibility of alternative conceptions of social reality may gain in adaptability what it loses in cohesiveness. A community that cannot do so becomes a community under siege. Language, in the form of rhetorical argument (Billig, 1985), then becomes vital for the communication of such alternative conceptions at a societal as well as individual level.

From this point of view, social psychological inquiry does not need to be confined either to the level of individual information-processing or to the level of corporate consensus. Whilst it is true that communities may tolerate or even encourage *some* diversity of opinion among their members, bounds may be set both to the kinds and to the extent of permissible diversity. At the same time, members of a community may *reason* for themselves not only about the general *truth* of common-sense notions, but also (one suspects more commonly and inevitably) about the *applicability* of such notions to specific practical circumstances. Since not all community members will reason in the same way or to the same extent, they will participate in different ways in the common-sense understanding of events which social representations should provide. Instead of 'consensual universes', therefore, one may end up with something rather closer to what Moscovici calls 'reified universes', within which 'society views itself as a system with different roles and categories, whose occupants are not equally entitled to represent it and speak in its name' (Moscovici, 1981: 187).

Moscovici attempts to steer social psychology away from what he sees as an attempt to model society as a 'reified universe' through constructing 'a map of the forces, objects and events unaffected by our desires and consciousness' (Moscovici, 1981: 187). However, the study of the influence of desires and collective consciousness on societal processes does not need to exclude the study of individual reactions to, and representations of, such processes. As the following two chapters will show, there are large areas of research which point not merely to how 'different roles and categories' may shape social cognition and behaviour, but also to how such roles and categories are subjectively *represented* by the participants involved.

Conclusions

Research on decisions and representations spans many different theoretical and methodological approaches. A common question, however, concerns how people react to situations of uncertainty and unfamiliarity as compared with situations where events closely match their expectations, and are easily understood in terms of existing knowledge. At the beginning of this chapter, I considered the applicability of normative models of 'rational' decision-making involving the notion of expected value. It is clear that human beings make many decisions that do not serve the function of maximizing expected value, but it is far less clear that departures from the precepts of normative models necessarily involve 'irrationality' in the sense of dysfunctional decision-making. Much attention has been paid in recent years to the notion of cognitive heuristics, which appear from experimental studies in the form of biases that leave decision-makers prone to error. Again, though, if one considers such heuristics as embodying hypotheses about the information presented, and the consequences of decisions, such heuristics may allow decision-makers to make quick judgements that may very frequently be correct in real-life circumstances.

Another line of research has considered the ways that judgements and decisions may be influenced by the manner in which information is stored in memory. This has emphasized the importance both of the context within which the information was initially acquired, and also the facilitative and inhibitory effects of associated stimuli. Of special importance here is evidence that recall and judgements may be influenced by mood states, and also by linguistic labels, when these are used as priming stimuli. This adds force to the general argument that human decision-making depends on the *selective* processing and use of information, whilst giving some indication of ways in which such selectivity may be shaped.

The notion of selectivity leads on to structure. The main issue here has been how pre-existing cognitive structures or schemata guide the interpretation and processing of information. Although derived from cognitive psychological research on memory, the concept of schemata has been applied to a broader range of topics, including stereotyping and the self-concept. Such research, though, may be open to the criticism that it says little about where schemata come from, and does not properly explore the implications of the fact that schemata may be shared in common by different individuals.

Research on social representations seeks to correct this imbalance, and in so doing offers hypotheses about the generation and reproduction of 'common-sense' knowledge and explanatory schemata within a group or community. Serious ambiguities remain with respect to the criteria for determining whether linguistic discourse adequately expresses such representations, and whether any specific representation reflects the consensual view of different members of a community, and indeed whether different individuals do in fact constitute a group or community in psychological terms. Nonetheless, a social psychological analysis of decision-making and representations must address the issue of the social origins and functions of the decision rules, heuristics and schemata by which our judgements and experiences are shaped.

8
Justice, roles and obligations

The notion of equity

An emerging theme throughout the last few chapters has been the extent to which individuals judge their outcomes from an interaction in comparison with what they feel they deserve. This is implicit in Nuttin's (1975) challenge to cognitive dissonance theory, with regard to the finding that inequitably high or low rewards for a task can lead to 'dissonance' effects. It is implicit in the definition of comparison level (CL) proposed by Thibaut and Kelley (1959; see Chapter 5, p. 130). The importance of the concept of deservedness for social psychological theory may be difficult to over-estimate. It allows us to deal with the fact that individuals decide on a course of action at least partly because of what they expect to get out of it, but does not require us to assume that the law of effect applies to social interaction deterministically and without regard to personal norms and values. It allows for a motivational analysis, but also enables the relevant motives to be treated as potentially under cognitive control.

Stimulated by such considerations, researchers have recently paid increasing attention to the issue of how people judge what is just, fair, deserved, or equitable, and how such judgements influence behaviour. Corporately this research has adopted the name of 'equity theory'. At present, however, the 'theory' consists for the most part of rather loosely formulated predictions and generalizations, and is in need of more precise definitions and empirical validation (Berkowitz and Walster, 1976).

The fundamental question of equity research is that of how a desired resource should be distributed. This resource will often be limited, as in the case of money, employment, admission to a university, membership of a sports team, helpings of food or drink, the company of a mutual friend, and so on. In such cases, there is a potential conflict of interest between the participants in a relationship, and the function of an equity norm is to provide a guideline for its resolution. By extension, the same norm is treated as applicable to cases where one or more of the participants is deprived of certain resources, or receives undesirable outcomes, through accident, malice, neglect, or punishment.

A simple solution to the issue of resource allocation is that all participants should receive the same. So, in a situation involving two people, A and B, an equitable relationship might be assumed to exist if:

$$O_A = O_B \tag{8.1}$$

where O_A represents A's outcomes and O_B represents B's outcomes. This simple formula may be termed a 'parity' principle. As can be seen, it deals only with outcomes, and takes no account of the respective *inputs* of the participants, i.e. what they each contribute to the relationship or achieve through effort or quality of performance. Developmental evidence suggests that a feature of socialization may be a shift from a reliance on parity towards greater consideration of relative inputs (Eiser and Eiser, 1976; Lerner, 1974). Brickman and Bryan (1978) have also suggested that principles of parity and equity may 'operate independently and simultaneously' in determining children's moral judgements of various acts and exchanges.

A possible solution which also takes account of the relative inputs (I_A and I_B) of the two participants was proposed by Adams (1963, 1965). This basic formulation of an 'equity' principle assumes that a relationship will be seen as equitable if the ratio of all participants' outcomes to their inputs are equal. Thus:

$$\frac{O_A}{I_A} = \frac{O_B}{I_B} \tag{8.2}$$

For example, in an industrial setting, an employee's outcomes (pay, prestige, etc.) would be seen as more or less equitable depending on their relation to his or her inputs (skill, training, experience, productivity, responsibility, danger, and discomfort endured, etc.) when set against the outcomes and inputs of other employees. Disputes over 'differentials' involve just this sort of comparison. The fact that there are such disputes implies that the relative importance of different kinds of inputs and outcomes may not be viewed in the same way by all participants. In any context, there are likely to be powerful cultural and personal norms operating to define how any individual's outcomes, and especially inputs, should be evaluated.

Notwithstanding such considerations, attempts have been made to improve the Adams formula. Walster, Berscheid and Walster (1976) point out that the formula cannot handle situations involving negative inputs, i.e. relationships where one or more of the participants' contributions may be directly damaging. According to Formula 8.2, a relationship could still be defined as equitable if person A contributed positive inputs but had negative outcomes, while person B gained positive outcomes in spite of negative inputs. For example, if $O_A = -10$, $I_A = 5$, $O_B = 10$, and $I_B = -5$, both sides of the equation would equal -2, which would imply that the relationship was equitable, which it clearly is not. To deal with such anomalies, Walster *et al.* therefore proposed the following revision of the formula, whereby, if

$$k_A = \text{sign}\,(I_A) \times \text{sign}\,(O_A - I_A)$$

and

$$k_B = \text{sign}\,(I_B) \times \text{sign}\,(O_B - I_B)$$

then a relationship is said to be equitable if

$$\frac{O_B}{O_A\ O_B} \qquad \frac{I_B}{I_A\ I_B} \tag{8.4}$$

A simpler, and interestingly different, definition of equity has been proposed by Anderson (1976). He leaves aside the problem of negative inputs, and instead turns Adams's formula around to read as follows:

$$\frac{O_B}{O_A + O_B} = \frac{I_B}{I_A + I_B} \tag{8.4}$$

This means that a relationship is said to be equitable if each participant's proportionate share of the outcomes equals his or her proportionate share of the inputs. Discussing the difference between Formula 8.2 and Formula 8.4, Anderson (1976: 293) writes:

> The contrast between them highlights a basic structural assumption. In general equity judgements require two comparison processes, one between input and outcome, the other between persons. [Formula 8.2] implies that an initial comparison is made between outcome and input within each person separately, and a second comparison is then made between persons on these two outcome/input ratios. [Formula 8.4] implies a reverse order of comparisons, first between persons for input and outcome separately and then between these interpersonal ratios.

Anderson reports data which show that his model is reasonably successful at predicting how subjects allocate hypothetical monetary rewards to two imaginary people on the basis of information given about their performance on a task, the best fit being obtained when subjects were constrained to divide a fixed sum between the two people. He then attempts to deal with two conceptual problems. The first, which has already been mentioned, is that of negative inputs. Anderson makes no attempt to revise the basic equity equation to take account of negative inputs, but proposes a separate 'justice' equation:

$$O = kI \tag{8.5}$$

in which the punishment O fits the crime I. He does not regard this as an equity equation since 'it exhibits no interpersonal comparison structure' (p. 296), and suggests that 'it might not overstate the case too far to say that equity theory does not apply to negative input' (p. 296).

The second conceptual problem considered by Anderson (1976) concerns the distinction between equity and inequity. His recommendation is that the emphasis should shift from attempts to model equity (which he sees as an ideal rarely attained by everyday interaction) to attempts to model inequity. In other words, what is important is to be able to specify the extent to which any given situation will be judged as inequitable: 'Each person's accomplishments, efforts, needs, and aspirations are more salient to himself than to another, and so he will rate his own input higher than will the other. Any objectively fair division will, therefore, tend to leave all parties dissatisfied' (p. 297).

In fact, it is only really when it comes to defining the degree of inequity that the distinction between Formulae 8.2 and 8.4 becomes important. For the ideal state of equity, the two formulae are mathematically equivalent. In situations of relative inequity, derivations from Formula 8.4 are found to be predictively superior (Anderson and Farkas, 1975). Most social psychological research on 'equity theory' has not, as yet, been designed so as to discriminate between different formulations. Nonetheless, Anderson's reformulation makes good intuitive sense regarding the order in which the different comparison processes are assumed to operate. It seems implausible that one typically compares one's absolute outcomes with one's absolute inputs, as Adams's (1963, 1965) formula implies, except in situations where one has already compared one's outcomes and inputs with those of others.

It should, of course, be remembered that such attempts to define perceived equity and inequity mathematically make no prescriptions concerning what people *ought* to feel or do. We may regard a moral commitment to principles of justice and equity as a major civilizing force in our society – something, perhaps, that distinguishes us from 'lower' forms of animal life. If we believe this, though, we should beware. As we shall see later in this chapter, the motivation to believe that the world is fundamentally just can lead to forms of social behaviour of which we should be anything but proud. Moreover, the equity principle does *not* seem to be exclusively human. In fact, Anderson's (1976) Formula 8.4 is formally identical to the 'matching law' devised by Herrnstein (1961, 1974) in the field of animal learning. What Herrnstein's matching law predicts is that animals who have a choice between differently reinforced responses will match proportionate response strengths (inputs) to proportionate reward probabilities (outputs); for instance, pigeons peck more at keys associated with more frequent rewards.

In pointing out this parallel, I am not trying to suggest that pigeons have as much moral sense as people, or that they have the cognitive capacity to protest against oppression, or to pass sentences in a court of law. The word 'justice' carries evaluative and moral connotations, but to what precisely does it refer? That may be a question for ethics and for jurisprudence, not for psychology. However, if we take *any* mathematical formulation of *perceived* equity or inequity as a definition of what justice *is*, we surpass Herrnstein's pigeons only in the scope of our self-delusion. Pigeons may follow a kind of profit principle simply to survive, but we need better arguments than that, if we are to assign to such a definition of equity the force of a *moral* imperative.

Intervention in emergencies

A central assumption of the various applications of equity theory is that people who perceive themselves or others to be receiving inequitable outcomes will attempt to resolve this apparent inequity, either by acting directly to bring the level of outcomes back to what would be equitable, or by finding justifications for the outcomes experienced or observed. An important instance where this should apply is when one observes another person who has suffered from some kind of accidental misfortune, for example, physical injury or assault. There appears to be a generally accepted moral obligation to help others in emergencies, if one is in a position to do so. However, this obligation is not always followed in real life, as is shown by incidents such as the frequently cited assault and murder of Kitty Genovese in New York City, passively witnessed by 38 onlookers (Rosenthal, 1964).

As with many problems that are 'important' in a broad sense, it took social psychologists some time to identify questions that could be meaningfully submitted to empirical investigation. An approach which showed considerable early promise was the 'diffusion of responsibility' notion proposed by Darley and Latané (1968). They suggest that, when there is a large number of people who are all in a position to offer help, the responsibility for any individual actually doing so appears to be reduced. Any single individual can say, 'I don't have to do anything. Someone else can.' This suggests that any single individual within a group will be less likely to offer help than if he or she were alone. Darley and Latané (1968) found support for this prediction in an experiment which involved subjects supposedly having a discussion with one, two or five other students over an intercom system. When another discussant appeared to have an epileptic fit, the speed and likelihood of subjects going to seek help was inversely related to the supposed size of the group. Other factors of importance include subjects' apparent ability to help (Bickman, 1971), and the apparent seriousness of the incident (Bickman, 1971; Clark and Word, 1972).

The ambiguity of an emergency seems to be an important factor inhibiting bystanders from intervening, and it seems plausible that individuals will rely upon the reactions of others as a means of resolving such ambiguity. This was demonstrated clearly by Ross and Braband (1973). The subjects in their study were required to work on a task alone, or in the presence of a confederate, who was either obviously normally-sighted, or disguised as a blind person. After the experimenter had left, one of two emergencies occurred. A 'scream' emergency consisted of the sound of a workman hurting himself and screaming, and the alternative 'smoke' emergency consisted of the sound of glass breaking followed by smoke pouring into the experimental room. In none of the conditions was there any reaction from the confederate. If the important factor was diffusion of responsibility, then only the presence of the sighted confederate would be expected to inhibit helping, regardless of the type of emergency. An apparently blind confederate could not reasonably be expected to offer help, and might well be in need of protection himself. On the other hand, the failure of the blind confederate to react could well provide subjects with the cue that 'nothing serious' had happened, but only, of course, in the 'scream' condition. The blind confederate would have heard the scream, but could not have noticed the smoke. The results support the interpretation that subjects used the confederate's behaviour as a cue. The presence of the confederate inhibited subjects from going to seek help in the 'scream' but not in the 'smoke' condition.

It is important to remember that there are potentially two kinds of ambiguity that subjects, or witnesses of real-life emergencies, may need to resolve. The first is ambiguity over what is happening. Until this is resolved, the would-be helper cannot plan effective action. Removing this ambiguity, however, does not immediately open the way for intervention if the would-be helper is still uncertain over what should be done. The failure of others to react in any way to an emergency, when they are capable both of noticing the emergency and of offering assistance, may provide cues which imply both that nothing serious has happened, and that the most appropriate reaction is to do nothing. Even where it is quite obvious that something untoward has happened, however, the inactivity of others may still be enough to inhibit subjects from taking the initiative by going to help or investigate.

As will be clear, experiments of the kind just described require the efficient stage-management of elaborate deceptions. As elsewhere in social psychology, there are no doubt experimenters who can make the most bizarre procedures convincing for their subjects, and others who manage to arouse their subjects' suspicions even before a single half-truth has been spoken. There are also likely to be differences in gullibility between individual subjects. Although experimenters attempt to elicit from their subjects (during ethically obligatory debriefings) the extent to which they may have seen through any experimental deception, there may yet be a number of subjects who may have felt that there was something strange going on, but have not tumbled to the fact that the emergency was actually contrived by the experimenter. Combined with the possibility that some subjects may see through the deception, but not want to hurt the experimenter's feelings (or data) by saying so, and that others may on principle distrust indiscriminately any instructions given to them during a social psychology experiment, we end up with a situation in which an artefactual bias may be operating to reduce the possibility of experimental subjects reacting as quickly as they might in a genuine emergency. This would not matter too much if it operated evenly in all conditions, but it might well interact with experimental manipulations, becoming more acute as more elaborate stage-management is called for. The acting skills of experimental confederates are not easy to assess from typical experimental reports, which is why face-to-face interactions may require more subtle handling than simulated interactions over intercoms.

The costs of helping

Some of the theoretically most provocative studies in the area have in fact used field situations, rather than laboratory deceptions. Among these are a number relevant to another of the predictions by Darley and Latané (1970), namely that a person's preparedness to help another will be a function of the costs of risks incurred in doing so. Such costs might include consequences such as physical injury, monetary loss or sacrifice, loss of time, embarrassment, and so on.

Piliavin, Rodin and Piliavin (1969) observed the response of travellers on the New York subway to a 'victim' who collapsed onto the floor of the train, where he remained staring at the ceiling. In some cases, the 'victim' smelt of alcohol and was carrying a bottle of liquor; in other cases, he carried a cane so as to give the appearance of being an invalid. Four different male stooges (three white and one black) took the part of the victim. The performance was convincing enough to elicit help about 60 per cent of the time from the other passengers, with little effect due to the number of bystanders. Males tended to offer help more frequently than females, and when the victim appeared drunk, he was more likely to be helped by members of his own race. Overall, when the victim appeared to be an invalid, he received more help than when he appeared drunk. In sequels to this study, a victim who 'bled' from the mouth after falling was less likely to be helped, or was helped more slowly, than one who did not bleed (Piliavin and Piliavin, 1972), as was a victim with a disfiguring birthmark (Piliavin, Piliavin and Rodin, 1975).

Darley and Latané (1970) cite a similar study by Allen again conducted on the New York subway. The reactions of passengers were observed when they heard one fellow-passenger ask in which direction the train was going, and another reply with what was obviously the wrong answer. The issue was whether the genuine traveller would interrupt to correct the stooge who had given the false information. It was found that travellers would be more likely to correct the stooge if the request for directions had been addressed to them specifically (so that it was the stooge who had interrupted), rather than to the occupants of the carriage generally. They were also less likely to intervene if the stooge who had given the wrong information was made to look like a dangerous character. This was achieved by his having previously looked up from a magazine on muscle-building and shouted threats of physical assault at a fourth traveller (another stooge) who tripped over his feet!

Darley and Latané also report data from observations of the responses of passers-by to requests from a stranger for very minimal amounts of help. Requests which cost the giver nothing, such as to tell the time, or to give simple street directions, were granted more readily than requests for even minimal amounts of money (10c.). It should be noted, though, that even when no reason was given for the request, 34 per cent of the passers-by who were approached handed over the 10c. This percentage rose to 64 per cent when the person making the request explained that he needed to make a telephone call, and to 72 per cent when he explained that his wallet had been stolen.

An implication which Darley and Latané draw from such findings is that it is more reasonable to look for the mediating influence of self-interest on helping than to seek to explain helping by postulating the presence of norms to act altruistically. Discussing how variations in costs to the helper influence whether or not help will be given, they argue that 'any serious attempt to deal with the various response rates in normative terms must involve the postulation of a proliferation of norms' (1970: 99).

Clearly it is not much good, whenever any new instances of behaviour come up for explanation, simply to say that 'this behaviour is determined by a norm' and to assume that one has thereby explained it. Equally, though, it is not much good simply to say that 'this behaviour is determined by self-interest'. What is important is how self-interest may operate within norma-tive constraints, and how self-interest may set limits to the viability of norms. Furthermore, one does not need a 'proliferation of norms' to allow for situational variation within an approach that includes consideration of normative factors. All one needs to assume is that the perceived applica-bility or salience of any norm or moral principle will depend on the specific situation in question. To assume instead that all requests for help or all apparent emergencies are equally obligating from an ethical point of view – or, alternatively, that no principles can be found on the basis of which to predict any variations in the perceived level of obligation – is greatly to oversimplify the ways in which norms can operate.

There is no reason to view normative explanations as necessarily incompatible with the operation of a principle of self-interest. While the studies described by Darley and Latané (1970) show how response rates may vary as a function of the helper's costs, they do not provide a clear answer to the question of why people should give any help at all if it is not in their interest to do so. One possible explanation is that giving help is self-gratifying, in other words, that it makes one 'feel good'. There is evidence, for instance, that generosity may be determined by the mood of the helper (e.g. Isen, 1970). This is consistent with the notion that mood can 'prime' a variety of cognitive and decision processes (Bower, 1981; see also Chapter 7, pp. 232–4). However, this effect depends on various factors. It decays with time following the induction of mood (Isen, Clark and Schwartz, 1976). It may also depend on age. Cialdini and Kenrick (1976) had subjects of various ages from 6 up to 18 years old think of either neutral or depressing events, before being given the opportunity to be privately generous by giving up prize coupons in favour of their fellow-students. Whereas the youngest subjects tended to be less generous when they had been thinking about depressing events, this difference was reversed in the case of the older subjects, consistent with the notion that they had been socialized into finding altruistic behaviour self-gratifying and hence could use it to relieve a negative mood.

Pomazal and Jaccard (1976) applied the Fishbein and Ajzen (1975) model of attitude and behavioural intention to the problem of predicting who would donate blood during a 'blood drive' on a university campus. According to the model, one's attitude towards performing an altruistic act, in this case giving blood, would depend on one's evaluative beliefs about the consequences of doing so. In comparison with those who said that they intended to give blood, those who said that they did not intend to do so were significantly more likely to say that they thought that giving blood would make them feel anxious, tired or faint, or would take up too much of their time. In addition, however, they found that predictions of intention were significantly improved when account was taken of subjects' levels of agreement with the statement, 'I personally feel I have a moral obligation to donate blood at the upcoming drive', indicating the importance of a 'moral norm' over and above a consideration of the pleasantness of the personal consequences.

The need for help and the legitimacy of demands

It is, of course, one thing to posit a general norm or moral obligation to help others, and quite another to define the principles in terms of which an individual will decide whether this norm is applicable to a given situation. It is here that equity theory has an important part to play. The finding that people are less likely to help when helping can be costly is quite compatible with equity theory. If one believes that one's own outcomes, possessions, status, freedom from hazard or injury, etc., are no more than what one is equitably entitled to, then depriving oneself of any of these benefits by giving help to another person may be seen to produce a new inequity. Indiscriminate altruism is thus not predicted by equity theory.

Even in the data which Darley and Latané (1970) cite in support of a reward–cost analysis of helping behaviour, however, there is evidence of the importance of an additional factor – how much the victim, or the person making the request, needs or deserves to be helped. The finding by Piliavin *et al.* (1969) that a 'drunk' victim was helped less readily than an 'ill' victim could be explained in these terms, though the inhibitory effects of blood (Piliavin and Piliavin, 1972) seem to go against this. A drunk might appear less deserving of help, and less likely to come to serious harm if left to 'sleep it off', as compared with someone who passed out when apparently ill. The moral obligation to help an ill person in distress, related as it may be to apparent urgency, would seem to be at least as important a factor as the possibility of being hurt by a barely conscious inebriate. Similarly, the finding by Darley and Latané that passers-by would be much more likely to give 10c. to a stranger who gave reasons for his request, suggests that even minimal help of this kind may be given in proportion to its perceived need. The experimental studies that have manipulated the ambiguity of an emergency (e.g. Bickman, 1972; Clark and Word, 1972) may also be interpreted as showing that help is less likely to be given if the victim's need for help is uncertain.

In a study that foreshadows later work on mindfulness/mindlessness (see Chapter 7, pp. 226–9), Langer and Abelson (1972) have shown that the wording of a request for help can strongly influence a person's willingness to give assistance if approached. They distinguish in the first place between appeals which are 'victim-oriented', which evoke sympathy by stressing the victim's urgent personal need, and those which are 'target-oriented', where emphasis is placed on the responsibility of the person approached to help the victim. This distinction may be conveyed by opening phrases such as: 'I've hurt myself', as opposed to: 'Would you do something for me?' and Langer and Abelson manipulated this variable by simply changing the order of phrases in the appeal. The second distinction is that between 'legitimate' and 'illegitimate' requests, which essentially relates to the difference between cases of genuine need and others where the request is an imposition.

Langer and Abelson (1972) report the results of two field experiments in which passers-by were confronted with appeals for help worded so as to be victim- or target-oriented, and legitimate or illegitimate. The two factors were found to interact, with legitimate requests eliciting more help than illegitimate requests only when they were victim-oriented. Langer and Abelson conclude that victim-oriented appeals focus attention on the victim's state of need, and will tend to elicit more help if the need seems genuine. 'But there is also a strong cultural imperative ("rugged individualism") that people should not let others take illegitimate advantage of them' (p. 31). This 'cultural imperative' could just as easily be called a norm. These results therefore imply that an approach which takes account of normative factors is quite capable of dealing with situational variations in levels of helping without, as Darley and Latané (1970) argue, needing to postulate a new norm for each situation.

A field study by Dorris (1972) provides evidence of the operation of a norm to act equitably towards others in a vulnerable position, and shows that this norm can be made more or less salient depending on how an appeal is phrased. Dorris approached a number of coin dealers with a set of rare coins which he said he had just inherited from his grandfather. He explained that he wanted to sell the coins, but that he knew nothing about how much they were worth. Through this admission of ignorance, therefore, he left himself open to exploitation, if the dealer wished to offer an unfairly low price.

In the 'neutral-appeal' condition, the experimenter then simply continued by saying that he had no wish to become a collector, and that he did not want to take a lot of time over getting different estimates, so he was ready to sell the coins for whatever he was offered. Contrasted with this was a 'moral-appeal' condition, in which the experimenter explained that he was afraid that he might get exploited when selling them, and so he had asked a stamp collector friend, who had recommended the dealer as someone he could trust to give a fair price. He then explained: 'Normally I wouldn't sell the coins, but I'm in a kind of jam; I need to buy some textbooks for my summer-school class to get ready for exams, and for some reason my check got held up at work' (p. 389).

The average initial offer from dealers who received the moral appeal was 56 per cent higher than from those who received the neutral appeal. Also, when making their offer, those in the moral-appeal condition maintained more eye-contact, and stood closer to the experimenter.

Although this study is concerned with exploitation or non-exploitation rather than with clear-cut altruism, the results reinforce those of Langer and Abelson (1972). The 'moral appeal' emphasized the personal circumstances of the experimenter, the fact that he needed the money urgently for the 'worthy cause' of buying textbooks for his studies, and the fact that his present temporary insolvency was no fault of his own. The effects of this appeal are notable in that the role of the dealer was already defined, his relationship with the experimenter involved no more than an ordinary business transaction, and that there were other dealers also in the position to buy the coins if they wished. It may be that the appeal functioned partly so as to invite the dealer to distance himself from the role of the profiteer. What is clear, however, is that dealers in the moral appeal condition to some extent resisted the opportunity to increase their own outcomes at the experimenter's expense, owing to features of the appeal that implied that it would be inequitable for them to do so.

Although these findings can be interpreted without the help of any of the mathematical formulations of equity theory discussed at the beginning of this chapter, they clearly demonstrate the importance of some kind of equity principle in moderating the demands of immediate self-interest. This principle or norm is not invoked indiscriminately. What counts as fair or equitable in a given situation may depend upon quite subtle features of the interaction that takes place. At the same time, however, an equity principle can act as a protection against demands for help that are themselves exploitative. The issue of whether a request for help is, or is not, an imposition, seems to depend primarily upon a consideration of the needs of the victim and the costs of the helper. If nothing particularly terrible is likely to happen to the victim if he or she does not receive help, then it is unreasonable to expect the helper to go to any great pains on the victim's behalf. To do so would be to create a new imbalance in outcomes in favour of the victim and to the detriment of the helper. The fact that such comparisons between outcomes can be made quite readily is consistent with Anderson's (1976) suggestion that the primary comparisons in equity judgements are interpersonal rather than intrapersonal, although it is far short of being a proof of his formulation.

Although the terms are sometimes used interchangeably, the deservedness of the victim should be distinguished from the victim's need for help. Deservedness seems to be more appropriately construed in terms of inputs rather than outcomes, in that it depends on the victim's attributes and previous behaviour, i.e. on why he or she comes to be in need of help. A 'good' person, who has not acted selfishly or carelessly, may be seen to be entitled to better outcomes, and hence more help if in distress, than a 'bad' person who appears to be responsible for his or her own misfortunes. This again may imply an interpersonal comparison, in that would-be helpers may consider their own attributes and entitlement to their relatively happy position. The less deserving they consider the victim to be in comparison to themselves, the less obliged will they feel to help the victim out of considerations of equity. Granted a tendency for individuals to over-evaluate their own relative inputs, therefore the principle of equity may frequently serve as a justification for self-interested, as well as altruistic, behaviour.

Limits to social obligations – the 'just world' hypothesis

Emphasis on individuals' perception of their own inputs and entitlements is central to a version of equity theory, proposed by Lerner (1970; Lerner, Miller and Holmes, 1976), referred to as the 'just world' hypothesis. In contrast to the attempts by writers such as Anderson (1976) and Walster *et al.* (1976) to formulate the notions of equity and inequity in more precise mathematical terms, Lerner's approach is more 'broad brush', highlighting paradoxes in the definition of the principle itself.

An individual is assumed to develop a sense of deserving and justice during socialization and in so doing makes a 'personal contract':

> to orient himself to the world on the basis of what he earns or deserves via his prior investments rather than on the basis of what he can get at any given

moment. He learns and trusts that his world is a place where additional investments often entitle him to better outcomes, and that 'earning' or 'deserving' is an effective way of obtaining what he desires. (Lerner *et al.*, 1976: 135)

This notion, highly reminiscent of the 'Protestant Ethic' (Weber, 1958) has implications for how a person will evaluate others also, since: 'We want to believe we live in a world where people get what they deserve or, rather, deserve what they get' (Lerner, 1970: 207).

This belief in a 'just world' is threatened, however, whenever individuals come across others in greater need than themselves who clearly do not deserve their misfortunes. One possibility, directly predicted by other equity theorists (e.g. Walster *et al.*, 1976), is that they will attempt to remove the inequity by compensating those in need. They thus may give donations to charity, pay taxes to support welfare services, do voluntary work in their spare time, and so on. However, as Lerner rightly emphasizes, while such altruistic acts might discharge one's social obligation, they rarely go very far towards removing the inequality of outcomes. To prepare a positive self-evaluation in the face of evident injustice, Lerner suggests a form of social comparison, based on the principle: 'I deserve what others who are like me have' (Lerner *et al.*, 1976). Basically, this is analogous to the problem of relevance of judgemental standards, which were considered in Chapter 5 (see p. 128). Judgements of stimuli may be influenced by the presence of qualitatively similiar, but not dissimilar, standards (Brown, 1953). Knowledge of the plight of starving millions in a far-off country may thus have less impact on the level of outcomes to which one feels personally entitled than extremely minor discrepancies in salary or possessions that may differentiate one from one's neighbours or colleagues. Unilateral altruism is thus likely to reduce one's outcomes to below those of others whom one has chosen as relevant standards for social comparison, so that a demand for such altruism, even if justified by the needs of the victim, would appear 'unfair' – unless, that is, it was also addressed to others like oneself. If others like oneself also answered the appeal, even quite large sacrifices might be tolerable if the individuals who made them did not feel that they were thereby depriving themselves or their dependants below the level enjoyed by comparable others, that is to say, below their comparison level.

The aspect of appeals for help that can be most threatening to the person's concept of a 'just world' is their potential open-endedness. Once we have admitted the entitlement of one victim to receive help, how can we then deny help to another, no less deserving? One way in which it may be possible to elicit higher levels of altruism, therefore, is if we can define the situation as one in which our altruism would not imply any such open-ended commitment. This may be achieved if the appeal for help is presented under the guise of a trade or exchange, or more generally in situations where we can feel that we are gaining some positive outcomes, which may partially compensate for the help we have given. Answering such appeals does not imply a commitment to answer other appeals where one gets nothing in return.

These notions were explored in an experiment by Holmes, Miller and Lerner (cited by Lerner *et al.*, 1976: 151–2). The experimenters approached students on a university campus, offering candles for sale as part of a supposed fund-raising activity on behalf of either a deserving, or less deserving, cause (respectively, handicapped children or a children's sports team). The candles were offered for $3 each, and subjects were told that $1 of this would go to the cause in question. They were also told that the candles sold for $2, $3, or $4 in most stores.

Subjects showed little interest in buying the candles to help the less deserving cause. (Incidentally, it was not the Christmas season.) On the other hand, more than half of those approached were prepared to buy the candles to help the handicapped children, provided they were told that they would be getting the candles at a fair or bargain price. In these conditions, they were able to respond to the perceived need of the handicapped children without taking action which implied that the children had an unqualified claim upon their resources. They could act as though they were simply making a fair economic transaction. Far fewer subjects were prepared to buy the candles if they were given to believe that they would be paying more than the candles were worth.

People's willingness to improve others' outcomes at their own expense may also be inhibited by normative factors relating to what Lerner and Lichtman (1968) refer to as 'justified self-interest'. These 'imply equal opportunity and risk among the participants as well as the pursuit of self-interest within the rules of what is fair and equal' (p. 226). Running counter to these are other norms which may be elicited by a plea for special help or consideration ('the participant confesses he is not able to compete on an equal basis', p. 226), or by an intentionally gracious act ('It is possible for a participant clearly and openly to refuse to profit from a fortuitous opportunity and at the same time to establish the expectation that . . . the other competitors should not take advantage of any fortuitous opportunities which may become available to them', pp. 226–7).

Lerner and Lichtman (1968) conducted their study on pairs of female students who had volunteered for a learning experiment. On arrival, subjects were told that one of them, depending on a draw, would be in a condition in which she would receive electric shocks which would be 'painful', but would cause no 'permanent damage', whereas the other would receive no shocks. Subjects then drew numbers to determine who would have the choice of condition, and were taken to separate cubicles before being told the outcome of the draw. The experimenter then informed each subject individually about the supposed outcome of the draw.

In a 'justified self-interest' condition, each subject was told that she had won the draw and could choose the condition she preferred. Naturally, if she chose the control condition, the other subject would supposedly be put in the shock condition. Only 9 per cent of these subjects chose the shock condition for themselves. This was compared with four other conditions. A 'gracious-act' condition involved the subject being told that her partner had won the draw, but asking for the choice to be given to the subject instead. Here 88 per cent of the subjects chose the shock condition for themselves. A 'plea-for-help' condition, in which the subject was told that her partner was really scared about the shocks, led to 72 per cent of the subjects choosing the shocks for themselves. An 'illicit-gracious-act' condition was designed so that the partner's 'gracious act' appeared to be a piece of manipulative calculation, and here only 22 per cent chose the shock condition. Finally, an 'illicit-plea-for-help' condition involved the experimenter arbitrarily over-ruling the draw, and putting the partner, who seemed 'really scared', into the control condition. Subjects were offered the right to object to being put into the shock condition, but 86 per cent acquiesced. However, when asked to rate their partner, subjects gave far more negative evaluations in this condition than in any of the other four.

In a replication of this study using male students, Lerner (1971) found that subjects were almost as likely to choose the shock as the control condition for themselves under 'justified self-interest' instructions. Presumably, Lerner argues, it was not appropriate for men to use the wish to avoid pain as a justification for causing another person to suffer. However, when the control condition was rendered even more attractive by turning it into a positive reinforcement condition, involving the chance of considerable monetary reward, the principle of justified self-interest reasserted itself.

The quite remarkable variations in choice rates in the Lerner and Lichtman study (1968) testify to the influence that norms of fairness and justice have on both 'altruistic' and 'selfish' behaviour. In some situations, it is culturally defined as fair and equitable for one person to preserve or improve his or her own outcomes at another's expense. In other situations it is not. The results just described provide some indications of how such situations might be discriminated. The important contribution of equity theory in this context is thus the demonstration that classes of behaviour which might be viewed as complete opposites of each other may be accounted for within a common framework. These results also give further support to the generalization that some of the most powerful manipulations employed in experimental social psychology are those that influence subjects' interpretations of the experimental situation through increasing the salience of specific extra-experimental norms and values.

Justification and derogation

So far, I have concentrated on responses to perceived inequity that take the form of redistribution of outcomes. In other words, subjects have been placed in situations where they have been given the opportunity to intervene on behalf of the victim, or to compensate the victim through donations or other favours, or through turning down the chance to increase their own outcomes at the victim's expense. The importance of the perceived need or deservedness of the victim, however, stresses the fact that equity theory is concerned not only with interpersonal comparisons of outcomes, but also with how people will evaluate others' inputs in comparison to their own. An unequal distribution of outcomes may thus be seen as equitable if those with lower outcomes contributed lower inputs – if, in other words, victims deserved their misfortunes, either through defects of character, errors of judgement, or reproachable behaviour. As Walster *et al.* (1976) have hypothesized: 'Harmdoers tend either to compensate their victims (and so restore actual equity) or to justify the victim's deprivation (and so restore psychological equity). Harmdoers rarely use both techniques in concert; compensation and justification seem to be alternative, rather than supplementary, techniques for restoring equity' (p. 12).

It should be stressed that this prediction concerns the reactions of people who have actually harmed another individual. From this point of view, there is no particular need for the 'just world' hypothesis, over and above notions such as dissonance reduction and defensive attribution (Shaver, 1970a). Presumably the cognition that one has inequitably harmed another person is dissonance-arousing. If this is so, then dissonance may be reduced by either making amends through compensation or denying one's own responsibility for the harm done, and instead attributing responsibility to the victim, through either blame or derogation. Walster and Prestholdt (1966), for instance, led trainee social workers to harm their clients inadvertently, and then gave them the chance to volunteer to help their clients in their free time. The more positively subjects evaluated their clients, the more time they were prepared to volunteer. Derogation could thus be a technique for justifying the original harmful act and the failure to offer compensation.

Whereas such results are unsurprising in view of the weight of experimental evidence and everyday knowledge which points to the importance of processes of self-justification, the predictions derived from the 'just world' hypothesis are less obvious. What should matter, in terms of Lerner's approach, is not that one has oneself harmed another person, but that an unjust incident has occurred. If a victim has been harmed inequitably, this is offensive to one's belief in a just world, regardless of the identity of the perpetrator. Observers should be as likely to derogate victims whom they cannot compensate as are the inadvertent perpetrators of the harm which the victims suffer. Lerner (1970) also proposes that there is a kind of 'trade-off' function between attributing responsibility to a victim ('It was his own fault') and derogation ('He's such a nasty person that he deserved to have it happen to him'). Derogation should thus be negatively related to blame, as well as to compensation. Similarly, positive outcomes may be justified by reference to a person's efforts, or attractiveness, but not both.

In support of the 'just world' position, there is evidence that observers will rate the recipients of fortuitous rewards as deserving their good fortune by virtue of their task performance, or as being generally more attractive. Even here, though, rated attractiveness and entitlement to rewards tend, if anything, to be positively related (Lerner, 1965; Apsler and Friedman, 1975). The reactions of observers to victims of misfortune, however, present a varied picture. Jones and Aronson (1973) presented male and female students with written accounts of a rape case, and then asked them to recommend a sentence for the convicted rapist, and to say how much they considered the crime to be the victim's fault. Varied details in the case accounts informed subjects that the victim was either a divorcee, a married woman, or a virgin. More fault was attributed to the victim when she was a divorcee than when she was married, or a virgin.

This result was interpreted as consistent with the 'just world' hypothesis, on the assumption that divorcees are less respectable than married women or virgins (which is itself a revealing assumption from a 'just world' perspective). It seems that subjects were less willing to accept that chance catastrophes happen to good or respectable people, since this would imply that they themselves (as good and respectable people, of course) might also be vulnerable to disasters beyond their control. To be able to see the rape as at least partly the victim's fault allows one to retain the belief that bad things don't 'just happen' to good people if they behave correctly. Such an attribution thus restores one's feeling of personal control over one's environment and with it one's sense of relative security. No such attribution is needed, on the other hand, when the victim is less respectable, in that it is seen as less offensive to notions of justice for bad things to happen to bad people, even if they are in no way responsible. However, Jones and Aronson (1973) still found that lighter sentences were recommended when the victim was a divorcee. If punishment of the rapist can be interpreted as a kind of compensation for the victim, these results do not support the Walster *et al.* (1976) prediction that compensation and justification (in this case, through attribution of responsibility) should be inversely related.

Probably the most influential study in this field is that by Lerner and Simmons (1966). The basic procedure of this study involved groups of female students taking part in an experiment supposedly to do with the perception of emotional cues. On arrival at the laboratory they were introduced to another 'subject' who was supposedly taking part in a learning experiment. It was explained that it had been arranged that subjects in the learning experiment should also serve as target persons for the emotional cues experiment: their performance on the learning task would be observed, as it occurred, over a closed-circuit television system by the remaining subjects. Actually, what subjects saw was a standard videotape which showed the target person apparently receiving several painful electric shocks for wrong responses.

After subjects had viewed the tape, they were given differing sets of instructions. In the 'midpoint' condition, they were told that they were now halfway through the experiment, and that, after they had made some ratings, there would be another negative reinforcement session for the same 'victim'. In the 'reward' condition, subjects were also told that there would be a second session; but they were then asked to vote on whether the victim should continue in the negative reinforcement condition, or be transferred to a control or a reward condition for the second session. The experimenter then announced that the group had chosen the reward condition for the victim, and then asked them to give their ratings. In the 'reward-decision' condition, the procedure was identical, except that subjects gave their ratings before the experimenter told them of the outcome of the vote. (Almost all subjects did in fact vote for the second session to be a reward treatment.)

In the 'end-point' condition, subjects were told that the learning experiment was now over, and no mention was made of a second session. In the 'past-event' condition, subjects were told that what they would see would in fact be a videotape of someone who had been shocked in the past. They were given an opportunity to meet the victim to determine that she was now fine and had been paid for her participation. Finally, in the 'martyr' condition, the procedure was similar to that for the 'end-point' condition, except that, before the 'learning experiment' started, an argument took place between the victim and her 'experimenter' in front of the subjects, in which the victim protested against being put in the negative reinforcement condition, but then withdrew her refusal so that the subjects could receive their experimental course credits for taking part in the emotional cues experiment. After subjects had given their ratings, following what they believed to be the first or only session, the experiment was terminated.

The task required of the subjects in each condition was to rate the victim on a number of scales. The main dependent variable was a composite measure of the perceived attractiveness of the victim, minus the subject's self-ratings, and negative scores were taken as a sign of derogation. The means for each condition were: 'midpoint' −26, 'reward' −5, 'reward decision' −25, 'end-point' −13, 'past event' −11, and 'martyr' −34, compared with a maximum possible derogation score of −120.

With the exception of the 'martyr' condition, these results show that the victim was derogated less in conditions where her suffering was at an end than when subjects believed it would continue ('midpoint') or could continue ('reward decision'). Most derogation, however, occurred in the 'martyr' condition, and Lerner and Simmons (1966) regard this as particularly strong vindication of the 'just-world' hypothesis: 'the suffering of someone who has acted out of altruistic motives should be most threatening to the belief in a just world. If this is true, then the observer should reject the willing martyr even more than the innocent victim' (p. 205).

As has been pointed out, the 'just world' hypothesis predicts derogation of victims by observers, and not just by perpetrators, of injustice. Subsequent research, as well as critiques of the Lerner and Simmons (1966) study, have questioned whether derogation in fact occurs, other than in conditions where the subjects (observers) feel that they are in some way responsible for the victim's suffering. Subjects in the 'martyr' condition might have felt particularly responsible, since the victim explicitly chose to go on with the experiment so that they could obtain their experimental credits. As was seen, this was the condition in which most derogation occurred. Some feelings of responsibility might still have been present among subjects in the other conditions, however, since the 'emotional-cues' experiment still required the victim to serve as a target person.

Lerner and Matthews (1967) in fact manipulated personal responsibility using a modification of the Lerner and Lichtman (1968) procedure, involving a rigged draw to determine whether the subject or her partner was put in the shock condition of a learning experiment. The crucial comparison was between a condition where the subject drew before her partner, with the result that she was in a control or reward condition while her partner was in the shock condition, and a condition where her partner drew first, drawing the shock condition for herself and leaving the control or reward condition for the subject. Apparently, the order of the draw was sufficient to produce an illusion of differential responsibility. The results showed derogation of the partner (compared with ratings of the 'average college student') in the former but not the latter condition.

Lerner and Matthews (1967) interpret these results as consistent with the 'just world' hypothesis, on the grounds that blame and derogation should be inversely related to each other. If one can point to something the victim did which led to her suffering, one does not need to derogate her as a person. Apparently, when the victim had supposedly drawn first and put herself in the shock condition, she 'was perceived as responsible for her own suffering, and the subject's need to believe in a just world was not threatened' (p. 324). On the other hand, an equally plausible interpretation of these data is that one only derogates victims if one feels oneself to be in some way responsible for their suffering.

A number of studies have attempted to define the limiting conditions of victim derogation through modified replications of the Lerner and Simmons (1966) experiment. Aderman, Brehm and Katz (1974) showed female students a ten-minute videotape of a victim receiving shocks as part of a negative reinforcement learning experiment. Derogation occurred when subjects were instructed to 'watch' or 'observe' the victim (as in the Lerner and Simmons experiment), but not when they were told to imagine how they would feel if they were the victim.

Sorrentino and Boutelier (1974) had subjects observe a victim suffering under a negative reinforcement schedule in either a 'similar-fate' condition, in which they believed they might have to undergo the same experience, or a 'dissimilar-fate' condition, when they knew they would not. The victim was rated as more attractive than 'the average university student' in the 'similar-fate' condition, but was derogated in the 'dissimilar-fate' condition. This difference was only significant, however, among subjects who regarded the experiment as unfair. This last finding is somewhat troublesome for the 'just world' hypothesis. The unfair suffering of another person would offend one's notions of a 'just world' more than suffering which is perceived as fair, and so should lead to more derogation. Once derogation has occurred, however, presumably there is less need to see the situation as unfair. Also, such unfair suffering should be particularly threatening to one's belief in a 'just world' if one anticipated the possibility of a similar fate oneself. Yet subjects in the 'similar-fate' condition did not derogate the victim – presumably because this would imply the potential derogation of themselves.

Very similar conclusions were reached by Chaikin and Darley (1973), who had pairs of male students view a videotape of what was supposedly a previous trial of an experiment in which they would be participating later. The tape showed two students acting as a 'worker–supervisor team' on a communication task which required the worker to build several stacks of blocks according to the supervisor's instructions. The worker's output was measured by the number of blocks stacked. At the end of the session, the supervisor accidentally knocked over the worker's blocks as he stood up. This had either mild consequences for the worker (he could be compensated), or severe consequences (he could not). Half the subjects were told that they would later be taking the part of the supervisor, and half that they would be taking that of the worker.

Derogation of the worker was shown only by future supervisors when the consequences were severe. Future workers saw the supervisor as clearly responsible for the accident, particularly when the consequences were severe. Chaikin and Darley (1973) interpret their data as evidence of defensive attribution, rather than as support for the 'just world' hypothesis, arguing that individuals are more concerned with making attributions for harmful accidents so as to avoid seeing themselves as potentially responsible for any similar mishap, than they are with defending any belief that the world is 'just'.

Such results lead one to ask what kind of attributions might have been made by subjects in the different conditions of the Lerner and Simmons (1966) study. Was the learner in fact seen as an 'innocent victim', or as someone who was responsible for her own suffering because of her poor performance on the learning task? Did subjects see themselves as mere 'observers', or did they feel responsible for the learner's suffering, in that she had to go through this procedure so that they could complete their own experiment? Piliavin, Hardyck and Vadum (1967) failed to find derogation of the victim in a replication of the Lerner and Simmons 'midpoint' condition, as compared with the 'end-point' condition, when subjects were informed that the machine controlling the shocks had been wrongly pro-grammed, so that the victim was completely helpless, and unable to avoid the shocks even by giving correct responses. This situation should of course be even more threatening to one's belief in a 'just world'. On the other hand, it poses no problems from a defensive attribution point of view, since the experimental equipment was clearly to blame, and so no responsibility need be attached to either observers or victim.

Similarly, comparing the effects of the Lerner and Simmons 'midpoint' and 'past-event' conditions under different experimental instructions, Simons and Piliavin (1972) found evidence of relative derogation in the 'midpoint' condition only, as in the original study, when subjects were kept in ignorance of the true purpose of the experiment, and of the fact that the victim was only pretending to be shocked. When told that the purpose of the experiment was to study reactions to victims of misfortune, subjects did not derogate the victim, regardless of whether or not they were told that the shocks were only simulated. Apparently, seeing the learner as a 'victim of misfortune' was enough to inhibit derogation. The concept of 'misfortune' seems to invoke a different kind of attributional set from that which is required for victim derogation.

Even more directly, Cialdini, Kenrick and Hoerig (1976) have argued that victim derogation by observers in the Lerner and Simmons (1966) paradigm is not due to a wish to restore their belief in a 'just world', but is instead a means of justifying their complicity in the victim's suffering. 'After all, they discover themselves to be willing and nonprotesting participants in a procedure that seems to involve the instigation of another's suffering' (pp. 719–20). Cialdini *et al.* therefore replicated the 'midpoint' condition with the Lerner and Simmons instructions, and also with these instructions modified to reduce subjects' perceived complicity. Subjects in this latter condition were told that the learning experiment they would be viewing was taking place in another department, that it had been going on for some time but had only recently come to the attention of the experimenters running the 'emotional-cues' study, and that these experimenters, and the psychology department generally, were relatively unfamiliar with the procedures involved. Orthogonally with this manipulation, half the subjects observed the learner undergoing a shock schedule, and half saw her perform under a schedule involving no shocks. The prediction derived from the 'just world' hypothesis, for derogation of the learner in the 'shock' but not in the 'no-shock' condition, was supported only under the original instructions, when subjects could have felt in some way responsible for the victim's fate.

The assumption of a trade-off function between derogation and compen-sation also requires some qualification in the light of a study by Kenrick, Reich and Cialdini (1976). They used a modification of the Lerner and Simmons 'midpoint' condition, with half the subjects seeing the learner receive shocks for incorrect responses on a serial learning task, and half seeing her receive no shocks (errors instead being identified by a buzzer). Half the subjects then made evaluative ratings of the learner, and then were asked to vote on how much compensation (from 50c. to $5) she should receive 'for her effort'. The remaining subjects were given the opportunity to compensate the learner before rating her. Derogation occurred in the 'shock' and not in the 'no-shock' condition, but was far less marked when subjects made their ratings after voting for compensation. This suggests that compensation does, indeed, inhibit derogation. However, the reverse relationship did not hold. Subjects voted for about $4.50 compensation for the learner in the 'shock' condition (as compared with about $3 in the 'no-shock' condition) regardless of whether they had already rated her. Within the 'shock' condition, there was no correlation ($r=0.02$) between compensation and evaluation for subjects who gave their ratings first, but there was a strong correlation ($r=0.81$) when they gave their ratings after compensating the victim.

On balance, therefore, there seems little evidence for the more 'non-obvious' predictions from the 'just world' hypothesis. It does indeed seem to be the case that the perception of inequity has important implications for both social interaction and social cognition. If inequity cannot be removed by redistribution or compensation, some kind of 'cognitive work' will ensue to find a justification. When people receive unjustified rewards, there is some limited evidence that observers will still try to see their good fortune as earned or deserved, although it seems unlikely that this would apply to all kinds of windfalls. On the other hand, there seems to be no real evidence that observers will derogate innocent victims except when they feel in some way responsible for their fate.

If one does indeed believe the world to be a just place, then the suffering of others is undoubtedly distressing and threatening. Even without such a 'world view', however, one does not wish to see the suffering of others left unexplained, since what is unexplained is also less predictable. Observers, therefore, seem prepared to undertake an attributional inquiry until they can find a cause or culpable agent for the victims' suffering. In some cases, observers might blame the victim's own judgement – they should have been more careful, but it was a mistake anyone might make – but such an attribution places relatively little emphasis on the personal distinctiveness of the victim's behaviour and hence stops short of derogation of their character. But suppose one feels oneself to be responsible for the victim's suffering, even if only indirectly? In a sense, the attributional inquiry has been completed but its recommendations have been vetoed. As a just person, one cannot possibly see oneself as responsible for the unjust suffering of another individual. Either someone or something else must be responsible, or the suffering itself has to be seen as justified by the kind of person the victim really is. For a good person to do harm to a bad person, in terms of balance theory or any of its derivatives, is cognitively more acceptable than for a good person to do harm to a good person. It appears, therefore, that when derogation occurs, this is not necessarily due to a belief in a 'just world', but rather to a belief in a 'just self'.

Lerner's theory, and the empirical research derived from it, thus highlights the potentially self-serving nature of the application of moral principles. What is special about just world beliefs is that they offer justifications for personal attitudes and behaviour by appeal to factors and values *external to the self*. This involves notions of attribution of cause and responsibility at least as much as those of dissonance or inconsistency reduction. As Lerner (1980: 180) emphasizes:

> people can justify causing others to suffer if they can locate the 'cause' of their acts within a set of norms which assumes that all people have a right, a need, to look out for themselves regardless of the cost to others (who are presumably doing the same thing).

The norm of justified self-interest and the process of victim derogation point to a central paradox in the just world theory: people do not *simply* believe the world is just; they also accept the existence of injustice. Nor does this inconsistency necessarily lead to cognitive change, *except when they personally feel held to account* for such injustice. What is more, even when cognitive change *does* occur, it does not necessarily take the form of a *resolution* of the inconsistency, so much as of an isolation or insulation of the potentially contradictory elements from one another, so that they are not considered in terms of a common frame of reference.

As Lerner (1980: 180) goes on to say:

> I can *ignore* the considerations of what I do to you, or fail to do to you, as I pursue my own interests, as long as I can locate the basis of my actions within this normative context. (emphasis added)

As we shall see, this may be one of the most important aspects of norms and role-definitions: they do not simply guide our behaviour but also the *cognitions* we have about our behaviour. They distinguish the 'relevant' aspects of our behaviour to which we need to attend from the 'irrelevant' aspects we are entitled to ignore.

Obedience

In the studies on victim derogation just described, subjects have typically been asked to make attributions after they have observed the victim's suffering, with the expectation that it has now finished, and nothing can be done about it, or alternatively that the suffering will continue in a later session. Depending upon the conditions, subjects appear to feel some measure of responsibility, even though they themselves do not administer the electric shocks which the victim receives. Even in the Lerner and

Lichtman (1968) study, where subjects chose to assign their partner to the shock condition, they did not actually administer the shocks themselves. They merely put her into a condition where she would receive shocks from the experimenter, if she made errors. Once the 'learning experiment' was under way, the subject, however remorseful, was a helpless observer. The focus of Milgram's (1963, 1964, 1974) research, however, has been on identifying the conditions under which subjects will obey an instruction knowingly to inflict pain, and possibly physical damage, on another individual.

A part at least, of the political significance of this question is all too obvious. In war, ordinary soldiers will obey orders which will lead to the death or injury of enemy combatants and civilians. Under oppressive regimes, ordinary officials will condemn citizens of an 'undesirable' race or political persuasion to death, torture, or imprisonment. Such acts, when revealed, are often 'justified' in terms of some supposedly noble ideal, such as preservation of national security, racial identity, law and order, democracy, the revolution, civilization and so on and so forth. The invocation of such value-laden concepts is the cornerstone of political propaganda, of whatever orientation, and it enables ordinary citizens of the states concerned to 'sleep soundly in their beds' reassured that Right, however, defined, is on their side. But what of the individuals who actually carry out the acts of cruelty or carnage? One possibility is that they are sadists of dubious sanity who deliberately choose the role of executioner or torturer, or who are deliberately recruited by some government agency wishing to capitalize on their perversions. No doubt such individuals exist, and may occasionally be thrown into prominence. To attribute the generality of institutionalized cruelty to such individual perversions, however, is no more persuasive or illuminating than attempts to reduce the causes of group conflict to the irrational motives or drives of individuals (Billig, 1976).

The alternative viewpoint, favoured by Milgram, is that most acts of inhumanity are in fact carried out by quite ordinary people, who are simply doing their job. Their role, as defined within a political or organizational system, or a military command structure, is perceived to oblige them to carry out instructions received from higher up the hierarchy. It is not their place to question the decision of their 'superiors'. Disobedience, within such organizations, carries its own penalties, which may well be severe, but such penalties may not be absolutely necessary for authority to be obeyed. Milgram's studies claim to demonstrate 'obedience that is willingly assumed in the absence of threat of any sort, obedience that is maintained through the simple assertion by authority that it has the right to exercise control over the person' (Milgram, 1974: xiii).

Milgram's basic procedure is as follows: two people come to the laboratory to take part in a study which, the experimenter explains, is concerned with the effects of punishment on learning. One of them is assigned the role of the 'learner' and the other that of the 'teacher'. The learner is taken into a room and, watched by the teacher, is strapped into a chair and an electrode is attached to his wrist. He is told that his task is to learn a list of word pairs, and that any errors he makes will be punished by the teacher with electric shocks of increasing intensity.

The learner is then seated (usually in another room) in front of a simulated shock generator with a row of 30 switches, ranging from 15 volts to 450 volts in 15-volt increments. The switches also bear verbal labels from 'slight shock' to 'danger – severe shock'. When the learner responds correctly, the teacher goes on to the next item in the test, but when the learner makes a mistake, the teacher is supposed to give him an electric shock, starting with the lowest voltage, but increasing the voltage level by 15 volts with each further error. In fact, only the teacher is a genuine subject. The learner is a paid actor, who deliberately makes errors so that the teacher is put in the position of having either to administer the shocks or to disobey the experimenter. Unknown to the teacher, no shocks are felt by the learner.

Of crucial importance are the learner's reactions to the shocks, which are coordinated with the supposed levels. Thus, in the condition described by Milgram (1974: 23), the learner indicated no discomfort below 75 volts; shocks from 75 to 105 volts produced grunts; 120 volts produced a shout of complaint; 135 volts a painful groan; and 150 volts a demand to be released from the experiment. Such demands and painful groans persisted with rising intensity until 300 volts, when the learner shouted desperately that he refused to provide any more answers to the test. The teacher would then usually turn to the experimenter for guidance, and would be told to treat the absence of a response as a wrong answer, and continue to administer shocks with increasing intensity. The 315-volt shock produced a violent scream and a repeated refusal to give more responses, and after 330 volts, the learner remained silent and gave no responses to the test items.

While this was going on, the subject would frequently turn to the experimenter to ask whether he should continue, or to say that he did not wish to. The experimenter responded to such queries or protests with a series of standard 'prods', as follows: 'Please continue' or 'Please go on'; 'The experiment requires that you continue', 'It is absolutely essential that you continue'; 'You have no other choice, you must go on'. If the subject expressed concern about possible injury to the learner, this sequence started with, 'Although the shocks may be painful, there is no permanent tissue damage, so please go on.' If the subject pointed to the learner's unwillingness to continue, the experimenter responded, 'Whether the learner likes it or not you must go on until he has learned all the word pairs correctly. So please go on.' If, in spite of these 'prods', the subject insisted that he was not going to administer any more shocks to the learner, his refusal was accepted, and he was then debriefed and allowed to meet the learner again, who, of course, was perfectly well and in good spirits.

Milgram (1974) starts by reporting, not subjects' actual behaviour, but the predictions made by three groups (psychiatrists, college students and middle-class males) as to how far they themselves would go if they had to serve as 'teachers'. All these subjects predicted that they would defy the experimenter and refuse to administer shocks beyond a given level. The modal break-off point was around 150 volts, and no subjects were prepared to say that they would go beyond 300 volts. These predictions were in marked contrast to the levels of obedience observed among real subjects, recruited from adult male members of the general public who responded to an advertisement in a local newspaper. In the standard condition already described, 62.5 per cent of subjects obeyed the experimenter all the way through to the maximum shock level of 450 volts, and none showed defiance before the 135-volt level. The results were even more chilling in a 'remote' condition, in which there was no vocal feedback from the learner, but in which he was heard to pound the laboratory walls in protest at 300 volts, falling silent after 315 volts. Here 65 per cent of subjects showed complete obedience, and no subject broke off before the 300-volt level. Complete obedience was reduced to 40 per cent in a 'proximity' condition in which the subject could not only hear the learner, but see him also, as he was seated in the same room. A 'touch-proximity' condition was also run, which involved the teacher having to hold the learner's hand down onto the electric shock plate. As might be imagined, this condition produced lower levels of compliance, but nonetheless 30 per cent of subjects still obeyed right through to the maximum shock level. Of those who disobeyed the experimenter in this condition, most did so at 150 volts, which was the point at which the learner demanded to be let free and refused to leave his hand on the shock plate, and at which the experimenter told the teacher to keep the learner's hand in position by force.

A series of modified replications was then conducted. A new base-line condition was run, in which the learner asked the experimenter before the session started whether the shocks were dangerous, as he had 'a slight heart condition'. The experimenter then replied, 'in a confident, somewhat dismissive tone that although the shocks may be painful, they cause no permanent tissue damage' (p. 56). The vocal feedback from the learner during the experiment was also modified to contain references to this heart condition ('My heart's bothering me'). A less elegant room was also used as the laboratory. In spite of these modifications, 65 per cent of subjects were completely obedient.

Women were also used as subjects in the base-line condition, though with a male experimenter and learner. Again 65 per cent showed complete obedience, although Milgram refers to certain stylistic differences in their behaviour during the session and post-experimental interview. Many more women than men 'related their experience to problems of rearing children' (p. 63). Additional manipulations were introduced to remove some of the experimenter's authority. If the experimenter no longer remained in the same room as the teacher, but instead gave his instructions by telephone, the number of completely compliant subjects dropped sharply to 22.5 per cent. Rather more (40 per cent) remained obedient throughout in a variation of the base-line condition, which involved the learner stating at the outset (when signing a release form absolving the university from legal liability): 'I'll agree to be in it, but only on condition that you let me out when I say so; that's the only condition.'

A particularly important variation sought to divest the experimenter of the prestige and respectability of Yale University, by conducting the study in a nearby industrial city 'in a three-room office suite in a somewhat rundown commercial building located in the downtown shopping area' (p. 68) in the name of a fictitious organization called Research Associates of Bridgeport. The reduction in compliance was very slight. Although 5 per cent refused to administer any shocks at all, 47.5 per cent remained completely obedient. These results contrast sharply with those in a condition in which subjects were free to choose the level of shock they wanted to administer to the learner on any trial. With the requirement of escalation removed, only 1 subject out of 40 went as high as the 450-volt maximum, another went to 375 volts, but the remaining 38 gave shocks of 150 volts or below.

Further conditions were introduced to try to reduce compliance by putting the subject in situations where his obligation to complete the experiment conflicted with his acceptance of the experimenter's authority. In one condition, the learner insisted, at 150 volts, that he wanted to go on, even though the shocks were painful. However, the experimenter instructed the teacher to break off the experiment regardless, and all subjects indeed did so at this point. Another variation involved the experimenter taking on the role of the learner, while a third person, supposedly another subject, took on the experimenter's role, instructing the teacher to continue. All subjects in this condition broke off at 150 volts, when the experimenter, in the role of the learner, demanded to be let out, even though the 'ordinary man' who had been told to give them orders instructed them to continue. When two confederates were used, so that the teacher received his orders from an 'ordinary man' with the experimenter out of the room, and with the learner also being an 'ordinary man' recruited like himself, only 20 per cent continued to the maximum shock level. However, of those who disobeyed their instructor at some point, fewer than one in three interfered with his taking over their role as teacher and administering the shocks himself up to the maximum level. When two experimenters instructed the teacher, with the learner supposedly being another subject, but gave contradictory instructions when the learner protested, all subjects refused to proceed beyond 165 volts. When two experimenters were used, and one took the role of the learner, 65 per cent of subjects remained completely obedient to the experimenter who instructed them to continue. When subjects did not have to administer the shocks themselves, but instead fulfilled a subsidiary role while another 'subject' did so, only 7.5 per cent interfered to stop the experimenter continuing. However, if the teacher was required to administer the shocks with the assistance of two other 'subjects' who rebelled against the experimenter and refused to carry on, obedience to the experimenter was considerably reduced: 62.5 per cent broke off at, or before, the 210-volt level, but 10 per cent remained obedient to the experimenter throughout.

Roles and responsibility

Milgram's results are certainly some of the most challenging and provocative in experimental social psychology. At their face value, they imply that individuals will perform actions that appear to severely hurt an innocent person, who has been recruited in the same way as themselves, even to the point of possibly precipitating a heart attack, for no better reason than because the experimenter told them to do so. Somehow, the experimenter is accepted as a legitimate authority who can command behaviour which, in almost any context, would be regarded as offensive and immoral. In addition to giving commands, the experimenter defines the situation for the subject. 'There is a propensity for people to accept definitions of action provided by legitimate authority. That is, although the subject performs the action, he allows authority to define its meaning' (Milgram, 1974: 145). Milgram interprets his results as showing that the subject takes on the role of an 'agent' so that he 'feels responsible to the authority directing him but feels no responsibility for the content of the actions that the authority prescribes' (p. 145–6). The notion of perceived responsibility is thus central to Milgram's analysis. Subjects may be deeply concerned and distressed about the possible consequences of their actions for the victim, but they do not tend to see these actions as *their* actions, in the sense of being their responsibility.

Evidence of the harmful consequences for the victim of their performance of their role as 'agents' is said to produce 'strain', which may lead some of the subjects to disobey, i.e. to refuse to be 'agents' any more. Such an act of refusal, however, is not undertaken lightly. It involves the subject breaking his or her initial promise to help the experimenter, and offering a personal affront to the experimenter by negating his definition of the situation. 'The experimental situation is so constructed that there is no way the subject can stop shocking the learner without violating the experimenter's self-defini-tion' (p. 150). As Milgram points out, in terms of Goffman's (1959) approach, there is a 'moral demand' or social obligation, on individuals to respect each other's self-definitions.

It is nonetheless fair to say that the weight of Milgram's contribution has been empirical, rather than more broadly theoretical. The notion of perceived responsibility is emphasized, but is not related to the wider literature on attribution processes. Explanations based upon assumptions of aggressive instincts are mentioned but quickly dismissed. Milgram presents his findings as evidence that ordinary people will tend to carry out 'immoral' orders if they perceive their roles as requiring them to do so, and apart from identifying certain limiting conditions and drawing comparisons with real-life atrocities, he seems content to let his experiments speak for themselves. This interpretation, however, has not gone unchallenged.

An extensive critique of Milgram's research has been published by Mixon (1972). Mixon's thesis seems to contain three distinct, but purportedly related, themes: a general metatheoretical argument concerning the nature of explanation and investigation in social psychology; a more methodological part involving the advocacy of a particular role-playing technique as an alternative to experimental deception; and a more speculative, but nonetheless more directly relevant, reinterpretation of Milgram's results.

The general metatheoretical position adopted by Mixon is shared by Harré and Secord (1972). Central to this position is a distinction between 'role/rule governed behaviour' and 'performance' within a given role/rule context. It is argued that an understanding of social interaction requires consideration not only of differences in performance, but also of the roles and rules which apply to the interaction and provide the context within which individuals may differ stylistically in performing the roles which they adopt. It is alleged that psychology has traditionally been concerned only with 'the effects of treatments on performance within a single role/rule context – that of the psychological experiment' (Mixon, 1972: 168), and has ignored the roles and rules which define the social context of such performance.

To imply that the role of the experimental subject is the same in all psychological experiments is, however, a gross over-simplification. Mostly the experimenter gives instructions to the subjects and the subjects attempt to carry them out, but this does not necessarily entail that the subjects see themselves in a subservient or inferior role. In experiments on recognition and recall, or on visual and auditory discrimination, the ground rules of the encounter imply that the experimenter is deliberately trying to stretch the subject's cognitive and perceptual abilities to their limit. Similarly in studies of communication accuracy (e.g. Mehrabian and Reed, 1968), the experimenter exerts little direct control, after explaining the purpose of the task and providing the stimulus materials. Again, there are many procedures in which the subject's role comes close to that of an 'expert witness'. Many social-judgement studies involve the implicit theme that: 'We want to know what people like you think about these statements.' The subjects' extra-experimental status, be it as a pupil, student, male or female, member of a particular age, occupational, political, religious, or ethnic group, makes him or her in an important way special and respected.

It is even debatable whether, in many paradigms, a 'single role/rule context' operates across different conditions of the same experiment. What is intriguing about experimental social psychological research is the way in which individual subjects define their own roles and rules of conduct, do so differently under different treatments, but yet often do so in a manner predictable from theory. A few studies have attempted explicitly to introduce extra-experimental norms into the experimental situation, simply by varying the information given to subjects concerning the supposed purpose of the experiment (e.g. Eiser and Bhavnani, 1974; Simons and Piliavin, 1972). More generally, the implicit norms involved in most social psychological experiments, that one should behave in a way that appears to others, if not to oneself, to be reasonable, ethical and justifiable, do not appear to be the manufactured product of social psychologists, nor their sole discovery.

Milgram's general criticisms of the social psychology experiment, though, are particularly inappropriate in the case of Milgram's research. It is precisely because disobedience is 'an act uncharacteristic of laboratory behaviour' (Mixon, 1972: 169), that the experimenter–subject relationship can be used as a plausible analogue of superordinate–subordinate relationships outside the laboratory. In hierarchical social systems, disobedience may not only be uncharacteristic, it may carry severe punishments or reprimands. The presumed absence of such sanctions in the laboratory experiment makes Milgram's results all the more compelling.

The methodological part of Mixon's paper presents a distinction between 'active' and 'non-active' role-playing. Mixon argues that what typically passes for role-playing – when subjects are given an outline description of a procedure and asked to predict how they would respond – is 'non-active' and insufficiently involving. In 'active' role-playing situations, however, the subject goes through a simulation of the same procedure as a 'real' subject, and is asked to pretend that the situation is real. Using this technique, Mixon reports a number of modified replications of Milgram's basic paradigm.

The levels of pretended obedience found by Mixon were, in general, comparable to the levels of actual obedience found by Milgram, but varied as a function of the script read out by the experimenter. For instance, 'obedience' increased with more reassurance that the shocks were not dangerous. The implications of these results depend on whether one believes, as Mixon argues, that the behaviour of 'active' role-playing subjects will generally be the same as that of deceived subjects in actual experiments with the same 'script'. Unfortunately, the details of procedure given are so scanty one simply cannot tell whether Mixon's various scripts were adequate simulations of any of Milgram's conditions, and Mixon does not put their adequacy directly to the test himself by running them under Milgram-type deception procedures to compare the results.

If we set Mixon's general theoretical and methodological viewpoints to one side, his specific interpretation of Milgram's results is in fact quite simple. Subjects tend to do what experimenters tell them, however bizarre or dangerous it might appear, so long as they believe that 'safeguards are in place', that is, so long as they can maintain their initial expectation that people do not get hurt in psychological experiments. In Milgram's experiments, subjects did in fact have considerable evidence of the victim's suffering – the feedback from the victim, the voltages indicated on the shock generator, and the verbal labels (e.g. 'danger – severe shock') which explained the different voltage levels. On the other hand, this evidence was contradicted by continued reassurance from the experimenter, implying that everything was under control. Subjects were thus faced with contradictory interpretations of the situation, and their compliance or disobedience might therefore be explained on the assumption that they gave greater or less weight to the cues provided by the experimenter rather than the victim. Mixon argues that his own results support this view, since manipulations designed to vary the salience of the conflicting types of information resulted in the changes in 'obedience' that would be expected.

Attractively simple though this might be, a number of problems still remain. First, if obedient subjects attach more weight to the cues provided by the experimenter, why should this be so? Mixon assumes that subjects will have clear 'background expectations' about what happens in experiments, but it will be remembered that Milgram deliberately recruited members of the general public for his studies, and also controlled for the perceived expertise and respectability of the experimenter. Second, Milgram's subjects continued to obey even after they had begun to doubt the credibility of the experimenter's assurances – at least, this seems to be the clear implication of the individual protocols presented by Milgram (1974), and of the available film records. Third, in his emphasis on subjects' expectations about the effects on the victim, Mixon pays little attention to the issue of perceived *responsibility* for such effects. Central to Milgram's analysis is the assumption that subordinates do not tend to see themselves as responsible for the effects of their actions when they are acting under instructions. Perhaps in real life, just as in experiments, people do not expect that anything they are instructed to do will involve seriously harming another person, but this does not mean that they will necessarily disobey their instructions as soon as such expectations are disconfirmed. Instead, they might assume that there must be some good reason for the instructions they have been given, and thus might see their actions as justifiable in terms of a wider context of which they cannot be blamed for being unaware.

Milgram, no less than Mixon, realizes that it is part of the role of the experimental subject, within certain paradigms, to obey the experimenter without being entitled to an explanation of the instructions until after the experiment is completed. The extraordinary thing about Milgram's results is the extent to which subjects find it difficult to break out from their roles, even when obviously distressed by the functions they are instructed to perform. In the next chapter (pp. 295–8) I shall describe an even more striking example of this phenomenon, the simulated prison experiment at Stanford, in which young male volunteers took on the roles of prisoners and guards (Haney, Banks and Zimbardo, 1973). As will be seen, the participants in this study, even including the senior investigators, became so engrossed in their roles that it ceased to be just a simulation, but instead an experience with brutalizing effects which were all too real. Ambiguity of cues may be an important feature of Milgram's procedures, but this by itself would not seem to be a sufficient, and perhaps not even a necessary, condition of people's preparedness to carry out instructions, even when to do so may seem to cause distress or pain to another person. If there is some room for doubt concerning the negative effects of the actions a person is instructed to perform, it appears that this will inhibit defiance and disobedience. Even where there is no reasonable doubt, however, experimental subjects, and others in defined roles, may cling on to the excuse that they are 'only doing their job' and hence are not personally responsible.

Games and roles

The debate between Milgram and his critics raises fundamental issues. Much turns on the question of whether Milgram's subjects took the experimental situation seriously, or were just pretending to do so. Were their actions 'real', or did they just reflect convincing game-playing or play-acting? Milgram seems to argue mainly that subjects' behaviour should be regarded as 'real' because they appeared to experience 'real' emotional distress and so on. Mixon seems to argue that the context is still that of an artificial experiment. Milgram is more inclined to the traditional view that human social behaviour is determined by factors that are common to both 'real' and 'artificial' situations. However, neither has properly articulated what it is that constitutes 'reality' as opposed to 'artificiality'. What underlies people's decisions to take interactions seriously or not?

Another important aspect of the debate centres on the notion of role. Mixon talks about the role of the subject in a social psychological experiment as though all such experiments were equivalent in their role demands. Milgram talks of the 'agentic role' and its associated responsibilities, but really says very little that bears on how such a role is supposedly generated, how it is recognized as applicable, why it is chosen (if and when it is) in preference to any applicable alternatives, and how it is interpreted as demanding a particular kind of performance. Yardley (1984), moreover, has severely criticized the definition of 'role-play' incorporated in many experiments, including Mixon's (1972). She argues that such experimental techniques have typically been derived from a deterministic view of behaviour as dictated by particular roles, such as those in terms of which a social or societal structure may be described. As a result, 'subjects are discouraged from active construction' so that 'the actor is replaced by the puppet'. This kind of 'role-play' is fundamentally different, Yardley points out, from the skills of an actor in the theatre whose task

> is not objectively to declaim that which is given (even if this were possible) but to *embody* and elaborate the 'role', 'character', to personhood using certain expressive conventions appropriate to the social context of the event . . . To put matters another way, the actor must find the situation ecologically valid, and the audience must perceive persons and situations, not roles and scenarios. (p. 119)

The important point here is that terms like 'games' and 'roles', whilst widespread in the social science literature, constitute a metaphor, rather than a reference to specific entities. What is more, such terms may often be used, as Yardley (1984) points out, in ways that betray misconceptions about play-acting in a more literal sense. This metaphor is nonetheless one of the most fertile in the social sciences, bringing together, among others, such unlikely companions as therapists involved in 'transactional analysis' (Berne, 1968); cognitive scientists concerned with script theory (Schank and Abelson, 1977); social psychologists and philosophers concerned with 'ethogenics' and 'dramaturgical' explanations (Ginsburg, 1979); those, such as Bem (1965) and Mixon (1972) who, for very different reasons, advocate role-playing as an alternative experimental methodology; those studying cooperation and competition by means of experimental games such as the Prisoner's Dilemma (e.g. Colman, 1982); and a whole gamut of workers using social simulations in fields as diverse as management training, group psychotherapy, conflict resolution and so on.

There is thus a curious contradiction between, on the one hand, a tendency to dismiss game-like behaviour as something not to be taken seriously and, on the other hand, a widespread tendency to use the notions of games and roles as the basic building blocks of theory and methodology. Probably the best worked-out analysis of this contradiction is that by Goffman. An important concept in Goffman's writings is that of *face-work* (Goffman, 1955). In broad terms this refers to the devices people will adopt in order to present themselves to others in a socially acceptable manner. In *The presentation of self in everyday life* (Goffman, 1959) numerous examples are given of more or less successful social 'performances', while in *Asylums* (1961) and *Stigma* (1963) Goffman deals, among related issues, with the problems of self-presentation posed for specific groups, such as psychiatric patients and persons with physical deformities. In *Strategic interaction* (1970) he goes into detail regarding the performances required of spies and diplomats. Role-enactment, then, is seen as relevant to a wide range of social encounters. By examining the structure of particular relationships, one can draw inferences about the processes involved in role-enactment generally, and how such processes interact with structure.

Of particular relevance to the present discussion are the two papers published together in Goffman's volume *Encounters* (1972). In *Fun in games* Goffman presents a powerful argument against dismissing game-playing as something which is trivial and unilluminating about social encounters in general. This argument is not based on a contention that the superficial structure of games is like that of more 'serious' interactions, but rather that the question of why any game is fun is a question which deserves to be taken seriously. Games are defined in the first instance by 'rules of relevance and irrelevance'. These define what should, or should not be, attended to in the game. In a football match, the colour of each team's strip is relevant, in that it is something that players and spectators can attend to so as to determine which side a player is on. The colour of their skin is not. Similarly, although the official rules of football lay down details of how many players constitute a team, the size and separation of goalposts, etc., these rules may often be amended by local contract, as one can see on any park or common. When a pair of coats are put down on the ground to serve as goalposts, their attributes as coats cease to be relevant to the game. The fact that they are coats rather than 'real' goalposts can easily be seen, but this fact is ignored through 'selective inattention'.

Goffman argues that a game will be fun for the players, to the extent that it defines a reality for them in which they can become engrossed. Violation of rules of irrelevance can threaten this engrossment, by diverting players' attention away from the game itself to aspects of external reality. The boy who starts complaining that his coat, which is being used as a goalpost, has been trampled on and is getting muddy will not be thanked for reminding his friends that they are not playing 'proper' football. It doesn't matter if 'proper' goalposts get muddy. Goffman talks of games being separated from external reality by a 'membrane' which can easily be punctured, and much of his discussion concerns the means adopted by players to preserve this membrane or to repair it if it is punctured. Typically, this requires a tacit recognition of aspects of external reality that are officially ruled to be irrelevant to the game itself. The question of who gets on well with whom may need to be taken into account in choosing partners for a game, if the game is to be fun. Similarly, for experienced bridge players, it will make an important difference to the kind of game being played whether or not husbands and wives are supposed to partner one another.

It is also important that games should be played with a certain degree of seriousness if they are to be fun. Blatantly to show that one doesn't care about the result will undermine one's opponent's fun, whatever the result may be. On the other hand, to appear over-exultant at winning or depressed at losing may similarly destroy the 'membrane' that keeps the game in its place. Stakes at poker are thus set at a level where players will try to win, but will (hopefully) not lose more than they can reasonably afford. On this point, what Goffman has to say is of direct relevance to the criticism often made of social psychological experiments involving games, namely that such games are not taken seriously by subjects. He argues that whether an activity is taken seriously depends primarily not on whether it is categorized as work or recreation, but on 'whether external pulls upon one's interest can be selectively held in check so that one can become absorbed in the encounter as a world in itself. The problem of too-serious or not-serious-enough arises in gaming encounters not because a game is involved but because an encounter is involved' (1972: 63).

Role distance

The second paper in the same volume is entitled *Role distance*, and to a large extent follows on from the preceding discussion, by showing how people who may be performing a particular role give notice to others that they do not fully identify with the role, to the point that they could be accused of taking it too seriously. Graphic descriptions are given of how people of different ages, from toddlers to young adults, will set about the business of riding a merry-go-round horse. As just remaining in the saddle becomes less of an achievement, it also becomes increasingly necessary for the riders to make it clear to their spectators that they do not expect to be judged simply on the basis of that achievement. Another example is of a group of high-school girls, 'not of the horsey set', on a pony-trek, who manifest 'role distance' by generally larking around so that nobody could think they were really trying: 'Whatever their showing, they avoid having to be humbled before those who are socially placed to make a much better showing' (1972: 99).

The manifestations of role distance, however, may do much more than allow the performers of a role to protect themselves against personal criticism for failure. Surgery teams are used as an example of how distancing oneself from a role may serve as a kind of safety valve, which allows for better performance both by oneself and the people around one. Just as games are less fun and more tension-provoking as rules of irrelevance come under pressure, so even something as serious as a surgical operation can run less efficiently if it is taken too seriously. The problem again is one of selective inattention. To try and deny that there is a world outside the theatre, faces behind the masks or bodies beneath the gowns, is to put a strain on the 'situated-activity system' of the operation which not all of the individuals involved may be able to sustain. For this reason, although surgeons are entitled by virtue of their authority to expect the junior members of their teams to carry out their orders as orders and not as requests, and to do so in a manner of high seriousness, medical etiquette requests that they phrase instructions as requests and thank their juniors for their help. It is also clear from Goffman's observations that a certain measure of good-humoured irreverence and teasing, if the surgeon gives the lead, can be a fairly typical part of how the different roles on the surgical team are performed, although not a part of the roles themselves. Such irreverence essentially takes the form of limited violation of rules of irrelevance, and itself follows predictable patterns depending on the status of the performer.

The phenomenon of role distance thus shows, not just that people engaged in social interaction can be described as performing roles, but that, even as they identify with the activities they are performing, they are aware of their roles as roles – as only a specific part of their identity set apart from wider considerations by accepted rules which define which of their attributes are or are not relevant to their place in the interaction. However, the fact that no game or role can usually claim to represent the total reality of a social relationship or of an individual's identity does not mean that it can be lightly dismissed. It is in fact the selective aspect of games and roles that enables us to take them seriously.

Contradiction, choice and identity

The concepts of role distance, however, may touch on something even more general and fundamental. Role demands may contain within themselves their own contradiction. It may not be merely that there is a balance that needs to be struck between the identity demands of the individual and the role demands of society. It is that society itself may impose (that is, teach us) both norms and counternorms – such as the demands on medical staff to be simultaneously cool and 'scientific' and warm and personally attentive.

According to such a view, ambivalence and contradiction may be *typical* of human thought and experience, at least in our society. Faced with a complex world, individuals may try to impose a consistency through the denial of contradiction, but to do this is to aspire more to the rigidity of authoritarianism than to any ideal of rationality. More adaptive than a notion of 'balance-as-consistency' may be what Billig (1982: 161) terms 'balance-as-counterweight'. People may *typically* hold potentially contradictory cognitions, without apparently feeling the need to resolve such ambivalence. Indeed, it may take rather special kinds of instructions to make people bring their capacities for syllogistic reasoning to bear on what is defined for them as a problem in need of solution (cf. McGuire, 1960; Wyer, 1974).

This idea of 'built-in ambivalence' has a venerable history. Aristotle's advocacy of the virtues of moderation over deficiency and excess finds contemporary evidence in the value connotations of different descriptive labels (see Chapter 5, pp. 165–9). Adam Smith, in *The theory of moral sentiments* (1759; 1892) cited by Billig (1982: 169–70), relates the same notion more directly to that of social roles:

> in each rank, or, if I may say so, in each species of men, we are particularly
> pleased if they have neither too much nor too little of the character which

usually accompanies their particular condition and situation. A man, we say, should look like his trade and profession yet the pedantry of every profession is disagreeable.

Adam Smith is convinced, too, that moderation, ambivalence, and hence adaptability are functional:

> the propriety of a person's behaviour depends not upon its suitableness to any one circumstance of his situation, but to all the circumstances which, when we bring his case home to ourselves, we feel should naturally call upon his attention.

Ambivalence, in the sense of conflicting *emotional* reactions within an individual, plays an important part, too, in Freud's (e.g. 1922) psychodynamic theory; but what is more relevant to the notion of conflicting roles is what Merton and Barber (1976) term 'sociological ambivalence'. This, they say, is the kind of ambivalence that is 'built into the very structure of social relations'. In their view, the acceptable performance of a whole range of social roles involves satisfying as far as possible 'incompatible normative demands'.

One contemporary example comes from the Federal Republic of Germany, where reform of penal law in 1977 stipulated that the primary aim of the prison or 'correctional' system should be resocialization and rehabilitation rather than retribution or restraint. As Lösel (1985) describes, this has placed prison officers in a situation of conflicting demands. The internal demands of the system, often from superiors, require an authoritarian and disciplinarian version of efficiency, with the needs of security and good order paramount. Demands from social services, the law and prisoners themselves, require a more pastoral and caring style responsive to the needs of prisoners as individuals.

In the light of this more complex view of roles and social obligations, what can be said of social psychological findings such as Lerner's (1971) demonstrations of 'justified self-interest' and Milgram's (1974) demonstrations of 'destructive obedience'? Both essentially involve an attempt to account for arguably amoral or immoral behaviour through an appeal to social or societal norms, rules and conventions. For Lerner, such norms are seen as functional for the individual, but the ethical and emotional ambivalence of reactions to others' misfortunes is never completely disguised. Milgram, however, seems to try to make a more contentious point – that the situation and the normative demands are so strong that the individual is not really to blame. Ambivalence is there in the emotional distress of the 'teacher' subjects, but it is *not* built into the 'agentic role' itself. This role is seen as requiring administration of a superior's instructions, without feelings of personal responsibility for their consequences, at least so long as such instructions are unambiguous. Yet the important point is that roles can only be performed with total commitment by means of selective inattention to conflicting demands and cues, at least during the course of the performance. To take role performance as a negation of individual choice is, in effect, to deny the distinction between the activity and a broader reality. Sartre terms this form of denial 'bad faith'. Part of what he means by this phrase may be illustrated in the following example:

> Let us consider this waiter in the cafe. His movement is quick and forward, a little too precise, a little too rapid . . . He bends forward a little too eagerly; his voice, his eyes, express an interest a little too solicitous for the order of the customer. Finally there he returns, trying to imitate in his walk the inflexible stiffness of some kind of automaton while carrying his tray with the recklessness of a tight-rope walker . . . All his behaviour seems to us a game . . . He is playing, he is amusing himself. But what is he playing? We need not watch long before we can explain it: he is playing at *being* a waiter in a cafe. (1943; translated 1969: 59)

The 'bad faith' comes from denying the contradiction involved in the idea of *being* a waiter, and hence denying one's consciousness of oneself as an active, reflective individual. Society demands that waiters and others perform their roles predictably 'as a ceremony'. However, 'the waiter in the cafe cannot be immediately a cafe waiter in the sense that this inkwell *is* an inkwell, or the glass is a glass. It is by no means that he can not form reflective judgements or concepts concerning his condition. He knows well what it "means" ' (pp. 59–60).

To fail to distinguish one's self from the activity or role that one is performing constitutes, for Sartre, therefore, a denial of the self. On the one hand, society demands that we perform roles efficiently, but the needs of personal identity require that we are capable of distancing ourselves from our roles. It may be added that society, too, demands such a capacity for role distance from us, to the extent that social obligations are defined as obligations between moral beings, not between automata.

What implications do these notions have for the empirical research reviewed in this chapter? In studies of altruism, derogation of victims, and obedience, we are dealing with behaviour that has clear moral overtones. The answer to the question, 'Why do people behave like this?' is therefore at least partly rephraseable as, 'Why do people have the conceptions of morality that allow or encourage them to behave like this?' This question is a vast one, and we should not be disappointed if social psychology can only provide part of an answer.

Milgram (1974) proposes that the reason for destructive obedience lies primarily in the demands of 'agentic' roles. However, the implication of the ideas just described is that such an appeal to a role as a deterministic account of behaviour constitutes 'bad faith'. Milgram's obedient subjects were so intent on *being* good subjects that they denied not only individual responsibility but also their *identity* as distinct from their roles. Mixon argues that the role/rule context of the psychological experiment is a particularly authoritarian one. This may be disputed. Right or wrong, though, Mixon's assertion is beside the point. The central problem is not what assumptions people have of how particular roles should be performed, but whether the demands of *any* role constitute a deterministic *cause* of behaviour to the extent that all individual responsibility can be denied.

As has been seen, in many situations many people may appeal subjectively to concepts of 'what's normally expected of them' to guide and excuse their behaviour – whether they are inactive bystanders, reluctant donors, victim derogators or punitive experimental assistants. Such subjective expectations do *not*, however, *determine* their behaviour. The choice is still there, at an individual level, of whether to let oneself be guided by these norms, or by the *counternorms* that are also there, if perhaps slightly below threshold, to the effect that, *as a human being*, one should give help and show compassion to those in need, and avoid hurting others who are in one's power.

I have been arguing that the typical role is not one that contains unambiguous normative demands, but rather one where normative demands are checked and balanced by counternorms. The question, though, remains: why are such checks and balances sometimes heeded and sometimes not? Social psychologists are clever enough at contriving variations in the immediate situation, but what they cannot manipulate are the personalities of their subjects or the political ideology of society as a whole. The attempt by Adorno, Frenkel-Brunswik, Levinson and Sanford (1950), in *The authoritarian personality*, to describe the personality characteristics of the potential fascist still contains important lessons. One of their conclusions – that authoritarians will attempt to deal with contradictory information through denial – has echoes in the ideology of contemporary fascism (Billig, 1978). At the same time, authoritarian political systems may maintain themselves by the denial of the legitimacy of opposition, and, of course, by suppression of the diversity implied by treating religious and ethnic minorities as equals.

We may therefore take to heart the central lesson of this research, that 'ordinary people' and not just psychopaths may deny help to those in need, or may hurt others because they have been told to do so. However, 'ordinary people' can be very different from one another in the roles they choose, the ways they perform their chosen roles, and the extent to which they distance themselves from such roles, rather than letting such roles become their whole being. Societies also differ in the roles they demand, the ways they demand that such roles are performed, and the extent to which they admit counternormative checks and balances as legitimate. How do such societies impose their authority? By simple terror? Partly, perhaps, but also possibly by making ordinary people commit first mild and then more sinister acts of 'bad faith', i.e. of denial of individuality and responsibility, in the performance of their roles. They may then become forced into a vicious cycle of embracing the authority of their masters or leaders rather than admitting the contradictory nature of their own behaviour. One example of this is that against which Jeremy Bentham protested at the beginning of the last century. Students at Oxford University were required to swear a number of religious oaths, inconsistent with many of their personal beliefs. These, Bentham argued, paved the way for submission to authority, through teaching the students the practice of hypocritical compliance (see Billig, 1982: 148). The systematic escalation from relatively harmless to more sinister demands for compliance may be an important feature both of Milgram's experimental paradigm and of the slide towards totalitarianism, as in Nazi Germany.

Milgram's conclusion about human nature and society is chillingly pessimistic (1974: 188):

> Each individual possesses a conscience which to a greater or lesser degree serves to restrain the unimpeded flow of impulses destructive to others. But when he merges his person into an organizational structure, a new creature replaces autonomous man, unhindered by the limitations of individual morality, freed of humane inhibition, mindful only of the sanctions of authority.

But are we necessarily doomed to such loss of autonomy? In this quotation, is Milgram not coming close to merely repeating the representation of war criminals and such like as ogres and monsters – the 'Beast of Belsen', etc. (beyond, of course and importantly, attributing monstrosity to the situation rather than the person)? An alternative interpretation is that such a state of monstrosity can only be attained through hypocrisy, 'bad faith', and selective inattention to all those personal and social demands that run counter to the dominant requirements of the role. Those who deny such contradictory demands are essentially denying their individual identity. When such identity is denied, what happens? Not necessarily the bursting of any psychodynamic floodgates that restrain 'the flow of impulses destructive to others', *for the individual's own impulses have now been ruled irrelevant*; rather the blinkered, non-reflective, playing at *being* a subject or a soldier, an executive or an executioner.

Conclusions

This chapter started with a description of the notions of equity and inequity as used in psychological research. People's judgements of equity and inequity are in the first place *interpersonal* judgements, and this allows us to consider the social and contextual factors that influence how they are made and acted upon.

A good case can be made that both the giving and the withholding of help stem from a common source – the notion that people's relative outcomes should not fall too far out of line with their relative worth or with what they may have seemed to earn through their behaviour. On the one hand, this resembles a general principle that governs the performance of instrumental behaviour. On the other hand, it evokes broader systems of values which must be culturally relative in many kinds of ways.

The obligations we feel to help others in need or distress will likewise reflect the culture in which we live, and all cultures contain their contradictions. A culture that can encourage individual and corporate acts of charity can also predispose people to find reasons for victims' suffering in the character and/or behaviour of the victims themselves. Such a process of derogation may serve to deflect responsibility for such suffering from the derogators themselves.

A dramatic example of deflection of personal responsibility is provided by Milgram's (1974) experimental research on obedience. To understand the acquiescence of Milgram's subjects with instructions to act in an apparently destructive and callous fashion, we must consider the way they interpret the responsibilities and obligations of their role. However, knowing that Milgram's subjects *were* participating in research does not make their behaviour any less disturbing. The reason for this is that we do *not* tend to take role obligations as complete explanations for such behaviour, since the performance of any role is influenced both by norms and counternorms. The plea, 'I was only doing my job', is never *quite* a perfect excuse, since one's job, even if it allows little room for individual discretion, is not the *only* thing one is obliged to do.

9
Social identity and intergroup processes

Deindividuation

The previous chapter contained many examples of *individuals* responding in unedifying ways, whether out of a reluctance to take responsibility, a wish to preserve what they see as deserved better fortune, or a willingness to accept the directions of another person in authority. But what of the behaviour of *groups*, and the actions of individuals as members of a group?

An approach which seems to start from the assumption that group behaviour is qualitatively different from other social psychological phenomena is that of Zimbardo (1969a, b). His basic distinction is between 'individuated' and 'deindividuated' behaviour. The individuated person is viewed as acting rationally and consistently, in control of his or her own behaviour and, as far as possible, of the environment: 'consistency becomes a self-imposed principle in order for the individual to maintain a conception of himself as a normal member of society who, in behaving as others expect him to, gains their social recognition (the most potent of all reinforcers) as a rational decision-maker, whose decisions help him to control his environment' (1969a: 280).

This familiar picture is contrasted with that of the deindividuated person, acting on unrestrained primitive impulses, engaging in orgies of rape, murder, torture, theft and vandalism, or indeed any evil or delinquent act that is not easily explained in other ways (Zimbardo, 1969b). Although not proposed as an absolutely necessary, let alone sufficient, condition for these effects, anonymous membership of a group is assumed to be an important antecedent of the 'deindividuation process'. This process is supposed to involve a minimization of self-observation and concern for social evaluation, followed by a weakening of controls based upon guilt, shame, fear and commitment, and a lowered threshold for expressing inhibited behaviours. The person may then get 'carried away' by the contagious arousal of group activity, and enter a chain reaction of destruction and brutality. Although the debt to Freud is not acknowledged in Zimbardo's (1969b) paper, the notion of primitive impulses (the id?) held in check by rational control (the ego?) and socialized ideals and moral norms (the superego?) is by no means innovatory. Perhaps, though, these older ideas are the right ones after all: so what is Zimbardo's evidence?

The evidence which Zimbardo presents can be crudely summarized as follows: that (1) acts of brutality by individuals acting in groups are a feature of modern life, and (2) acts of brutality can also be performed by experimental subjects, granted suitably 'deindividuating' conditions. The first of these points is never in dispute, although it is for historians to judge whether things are better or worse than they used to be: what is problematic is how such events are to be explained. The second point is more provocative, although by now you will be familiar with the experiments on obedience and victim derogation described in Chapter 8. The data which Zimbardo (1969b) presents are in fact obtained from a very similar paradigm, with naive subjects being put in the situation where they have the opportunity to deliver electric shocks to a victim. Zimbardo's innovation was to run subjects in groups, and, in the critical experimental condition, have them wear over-sized lab coats and hoods over their heads, making them look strikingly similar to members of the Ku-Klux-Klan, and, of course, unidentifiable by each other. Female college students administered longer durations of electric shock to a simulated victim when thus 'deindividuated' than when identifiable by each other. Contrary to expectations, however, opposite results were obtained using Belgian soldiers as subjects. Zimbardo explains this contradiction by suggesting that the soldiers in the 'deindividuated' condition in fact felt *more* alone than those who were not required to wear a hood, but instead were tested together with their friends (who were all uniformed anyway).

This leaves the rather unsatisfactory state of affairs that the principal experimental manipulation can have opposite effects, depending on its meaning for the particular group of subjects used, and this meaning is inferred *post hoc*. Decreased self-consciousness should lead to greater aggression, but the bizarre business of donning a hood could make subjects feel more, not less, self-conscious. To attempt to clarify this problem, therefore, Zimbardo repeated his first experiment, with one change: subjects were tested alone. What happened as a result was that the hooded subjects were *less* aggressive than those not made to wear a hood. The inference is that a manipulation that makes subjects feel anonymous within a group can set the 'deindividuation process' in motion and lead to less inhibition of aggressive acts, but if the same manipulation makes subjects feel alone, it can have the reverse effect. There are nonetheless some untidy loose ends to this argument. Why should the soldiers have acted more aggressively when identifiable by their peers, whereas the reverse was true of the college students? Because they were already uniformed? Because they were a more cohesive group in terms of previous acquaintanceship? Because of their military training? The list is almost endless. There is also the obvious confounding of sex, which, though not necessarily important, would have been easy to control.

The aggression shown by these subjects was, nonetheless, only simulated and was administered at a distance. Not so in Zimbardo's most controversial study, commonly known as the Stanford prison experiment. The most complete account of the data obtained in this study is to be found in Haney, Banks and Zimbardo (1973), but a more vivid impression of what went on is conveyed by the photographs and accompanying recordings which have been edited and marketed as a teaching package. The study was an attempt to look at 'interpersonal dynamics in a prison environment', using what the authors term a 'functional' simulation of a prison, in which male students played the roles of prisoners and guards for an extended period of time. Activities and experiences were created, which, while not 'literal' simulations of actual prison life, 'were expected to produce qualitatively similar psychological reactions in our subjects – feelings of power and powerlessness, of control and oppression, of satisfaction and frustration, of arbitrary rule and resistance to authority, of status and anonymity, of machismo and emasculation' (p. 72).

Subjects were male students who answered a newspaper advertisement for volunteers for a psychological study of prison life, in return for payment of $15 per day. The final sample consisted of 10 'prisoners' and 11 'guards', whose roles were assigned on a random basis. The mock prison was built in a basement corridor of the Stanford University psychology building, and included three small cells (6ft × 9ft) in which the prisoners slept in threes, as well as a solitary confinement room (2ft × 2ft × 7ft). The prisoners remained in the prison 24 hours a day, wore nylon stocking caps on their head (to simulate having their hair cut short), a loosely fitting muslin smock with an identification number in front, no underclothes, rubber sandals on their feet and a chain and lock around one ankle. The guards wore plain khaki shirts and trousers, reflecting sun glasses (to prevent eye-contact), and carried whistles and wooden batons, and attended in shifts. Various other details of the initial set-up also served to stress the inferiority of the prisoners such as a 'delousing' procedure, and the rule that they could refer to each other only by a number. They also had all been unexpectedly 'arrested' with the cooperation of the local police and charged with suspicion of burglary or armed robbery 'often as curious neighbours looked on' (p. 76).

Apart from some minor restrictions, the guards were given extremely wide discretion in the methods they could devise to keep order in the prison. Very quickly, however, the guards' use of their arbitrary authority escalated as they were faced first with taunts, and then more hostile resistance from the prisoners, until the prisoners' will was broken.

A very clear picture emerges of almost everyone involved losing touch with the reality that it was only a simulation, and being completely consumed by their roles. Essentially, the experiment got completely out of hand, to the point where five of the prisoners had to be released 'because of extreme emotional depression, crying, rage, and acute anxiety' (p. 81). Finally: 'When the experiment was terminated prematurely after only six days (it had originally been scheduled for two weeks), all the remaining prisoners were delighted by their unexpected good fortune. In contrast, most of the guards seemed to be distressed by the decision' (p. 81).

Was it all worth it? This question has to be considered in two parts. The first is whether it served a useful social purpose. Certainly the experiment attracted sufficient publicity to allow it to provide a springboard for a more general criticism of penal institutions. Yet this criticism is weakened considerably by the fact that so many departures from actual prison procedure were employed that the very people whom Zimbardo might have wished to persuade could well say to themselves, 'That wouldn't happen in a real prison.' Indeed, the fact that things got so out of hand might even be used as a justification for existing practices. The authors talk of ethical and legal considerations which led them to devise a 'functional' rather than a 'literal' simulation. The end-product does not strike me personally as noticeably more ethical than the real thing. Moreover, there seems to have been no ethical, legal, or practical imperative (at least, none that is explained) that required a simulation study rather than a naturalistic observation study, or even a participant observation study of the kind courageously performed by Rosenhan (1973) in psychiatric hospitals. The main justification seems to lie in the need felt by the authors to disprove the 'dispositional hypothesis' that 'the state of the social institution of prison is due to the "nature" of the people who administer it, or the "nature" of the people who populate it, or both' (Haney, Banks and Zimbardo, 1973: 70). Indeed, the battery of personality measures administered to subjects before the start of the simulation predicted little of their behaviour.

The second aspect to the question, 'Was it worth it?', concerns the value of any findings from a scientific point of view. Apart from the 'dispositional hypothesis' just mentioned, the analysis does not set out to test specific hypotheses. About all that can be said is that a very strong and unpleasant experimental procedure had some very strong and unpleasant effects, but no real attempt can be made to try to separate out which aspects of the situation had the greatest influence. In this respect, this study compares unfavourably with the much more systematic approach of Milgram (1974).

Was deindividuation the crucial factor? We simply cannot say. Certainly the guards thought of themselves as guards, and seemed to lose any initial self-consciousness about playing their roles, to the point where the roles became reality. On the other hand, the anonymity imposed on the prisoners does not seem to have facilitated the expression of similar aggressive 'impulses', except perhaps towards themselves. In neither case, however, does there seem to be particularly strong evidence of the kind of irrational frenzy postulated by Zimbardo (1969b). The prisoners' depression may be seen as a quite 'rational' response to their loss of control over their environment. The escalation of punitiveness on the part of the guards until resistance to their authority was crushed may also be seen as a quite 'rational' response to a situation in which they may have believed that, if they were soft, they would have a riot on their hands. Both groups seem to have been searching for some meaning and consistency in the situation, and found it in the administration and observation of the prison rules.

Even, therefore, where one has people from normal, healthy backgrounds acting in a destructive or self-destructive way, it cannot be definitely said that this is the result of deindividuation. If the individuated person is someone who attempts to gain the social recognition of others by behaving in accordance with their expectations, then the same could be said of the guards and prisoners in this study, as well as of people indulging in the kinds of 'deindividuation' behaviour which Zimbardo (1969b) describes. The difference between individuated and deindividuated behaviour, as postulated by Zimbardo, seems to depend on the *particular* social expectations involved and the *particular* kind of social recognition that is being sought, rather than on the presence or absence of a group, or on the rationality or irrationality of the thought processes of the individuals involved. Even frenzied behaviour may be susceptible to cognitive analysis, and by no means all or most acts of intergroup hostility are frenzied. Simply invoking the concept of punitive, destructive impulses, therefore, makes little contribution to the understanding of intergroup behaviour.

Later research has therefore attempted to identify some of the cognitive and situational factors responsible for such displays of aggressive behaviour. Diener, Dineen, Endresen, Beaman and Fraser (1975) gave male students the opportunity to assault a confederate playing the role of a passive target, with reasonably harmless weapons, including paper balls, rubber bands, sponge bricks and foam swords. Observed levels of aggression were higher when subjects had watched a film of a previous subject acting aggressively in the same situation, when they were told to regard it as a 'game' rather than as though they were 'a person in the army', and when the experimenter assumed full responsibility for their actions as opposed to stressing that they were still personally responsible. Following a similar procedure, Diener (1976) found heightened aggression when subjects had previously engaged in throwing rocks and bottles against a concrete wall, as compared with the more calming activity of painting an ecology sign. The justification for this procedure is interesting:

> activity-induced arousal was manipulated in a way designed to simulate the activities of members of some crowds. Participants were asked to throw rocks and bottles as fast as they could, simulating the throwing of objects that may occur in mobs. Such an activity presumably aroused participants through the physical exercise involved and through the feedback of noise and destruction. A spiralling rate of nonrestrained behaviour is alluded to by Zimbardo (1969 [b]), and the present arousal manipulation was designed in an attempt to maximize the possibility that such aggressive disinhibitions would occur. (p. 498)

This is by no means a value-free study, therefore, either in its assumption about what real crowds (or 'mobs') are like, or in the content of the manipulation. Painting an ecology sign, for instance, may not have just left the subjects non-aroused, it may have made salient a value for pacificism. Once again, therefore, we have a strong behavioural effect as the result of a conceptually ambiguous manipulation. Other features of the design had less impact. Aggression was not significantly reduced by leading subjects to believe that the passive target person knew their identities, but, contrary to predictions, was slightly higher when subjects acted alone rather than in groups of three. In all conditions, the experimenter informed subjects: 'I am completely responsible for what goes on here. None of you are responsible at all' (p. 499).

Reicher (1984a) looked at how the supposedly 'deindividuating' procedure used by Zimbardo (1969b) depended on whether subjects were tested as individuals or as members of groups. The experiment was introduced as a study of the relationship between attitudes and behaviour on the issue of vivisection. In the first part the subjects, who included science and social science students, were shown the results of a survey supposedly showing that scientists were consistently pro-vivisection and social scientists anti-vivisection. In the second part, subjects filled in attitude and behavioural intention responses on the issue, under conditions where (a) they were either tested altogether 'as individuals' or were divided up into scientists and social scientists and tested 'as members of their faculty group and not as individuals'; and (b) they either wore baggy white overalls and cloth masks (which were the same colour for everyone in the 'individual' condition and different colours for scientists and social scientists in the 'group' condition), or were tested with no alteration to their dress.

Reicher presents three separate analyses on different sets of responses. In all three, scientists gave more pro-vivisection responses under group than individual conditions, whereas social scientists gave more anti-vivisection responses under group conditions. The deindividuation (hood) manipulation interacted with the grouping manipulation but only in one analysis (on attitude scores) and only for the science students (who responded more pro under group than individual conditions when hooded but not when in normal dress). Reicher interprets these findings as due to differences in the salience of social identity. Division of subjects into groups made their social identity as members of such groups more salient, and they responded more in accordance with the presumed norms of their group. When the salience of social identity is directly manipulated, therefore, procedures such as Zimbardo's may have less consistent influence. Reicher argues, however, that the effects of deindividuation procedures generally should be interpreted in identity terms:

the consequence of decreasing personal identifiability is not to destroy identity but rather to increase the salience of social identity. In other words, de-individuation gains its effects by altering the relative salience of personal and social identity and consequently by manipulating adherence to personal standards or social norms. (p. 342)

Reicher (1984b; Reicher and Potter, 1985) goes on to challenge the tradition of social and political thought that views crowds and mass action in terms of the disinhibitions of irrational primitive and destructive impulses when individuals become 'submerged' within a crowd. The classic expression of this viewpoint, the 'group mind' theory of Le Bon (1895) gained prominence, according to Reicher (1984b) merely 'through its conscious attempt to advise the establishment on how to contain crowds or even use them against the socialist opposition' (p. 2). Reicher presents detailed evidence from a remarkable investigation of participants' definitions of events that occurred on 2 April 1980 in the St Paul's district of the city of Bristol, England.

St Paul's is a relatively deprived inner-city area consisting predominantly of Victorian working-class housing (in a city where the housing stock is generally old). Whereas the term 'ghetto' would give a misleading impression of exclusivity, for many years it has been the main residential area of the black community. The events known as the 'St Paul's riots' started after police raided a café in the mid-afternoon to investigate allegations of illegal drinking, and arrested the owner and another man. The café (The Black and White) was very much a social centre for the neighbourhood. About an hour later bricks started to be thrown, and the police who were there retreated into The Black and White. Police reinforcements who came to relieve them came under further attack from a crowd that had swollen to about two or three thousand. By the time all police left the area a few hours later, in disarray, a number of police cars had been overturned and set on fire and there was a limited amount of other damage.

From accounts offered by various observers and participants, Reicher persuasively concludes that the violence, while in no way orchestrated, was sharply defined in terms of rules of selectivity and restraint. The violence did not spread outside St Paul's, and (apart from some accidental damage from stray missiles) there was no general attack on property, with the exception of a bank. The police and their cars were the only real target, although a few other cars that might have been mistaken for unmarked police cars were also damaged. According to Reicher, the participants 'saw themselves as ridding St Paul's of an illegitimate and alien police presence' (p. 13). Actions that went beyond these limits (e.g. a bus had a window broken) were quickly stopped, and obvious strangers to the area were warned away from particular roads.

The theoretical interpretation proposed by Reicher is that what happened, and equally importantly, what did *not* happen, cannot be explained by reference to any notion of deindividuation or 'group mind'. Rather, participants' actions were governed by the salience to them of their social identity as members of the St Paul's community – a community whose basic individuality was seen as threatened by the police raid. Individual decisions would be made with reference to what actions were seen as compatible with the social category of the St Paul's community. Thus reactions of others 'seen clearly as ingroup members . . . such as older black youths are looked to. However, actions can only be seen to translate social identity into specific situational norms if they are congruent with that identity. Hence, the limits of crowd behaviour' (pp. 18–19).

In acting as members of a group or community rather than as individuals, moreover, crowd members may 'discover' a sense of social identity and pride in their group that previously was dormant. Far from being irrational and unrestrained, therefore, crowd action may appear to those who participate in it as subjectively rational and measured, granted their self-definition as members of a group. The question of 'objective' rationality and justification for any mass action, or for any side in any conflict, then becomes an ethical or political value judgement, and not one that can be resolved by appeals to psychological theories of motivation. The conditions that gave rise to such conflict, however, are still with us, as shown by the many resemblances between what happened in St Paul's and subsequent street disturbances in Liverpool, Birmingham and London.

The minimal conditions for intergroup discrimination

It does not require social psychological experiments to show that groups, classes, races and nations discriminate against one another, both at the level of hostile actions and at the level of negative stereotypes. Often there is a history of conflict of interest between opposing groups to which such behaviour and attitudes can be attributed. But can discrimination still occur in the absence of any such 'realistic' conflict? Is conflict perhaps sometimes the effect rather than the cause of a perception of difference between one's own and another group? Might even the mere presence of another group, different from one's own in some way, be sufficient to trigger discrimination? To answer such questions, a number of researchers have attempted to create group divisions experimentally from individuals with no previous history of conflict, in order to observe the effects of such group divisions on judgements and behaviour.

Early studies of this kind were conducted by Sherif (1951; Sherif and Sherif, 1953), on boys attending American summer camps, who were quite unaware that an experiment was going on. For the first period after they arrived at the camp, the boys mixed freely with each other, establishing friendships, etc. After about a week, however, the camp organizers divided the boys into two groups (taking care to split up previously established friendship pairs). As a result, each group developed its own separate hierarchy and miniature culture. After this, the two groups were put into competition with each other in sports activities, which had the effect of producing strong overt hostility between them. In a later study, Sherif (1966) added a fourth stage, in which the groups were brought together to perform cooperative tasks (e.g. combining to pull a broken-down food truck), and the introduction of such 'superordinate goals' helped to relieve the intergroup tension that had been created.

Since Sherif's original study, a number of studies have been designed to identify the minimal conditions under which intergroup discrimination can occur. Subjects' assignment to groups in these studies has typically been extremely short-term, relating merely to performance of experimental tasks, and not extending through whole days and nights as in the Sherif studies, or the Stanford prison experiment. Nonetheless, clear evidence of intergroup rivalry is often observed. Ferguson and Kelley (1964), for instance, had pairs of groups perform tasks within sight of one another, but without any formal competition between them having been introduced. Subjects still consistently overvalued the products of their own group and undervalued those of the other group.

Rabbie and Horwitz (1969) tested a hypothesis derived from Lewin (1948), that the main criterion for feeling that one belongs to a group is interdependence of fate with the other group members. To this end, equal numbers of boys and girls of about 15 years old were tested in groups of eight, and were randomly subdivided into groups of four. After some preliminary tasks, the experimenter announced that he would like to give them a reward for participating, a transistor radio, but unfortunately he only had four radios to give away, instead of eight. He then arbitrarily gave the radios to one of the two subgroups, or alternatively did so on the toss of a coin, or else arbitrarily let one of the two subgroups decide, and led subjects to believe that the subgroup had decided in its own favour. Half the subjects thus experienced reward and half relative deprivation by virtue of their membership of one of the experimentally created groups. They then each had to rate the impressions of the other subjects in their session, who came from different schools and were, therefore, not previously acquainted with one another. Disregarding some minor variations between conditions and different dependent variables, the overall picture that emerges is one of subjects rating members of their own subgroup more favourably than members of the other subgroup, whether they were themselves rewarded or not, and whether the cause of their deprivation was chance, the experimenter, or the decision of their own or the other group. No such ingroup bias was observed in a control condition without any reward manipulation. Rabbie and Wilkens (1971) similarly found greater evidence of ingroup bias among subjects who anticipated working together as a group, particularly when this would be in competition with another group, than when they were given no such expectation.

The absence of a bias by subjects in favour of their own group in the control condition of these two experiments might imply that the mere presence of an outgroup is not enough to elicit discrimination, or ingroup favouritism. Some details of these conditions, however, should be borne in mind. Subjects were divided at random into the two groups, and the two groups were seated on opposite sides of a screen so that they could not see each other. Subjects were told that the division was 'for administrative reasons only' and that they would not work together in any way. The two groups were labelled as 'Greens' and 'Blues', but were not addressed as the green or blue *group*. It is, therefore, possible that the cues of group membership were so weak that subjects did not see the situation as involving any kind of intergroup comparison. Rabbie and Horwitz (1969: 272) concluded that: 'Group classification *per se* appears to be insufficient to produce discriminatory evaluations.' One might ask, though, whether any group classification *was* perceived by the control subjects.

Very different conclusions were reached by Tajfel, Flament, Billig and Bundy (1971). Their concern was with whether 'the very act of social categorization' could lead to discriminatory behaviour against an outgroup and in favour of one's ingroup. The emphasis is very much on the cognitive functions that intergroup categorization could serve, in terms of simplifying individuals' perception of their social world and providing guidelines for social action. Their experiments were, therefore, designed to satisfy six criteria, so as to be able to say whether the mere perception of a difference between one's own group and another was sufficient to lead to discriminatory behaviour in favour of the ingroup. These criteria were that there should be: (1) no face-to-face interaction between subjects, either within or between groups, (2) complete anonymity of group membership, and (3) no connection between the basis on which subjects are categorized into groups and the kind of ingroup and outgroup responses they are asked to make. Also, these responses should: (4) have no utilitarian value to the individual making them, (5) pose a direct conflict between a strategy of differentiation in favour of the ingroup and against the outgroup, and other more 'rational' strategies, such as the production of maximum benefit for all, and finally (6) be made as important as possible to the subjects.

The two experiments reported by Tajfel *et al.* (1971) shared the following basic paradigm. Subjects (all of them boys of 14 to 15 years old) are brought from school together in small parties to the university's psychology department. Since all of those in a party come from the same class at school, they are well-acquainted with each other before the experiment starts. The first phase of the experiment then consists of their being shown a number of visual stimuli projected onto a screen. Supposedly on the basis of their individual responses to these stimuli (but in fact randomly), the subjects are then divided into two groups, but in such a way that they do not know the composition of the two groups. Each subject is taken individually into a separate room and seated in a cubicle, and is told which of the two groups he belongs to. This division into groups and the task which follows it are introduced in a way that seems intended to lead subjects to believe that they are taking part in a second study which is separate from the first phase. It is not clear, though, how convincing the instructions would have been on this point. They then perform a task that they are told consists of giving real money rewards and penalties to others. In no case do they assign money to themselves. In fact they have to make quite a number of reward assignments, which in all cases involve a comparative choice between two other boys from their party. Sometimes the two recipients of the rewards are both members of the same group to which the subject himself was assigned, sometimes they are both members of the other group, and sometimes one of them is a member of the subject's own group and the other a member of the other group. It is this last category – that of ingroup–outgroup choices – that is the main focus of interest. Subjects are told that after completing this task, they will be taken back into the first room and given the money that the others have assigned to them.

The form in which these reward assignments are made is fairly complex, and requires subjects, on each trial, to choose one column or 'box' in a two-row matrix. The numbers in the top row refer to the rewards to be assigned to one person, and those in the bottom row refer to the other person's rewards. Examples of two such matrices are shown in Table 9.1. The numbers represent units of 0.1d. (one-tenth of an old penny). The matrices are designed to assess, in the case of ingroup–outgroup choices, the relative 'pull' of different strategies which subjects might adopt. Specifically, those compared are:

MJP – 'maximum joint profit' – responding so as to maximize the total amount given to the two others combined.

MIP – 'maximum ingroup profit' – responding so as to maximize the individual outcomes of the member of the subject's ingroup.

MD – 'maximum difference' – responding so as to maximize the relative difference between the outcomes of the two others, to the advantage of the ingroup member and to the disadvantage of the outgroup member.

On the type A matrix, the MIP and MD strategies both exert a pull towards the left-hand extreme, while the MJP strategy exerts a pull to the right, if the top row represents the outcomes of the ingroup member and the bottom row the outcome of the outgroup member. However, if the outgroup members' outcomes are on top, and those of the ingroup member on the bottom, all three strategies pull to the right. On the type B matrix, MJP and MIP pull to the right, and MD pulls to the left when the ingroup member's outcomes are on top, while all three strategies pull to the right if the ingroup member's outcomes are on the bottom. By comparing each subject's responses over a series of different matrices, scores can be derived which represent the relative strengths of these different strategies.

Table 9.1. *Examples of response matrices used by Tajfel et al. (1971)*

A

19	18	17	16	15	14	13	12	11	10	9	8	7
1	3	5	7	9	11	13	15	17	19	21	23	25

B

7	8	9	10	11	12	13	14	15	16	17	18	19
1	3	5	7	9	11	13	15	17	19	21	23	25

In the first of the Tajfel *et al.* (1971) experiments, subjects were required to estimate the number of dots in a series of slides, and were divided into those who were supposedly more and less accurate, or who tended to over- and under-estimate. In the second experiment, subjects were shown slides of paintings by Klee and Kandinsky, and were split into groups, supposedly on the basis of their preferences for either one of the painters. In both experiments, the division was actually made on a random basis, and in both, subjects assigned 'rewards' which favoured the members of their own group over the members of the outgroup, typically choosing responses which represented a compromise between complete fairness (the middle box in the matrix) and complete bias in favour of the ingroup.

Particularly challenging are the results of the second experiment. On matrices of type A, subjects consistently responded to increase the absolute (MIP) and relative (MD) outcomes of the ingroup, and this tendency was not significantly affected by a consideration of joint outcomes (MJP). On matrices of type B, subjects' responses reflected an apparent wish to give more to the ingroup than to the outgroup member (MD), even when this was incompatible with giving a larger absolute amount to the ingroup member (MIP) or to the ingroup and outgroup member combined (MJP).

A sequel to these experiments was conducted by Billig and Tajfel (1973), to provide an even more stringent test of the assumption that social categorization – explicit division of subjects into groups – is sufficient to lead to ingroup bias. Even though the bias for division into groups used by Tajfel *et al.* (1971) might appear to be essentially trivial, subjects were still given to believe that there was some real similarity between themselves and the other members of their own group which was not shared by members of the outgroup. The perceptual judgements which subjects had to make might not have seemed that important in themselves, but from the subjects' point of view, they must have been of interest to the experimenter or why would they have been included in the experimental task at all? Effectively, the Tajfel *et al.* experiments confounded social categorization with perceived similarity in terms of an attribute to which some implicit importance has been attached by the experimenters. In view of the literature on similarity and interpersonal attraction (see Chapter 2, pp. 21–4) the finding of ingroup bias may be less surprising than it at first appears.

Billig and Tajfel, therefore, manipulated the variables of social categorization and similarity in a simple 2×2 design. In the 'categorization–similarity' condition, subjects were divided into groups on the basis of their supposed preferences for Klee and Kandinsky pictures, as in the second experiment by Tajfel *et al.* (1971). The response matrices were labelled so that, e.g., the top row might refer to rewards for 'Member No. 49 of the Kandinsky group', and the bottom row to rewards for 'Member No. 79 of the Klee group'. The 'noncategorization–similarity' condition followed the same procedure, except that the word 'group' was carefully avoided. Subjects were told that they would know only the code numbers of the other subjects to whom they were awarding money. They were told in an off-hand way that some of the code numbers were in the forties and some were in the seventies, and that those with numbers in the forties had tended to prefer the Kandinsky pictures, and those with numbers in the seventies had preferred the Klee pictures. In the 'categorization–nonsimilarity' condition, subjects were told that the two parts of the experiment had nothing to do with each other, and that for the second part they would be divided into 'group X' and 'group W' on the toss of a coin. The response matrices were labelled with these group designations (e.g. 'Member No. 49 of the W group'). Finally, in the 'noncategorization–nonsimilarity' condition, the word 'group' was avoided, subjects being told that their code numbers, some of which would be in the forties and some in the seventies, had been allocated to them on the toss of a coin. The results showed that ingroup favouritism increased as a function of both categorization and similarity, being strongest in the 'categorization–similarity' condition and weakest in the 'noncategor-ization–nonsimilarity' condition. In other words, categorization *per se* seems to have an effect, over and above any due to similarity.

Deschamps and Doise (1978) have explored the effects of categorization on ingroup favouritism from a slightly different perspective. Their concern is with the fact that, in real life, there are many alternative criteria for dividing people up into categories, which are, to a large extent, independent of one another. Their first experiment, using girls aged between 13 and 15 years as subjects, required judgements in terms of 32 traits of the four concepts: 'people of the female sex', 'people of the male sex', 'young people', and 'adults' in the *simple* categorization condition, and of the four concepts: 'young people of the female sex', 'young people of the male sex', 'female adults' and 'male adults' in the *crossed* categorization condition. In the simple categorization condition, the girls rated males as more different from females, and young people more different from adults, than when they had to deal with both age and sex categories independently. In a second experiment, they used a similar design with subjects of both sexes, and with the categories being sex and an experimentally imposed group division (into a 'group of reds' seated on one side of a table, and a 'group of blues' on the other side). Interpersonal evaluations generally showed greater bias in favour of subjects' own sex, or own group, when subjects had to consider only one criterion of classification than when they had to consider the two independent criteria simultaneously.

Discrimination between minimal groups: what function does it serve?

In many ways, the longer one thinks about the Tajfel *et al.* (1971) and Billig and Tajfel (1973) findings, the stranger they seem. We all know that discrimination takes place in the outside world, so at one level it might not seem too surprising that it can be reproduced in the laboratory. Also, we know that categorization is an extremely important process in both social and perceptual judgements, so perhaps the special place accorded to this process by these studies is not all that extraordinary. But however irrational and arbitrary the criteria for discrimination in the outside world may be, the discrimination itself usually seems interpretable as an attempt by the discriminating group to protect or enhance its own interests or integrity. In the minimal group, it is difficult to see what subjects possibly hope to get out of discriminating, particularly when it does not serve their own individual interests to do so.

One possibility, albeit rather an anticlimactic one, is that subjects discriminate because they feel that that is what the experimenter wants them to do. Criticizing the Tajfel *et al.* (1971) experiments, Gerard and Hoyt (1974: 837) argue: 'Faced with the forced-choice situation of favoring one or the other of two groups, . . . it is not surprising that the subject distributed outcomes with regard to the ingroup–outgroup distinction . . . indeed, Tajfel *et al.* recognized that the subject saw the situation as one "in which social categorization *ought* to lead to discriminatory behaviour . . .".'

Gerard and Hoyt overstate their case by talking of a 'forced-choice situation'. It is worth noting that they do not complete the sentence which they quote from Tajfel *et al.* The fuller context is as follows:

> It will be clear that we interpret our results in terms of a 'generic' social norm of ingroup–outgroup behaviour which guided the Ss' choices. This was so because they classified the social situation in which they found themselves as one to which this norm was pertinent, in which social categorization *ought* to lead to discriminatory intergroup behaviour *rather than to behaviour in terms of alternatives that were offered to them.* (1971: 174; italics added to last phrase)

The Tajfel *et al.* position is that, because of the way in which the response matrices were constructed, subjects were *not* forced to choose which of the two groups to favour at the expense of the other. In other words, they were not forced to base their responses on a strategy of MD or even MIP rather than MJP. Gerard and Hoyt do not comment on this feature of the experiments. Nor is the concept of an experimenter effect (e.g. Orne, 1962), which is implicit in the Gerard and Hoyt criticism, ignored by Tajfel *et al.* (1971). In the paragraph which follows the passage just quoted, Tajfel *et al.* explain:

> The experimenter effect can be defined for present purposes as the use of

experimental procedures which may have caused the Ss to entertain certain hypotheses as to how the experimenters expected them to behave, and then to conform to these expectations. There is no doubt that this was an important aspect of the situation. The term 'group' was used extensively in the instructions to the Ss preceding their choices and on the pages of the booklets of matrices which they found in their cubicles. The experimenter effect is not, however, a concept which presents a theoretical alternative to the interpretation of the findings presented here. The point of the experiments was to activate for the Ss the norm of 'groupness' under certain specified conditions . . . what does seem theoretically important is the fact that a few references to 'groupness' in the instructions were sufficient to release the kind of behaviour that was observed despite its 'non-rational', 'non-instrumental' and 'non-utilitarian' character, despite the flimsy criteria for social categorization that were employed, and despite the possibility of using alternative and in some ways 'better' strategies. (1971: 174)

If there is any basis to the Gerard and Hoyt (1974) argument, it lies in the fact that responding in accordance with the MD strategy rather than any other was the only means whereby subjects could express an intergroup *comparison*. The MIP and MJP strategies are non-comparative. If subjects saw the situation as one involving intergroup comparison, then indeed there is some sense in the argument that MD was the only appropriate strategy available to them. By implication, then, part of any norm of 'groupness' activated in the experimental situation should be the tendency to engage in intergroup comparison. This point is quite crucial, but it is by no means one with which Tajfel would disagree. On the contrary, the central assumption of Tajfel's approach is that individuals are attracted to a group to the extent that it provides them with a positive 'social identity' through comparisons with other groups (Tajfel, 1978).

But again we return to the basic question of why this should happen in *minimal* groups. This question has been considered at some length by Turner (1975). Turner proposes a basic distinction between 'conflict of interests' and what he terms 'social competition', which depends primarily on the individuals' desire to be able to evaluate themselves positively in comparison with others. If they are members of a group which can prove itself 'better' than another group on some dimension of comparison, then that group and that dimension will be salient to their self-concept and 'social identity'. The minimal group situation thus provides subjects with the opportunity of being the 'winners', if they respond discriminatively in favour of their ingroup and against the outgroup, and with the threat of coming out the 'losers' if they do not. The monetary rewards, according to this analysis, are not an end in themselves, but merely a symbolic means to enhance one's self-image.

To test these assumptions, Turner conducted an experiment which closely followed the Tajfel *et al.* (1971) paradigm, with two innovatory manipulations. The first of these was that half the subjects allocated real money rewards in terms of the matrices, whereas for the other half of the subjects, the points had only symbolic value. Discrimination in favour of the ingroup was even stronger when symbolic rewards were used, suggesting that in this condition the motivation to do 'better' than the outgroup was even less encumbered by a consideration of the absolute level of outcomes (cf. Oskamp and Kleinke, 1970).

The second manipulation involved half the subjects first allotting rewards, as in the Tajfel *et al.* (1971) experiments, to two subjects other than themselves ('other–other' choices), but then also allotting rewards between themselves and another subject, who could be either a member of the ingroup or a member of the outgroup ('self–other' choices). In this condition, subjects still showed evidence of intergroup discrimination even in their self–other choices. In other words, their responses were more discriminatory in their own favour when they allotted rewards between themselves and an outgrouper than when they did so between themselves and another member of their own group. For the other subjects, the order of tasks was reversed, so that they made their self–other choices first. In this condition, subjects showed about the same levels of discrimination in their own favour whether the other was an ingrouper or outgrouper. In other words, the distinction between the two groups was only used by subjects as a basis for discrimination in their self–other choices if they had *already* used it in their other–other choices. The task order manipulation had no significant effect on the extent of intergroup discrimination in subjects' other–other choices. Turner (1975) concludes that:

> subjects will identify with a social category to the extent that such identification enables them to achieve value significance, to the extent that it is the category most relevant to the desire for positive self-evaluation in the experimental situation. Thus it can be said that in the experiment by Tajfel *et al.* it was not the *division into groups which caused discrimination* but rather that the group dichotomy was the only existing categorization through which a more basic motivation might be expressed – the subjects therefore *had* to use the categories provided. (pp. 19–20)

Comparisons between unequal groups

If what attracts individuals to groups is the hope of achieving a 'positive social identity', then it would seem, at first sight, that some real-life groups should be much more attractive to their members than others. I say 'at first sight' because, as we shall see later in this chapter, things are not quite so simple. Nonetheless, it is undeniable that differences do exist between groups on conventionally accepted dimensions of status, power, achievement, numerical strength, etc., and perhaps the most significant question that can be asked of research on intergroup behaviour concerns how groups which are unequal in terms of such criteria relate to one another.

Shortly, I shall be describing a major attempt at a theoretical synthesis of this area, but first let us consider some of the relevant experimental data. Two of the experiments already described contained manipulations which *might* be construed as relevant to the question of whether high or low status groups show different levels of intergroup discrimination. In the Rabbie and Horwitz (1969) study, half the experimental subjects were rewarded, and half relatively deprived by virtue of their membership of an arbitrary group. One might have expected different levels of discriminatory behaviour between the rewarded and deprived groups, but no clear effects were found. Similarly, in the first of the Tajfel *et al.* experiments, some subjects were told that they were more accurate, and others that they were less accurate, in their estimates of numbers of dots, but both groups showed comparable levels of ingroup favouritism.

Differences are found, however, when one looks at real-life social groups. Doise and Sinclair (1973) conducted a study within the context of the Swiss secondary education system, in which a higher status is conventionally attributed to the more academically oriented *collégiens* than to the more technically oriented *apprentis*. Subjects drawn from both these groups were asked to rate both their own and the other group on a series of attributes. In a 'no-encounter' condition, subjects first rated the characteristics of their own group, and then those of the other group, but were not told until after they had made their ingroup ratings that they would also have to describe the other group. In a 'symbolic-encounter' condition, subjects were told from the outset that they would have to rate both *collégiens* and *apprentis*. In an 'individual-encounter' condition, subjects were tested in pairs consisting of one *collégien* and one *apprenti*, and in a 'collective-encounter' condition, subjects were tested in fours, with two from each group. In these last two conditions, ratings were obtained before and after discussion.

In the 'no-encounter' condition the ingroup evaluations which subjects made (when they did not know they would also have to rate the other group) were evaluatively neutral rather than favourable. In the 'symbolic-encounter' condition, however, subjects gave much more favourable ratings of their ingroup (so that their ingroup came out 'better' than the outgroup) than did subjects in the 'no-encounter' condition. The difference between the two conditions is stronger for *collégiens* than for *apprentis*, among whom some gave very favourable, and others less favourable, ingroup ratings. The last two conditions confirmed a stronger tendency for the *collégiens* to evaluate their ingroup more favourably, and the outgroup less favourably, than was the case in the ratings given by the *apprentis*. Overall, bias in favour of the ingroup was stronger in the 'collective' than in the 'individual-encounter' condition. In general the *collégiens* rated the ingroup more favourably than the outgroup, whereas the reverse was true in the case of the *apprentis* (to which one should add the important qualification: *on the specific attributes presented*).

These findings do not allow us to conclude that, in general, higher status groups show more ingroup bias, since the results of a study by Branthwaite and Jones (1975) appear to point in exactly the opposite direction. They used the issue of national attitudes between the Welsh and English. In the context of their historical position of political and economic pre-eminence, and their majority status within the United Kingdom, the English were regarded as having the higher status of the two national groups. Subjects in this study were undergraduate students at University College, Cardiff, who unambiguously categorized themselves as English or Welsh. The experimental procedure was modelled after that of Tajfel *et al.* (1971) and involved the allocation of rewards to others in terms of the same response matrices. The crucial feature of this experiment was that subjects were explicitly divided on the basis of nationality, so that the response booklet contained references to, e.g., 'Member No. 32 of Welsh group', and 'Member No. 22 of English group'. Although, overall, about one-third of the subjects responded so as to give equal outcomes to the two groups, the Welsh tended to show more discrimination against the English than the English did against the Welsh. Conversely, discrimination in favour of the *outgroup* was more common on the part of the English. (As a warning against too broad a generalization from these data, however, it should be pointed out that *if* any English students were negatively disposed towards the Welsh, they would be unlikely to choose to go to university in Cardiff.)

Even without using broader social categories of this kind, differences in the level of *ingroup* bias can be produced experimentally by varying the numerical size of the ingroup compared with the outgroup. Gerard and Hoyt (1974) divided subjects into those who were supposedly 'overestimators' and those who were supposedly 'underestimators' on a visual estimation of number task. Subjects were told that 'estimation tendencies are an interesting and important personality attribute, although it's not "better" to be one way or the other' (p. 839). Groups of ten subjects were led to believe that they had been split either into two subgroups of five, or into one subgroup of eight and one of two. Subjects then had to evaluate two essays, one supposedly written by another member of their ingroup and one by a member of their outgroup. Both male and female subjects were used, and when the results for both sexes are combined, they show a tendency for ingroup bias to decrease with the size of the ingroup. Subjects who believed they were in a minority of two evaluated the ingroup essay more favourably than the outgroup essay – very slightly so in the case of females but strongly so in the case of males. When the groups were supposedly of equal size, both male and female subjects were somewhat more favourable in their ratings of the outgroup than the ingroup essay. When subjects believed that they were in the majority, males indicated a slight preference, and females a strong preference, for the outgroup essay. Females were thus, overall, more favourable in their ratings of the outgroup essay relative to the ingroup essay than were males, although this effect was only marginally significant ($p < 0.1$).

Once again, though, results can be found that support the opposite conclusion: that majorities discriminate more than minorities. Moscovici and Paichelier (1978), using first-year university students as students, replicated the main condition of the Tajfel *et al.* (1971) study, with subjects being split into equal groups on the basis of their supposed preference for pictures by Klee or Kandinsky, and compared this 'control' condition with a 'majority' condition, in which they were told that their preferences were shared by just over 80 per cent of the total subject population, and a 'minority' condition in which they were told that their preferences put them in a minority of under 20 per cent. Subjects then filled out the standard response matrices allotting rewards to members of the Klee and Kandinsky groups. The data are presented in the form of the percentages of responses demonstrating ingroup favouritism, fairness, or outgroup favouritism. For the control group, these percentages were respectively 32, 47, and 21. For subjects who thought they were in the majority, they were 70, 14 and 16; for those who thought they were in the minority, 44, 29 and 27. In other words, the 'majority' subjects were the most discriminatory in their own favour. The 'control' subjects seem to have been less discriminatory than would have been expected on the basis of the Tajfel *et al.* data, although the different ages of the subjects might have played some part.

These last two experiments, however, do not deal directly with the issue of whether belonging to a majority or minority has positive or negative value for the individual, so it is possible that some such variable might account for the discrepancy between the results. A difference in value might explain the low levels of ingroup favouritism shown by the *apprentis* in the Doise and Sinclair (1973) study, but the relatively higher levels shown by the Welsh students in the Branthwaite and Jones (1975) study. To test this possibility, Moscovici and Paichelier conducted a second experiment in which subjects were again led to believe that they were in a majority or minority group, but this time the division was supposedly made on the basis of their scores on a test of creativity, and subjects were also given feedback which implied that they were personally high or low in creativity. As can be seen in Table 9.2, most ingroup favouritism was shown by subjects who believed they were high in creativity and in a minority, or low in creativity and in a majority. The value attached to group membership and the minority–majority status of the group thus appear to have interactive effects on the level of discrimination. Although such an interpretation would be entirely *post hoc*, it is possible that the criteria for group division led to Gerard and Hoyt's (1974) subjects having a more positive image of their ingroup than was the case in the first of the Moscovici and Paichelier experiments. Similarly, one might suppose, on a more substantial basis, that the Welsh students in the Branthwaite and Jones study valued their own group more positively than did the *apprentis* in the Doise and Sinclair study.

Moscovici and Paichelier discuss these results in the context of Moscovi-

Table 9.2. *Percentages of ingroup favouritism, fairness, and out-group favouritism responses as a function of self-image and minority–majority status, found by Moscovici and Paichelier (1978)*

	Positive self-image (high creativity)		Negative self-image (low creativity)	
	Minority	Majority	Minority	Majority
Ingroup favouritism	61	29	46	62
Fairness	24	56	38	24
Outgroup favouritism	15	15	17	14

ci's (1976b) distinction between 'nomic' and 'anomic' groups. Broadly speaking, 'nomic' groups are sure of their position and opinions and have experience of success. 'Nomic' majorities can afford to tolerate minorities and act equitably towards them, while 'nomic' minorities will tend to assert their differences from the majority and hence show strong ingroup bias. By contrast, 'anomic' groups are unsure of their positions and have experience of failure. 'Anomic' majorities will avoid comparisons with the minority and will show strong ingroup favouritism, whereas 'anomic' minorities will tend to identify more with the majority outgroup, which is seen as conforming to accepted norms.

This highlights an important distinction between the position of a group on some valued dimension, such as status, and the stability of that position. An attempt to manipulate these as independent factors has been made by Turner (1978). Groups of students were presented with the task of improving a passage of prose. There were two groups of subjects in each session, and they each read out their revised versions and rated each other's performance. The instructions introduced the task as a measure of verbal intelligence, related to linguistic and literary skills, as distinct from spatial-motor intelligence, related to scientific and technical skills. Subjects were drawn from either the Arts or the Science faculty of the university. In the 'unstable' condition, they were told that verbal intelligence was more important for Arts students, and spatial-motor intelligence for Science students. In the 'stable' condition, they were told explicitly that Arts students were definitely superior to Science students in verbal intelligence, but inferior to them in spatial-motor intelligence. The intended implication of this rather subtle distinction seems to be that, in the 'unstable' condition, Science students were likely to do worse than Arts students, in that the task required skills which were 'less important' to them, but this result was not inevitable. Ratings were obtained of the respective merits of the two groups' performances, subjects' preferences for belonging to either group, and perceived task importance.

When both groups were drawn from the same faculty, Arts students were more likely to evaluate their own group's performance more highly than that of the outgroup, whereas Science students were more likely to rate the task as unimportant, particularly under 'stable' instructions. When the two groups were drawn from different faculties, the only subjects who consistently rated their own group's performance more highly than that of the other group were the Arts students under 'unstable' instructions. The Arts students who received the 'stable' instructions, and therefore knew that they were anyway 'definitely' superior, acted more as though they felt that they could afford to 'give credit where credit was due'. Arts students, under either set of instructions, were not at all keen to change groups for another similar task, whereas Science students were not too bothered if they changed groups or not. The task was rated as less important by Science students under 'stable' instructions.

These results suggest that comparisons between unequal groups differ from those between equal groups in a way that depends upon the stability of that inequality. In particular, groups in a position of unstable superiority seem to discriminate more than those in a position of stable superiority. One has to be careful, though, to remember what was meant by 'superior' and 'inferior' in this context. Science students do not necessarily perceive themselves as 'inferior' to Arts students. Superiority and inferiority were manipulated purely by instructions which gave information about the nature of the task. This information related, on the one hand, to expected levels of performance and, on the other hand, to the relevance of the task to the subject's self-evaluation. It is by no means clear that the stability manipulation in fact succeeded in manipulating perceived *stability* of status inequality (i.e. inequality of the relevant skills) independently of the perceived *size* of that inequality. In addition, it seems quite plausible that the 'stable' instructions may have further increased the perceived relevance of the task as a dimension of self-evaluation in the case of the Arts students, and decreased it further in the case of the Science students. It is an experiment where the conceptual distinctions are clearer at a theoretical than at an operational level.

A similar procedure was employed by Turner and Brown (1978) in an experiment designed to distinguish the stability of a perceived difference in status (i.e. task ability) from its perceived *legitimacy*. The meaning of legitimacy in this context will be best understood if the experimental design is first described. Subjects were 48 male students, half from the Arts and half from the Science faculty. Sixteen experimental sessions were run, each with a single group of three subjects, all from the same faculty. Subjects were told that the experiment was an investigation of reasoning skills, and they would be required to work on a group task which consisted of discussing for 20 minutes the statement: 'No individual is justified in committing suicide.' They were told that research had shown either that Arts students, or that Science students, tended to do better. This information was manipulated orthogonally with subjects' faculty membership, so that half the students from each faculty were led to expect that they would do relatively well ('high status'), and half that they would do relatively badly ('low status'). This was achieved by giving different instructions in the 'legitimate' and 'illegitimate' conditions. In the 'legitimate' conditions, subjects who were told that Art students did better were told that this was 'not surprising', as the task was probably influenced by 'verbal intellectual skills', and this was 'widely recognized by psychologists. So it does not amount to any kind of handicap for Science students.' When it was the Science students who were supposed to do better, the instructions were changed appropriately with the phrase 'mathematicodeductive skills' replacing 'verbal intellectual skills'. In the 'illegitimate' conditions, the difference was instead described as 'worrying' and 'not sufficiently well recognized by psychologists', and subjects were told that the bias 'undoubtedly amounts to quite a handicap for people like Science (Arts) students'. In the 'stable' conditions, subjects were told that the differences were 'a high consistent finding', whereas those in the 'unstable' conditions were told the opposite. Collapsing over subjects' faculty membership, the three independent variables of status, legitimacy, and stability constituted a $2 \times 2 \times 2$ factorial design.

After subjects had held their group discussion, which was recorded, the experimenter told them that he wanted to know how well they thought they had done, and would play them a recording of an earlier group, 'so that they had a standard against which to compare their work'. This tape was in fact constant for all conditions, but was introduced to subjects as being that of a group from the *other* faculty from their own. They then had to evaluate the 'relative merits' of the two groups' performances on response matrices adapted from Tajfel *et al.* (1971), and also had to assess their own and the other group on a number of rating scales. 'Creativity' measures were also included, in which subjects were invited to list other methods they could think of for measuring 'reasoning skills', and other factors which they thought were important and ought to be 'taken into account in assessing overall intellectual ability'.

Ignoring the results of an unreliable factor analysis, the familiar measure of ingroup favouritism derived from the Tajfel *et al.* (1971) matrices showed significant main effects with high-status subjects showing more ingroup bias than low-status subjects, and more ingroup bias being shown by subjects in the illegitimate than legitimate conditions. Contrary to prediction, there was no overall tendency for 'unstable' instructions to produce more ingroup bias than 'stable' instructions, but instead a three-way interaction occurred, as can be seen in Table 9.3. As shown by the group means, the low-status subjects tended to be more favourable to the out-group than towards their own group when allocating points for perform-ance, except in the illegitimate unstable condition. The high-status subjects, who perceived their superiority to be both legitimate and stable, showed no bias (as predicted), but those who perceived their superiority to be neither legitimate nor stable, and who thus should be the most 'anomic' in

Table 9.3. *Ingroup bias as a function of status, legitimacy, and stability, found by Turner and Brown (1978)*

	Legitimate		Illegitimate	
	Stable	Unstable	Stable	Unstable
High status	0.1	2.3	3.6	0.9
Low status	1.2	2.1	0.9	1.1

Note: Figures are mean scores with a range from 12 (maximum discrimination in favour of the ingroup) to 12 (maximum discrimination in favour of the outgroup).

Moscovici's (1976b) terms, showed far less bias than Turner and Brown predicted. Perhaps there comes a point when groups in a superior position perceive their superiority to be so unreliable and indefensible that they no longer seek to differentiate themselves from others in an 'inferior' position on the relevant dimension.

Among the remaining data of this experiment, perhaps the most interesting finding is that low-status subjects tended to be more 'creative', in the sense of suggesting more methods for measuring reasoning ability and more factors of relevance to general intelligence, when they perceived their inferiority to be illegitimate. High-status subjects tended to be somewhat more 'creative' under 'unstable' instructions.

Tajfel's theory of intergroup behaviour

One of the most ambitious undertakings in research on group processes has been Tajfel's attempt to develop a theory of intergroup behaviour from a cognitive social psychological perspective. The theory and related research is presented in detail in Tajfel's (1978) volume. It should be stressed that the theory is not just an attempt to synthesize established experimental findings, but is intended to be applicable to the analysis of more large-scale phenomena of societal change and social movements. As a result of this deliberately wide-ranging approach, a number of specific issues remain in need of attention, not least of which is a methodological one – that of validly and unambiguously operationalizing the conceptual distinctions to which Tajfel draws attention.

Tajfel sees the various issues of intergroup relations as turning on individuals' sense of belonging to, or identification with, their group. Definitions of what is or is not a group thus depend on this process of identification, rather than on any other single factor. As an illustration of this point, Tajfel cites the definition of a 'nation' offered by the historian Emerson (1960: 102): 'The simplest statement that can be made about a nation is that it is a body of people who feel that they are a nation; and it may be that when all the fine-spun analysis is concluded this will be the ultimate statement as well.'

The salience of individuals' identification with their group (and indeed the particular group with which they identify) will not be constant across all situations. On the contrary, social situations can be characterized as lying on a continuum from the extremely interpersonal to the extremely intergroup. Towards the interpersonal extreme (which may be rarely if ever reached) individuals relate to each other purely as individuals, without regard to their membership of any social categories. Towards the intergroup extreme, individual attributes of the participants lose relevance, interactions being based purely on people's membership of social categories. The major common features of behaviour in intergroup rather than interpersonal situations are a shared ingroup affiliation of the individuals concerned, and a shared interpretation of the relations between the ingroup and outgroup as applied to the particular situation. The corollary of this interpersonal–intergroup continuum is a continuum of variability–uniformity of behaviour in the ingroup and of its treatment of members of the outgroup; in other words, as one approaches the intergroup extreme, different members of the ingroup will adopt similar behaviour towards the outgroup, and no differentiations will be made by them between individual outgroup members. The interesting and important departure in this argument from similar interpretations of earlier research on prejudice and stereotypes (see Chapter 5) is that these phenomena are treated as a function of the specific social *situation*, rather than of individuals' deep-seated drives and dispositions.

Of crucial relevance to the extent of differentiation between and within groups is assumed to be the perceived permeability of the boundaries between the groups. The basic condition for extreme forms of intergroup behaviour is said to be the belief that the boundaries are sharply drawn and immutable, so that it is impossible, or extremely difficult, for individuals to pass from one group to the other. Similarly, the basic condition for predominantly interpersonal behaviour is the belief that the boundaries are flexible and that individuals can pass through them with no special difficulty. This becomes particularly important, in terms of generalizations to society at large, if one is considering the relations between groups which occupy different positions in some status hierarchy. To preserve or improve their status, can individuals just look after themselves, or must they act as members of their group? Tajfel discusses some of the ways in which social stratifications may present themselves in psychological terms:

> We can distinguish *a priori* between several major sets of social psychological attributes of these stratifications which are likely to determine different forms of social behaviour relating to them. The first consists of the consensus in *all* the groups involved that the criteria for the stratification are both legitimate and stable (i.e., incapable of being changed). The second consists of the consensus existing (or developing) in one or more groups that the criteria are neither legitimate nor incapable of change. The third arises when one or more groups believe that the criteria are illegitimate but unchangeable

(because of, e.g., drastic differences in power between the groups). And the fourth – conversely – when they are believed to be legitimate but unstable (i.e., capable of change). The third and fourth sets of attributes most probably interact in many cases – in the sense that perceived illegitimacy is likely to determine, sooner or later, attempts to change the situation; and the perceived instability (which can be translated as the development in a group of the awareness of cognitive alternatives to the existing situation) is likely to be associated, sooner or later, with the decrease in that group of the perceived legitimacy of the situation. It will be obvious that a combination of illegitimacy and instability would become a powerful incitement for attempts to change the intergroup *status quo* or to resist such changes on the part of the groups which see themselves as threatened by them. (Tajfel, 1978: 51–2)

Tajfel summarizes this position by assuming another corollary to the interpersonal–intergroup continuum. This is the 'social mobility–social change' continuum which refers to differences in individuals' beliefs concerning the nature of intergroup relations (or, more specifically, intergroup stratifications). At the 'social mobility' end, the basic assumption is that the social system is flexible and permeable, and allows improvement of individual status on the basis of luck, effort, ability, etc. At the 'social change' end, the basic assumption is that the only way individuals can change or preserve their status and conditions is together with their group as a whole. Implicit or explicit in much of Tajfel's argument is the thought that the bulk of social psychological research on groups has been premised on a 'social-mobility' rather than a 'social-change' conception of intergroup relations, and the correspondence between this conception and the traditional American ethos of 'rugged individualism' is seen as no coincidence. Tajfel's position is that intergroup discrimination and hostility cannot be adequately understood unless the structure of beliefs at the 'social change' end is more directly examined.

The three main 'independent variables' of the theory thus emerge as being those of *status, legitimacy* and *stability*. All three relate to the structure of the relationship between any pair of groups *as perceived by the group members*. At a conceptual level, it is freely admitted that these three classes of perception can influence each other, so that, for instance a superior group might be more likely to perceive its status as legitimate, and unstable relations might also tend to be seen as illegitimate. A very real methodological problem to which this gives rise, though, is the difficulty of manipulating these perceptions as truly *independent* factors within an experimental design (as in the studies by Turner, 1978, and Turner and Brown, 1978), which can lead to ambiguities in the interpretation of results.

The concept of stability also needs additional clarification. Tajfel seems to use the term 'stability' to refer both to the stability of the status differences between groups, and to the rigidity, as opposed to the permeability, of the intergroup boundaries. A clearer differentiation between the effects of stability and permeability appears to be called for. One can easily think of situations in which the boundaries between groups (e.g. nations) are clearly defined and impermeable, but where the status differences are quite unstable. In other words, it is possible to envisage changes in the status positions of groups as a whole without any implication that the boundaries between the groups are permeable. Indeed, this is precisely what Tajfel means by a 'social change' system of beliefs. Increasing the permeability of intergroup boundaries, on the other hand, would seem to encourage individuals to adopt a 'social mobility' system of beliefs. Arguments against calls for radical social change (at least in Western democracies) are rarely, if ever, premised on the untenable assumption that class differences are non-existent. Instead, some argue that the class boundaries are permeable (i.e. there is equality of opportunity), so that the class differences that do (or will) exist are not really *class* differences at all, but differences between achieving and non-achieving *individuals*. Permeability, actual or perceived, may thus legitimate a social system containing inequalities of status, and hence contribute to its stability.

Having dealt with the relations between groups in terms of status, legitimacy and stability, Tajfel then discusses the probable effects of these variables on the individual's commitment to the group. The basic assumptions are as follows:

> (a) It can be assumed that an individual will tend to remain a member of a group and seek membership of new groups if these groups have some contribution to make to the positive aspects of his social identity; i.e., to those aspects of it from which he derives some satisfaction.
> (b) If a group does not satisfy this requirement, the individual will tend to leave it *unless*:
> (i) leaving the group is impossible for some 'objective' reason, or,
> (ii) it conflicts with important values which are themselves a part of his acceptable self image.
> (c) If leaving the group presents the difficulties just mentioned, then at least two solutions are possible:
> (i) to change one's interpretations of the attributes of the group so that its unwelcome features (e.g., low status) are either justified or made acceptable through a reinterpretation; or,
> (ii) to accept the situation for what it is and engage in social action which would lead to desirable changes in the situation.
> (d) No group lives alone – all groups in society live in the midst of other groups. In other words, the 'positive aspects of social identity' and the reinterpretation of attributes and engagement in social action only acquire meaning in relation to, or in comparisons with, other groups. (Tajfel, 1978: 64)

The similarity of this part of the theory to the ideas proposed by Thibaut and Kelley (1959; see Chapter 5, p. 130) is quite striking. According to Thibaut and Kelley, individuals should remain in a group so long as their outcomes derived from membership do not fall below their comparison level (CL). The concept of CL has at least two distinct advantages in this context. First, since CL is defined as the level of outcomes to which one feels one is *entitled*, it directly incorporates the notion of perceived legitimacy. Second, since CL is a judgemental standard, and standards shift with experience, it is an easy prediction that individuals will tend to adjust their CLs, and hence their levels of aspiration, to the levels of outcomes which they habitually experience, thus tending to adopt a relatively 'conservative' ideology. A possible criticism of the balance of Tajfel's theory is that, with its emphasis on the preconditions for social *change*, proportionately less attention tends to be given to the psychological basis of the inertia which any forces for change need to overcome, and to the processes underlying the continued perception of a system as legitimate and stable, in spite of inequalities.

The concept of CL is also relevant to the question of when individuals will leave or stay in their group. Individuals may remain in their group, even if it produces outcomes for them below their CL, if these outcomes are still above their CL, i.e. what they could expect to get from leaving the group. This would be equivalent to a system which was perceived as illegitimate but stable. On the other hand, in a system which allowed for upward individual social mobility, individual members' outcomes within a group could be below their CL, and under such circumstances they would be motivated to leave their group. Whereas Tajfel's theory is phrased in terms of 'positive social identity', that of Thibaut and Kelley is phrased in terms of 'outcomes', but that is no problem – a contribution to a person's positive social identity can be easily regarded as an outcome.

One of the most important aspects of Tajfel's theory, however, is the assumed dependence of a person's social identity, or self-evaluation, on processes of social comparison (cf. Festinger, 1954). Whereas Thibaut and Kelley were more concerned with comparisons within a group, Tajfel stresses the role that intergroup comparisons play in a person's self-evaluation. It is through such comparisons that one acquires a better or worse image of oneself by virtue of one's group membership:

> The characteristics of one's group as a whole (such as its status, its richness or poverty, its skin colour or its ability to reach its aims) achieve more of their significance in relation to perceived differences from other groups, and the value connotation of these differences. For example, economic deprivation acquires its importance in social attitudes, intentions and actions mainly when it becomes 'relative deprivation' . . . the definition of a group (national, racial or any other) makes no sense unless there are other groups around. (Tajfel, 1978: 66)

From this follows the crux of Tajfel's argument: that *individuals will tend to engage in intergroup comparisons which are seen as likely to make a positive contribution to their social identity* (self-evaluation as group members), *and will tend to avoid intergroup comparisons which are seen as likely to make a negative contribution.* For intergroup comparisons to make any (positive) contribution of this kind, however, the other group must be seen as potentially similar or comparable to one's own. Yet in society comparisons will tend to be made between groups that are often quite dissimilar in terms of status. This is why it is necessary to take the variable of legitimacy into account:

> Social comparisons between groups which may be highly dissimilar are based on the perceived legitimacy of the perceived relationships between them. The concept of social identity . . . is linked to the need for a positive and distinctive image of the ingroup; this is why the perceived illegitimacy of an intergroup relationship transcends the limits of intergroup similarity in the relevant social comparison and reaches out wherever the causes of illegitimacy are thought to reside . . . The perceived legitimacy of an intergroup relationship presents no problems for a social comparison theory, based on the assumption of similarity, when the groups are (at least potentially) of similar status . . . Again, the assumption of similarity seems valid in the case of stable and clear-cut status differences which are perceived as legitimate, in the sense that dissimilarity implies here the *absence* of comparisons. The difficulties arise when this kind of a stable and legitimate intergroup system begins to break down . . . The important issue . . . is that the perceived illegitimacy of an existing relationship in status, power, domination or any other differential implies the development of *some* dimensions of comparability (i.e., underlying *similarity*) where none existed before . . . Paradoxically, this means that the perceived illegitimacy of the relationship between groups which are highly dissimilar leads to the acknowledgement or discovery of *new* similarities, actual or potential . . . The perceived illegitimacy of an intergroup relationship is thus socially and psychologically the accepted and acceptable lever for social action and social change in intergroup behaviour. (Tajfel, 1978: 74–6)

What is the link, finally, between individual's choice to engage (or not engage) in intergroup comparisons and behaviour in minimal groups and similar experimental situations? Ingroup bias, as shown by the 'pulls' of the MIP and (more directly) MD strategies on the response matrices, and also as shown by differential evaluations of group performance or attributes of ingroup and outgroup members, is taken as evidence that subjects are engaging in intergroup comparisons – that is, in behaviour towards the intergroup end of the interpersonal–intergroup continuum. Such bias is seen primarily as action designed to enhance subjects' social identity or self-image, in the sense of allowing them to feel, 'Our side won'. As distinct from how such bias might be viewed by writers such as Berkowitz (1962), who treats outgroup aggression as a response to individual frustration, or Zimbardo (1969b), who treats it as a result of deindividuation, it is not seen by Tajfel as an end in itself, but rather as a means through which individuals can enhance their self-evaluation as members of a group, through seeing their own group as both *distinctive* and also as *better* than the outgroup on the (only) available dimension of comparison.

This assumption is consistent with the findings of ingroup bias in those minimal group studies (e.g. Billig and Tajfel, 1973; Tajfel *et al.*, 1971) where the status variable has not been incorporated. Since the groups are comparable, subjects tend to make intergroup comparisons. Where status has been incorporated, as in the Turner (1978) and Turner and Brown (1978) studies, unequal status should reduce comparability and hence the degree of intergroup comparison (and hence bias) except where the status difference is presented as illegitimate and/or unstable. The results of these studies to date are partially, but not completely, consistent with this assumption (see Table 9.3, p. 316).

The results of minority–majority intergroup comparisons (Gerard and Hoyt, 1974; Moscovici and Paichelier, 1978) are also compatible with Tajfel's approach if one assumes that, in general, minorities will be more likely to compare themselves with majorities than vice versa. In conditions when the minority can evaluate themselves positively along a relevant dimension, the minority is likely to show bias against the outgroup, but in conditions where they are told that the majority is 'better' than they are on the relevant dimension, it is less in their interest to compare themselves directly with the majority. By the same token, a majority that is sure of its own merits stands to gain nothing by comparing itself with an inferior minority (it is 'on a hiding to nothing'), but is likely to show more bias if its 'normative' status is threatened by the possibility of being 'bettered' by the minority.

One remaining issue is the relationship of such effects to processes more traditionally studied within the framework of attribution theory and equity theory. Experiments on intergroup relations have frequently involved procedures with a family likeness to those used in studies of attributions for success and failure (see Chapter 6, pp. 198–203), or of equity principles (see Chapter 8, pp. 253–7) in the distribution of rewards on the basis of task performance. The term 'reward' appears throughout the Tajfel *et al.* matrices, and it is not necessarily an idle speculation to wonder whether the same results would have been obtained if the word 'gift' had been used instead.

As things stand, it seems quite reasonable to suppose that subjects saw their task, at least partly, as that of distributing money or points in accordance with what they felt was *deserved* by the different ingroup and outgroup members – indeed, where subjects have to evaluate ingroup and outgroup performance in terms of rating scales, this seems to be precisely what subjects would have thought was required of them. The importance of the comparative 'maximum difference' (MD) strategy is quite compatible with this argument, provided one goes along with Anderson's (1976) formulation of the equity principle that each participant's proportionate share of the outcomes should equal their proportionate share of the inputs. Equity, according to this view, is a matter primarily of interpersonal rather than intrapersonal comparisons. Furthermore, when one considers the factors which might effect such perceptions of deservedness, it seems more than a coincidence that 'ingroup bias' should be least marked where subjects are encouraged to attribute any differences in performance to stable and legitimate differences in the difficulty of the task for the different groups, rather than being led to expect that relative success or failure will be primarily determined by effort, or differences in ability not previously recognized.

Increasingly, researchers are looking at how social identification impinges on other processes, such as equity, judgement and attribution. van Knippenberg and van Oers (1984) conducted a study on how two groups of nurses in the Netherlands (the one with higher academic qualifications than the other) perceived the equitableness of each others' professional inputs and outcomes. A factor analysis on perceptions of input characteristics yielded three factors – practical skills, theoretical insight, and interpersonal relations. The more academically qualified group rated themselves higher than the other group on theoretical insight and (somewhat) on practical skills. The less-academic group rated their own practical and interpersonal skills much higher. Theoretical insight was rated as more important by the more-academic group, interpersonal relations by the less-academic group. As far as outputs are concerned, the tendency was for relatively more positive evaluations of the *intrinsic* rewards of one's own group (success, freedom, satisfaction) but more positive evaluations of the other group's *extrinsic* rewards (career opportunities, income and prestige).

Group membership can also have major influence on the kinds of attributions that people make for one another's behaviour with (for instance) ingroup bias being shown in attributions made for the behaviour of members of one's own group (Deschamps, 1983; Hewstone and Jaspars, 1984). Hewstone, Jaspars and Lalljee (1982) compared how schoolboys from public and comprehensive schools (i.e. for non-British readers, selective private and non-selective state schools, respectively) attributed the examination success or failure of pupils from either type of school. Public schoolboys attributed failure by one of their own group more to lack of effort, but failure by a comprehensive schoolboy more to lack of ability. Comprehensive schoolboys attributed success by a public schoolboy more to luck. Feather (1985) found that political conservatism and higher socio-economic status was associated with a greater tendency for Australian university and high school students to regard youth unemployment as the fault of the unemployed themselves, as opposed to defective government policies. Presumably 'the unemployed' would be more likely to constitute an outgroup for those from more economically privileged homes. Kelvin (1984) and Kelvin and Jarrett (1985) also consider explanations for (and other psychological effects of) unemployment from a more historical perspective.

Differentiation and deviance

Potentially one of the most exciting aspects of intergroup behaviour dealt with by Tajfel is the phenomenon that groups who find themselves in a disadvantaged position in terms of one dimension will tend to look for new dimensions of comparison along which they can achieve a distinctive and positive social identity. Many striking examples are provided by Giles (1978) of how national or ethnic minorities will use and perceive their own language (as in the case of the Welsh or the French Canadians), or dialect and accent (as in the case of American blacks), to differentiate themselves from a majority outgroup, the use of such differentiating language or speech markers being predictable from the intergroup dynamics implicit in any given social situation. Turner and Brown (1978) included their measure of 'creativity' (suggestions of new assessment methods) to see if illegitimately disadvantaged groups would be the more likely to challenge the existing dimensions of comparison, and the direction of differences accorded with this prediction.

Particularly relevant here is the work of Lemaine (1974; Lemaine, Kastersztein and Personnaz, 1978), who carried out a series of studies in children's summer camps. These involved two groups of children competing against each other for a single prize on tasks such as the construction of a hut in the woods. In each case, one of the groups was deprived of a resource vital to the completion of the task. This was done on a chance basis, after both groups had agreed to follow the 'rules of the game'. The main focus of interest was on how the disadvantaged group would react. In fact, a recognizable sequence was observed, with the disadvantaged group showing less efficient organization and division of labour, and with them, first of all, spending a lot of time watching the advantaged group. After a while, though, they set to work, but in doing so 'closed their frontiers' so as to keep away the children of the other group. Most interestingly, they then set about their task in a way which was deliberately different from the approach adopted by the advantaged group. For instance, when it was quite obvious that they could not build as good a hut as the other group, they diverted considerable energy towards making a garden around their hut – something not specifically prohibited under the rules.

Lemaine also observed comparable behaviour among older subjects in situations of interpersonal rather than intergroup competition. In one experiment, psychology students wrote a fictitious letter of application for a job in a marketing agency. At first they only believed that they would have to write one letter, but then were instructed to write a second letter, believing themselves to be competing with another candidate who was either: (1) similar to themselves, (2) had previous experience of the job in question, or (3) had a superior academic background to their own. Subjects changed the content of their letters more in conditions (2) and (3) than in condition (1), and whereas the changes made in condition (1) tended to be simple additions, those in the latter two conditions suggested that subjects sought to differentiate themselves from their hypothetical rival by stressing new dimensions of comparison. In another experiment, subjects performed a task involving painting in the presence of a confederate of the experimenters, who either claimed to have, or not to have, a talent for painting. The experiment was supposedly about people's subjective sense of colour, so the instructions were simply that subjects paint *colours*. Those paired with another person supposedly no better at painting than themselves obeyed these instructions, whereas those who felt the other person to be more expert paid attention to features of design and composition not mentioned in the instructions. Lemaine interprets such findings as part of a general tendency for individuals to attempt to differentiate themselves from others along dimensions which allow them to maintain a positive self-evaluation and hence a sense of identity.

Besides seeking positive distinctiveness for themselves, minorities and less powerful groups or individuals may still exert influence on the attitudes and behaviour of the dominant majority. In the experiments on social influence and conformity described in Chapter 2 (pp. 32–8), the focus was primarily on how individuals adjust to the pressures from other members of the group. In other words, the question of the relationship between groups and individuals, or between majorities and minorities, has been posed traditionally in terms of the influence of the group on the individual, or of the majority on the minority. Such an approach may provide insights into how individuals become socialized into a given system, but is arguably less relevant to the question of how that system may come to change. Moscovici has described this tradition: 'The phenomenon of deviance has been barely skimmed, and viewed only in relation to conformity. Very few studies have looked at the conditions in which a minority may take innovative initiatives and change group norms. Nor has the function of independence within the group been the object of any research' (1976b: 43).

Our attitude towards nonconformists often can be quite ambivalent. In Schachter's (1951) study, there was clear evidence of rejection of the stubborn deviate by the majority, but on the other side Gerard and Greenbaum (1962) interviewed subjects who had taken part in conformity studies, and found that they gave stereotypically negative judgements of other members of the group who appeared to yield to a majority norm. As Moscovici points out, such results are difficult to reconcile with a view that individuals conform in order to gain esteem, since 'the only advantage of conformity that might be gained was to change in the eyes of the others from the status of deviant to the status of sheep' (1974: 203). Innovation and originality receive acclaim just as surely as deviance and defiance cause offence. Historical examples abound where one person's hero has been another's heretic. Contemporarily, opposition to political systems from within may be seen as dissident or treacherous, radical or subversive. From a cynical point of view, it might be argued that nonconformists are admired only if they challenge *other people's* norms, or after history has 'proved them right'. But there is also a more positive possibility: that groups may themselves seek change, perhaps especially as desired goals appear more difficult to obtain, and therefore welcome or give prominence to those who will show them a new direction.

To deviate, in terms of its Latin derivation, means to 'leave the main road', and the metaphor can be quite revealing. If one can be sure that the main road is leading to where one wants to go, and that what is important is arriving at one's destination, then a suggestion that a better way of getting there would be to take another ('devious') route might seem stupid, inefficient or dangerous. By the same token, forced diversions (or, as the French say, *deviations*) can cause frustration and delay. The Roman *via* was not 'just a road', but a major highway, essential to commerce and political control, and often passing through potentially hostile country. It would also represent the shortest and straightest route to one's destination. A reasonable analogy might be the railroads of America a century ago. To the ordinary traveller, as opposed to the explorer or adventurer, territories away from the main route would be inhospitable – unknown, uncivilized, undefended. Yet at the same time, the destination of the *via*, like that of the railroad, was fixed. If new territories were to be acquired, at some point an expedition would need to leave the familiar route, and strike out in a new direction, and this would be when the services of guides or pathfinders, either from among the native population, or from the less conforming colonists, would be indispensable.

Lemaine (1974) relates the notion of psychological differentiation to aspects of both Durkheim's and Darwin's theories, and, in the latter case particularly, the territorial metaphor is still appropriate: 'Darwinian competition is above all competition between close relations, and natural selection comes into play when, in a given region, there exist what might be called *vacant places* which can be better occupied when some of the existing inhabitants have undergone certain modifications' (p. 18). The traditional conformity model, in terms of which the group is seen as the source of rewards (acceptance) and punishments (rejection), thus appears far too simplistic. Individuals can be in competition with the other members of their group for rewards such as those of status, recognition, or affection, and to achieve such rewards they must take the essentially risky option of differentiating themselves from the other members – in other words, they must find a 'vacant place' within the group where their presence will be valued, and of course they may fail in their search. Lemaine points to the diversification of research activity within the scientific community as being one of a number of real-life examples of this search for 'vacant places'. Scientific 'distinction' requires finding questions which others have not answered, and then answering them, and the rewards for doing so can far outweigh, at least symbolically, those for more conventional activity.

This need for individuals to differentiate themselves from others implies that they might *not* wish to see themselves, in all circumstances, as completely similar to the other members of their group. This may be so in spite of a general tendency for individuals to expect members of their own reference group to behave in similar ways to themselves, even to the extent of overestimating such similarity (Hansen and Donoghue, 1977; Ross, Greene and House, 1977; see Chapter 6, pp. 187–9). Codol (1975) presents an abundance of evidence that individuals tend to see their own behaviour as more 'normative' than that of other members of their group. Codol's use of the term 'normative' deliberately implies the operation of two kinds of norms: 'factual' norms, which refer to conventional practices or customs, and 'desirable' norms which refer to conventional values or ideals. Unfortunately, Codol does not commit himself with regard to the factors which may make either one of these two kinds of norms the more salient in any situation. Nonetheless, according to Codol, whether individuals are asked to compare themselves with other members of an experimentally created group or of a real-life social category to which they belong, they will tend to describe themselves as closer to the standard or ideal of the group than they describe the other group members. This tendency, which Codol calls 'superior conformity of the self', seems to imply that individuals set a positive value on their group membership. The interesting thing is that they can do so at the same time as they attempt to distinguish themselves from the rest of the group.

Minority influence

The contest for 'vacant places', may occur both within and between groups. Because of this, there will be many circumstances in which *groups need their deviants*, or active minorities. If a group is unsure of its own direction, it will be more likely to listen to someone who claims to know the way, even if that way is different. In an experimental context, what may be involved may be no more than the need to achieve a reasonable consensus on a group discussion topic, or a successful solution to a problem. Sometimes an element of intergroup competition is introduced explicitly, but even without this, a confident minority can have a marked influence on the behaviour of the majority. A question that arises, therefore, is how a minority presents itself as being confident of its position without permanently antagonizing the other group members.

Recognizing the dangers to group members who take an innovative stance, Hollander (1964) suggested that an individual would be more likely to be accepted as a leader if he or she accumulated 'credits' by first showing competence and conforming to expectations. Moscovici (1976b: 48) cites this as an example of research which is 'solely concerned with innovating behaviour and non-conformity at the top end of the social scale'. Contrary to Hollander's hypothesis, Wahrman and Pugh (1972) demonstrated that an *early* innovative stand can have greater influence. They had groups of four subjects perform a task which required them to decide on a common strategy before each trial. One member of each group was a confederate who showed varying degrees of disruptive or deviant behaviour, claiming to be better at the task than the other subjects. The timing of this deviant behaviour constituted the main manipulation, and it was found that the earlier the confederate started being assertive in this way, the more likely it was that the other subjects would accept his suggestions. On the other hand, Bray, Johnson and Chilstrom (1982), using a similar procedure, compared the influence on other members of a four-person group of a confederate who followed either a 'Hollander' strategy of conforming at first and deviating at the end, or a 'Moscovici' strategy of deviating consistently throughout. Bray *et al.* found the 'Hollander' strategy to be the more effective, but only for male subjects. For females, the two strategies were equally effective.

Wolf (1985) looked at the influence of a consistent or inconsistent deviant, compared with a consistent or inconsistent majority of three in a group of four, under conditions of high or low 'cohesiveness' (manipulated as the degree to which the group members supposedly liked each other). The group members had to play the role of jurors assigning damages in a suit brought to gain compensation for accidental injury. Following Moscovici's (1980) suggestion that minority influence tends to be more indirect, she included measures of assigned damages, and also ratings of the severity of two different compensation levels (cf. Upshaw, 1978; see also Chapter 5, pp. 154–5). Although cohesiveness enhanced majority influence on the more direct (assignment) measure, consistency failed to produce a reliable increase in minority influence on either type of measure.

There is considerable evidence, though, that consistent subgroups (not just single deviants) can influence majorities to change their position. In an experiment by Moscovici, Lage and Naffrechoux (1969), female subjects were tested in groups of six and were required to judge whether a series of colour slides was blue or green. In fact, all the slides were blue, but they varied in light intensity. In a control condition, only 0.25 per cent of subjects' responses were 'green'. However, in an experimental condition, where two of the subjects, acting as confederates, consistently said, 'green' on every trial, the total number of 'green' responses made by the naive subjects increased to 8.42 per cent. Nearly one in three of these subjects made at least one 'green' response. These judgements were made publicly in a group setting, but in a second part of the same experiment, each subject was presented privately with sixteen more slides to categorize as 'blue' or 'green'. Of these, three were unambiguously blue and three were unambiguously green, while the remainder were blue–green. Subjects who had been in the experimental conditions were more likely than the controls to judge these blue–green stimuli as 'green' rather than 'blue'. Interestingly, this tendency was even stronger among those subjects who had *not* given any judgements of 'green' in the group setting. On the basis of these data, public compliance would not seem to be a necessary condition of private change in judgement in response to social influence.

Nemeth, Swedlund and Kanki (1974) followed up this study with an investigation of the effects of the consistency of the minority's position. As in the Moscovici *et al.* (1969) study, the stimuli were blue slides varying in light intensity, and subjects were tested in groups of six which included two confederates. In the main phase of the experiment, the two confederates responded 'green' to half the stimuli and 'green' and 'blue' to the other half. In one condition, these responses were given in a random order, unrelated to the light intensity of the stimuli. In a second condition, the confederates responded 'green' to the dimmest half of the stimulus series and 'green' and 'blue' to the brightest half. In a third condition, the pattern of the confederates' responses was reversed. The naive subjects were influenced by the two confederates in the latter two conditions, to the extent that they gave 'green' responses on nearly a quarter of the trials. In the first condition, however, almost no 'green' responses were given, suggesting that majorities are unlikely to be influenced by minorities whose judgements appear inconsistent. These results confirm those of an additional experiment reported by Moscovici *et al.* in which naive subjects were not influenced by confederates who similarly responded 'green' to half the stimuli, and 'blue' to the other half, but in a random order.

The data prompt the question, is minority influence different in kind from the influence of majorities on minorities and individuals (as described in Chapter 2, pp. 32–8), or can both types of process be incorporated into a single model? Moscovici (1976b; 67) argues that: 'Every group member, irrespective of his rank, is a potential source and receiver of influence' and that: 'Both minorities and majorities always exert influence' (1980: 212). In accordance with this part of Moscovici's position, attempts have been made to consider social influence as a single process, whether emanating from individuals, minorities, or majorities.

Social impact theory (Latané, 1981; Latané and Wolf, 1981) describes the influence of sources on targets in terms of a general functional relationship whereby the amount of impact depends on: 'the strength(s) or intensity (status, power, ability) of the source persons . . . their immediacy (I) or proximity in space of time to the target, and the number (N) of source persons present' (Latané and Wolf, 1981: 440–1). If however, there is more than one target person, the amount of impact will become diversified among the targets. In other words, the amount of impact should depend on strength, immediacy and number of people in the source group relative to the strength, immediacy and number of people in the target group.

Tanford and Penrod (1984) develop a more precise mathematical statement of these notions, which they term a *social influence model*. This is based on a computer simulation of jury decision-making, but is then applied to the results of a large number of published studies on conformity, minority influence, and rejection of deviants. Their findings support the notion that these different types of influence may be described parsimoniously within a single model. As hypothesized by Moscovici, moreover, the consistency of any influence source emerged as a strong predictor of its effectiveness.

Moscovici (1980: 211), however, maintains that: 'There is a difference in kind between majority and minority influence, which can be seen in the asymmetry between compliance and conversion.' Tanford and Penrod (1984) concluded from their meta-analysis of previous studies that the distinction between responding in public rather than private made relatively little difference to the amount of social influence obtained. Similarly, Wolf (1985), as has been described, failed to find evidence of greater influence by an individual on the rest of the group when a supposedly more 'indirect' dependent measure was used. However, experiments by Mugny (1974) and Papastamou (1979) (cited by Moscovici, 1980; see also Mugny, 1982) show that messages (on the issue of pollution) that were attributed to a minority group or institution produced more change on 'indirect' items which 'related to the topic but were not explicitly contained in the message' than on 'direct' items which 'were nearly identical with those contained in the message'.

As regards *quantitative* predictions of the amount of impact of majorities and minorities on one another, therefore, there are good reasons to be attracted to the parsimony of approaches such as the social influence model of Tanford and Penrod (1984). Moscovici's hypothesis of *qualitative* differences between types of influence, however, requires a finer-grain investigation, and may be usefully considered in relation to the work of Petty and Cacioppo (1985; see Chapter 2, pp. 44–9) on cognitive responses to persuasion.

'Indirect' influence or 'conversion', in Moscovici's terms, may be essentially the same as what Petty and Cacioppo describe as the 'central' route to persuasion, and may depend on recipients elaborating their own arguments and inferences in response to a message or influence attempt. Indeed, the importance of elaboration for the stability of any change is quite compatible with the notion that 'conversion' should be deeper and more long-lasting than 'compliance'. In comparison, it is reasonable to suppose that influence from the majority, that will be by definition more normative (at least in a statistical sense) will be processed more peripherally or heuristically (Chaiken, 1980). In simple terms, one may be more prepared to accept the views of the majority than of the minority without considering them in great detail. Minorities or deviants, on the other hand, will be more salient and distinctive (see Chapter 5, pp. 135–6), and hence may prompt more active processing of a message. Mugny, Kaiser, Papastamou and Pérez (1984) reach a similar conclusion:

The mere fact that minority gains recognition as a possible alternative in a social field, notwithstanding its lack of direct influence, brings about a *cognitive activity* that reshuffles the field's categories and reassigns different characteristics to the various entities which have been newly identified and differentiated in this process. (p. 321; emphasis added)

Identity and influence

One ambiguity in discussions of majority and minority influence is whether one is simply considering pressures arising from divergences of opinion, however distributed, between individual members of a single group, or whether the division between majorities and minorities is perceived as an *intergroup* discrepancy. At what point does a minority cease to be simply a minority within a group, and become a separate 'minority group'. Since much of the experimental literature on 'minority influence' deals with minorities of *one* (e.g. Wolf, 1985) this is more than a semantic issue. The effects here may be quite different from those of attributing opinions to minorities in society (e.g. Mugny, 1982).

What this leads to is the need for classification of what one means by a 'social group'. Turner (1982) has proposed what he terms a 'cognitive redefinition of the social group'. His basic position is that 'a social group can be defined as two or more individuals who share a common social identification of themselves or, which is nearly the same thing, perceive themselves to be members of the same social category' (p. 15).

There are various implications of defining groups in terms of members' perceptions. Turner discusses the relationship of attraction to social identity as follows:

attraction to *individuals as individuals* does not create a group, but attraction to *individuals as group members*, which presupposes social categorization reinforces social identification by defining the common attributes of group membership as positive. (pp. 26–7, emphasis in original)

To account for how group membership relates to influence, Turner postulates a new concept of *referent informational influence*. This is seen as incorporating aspects of identification (Kelman, 1961), referent power (French and Raven, 1959) and informational influence (Deutsch and Gerard, 1955), and is seen as consisting of three stages:

(i) Individuals define themselves as members of a distinct social category.
(ii) Individuals form or learn the stereotypic norms of that category. They ascertain that certain ways of behaving are criterial attributes of category membership. Certain appropriate, expected or desirable behaviours are used to define the category as different from other categories.
(iii) Individuals using these norms to themselves in the same way that they assign other stereotypic characteristics of the category to themselves when

their category membership becomes psychologically salient. Thus their behaviour bcomes more normative (conformist) as their category membership becomes salient. (p. 31)

This form of social influence, then, will be strongest when people's group membership is most salient, and will occur when information is provided concerning criterial norms of their own group. For instance, an individual will be more likely to comply or agree with a source who is seen both as a member of the individuals' own group and as responding in a manner prototypical of that group.

For Turner, then, influence depends upon social identity. But what precisely *is* social identity? Many writers in this area are disconcertingly vague about their assumptions on this point. In Turner's work, two main themes are apparent. First, he draws a distinction between the *self-concept*, which he regards as a relatively enduring cognitive structure, and *self-images*, which reflect the functioning of that system at any point in time, may operate relatively independently of each other, and may be responsive to specific situational demands, reflecting the possibility 'that people have learnt to regulate their social behaviour in terms of different self-conceptions at different times' (1982: 20). Social identity is then defined as a 'subsystem of the self-concept' that 'seems to be "switched on" by certain situations' (1982: 21). The second part of Turner's definition of social identity is that it involves *self-categorization* (Turner, 1985), on the basis of criterial attributes, and that the way one categorizes oneself is what determines one's social behaviour.

Turner assumes an inverse relationship between the tendency to categorize oneself at a personal individual level on the one hand, and at the level of group membership on the other. He refers to the process of coming to perceive the self as a group member as 'depersonalization'. Situational factors can facilitate or impede this process of depersonalization, or in other words, make alternative individual or group dimensions of the self more salient. Reicher's (1984b) analysis of crowd behaviour thus provides an illustration, from Turner's perspective, of depersonalization (the definition of the self as group member) which is quite different from deindividuation (the loss of individual inhibitions over destructive impulses).

An issue to which Reicher (1984b) alludes, however, is whether particular events trigger the adoption of a self-categorization in group terms, which then motivates collective action, or whether involvement in collective action itself enables participants to think differently about themselves both as group members and individuals. Social identity may not just stimulate social behaviour, it may be learned and discovered *through* social behaviour.

Different situations may therefore 'switch on' personal or social identities. But can both personal *and* social definitions of the self be held in mind at the same time? Recall the discussion of the concepts of role distance and role choice at the end of Chapter 8. Group members who behave so as to *be* just members of the group and not individuals as well are engaging in a denial of self – an act of 'bad faith' (Sartre, 1943, translated 1969). By the same token, individuals who try to define themselves completely as individuals without reference to any broader social context are engaging in a converse form of existential denial. These different forms of denial have their parallels in collectivist and individualist ideologies – indeed, a fair definition of an idealogue is someone who achieves consistency by the denial or reinterpretation of contradiction. Yet, if we accept Billig's (1985) argument, contradiction may be an even more natural state of mind than consistency.

From social identity to social change

Perceived group membership has a major impact on most if not all the processes discussed elsewhere in this book – among them attitude change, social influence, self-esteem, attribution, equity, attraction, social judgement, and destructive behaviour. Indeed, it is tempting to argue that if one *completely* excludes the concept of groups and social identity from these different topic areas, what one is left with is something barely *social* psychological at all. But how far has research on social identity moved towards Tajfel's ultimate goal of a theoretical account of the psychological processes involved in social change *over time*?

Work such as that by Moscovici (1980) and Mugny (1982) on minority influence demonstrates change of a kind, but only change at the level of individual cognitive response. Changes in structural relationships within the group can at best be inferred, and interpretations of presumably similar societal changes require extrapolations by analogy. Unless, like Reicher (1984b), one can be ready with an applicable theory in one pocket and a notebook in the other for any sudden manifestation of the pressures for change within a society, one cannot realistically hope to study social change *as such* unless time is allowed within one's research design for such change to occur. Even when one has many years in which to gather data, however, many of the psychological variables which relate to more general theoretical concerns – attitudes, values, ingroup loyalty and such like – may sometimes prove remarkably stable over time (Himmelweit *et al.*, 1981).

There is, then, an inevitable mismatch between the empirical research methods typically used by social psychologists and the theoretical task of explaining change in the structure of relationships within society. On the other hand, this is no reason simply to give up the task of trying to achieve at least some improvement to our understanding of important events in what we revealingly term the 'real' world. Our methods, while imperfect, may be better than many, and their mismatch with our theoretical goals may be neither total, nor so wide than it cannot be bridged by a mixture of conceptual argument and fortuitous evidence.

A social psychological study of social change, therefore, needs to start from some basic assumptions that essentially have to be assumed *a priori*, and without which the research activity itself becomes pointless. We need to assume:

(1)   That actions directed at producing (or resisting) change in the structure of relationships within a society or social group depend at least partly on the motives of the individual actors concerned.

(2)   That such motives for action can be a function of how the actors interpret (parts of) the social system to which they belong, and their own relationship to it.

(3)   That such interpretations of the social system will be at least partly responsive to external events – either through events causing a change in the interpretations, or through making it more likely that different interpretations will be called to mind.

If we allow ourselves these assumptions, we can in fact proceed quite a long way without the need for further apology. We can start to ask what kinds of motives and interpretations prompt what kinds of actions, and what kinds of external events produce what kinds of cognitive change. In other words, there are plenty of issues on which empirical progress can yet be made.

Although Tajfel (1978) predicts motivation for social mobility or social change from differences in status and perceived legitimacy and stability of intergroup distinctions, he does not explicitly propose any sequence for changes in such variables. Taylor and McKirnan (1984), however, have attempted to do precisely this. Their 'five-stage model of intergroup relations' is illustrated in Figure 9.1.

Essentially, this assumes an historical progression from a situation of status differences perceived as both legitimate and stable (stage 1); to a perception of such differences as legitimate, but unstable in the sense of the class boundaries being increasingly permeable through individual social mobility (stages 2 and 3); to a stage when the legitimacy as well as the stability of the status difference is called into question (stage 4); and finally to a stage of collective action by the disadvantaged group for social change (stage 5).

There is much to be said both for and against stage theories in many branches of psychology. Certainly, for such a progression to occur at all, one must assume that reactionary efforts on the part of the advantaged group fail to achieve the goal of restoring a *status quo ante*. One must allow also for the possibility of external events, not necessarily under the control of either group, causing either a jump forward or backward in the system. For example, the need for a female workforce during the First World War has often been cited as a factor that accelerated women's political emancipation.

There is also the issue of the point at which one enters the system. Where do the status differences come from? If, as may often be the case, one is

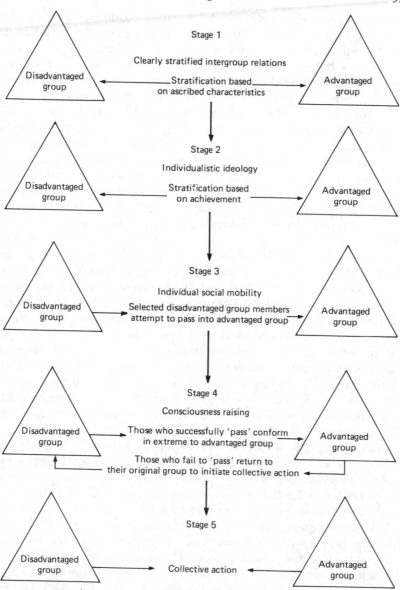

Figure 9.1. Stages in the dynamics of intergroup relations. (From D. M. Taylor and D. J. McKirnan, 'A five-stage model of intergroup relations', *British Journal of Social Psychology*, 23 (1984), 293. Copyright 1984 by the British Psychological Society. Reprinted with permission.)

dealing with groups of conquered and conquerors, or where the 'disadvantaged group' was shipped in chains from another continent, how can it be assumed that one *starts* with a stratification perceived to be legitimate? Even without explicit attribution to earlier group conflicts, differences of class still need explanation ('When Adam delved and Eve span, who was then the gentleman?'). If one can derive from Taylor and McKirnan (1984) any insight into the psychological bases of liberalization, liberation and revolution, this only reinforces the need to examine also the psychological bases of conservatism, oppression and reaction to which these are opposed.

Schemes such as that proposed by Taylor and McKirnan are most unlikely to capture the complexities of any specific historical change, yet, if they do nothing else, they may prompt social psychologists to be prepared to think in more historical terms. This does not need to involve only interpretation of past events, or extensive longitudinal studies of social movements (that need luck and/or foresight to ensure that the right social movements are selected for study). Empirical research can still be conducted to examine what is happening psychologically at a single point or stage within the system.

For instance, if, despite its limitations already mentioned, we take the Taylor and McKirnan scheme as a starting point, we can ask questions such as the following: At early stages, how do the disadvantaged group members interpret the stability of the status distinction? Is the distinction simply accepted, or do feelings of powerlessness lead to alienation? Is alienation itself a useful or unitary concept (Seeman, 1971)? At 'stage 3', what distinguishes the 'selected disadvantaged group members' who attempt to pass into the advantaged group? How does their behaviour reflect their self-categorization? At 'stage four' *how*, in terms of communication, is 'consciousness raised'? What changes in expectancy of success and ingroup evaluation occur, and what are the messages and events that bring such changes about?

In particular, is the model correct in predicting that successful 'passing' is associated with extreme conformity, with the implication of complete denial of one's previous social identity, whereas it is the *unsuccessful* 'passers' or climbers who 'return to their original group to initiate collective action'. This seems to put down the impetus for social change through collective action to a kind of 'sour grapes' disaffection. A contrary view may be that *successful* 'passers' may acquire the power and skills necessary to accelerate the emancipation of members of their original group, and may indeed take on the role of champions for the less advantaged members of their original group. Walker and Pettigrew (1984) allow for this possibility in their discussion of how individuals may feel 'fraternally deprived' even though they are more fortunate than others in their group.

A feeling of 'belongingness' to a group implies in no small part the appropriation of a representation of the group as an *historical* entity, so that memories, real or legendary, of the origins of one's group and its relationships to other groups are accepted as in some sense one's own, even if one has never oneself experienced the past agonies or glories which such representations describe. Such representations, moreover, may be invoked as a framework for the interpretation of current events and as an impetus for current action, even where they refer to events of years centuries or millenia before. Mere affluence or personal success may not by itself erase these aspects of a person's identity, though it may make them less accessible.

Thus, within a single psalm, one can find an historical evocation of group loyalty, a pledge of revenge, but still an admission of the temptation to forget:

> By the rivers of Babylon, there we sat down, yea, we wept, when we remembered Zion.
>
> Happy shall he be, that taketh and dasheth thy little ones against the stones.
>
> If I forget thee, O Jerusalem, let my right hand forget her cunning. (Psalm 137: 1, 9 and 5)

In much the same way may *émigrés* in many parts of the world nurture sentiments of liberation of their (or their forebears') homeland, while some pledge material support for armed struggle by those whom one side will see as terrorists and the other as freedom fighters. Beautiful and ugly sentiments can thus be simultaneously evoked by identification with a group, and different kinds of identification may be in tension with each other. Identity may not simply depend on the selection of situationally appropriate self-images from a larger repertoire. Rather, it may be the outcome of a *constructive* process of making sense of oneself, and of where one fits, socially and historically, into a larger scheme of things.

Both Tajfel (1978) and Turner (1982) clearly acknowledge that self-definitions in entirely personal or group terms are idealized abstractions that may rarely be present in their pure form. The remaining point at issue is whether most people's identities lie at intermediate points along a *single* continuum from more social to more personal, or whether most people learn somehow to live with potentially contradictory identities (to which they may attach varying importance at different times), some of which may be primarily 'social', some primarily 'personal', and some, for all we know, something else besides. In terms of Moscovici's (1984; see Chapter 7, pp. 243–50) approach, how 'consensual' is the universe that our social representations create? The assumption of a single social to personal continuum has an appealing simplicity, but perhaps, as someone once said, if you live in a pretzel-shaped universe, you need pretzel-shaped hypotheses.

Conclusions

Recent years have witnessed an important change in the emphasis and direction of research on group processes. Before, attention was focused mainly on the normalizing and stabilizing effects of group interaction, and, with the important exception of Sherif (1951), most researchers neglected the question of intergroup processes. Wider issues of intergroup relations tended to be discussed in the context either of individual attitudes, or of cooperation and competition between individuals. These more traditional approaches have since been balanced by a concern with processes of differentiation and innovation, and with intergroup as well as intragroup behaviour.

It is undoubtedly the case that groups may impose conditions and restrictions on their individual members, and that individuals will frequently defer to the norms of their group, and will validate their own judgements by reference to others. Yet any role has its rights as well as its responsibilities, and mere performance of a role is not by itself an adequate basis for a sense of identity. As Goffman (1972; see Chapter 8, pp. 287–8) argued in his discussion of 'role distance', it is important to individuals' sense of identity and personal worth to be able to feel and show that they are more than the role they perform. It is good to be a good team-member, but not good to be *just* a good team-member. It is good to belong, but not good to be type-cast, to have nothing personal to offer. Individuals will compare themselves with others, not simply to see how they can be the same, but also to see how they can be different.

Earlier work both on deindividuation and on discrimination between groups tended to stress the competitive and essentially destructive aspects of group behaviour. This was attributed either to disinhibition of primitive impulses or to conflict of interest between groups and community of interest within groups. The competitive aspects continue to be stressed, but the goal of such competition is not simply or necessarily material profit, so much as the attainment of a 'positive social identity' – the ability to evaluate oneself positively as a member of a distinct and positively valued group. Such an identity is assumed to depend upon comparison with other groups and to be more salient in some situations than others. As with all other comparisons, the crucial factors will be the standards available for comparison and the dimensions perceived as relevant. Not all aspects of a person's self-concept are likely to be consistent with each other, or to carry compatible implications for action. The capacity of individuals and groups to create and discover standards and dimensions of comparison appropriate to their identity remains one of the most fundamental aspects of human social behaviour. Social identification is a constructive process that can lay the psychological foundations for social change.

PART V

CONCLUSIONS

10
Achievements and prospects

Progress and fashion

A popular view of scientific research is that it is rather like a detective story. A crime is committed. The unimaginative police inspector puts a conventional interpretation on the more obvious clues and makes an arrest. Then along comes some eccentric who views the crime as an intellectual puzzle, worries about apparent trivia that fail to hang together, and, as one suspect after another is eliminated, comes up with the true answer, so that the innocent prisoner is freed and the murderer is handed over for punishment.

Up to a point, the analogy holds. At the level of trying to work out why a specific effect occurs, research can indeed seem like detection. Certainly, it involves an element of fussing over facts that seem not to fit with each other, and a preparedness to challenge conventional solutions if they do not seem quite conclusive. A large part of research design involves playing around with alternative possibilities, until one can crystallize one's reasoning along such lines as: 'if theory A is correct, then, under these conditions, this should happen. If theory B is correct, then, something else should happen.' One of the things that can be most fun about doing research is seeing some of these 'if–then' connections one imagined turn into actuality in the response of one's subjects.

The analogy starts to fail, however, as soon as one starts to move away from the confines of a specific paradigm to a choice of broader theoretical perspectives. It is rather as though we were simultaneously involved in a large number of different detective stories where some of the characters were the same and some were different, and where we could only guess, at first, whether the different stories related to each other in any reliable way. The fortune-hunting tennis coach, who, despite appearances, had not in fact disposed of the gardener in story one by practising his two-handed backhand with the garden spade, may still need to be considered as a serious suspect for the strangling of the maid in story two. When it comes to gaining evidence, moreover, we may still be able to do tests to confirm or disprove individual alibis for specific times and events, but, when examining witnesses, we may never feel entirely sure that we are hearing the truth, the whole truth and nothing but the truth.

Whilst it is relatively easy, then, to evaluate the comparative merits of different models and hypotheses as explanations of specific effects, it is much more difficult to decide whether, and if so why, one *type* of theory should be preferred to another. One cannot simply take the temporary ascendancy of a particular theoretical approach in social psychology as implying that it has been 'proved' superior to what has gone before, or that the dominant approaches of a few years earlier have been conclusively eliminated from investigation like so many fictional distractions.

The relative popularity and unpopularity of different theoretical approaches is a product of many factors. Intrinsic coherence and predictive power alone does not guarantee that a theory will be widely used. Research does not take place in a totally free environment. The resources on which research depends are limited, and in social psychology even more limited at the time of writing than even five or ten years ago. Funding agencies have their own priorities and even prejudices; so too may appointments and promotions committees, on whom the careers of researchers depend. Even when research is conducted, to make any impact it needs to be published. Typically, papers submitted for publication are evaluated by independent (unpaid) reviewers ideally with a special expertise in the area investigated by the authors. By and large, the great majority of reviewers are conscientious, non-vindictive and constructive, even if mistakes are sometimes made. Theirs can be a time-consuming and fairly thankless task. Nonetheless, however helpful reviewers are trying to be *according to their own lights*, they will tend to evaluate a new piece of research in relation to their own schema or interpretation of what constitute 'important issues' in the field. This is *not* to say that papers are easier to get published if they merely confirm what other people think. It is rather that quite a number of studies get published, even though they may be pretty pedestrian from the point of view of creativity, simply because they are seen to contribute to an 'ongoing debate'.

Thus, a set of contingencies is set up for reinforcing researchers, at least in the short term, for working on 'safer', more conventional topics and within the framework of more 'established' theoretical approaches. This is not altogether a bad thing. A point in its favour is that researchers need colleagues who share their interests, to whom they can explain their ideas without going back to first principles, and with whom they can collaborate. But what this can also lead to is the reinforcement and reproduction of fashions in method and theory. In short, there are bandwagons. What saves the system from mere sterile normativeness is that there is also a counter-norm, as Lemaine (1974) puts it, to seek out 'vacant places' so that individual researchers may gain recognition for more independent creativity. It may not be as easy, but it is still possible. On any bandwagon there will be some people who object to feeling crowded in, and will be on the look-out for a chance to jump off as soon as it looks like slowing down. This, though, can lead to sudden switches in fashion, so that the cycle begins again.

This may sound very cynical. That is not my intention. My point is that learning about social psychology is not just learning about some 'body of knowledge'. Read between the lines and what you will see is also a *social activity*. Those that perform this activity differ widely from one another in talent, skills, experience, style and influence; they are bound to and separated from each other by ties of institutional or national identity, by relationships of dependence and autonomy, collaboration and rivalry, affection and ambition, respect and neglect, admiration and indifference. The system is human. It has its faults, but also its strengths, and one thing at least unites us all: a wish to achieve a better understanding of human thought and behaviour.

How, then, are the products of this activity to be interpreted? As a steady linear progress from ignorance to enlightenment? As the whimsical spinning of some wheel of fortune? Neither picture is entirely fair. Research *does* add to the 'body of knowledge', but not in a steadily cumulative way. Today's social psychologists *have* learned from the work of ten or twenty years ago, and not simply from the mistakes that were made. But, there is still far too much tyranny of the here and now, of a discarding of ideas that derive from another time and place. Returning to the analogy of the detective story, we are bound to miss some vital clues if we assume that the early part of the story consists only of red herrings.

There are many reasons, then, why theoretical approaches gain or lose popularity, or are simply ignored. Even so, an important factor is still what an approach appears to offer, intrinsically, in terms of a new integration of existing findings and prospects for new research, against the background of what has gone before. Of course there is conformity, but there is much else besides. No single approach may encapsulate all the answers, but neither can we retreat to a kind of 'anything goes' agnosticism or solipsism, where we pretend that we have no way of telling whether ideas are good or bad, and where any crackpot speculation can command attention, regardless of the evidence. There may be contrary exceptions to every general theoretical principle in social psychology, but this does not mean that we should abandon theory, nor the rules of argument and rules of evidence upon which the building and testing of theory depends.

The experimental method

Viewed as a whole, social psychology research since the 1950s at least has been characterized, on the one hand methodologically, by a reliance on the laboratory experiment and on the other hand theoretically, by an almost relentless rise of the 'cognitive approach' in its various shapes and guises.

The use of the experimental method has played a large part in distinguishing social psychology from other social sciences, but it has also attracted familiar criticisms. Most social psychological experiments have involved a fairly small number of basic laboratory paradigms, frequently using a captive population of psychology students as subjects. The kinds of social interaction which can take place in such laboratory settings are often very restricted and artificial. Yet the experiment, for all its shortcomings, is more than a device to enable social psychologists to align themselves with other branches of psychology. What is often overlooked is that experiments *work*, and social psychologists have continued to use them because they work, rather than because of some deliberately endorsed philosophical or ideological stance. What I mean by this is not that experiments always confirm the experimenter's hypotheses, nor that experimental effects may not be subject to important limiting conditions, be these procedural, individual, cultural or historical. Nor do I deny that experimentation may demand a measure of skill and sensitivity which may be unequally shared or acquired. An experiment is like a radio: if we twiddle the knobs at random, there's no telling what we will find, nor any guarantee that it will be in a language we understand, even though the radio itself may be in perfect working order. On the other hand, if the radio is accurately tuned, we can expect to hear something, and also, which is especially important, we can expect others whose radios are similarly tuned to hear the same thing.

A basic assumption of the experimental method is that results are in principle reproducible, and that where apparent discrepancies occur, they should in principle be able to be resolved. If two experiments produce results which seem to conflict, it matters. Sometimes such discrepancies may lead to important theoretical advances, sometimes they may arise because one of the experiments was confounded, or was measuring something different from the other, but they are not to be simply shrugged off with an, 'Oh well, different people find different things.' The experiment provides both a testing ground for ideas and a language for debate. Without it, it is difficult to see how social psychology could have avoided veering off course towards either of the twin dangers of impressionistic invention or aimless head-counting that have characterized an unfortunately large proportion of what has passed for 'social research' over the years.

But of course, there are experiments and experiments. In their search for reproducible results, many experimenters have not worried too much about the correspondence between such results and behaviour outside the laboratory. Many have played safe, adding only minor variations to well-tried paradigms. Yet there has also been a trend, over recent years, away from rigidly controlled 'minimal' situations towards the study of behaviour both inside and, especially, outside the laboratory that has much more of a 'real-life' flavour. In a number of ways studies of this sort are not 'true' experiments, in that subjects may be allocated to conditions on the basis of prior attitudes or other characteristics, rather than by random selection from some homogeneous population, and procedures may be used which contain many aspects that cannot all, from a practical point of view, be controlled and manipulated independently. These studies, however, do not negate the value of the experimental method, but rather affirm the confidence that social psychologists now have in that method, which allows them to take a few risks and relax a few controls in the search for richer and more realistic social situations. Like radio broadcasts, laboratory experiments can only offer a selective account of social phenomena. One may need to check for oneself whether such selectivity is balanced, biased or misleading. Ultimately, the 'ideal' experiment, in which *all* non-manipulated variables are held constant, is only one means to an end, which is the disciplined comparison of effects under different conditions. Experiments are about *comparison*, at least as much as they are about control.

The cognitive approach

On the theoretical side, the cognitive approach to social psychology has been built upon a view of the individual as an *active processor of information*. The assumption has been that the effect of any stimulus depends on how it is categorized and interpreted by the perceiver, and that this interpretation depends both on attributes of the stimulus and on the perceiver's prior expectations and standards of comparison. Stimuli, in other words, are not reacted to in isolation, but in terms of their relation to previous learning and experience. This in turn leads on to assumptions about how social information is stored in memory, and how it can be recalled. The functions of such information-processing are variously considered in terms of the need to predict and/or explain one's environment, to be 'correct', to create selective and simplified representations of events so that decisions can be made with an economy of effort, and such like.

Within this general approach, theoretical debates have still gone on, of course. There have been issues of the importance to be afforded to consistency as an organizing principle, of whether stereotyping reflects illusion or the accentuation of marginal differences, of whether all attributions are causal, and so on. But through all this, cognition has seemed to reign supreme. Why? The answer is probably that a cognitive approach offered social (and other) psychologists an escape from the straightjacket of an unreconstructed behaviourism with little time or patience for mentalistic concepts such as attitudes, whilst at the same time avoiding the apparent non-empiricism of psychodynamic approaches. This is not to say that concepts from these other traditions have not occasionally leaked through. Bem's (1967) self-perception theory of attitudes carries a behaviourist flag, and Zimbardo (1969b) is prepared to talk of unrestrained primitive impulses in his attempt to explain crowd behaviour. The principal motif, though, has sounded through clearly: people act the way they do because they have decided to do so, and they make the decisions they do because of the way they process information.

In the last few years, though, there have been some potentially far-reaching shifts in direction, and an increasing questioning of the all-importance of cognition. Part of the impetus for this has come from demonstrations of the imperfect or 'bounded' nature of human rationality. Decision-makers we may be, but normatively 'rational' decision-makers we are not. Nisbett and Ross (1980) put forward probably the most eloquent statement of this position. Of course, the ripostes have come in fast: what looks 'irrational' in an experiment may be very adaptive in real life (Hogarth, 1981). Even so, the attack has not been entirely deflected. Cognitive processes in social psychology need to be seen in terms of their *functional* relationship to *behaviour*, not just in terms of their match or mismatch with some notion of symmetry or good form.

But quite what is the functional relationship of cognition to behaviour? This raises the issue of attitude–behaviour relations again. In a way, the early studies that showed little correlation between attitudes and behaviour gave cognitivists implicit licence to do whatever they wished with the attitude concept. Attitudes could be studied 'for their own sake'. Fishbein and Ajzen (1975) reestablished attitude as a major predictor of behaviour, but when they came to offer an *explanation* of the predictability that they observed, they produced a theory that is as unrepentantly cognitive and rationalistic as any that one is likely to find. But overlooked in much of this was the matter of the stability of behaviour over time. Not all decisions are new ones. Much behaviour is habitual, and when it is, attitudes, even though they may be predictably related to behaviour, may make no identifiable causal contribution.

Habit, that bland but dangerous concept, thus returns quietly into social psychology, and with it comes a reevaluation of the importance of deliberate decision-making and conscious monitoring of behaviour in social interaction. Langer's (1978) concept of 'mindlessness' is the most forthright expression of this tendency, but she is not alone in questioning the idea that people always think before they act, and that they can tell us what they think.

As habit comes in through one door, emotion has started knocking at the other. Some years ago, Manis (1977: 562) gave the following warning:

> Motivational variables are given scant consideration by many cognitive theories. This is doubtless a healthy corrective from an earlier tradition in which unconscious motives, fantasies, and unbridled emotional reactions were too-freely invoked to account for social phenomena. On the other hand, the recent popularity of 'cool' cognitive formulations like attribution theory should not blind us to the important role of motivation and emotion in social phenomena.

Up to a point, a number of the major areas of social psychology could be interpreted as indirect attempts to study emotional experience – for attitude read affect, for interpersonal attraction read love and friendship, and so on.

But although this is a partial defence, the point is still that cognitive processes have been assumed to be primary. Our beliefs supposedly *cause* our attitudes, the perception of another's attributes *causes* attraction, attribution of failure to uncontrollable factors *cause* depression, and so on. But just suppose the relationships can be the other way round, as Zajonc (1980) and others, in more moderate terms, have suggested. We would then need to treat beliefs and cognitions as effects, and not just as antecedents, which is something that dissonance researchers have long realized. (Indeed, the revitalization of dissonance research is a fascinating subplot illustrating this same theme.)

What effect have these intrusions had upon the inner sanctum of social cognition? As may be seen from the review by Fiske and Taylor (1984), the dominant tendency has been an attempt to accommodate these developments within a cognitive approach. At the same time, though, there has been a good deal of new energy directed towards applying the *methods* of cognitive psychology to problems in social psychology. This is evident in various studies of memory and recall, of the effects of priming, and in the use of reaction time measures. As paradigms for the study of naturally-occurring social behaviour, these experimental procedures have severe limitations. Even so, the conceptual contribution of these studies has been very important. In particular, the same story is told of the importance of previously learned associations, of stimuli influencing responses even without having been consciously monitored, and of mood and emotion influencing 'basic' cognitive processes.

We come back, then, to something rather reminiscent of the Rosenberg and Hovland (1960) distinction of affect, cognition and behaviour, but in a more general context than that of attitudes alone. We are dealing with areas of psychological functioning that each have their own learning history, but still impinge on one another. Claims for primacy are unnecessary and unlikely to be long substantiated. We are dealing with different classes of mutually interacting phenomena – not epiphenomena, not 'mental way-stations' – just phenomena.

Experience is social

At least as represented in the North American literature, social psychology remains as it has long been, a predominantly individualistic social science. Is this necessarily a criticism? Surely it is as silly to blame psychologists for not being sociologists as it is to blame sociologists (of a certain kind) for not being psychologists? This is fair enough up to a point, but we are special kinds of psychologists. We claim to have something to say about *social* behaviour, about *interaction* between groups and individuals.

But what changes does such a criticism demand? I cannot accept that we should simply throw away the study of individual thought and experience in the search for the collective and the supposedly consensual. Nonetheless, the kinds of questions we might ask about the psychological processes of individuals could sometimes be quite different if we take this criticism to heart.

Consider how this might apply in the field of attitude research. Attitudes are a form of subjective evaluative experience, and most theories have considered attitude organization in terms of psychic structures within the individual. Yet both the experience of attitudes and the various forms of their expression are socially conditioned. Consistency itself may be a social product, a style of thought and argumentation acquired because, but only insofar as, it is functional for communication and social relationships. Verbal expressions of attitude – often all we have as a sign of another's private experiences – are public acts depending on a shared system of representation, a shared set of assumptions concerning prior knowledge of the issue, and of the frame of reference within which any remark may be interpreted. Above all, the identification of *arguments* as a means of expression implies a context in which others may disagree. The simplest fact about attitudes, that people disagree with one another, is also the most problematic for conventional theories, which can predict one individual's attitude, and then go on to predict another's, but say little or nothing about the disagreement *as such*. Yet, at the level of individual experience and expression the possibility of disagreement is already acknowledged.

The importance of language for social psychology can hardly be overemphasized. It is not the only code of communication used by human beings but it is by far the most adaptable. This remarkable skill would not have evolved without a function, and this function is all to do with social relationships. It binds the self to the other, the private to the public, the personal to the communal, in an inextricable web of reciprocal links. Through language we communicate what we think and feel, but then because we have communicated, we *experience* our thoughts and feelings as shared, as having reference to objects and events beyond ourselves. We experience *ourselves*, too, as parts of an experience that others share. Our personhood involves an identity that is not ours alone but is both labelled *and experienced* as a classification that others share. Social identity involves not just seeing oneself as part of the group, but seeing the group as part of oneself.

It is because human beings communicate that what is individual is at the same time social. We are not looking at two sides of a fence, but at two sides of a coin. To attempt a synthesis is not easy. It is here, though, that we may find the best future for social psychology, and the best of its past.

References

Abelson, R. P. (1959). Modes of resolution of belief dilemmas. *Journal of Conflict Resolution, 3,* 343–52.

Abelson, R. P. (1976). Script-processing in attitude formation and decision making. In J. S. Carroll & J. W. Payne (eds.), *Cognition and Social Behavior.* Hillsdale, NJ: Erlbaum.

Abelson, R. P. (1981). Psychological status of the script concept. *American Psychologist, 36,* 715–29.

Abramson, L. Y., Seligman, M. E. P. & Teasdale, J. D. (1978). Learned helplessness in humans: critique and reformulation. *Journal of Abnormal Psychology, 87,* 49–74.

Adams, J. S. (1963). Toward an understanding of inequity. *Journal of Abnormal and Social Psychology, 67,* 422–36.

Adams, J. S. (1965). Inequity in social exchange. In L. Berkowitz (ed.), *Advances in experimental social psychology.* Vol. 2. New York: Academic Press.

Aderman, D. (1969). Effects of anticipating future interaction on the preference for balanced states. *Journal of Personality and Social Psychology, 11,* 214–19.

Aderman, D., Brehm, D. & Katz, L. B. (1974). Empathetic observation of an innocent victim: The just world revisited. *Journal of Personality and Social Psychology, 29,* 342–47.

Adorno, T. W., Frenkel-Brunswick, E., Levinson, D. J. & Sanford, R. N. (1950). *The authoritarian personality.* New York: Harper and Row.

Ager, J. W. & Dawes, R. M. (1965). The effect of judges' attitude on judgment. *Journal of Personality and Social Psychology, 1,* 533–8.

Ajzen, I. (1977). Intuitive theories of events and the effects of base-rate information on prediction. *Journal of Personality and Social Psychology, 35,* 303–14.

Ajzen, I. & Fishbein, M. (1969). The prediction of behavioral intentions in a choice situation. *Journal of Experimental Social Psychology, 5,* 400–15.

Ajzen, I. & Fishbein, M. (1970). The prediction of behavior from attitudinal and normative beliefs. *Journal of Personality and Social Psychology, 6,* 466–87.

Ajzen, I. & Fishbein, M. (1977). Attitude–behavior relations: A theoretical analysis and a review of empirical research. *Psychological Bulletin, 84,* 888–918.

Ajzen, I. & Fishbein, M. (1980). *Understanding attitudes and predicting social behavior.* Englewood Cliffs, NJ: Prentice-Hall.

Alexander, C. N. Jr., Zucker, L. G. & Brody, C. L. (1970). Experimental expectations and autokinetic experiences: Consistency theories and judgmental convergence. *Sociometry, 33,* 108–22.

Allais, M. (1953). Le comportement de l'homme rationnel devant le risque: Critique des postulats et axiomes de l'école americaine. *Econometrica, 21,* 503–46.

Allen, V. L. & Levine, J. M. (1968). Social support, dissent, and conformity. *Sociometry, 31,* 138–49.

Alloy, L. B., Peterson, C., Abramson, L. L. & Seligman, M. E. P. (1984). Attributional style and the generality of learned helplessness. *Journal of Personality and Social Psychology, 46,* 681–7.

Alloy, L. B. & Tabachnik, N. (1984). Assessment of covariation by humans and animals: The joint influence of prior expectations and current situational information. *Psychological Review, 91,* 112–49.

Allport, G. W. (1935). Attitudes. In C. Murchison (ed.), *Handbook of social psychology.* Vol. 2. Worcester, Mass.: Clark University Press.

Allport, G. W. (1958). *The nature of prejudice.* Garden City: Anchor Books.

Allport, G. W. & Odbert, H. S. (1936). Trait-names: A psycho-lexical study. *Psychological Monographs, 47* (Whole No. 211).

Anderson, N. H. (1965). Averaging versus adding as a stimulus-combination rule in impression formation. *Journal of Experimental Psychology, 70,* 394–400.

Anderson, N. H. (1968a). Application of a linear-serial model to a personality-impression task using serial presentation. *Journal of Personality and Social Psychology, 10,* 354–62.

Anderson, N. H. (1968b). Likeableness ratings of 555 personality-trait words. *Journal of Personality and Social Psychology, 9,* 272–9.

Anderson, N. H. (1970). Functional measurement and psychophysical judgment. *Psychological Review, 77,* 153–70.

Anderson, N. H. (1974). Cognitive algebra: Integration theory applied to social attribution. In L. Berkowitz (ed.), *Advances in experimental social psychology.* Vol. 7. New York: Academic Press.

Anderson, N. H. (1975). On the role of context effects in psychophysical judgment. *Psychological Review, 82,* 462–82.

Anderson, N. H. (1976). Equity judgments as information integration. *Journal of Personality and Social Psychology, 33,* 291–9.

Anderson, N. H. (1977). Some problems in using analysis of variance in balance theory. *Journal of Personality and Social Psychology, 35,* 140–58.

Anderson, N. H. & Farkas, A. J. (1975). Integration theory applied to models of inequity. *Personality and Social Psychology Bulletin, 1,* 588–91.

Anscombe, G. E. M. (1963). *Intention.* 2nd edition. Oxford: Blackwell.

Apsler, R. & Friedman, H. (1975). Chance outcomes and the just world: A comparison of observers and recipients. *Journal of Personality and Social Psychology, 31,* 887–94.

Arcuri, L. (1984). Memory for the statement-source relations: A development of Eiser, van der Pligt & Gossop's study. *British Journal of Social Psychology, 23,* 181–3.

Arkellin, D., Oakley, T. & Mynatt, C. (1979). Effects of controllable versus uncontrollable factors on responsibility attributions: A single-subject approach. *Journal of Personality and Social Psychology, 37,* 110–15.

Aronson, E. (1968). Dissonance theory: Progress and problems. In R. P. Abelson, E. Aronson, T. M. Newcomb, M. J. Rosenberg & P. H. Tannenbaum (eds.), *The cognitive consistency theories: A sourcebook.* Chicago: Rand McNally.

Aronson, E. (1969). The theory of cognitive dissonance: A current perspective. In L. Berkowitz (ed.), *Advances in experimental social psychology*. Vol. 4. New York: Academic Press.

Aronson, E. & Mills, J. (1959). The effects of severity of initiation on liking for a group. *Journal of Abnormal and Social Psychology, 59,* 177–81.

Asch, S. E. (1946). Forming impressions of personality. *Journal of Abnormal and Social Psychology, 41,* 258–90.

Asch, S. E. (1951). Effects of group pressure upon the modification and distortion of judgment. In H. Guetzkow (ed.), *Groups, leadership and men*. Pittsburg: Carnegie Press.

Asch, S. E. (1956). Studies of independence and conformity: A minority of one against a unanimous majority. *Psychological Monographs, 70,* No. 9 (Whole No. 416).

Asch, S. E. & Zukier, H. (1984). Thinking about persons. *Journal of Personality and Social Psychology, 46,* 1230–40.

Ashley, W. R., Harper, R. S. & Runyon, D. L. (1951). The perceived size of coins in normal and hypnotically induced economic states. *American Journal of Psychology, 64,* 564–72.

Atkinson, J. W. (1957). Motivational determinants of risk-taking behavior. *Psychological Review, 64,* 359–72.

Atkinson, J. W. (1964). *An introduction to motivation*. New York: Van Nostrand.

Ayer, A. J. (1959). Privacy. *Proceedings of the British Academy, 45,* 43–65.

Bagozzi, R. P. & Burnkrant, R. E. (1979). Attitude organization and the attitude–behavior relation. *Journal of Personality and Social Psychology, 37,* 913–29.

Bagozzi, R. P. & Burnkrant, R. E. (1985). Attitude organization and the attitude–behavior relation: A reply to Dillon and Kumar. *Journal of Personality and Social Psychology, 49,* 47–57.

Baltes, M. M. & Skinner, E. A. (1983). Cognitive performance deficits and hospitalization: Learned helplessness, instrumental passivity, or what? *Journal of Personality and Social Psychology, 45,* 1013–16.

Bandura, A. (1977). Self-efficacy: Toward a unifying theory of behavioral change. *Psychological Review, 84,* 191–215.

Bartlett, F. C. (1932). *Remembering*. Cambridge: Cambridge University Press.

Baumeister, R. F. (1982). A self-presentational view of social phenomena. *Psychological Bulletin, 91,* 3–26.

Beck, A. T. (1967). *Depression: Clinical, experimental, and theoretical aspects*. New York: Harper and Row.

Beck, A. T. (1976). *Cognitive therapy and the emotional disorders*. New York: International Universities Press.

Bem, D. J. (1965). An experimental analysis of self-persuasion. *Journal of Experimental Social Psychology, 1,* 199–218.

Bem, D. J. (1967). Self-perception: An alternative interpretation of cognitive dissonance phenomena. *Psychological Review, 74,* 183–200.

Bem, D. J. & McConnell, H. K. (1970). Testing the self-perception explanation of dissonance phenomena. *Journal of Personality and Social Psychology, 14,* 23–31.

Bem, S. L. (1974). The measurement of psychological androgyny. *Journal of Consulting and Clinical Psychology, 42,* 155–62.

Bem, S. L. (1981). Gender schema theory: A cognitive account of sex typing. *Psychological Review, 88,* 354–64.

Benson, J. S. & Kenelly, K. J. (1976). Learned helplessness: The result of uncontrollable reinforcements or uncontrollable aversive stimuli? *Journal of Personality and Social Psychology, 34,* 138–45.

Benson, P. L., Karabenic, S. A. & Lerner, R. M. (1976). Pretty pleases: The effects of physical attractiveness on race, sex, and receiving help. *Journal of Experimental Social Psychology, 12,* 409–15.

Bentler, P. M. & Speckart, G. (1979). Models of attitude–behavior relations. *Psychological Review, 86,* 452–64.

Bentler, P. M. & Speckart, G. (1981). Attitudes 'cause' behaviors: A structural equation analysis. *Journal of Personality and Social Psychology, 40,* 226–38.

Berger, P. & Luckmann, T. (1967). *The social construction of reality: A treatise in the sociology of knowledge.* Chicago: Aldine.

Berkowitz, L. (1962). *Aggression: A social psychological analysis.* New York: McGraw-Hill.

Berkowitz, L. & Walster, E. (eds.) (1976). *Advances in experimental social psychology. Vol. 9: Equity theory: Toward a general theory of social interaction.* New York: Academic Press.

Berlyne, D. E. (1960). *Conflict, arousal and curiosity.* New York: McGraw-Hill.

Berne, E. (1968). *Games people play: The psychology of human relationships.* Harmondsworth: Penguin.

Bernouilli, D. (1738). Specimen theoriad novae de mensura sortis. *Commentarii Academiae Scientiarum Imperiales Petropolitane, 5,* 175–92. Translated by L. Sommer, *Econometrica* (1954), *22,* 23–36.

Berscheid, E. & Walster, E. (1974). A little bit about love. In T. L. Huston (ed.), *Foundations of interpersonal attraction.* New York: Academic Press.

Bevan, W. & Pritchard, F. J. (1963). The anchor effect and the problem of relevance in the judgment of shape. *Journal of General Psychology, 69,* 147–61.

Beyle, H. C. (1932). A scale of measurement of attitude toward candidates for elective governmental office. *American Political Science Review, 26,* 527–44.

Bickman, L. (1971). The effect of another bystander's ability to help on bystander intervention in an emergency. *Journal of Experimental Social Psychology, 7,* 367–79.

Bickman, L. (1972). Social influence and diffusion of responsibility in an emergency. *Journal of Experimental Social Psychology, 8,* 438–45.

Billig, M. (1976). *Social psychology and intergroup relations.* London: Academic Press.

Billig, M. (1978). *Fascists: A social psychological view of the National Front.* London: Academic Press.

Billig, M. (1982). *Ideology and social psychology.* Oxford: Blackwell.

Billig, M. (1985). Prejudice, categorization and particularization: From a perceptual to a rhetorical approach. *European Journal of Social Psychology, 15,* 79–103.

Billig, M. & Tajfel, H. (1973). Social categorization and similarity in intergroup behaviour. *European Journal of Social Psychology, 3,* 27–52.

Birnbaum, M. H. (1974). Using contextual effects to derive psychophysical scales. *Perception and Psychophysics, 15,* 89–96.

Bonarius, J. C. J. (1965). Research in the personal construct theory of George A.

Kelly: Role construct repertory test and basic theory. In B. Maher (ed.), *Progress in experimental personality research.* Vol. 2. New York: Academic Press.

Borgida, E. & Campbell, B. (1982). Belief relevance and attitude–behavior consistency: The moderating role of personal experience. *Journal of Personality and Social Psychology, 42,* 239–47.

Bower, G. (1981). Mood and memory. *American Psychologist, 36,* 129–48.

Bower, G. (1984). Prime time in cognitive psychology. Paper presented to the 14th Annual congress of the European Association for Behaviour Therapy. Brussels, September, 1984.

Bower, G., Black, J. R. & Turner, T. (1979). Scripts in text comprehension and memory. *Cognitive Psychology, 11,* 177–220.

Bowman, C. H. & Fishbein, M. (1978). Understanding public reactions to energy proposals: An application of the Fishbein model. *Journal of Applied Social Psychology, 8,* 319–40.

Bradley, G. W. (1978). Self-serving biases in the attribution process: A reexamination of the fact or fiction question. *Journal of Personality and Social Psychology, 36,* 56–71.

Branthwaite, A. & Jones, J. E. (1975). Fairness and discrimination: English versus Welsh. *European Journal of Social Psychology, 5,* 323–38.

Bray, R. M., Johnson, D. & Chilstrom, J. T., Jr. (1982). Social influence by group members with minority opinions: A comparison of Hollander and Moscovici. *Journal of Personality and Social Psychology, 43,* 78–88.

Breckler, S. J. (1983). *Validation of affect, behavior and cognition as distinct components of attitude.* Unpublished doctoral dissertation. Ohio State University, Columbus.

Breckler, S. J. (1984). Empirical validation of affect, behavior and cognition as distinct components of attitude. *Journal of Personality and Social Psychology, 47,* 1191–205.

Brehm, J. W. (1962). An experiment on recall of discrepant information. In J. W. Brehm & A. R. Cohen (eds.), *Explorations in cognitive dissonance.* New York: Wiley.

Brehm, J. W. (1966). *A theory of psychological reactance.* New York: Academic Press.

Brehm, J. W. & Cohen, A. R. (1959). Reevaluation of choice alternatives as a function of their number and qualitative similarity. *Journal of Abnormal and Social Psychology, 58,* 373–8.

Brehm, J. W. & Cohen, A. R. (1962). *Explorations in cognitive dissonance.* New York: Wiley.

Brewer, M. B. (1977). An information-processing approach to attribution of responsibility. *Journal of Experimental Social Psychology, 13,* 58–69.

Brewin, C. R. (1985). Depression and causal attributions: What is their relation? *Psychological Bulletin, 98,* 297–309.

Brickman, P. & Bryan, J. H. (1976). Equity versus equality as factors in children's moral judgments of thefts, charity, and third-party transfers. *Journal of Personality and Social Psychology, 34,* 757–61.

Brigham, J. C. (1971). Ethnic stereotypes. *Psychological Bulletin, 76,* 15–38.

Brock, T. C. (1967). Communication discrepancy and intent to persuade as determinants of counterargument production. *Journal of Experimental Social Psychology, 3,* 269–309.

Brown, D. R. (1953). Stimulus-similarity and the anchoring of subjective scales. *American Journal of Psychology, 66,* 199–214.

Brown, G. W. & Harris, T. (1978). *Social origins of depression: A study of psychiatric disorder in women.* New York: Free Press.

Bruner, J. S. & Goodman, C. C. (1947). Value and need as organizing factors in perception. *Journal of Abnormal and Social Psychology, 42,* 33–44.

Bruner, J. S., Goodnow, J. L. & Austin, G. A. (1956). *A study of thinking.* New York: Wiley.

Bruner, J. S. & Postman, L. (1948). Symbolic value as an organizing factor in perception. *Journal of Social Psychology, 27,* 203–8.

Bruner, J. S. & Rodrigues, J. S. (1953). Some determinants of apparent size. *Journal of Abnormal and Social Psychology, 48,* 17–24.

Budd, R. J. (1986). Predicting cigarette use: The need to incorporate measures of salience in the theory of reasoned action. *Journal of Applied Social Psychology, 16,* 663–86.

Budd, R. J. (1987). Response bias and the theory of reasoned action. *Social Cognition.* In press.

Budd, R. J. & Spencer, C. (1984). Latitude of rejection, centrality and certainty: Variables affecting the relationship between attitudes, norms and behavioural intentions. *British Journal of Social Psychology, 23,* 1–8.

Budd, R. J. & Spencer, C. (1985). Exploring the role of personal normative beliefs in the theory of reasoned action: The problem of discriminating between alternative path models. *European Journal of Social Psychology, 15,* 299–313.

Budd, R. J. & Spencer, C. (1986). Lay theories of behavioural intention: A source of response bias in the theory of reasoned action? *British Journal of Social Psychology, 25,* 109–18.

Bulman, R. J. & Wortman, C. B. (1977). Attributions of blame and coping in the 'real world': Severe accident victims react to their lot. *Journal of Personality and Social Psychology, 35,* 351–63.

Burnstein, E. (1967). Sources of cognitive bias in the representation of simple social structures: Blame, minimal change, reciprocity and the respondent's own attitude. *Journal of Personality and Social Psychology, 7,* 36–48.

Buss, A. R. (1978). Causes and reasons in attribution theory: A conceptual critique. *Journal of Personality and Social Psychology, 36,* 1311–21.

Buss, A. R. (1979). On the relationship between causes and reasons. *Journal of Personality and Social Psychology, 37,* 1458–61.

Byrne, D. (1961). Interpersonal attraction and attitude similarity. *Journal of Abnormal and Social Psychology, 62,* 713–15.

Byrne, D. & Clore, G. L., Jr. (1966). Predicting interpersonal attraction toward strangers presented in three different stimulus modes. *Psychonomic Science, 4,* 239–40.

Byrne, D. & Clore, G. L., Jr. (1967). Effectance arousal and attraction. *Journal of Personality and Social Psychology Monograph, 6,* (4, Whole No. 638).

Byrne, D., Ervin, C. R. & Lamberth, J. (1970). Continuity between the experimental study of attraction and real life computer dating. *Journal of Personality and Social Psychology, 16,* 157–65.

Byrne, D. & Griffitt, W. (1966). A developmental investigation of the law of attraction. *Journal of Personality and Social Psychology, 4*, 699–702.

Byrne, D. & Nelson, D. (1965). Attraction as a linear function of proportion of positive reinforcements. *Journal of Personality and Social Psychology, 1*, 659–63.

Cacioppo, J. T. (1979). The effects of exogenous changes in heart rate on the facilitation of thought and resistance to persuasion. *Journal of Personality and Social Psychology, 37*, 489–98.

Cacioppo, J. T. & Petty, R. E. (1979). Effects of message repetition and position on cognitive responses, recall, and persuasion. *Journal of Personality and Social Psychology, 37*, 97–109.

Cacioppo, J. T. & Petty, R. E. (1982). The need for cognition. *Journal of Personality and Social Psychology, 42*, 116–31.

Cacioppo, J. T., Petty, R. E. & Kao, C. (1984). The efficient assessment of need for cognition. *Journal of Personality Assessment, 48*, 306–7.

Calder, B. J. & Staw, B. M. (1975). Self-perception of intrinsic and extrinsic motivation. *Journal of Personality and Social Psychology, 31*, 599–605.

Campbell, D. T. (1956). Enhancement of contrast as composite habit. *Journal of Abnormal and Social Psychology, 53*, 350–5.

Campbell, D. T. & Fiske, D. W. (1959). Convergent and discriminant validation by the multitrait–multimethod matrix. *Psychological Bulletin, 56*, 81–105.

Cantor, J., Zillman, D. & Bryant, J. (1975). Enhancement of experienced sexual arousal in response to erotic stimuli through misattribution of unrelated residual excitation. *Journal of Personality and Social Psychology, 32*, 69–75.

Cantril, H. (1946). The intensity of an attitude. *Journal of Abnormal and Social Psychology, 41*, 129–36.

Carlsmith, J. M., Collins, B. E. & Helmreich, R. L. (1966). Studies in forced compliance: I. The effect of pressure for compliance on attitude change produced by face-to-face role playing and anonymous essay writing. *Journal of Personality and Social Psychology, 4*, 1–13.

Carter, L. F. & Schooler, K. (1949). Value, need, and other factors in perception. *Psychological Review, 56*, 200–7.

Cartwright, D. & Harary, F. (1956). Structural balance: A generalization of Heider's theory. *Psychological Review, 63*, 277–93.

Chaiken, S. (1979). Communicator physical attractiveness and persuasion. *Journal of Personality and Social Psychology, 37*, 1387–97.

Chaiken, S. (1980). Heuristic versus systematic information processing and the use of source versus message cues in persuasion. *Journal of Personality and Social Psychology, 39*, 752–66.

Chaikin, A. L. & Darley, J. M. (1973). Victim or perpetrator? Defensive attribution of responsibility and the need for order and justice. *Journal of Personality and Social Psychology, 25*, 268–75.

Chanowitz, B. & Langer, E. J. (1981). Premature cognitive commitment. *Journal of Personality and Social Psychology, 41*, 1051–63.

Chapanis, N. J. & Chapanis, A. C. (1964). Cognitive dissonance: Five years later. *Psychological Bulletin, 61*, 1–22.

Chapman, L. J. (1967). Illusory correlation in observational report. *Journal of Verbal Learning and Verbal Behavior, 6*, 151–5.

Cialdini, R. B. (1971). Attitudinal advocacy in the verbal conditioner. *Journal of Personality and Social Psychology, 17,* 350–8.

Cialdini, R. B. (1984). Principles of automatic influence. In J. Jacoby & C. S. Craig (eds.), *Personal selling: Theory, research and practice.* Lexington, Mass.: D.C. Heath.

Cialdini, R. B., Braver, S. L. & Lewis, S. K. (1974). Attributional bias and the easily persuaded other. *Journal of Personality and Social Psychology, 30,* 631–7.

Cialdini, R. B. & Kenrick, D. T. (1976). Altruism as hedonism: A social development perspective on the relationship of negative mood state and helping. *Journal of Personality and Social Psychology, 34,* 907–14.

Cialdini, R. B., Kenrick, D. T. & Hoerig, J. H. (1976). Victim derogation in the Lerner paradigm: Just world or just justification? *Journal of Personality and Social Psychology, 33,* 719–24.

Cialdini, R. B. & Mirels, H. L. (1976). Sense of personal control and attributions about yielding and resisting persuasion targets. *Journal of Personality and Social Psychology, 33,* 395–402.

Cialdini, R. B., Petty, R. E. & Cacioppo, J. T. (1981). Attitude and attitude change. *Annual Review of Psychology, 32,* 357–404.

Clark, M. S. & Fiske, S. T. (eds.). (1982). *Affect and cognition: The 17th annual Carnegie symposium on cognition.* Hillsdale, NJ: Erlbaum.

Clark, M. S. & Isen, A. M. (1982). Toward understanding the relationship between feeling states and social behavior. In A. Hastorf & A. M. Isen (eds.), *Cognitive social psychology.* New York: Elsevier.

Clark, R. D., III & Word, L. E. (1972). Why don't bystanders help? Because of ambiguity? *Journal of Personality and Social Psychology, 24,* 392–400.

Cliff, K. S., Catford, J., Dillow, I. & Swann, C. (1980). Promoting the use of seat belts. *British Medical Journal, 381,* ii, 1477–8.

Codol, J. P. (1975). On the so-called 'superior conformity of the self' behavior: Twenty experimental investigations. *European Journal of Social Psychology, 5,* 457–501.

Codol, J. P. (1984). On the system of representations in an artificial social situation. In R. M. Farr & S. Moscovici (eds.), *Social representations.* Cambridge: Cambridge University Press.

Cohen, A. R. (1962). An experiment on small rewards for discrepant compliance and attitude change. In J. W. Brehm & A. R. Cohen (eds.), *Explorations in cognitive dissonance.* New York: Wiley.

Cohen, R. (1971). An investigation of the diagnostic processing of contradictory information. *European Journal of Social Psychology, 1,* 475–92.

Collins, B. E. & Hoyt, M. F. (1972). Personal responsibility-for-consequences: An integration and extension of the 'forced compliance' literature. *Journal of Experimental Social Psychology, 8,* 558–93.

Colman, A. (1982). *Game theory and experimental games.* Oxford: Pergamon Press.

Cook, S. W. (1975). A comment on the ethical issues involved in West, Gunn and Chernicky's 'Ubiquitous Watergate: An attributional analysis'. *Journal of Personality and Social Psychology, 32,* 66–8.

Cook, T. D. (1969). Competence, counterarguing, and attitude change. *Journal of Personality, 37,* 342–58.

Cooley, C. H. (1968). The social self: On the meanings of 'I'. In C. Gordon & K.

J. Gergen (eds.), *The self in social interaction. Vol. 1: Classic and contemporary perspectives*. New York: Wiley.

Coombs, C. H. (1950). Psychological scaling without a unit of measurement. *Psychological Review, 57*, 145–58.

Coombs, C. H. (1964). *A theory of data*. New York: Wiley.

Coombs, C. H. (1975). Portfolio theory and the measurement of risk. In M. F. Kaplan & S. Schwartz (eds.), *Human judgment and decision processes*. New York: Academic Press.

Coombs, C. H. & Huang, L. C. (1970). Tests of a portfolio theory of risk preference. *Journal of Experimental Psychology, 85*, 23–9.

Coombs, C. H. & Huang, L. C. (1976). Tests of the betweenness property of expected utility. *Journal of Mathematical Psychology, 13*, 323–37.

Cooper, J. (1971). Personal responsibility and dissonance: The role of foreseen consequences. *Journal of Personality and Social Psychology, 18*, 354–63.

Cooper, J. & Brehm, J. W. (1971). Prechoice awareness of relative deprivation as a determinant of cognitive dissonance. *Journal of Experimental Social Psychology, 7*, 571–81.

Cooper, J. & Fazio, R. H. (1984). A new look at dissonance theory. In L. Berkowitz (ed.), *Advances in experimental social psychology*. Vol. 17. New York: Academic Press.

Cooper, J. & Goethals, G. R. (1974). Unforeseen events and the elimination of cognitive dissonance. *Journal of Personality and Social Psychology, 29*, 441–5.

Cooper, J., Zanna, M. P. & Taves, P. A. (1978). Arousal as a necessary condition for attitude change following compliance. *Journal of Personality and Social Psychology, 36*, 1101–6.

Cooper, J. & Worchel, S. (1970). The role of undesired consequences in arousing cognitive dissonance. *Journal of Personality and Social Psychology, 16*, 199–206.

Cottrell, N. B., Ingraham, L. B. & Monfort, F. W. (1971). The retention of balanced and imbalanced cognitive structures. *Journal of Personality, 39*, 112–31.

Coyne, J. C. & Gotlib, I. H. (1983). The role of cognition in depression: A critical appraisal. *Psychological Bulletin, 94*, 472–505.

Crandall, V. C., Katkovsky, W. & Crandall, U. J. (1965). Children's beliefs in their own control of reinforcements in intellectual–academic achievement situations. *Child Development, 36*, 91–109.

Crocker, J., Fiske, S. T. & Taylor, S. E. (1984). Schematic bases of belief change. In J. R. Eiser (ed.), *Attitudinal judgment*. New York: Springer Verlag.

Crocker, J., Hannah, D. B. & Weber, R. (1983). Person memory and causal attributions. *Journal of Personality and Social Psychology, 44*, 55–66.

Crockett, W. H. (1974). Balance, agreement and subjective evaluations of the P–O–X triads. *Journal of Personality and Social Psychology, 29*, 102–10.

Cromwell, R. L. & Caldwell, D. F. (1962). A comparison of ratings based on personal constructs of self and others. *Journal of Clinical Psychology, 18*, 43–6.

Croyle, R. T. & Cooper, J. (1983). Dissonance arousal: Physiological evidence. *Journal of Personality and Social Psychology, 45*, 782–91.

Darley, J. M. & Berscheid, E. (1967). Increased liking as a result of the anticipation of personal contact. *Human Relations, 20*, 29–39.

Darley, J. M. & Latané, B. (1968). Bystander intervention in emergencies:

Diffusion of responsibility. *Journal of Personality and Social Psychology, 8,* 377–83.

Darley, J. M. & Latané, B. (1970). Norms and normative behavior: Field studies of social interdependence. In J. Macaulay & L. Berkowitz (eds.), *Altruism and helping behavior.* New York: Academic Press.

Davidson, A. R. & Jaccard, J. J. (1975). Population psychology: A new look at an old problem. *Journal of Personality and Social Psychology, 31,* 1037–82.

Davidson, A. R. & Jaccard, J. J. (1979). Variables that moderate the attitude–behavior relation: Results of a longitudinal survey. *Journal of Personality and Social Psychology, 37,* 1364–76.

Dawes, R. M., Singer, D. & Lemons, F. (1972). An experimental analysis of the contrast effect and its implications for intergroup communication and the indirect assessment of attitude. *Journal of Personality and Social Psychology, 21,* 281–95.

Deci, E. L. (1971). Effects of externally mediated rewards on intrinsic motivation. *Journal of Personality and Social Psychology, 18,* 105–15.

Deconchy, J. P. (1984). Rationality and social control in orthodox systems. In H. Tajfel (ed.), *The social dimension: European developments in social psychology.* Vol. 2. Cambridge: Cambridge University Press.

DeFleur, M. L. & Westie, F. R. (1958). Verbal attitudes and overt acts: An experiment on the salience of attitudes. *American Sociological Review, 23,* 667–73.

Delia, J. G. & Crockett, W. H. (1973). Social schemas, cognitive complexity and the learning of social structures. *Journal of Personality, 41,* 413–29.

Deschamps, J. C. (1983). Social attribution. In J. Jaspars, F. D. Fincham & M. Hewstone (eds.), *Attribution theory and research: Conceptual, developmental and social dimensions.* London: Academic Press.

Deschamps, J. C. & Doise, W. (1978). Crossed category memberships in intergroup relations. In H. Tajfel (ed.), *Differentiation between social groups: Studies in the social psychology of intergroup relations.* London: Academic Press.

Deutsch, M. & Gerard, H. B. (1955). A study of normative and informational social influences upon individual judgments. *Journal of Abnormal and Social Psychology, 51,* 629–36.

Deutsch, M. & Solomon, L. (1959). Reactions to evaluations of others as influenced by self-evaluations. *Sociometry, 22,* 93–112.

Deutscher, I. (1984). Choosing ancestors: Some consequences of the selection from intellectual traditions. In R. M. Farr & S. Moscovici (eds.), *Social representations.* Cambridge: Cambridge University Press.

Dickinson, A. (1980). *Contemporary animal learning theory.* Cambridge: Cambridge University Press.

Diener, E. (1976). Effects of prior destructive behavior, anonymity, and group presence on deindividuation and aggression. *Journal of Personality and Social Psychology, 33,* 497–507.

Diener, E., Dineen, J., Endresen, K. Beaman, A. L. & Fraser, S. C. (1975). Effects of altered responsibility, cognitive set, and modeling on physical aggression and deindividuation. *Journal of Personality and Social Psychology, 31,* 328–37.

Dillehay, R. C. (1965). Judgmental processes in response to a persuasive communication. *Journal of Personality and Social Psychology, 1,* 631–41.

Dillon, W. R. & Kumar, A. (1985). Attitude organization and the attitude–behavior relation: A critique of Bagozzi and Burnkrant's reanalysis of Fishbein and Ajzen. *Journal of Personality and Social Psychology, 49,* 33–46.

Dixon, N. F. (1976). *On the psychology of military incompetence.* London: Jonathan Cape.

Doise, W. & Sinclair, A. (1973). The categorization process in intergroup relations. *European Journal of Social Psychology, 3,* 145–57.

Dorris, J. W. (1972). Reactions to unconditional cooperation: A field study emphasizing variables neglected in laboratory research. *Journal of Personality and Social Psychology, 22,* 387–97.

Duck, S. W. (1973). *Personal relationships and personal constructs: A study of friendship formation.* London: Wiley.

Durkheim, E. (1898). Représentations individuelles et représentations collectives. *Revue de Métaphysique et de Morale, 6,* 273–302.

Dutton, D. G. (1972). Effect of feedback parameters on congruency versus positivity effects in reactions to personal evaluations. *Journal of Personality and Social Psychology, 24,* 366–71.

Dutton, D. G. & Aron, A. (1974). Some evidence for heightened sexual attraction under conditions of high anxiety. *Journal of Personality and Social Psychology, 30,* 510–17.

Eagly, A. H. & Chaiken, S. (1975). An attribution analysis of the effect of communicator characteristics on opinion change: The case of communicator attractiveness. *Journal of Personality and Social Psychology, 32,* 136–44.

Eagly, A. H. & Chaiken, S. (1984). Cognitive theories of persuasion. In L. Berkowitz (ed.), *Advances in experimental social psychology.* Vol. 17, New York: Academic Press.

Eagly, A. H., Wood, W. & Chaiken, S. (1978). Causal inferences about communicators and their effect on opinion change. *Journal of Personality and Social Psychology, 36,* 424–35.

Efran, M. G. & Patterson, E. W. J. (1976). *The politics of appearance.* Unpublished manuscript. University of Toronto.

Eiser, C. & Eiser, J. R. (1976). Children's concepts of a fair exchange. *British Journal of Social and Clinical Psychology, 15,* 357–64.

Eiser, J. R. (1971a). Categorization, cognitive consistency, and the concept of dimensional salience. *European Journal of Social Psychology, 1,* 435–54.

Eiser, J. R. (1971b). Comment on Ward's 'Attitude and involvement in the absolute judgment of attitude statements'. *Journal of Personality and Social Psychology, 17,* 81–3.

Eiser, J. R. (1971c). Enhancement of contrast in the absolute judgment of attitude statements. *Journal of Personality and Social Psychology, 17,* 1–10.

Eiser, J. R. (1973). Judgement of attitude statements as a function of judges' attitudes and the judgemental dimension. *British Journal of Social and Clinical Psychology, 12,* 231–40.

Eiser, J. R. (1978). Discrepancy, dissonance and the 'dissonant' smoker. *International Journal of the Addictions, 13,* 1295–305.

Eiser, J. R. (1982). Addiction as attribution: cognitive processes in giving up smoking. In J. R. Eiser (ed.), *Social psychology and behavioral medicine.* Chichester: Wiley.

Eiser, J. R. (1983). Attribution theory and social cognition. In J. M. F. Jaspars, F. D. Fincham & M. Hewstone (eds.), *Attribution theory and research: Conceptual, developmental and social dimensions.* London: Academic Press.

Eiser, J. R. (1985). Smoking: The social learning of an addiction. *Journal of Social and Clinical Psychology, 3,* 446–57.

Eiser, J. R. & Bhavnani, K. K. (1974). The effect of situational meaning on the behaviour of subjects in the Prisoner's Dilemma game. *European Journal of Social Psychology, 4,* 93–7.

Eiser, J. R. & Gossop, M. R. (1979). 'Hooked' or 'sick': Addicts' perceptions of their addiction. *Addictive Behaviors, 4,* 185–91.

Eiser, J. R. & Mower White, C. J. (1974). Evaluative consistency and social judgment. *Journal of Personality and Social Psychology, 30,* 349–59.

Eiser, J. R. & Mower White, C. J. (1975). Categorization and congruity in attitudinal judgment. *Journal of Personality and Social Psychology, 31,* 769–75.

Eiser, J. R. & Osmon, B. F. (1978). Judgmental perspective and the value connotations of response scale labels. *Journal of Personality and Social Psychology, 36,* 491–7.

Eiser, J. R. & Pancer, S. M. (1979). Attitudinal effects of the use of evaluatively biased language. *European Journal of Social Psychology, 9,* 39–47.

Eiser, J. R. & Ross, M. (1977). Partisan language, immediacy, and attitude change. *European Journal of Social Psychology, 7,* 477–89.

Eiser, J. R. & Stroebe, W. (1972). *Categorization and social judgement.* London: Academic Press.

Eiser, J. R. & Sutton, S. R. (1977). Smoking as a subjectively rational choice. *Addictive Behaviors, 2,* 129–34.

Eiser, J. R., Sutton, S. R. & Wober, M. (1978). 'Consonant' and 'dissonant' smokers and the self-attribution of addiction. *Addictive Behaviors, 3,* 99–106.

Eiser, J. R. & van der Pligt, J. (1979). Beliefs and values in the nuclear debate. *Journal of Applied Social Psychology, 9,* 524–36.

Eiser, J. R. & van der Pligt, J. (1982). Accentuation and perspective in attitudinal judgment. *Journal of Personality and Social Psychology, 42,* 224–38.

Eiser, J. R., van der Pligt, J. & Friend, P. (1983). Adolescents' arguments for or against smoking. *Journal of the Institute of Health Education, 21,* 73–8.

Eiser, J. R., van der Pligt, J. & Gossop, M. R. (1979). Categorization, attitude and memory for the source of attitude statements. *European Journal of Social Psychology, 9,* 243–51.

Eiser, J. R., van der Pligt, J., Raw, M. & Sutton, S. R. (1985). Trying to stop smoking: Effects of perceived addiction, attributions for failure and expectancy of success. *Journal of Behavioral Medicine, 8,* 321–41.

Emerson, R. (1960). *From empire to nation.* Cambridge, Mass.: Harvard University Press.

Exline, R. V., Gray, D. & Schuette, D. (1965). Visual behavior in a dyad as affected by interview content and sex of respondent. *Journal of Personality and Social Psychology, 1,* 201–9.

Eysenck, H. J. & Crown, S. (1949). An experimental study in opinion–attitude methodology. *International Journal of Opinion and Attitude Research, 3,* 47–86.

Farr, R. M. (1977a). Heider, Harré and Herzlich on health and illness. Some observations on the structure of 'représentations collectives'. *European Journal of Social Psychology, 7,* 491–504.

Farr, R. M. (1977b). On the nature of attributional artifacts in qualitative research: Herzberg's two-factor theory of work motivation. *Journal of Occupational Psychology, 50,* 3–14.

Farr, R. M. & Moscovici, S. (eds.) (1984). *Social representations.* Cambridge: Cambridge University Press.

Fazio, R. H. (1985). How do attitudes guide behavior? In R. M. Sorrentino & E. T. Higgins (eds.), *The handbook of motivation and cognition: Foundations of social behavior.* New York: Guilford Press.

Fazio, R. H., Chen, J., McDonel, E. C. & Sherman, S. J. (1982). Attitude accessibility, attitude–behavior consistency and the strength of the object-evaluation association. *Journal of Experimental Social Psychology, 18,* 339–57.

Fazio, R. H. & Cooper, J. (1983). Arousal in the dissonance process. In J. T. Cacioppo & R. E. Petty (eds.), *Social psychophysiology.* New York: Guilford Press.

Fazio, R. H. & Herr, P. M. (1984). On the role of selective perception in the attitude–behavior process. Unpublished data. Indiana University.

Fazio, R. H., Herr, P. M. & Olney, T. J. (1984). Attitude accessibility following a self-perception process. *Journal of Personality and Social Psychology, 47,* 277–86.

Fazio, R. H., Lenn, T. M. & Effrein, E. A. (1984). Spontaneous attitude formation. *Social Cognition, 2,* 217–34.

Fazio, R. H., Powell, M. C. & Herr, P. M. (1983). Toward a process model of the attitude–behavior relation: Accessing one's attitude upon mere observation of the attitude object. *Journal of Personality and Social Psychology, 44,* 723–35.

Fazio, R. H. & Zanna, M. P. (1978). Attitudinal qualities relating to the strength of the attitude–behavior relationship. *Journal of Experimental Social Psychology, 14,* 398–408.

Fazio, R. H. & Zanna, M. P. (1981). Direct experience and attitude–behavior consistency. In L. Berkowitz (ed.), *Advances in experimental social psychology.* Vol. 14. New York: Academic Press.

Fazio, R. H., Zanna, M. P. & Cooper, J. (1977). Dissonance and self-perception: An integrative view of each theory's proper domain of application. *Journal of Experimental Social Psychology, 13,* 464–79.

Feather, N. T. (1985). Attitudes, values and attributions: Explanations for unemployment. *Journal of Personality and Social Psychology, 48,* 876–89.

Fechner, G. T. (1860). *Elemente der Psychophysik.* Leipzig: Breitkopf & Hartel.

Federoff, N. A. & Harvey, J. H. (1976). Focus of attention, self-esteem and attribution of causality. *Journal of Research in Personality, 10,* 336–45.

Fehrer, E. (1952). Shifts in scale values of attitude statements as a function of the composition of the scale. *Journal of Experimental Psychology, 44,* 179–88.

Felipe, A. I. (1970). Evaluative and descriptive consistency in trait inferences. *Journal of Personality and Social Psychology, 16,* 627–38.

Ferguson, C. K. & Kelley, H. H. (1964). Significant factors in over-evaluation of own group's product. *Journal of Abnormal and Social Psychology, 69,* 223–8.

Ferguson, L. S. (1935). The influence of individual attitudes on construction of an attitude scale. *Journal of Social Psychology, 6,* 115–17.

Festinger, L. (1950). Informal social communications. *Psychological Review, 57,* 271–82.

Festinger, L. (1954). A theory of social comparison processes. *Human Relations, 7,* 117–40.

Festinger, L. (1957). *A theory of cognitive dissona~ce.* Evanston, Ill.: Row, Peterson.

Festinger, L. & Carlsmith, J. M. (1959). Cognitive consequences of forced compliance. *Journal of Abnormal and Social Psychology, 58,* 203–10.

Festinger, L., Schachter, S. & Back, K. (1950). *Social pressures in informal groups: A study of human factors in housing.* New York: Harper & Row.

Fincham, F. D. & Jaspars, J. M. F. (1980). Attribution of responsibility: From man the scientist to man as lawyer. In L. Berkowitz (ed.), *Advances in experimental social psychology.* Vol. 13. New York: Academic Press.

Fischhoff, B. (1983). Predicting frames. *Journal of Experimental Psychology: Learning, Memory and Cognition, 9,* 103–16.

Fishbein, M. (1967). Attitude and the prediction of behavior. In M. Fishbein (ed.), *Readings in attitude theory and measurement.* New York: Wiley.

Fishbein, M. (1982). Social psychological analysis of smoking behavior. In J. R. Eiser, (ed.), *Social psychology and behavioral medicine.* Chichester: Wiley.

Fishbein, M. & Ajzen, I. (1973). Attribution of responsibility: A theoretical note. *Journal of Experimental Social Psychology, 9,* 148–53.

Fishbein, M. & Ajzen, I. (1974). Attitudes toward objects as predictors of single and multiple behavioral criteria. *Psychological Review, 81,* 59–74.

Fishbein, M. & Ajzen, I. (1975). *Belief, attitude, intention and behavior: An introduction to theory and research.* Reading, Mass.: Addison-Wesley.

Fishbein, M. & Ajzen, I. (1980). Predicting and understanding consumer behavior: Attitude–behavior correspondence. In I. Ajzen & M. Fishbein (eds.). *Understanding attitudes and predicting social behavior.* Englewood Cliffs, NJ: Prentice-Hall.

Fiske, S. T. & Taylor, S. E. (1984). *Social cognition.* Reading, Mass.: Addison-Wesley.

Folkes, V. S. (1985). Mindlessness or mindfulness: A partial replication and extension of Langer, Blank, and Chanowitz. *Journal of Personality and Social Psychology, 48,* 600–4.

Fontaine, G. (1974). Social comparison and some determinants of expected personal control and expected performance in a novel task situation. *Journal of Personality and Social Psychology, 29,* 487–96.

Fredricks, A. J. & Dossett, D. L. (1983). Attitude–behavior relations: A comparison of the Fishbein–Ajzen and the Bentler–Speckart models. *Journal of Personality and Social Psychology, 45,* 501–12.

Freedman, J. L. (1963). Attitudinal effects of inadequate justification. *Journal of Personality, 31,* 371–85.

French, K. & Raven, B. H. (1959). The bases of social power. In D. Cartwright (ed.), *Studies in social power.* Ann Arbor, MI: Institute for Social Research.

Freud, S. (1922). *Introductory lectures on psycho-analysis.* London: George Allen & Unwin.

Frey, D. & Wicklund, R. A. (1978). A classification of selective exposure: The impact of choice. *Journal of Experimental Social Psychology, 14,* 132–9.

Gabrielcik, A. & Fazio, R. H. (1984). Priming and frequency estimation: A strict test of the availability heuristic. *Personality and Social Psychology Bulletin, 10,* 85–9.

Gaes, G. G., Kalle, R. J. & Tedeschi, J. T. (1978). Impression management in the forced compliance situation: Two studies using the bogus pipeline. *Journal of Experimental Social Psychology, 14,* 493–510.

Gammage, P. (1974). Socialisation, schooling, and locus of control. Unpublished Ph.D. Thesis. University of Bristol.

Gerard, H. B. & Fleischer, L. (1967). Recall and pleasantness of balanced and imbalanced cognitive structures. *Journal of Personality and Social Psychology, 7,* 332–7.

Gerard, H. B. & Greenbaum, C. U. (1962). Attitudes toward an agent of uncertainty reduction. *Journal of Personality, 30,* 485–95.

Gerard, H. B. & Hoyt, M. F. (1974). Distinctiveness of social categorization and attitude toward ingroup members. *Journal of Personality and Social Psychology, 29,* 836–42.

Giles, H. (1978). Linguistic differentiation in ethnic groups. In H. Tajfel (ed.), *Differentiation between social groups: Studies in the social psychology of intergroup relations.* London: Academic Press.

Ginsburg, G. P. (ed.) (1979). *Emerging strategies in social psychological research.* Chichester: Wiley.

Goethals, G. R., Cooper, J. & Naficy, A. (1979). Role of foreseen, foreseeable, and unforeseeable behavioral consequences in the arousal of cognitive dissonance. *Journal of Personality and Social Psychology, 37,* 1179–85.

Goffman, E. (1955). On face-work: An analysis of ritual elements in social interaction. *Psychiatry, 18,* 213–31.

Goffman, E. (1959). *The presentation of self in everyday life.* New York: Doubleday Anchor Books.

Goffman, E. (1961). *Asylums: Essays on the social situation of mental patients and other inmates.* New York: Doubleday Anchor Books.

Goffman, E. (1963). *Stigma: Notes on the management of spoiled identity.* Englewood Cliffs, NJ: Prentice-Hall.

Goffman, E. (1970). *Strategic interaction.* Oxford: Blackwell.

Goffman, E. (1972). *Encounters: Two studies in the sociology of interaction.* Harmondsworth: Allan Lane.

Goldberg, G. N., Kiesler, C. A. & Collins, B. E. (1969). Visual behavior and face-to-face distance during interaction. *Sociometry, 32,* 43–53.

Goldberg, L. R. (1978). Differential attribution of trait-descriptive terms to oneself as compared to well-liked neutral and disliked others: A psychometric analysis. *Journal of Personality and Social Psychology, 36,* 1012–28.

Goldman, R., Jaffa, M. & Schachter, S. (1968). Yom Kippur, Air France, dormitory food, and the eating behavior of obese and normal persons. *Journal of Personality and Social Psychology, 10,* 117–23.

Gollob, H. F. (1974). The subject–verb–object approach to social cognition. *Psychological Review, 81,* 286–321.

Gossop, M. R., Eiser, J. R. & Ward, E. (1982). The addict's perception of their own drug-taking: Implications for the treatment of drug dependence. *Addictive Behaviors, 7,* 189–94.

Greene, D., Sternberg, B. & Lepper, M. R. (1976). Overjustification in a token economy. *Journal of Personality and Social Psychology, 34,* 1219–34.

Greenwald, A. G. (1968a). Cognitive learning, cognitive responses to persuasion, and attitude change. In A. G. Greenwald, T. C. Brock & T. M. Ostrom (eds.), *Psychological foundations of attitudes.* New York: Academic Press.

Greenwald, A. G. (1968b). On defining attitude and attitude theory. In A. G. Greenwald, T. C. Brock & T. M. Ostrom (eds.), *Psychological foundations of attitudes.* New York: Academic Press.

Greenwald, A. G. (1975). On the inconclusiveness of 'crucial' cognitive tests of dissonance versus self-perception theories. *Journal of Experimental Social Psychology, 11,* 490–9.

Gregory, W. S. (1939). Ideology and affect regarding 'law' and their relation to law-abidingness. Part I. *Character and Personality, 7,* 265–84.

Gullahorn, J. T. (1952). Distance and friendship as factors in the gross interaction matrix. *Sociometry, 15,* 123–34.

Gurwitz, S. B. & Panciera, L. (1975). Attributions of freedom by actors and observers. *Journal of Personality and Social Psychology, 32,* 531–9.

Hadamovsky, E. (1933, 1972). *Propaganda and nationale Macht.* Oldenburg: 1933. Translated by A. Mavrogordato & I. De Witt as *'Propaganda and national power'.* Reprint edition. New York: Arno Press.

Hamilton, D. L. (1976). Cognitive biases in the perception of social groups. In J. S. Carroll and J. W. Payne (eds.). *Cognition and social behavior.* Hillsdale, NJ: Erlbaum.

Hamilton, D. L. & Gifford, R. K. (1976). Illusory correlation in interpersonal perception: A cognitive basis of stereotypic judgments. *Journal of Experimental Social Psychology, 12,* 392–407.

Hamilton, D. L., Dugan, P. M. & Trolier, T. K. (1985). The formation of stereotypic beliefs: Further evidence for distinctiveness-based illusory correlations. *Journal of Personality and Social Psychology, 48,* 5–17.

Haney, C., Banks, C. & Zimbardo, P. (1973). Interpersonal dynamics in a simulated prison. *International Journal of Criminology and Penology, 1,* 69–97.

Hansen, R. D. & Donoghue, J. M. (1977). The power of consensus: Information derived from one's own and others' behavior. *Journal of Personality and Social Psychology, 35,* 294–302.

Harackiewicz, J. M., Manderlink, G. & Sansone, C. (1984). Rewarding pinball wizardry: Effects of evaluation and cue value on intrinsic interest. *Journal of Personality and Social Psychology, 47,* 287–300.

Harding, C. M., Eiser, J. R. & Kristiansen, C. M. (1982). The representations of mortality statistics and the perceived importance of causes of death. *Journal of Applied Social Psychology, 12,* 169–81.

Harré, R. & Secord, P. F. (1972). *The explanation of social behaviour.* Oxford: Blackwell.

Harris, M. J. & Rosenthal, R. (1985). Mediation of interpersonal expectancy effects: 31 meta-analyses. *Psychological Bulletin, 97,* 363–86.

Harris, P. R. (1985). Asch's data and the 'Asch effect': A critical note. *British Journal of Social Psychology, 24,* 229–30.

Hart, H. L. & Honoré, A. M. (1959). *Causation in the law.* Oxford: Oxford University Press.

Harvey, J. H., Harris, B. & Barnes, R. D. (1975). Actor–observer differences in the perception of responsibility and freedom. *Journal of Personality and Social Psychology, 32,* 22–8.

Harvey, J. H., Ickes, W. J. & Kidd, R. F. (eds.) (1976). *New directions in attribution research.* Vol. 1. Hillsdale, NJ: Erlbaum.

Harvey, J. H. & Tucker, J. A. (1979). On problems with the cause–reason distinction in attribution theory. *Journal of Personality and Social Psychology. 37,* 1441–6.

Harvey, O. J. & Ware, R. (1967). Personality differences in dissonance resolution. *Journal of Personality and Social Psychology, 7,* 227–30.

Hastie, R. (1984). Causes and effects of causal attribution. *Journal of Personality and Social Psychology, 46,* 44–56.

Hastie, R. & Kumar, P. A. (1979). Person memory: Personality traits as organising principles in memory for behaviors. *Journal of Personality and Social Psychology, 37,* 25–38.

Heesacker, M., Petty, R. E. & Cacioppo, J. T. (1983). Field dependence and attitude change: Source credibility can alter persuasion by affecting message-relevant thinking. *Journal of Personality and Social Psychology, 51,* 653–66.

Heider, F. (1944). Social perception and phenomenal causality. *Psychological Review, 51,* 358–74.

Heider, F. (1946). Attitudes and cognitive organization. *Journal of Psychology, 21,* 107–12.

Heider, F. (1958). *The psychology of interpersonal relations.* New York: Wiley.

Helson, H. (1947). Adaptation-level as frame of reference for prediction of psychophysical data. *American Journal of Psychology, 60,* 1–29.

Helson, H. (1964). *Adaptation-level theory.* New York: Harper & Row.

Hensley, V. & Duval, S. (1976). Some perceptual determinants of perceived similarity, liking, and correctness. *Journal of Personality and Social Psychology, 34,* 159–68.

Herr, P. M., Sherman, S. J. & Fazio, R. H. (1983). On the consequences of priming: Assimilation and contrast effects. *Journal of Experimental Social Psychology, 19,* 323–40.

Herrnstein, R. J. (1961). Relative and absolute strength of response as a function of frequency of reinforcement. *Journal of the Experimental Analysis of Behavior, 4,* 267–74.

Herrnstein, R. J. (1974). Formal properties of the matching law. *Journal of the Experimental Analysis of Behavior, 21,* 159–64.

Herzberg, F., Mausner, B. & Snyderman, B. B. (1959). *The motivation to work.* 2nd edition. New York: Wiley.

Herzlich, C. (1973). *Health and illness: A social psychological analysis.* London: Academic Press.

Hewstone, M. & Jaspars, J. M. F. (1984). Social dimensions of attribution. In H. Tajfel (ed.), *The social dimension: European developments in social psychology.* Vol. 2. Cambridge: Cambridge University Press.

Hewstone, M., Jaspars, J. M. F. & Lalljee, M. (1982). Social representations, social attribution and social identity: The intergroup images of 'Public' and 'Comprehensive' schoolboys. *European Journal of Social Psychology, 12,* 241–69.

Higgins, E. T. & Lurie, L. (1983). Context, categorization, and recall: The 'change-of-standard' effect. *Cognitive Psychology, 15,* 525–47.

Higgins, E. T. & McCann, C. D. (1984). Social encoding and subsequent attitudes, impressions, and memory: 'Context-driven' and motivational aspects of processing. *Journal of Personality and Social Psychology, 47,* 26–39.

Higgins, E. T., Rhodewalt, F. & Zanna, M. P. (1979). Dissonance motivation: Its nature, persistence and reinstatement. *Journal of Experimental Social Psychology, 15,* 16–34.

Higgins, E. T. & Rholes, W. S. (1978). 'Saying is believing': Effects of message modification on memory and liking for the person described. *Journal of Experimental Social Psychology, 14,* 363–78.

Higgins, E. T., Rholes, W. S. & Jones, C. R. (1977). Category accessibility and impression formation. *Journal of Experimental Social Psychology, 13,* 141–54.

Himmelfarb, S. & Eagly, A. H. (eds.) (1974). *Readings in attitude change.* New York: Wiley.

Himmelweit, H. T., Humphreys, P., Jaeger, M. & Katz, M. (1981). *How voters decide: A longitudinal study of political attitudes and voting extending over fifteen years.* London: Academic Press.

Hinckley, E. D. (1932). The influence of individual opinion on construction of an attitude scale. *Journal of Social Psychology, 3,* 283–96.

Hiroto, D. S. & Seligman, M. E. P. (1975). Generality of learned helplessness in man. *Journal of Personality and Social Psychology, 81,* 311–27.

Hogarth, R. M. (1981). Beyond discrete biases: Functional and dysfunctional aspects of judgmental heuristics. *Psychological Bulletin, 90,* 197–217.

Hollander, E. P. (1964). *Leaders, groups and influence.* Oxford: Oxford University Press.

Holmes, J. G. & Strickland, L. H. (1970). Choice freedom and confirmation of incentive expectancy as determinants of attitude change. *Journal of Personality and Social Psychology, 14,* 39–45.

Holzkamp, K. (1965). Das Problem der 'Akzentuierung' in der sozialen Wahrnehmung. *Zeitschrift für experimentelle und angewandte Psychologie, 12,* 86–97.

Holzkamp, K. & Perlwitz, E. (1966). Absolute oder relative Grossenakzentuierung? Eine experimentelle Studie zur sozialen Wahrnehmung. *Zeitschriuft für experimentelle und angewandte Psychologie, 13,* 390–405.

Hovland, C. I., Harvey, O. J. & Sherif, M. (1957). Assimilation and contrast effects in reactions to communication and attitude change. *Journal of Abnormal and Social Psychology, 55,* 244–52.

Hovland, C. I. & Sherif, M. (1952). Judgmental phenomena and scales of attitude measurement: Item displacement in Thurstone Scales. *Journal of Abnormal and Social Psychology, 47,* 822–32.

Hoyt, M. F., Henley, M. D. & Collins, B. E. (1972). Studies in forced compliance: The confluence of choice and consequences on attitude change. *Journal of Personality and Social Psychology, 23,* 205–10.

Hunt, W. A. & Matarazzo, J. D. (1973). Three years later: Recent developments in the experimental modification of smoking behavior. *Journal of Abnormal and Social Psychology, 81,* 107–14.

Huston, T. L. (1973). Ambiguity of acceptance, social desirability, and dating choice. *Journal of Experimental Social Psychology, 9,* 32–42.

Insko, C. A. (1984). Balance theory, the Jordan paradigm and the Wiest tetrahedron. In L. Berkowitz (ed.), *Advances in experimental social psychology.* Vol. 18. New York: Academic Press.

Insko, C. A., Sedlak, A. J. & Lipsitz, A. (1982). A two-valued logic or two-valued balance resolution of the challenge of agreement and attraction effects in *p-o-x* triads, and a theoretical perspective on conformity and hedonism. *European Journal of Social Psychology, 12,* 143–67.

Insko, C. A., Songer, E. & McGarvey, W. (1974). Balance, positivity and agreement in the Jordan paradigm: A defense of balance theory. *Journal of Experimental Social Psychology, 10,* 53–83.

Isen, A. M. (1970). Success, failure, attention and reactions to others: The warm glow of success. *Journal of Personality and Social Psychology, 15,* 294–301.

Isen, A. M., Clark, M. & Schwartz, M. F. (1976). Duration of the effect of good mood on helping: 'Footprints on the sands of time'. *Journal of Personality and Social Psychology, 34,* 385–93.

Isen, A. M. & Daubman, K. A. (1984). The influence of affect on categorization. *Journal of Personality and Social Psychology, 47,* 1206–17.

Jaccard, J. J. & Davidson, A. R. (1972). Toward an understanding of family planning behaviors: An initial investigation. *Journal of Applied Social Psychology, 2,* 228–35.

James, W. (1968). The self. In C. Gordon & K. J. Gergen (eds.), *The self in social interaction. Vol. 1: Classic and contemporary perspectives.* New York: Wiley.

Janis, I. L. (1972). *Victims of groupthink.* Boston, Mass.: Houghton Mifflin.

Janis, I. L. (1983). Groupthink. In H. H. Blumberg, A. P. Hoare, V. Kent & M. J. F. Davies (eds.). *Small groups and social interaction.* Vol. 2. Chichester: Wiley.

Jaspars, J. M. F. (1965). On social perception. Unpublished Ph.D. Thesis. University of Leiden.

Jaspars, J. M. F., Hewstone, M. & Fincham, F. D. (1983). Attribution theory and research: The state of the art. In J. M. F. Jaspars, F. D. Fincham & M. Hewstone (eds.), *Attribution theory and research: Conceptual, developmental and social dimensions.* London: Academic Press.

Jodelet, D. (1984). Représentation sociale: phénomènes, concept et théorie. In S. Moscovici (ed.), *Psychologie sociale.* Paris: Presses Universitaires de France.

Johnson, E. J. & Tversky, A. (1983). Affect, generalization and the perception of risk. *Journal of Personality and Social Psychology, 45,* 20–31.

Johnson, T. J., Feigenbaum, R. & Weiby, M. (1964). Some determinants and consequences of the teacher's perception of causation. *Journal of Educational Psychology, 55,* 237–46.

Jones, C. & Aronson, E. (1973). Attribution of fault to a rape victim as a function of respectability of the victim. *Journal of Personality and Social Psychology, 26,* 415–19.

Jones, E. E. & Davis, K. E. (1965). From acts to dispositions: The attribution process in person perception. In L. Berkowitz (ed.), *Advances in experimental social psychology.* Vol. 2. New York: Academic Press.

Jones, E. E., Davis, K. E. & Gergen, K. J. (1961). Role playing variations and their informational value for person perception. *Journal of Abnormal and Social Psychology*, *63*, 302–10.

Jones, E. E. & Goethals, G. R. (1971). Order effects in impression formation: Attribution context and the nature of the entity. In E. E. Jones, D. E. Kanouse, H. H. Kelley, R. E. Nisbett, S. Valins & B. Weiner (eds.), *Attribution: Perceiving the causes of behavior*. Morristown, NJ: General Learning Press.

Jones, E. E. & Harris, V. A. (1967). The attribution of attitudes. *Journal of Experimental Social Psychology*, *3*, 1–24.

Jones, E. E. & Nisbett, R. E. (1971). The actor and observer: Divergent perceptions of the causes of behavior. In E. E. Jones, D. E. Kanouse, H. H. Kelley, R. E. Nisbett, S. Valins & B. Weiner (eds.), *Attribution: Perceiving the causes of behavior*. Morristown, NJ: General Learning Press.

Jones, E. E. & Sigall, H. (1971). The bogus pipeline: A new paradigm for measuring affect and attitude. *Psychological Bulletin*, *76*, 349–64.

Jones, E. E., Worchel, S., Goethals, G. R. & Grumet, J. F. (1971). Prior expectancy and behavioural extremity as determinants of attitude attribution. *Journal of Experimental Social Psychology*, *7*, 59–80.

Jones, R. A., Linder, D. E., Kiesler, C. A., Zanna, M. P. & Brehm, J. W. (1968). Internal states or external stimuli: Observers' attitude judgments and the dissonance theory–self-persuasion controversy. *Journal of Experimental Social Psychology*, *4*, 247–69.

Jordan, N. (1953). Behavioral forces that are a function of attitudes and cognitive organization. *Human Relations*, *6*, 273–87.

Jøreskog, K. G. (1971). Statistical analysis of sets of congeneric tests. *Psychometrika*, *36*, 109–33.

Jøreskog, K. G. & Sorbom, D. (1981). *LISREL V*. Chicago: National Educational Resources.

Kahneman, D. & Tversky, A. (1972). Subjective probability: A judgment of representativeness. *Cognitive Psychology*, *3*, 430–54.

Kahneman, D. & Tversky, A. (1973). On the psychology of prediction. *Psychological Review*, *80*, 237–51.

Kahneman, D. & Tversky, A. (1979). Prospect theory: An analysis of decision under risk. *Econometrica*, *47*, 263–91.

Kamin, L. J. (1969). Predictability, surprise, attention and conditioning. In B. A. Campbell & R. M. Church (eds.), *Punishment and aversive behavior*. New York: Appelton-Century-Crofts.

Kanouse, D. E. & Hanson, L. R., Jr. (1971). Negativity in evaluations. In E. E. Jones, D. E. Kanouse, H. H. Kelley, R. E. Nisbett, S. Valins & B. Weiner (eds.), *Attribution: Perceiving the causes of behavior*. Morristown, NJ: General Learning Press.

Kelley, H. H. (1967). Attribution theory in social psychology. *Nebraska Symposium on Motivation*, *15*, 192–238.

Kelley, H. H. (1971). Causal schemata and the attribution process. In E. E. Jones, D. E. Kanouse, H. H. Kelley, R. E. Nisbett, S. Valins & B. Weiner (eds.), *Attribution: Perceiving the causes of behavior*. Morristown, NJ: General Learning Press.

Kelley, H. H. & Michela, J. L. (1980). Attribution theory and research. *Annual Review of Psychology, 31,* 457–501.

Kelley, H. H. & Stahelski, A. J. (1970a). Errors in perception of intentions in a mixed-motive game. *Journal of Experimental Social Psychology, 6,* 379–400.

Kelley, H. H. & Stahelski, A. J. (1970b). Social interaction basis of cooperators' and competitors' beliefs about others. *Journal of Personality and Social Psychology, 16,* 66–91.

Kelley, G. A. (1955). *The psychology of personal constructs.* New York: Norton.

Kelman, H. C. (1961). Processes of opinion change. *Public Opinion Quarterly, 25,* 57–78.

Kelvin, P. (1984). The historical dimension of social psychology: The case of unemployment. In H. Tajfel (ed.), *The social dimension: European developments in social psychology.* Vol. 2. Cambridge: Cambridge University Press.

Kelvin, P. & Jarrett, J. E. (1985). *Unemployment: Its social psychological effects.* Cambridge: Cambridge University Press.

Kenrick, D. T. & Cialdini, R. B. (1977). Romantic attraction: Misattribution versus reinforcement explanations. *Journal of Personality and Social Psychology, 35,* 381–91.

Kenrick, D. T., Reich, J. W. & Cialdini, R. B. (1976). Justification and compensation: Rosier skies for the devalued victim. *Journal of Personality and Social Psychology, 34,* 654–7.

Kiesler, C. A., Collins, B. E. & Miller, N. (1969). *Attitude change.* New York: Wiley.

Kiesler, C. A., Nisbett, R. E. & Zanna, M. P. (1969). On inferring one's beliefs from one's behavior. *Journal of Personality and Social Psychology, 11,* 321–7.

Kinder, D. R., Smith, T. & Gerard, H. B. (1976). The attitude-labeling process outside of the laboratory. *Journal of Personality and Social Psychology, 33,* 480–91.

Klein, D. C., Fencil-Morse, E. & Seligman, M. E. P. (1976). Learned helplessness, depression, and the attribution of failure. *Journal of Personality and Social Psychology, 33,* 508–16.

Klein, G. S., Schlesinger, H. J. & Meister, D. E. (1951). The effect of values on perception: An experimental critique. *Psychological Review, 58,* 96–112.

Kosterlitz, H. W. & Hughes, J. (1977). Opiate receptors and endrogenous opioid peptides in tolerance and dependence. In M. M. Gross (ed.), *Alcohol intoxication and withdrawal.* New York: Plenum.

Kothandapani, V. (1971). Validation of feeling, belief, and intention to act as three components of attitude and their contribution to prediction of contraceptive behavior. *Journal of Personality and Social Psychology, 19,* 321–33.

Kruglanski, A. W. (1979). Causal explanation, teleological explanation: On radical particularism in attribution theory. *Journal of Personality and Social Psychology, 37,* 1447–57.

Kruglanski, A. W., Alon, S. & Lewis, T. (1972). Retrospective misattribution and task enjoyment. *Journal of Experimental Social Psychology, 8,* 493–501.

Kruglanski, A. W. & Cohen, M. (1973). Attributed freedom and personal causation. *Journal of Personality and Social Psychology, 26,* 245–50.

Kruglanski, A. W., Friedman, I. & Zeevi, G. (1971). The effects of extrinsic incentives on some qualitative aspects of task performance. *Journal of Personality, 39,* 606–17.

Kuhlman, D. & Wimberley, D. L. (1976). Expectations of choice behavior held by cooperators, competitors, and individualists across four classes of experimental game. *Journal of Personality and Social Psychology, 34,* 69–81.

Kutner, B., Wilkins, C. & Yarrow, P. R. (1952). Verbal attitudes and overt behavior involving racial prejudice. *Journal of Abnormal and Social Psychology, 47,* 649–52.

Landfield, A. W. (1968). The extremity rating revisited within the context of personal construct theory. *British Journal of Social and Clinical Psychology, 7,* 135–9.

Langer, E. J. (1975). The illusion of control. *Journal of Personality and Social Psychology, 32,* 311–28.

Langer, E. J. (1978). Rethinking the role of thought in social interaction. In J. H. Harvey, W. J. Ickes & R. F. Kidd (eds.), *New directions in attribution research.* Vol. 2. Hillsdale, NJ: Erlbaum.

Langer, E. J. & Abelson, R. P. (1972). The semantics of asking a favor: How to succeed in getting help without really dying. *Journal of Personality and Social Psychology, 24,* 26–32.

Langer, E. J., Bashner, R. S. & Chanowitz, B. (1985). Decreasing prejudice by increasing discrimination. *Journal of Personality and Social Psychology, 49,* 113–20.

Langer, E., Blank, A. & Chanowitz, B. (1978). The mindlessness of ostensibly thoughtful action: The role of 'placebic' information in interpersonal interaction. *Journal of Personality and Social Psychology, 36,* 635–42.

Langer, E. J., Chanowitz, B. & Blank, A. (1985). Mindlessness–mindfulness in perspective: A reply to Valerie Folkes. *Journal of Personality and Social Psychology, 48,* 605–7.

Langer, E. J. & Imber, L. G. (1979). When practice makes imperfect: Debilitating effects of overlearning. *Journal of Personality and Social Psychology, 37,* 2014–24.

Langer, E. J. & Imber, L. G (1980). Role of mindlessness in the perception of deviance. *Journal of Personality and Social Psychology, 39,* 360–7.

Langer, E. J., Rodin, J., Beck, P., Weinman, C. & Spitzer, L. (1979). Environmental determinants of memory improvement in late adulthood. *Journal of Personality and Social Psychology, 37,* 2005–13.

LaPiere, R. T. (1934). Attitudes vs. actions. *Social Forces, 13,* 230–7.

Latané, B. (1981). Psychology of social impact. *American Psychologist, 36,* 343–56.

Latané, B. & Wolf, S. (1981). The social impact of majorities and minorities. *Psychological Review, 88,* 438–53.

Lawrence, D. H. & Festinger, L. (1962). *Deterrents and reinforcement.* Stanford, California: Stanford University Press.

Lea, S. E. G., Tarpy, R. M. & Webley, P. (1986). *The individual in the economy.* Cambridge: Cambridge University Press.

Le Bon, G. (1895) (translated 1947). *The crowd: A study of the popular mind.* London: Ernest Benn.

Lefcourt, H. M. (1972). Recent developments in the study of locus of control. In B. Maher (ed.), *Progress in experimental personality research.* Vol. 6. New York: Academic Press.

Lemaine, G. (1974). Social differentiation and social originality. *European Journal of Social Psychology, 4,* 17–52.

Lemaine, G., Kastersztein, J. & Personnaz, B. (1978). Social differentiation. In H. Tajfel (ed.), *Differentiation between social groups: Studies in the social psychology of intergroup relations*. London: Academic Press.

Lepper, M. R. & Greene, D. (1975). Turning play into work: Effects of adult surveillance and extrinsic rewards on children's intrinsic motivation. *Journal of Personality and Social Psychology, 31*, 479–86.

Lepper, M. R. & Greene, D. (1976). On understanding 'overjustification': A reply to Reiss and Sushinsky. *Journal of Personality and Social Psychology, 33*, 25–35.

Lepper, M. R., Greene, D. & Nisbett, R. E. (1973). Undermining children's intrinsic interest with extrinsic reward: A test of the 'overjustification' hypothesis. *Journal of Personality and Social Psychology, 28*, 129–37.

Lerner, M. J. (1965). Evaluation of performance as a function of performer's reward and attractiveness. *Journal of Personality and Social Psychology, 1*, 355–60.

Lerner, M. J. (1970). The desire for justice and reactions to victims. In J. Macaulay & L. Berkowitz (eds.), *Altruism and helping behavior*. New York: Academic Press.

Lerner, M. J. (1971). Justified self-interest and the responsibility for suffering. *Journal of Human Relations, 19*, 550–9.

Lerner, M. J. (1974). The justice motive: 'Equity' and 'parity' among children. *Journal of Personality and Social Psychology, 29*, 539–50.

Lerner, M. J. (1980). *The belief in a just world: A fundamental delusion*. New York: Plenum.

Lerner, M. J. & Lichtman, R. R. (1968). Effects of perceived norms on attitudes and altruistic behavior toward a dependent other. *Journal of Personality and Social Psychology, 9*, 226–32.

Lerner, M. J. & Matthews, G. (1967). Reactions to suffering of others under conditions of indirect responsibility. *Journal of Personality and Social Psychology, 5*, 319–25.

Lerner, M. J., Miller, D. T. & Holmes, J. G. (1976). Deserving and the emergence of forms of justice. In L. Berkowitz & E. Walster (eds.), *Advances in experimental social psychology. Vol. 9. Equity theory: Toward a general theory of social interaction*. New York: Academic Press.

Lerner, M. J. & Simmons, C. H. (1966). Observer's reaction to the 'innocent victim': Compassion or rejection? *Journal of Personality and Social Psychology, 4*, 203–10.

Leventhal, H. (1980). Toward a comprehensive theory of emotion. In L. Berkowitz (ed.), *Advances in experimental social psychology*. Vol. 13. New York: Academic Press.

Leventhal, H. (1984). A perceptual-motor theory of emotion. In L. Berkowitz (ed.), *Advances in experimental social psychology*. Vol. 17. New York: Academic Press.

Lewin, K. (1936). *Principles of topological psychology*. New York: McGraw-Hill.

Lewin, K. (1948). *Resolving social conflicts*. New York: Harper.

Lichtenstein, S., Slovic, P., Fischhoff, B., Layman, M. & Combs, B. (1978). Judged frequency of lethal events. *Journal of Experimental Psychology: Human Learning and Memory, 4*, 551–78.

Likert, R. (1932). A technique for the measurement of attitudes. *Archives of Psychology*, 22 (Whole No. 140).

Lilli, W. (1970). Das Zustandekommen von Stereotypen über einfache und komplexe Sachverhalte: Experimente zum klassifizierenden Urteil. *Zeitschrift für Sozialpsychologie*, 1, 57–79.

Linder, D. E., Cooper, J. & Jones, E. E. (1967). Decision freedom as a determinant of the role of incentive magnitude in attitude change. *Journal of Personality and Social Psychology*, 6, 245–54.

Litton, I. & Potter, J. (1985). Social representations in the ordinary explanation of a 'riot'. *European Journal of Social Psychology*, 15, 371–88.

Lloyd-Bostock, S. (1983). Attributions of cause and responsibility as social phenomena. In J. M. F. Jaspars, F. D. Fincham & M. Hewstone (eds.), *Attribution theory and research: Conceptual, developmental and social dimensions*. London: Academic Press.

Lombardo, J. L., Weiss, R. F. & Buchanan, W. (1972). Reinforcing and attracting functions of yielding. *Journal of Personality and Social Psychology*, 21, 359–68.

Lord, C. G., Lepper, M. R. & Mackie, D. (1984). Attitude prototypes as determinants of attitude–behavior consistency. *Journal of Personality and Social Psychology*, 46, 1254–66.

Lösel, F. (1985). An empirical study on organisational assessment and personnel development in correctional treatment. Paper presented to colloquium: 'Applied Social Psychology in Practice'. Paris: Maison des Sciences de l'Homme.

Lott, A. J. & Lott, B. E. (1961). Group cohesiveness, communication level, and conformity. *Journal of Abnormal and Social Psychology*, 62, 408–12.

Lysak, W. & Gilchrist, J. C. (1955). Value equivocality and goal availability. *Journal of Personality*, 23, 500–1.

McArthur, L. A. (1970). Luck is alive and well in New Haven: A serendipitous finding on perceived control of reinforcement after the draft lottery. *Journal of Personality and Social Psychology*, 16, 316–18.

McArthur, L. A. (1972). The how and what of why: Some determinants and consequences of causal attribution. *Journal of Personality and Social Psychology*, 22, 171–93.

McArthur, L. Z. (1976). The lesser influence of consensus than distinctiveness information on causal attributions: A test of the person–thing hypothesis. *Journal of Personality and Social Psychology*, 33, 733–42.

McGuire, W. J. (1960). A syllogistic analysis of cognitive relationships. In C. I. Hovland & M. J. Rosenberg (eds.), *Attitude organization and change: An analysis of consistency among attitude components*. New Haven, Conn.: Yale University Press.

McGuire, W. J. (1964). Inducing resistance to persuasion: Some contemporary approaches. In L. Berkowitz (ed.), *Advances in experimental social psychology*. Vol. 1. New York: Academic Press.

McGuire, W. J. (1968). Résumé and response from the consistency theory viewpoint. In R. P. Abelson, E. Aronson, W. J. McGuire, T. M. Newcomb, M. J. Rosenberg & P. H. Tannenbaum (eds.), *Theories of cognitive consistency: A sourcebook*. Chicago: Rand McNally.

McGuire, W. J., McGuire, C. V., Child, P. & Fujioka, T. (1978). Salience of ethnicity in the spontaneous self-concept as a function of one's ethnic distinctiveness in the social environment. *Journal of Personality and Social Psychology, 36,* 511–20.

McGuire, W. J. & Millman, S. (1965). Anticipatory belief lowering following forewarning of a persuasive attack. *Journal of Personality and Social Psychology, 2,* 471–9.

McGuire, W. J. & Padawer-Singer, A. (1976). Trait salience in the spontaneous self-concept. *Journal of Personality and Social Psychology, 33,* 743–54.

McKennell, A. C. & Thomas, R. K. (1967). *Adults' and adolescents' smoking habits and attitudes.* Government Social Survey (SS353/B). London: HMSO.

McMahan, I. D. (1973). Relationships between causal attributions and expectancy of success. *Journal of Personality and Social Psychology, 28,* 108–14.

Maddi, S. R. (1968). The pursuit of consistency and variety. In R. P. Abelson, E. Aronson, W. J. McGuire, T. M. Newcomb, M. J. Rosenberg & P. H. Tannenbaum (eds.), *Theories of cognitive consistency: A sourcebook.* Chicago: Rand McNally.

Malpass, R. & Kravitz, L. (1969). Recognition for faces of own and other race. *Journal of Personality and Social Psychology, 13,* 330–4.

Manis, J. G. & Meltzer, B. N. (eds.) (1972). *Symbolic interaction.* Boston: Allyn & Bacon.

Manis, M. (1960). The interpretation of opinion statements as a function of recipient attitude. *Journal of Abnormal and Social Psychology, 60,* 340–4.

Manis, M. (1961). The interpretation of opinion statements as a function of message ambiguity and recipient attitude. *Journal of Abnormal and Social Psychology, 63,* 78–81.

Manis, M. (1964). Comment of Upshaw's 'Own attitude as an anchor in equal-appearing intervals'. *Journal of Abnormal and Social Psychology, 68,* 689–91.

Manis, M. (1977). Cognitive social psychology. *Personality and Social Psychology Bulletin, 3,* 550–66.

Manis, M., Paskewitz, J. & Cotler, S. (1986). Stereotypes and social judgment. *Journal of Personality and Social Psychology, 50,* 461–73.

Manstead, A. S. R., Proffitt, C. & Smart, J. L. (1983). Predicting and understanding mothers' infant-feeding intentions and behavior: Testing the theory of reasoned action. *Journal of Personality and Social Psychology, 44,* 657–71.

Marchand, B. (1970). Auswirkung einer emotional wertvollen und einer emotional neutralen Klassifikation auf die Schätzung einer Stimulusserie. *Zeitschrift für Sozialpsychologie, 1,* 264–74.

Markus, H. (1977). Self-schemata and processing information about the self. *Journal of Personality and Social Psychology, 35,* 63–78.

Markus, H., Crane, M., Bernstein, S. & Siladi, M. (1982). Self-schemas and gender. *Journal of Personality and Social Psychology, 42,* 38–50.

Marshall, G. & Zimbardo, P. G. (1979). Affective consequences of inadequately explained physiological arousal. *Journal of Personality and Social Psychology, 37,* 970–88.

Martin, L. K. & Riess, D. (1969). Effects of US intensity during previous discrete delay conditioning on conditioned acceleration during avoidance extinction. *Journal of Comparative and Physiological Psychology, 69,* 196–200.

Martin, L. L. (1985). *Categorization and differentiation: A set, re-set, comparison analysis of the effects of context on person perception.* New York: Springer-Verlag.

Martin, L. L. (1986). Set/re-set: Use and disuse of concepts in impression formation. *Journal of Personality and Social Psychology, 51*, 493–504.

Maslach, C. (1979). Negative emotional biasing of unexplained arousal. *Journal of Personality and Social Psychology, 37*, 953–69.

Mead, G. H. (1934). *Mind, self and society: From the standpoint of a social behaviorist.* Edited with an introduction by C. W. Morris. Chicago: University of Chicago Press.

Mead, G. H. (1968). The genesis of the self. In C. Gordon & K. J. Gergen (eds.), *The self in social interaction. Vol. 1: Classic and contemporary perspectives.* New York: Wiley.

Mehrabian, A. (1969). Measures of the achieving tendency. *Educational and Psychological Measurement, 29*, 445–51.

Mehrabian, A. & Reed, H. (1968). Some determinants of communication accuracy. *Psychological Bulletin, 70*, 365–80.

Merton, R. K. & Barber, E. (1976). Sociological ambivalence. In R. K. Merton (ed.), *Sociological ambivalence and other essays.* New York: Free Press.

Messick, D. M. & Reeder, G. (1972). Perceived motivation, role variations, and the attribution of personal characteristics. *Journal of Experimental Social Psychology, 8*, 482–91.

Meyer, W. U. (1970). Selbstverantworklichkeit und Leistungsmotivation. Unpublished Ph.D. Thesis. Ruhr-Universität Bochum.

Milgram, S. (1963). Behavioral study of obedience. *Journal of Abnormal and Social Psychology, 67*, 371–8.

Milgram, S. (1964). Group pressure and action against a person. *Journal of Abnormal and Social Psychology, 69*, 137–43.

Milgram, S. (1974). *Obedience to authority.* London: Tavistock.

Miller, C. T. (1984). Self-schemas, gender, and social comparison: A clarification of the related attributes hypothesis. *Journal of Personality and Social Psychology, 46*, 1222–9.

Miller, D. T. & Holmes, J. G. (1795). The role of situational restrictiveness on self-fulfilling prophecies: A theoretical and empirical extension of Kelley and Stahelski's Triangle Hypothesis. *Journal of Personality and Social Psychology, 31,* 661–73.

Miller, D. T. & Ross, M. (1975). Self-serving biases in the attribution of causality: Fact or fiction? *Psychological Bulletin, 82*, 213–25.

Miller, G. A. (1956). The magical number seven; plus or minus two: Some limits on our capacity for processing information. *Psychological Review, 63*, 81–97.

Miller, N. (1965). Involvement and dogmatism as inhibitors of attitude change. *Journal of Experimental Social Psychology, 1*, 121–32.

Miller, R. L., Brickman, P. & Bolen, D. (1975). Attribution versus persuasion as a means for modifying behavior. *Journal of Personality and Social Psychology, 31,* 430–41.

Mirels, H. L. (1970). Dimensions of internal versus external control. *Journal of Consulting and Clinical Psychology, 34*, 226–8.

Mischel, W. (1968). *Personality and assessment.* New York: Wiley.

Mischel, W. (1974). Processes in delay of gratification. In L. Berkowitz (ed.), *Advances in experimental social psychology*. Vol. 7. New York: Academic Press.

Mixon, D. (1972). Instead of deception. *Journal for the Theory of Social Behaviour, 2*, 145–78.

Monk, A. F. & Eiser, J. R. (1980). A simple, bias-free method for scoring attitude scale responses. *British Journal of Social and Clinical Psychology, 19*, 17–22.

Moscovici, S. (1973). Foreword. In C. Herzlich, *Health and illness: A social psychological analysis*. London: Academic Press.

Moscovici, S. (1974). Social influence, I: Conformity and social control. In C. Nemeth (ed.), *Social psychology: Classic and contemporary integrations*. Chicago: Rand McNally.

Moscovici, S. (1976a). *La psychanalyse, son image et son public*. 2nd edition. Paris: Presses Universitaires de France.

Moscovici, S. (1976b). *Social influence and social change*. London: Academic Press.

Moscovici, S. (1980). Toward a theory of conversion behavior. In L. Berkowitz (ed.), *Advances in experimental social psychology*, Vol. 13. New York: Academic Press.

Moscovici, S. (1981). On social representation. In J. P. Forgas (ed.), *Social cognition: Perspectives on everyday understanding*. London: Academic Press.

Moscovici, S. (1984). *The phenomenon of social representations*. In R. M. Farr (ed.), *Social representations*. Cambridge: Cambridge University Press.

Moscovici, S., (1985). Comment on Potter and Litton. *British Journal of Social Psychology, 24*, 91–2.

Moscovici, S., Lage, E. & Naffrechoux, M. (1969). Influence of a consistent minority on the responses of a majority in a color perception task. *Sociometry, 32*, 365–80.

Moscovici, S. & Paichelier, G. (1978). Social comparison and social recognition: Two complementary processes of identification. In H. Tajfel (ed.), *Differentiation between social groups: Studies in the social psychology of intergroup relations*. London: Academic Press.

Mouton, J. S., Blake, R R. & Olmstead, J. A. (1956). The relationship between frequency of yielding and the disclosure of personal identity. *Journal of Personality, 24*, 339–47.

Mower White, C. J. (1974). Positivity and consistency in attitude organization and judgement. Unpublished Ph.D. Thesis. University of Bristol.

Mower White, C. J. (1982). *Consistency in cognitive social behaviour: An introduction to social psychology*. London: Routledge & Kegan Paul.

Mugny, G. (1974). Négociation et influence minoritaire. Unpublished dissertation. University of Geneva.

Mugny, G. (1982). *The power of minorities*. London: Academic Press.

Mugny, G., Kaiser, C., Papastamou, S. & Pérez, J. A. (1984). Intergroup relations, identification and social influence. *British Journal of Social Psychology, 23*, 317–22.

Neely, J. H. (1976). Semantic priming and retrieval from lexical memory: Evidence for facilitatory and inhibitory processes. *Memory and Cognition, 4*, 648–54.

Neisser, U. (1967). *Cognitive psychology*. New York: Appleton-Century-Crofts.

Nemeth, C., Swedlund, M. & Kanki, B. (1974). Patterning of the minority's responses and their influence on the majority. *European Journal of Social Psychology, 4*, 53–64.

Newcomb, T. M. (1943). *Personality and social change: Attitude formation in a student community*. New York: Dryden Press.

Newcomb, T. M. (1956). The prediction of interpersonal attraction. *American Psychologist, 11*, 575–86.

Newcomb, T. M. (1961). *The acquaintance process*. New York: Holt, Rinehart & Winston.

Newcomb, T. M. (1968). Interpersonal balance. In R. P. Abelson, E. Aronson, W. J. McGuire, T. M. Newcomb, M. J. Rosenberg & P. H. Tannenbaum (eds.), *Theories of cognitive consistency: A source book*. Chicago: Rand McNally.

Newcomb, T. M. (1981). Heiderian balance as a group phenomenon. *Journal of Personality and Social Psychology, 40*, 862–7.

Nisbett, R. E. (1968). Taste, deprivation, and weight determinants of eating behavior. *Journal of Personality and Social Psychology, 10*, 107–16.

Nisbett, R. E. & Borgida, E. (1975). Attribution and the psychology of prediction. *Journal of Personality and Social Psychology, 32*, 932–43.

Nisbett, R. E., Borgida, E., Crandall, R. & Reed, H. (1976). Popular induction: Information is not always informative. In J. S. Carroll & J. W. Payne (eds.), *Cognition and social behavior*. Hillsdale, NJ: Erlbaum.

Nisbett, R. E., Caputo, C., Legant, P. & Maracek, J. (1973). Behavior as seen by the actor and as seen by the observer. *Journal of Personality and Social Psychology, 27*, 154–64.

Nisbett, R. E. & Ross, L. (1980). *Human inference: Strategies and shortcomings of social judgment*. Englewood Cliffs, NJ: Prentice-Hall.

Nisbett, R. E. & Wilson, T. D. (1977). Telling more than we can know: Verbal reports on mental processes. *Psychological Review, 84*, 231–59.

Nowell-Smith, P. H. (1956). *Ethics*. Harmondsworth: Penguin.

Nuttin, J. M. Jr. (1975). *The illusion of attitude change: Towards a response contagion theory of persuasion*. London: Academic Press.

Orne, M. T. (1962). On the social psychology of the psychological experiment: With particular reference to demand characteristics and their implications. *American Psychologist, 17*, 776–83.

Osgood, C. E., Suci, G. J. & Tannenbaum, P. H. (1957). *The measurement of meaning*. Urbana, Illinois: University of Illinois Press.

Osgood, C. E. & Tannenbaum, P. H. (1955). The principle of congruity in the prediction of attitude change. *Psychological Review, 62*, 42–55.

Oskamp, S. & Kleinke, C. (1970). Amount of reward as a variable in the Prisoner's Dilemma game. *Journal of Personality and Social Psychology, 16*, 133–40.

Ostrom, T. M. (1969). The relationship between the affective, behavioral and cognitive components of attitude. *Journal of Experimental Social Psychology, 5*, 12–30.

Ostrom, T. M. (1970). Perspective as a determinant of attitude change. *Journal of Experimental Social Psychology, 6*, 280–92.

Ostrom, T. M. & Upshaw, H. S. (1968). Psychological perspective and attitude change. In A. G. Greenwald, T. C. Brock & T. M. Ostrom (eds.), *Psychological foundations of attitudes*. New York: Academic Press.

O'Sullivan, C. S. & Durso, F. T. (1984). Effect of schema-incongruent information on memory for stereotypical attributes. *Journal of Personality and Social Psychology, 47,* 55–70.

Pagel, M. D. & Davidson, A. R. (1984). A comparison of three social-psychological models of attitude and behavioral plan: Prediction of contraceptive behavior. *Journal of Personality and Social Psychology, 47,* 517–33.

Pancer, S. M. & Eiser, J. R. (1977). Expectations, aspirations, and evaluations as influenced by another's attributions for success and failure. *Canadian Journal of Behavioral Science, 9,* 252–64.

Papastamou, S. (1979). Stratégies d'influence minoritaires et majoritaires. Unpublished dissertation. University of Geneva.

Parducci, A. (1963). Range–frequency compromise in judgment. *Psychological Monographs, 77,* (2, Whole No. 565).

Parducci, A. (1974). Contextual effects: A range–frequency analysis. In E. C. Carterette & M. P. Friedman (eds.), *Handbook of perception.* Vol. 2. New York: Academic Press.

Parducci, A. (1984). Value judgments: Toward a relational theory of happiness. In J. R. Eiser (ed.), *Attitudinal judgment.* New York: Springer-Verlag.

Parducci, A. & Marshall, L. M. (1962). Assimilation versus contrast in the anchoring of perceptual judgment of weight. *Journal of Experimental Psychology, 63,* 426–37.

Parducci, A. & Perrett, L. F. (1971). Category rating scales. *Journal of Experimental Psychology, 89,* 427–52.

Peabody, D. (1967). Trait inferences: Evaluative and descriptive aspects. *Journal of Personality and Social Psychology Monographs, 7* (2, Pt. 2, Whole No. 642).

Peabody, D. (1968). Group judgments in the Philippines: Evaluative and descriptive aspects. *Journal of Personality and Social Psychology, 10,* 290–300.

Peabody, D. (1970). Evaluative and descriptive aspects in personality perception: A reappraisal. *Journal of Personality and Social Psychology, 16,* 639–46.

Peabody, D. (1985). *National characteristics.* Cambridge: Cambridge University Press.

Peevers, B. H. & Secord, P. F. (1973). Developmental changes in attribution descriptive concepts to persons. *Journal of Personality and Social Psychology, 27,* 120–8.

Perrin, S. & Spencer, C. (1981). Independence or conformity in the Asch experiment as a reflection of cultural and situational factors. *British Journal of Social Psychology, 20,* 205–9.

Peterson, C. & Raps, C. S. (1984). Helplessness and hospitalization: More remarks. *Journal of Personality and Social Psychology, 46,* 82–3.

Petty, C. & Cacioppo, J. T. (1977). Forewarning, cognitive responding, and resistance to persuasion. *Journal of Personality and Social Psychology, 35,* 645–55.

Petty, R. E. & Cacioppo, J. T. (1979). Issue-involvement can increase or decrease persuasion by enhancing message-relevant cognitive responses. *Journal of Personality and Social Psychology, 37,* 1915–26.

Petty, R. E. & Cacioppo, J. T. (1985). The elaboration likelihood model of persuasion. In L. Berkowitz (ed.), *Advances in experimental social psychology.* Vol. 19. New York: Academic Press.

Petty, R. E., Harkins, S. G. & Williams, K. D. (1980). The effects of group diffusion of cognitive effort on attitudes: An information processing view. *Journal of Personality and Social Psychology, 38,* 81–92.

Petty, R. E., Wells, G. L. & Brock, T. C. (1976). Distraction can enhance or reduce yielding to propaganda: Thought disruption versus effort justification. *Journal of Personality and Social Psychology, 34,* 874–84.

Piliavin, I. M., Hardyck, J. & Vadum, A. (1967). Reactions to the victim in a just or non-just world. Paper presented at the meeting of the Society of Experimental Social Psychology, Bethesda, Maryland.

Piliavin, I. M., Piliavin, J. A. & Rodin, J. (1975). Costs, diffusion and the stigmatized victim. *Journal of Personality and Social Psychology, 32,* 429–38.

Piliavin, I. M., Rodin, J. & Piliavin, J. A. (1969). Good Samaritan: An underground phenomenon? *Journal of Personality and Social Psychology, 13,* 289–99.

Piliavin, J. A. & Piliavin, I. M. (1972). Effect of blood on reactions to a victim. *Journal of Personality and Social Psychology, 23,* 353–61.

Piliavin, J. A., Piliavin, I. M., Loewenton, E. P., McCauley, C. & Hammond, P. (1969). On observers' reproductions of dissonance effects: The right answers for the wrong reasons? *Journal of Personality and Social Psychology, 13,* 98–106.

Pintner, R. & Forlano, G. (1937). The influence of attitude upon scaling of attitude items. *Journal of Social Psychology, 8,* 39–45.

Podsakoff, P. M. & Schriesheim, C. A. (1985). Field studies of French and Raven's bases of power: Critique, reanalysis and suggestions for future research. *Psychological Bulletin, 97,* 387–411.

Pollis, N. P. (1967). Relative stability of scales formed in individual togetherness and group situations. *British Journal of Social and Clinical Psychology, 6,* 249–55.

Pollis, N. P. & Montgomery, R. L. (1968). Individual judgmental stability and the natural group. *Journal of Social Psychology, 74,* 75–81.

Pomazal, R. P. & Jaccard, J. J. (1976). An informational approach to altruistic behavior. *Journal of Personality and Social Psychology, 33,* 317–26.

Potter, J. & Litton, I. (1985). Some problems underlying the theory of social representations. *British Journal of Social Psychology, 24,* 81–90.

Powell, M. C. & Fazio, R. H. (1984). Attitude accessibility as a function of repeated attitudinal expression. *Personality and Social Psychology Bulletin, 10,* 139–48.

Press, A. N., Crockett, W. H. & Rosenkrantz, P. S. (1969). Cognitive complexity and the learning of balanced and unbalanced social structures. *Journal of Personality, 37,* 541–53.

Pretty, G. H. & Seligman, C. (1984). Affect and the overjustification effect. *Journal of Personality and Social Psychology, 46,* 1241–53.

Price, K. O., Harburg, E. & Newcomb, T. M. (1966). Psychological balance in situations of negative interpersonal attitudes. *Journal of Personality and Social Psychology, 3,* 265–70.

Prociuk, T. J. & Breen, L. J. (1975). Defensive externality and its relation to academic performance. *Journal of Personality and Social Psychology, 31,* 549–56.

Pruitt, D. G. & Kimmel, M. J. (1977). Twenty years of experimental gaming: Critique, synthesis, and suggestions for the future. *Annual Review of Psychology, 28,* 363–92.

Quattrone, G. A. (1985). On the congruity between internal states and action. *Psychological Bulletin, 98,* 3–40.

Rabbie, J. M. & Horwitz, M. (1969). Arousal of ingroup–outgroup bias by a chance win or loss. *Journal of Personality and Social Psychology, 13,* 269–77.

Rabbie, J. M. & Wilkens, G. (1971). Intergroup competition and its effect on intragroup and intergroup relations. *European Journal of Social Psychology, 1,* 215–34.

Raps, C. S., Peterson, C., Jonas, M. & Seligman, M. E. P. (1982). Patient behavior in hospitals: Helplessness, reactance, or both? *Journal of Personality and Social Psychology, 42,* 1036–41.

Raven, B. H. (1959). Social influence on opinions and the communications of related content. *Journal of Abnormal and Social Psychology, 58,* 119–28.

Raven, B. H. (1974). The Nixon group. *Journal of Social Issues, 30,* 297–320.

Raven, B. H. & Haley, R. W. (1982). Social influence and compliance of hospital nurses with infection control policies. In J. R. Eiser (ed.), *Social psychology and behavioral medicine.* Chichester: Wiley.

Regan, D. T. & Fazio, R. H. (1977). On the consistency between attitudes and behavior: Look to the method of attitude formation. *Journal of Experimental Social Psychology, 13,* 28–45.

Regan, D. T. & Totten, J. (1975). Empathy and attribution: Turning observers into actors. *Journal of Personality and Social Psychology, 32,* 850–6.

Reicher, S. D. (1984a). Social influence in the crowd: Attitudinal and behavioural effects of deindividuation in conditions of high and low group salience. *British Journal of Social Psychology, 23,* 341–50.

Reicher, S. D. (1984b). The St Paul's riot: An explanation of the limits of crowd action in terms of a social identity model. *European Journal of Social Psychology, 14,* 1–21.

Reicher, S. D. & Potter, J. (1985). Psychological theory as intergroup perspective: A comparative analysis of 'scientific' and 'lay' accounts of crowd events. *Human Relations, 38,* 167–89.

Reingen, D. H. (1982). Test of a list procedure for inducing compliance with a request to donate money. *Journal of Applied Psychology, 67,* 110–18.

Reisenzein, R. (1983). The Schachter theory of emotion: Two decades later. *Psychological Bulletin, 94,* 239–64.

Reiss, S. & Sushinsky, L. W. (1975). Overjustification, competing responses, and the acquisition of intrinsic interest. *Journal of Personality and Social Psychology, 31,* 1116–25.

Reiss, S. & Sushinsky, L. W. (1976). The competing response hypothesis of decreased play effects: A reply to Lepper and Greene. *Journal of Personality and Social Psychology, 33,* 233–44.

Rescorla, R. S. (1968). Probability of shock in the presence and absence of CS in fear conditioning. *Journal of Comparative and Physiological Psychology, 66,* 1–5.

Rescorla, R. S. & Solomon, R. L. (1967). Two-process learning theory: Relationships between Pavlovian conditioning and instrumental learning. *Psychological Review, 74,* 151–82.

Robins, L. N., Davis, D. H. & Goodwin, D. W. (1974). Drug use by U.S. Army enlisted men in Vietnam: A follow-up on their return home. *American Journal of Epidemiology, 99,* 235–49.

Robinson, D. (1972). The alcohologist's addiction: Some implications of having lost control over the disease concept of alcoholism. *Quarterly Journal of Studies on Alcohol, 33,* 1028–42.

Rodrigues, A. (1967). Effects of balance, positivity and agreement in triadic social relations. *Journal of Personality and Social Psychology, 5,* 472–6.

Rodrigues, A. (1968). The biasing effect of agreement in balanced and unbalanced triads. *Journal of Personality, 36,* 138–53.

Romer, D. (1983). Effects of own attitude on polarization of judgment. *Journal of Personality and Social Psychology, 44,* 273–84.

Rosch, E. & Lloyd, B. (eds.) (1978). *Cognition and categorization.* Hillsdale, NJ: Erlbaum.

Rosenberg, M. J. (1965). When dissonance fails: On eliminating evaluation apprehension from attitude measurement. *Journal of Personality and Social Psychology, 1,* 28–42.

Rosenberg, M. J. & Abelson, R. P. (1960). An analysis of cognitive balancing. In C. I. Hovland & M. J. Rosenberg (eds.), *Attitude organization and change: An analysis of consistency among attitude components.* New Haven, Conn.: Yale University Press.

Rosenberg, M. J. & Hovland, C. I. (1960). Cognitive, affective and behavioral components of attitudes. In C. I. Hovland & M. J. Rosenberg (eds.), *Attitude organization and change: An analysis of consistency among attitude components.* New Haven, Conn.: Yale University Press.

Rosenberg, S. & Olshan, K. (1970). Evaluative and descriptive aspects in personality perception. *Journal of Personality and Social Psychology, 16,* 619–26.

Rosenhan, D. L. (1973). On being sane in insane places. *Science, 179,* 250–8.

Rosenthal, A. M. (1964). *Thirty-eight witnesses.* New York: McGraw Hill.

Rosenthal, R. (1973). The mediation of Pygmalion effects: A four-factor 'theory'. *Papua New Guinea Journal of Education, 9,* 1–12.

Rosenthal, R. & Jacobson, L. (1968). *Pygmalion in the classroom.* New York: Holt, Rinehart & Winston.

Ross, A. S. & Braband, J. (1973). Effect of increased responsibility on bystander intervention. II: The cue value of a blind person. *Journal of Personality and Social Psychology, 25,* 254–8.

Ross, L., Greene, D. & House, P. (1977). The 'false consensus effect': An egocentric bias in social perception and attribution processes. *Journal of Experimental Social Psychology, 13,* 279–301.

Ross, M. (1975). Salience of reward and intrinsic motivation. *Journal of Personality and Social Psychology, 32,* 245–54.

Ross, M. (1976). The self-perception of intrinsic motivation. In J. H. Harvey, W. J. Ickes & R. F. Kidd (eds.), *New directions in attribution research.* Hillsdale, NH: Erlbaum.

Ross, M., Insko, C. A. & Ross, H. S. (1971). Self-attribution of attitude. *Journal of Personality and Social Psychology, 17,* 292–7.

Ross, M., Karniol, R. & Rothstein, M. (1976). Reward contingency and intrinsic motivation in children: A test of the delay of gratification hypothesis. *Journal of Personality and Social Psychology, 33,* 442–7.

Ross, M. & Shulman, R. F. (1973). Increasing the salience of initial attitudes:

Dissonance versus self-perception theory. *Journal of Personality and Social Psychology, 28,* 138–44.

Rossman, B. B. & Gollob, H. F. (1976). Social inference and pleasantness judgments involving people and issues. *Journal of Experimental Social Psychology, 12,* 374–91.

Roth, H. G. & Upmeyer, A. (1985). Matching attitudes towards cartoons across evaluative judgments and non-verbal evaluative behavior. *Psychological Research, 47,* 173–83.

Rothbart, M., Evans, M. & Fulero, S. (1979). Recall for confirming events: Memory processes and the maintenance of social stereotypes. *Journal of Experimental Social Psychology, 15,* 343–55.

Rotter, J. B. (1966). Generalized expectancies for internal versus external control of reinforcement. *Psychological Monographs, 80,* (1, Whole No. 609).

Rotter, J. B., Chance, J. E. & Phares, E. J. (1972). *Applications of a social learning theory of personality.* New York: Holt Rinehart & Winston.

Rubin, Z. & Zajonc, R. B. (1969). Structural bias and generalization in the learning of social structures. *Journal of Personality, 37,* 310–24.

Rundquist, E. A. & Sletto, R. F. (1936). *Personality in the depression.* Minneapolis: University of Minnesota Press.

Russell, M. A. H. (1976). Tobacco smoking and nicotine dependence. In R. J. Gibbins *et al.* (eds.), *Research advances in alcohol and drug problems.* New York: Wiley.

Rutter, D. R. (1984). *Looking and seeing: The role of visual communication in social interaction.* Chichester: Wiley.

Saltzer, E. B. (1981). Cognitive moderators of the relationship between behavioral intentions and behavior. *Journal of Personality and Social Psychology, 41,* 260–71.

Sampson, E. E. & Insko, C. A. (1964). Cognitive consistency and performance in the autokinetic situation. *Journal of Abnormal and Social Psychology, 68,* 184–92.

Sartre, J. P. (1943) (translated, 1969). *L'Être et le Néant.* Translated as: *Being and nothingness.* London: Methuen.

Schachter, S. (1959). *The psychology of affiliation.* Stanford, CA: Stanford University Press.

Schachter, S. (1951). Deviation, rejection, and communication. *Journal of Abnormal and Social Psychology, 46,* 190–207.

Schachter, S. (1982). Recidivism and self-cure of smoking and obesity. *American Psychologist, 37,* 436–44.

Schachter, S. & Gross, L. (1968). Manipulated time and eating behavior. *Journal of Personality and Social Psychology, 10,* 98–106.

Schachter, S., Silverstein, B., Kozlowski, L. T., Perlick, D., Herman, C. P. & Liebling, B. (1977). Studies of the interaction of psychological and pharmacological determinants of smoking. *Journal of Experimental Social Psychology: General, 106,* 3–40.

Schachter, S. & Singer, J. E. (1962). Cognitive, social and physiological determinants of emotional state. *Psychological Review, 69,* 379–99.

Schachter, S. & Singer, J. (1979). Comments on the Maslach and Marshall-Zimbardo experiments. *Journal of Personality and Social Psychology, 37,* 989–95.

Schaffner, P. E. (1985). Specious learning about reward and punishment. *Journal of Personality and Social Psychology, 48,* 1377–86.

Schank, R. C. & Abelson, R. P. (1977). *Scripts, plans, goals, and understanding: An inquiry into human knowledge structures.* Hillsdale, NJ: Erlbaum.

Schlegel, R. P., Crawford, C. A. & Sanborn, M. D. (1977). Correspondence and mediational properties of the Fishbein model: An application to adolescent alcohol use. *Journal of Experimental Social Psychology, 13,* 421–30.

Schlenker, B. R. (1980). *Impression management: The self-concept, social identity, and interpersonal relations.* Monterey, Calif.: Brooks/Cole.

Schlenker, B. R. (1982). Translating actions into attitudes: An identity-analytic approach to the explanation of social conduct. In L. Berkowitz (ed.), *Advances in experimental social psychology.* Vol. 15. New York: Academic Press.

Schneider, D. J. & Blankmeyer, B. L. (1983). Prototype salience and implicit personality theories. *Journal of Personality and Social Psychology, 44,* 712–22.

Schopler, J. & Layton, B. (1972). Determinants of the self-attribution of having influenced another person. *Journal of Personality and Social Psychology, 22,* 326–32.

Schwartz, S. & Griffin, T. (1986). *Medical thinking: The psychology of medical judgment and decision making.* New York: Springer-Verlag.

Secord, P. F. (1959). Stereotyping and favorableness in the perception of Negro faces. *Journal of Abnormal and Social Psychology, 59,* 309–15.

Secord, P. F. & Backman, C. W. (1965). An interpersonal approach to personality. In B. Maher (ed.), *Progress in experimental personality research.* Vol. 2. New York: Academic Press.

Secord, P. F., Bevan, W. & Katz, B. (1965). The Negro stereotype and perceptual accentuation. *Journal of Abnormal and Social Psychology, 53,* 78–83.

Seeman, M. (1971). The urban alienations: Some dubious theses from Marx to Marcuse. *Journal of Personality and Social Psychology, 19,* 135–43.

Segall, M. H. (1959). The effect of attitude and experience on judgments of controversial statements. *Journal of Abnormal and Social Psychology, 58,* 366–72.

Seligman, M. E. P. (1972). Learned helplessness. *Annual Review of Medicine, 23,* 407–12.

Seligman, M. E. P. (1975). *Helplessness.* San Francisco: Freeman.

Seligman, M. E. P., Abramson, L. Y., Semmel, A. & von Baeyer, C. (1979). Depressive attributional style. *Journal of Abnormal and Social Psychology, 88,* 242–247.

Seligman, M. E. P. & Maier, S. F. (1967). Failure to escape traumatic shock. *Journal of Experimental Psychology, 74,* 1–9.

Selltiz, C., Edrich, H. & Cook, S. W. (1965). Ratings of favorableness about a social group as an indication of attitude toward the group. *Journal of Personality and Social Psychology, 2,* 408–15.

Sermat, V. (1970). Is game behavior related to behavior in other interpersonal situations? *Journal of Personality and Social Psychology, 16,* 92–109.

Shaffer, D. R. (1975). Some effects of consonant and dissonant attitudinal advocacy on initial attitude salience and attitude change. *Journal of Personality and Social Psychology, 32,* 160–8.

Shaver, K. G. (1970a). Defensive attribution: Effects of severity and relevance on the responsibility assigned for an accident. *Journal of Personality and Social Psychology, 14,* 101–13.

Shaver, K. G. (1970b). Redress and conscientiousness in the attribution of responsibility for accidents. *Journal of Experimental Social Psychology, 6,* 100–10.

Shaw, J. I. & Skolnick, P. (1971). Attribution of responsibility for a happy accident. *Journal of Personality and Social Psychology, 18,* 380–3.

Shaw, M. E. & Sulzer, J. L. (1964). An empirical test of Heider's levels in attribution of responsibility. *Journal of Abnormal and Social Psychology, 69,* 39–46.

Shaw, M. E. & Wright, J. M. (1967). *Scales for the measurement of attitudes.* New York: McGraw-Hill.

Sherif, C. W., Sherif, M. & Nebergall, R. E. (1965). *Attitude and attitude change: The social judgment-involvement approach.* Philadelphia: Saunders.

Sherif, M. (1935). A study of some social factors in perception. *Archives of Psychology, 22,* No. 187.

Sherif, M. (1951). A preliminary experimental study of intergroup relations. In J. H. Rohrer & M. Sherif (eds.), *Social psychology at the crossroads.* New York: Harper.

Sherif, M. (1966). *Group conflict and cooperation: Their social psychology.* London: Routledge & Kegan Paul.

Sherif, M. & Hovland, C. I. (1961). *Social judgment: Assimilation and contrast effects in communication and attitude change.* New Haven, Conn.: Yale University Press.

Sherif, M. & Sherif, C. W. (1953). *Groups in harmony and tension.* New York: Harper.

Sherif, M. & Sherif, C. W. (1969). *Social psychology.* New York: Harper & Row.

Sherif, M., Taub, D. & Hovland, C. I. (1958). Assimilation and contrast effects of anchoring stimuli on judgment. *Journal of Experimental Psychology, 55,* 150–5.

Sherman, S. J. (1970). Effects of choice and incentive on attitude change in a discrepant behavior situation. *Journal of Personality and Social Psychology, 15,* 245–52.

Simons, C. W. & Piliavin, J. A. (1972). The effect of deception on reactions to a victim. *Journal of Personality and Social Psychology, 21,* 56–60.

Skolnick, P. (1971). Reactions to personal evaluations: A failure to replicate. *Journal of Personality and Social Psychology, 18,* 62–7.

Slovic, P., Fischhoff, B. & Lichtenstein, S. (1976). Cognitive processes and societal risk taking. In J. S Carroll & J. W. Payne (eds.), *Cognition and social behavior.* Hillsdale, NJ: Erlbaum.

Slovic, P., Fischhoff, B. & Lichtenstein, S. (1977). Behavioral decision theory. *Annual Review of Psychology, 28,* 1–39.

Smith, A. (1759; 1892). *The theory of moral sentiments.* London: George Bell and Sons.

Snyder, M. (1974). The self-monitoring of expressive behavior. *Journal of Personality and Social Psychology, 30,* 526–37.

Snyder, M. & Ebbesen, E. (1972). Dissonance awareness: A test of dissonance theory versus self-perception theory. *Journal of Experimental Social Psychology, 8,* 502–17.

Snyder, M. & Kendzierski, D. (1982). Acting on one's attitudes: Procedures for linking attitudes and behavior. *Journal of Experimental Social Psychology, 18,* 165–83.

Snyder, M. L., Stephan, W. G. & Rosenfield, D. (1976). Egotism and attribution. *Journal of Personality and Social Psychology, 33,* 435–41.

Snyder, M. & Swann, W. B. Jr. (1976). When actions reflect attitudes: The politics of impression management. *Journal of Personality and Social Psychology, 34,* 1034–42.

Snyder, M. & Swann, W. B. Jr. (1978). Behavioral confirmation in social interaction: From social perception to social reality. *Journal of Experimental Social Psychology, 14,* 148–62.

Sogin, S. R. & Pallak, M. S. (1976). Bad decisions, responsibility, and attitude change: Effects of volition, foreseeability, and locus of causality of negative consequences. *Journal of Personality and Social Psychology, 33,* 300–6.

Solley, C. M. & Lee, R. (1955). Perceived size: Obscure versus symbolic value. *American Journal of Psychology, 68,* 142–4.

Solomon, R. L. (1980). The opponent-process theory of acquired motivation: The cost of pleasure and the benefits of pain. *American Psychologist, 35,* 691–712.

Songer-Nocks, E. (1976). Situational factors affecting the weighting of predictor components in the Fishbein model. *Journal of Experimental Social Psychology, 12,* 56–69.

Sorrentino, R. M. & Boutelier, R. C. (1974). Evaluation of a victim as a function of fate similarity/dissimilarity. *Journal of Experimental Social Psychology, 10,* 83–92.

Spears, R., van der Pligt, J. & Eiser, J. R. (1985). Illusory correlation in the perception of group attitudes. *Journal of Personality and Social Psychology, 48,* 863–75.

Spears, R., van der Pligt, J. & Eiser, J. R. (1986). Generalizing the illusory correlation effect in social perception. *Journal of Personality and Social Psychology.* In press.

Sperling, H. G. (1946). An experimental study of psychological factors in judgment. Unpublished Master's thesis. N.S.S.R.

Stern, L. D., Marrs, S., Millar, M. G. & Cole, E. (1984). Processing time and the recall of inconsistent and consistent behaviors of individuals and groups. *Journal of Personality and Social Psychology, 47,* 253–62.

Stevens, L. & Jones, E. E. (1976). Defensive attribution and the Kelley cube. *Journal of Personality and Social Psychology, 34,* 809–20.

Stevens, S. S. (1957). On the psychophysical law. *Psychological Review, 64,* 153–81.

Stevens, S. S. (1958). Adaptation-level versus the relativity of judgment. *American Journal of Psychology, 71,* 633–46.

Stevens, S. S. (1966). A metric for the social consensus. *Science, 151,* 530–41.

Stevens, S. S. (1975). *Psychophysics: Introduction to its perceptual, neural, and social prospects.* New York: Wiley.

Stewart, J. E. (1980). Defendant's attractiveness as a factor in the outcome of trials. *Journal of Applied Social Psychology, 10,* 348–61.

Storms, M. D. (1973). Videotape and the attribution process: Reversing actors' and observers' points of view. *Journal of Personality and Social Psychology, 27,* 165–75.

Streufert, S. & Streufert, S. C. (1978). *Behavior in the complex environment.* Washington, D.C.: Winston.

Stroebe, W. (1977). Self-esteem and interpersonal attraction. In S. Duck (ed.), *Theory and practice in interpersonal attraction*. London: Academic Press.

Stroebe, W., Eagly, A. H. & Stroebe, M. S. (1977). Friendly or just polite? The effect of self-esteem on attributions. *European Journal of Social Psychology, 7,* 265–74.

Stroebe, W., Insko, C. A., Thompson, V. D. & Layton, B. D. (1971). Effects of physical attractiveness, attitude similarity and sex on various aspects of interpersonal attraction. *Journal of Personality and Social Psychology, 18,* 79–91.

Stroebe, W., Thompson, V. D., Insko, C. A. & Reisman, S. R. (1970). Balance and differentiation in the evaluation of linked attitude objects. *Journal of Personality and Social Psychology, 16,* 38–47.

Stults, D. M., Messé, L. A. & Kerr, N. L. (1984). Belief discrepant behavior and the bogus pipeline: Impression management or arousal attribution? *Journal of Experimental Social Psychology, 20,* 47–54.

Sutton, S. R. & Eiser, J. R. (1984). The effect of fear-arousing communications on cigarette smoking: An expectancy-value approach. *Journal of Behavioral Medicine, 7,* 13–33.

Tajfel, H. (1957). Value and the perceptual judgment of magnitude. *Psychological Review, 64,* 192–204.

Tajfel, H. (1959a). Quantitative judgement in social perception. *British Journal of Psychology, 50,* 16–29.

Tajfel, H. (1959b). The anchoring effects of value in a scale of judgements. *British Journal of Psychology, 50,* 294–304.

Tajfel, H. (1969). Cognitive aspects of prejudice. *Journal of Social Issues, 25,* 79–97.

Tajfel, H. (ed.) (1978). *Differentiation between social groups: Studies in the social psychology of intergroup relations*. London: Academic Press.

Tajfel, H., Flament, C., Billig, M. G. & Bundy, R. P. (1971). Social categorisation and intergroup behavior. *European Journal of Social Psychology, 1,* 149–78.

Tajfel, H., Sheikh, A. A. & Gardner, R. C. (1964). Content of stereotypes and the inference of similarity between members of stereotyped groups. *Acta Psychologica, 22,* 191–201.

Tajfel, H. & Wilkes, A. L. (1963). Classification and quantitative judgement. *British Journal of Psychology, 54,* 101–14.

Tajfel, H. & Wilkes, A. L. (1964). Salience of attributes and commitment to extreme judgements in the perception of people. *British Journal of Social and Clinical Psychology, 3,* 40–9.

Tanford, S. & Penrod, S. (1984). Social influence model: A formal integration of research on majority and minority influence processes. *Psychological Bulletin, 95,* 189–225.

Tarpy, R. M. (1982). *Principles of animal learning and motivation*. Glenview, Ill.: Scott, Foresman.

Taylor, D. M. & McKirnan, D. J. (1984). A five-stage model of intergroup relations. *British Journal of Social Psychology, 23,* 291–300.

Taylor, S. E. & Fiske, S. T. (1975). Point of view and perceptions of causality. *Journal of Personality and Social Psychology, 32,* 439–45.

Taylor, S. E. & Fiske, S. T. (1978). Salience, attention and attribution: Top of the head phenomena. In L. Berkowitz (ed.), *Advances in experimental social psychology*. Vol. 11. New York: Academic Press.

Taylor, S. E., Fiske, S. T., Etcoff, N. L. & Ruderman, A. J. (1978). Categorical and contextual bases of person memory and stereotyping. *Journal of Personality and Social Psychology, 36*, 778–93.

Taylor, S. E., Lichtman, R. R. & Wood, J. V. (1984). Attributions, beliefs about control, and adjustment to breast cancer. *Journal of Personality and Social Psychology, 46*, 489–502.

Taylor, S. E. & Thompson, S. C. (1982). Stalking the elusive 'vividness' effect. *Psychological Review, 89*, 155–81.

Tedeschi, J. T. & Rosenfeld, P. (1981). Impression management theory and the forced compliance situation. In J. T. Tedeschi (ed.), *Impression management theory and social psychological research.* New York: Academic Press.

Tedeschi, J. T., Schlenker, B. R. & Bonoma, T. V. (1971). Cognitive dissonance: Private ratiocination or public spectacle? *American Psychologist, 26*, 685–95.

Tetlock, P. E. (1979). Identifying victims of groupthink from public statements of decision makers. *Journal of Personality and Social Psychology, 37*, 1314–24.

Tetlock, P. E. (1983). Accountability and complexity of thought. *Journal of Personality and Social Psychology, 45*, 74–83.

Tetlock, P. E. & Manstead, A. S. R. (1985). Impression management versus intrapsychic explanations in social psychology: A useful dichotomy? *Psychological Review, 92*, 59–77.

Thibaut, J. W. & Kelley, H. H. (1959). *The social psychology of groups.* New York: Wiley.

Thomson, J. A. K. (transl.) (1955). *The Ethics of Aristotle.* Harmondsworth: Penguin.

Thurstone, L. L. (1928). Attitudes can be measured. *American Journal of Sociology, 33*, 529–54.

Thurstone, L. L. (ed.) (1931) *Scales for the measurement of social attitudes.* Chicago: University of Chicago Press.

Thurstone, L. L. & Chave, E. J. (1929). *The measurement of attitude.* Chicago: University of Chicago Press.

Tolman, E. C. (1959). Principles of purposive behavior. In S. Koch (ed.), *Psychology: A study of science.* Vol. 2. New York: McGraw-Hill.

Tom, G. & Rucker, M. (1975). Fat, full and happy: Effects of food deprivation, external cues and obesity on preference ratings, consumption, and buying intentions. *Journal of Personality and Social Psychology, 32*, 761–6.

Torgerson, W. S. (1958). *Theory and methods of scaling.* New York: Wiley.

Tresselt, M. E. (1948). The effect of experience of contrasted groups upon the formation of a new scale. *Journal of Social Psychology, 27*, 209–16.

Triandis, H. C. (1964). Exploratory factor analysis of the behavioural components of social attitudes. *Journal of Abnormal and Social Psychology, 68*, 420–30.

Triandis, H. C. (1967). Towards an analysis of the components of interpersonal attitudes. In C. W. Sherif & M. Sherif (eds.), *Attitudes, ego involvement, and change.* New York: Wiley.

Turner, J. C. (1975). Social comparison and social identity: Some prospects for intergroup behavior. *European Journal of Social Psychology, 5*, 5–34.

Turner, J. C. (1978). Social comparison, similarity and ingroup favouritism. In H. Tajfel (ed.), *Differentiation between social groups: Studies in the social psychology of intergroup relations.* London: Academic Press.

Turner, J. C. (1982). Towards a cognitive redefinition of the social group. In H. Tajfel (ed.), *Social identity and intergroup relations*. Cambridge: Cambridge University Press.

Turner, J. C. & Brown, R. (1978). Social status cognitive alternatives and intergroup relations. In H. Tajfel (ed.), *Differentiation between social groups: Studies in the social psychology of intergroup relations*. London: Academic Press.

Turner, J. C. (1985). Social categorization and the self-concept: A social cognitive theory of group behaviour. In E. J. Lawler (ed.), *Advances in group processes: Theory and research*. Vol. 2. Greenwich, CT: JAI Press.

Tversky, A. (1972). Elimination by aspects: A theory of choice. *Psychological Review, 79*, 281–99.

Tversky, A. & Kahneman, D. (1973). Availability: A heuristic for judging frequency and probability. *Cognitive Psychology, 5*, 207–32.

Tversky, A. & Kahneman, D. (1974). Judgment under uncertainty: Heuristics and biases. *Science, 185*, 1124–31.

Tversky, A. & Kahneman, D. (1980). Causal schemas in judgments under uncertainty. In M. Fishbein (ed.) *Progress in social psychology*. Vol. 1. Hillsdale, NJ: Erlbaum.

Tversky, A. & Kahneman, D. (1981). The framing of decisions and the psychology of choice. *Science, 211*, 453–8.

Tversky, A. & Sattath, S. (1979). Preference trees. *Psychological Review, 86*, 542–73.

Upshaw, H. S. (1962). Own attitude as an anchor in equal-appearing intervals. *Journal of Abnormal and Social Psychology, 64*, 85–96.

Upshaw, H. S. (1965). The effect of variable perspectives on judgments of opinion statements for Thurstone scales: Equal-appearing intervals. *Journal of Personality and Social Psychology, 2*, 60–9.

Upshaw, H. S. (1969). The personal reference scale: An approach to social judgment. In L. Berkowitz (ed.), *Advances in experimental social psychology*. Vol. 4. New York: Academic Press.

Upshaw, H. S. (1976). Out of the laboratory and into wonderland: A critique of the Kinder, Smith and Gerard adventure with perspective theory. *Journal of Personality and Social Psychology, 34*, 699–703.

Upshaw, H. S. (1978). Social influence on attitudes and on anchoring of congeneric attitude scales. *Journal of Experimental Social Psychology, 14*, 327–39.

Upshaw, H. S. & Ostrom, T. M. (1984). Psychological perspective in attitude research. In J. R. Eiser (ed.), *Attitudinal judgment*. New York: Springer-Verlag.

Upshaw, H. S., Ostrom, T. M. & Ward, C. D. (1970). Content versus self-rating in attitude research. *Journal of Experimental Social Psychology, 6*, 272–9.

Valins, S. (1966). Cognitive effects of false heart-rate feed-back. *Journal of Personality and Social Psychology, 4*, 400–8.

Valins, S. (1972). Persistent effects of information about internal reactions: Ineffectiveness of debriefing. In H. London & R. E. Nisbett (eds.), *The cognitive alteration of feeling states*. Chicago: Aldine.

van der Pligt, J. (1981). Actors' and observers' explanations: Divergent perspectives or divergent evaluations? In C. Antaki (ed.), *The psychology of ordinary explanations of social behaviour*. London: Academic Press.

van der Pligt, J. (1984). Attributions, false consensus, and valence: Two field studies. *Journal of Personality and Social Psychology, 46, 57–8*.

van der Pligt, J., Eiser, J. R. & Spears, R. (1986). Construction of a nuclear power station in one's locality: Attitudes and salience. *Basic and Applied Social Psychology, 7, 1–15*.

van der Pligt, J. & van Dijk, J. A. (1979). Polarization of judgment and preference for judgmental labels. *European Journal of Social Psychology, 9, 233–42*.

van Knippenberg, A. & van Oers, H. (1984). Social identity and equity concerns in intergroup perceptions. *British Journal of Social Psychology, 23, 351–61*.

Vannoy, J. S. (1965). Generality of cognitive complexity–simplicity as a personality construct. *Journal of Personality and Social Psychology, 2, 385–96*.

Velten, E. (1968). A laboratory task for induction of mood states. *Behavior Research and Therapy, 6, 473–82*.

Verhaeghe, H. (1976). Mistreating other persons through simple discrepant role playing: Dissonance arousal or response contagion. *Journal of Personality and Social Psychology, 34, 125–37*.

Volkmann, J. (1951). Scales of judgment and their implications for social psychology. In J. H. Rohrer & M. Sherif (eds.), *Social psychology at the crossroads*. New York: Harper.

von Cranach, M. & Vine, I. (eds.) (1973). *Social communication and movement: Studies of interaction and expression in man and chimpanzee*. London: Academic Press.

von Wright, G. H. (1965). *The logic problem of induction*. 2nd edition. Oxford: Blackwell.

Wahrman, R. & Pugh, M. D. (1972). Competence and conformity: Another look at Hollander's study. *Sociometry, 35, 376–86*.

Walker, I. & Pettigrew, T. F. (1984). Relative deprivation theory: An overview and conceptual critique. *British Journal of Social Psychology, 23, 301–10*.

Walster, E. (1966). Assignment of responsibility for an accident. *Journal of Personality and Social Psychology, 3, 73–9*.

Walster, E. (1967). 'Second guessing' important events. *Human Relations, 20, 239–50*.

Walster, E., Aronson, V., Abrahams, D. & Rottman, L. (1966). Importance of physical attractiveness in dating behavior. *Journal of Personality and Social Psychology, 4, 508–16*.

Walster, E., Berscheid, E. & Walster, G. W. (1976). New directions in equity research. In L. Berkowitz & E. Walster (eds.), *Advances in experimental social psychology. Vol. 9: Equity theory: Toward a general theory of social interaction*. New York: Academic Press.

Walster, E. & Prestholdt, P. (1966). The effect of misjudging another: Over-compensation or dissonance reduction? *Journal of Experimental Social Psychology, 2, 85–97*.

Ward, C. D. (1966). Attitude and involvement in the absolute judgment of attitude statements. *Journal of Personality and Social Psychology, 4, 465–76*.

Ware, R. & Harvey, O. J. (1967). A cognitive determinant of impression formation. *Journal of Personality and Social Psychology, 5,* 38–44.

Warr, P. & Jackson, P. (1975). The importance of extremity. *Journal of Personality and Social Psychology, 32,* 278–82.

Warr, P. B. & Smith, J. S. (1970). Combining information about people: Comparisons between six models. *Journal of Personality and Social Psychology, 16,* 55–65.

Weber, M. (1958). *The Protestant ethic and the spirit of capitalism* (translated by T. Parsons). New York: Scribners.

Weiner, B. (1979). A theory of motivation for some classroom experiences. *Journal of Educational Psychology, 71,* 3–25.

Weiner, B. (1985). 'Spontaneous' causal thinking. *Psychological Bulletin, 97,* 74–84.

Weiner, B., Frieze, I., Kukla, A., Reed, L., Rest, S. & Rosenbaum, R. M. (1971). Perceiving the causes of success and failure. In E. E. Jones, D. E. Kanouse, H. H. Kelley, R. E. Nisbett, S. Valins & B. Weiner (eds.), *Attribution: Perceiving the causes of behavior.* Morristown, NJ: General Learning Press.

Weiner, B., Heckhausen, H., Meyer, W. & Cook, R. E. (1972). Causal ascriptions and achievement behavior: The conceptual analysis of effort. *Journal of Personality and Social Psychology, 21,* 239–48.

Weiner, B. & Kukla, A. (1970). An attributional analysis of achievement motivation. *Journal of Personality and Social Psychology, 15,* 1–20.

Weiner, B., Russell, D. & Lerman, D. (1978). Affective consequences of causal ascriptions. In J. H. Harvey, W. J. Ickes & R. F. Kidd (eds.), *New directions in attribution research.* Vol. 2. Hillsdale, NJ: Erlbaum.

Weiner, B., Russell, D. & Lerman, D. (1979). The cognition–emotion process in achievement-related contexts. *Journal of Personality and Social Psychology, 37,* 1211–20.

Weiner, B. & Sierad, J. (1975). Misattribution for failure and enhancement of achievement strivings. *Journal of Personality and Social Psychology, 31,* 415–21.

Wells, G. L. & Harvey, J. H. (1977). Do people use consensus information in making causal attributions? *Journal of Personality and Social Psychology, 35,* 279–93.

West, S. G., Gunn, S. P. & Chernicky, P. (1975). Ubiquitous Watergate: An attributional analysis. *Journal of Personality and Social Psychology, 32,* 55–65.

Whitney, R. E. (1971). Agreement and positivity in pleasantness ratings of balanced and unbalanced social situations: A cross-cultural study. *Journal of Personality and Social Psychology, 17,* 11–14.

Wicker, A. W. (1969). Attitudes versus actions: The relationships of overt and behavioral responses to attitude objects. *Journal of Social Issues, 25,* 41–78.

Wicklund, R. A. & Brehm, J. W. (1976). *Perspectives on cognitive dissonance.* Hillsdale, NJ: Erlbaum.

Winter, L. & Uleman, J. S. (1984). When are social judgments made? Evidence for the spontaneousness of trait inferences. *Journal of Personality and Social Psychology, 47,* 237–52.

Wishner, J. (1960). Reanalysis of 'impressions of personality'. *Psychological Review, 67,* 96–112.

Wolf, S. (1985). Manifest and latent influence of majorities and minorities. *Journal of Personality and Social Psychology, 48,* 899–908.

Wong, P. T. P. & Weiner, B. (1981). When people ask 'why' questions, and the heuristics of attributional search. *Journal of Personality and Social Psychology*, 40, 650–63.

Wortman, C. B. & Dintzer, L. (1978). Is an attributional analysis of the learned helplessness phenomenon viable?: A critique of the Abramson–Seligman–Teasdale reformulation. *Journal of Abnormal and Social Psychology*, 87, 75–90.

Wortman, C. B. & Linder, D. E. (1973). Attribution of responsibility for an outcome as a function of its likelihood. *American Psychological Association 81st Annual Convention*. Montreal.

Wyer, R. S., Jr. (1974). *Cognitive organization and change: An information processing approach*. Potomac, Md.: Erlbaum.

Yardley, K. M. (1984). A critique of role play terminology in social psychology experimentation. *British Journal of Social Psychology*, 23, 113–20.

Yuker, H. E., Block, J. R. & Campbell, W. J (1960). *A scale to measure attitudes toward disabled persons*. Study No. 5, Albertson, NY: Human Resources Foundation.

Zajonc, R. B. (1965). Social facilitation. *Science*, 149, 269–74.

Zajonc, R. B. (1968a). Attitudinal effects of mere exposure. *Journal of Personality and Social Psychology Monograph Supplement*, 9, 2, pt 2, 1–27.

Zajonc, R. B. (1968b). Cognitive theories in social psychology. In G. Lindzey & E. Aronson (eds.), *Handbook of social psychology*. Vol. 1. Reading, Mass.: Addison-Wesley.

Zajonc, R. B. (1980). Feeling and thinking: Preferences need no inferences. *American Psychologist*, 35, 151–75.

Zajonc, R. B. & Burnstein, E. (1965). The learning of balanced and unbalanced social structures. *Journal of Personality*, 33, 153–63.

Zajonc, R. B. & Sherman, S. J. (1967). Structural balance and the induction of relations. *Journal of Personality*, 35, 635–50.

Zanna, M. P. & Cooper, J. (1974). Dissonance and the pill: An attribution approach to studying the arousal properties of dissonance. *Journal of Personality and Social Psychology*, 29, 703–9.

Zanna, M. P. & Cooper, J. (1976). Dissonance and the attribution process. In J. H. Harvey, W. J. Ickes & R. F. Kidd (eds.), *New directions in attribution research*. Vol. 1. Hillsdale, NJ: Erlbaum.

Zanna, M. P., Goethals, G. R. & Hill, J. F. (1975). Evaluating a sex-related ability: Social comparison with similar others and standard setters. *Journal of Experimental Social Psychology*, 11, 86–93.

Zanna, M. P., Higgins, E. T. & Taves, P. A. (1976). Is dissonance phenomenologically aversive? *Journal of Experimental Social Psychology*, 12, 530–8.

Zavalloni, M. & Cook, S. W. (1965). Influence of judges' attitudes on ratings of favorableness of statements about a social group. *Journal of Personality and Social Psychology*, 1, 43–54.

Zeigarnik, B. (1927). Das Behalten erledigter und underledigter Handlungen. *Psychologische Forschung*, 9, 1–85.

Zimbardo, P. G. (1969a). *The cognitive control of motivation*. Glenview, Ill.: Scott, Foresman.

Zimbardo, P. G. (1969b). The human choice: Individuation, reason and order versus deindividuation, impulse and chaos. *Nebraska Symposium on Motivation, 17*, 237–307.

Zimbardo, P. G., Weisenberg, M., Firestone, I. J. & Levy, B. (1965). Communicator effectiveness in producing public conformity and private attitude change. *Journal of Personality, 33*, 233–55.

Author index

Subject index

accentuation theory: and attitude judgement, 156–70, 245; and interpersonal judgement, 133–6, 141–4; and psychophysical judgement, 131–3, 139–43
adaptation level, 126–30, 150, 231
affect: affective-cognitive consistency, 29–30, 98; and cognition, 203–7, 232–4
anchor effects, 125–30, 153–4, 168–70
anticipatory belief change, 46–7
arousal: and dissonance, 106–11, 117–22; and emotion, 119–20, 131, 193–8; misattribution and attraction, 195–6
aspiration level, 130, 202
assimilation–contrast: and attitude change, 152–3; and attitude judgement, 148–51; and priming, 236–7; and psychophysical judgement, 150–1
attitude: accessibility, 72–6, 106; and behaviour, 52–83; change, 29–51; components of, 53–61; judgement, 145–70; as latent variable, 55–7, 155–6; measurement, 12, 55–60, 80, 145–6; organization, 13–19, 29–32, 79–82
attraction: and arousal (*see* arousal); and attitude similarity, 21–5, 305–6; and physical attractiveness, 24–6; and self-evaluation; 26–9
attribution: and achievement, 89, 184, 198–203, 209–10, 322–3; actor–observer differences in, 183–9; and addiction, 92, 207–10; defensive, 180–1, 268; and depression, 204–7; of intention, 174–83; and prediction, 211–13; of responsibility, 180–3; self-, 101–6, 183–9, 193–210, 213
authoritarianism, 143–4, 231, 291

'bad faith', 290–3, 333
balance theory, 14–19, 27–32, 50, 81–2, 211
base-rate probability, 137–9, 220–6
bias: agreement, 18–19; experimenter, 307–8; positivity, 17–19
'bogus pipeline', 100–1, 120
bystander intervention, 257–9

categorization, *see* accentuation theory
clinical applications/examples, 87–8, 204–7,

246–7; *see also* health applications/ examples
clinical judgement, 141–3, 172–3, 216
cognitive complexity, 19–21, 288–92, 337
cognitive dissonance, *see* dissonance
comparison level, 130–1, 220, 253, 319–20
conformity: and ambiguity, 32–4; public vs private, 37–8; and unanimity of majority, 35–6
congeneric scales, 155–6
congruity, 30–2, 41, 173; social congruity theory, 27–9
contrast effects: in attitudinal judgement, 146–8, 153–6, 165–70: in psychophysical judgement, 126–30; *see also* adaptation level, assimilation-contrast
control: illusion of, 224; locus of, 198–9
creativity, 315, 324–7
crowds, 249, 298–301, 332

deindividuation, 294–301, 332
depression, *see* attribution
deprivation: fraternal, 336; relative, 107–8, 115, 120, 310, 320; *see also* legitimacy
deviants: influence of, 325–8; rejection of, 37, 228–9
direct vs indirect experience, 56, 75
discrimination: intergroup, 301–23; and stereotyping, 133–9, 143–4, 170, 228–9, 240–2; strategies of, 304–5
dissonance: and arousal, 108–11, 117–21; and aversive consequences, 109, 114, 120–2; and choice, 91–2, 107, 111–15; and 'evaluation apprehension', 98; and forced compliance, 92–7; and foreseeability, 92, 114–17; and incentive magnitude 97–9, 107–9

emotion, *see* arousal, mood
equity, 253–7, 261–4, 292, 322–3
expectancy, 77, 191–3, 198–213, 336; *see also* learning
expected value, 61–72, 214–20, 250

'face-work', 285; *see also* impression management
'false consensus', 187–9, 327